THE SPIN MODEL CHECKER

Primer and Reference Manual

THE SPIN MODEL CHECKER

Primer and Reference Manual

Gerard J. Holzmann

✦ Addison-Wesley

Boston • San Francisco • New York • Toronto • Montreal
London • Munich • Paris • Madrid • Capetown
Sydney • Tokyo • Singapore • Mexico City

The publisher offers discounts on this book when ordered in quantity for special sales. For more information, please contact:

U.S. Corporate and Government Sales: (800) 382-3419

corpsales@pearsontechgroup.com

For sales outside the U.S., please contact:

International Sales: (317) 581-3793

international@pearsontechgroup.com

Visit Addison-Wesley on the Web at: awprofessional.com

Library of Congress Cataloging-in-Publication Data

```
Holzmann, Gerard J.
  The Spin model checker: primer and reference manual / Gerard J. Holzmann
  p. cm
  Includes bibliographical references and index.
  ISBN 0-321-22862-6
  1. Systems engineering--Mathematical models. 2. Computer programs--
  Testing. I. Title.
  TA168.H65 2003
  620'.001'171--dc22                                        2003057704
                                                                   CIP
```

This book was written, designed, and typeset by the author while affiliated with the Computing Sciences Research Center at Bell Laboratories. His current affiliation is with the Laboratory for Reliable Software at NASA's Jet Propulsion Laboratory / California Institute of Technology.

For information on obtaining permission to use material from this work, submit a request to:

Pearson Education, Inc.

Rights and Contracts Department

75 Arlington Street, Suite 300

Boston, MA 02116

Fax: (617) 848-7047

ISBN 0-321-22862-6

Text printed on recycled paper

First printing, September 2003

Contents

*"If you don't know where you're going,
it doesn't really matter which path you take."*
(Lewis Carroll, 1832–1898)

v

Foundation

Practice

*"You got to be careful if you don't know where you're going,
because you might not get there."*
(Yogi Berra, 1925–)

PREFACE

*"The worst thing about new books is that
they keep us from reading the old ones."*
(Joseph Joubert, 1754–1824)

A system is correct if it meets its design requirements. This much is agreed. But if the system we are designing is a piece of software, especially if it involves concurrency, how can we show this? It is not enough to merely show that a system *can* meet its requirements. A few tests generally suffice to demonstrate that. The real test is to show that a system cannot *fail* to meet its requirements.

Dijkstra's well-known dictum on testing[1] applies especially to concurrent software: the non-determinism of concurrent system executions makes it hard to devise a traditional test suite with sufficient coverage. There are fundamental problems here, related to both the limited controllability of events in distributed system executions and to the limited observability of those events.[2]

A well-designed system *provably* meets its design requirements. But, if we cannot achieve this degree of certainty with standard test methods, what else can we do? Using standard mathematics is not much of an option in this domain. A thorough hand proof of even simple distributed programs can challenge the most hardened mathematician. At first blush, mechanical proof procedures also do not seem to hold much promise: it was shown long ago

---

1. The quote *"Program testing can be used to show the presence of bugs, but never to show their absence"* first appeared in Dijkstra [1972], p. 6. The quote has a curious pendant in Dijkstra [1965] that is rarely mentioned: *"One can never guarantee that a proof is correct, the best one can say is: "I have not discovered any mistakes.""*

2. For instance, process scheduling decisions made simultaneously by different processors at distinct locations in a larger network.

that it is fundamentally impossible to construct a general proof procedure for arbitrary programs.[3] So what gives?

Fortunately, if some modest conditions are met, we *can* mechanically verify the correctness of distributed systems software. It is the subject of this book to show what these "modest conditions" are and how we can use relatively simple tool-based verification techniques to tackle demanding software design problems.

LOGIC MODEL CHECKING

The method that we will use to check the correctness of software designs is standard in most engineering disciplines. The method is called *model checking*. When the software itself cannot be verified exhaustively, we can build a simplified model of the underlying design that preserves its essential characteristics but that avoids known sources of complexity. The design model can often be verified, while the full-scale implementation cannot.

Bridge builders and airplane designers apply much the same technique when faced with complex design problems. By building and analyzing models (or prototypes) the risk of implementing a subtly flawed design is reduced. It is often too expensive to locate or fix design errors once they have reached the implementation phase. The same is true for the design of complex software.

The modeling techniques that we discuss in this book work especially well for concurrent software, which, as luck will have it, is also the most difficult to debug and test with traditional means.

The models we will build can be seen as little programs, written in, what may at first look like, a strangely abstract language. The models that are written in this language are in fact *executable*. The behaviors they specify can be simulated and explored exhaustively by the model checker in the hunt for logic errors. Constructing and executing these high-level models can be fun and insightful. It often also gives a sufficiently different perspective on a programming problem that may lead to new solutions, even before any precise checks are performed.

A logic model checker is designed to use efficient procedures for characterizing *all* possible executions, rather than a small subset, as one might see in trial executions. Since it can explore all behaviors, the model checker can apply a range of sanity checks to the design model, and it can successfully identify unexecutable code, or potentially deadlocking concurrent executions. It can even check for compliance with complex user-defined correctness criteria. Model checkers are unequalled in their ability to locate subtle bugs in system designs, providing far greater control than the more traditional methods based

---

3. The unsolvability of the *halting problem*, for instance, was already proven in Turing [1936].

on human inspection, testing, or random simulation.

Model checking techniques have been applied in large scale industrial applications, to reduce the reliance on testing, to detect design flaws early in a design cycle, or to prove their absence in a final design. Some examples of these applications are discussed in this book.

THE SPIN MODEL CHECKER

The methodology we describe in this book centers on the use of the model checker SPIN. This verification system was developed at Bell Labs in the eighties and nineties and is freely available from the Web (see Appendix D). The tool continues to evolve and has over many years attracted a fairly broad group of users in both academia and industry. At the time of writing, SPIN is one of the most widely used logic model checkers in the world.

In 2002 SPIN was recognized by the ACM (the Association for Computing Machinery) with its most prestigious *Software System Award*. In receiving this award, SPIN was placed in the league of truly breakthrough software systems such as UNIX, TeX, Smalltalk, Postscript, TCP/IP, and Tcl/Tk. The award has brought a significant amount of additional attention to the tool and its underlying technology. With all these developments there has been a growing need for a single authoritative and comprehensive user guide. This book is meant to be that guide.

The material in this book can be used either as classroom material or as a self-study guide for new users who want to learn about the background and use of logic model checking techniques. A significant part of the book is devoted to a comprehensive set of reference materials for SPIN that combines information that both novice and experienced users can apply on a daily basis.

BOOK STRUCTURE

SPIN can be used to thoroughly check high-level models of concurrent systems. This means that we first have to explain how one can conveniently model the behavior of a concurrent system in such a way that SPIN can check it. Next, we have to show how to define correctness properties for the detailed checks, and how to design abstraction methods that can be used to render seemingly complex verification problems tractable. We do all this in the first part of this book, Chapters 1 to 5.

The second part, Chapters 6 to 10, provides a treatment of the theory behind software model checking, and a detailed explanation of the fundamental algorithms that are used in SPIN.

The third part of the book, Chapters 11 to 15, contains more targeted help in getting started with the practical application of the tool. In this part of the book we discuss the command line interface to SPIN, the graphical user interface XSPIN, and also a closely related graphical tool that can be used for an intuitive specification of correctness properties, the Timeline editor. This part is concluded with a discussion of the application of SPIN to a range of standard problems in distributed systems design.

Chapters 16 to 19, the fourth and last part of the book, include a complete set of reference materials for SPIN and its input language, information that was so far only available in scattered form in books, tutorials, papers, and Web pages. This part contains a full set of manual pages for every language construct and every tool option available in the most recent versions of SPIN and XSPIN.

The Web site `http://spinroot.com/spin/Doc/Book_extras/` contains online versions of all examples used in this book, some lecture materials, and an up to date list of errata.

For courses in model checking techniques, the material included here can provide both a thorough understanding of the theory of logic model checking and hands-on training with the practical application of a well-known model checking system. For a more targeted use that is focused directly on the practical application of SPIN, the more foundational part of the book can be skipped.

A first version of this text was used for several courses in formal verification techniques that I taught at Princeton University in New Jersey, at Columbia University in New York, and at the Royal Institute of Technology in Stockholm, Sweden, in the early nineties. I am most grateful to everyone who gave feedback, caught errors, and made suggestions for improvements, as well as to all dedicated SPIN users who have graciously done this throughout the years, and who fortunately continue to do so.

I especially would like to thank Dragan Bosnacki, from Eindhoven University in The Netherlands, who read multiple drafts for this book with an unusually keen eye for spotting inconsistencies, and intercepting flaws. I would also like to thank Al Aho, Rajeev Alur, Jon Bentley, Ramesh Bharadwaj, Ed Brinksma, Marsha Chechik, Costas Courcoubetis, Dennis Dams, Matt Dwyer, Vic Du, Kousha Etessami, Michael Ferguson, Rob Gerth, Patrice Godefroid, Jan Hajek, John Hatcliff, Klaus Havelund, Leszek Holenderski, Brian Kernighan, Orna Kupferman, Bob Kurshan, Pedro Merino, Alice Miller, Doug McIlroy, Anna Beate Oestreicher, Doron Peled, Rob Pike, Amir Pnueli, Anuj Puri, Norman Ramsey, Jim Reeds, Dennis Ritchie, Willem-Paul de Roever, Judi Romijn, Theo Ruys, Ravi Sethi, Margaret Smith, Heikki Tauriainen, Ken Thompson, Howard Trickey, Moshe Vardi, Phil Winterbottom, Pierre Wolper, Mihalis Yannakakis, and Ozan Yigit, for their often profound influence that helped to shape the tool, and this book.

Gerard J. Holzmann
gholzmann@acm.org

FINDING BUGS IN CONCURRENT SYSTEMS 1

*"For we can get some idea of a whole from a part,
but never knowledge or exact opinion."
(Polybius, ca. 150 B.C., Histories, Book I:4)*

SPIN can be used to verify correctness requirements for systems of concurrently executing processes. The tool works by thoroughly checking either hand-built or mechanically generated models that capture the essential elements of a distributed systems design. If a requirement is not satisfied, SPIN can produce a sample execution of the model to demonstrate this.

There are two basic ways of working with SPIN in systems design. The first method, and the primary focus of this book, is to use the tool to construct verification models that can be shown to have all the required system properties. Once the basic design of a system has been shown to be logically sound, it can be implemented with confidence. A second, less direct, method is to start from an implementation and to convert critical parts of that implementation mechanically into verification models that are then analyzed with SPIN. Automated model extraction tools have been built to convert programs written in mainstream programming languages such as Java and C into SPIN models. A discussion of the latter approach to software verification is given in Chapter 10, and the constructs in SPIN that directly support model extraction techniques are discussed in Chapter 17.

We begin by considering in a little more detail what makes it so hard to test concurrent software systems, and why there is a need for tools such as SPIN.

It is worth noting up front that the difficulty we encounter when trying to reason about concurrent systems is not restricted to software design. Almost everything of interest that happens in our world involves concurrency and access to shared resources. In the supermarket, customers compete for shared resources, both consumable ones (such as food items) and non-consumable ones (such as checkout clerks). Customers follow simple, and very ancient, protocols for breaking ties and resolving conflicts. On the road, cars compete for access to road intersections and parking spots. In telephone systems, similarly, large numbers of simultaneous users compete for shared resources, this time with the unique feature that the users themselves are among the resources being shared. Problems of interaction occur in all these cases, and any new and untried set of rules that we may come up with to solve these problems can backfire in unexpected, sometimes amusing, and sometimes disastrous, ways.

CIRCULAR BLOCKING

As a simple example, we can look at the protocol rules that regulate the movements of cars across intersections. There is no unique solution, or even a best solution to this problem, as testified by the widely different standards that have been adopted in different countries around the world. In the U.S., when two roads intersect, one direction of traffic always explicitly has priority over the other direction, as indicated by markings on the pavement and by road-signs. At traffic circles, however, an implicit rule applies, rarely explicitly indicated, giving priority to traffic inside the circle. The implicit rule for circles is sensible, since it gives priority to cars leaving the circle over cars trying to enter it, which can avoid congestion problems.

In some European countries, the implicit and explicit rules are reversed. In the Netherlands, for instance, an implicit rule states that at otherwise unmarked intersections cars approaching from one's right have the right of way. The rule for traffic circles is explicitly marked to override this rule, again giving priority to traffic inside the circle. The implicit rule for unmarked intersections is simple and effective. But this rule can have unexpected consequences under heavy traffic conditions, as illustrated in Figure 1.1. It is not even true that we could avoid this problem with traffic lights that regularly reverse priority rules. One visit to a sufficiently large city will suffice to make it clear that this cannot prevent the problem. A fixed priority rule is not preferable either, since it will allow one direction of traffic to deny access to the other direction for any length of time. On the road, the occurrence of these conditions is typically accepted as just another fact of life. When they occur, they can often only be resolved by breaking the otherwise agreed upon rules. It will be clear that in software systems we cannot rely on such resolutions: The rules must cover all conceivable cases, and unfortunately, they must also cover all the humanly inconceivable ones.

DEADLY EMBRACE

As another everyday example, to make a person-to-person call, a user must secure exclusive access to at least two shared resources in the telephone

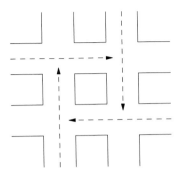

Figure 1.1 Circular Blocking

system: the line of the calling party and the line of the called party. The resources are allocated in a fixed order. Access is always first granted to the calling party's line and only then to the called party's line. Normally this causes no hardship, but when two subscribers A and B simultaneously attempt to establish a connection to each other, the access rules will prevent this. If both parties repeatedly pick up the receiver simultaneously to dial the connection, and refuse to give up until access is granted, they will repeatedly fail. This is especially curious because the two requests do not actually conflict: both subscribers desire the connection.

A very similar problem is encountered in the management of shared resources in operating systems. Virtually every textbook on operating systems contains a description of the problem. In the example used there, the shared resources are typically a line printer (A) and a card reader (B); the example is indeed that old. Two user processes then compete for exclusive access to these resources, both of which may be needed simultaneously, for instance to print a deck of punchcards. A deadly embrace is entered when both processes succeed in obtaining access to one of the two resources and then decide to wait indefinitely for the other. Of course it will not do to just require the processes to yield resources back to the operating system while waiting for more resources to become available.

The generic sequence of steps leading into the deadly embrace is illustrated in Figure 1.2. The solid arrows indicate the control-flow order in the two user processes. Once the two dashed states are reached simultaneously, there is no way to proceed. The dotted arrows indicate the dependency relations that prevent progress. Before device B can be obtained by the first process, it must first be released by the second process, and before device A can be obtained

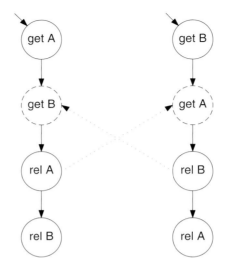

Figure 1.2 Deadly Embrace

by the second process, it must first be released by the first. The circular dependencies illustrate the deadly embrace.

MISMATCHED ASSUMPTIONS

It is a trusted premise of systems engineering that large systems should be built from smaller components, each of which can be designed and tested with a high degree of confidence. Ideally, the final system is then only assembled when all the smaller pieces have been proven correct. Some design problems, though, only become evident at the system level, and the absence of reliable methods for testing system level problems can sometimes take us by surprise. Decisions that are perfectly legitimate at the component level can have unexpected, and sometimes dramatic consequences at the system level.

A good illustration of this phenomenon is what happened September 14, 1993 on the runway at Warsaw airport in Poland.[1] A Lufthansa Airbus A320-200 with 72 people on board was landing in heavy rain. The plane was not getting much traction from the wheels in the landing gear on the wet runway, but the pilots knew that they could count on the thrust reversers on the main engines

---

1. A description of this accident can be found on the Web site www.crashdatabase.com.

to bring the plane to a stop. As it happened, the thrust reversers failed to deploy in time, and the plane overshot the end of the runway.

A thrust reverser should, of course, never be activated when a plane is in flight. Most planes, therefore, have elaborate protection built-in to prevent this from happening. This includes, for instance, that the thrust reversers cannot be deployed unless three conditions are met: the landing gear must be down, the wheels must be turning, and the weight of the plane must be carried on the wheels. In this case the landing gear was down, but the wheels were hydroplaning, and an unexpected tailwind provided enough lift on the wings that the control software did not decide until nine seconds after touchdown that the plane had landed. Two people lost their lives when the plane went off the end of the runway.

The most fascinating aspect of an accident like this is that no one really made any mistakes in the design or operation of this plane. All components were designed in a very sensible manner. The control software for the thrust reversers, though, was not designed to cope with the unexpected combination of events that occurred. This software formed one component in a complex system with many other interacting parts, including the dominant weather conditions that can affect a plane's operation.

When complex systems fail, the scenarios that trigger the failures usually could not easily have been imagined by any sensible human designer. For every one failure scenario that is considered, there are a million others that may be overlooked. In cases like this, it is invaluable to have design tools that can hunt down the potential error scenarios automatically, working from a sober description of the individual piece parts that together form a more complex integrated system. Automated tools have no trouble constructing the bizarre scenarios that no sane human could image—just the type of scenario that causes real-life systems to crash.

> *"The most pernicious and subtle bugs are system bugs arising from mismatched assumptions made by the authors of various components."*
> *(Fred Brooks, The Mythical Man-Month, p.142)*

FUNDAMENTAL PROBLEMS OF CONCURRENCY

The purpose of these few examples is to convince you of two things. First, concurrency-related problems are not rare oddities that appear only in obscure corners of software engineering. They are a fundamental part of life, and they can and do turn up almost everywhere. Secondly, it can be uncommonly hard to predict in advance where the problems in the various schemes can hide. Even the most obvious rules can have unexpected consequences. To find these problems, it never suffices to take a system apart, to study the individual components, and prove them correct. These types of problems have to do uniquely with the interaction of multiple, concurrently executing components. They are caused by the way in which the components are put together.

These types of problems are also extraordinarily hard to identify with standard system testing techniques. To test a piece of code, it should be possible to administer a series of reproducible tests and to evaluate the results. The keyword here is *reproducible*. Many aspects of the execution in a concurrent system are beyond the control of a tester. This lack of controllability makes it hard, if not impossible, to administer tests in a reproducible manner. This applies especially to the details of process execution and process interleaving that are in part determined by process schedulers, often running on independently executing hosts. The details of process interleaving, and even such subtle things as the relative speed of execution of asynchronously executing processes, can easily affect the outcome of a test. Even if the tester could know exactly how the process executions had to be interleaved in time to reproduce an error scenario, it is in general not possible to enforce such a schedule in a system test.

Limited observability and limited controllability normally restrict a tester's ability to thoroughly exercise concurrent system behaviors. As a result, some of the most difficult to diagnose bugs can slip through and hide as residual defects in production code, with the potential of striking at the least opportune moment in the lifetime of a system. To find these types of problems in a more systematic way, we need a different type of verification method. In the next chapter we begin the description of such a method with a tutorial overview of the language that is used to describe verification models in SPIN.

Traditional methods for testing software systems focus their energy on system description at the lowest level of detail, where higher level design errors are the hardest to find and the most costly to fix. By using verification models, we will be able to describe and verify complex system behavior at any desired level of abstraction, tracking it from concept to code. As noted, in larger systems it is not just the outright blunders that can cause system failure. Every single part of a system may have been designed correctly when considered in isolation. But if in the design of the various parts the system requirements were interpreted in just slightly different ways, the system as a whole can still fail. As system designers, we need tools that can catch all these types of design errors.

BUILDING
VERIFICATION MODELS 2

*"Measure what is measurable, and
make measurable what is not so."*
(Galileo Galilei, 1564–1642)

To verify a system we need to describe two things: the set of facts we want to verify, and the relevant aspects of the system that are needed to verify those facts. We investigate the types of facts we may want to prove about distributed systems in the next chapter. Here, we start with a gentle introduction to the art of describing distributed systems behavior at a relatively high level of abstraction, so that an automated verification of salient system facts becomes possible. We call such descriptions *verification models*.

SPIN

The tool that we will use to check verification models is called SPIN, and the specification language that it accepts is called PROMELA . The name SPIN was originally chosen as an acronym for *Simple PROMELA Interpreter*. The tool has arguably outgrown at least two of these three descriptive terms, but the name has stuck. SPIN can be used in two basic modes: as a simulator and as a verifier. In simulation mode, SPIN can be used to get a quick impression of the types of behavior that are captured by a system model, as it is being built. SPIN's graphical user interface, XSPIN (discussed in Chapter 12, p. 267), can conveniently visualize simulation runs, which can be of considerable help in the debugging of models. We use the term *debugging* intentionally here. No amount of simulation can *prove* the facts we may be interested in; only a verification run can do so. Nonetheless, when the verifier finds a counterexample to a correctness claim, it relies on the SPIN simulator to display the error trace using guided simulation. Simulation and verification are therefore tightly coupled in SPIN.

In this introductory chapter, we use SPIN primarily in simulation mode, only briefly illustrating how verifications can be set up in some common cases. To keep things simple, we also use the tool only in its basic command-line mode here, and resist the use of the graphical user interface for now. When we do discuss the graphical user interface, it will be a definite advantage if the user already knows the basic operation of SPIN itself, and the most important set of command-line options.

The focus on model building and simulation in this chapter leaves a lot to be explored in the rest of this book. The specification of correctness properties, for instance, is covered in Chapters 4 and 13. The use of SPIN for system verification is discussed in Chapters 11 and 14. And, finally, SPIN's graphical user interface, XSPIN, is discussed in Chapter 12.

PROMELA

PROMELA is an acronym for *Process Meta-La*nguage. The use of the term *meta* is significant in this context. As we shall see, abstraction is often key to successful verification. The specification language is intended to make it easier to find good abstractions of systems designs. PROMELA is not meant to be an implementation language but a systems description language. To make this possible, the emphasis in the language is on the modeling of process synchronization and coordination, and not on computation. The language is also targeted to the description of concurrent *software* systems, rather than the description of hardware circuits (which is more common for model checking applications).

The basic building blocks of SPIN models are asynchronous processes, buffered and unbuffered message channels, synchronizing statements, and structured data. Deliberately, there is no notion of time, or of a clock; there are no floating point numbers, and there are only few computational functions. These restrictions make it relatively hard to model the computation of, say, a square root in this language (cf. p. 325), but relatively easy to model and verify the behavior of clients and servers in networks of processors (cf. p. 299).

EXAMPLES

To get started, we discuss a few small examples of PROMELA specifications. We will prompt you for the things that are worth observing in these models, and for some experiments you can do to explore them further. We do not intend to define the language in full detail here; only to convey the style of system specifications in PROMELA. A more systematic treatment of various aspects of the language can be found, or skipped, in Chapters 3, 7, 16, and 17.

HELLO WORLD

The quintessential first program that prints a string on the user's terminal is, of course, *hello world*. The example dates from the first C programming language manual, Kernighan and Ritchie [1978]. It has been duplicated in virtually every language manual since then. We can specify this famous little first program as a PROMELA model as follows:

```
active proctype main()
{
        printf("hello world\n")
}
```

To simulate an execution of this model, assuming that we store it in a file named `hello.pml`, we can type the following, on a UNIX or UNIX-like system, at the shell prompt:

```
$ spin hello.pml
hello world
1 process created
```

and be rewarded with the gratifying result. The output, which is from SPIN's simulator, also contains a short reminder that PROMELA is a process modeling language, not a programming language. One process was created to simulate the execution of the model; there will usually be many more in a verification model.

The filename extension `.pml` is not required. SPIN is equally accommodating if other extensions, or none at all, are used.

If you have done some programming in C, all this will look familiar, as will many other features of the language that we encounter later. But there are some important differences. To begin with a few notable ones from this first example: `active` and `proctype` are keywords in the language, but `main` is not. That is, we could have used any other non-reserved word instead of `main` in this context. Next, there is no semicolon at the end of the `printf` statement, where in C this would be required. The reason is that the semicolon is defined as a statement *separator* in our new language, not as a statement *terminator*. This minor detail can of course quickly become a nuisance, so SPIN's parser is lenient on this issue. If you happen to type a semicolon where none is required, the parser will forgive you and quietly ignore it.

If it is not particularly important that the initial process is named, we can also use a shorthand notation to declare and instantiate an anonymous one, as follows:

```
init {
        printf("hello world\n")
}
```

Clearly, this works for only one single process, so in almost all cases of interest the use of a `proctype` declaration will be more useful. The keyword init, though, is a reserved word in the language and cannot be used for any other purpose, that is, it cannot be used for variable names or for proctype names.

A SPIN model is used to describe the behavior of systems of potentially inter-acting processes: multiple, asynchronous threads of execution. The primary unit of execution in a SPIN model is therefore a process, and not a C-style pro-cedure. The keyword proctype in the *hello world* example denotes that the identifier main that follows, introduces a name for a new *type* of process. Note carefully that the name does not identify a *process*, but a *process type*, that is, it defines the behavior for a process, but that definition does not auto-matically imply its execution. To execute a process, a named proctype must be instantiated explicitly. There can be multiple instantiations of any single process type.

The use of the optional prefix active in front of a proctype declaration tells SPIN that we want one process to be instantiated from the proctype dec-laration that follows. If that prefix is omitted, no instantiations of the proc-type are created by default. We will see shortly how processes can also be instantiated within the model itself, via a different mechanism.

The definition of printf is pretty much the same in PROMELA as it is in C. Many of the standard conversion formats are recognized, such as %c, %d, %u, %o, and %x, and special characters such as \t, and \n have the same meaning as in C.

PRODUCERS AND CONSUMERS

The *hello world* example includes just one single process, so there is not much opportunity there to experiment with process interaction. Our next example, shown in Figure 2.1, is a little system of two processes that do inter-act, by coordinating their actions with the help of a shared global variable.

The first line of the model declares two symbolic names, P and C. The effect of this declaration is very much like an enum declaration in a C program: the SPIN parser assigns a unique, positive integer value to each name, which repre-sents it internally. As the typename suggests, this type of declaration is often used to define the names of a range of message types used in interprocess message exchanges.

Following the mtype declaration, we find a global declaration of a variable named turn of type mtype. The variable can take any of the values from the mtype declaration, which in this case means that it can be assigned the sym-bolic values P and C. If left uninitialized, the value of the variable is zero, which is outside the range of possible mtype values. To avoid this, we assigned the initial value P. Next, we see two proctype declarations, both with the prefix active, defining that one process of each type is to be instan-tiated automatically.

```
mtype = { P, C };

mtype turn = P;

active proctype producer()
{
        do
        :: (turn == P) ->
                printf("Produce\n");
                turn = C
        od
}

active proctype consumer()
{
        do
        :: (turn == C) ->
                printf("Consume\n");
                turn = P
        od
}
```

Figure 2.1 Simple Producer Consumer Example

The control structure within each `proctype` is the same: both contain a loop. A PROMELA loop starts with the keyword `do` and ends with `od`. The loop body should contain one or more option sequences, with each separate option sequence preceded by a double colon `::`. In this case, the loops have just one single option sequence each. Each of these sequences has three, not two, statements, as we shall soon see.

The first statement after a double colon has special significance: it is called the *guard* statement, and it alone determines whether or not the execution sequence that follows is selectable for execution. In the case of the `pro-ducer` process, the one option for execution is guarded by the condition `(turn==P)`. This means that the statements that follow this guard can only be executed if and when the variable `turn` has the value P. PROMELA uses the double equals for the boolean equals operator and single equals for assignment, as in the C language.

The PROMELA loop is similar to another PROMELA control-flow construct: the selection statement. If we write the loop from the producer process with a selection statement, for instance, and use a jump and a label to execute it repeatedly, it looks as follows:

```
active proctype producer()
{
again:   if
         :: (turn == P) ->
                 printf("Produce\n");
                 turn = C
         fi;
         goto again
}
```

The rules for the execution of option sequences are the same as before. The one difference between a selection and a repetition structure (i.e., a PROMELA do loop) is that a loop is automatically repeated from the start when the execution of an option completes, while for a selection statement execution moves on to the next statement, which in this case is a jump that brings us back to the start of the selection in a different way. The execution of a loop can only be broken by either transferring control explicitly with a goto statement, or by executing a break statement. As in C, executing a break statement immediately terminates the execution of the innermost loop.

If all guard conditions in a loop construct evaluate to *false* (there is only one guard condition in our examples so far), then there is no available option for execution and the executing process *block*s. These semantics allow us to express process synchronization in a concise and clean way. Notice, for instance, that instead of encoding a busy wait cycle as in:

```
wait:   if
        :: (turn == P) -> ...
        :: else -> goto wait
        fi;
        ...
```

it suffices to write in PROMELA:

```
(turn == P) -> ...
```

Arrows and semicolons are equivalent in PROMELA, so the one statement above (yes, a condition is a full-fledged statement in PROMELA) can also be written:

```
(turn == P); ...
```

assuming of course that more statements follow. In the usual style of specification, only potentially blocking statements are followed by an arrow as a statement separator, and all other types of statements are followed by a semicolon, but this is purely a matter of style, not of grammar.

We quietly introduced another PROMELA keyword: else. The use of this keyword as a guard statement in a selection or repetition structure defines a condition that is *true* if and only if all other guard conditions in the same structure evaluate to *false*. So, in the earlier example, the use of else is equivalent to writing

```
!(turn == P)
```

Note that multiple guard conditions in the same structure could also evaluate to *true* simultaneously. In that case, SPIN selects one of these guards non-deterministically for execution. There can, however, be no more than one else per if or do construct, and therefore when an else option is selected it is necessarily the only executable option.

Another point worth observing is that when the else option is deleted from a selection, execution necessarily *blocks* until at least one guard condition evaluates to *true*. This temporary (or permanent) blocking provides a convenient means for modeling interprocess synchronization.

The use of *non-determinism* within a process definition allows for a considerable amount of freedom in the construction of a verification model. By saying that two possible events are possible at a particular point in the execution, we can remove unnecessary detail from the model and verify effectively that the correctness of the design is independent of such detail. There is also a second type of non-determinism in a PROMELA model. If at any point in an execution more than one process has an executable statement and could proceed, then the semantics of PROMELA state that any one of these processes may be selected for execution: the choice itself is a non-deterministic one. In essence, this system-level non-determinism means that we make no *a priori* assumptions about the behavior of process schedulers. Note, for instance, that the asynchronous processes are often under the control of independent process schedulers, executing on distinct hardware in a network of processors. Assumptions about process scheduling, even on a single system, are inherently suspect and unnecessarily limit the scope of a verification.

Returning to our *producer/consumer* example, we can note that, since this is a concurrent environment with potentially many executing processes, the value of turn could well change immediately after the producer process evaluates its guard condition.

The initial value for turn is P, so at least one producer process will find that its guard condition evaluates to *true*, and it can execute the next two statements. The first of these statements prints a string, and the second sets variable turn to C, thereby blocking the producer process from repeating the loop sequence, but enabling the guard condition in its peer process of type consumer. Simulating the execution of this model produces the following output:

```
$ spin prodcons.pml | more
Produce
        Consume
Produce
        Consume
  . . .
```

We forced the two processes to execute in strictly alternating order, *ad infinitum*. We therefore took the precaution to filter the output through the UNIX (or cygwin) `more` program, to avoid being swamped in output. Another method, that does not rely on the use of UNIX commands, is to use the SPIN option `-uN` to limit the simulation run to a maximum of N steps (see p. 513). The output would then look as follows:

```
$ spin -u14 prodcons.pml
       Produce
             Consume
       Produce
             Consume
    -------------
depth-limit (-u14 steps) reached
...
```

The simulation is now terminated after fourteen steps. We only see four lines produced by print statements, which means that ten non-print statements were also executed in the above run. Some more information is normally printed about the state of the system that is now reached, but we will ignore that for now.

EXTENDING THE EXAMPLE

What will happen to our little device to enforce the alternation between producer and consumer if we instantiate a few more processes of each type? We can do so most easily by adding the desired number of processes to be instantiated to the `proctype` declarations, as follows:

```
active [2] proctype producer() { ... }
```

Suppose we still wanted to enforce a strict alternation of execution of one of multiple running `producer` processes and one of multiple `consumer` processes. The earlier solution no longer works, because it is now possible that immediately after a first process of type `producer` evaluates the guard condition (`turn==P`) and finds it *true*, a second process of the same type comes to the same conclusion and also proceeds with its execution, potentially causing havoc.

To avoid this problem, we have to add a little more mechanism. First, we add one more symbolic value that we can use to record that the variable `turn` is neither P nor C. Let's call this value N. This changes the `mtype` declaration into:

```
mtype = { P, C, N };
```

We could equally well have added the extra definition in a separate declaration, for instance, as:

```
mtype = { P, C };
mtype = { N };
```

The declaration and initialization of variable `turn` itself remains as it was, but we add one extra global variable for bookkeeping purposes. The variable will record the identity of the process that is currently executing as either a producer or a consumer.

```
pid    who;
```

The type of this new variable is `pid`, and its name is `who`. We have left the variable uninitialized, since its initial value does not matter much to us here. If no explicit initial value is specified, the variable is by default initialized to zero.

The new declaration for the `producer` processes is as follows:

```
active [2] proctype producer()
{
        do
        :: request(turn, P, N) ->
                printf("P%d\n", _pid);
                assert(who == _pid);
                release(turn, C)
        od
}
```

We have added an argument to the print statement so that each process can print its process instantiation number when it executes. That number is available in the predefined, read-only, local variable named `_pid`.

Inside the loop, we have changed the guard condition into what at first sight would appear to be a function call: `request(turn,P,N)`. This is in fact an `inline` definition, which is a stylized version of a macro that PROMELA supports. The `inline` represents a condition here that, if *true*, allows the producer to continue with the execution of the code that follows. At the end of the execution sequence we see another `inline`, called `release(turn,C)`, which serves to yield back the access permission that was obtained so that other processes, presumably a `consumer`, can now run.

A PROMELA `inline` is very similar to a C-style macro definition. The SPIN parser performs a textual substitution of the body of each `inline` definition at each point in the PROMELA code where it is invoked. Doing so, the parser also applies a direct *textual* substitution of all actual parameter names that are provided at the point of invocation for the formal names that are used in the definition.

The definition of the `inline request` can be written as follows:

```
inline request(x, y, z) {
        atomic { (x == y) -> x = z; who = _pid }
}
```

Note that the formal parameters have no type designation: they are simply place holders for the actual variable names that are inserted when the `inline` is invoked. That is, if the `inline` is invoked as

```
request(turn, P, N)
```

then the code that is inserted into the model at the point of invocation is

```
atomic { (turn == P) -> turn = N; who = _pid }
```

The body of an `inline` definition can contain declarations for local variables, but these are not treated any differently than the remainder of the `inline` body: they will be included in the text segment that is inserted at each point of invocation, and therefore their scope depends on the point of invocation of the `inline`, and is not restricted to the body of the `inline` itself.

The guard condition in our example turned into an execution sequence of three statements. The sequence is designated as an `atomic` sequence, which means that once it starts, *all* steps in the sequence will complete before any other process is given the chance to execute. The executability of that atomic sequence is again determined by its first statement: the guard of the sequence. The atomicity of the three statements in the sequence will prevent multiple producer processes from evaluating the guard `(turn==P)` in quick succession, before the value of `turn` can be updated.

As noted, the execution of an `atomic` sequence can be initiated only when its guard condition (the executability condition of the first statement in the sequence) evaluates to *true*. As expected, in our example this means that `(turn==P)` must evaluate to *true*. Once execution starts, in one atomic action, variable `turn` is set to the value `N`, and the process identity of the `producer` process is recorded in global variable `who`.

Once a producer process gains access by completing the execution of the `atomic` sequence, it prints some output, and then checks an assertion. The assertion verifies that the value of global variable `who` matches the value the process assigned to it before. If, despite our efforts, it is still possible for multiple producer processes to reach this piece of code simultaneously, the assertion can fail for at least one of them. Luckily, the SPIN verifier will be able to prove decisively if this is possible or not.

Following the assertion, the second `inline` is executed. It is defined as follows:

```
inline release(x, y) {
        atomic { x = y; who = 0 }
}
```

This means that the call `release(turn,C)` translates into the inlined piece

```
mtype = { P, C, N };

mtype turn = P;
pid   who;

inline request(x, y, z) {
        atomic { x == y -> x = z; who = _pid }
}

inline release(x, y) {
        atomic { x = y; who = 0 }
}

active [2] proctype producer()
{
        do
        :: request(turn, P, N) ->
                printf("P%d\n", _pid);
                assert(who == _pid);
                release(turn, C)
        od
}

active [2] proctype consumer()
{
        do
        :: request(turn, C, N) ->
                printf("C%d\n", _pid);
                assert(who == _pid);
                release(turn, P)
        od
}
```

Figure 2.2 Revised Producer Consumer Example

of code

```
atomic { turn = C; who = 0 }
```

The guard condition in this case is always *true*, since the first statement of the atomic sequence is now an assignment statement and not an expression. Executing the sequence indirectly passes control to a consumer process by changing the value of variable turn, and it also resets the value of who to its initial zero state. (Technically, the zero value can match a process instantiation number, but that will not impede the effectiveness of the assertion in this example.) The new model, with two producers and two consumers, is shown in Figure 2.2.

If we simulate this model with SPIN, we may now see the following output:

```
$ spin prodcons2.pml | more
        P1
                        C2
        P1
                                C3
    P0
                                C3
        P1
                                C3
    . . .
```

There is some non-determinism in this model, since both producers and both consumers share the same guard conditions that can trigger their actions. The first process to reach a print statement, for instance, can be either P0 or P1. In this example it is the latter.

The simulation seems to confirm that we have succeeded in achieving alternate executions of producers and consumers. No assertion violations are reported in this simulation run: an assertion violation would abort the execution with a diagnostic message. For instance, executing the model

```
init { assert(false) }
```

produces:

```
$ spin false.pml
spin: line   1 "false.pml", Error: assertion violated
. . .
```

Of course, the fact that no assertion violations are encountered in a simulation run does not prove that all assertion violations are also impossible. To prove that we have to invoke SPIN in *verification* mode. Without getting into too many details on verification just yet, a basic verification run for this model would proceed as follows. First, the source text for a model-specific verifier is generated by SPIN, and that source text is then compiled to generate the executable verifier itself.

```
$ spin -a prodcons2.pml # generate a verifier
$ cc -o pan pan.c       # compile the verifier
```

The executable verifier can now be invoked, producing the following result:[1]

---

1. Sometimes, typing just pan also works. Typing ./pan, or .\pan on a PC, may be needed if your default search path for commands does not include the current directory. We will consistently use ./pan in this book. Similarly, the precise compilation command to be issued depends on the C compiler that is used. Popular alternatives to cc include the Gnu C compiler gcc, which is available from http://cygwin.com/, and the Microsoft compiler cl. We will consistently use cc in all examples that follow.

```
$ ./pan                          # perform the verification
(Spin Version 4.0.7 -- 1 August 2003)
        + Partial Order Reduction

Full statespace search for:
        never claim              - (none specified)
        assertion violations     +
        acceptance   cycles      - (not selected)
        invalid end states       +

State-vector 28 byte, depth reached 7, errors: 0
       14 states, stored
        3 states, matched
       17 transitions (= stored+matched)
        0 atomic steps
  . . .
```

We can see that the state-space that the verifier had to search to verify this model was very small, counting merely fourteen states. No errors, and in particular no assertion violations, are reported here. We will shortly see what we might do if errors had been reported by the verifier. In later chapters we will also look in more detail at the meaning of all other output that is generated by the verifier (e.g., cf. p. 540), most of which we have deleted here.

MUTUAL EXCLUSION

Perhaps the best illustration of the difficulty of designing correct coordination schemes for asynchronously executing processes is the classic *mutual exclusion* problem. The problem here is to find a way to grant mutually exclusive access to a shared resource while assuming only the indivisibility of read and write operations. That is, to solve this problem we cannot assume the availability of atomic sequences to make a series of test and set operations indivisible. One of the first attempted solutions of the problem was described by Edsger Dijkstra in Dijkstra [1965]. Dijkstra gives credit for the algorithm to the Dutch mathematician T.J. Dekker, who first devised it in 1962. It solves the problem for two processes only. The PROMELA version of this algorithm can be written as shown in Figure 2.3.

The algorithm uses a bit variable named turn with a similar function as in our previous *producer/consumer* example. Since there are just two processes in the system, the turn variable can point to one or the other using just a zero or a one. Note, though, that this time we cannot assume that the two processes will be content to alternate their access to the critical part of the code where the shared resource is accessed. If only one of the two processes needs access, it should be able to acquire it arbitrarily often. This makes the problem much harder to solve correctly. Dekker's algorithm uses an array of two booleans called flag to track the progress of the two processes. In our PROMELA model we have also added a global variable cnt of type byte to count how many processes can succeed in accessing the critical section in the

```
bit     turn;
bool    flag[2];
byte    cnt;

active [2] proctype mutex()
{   pid i, j;

    i = _pid;
    j = 1 - _pid;
again:
    flag[i] = true;
    do
    :: flag[j] ->
        if
        :: turn == j ->
            flag[i] = false;
            (turn != j) ->        /* wait until true  */
            flag[i] = true
        :: else ->
            skip                  /* do nothing       */
        fi
    :: else ->
        break                     /* break from loop  */
    od;

    cnt++;
    assert(cnt == 1);             /* critical section */
    cnt--;

    turn = j;
    flag[i] = false;
    goto again
}
```

Figure 2.3 Dekker's Mutual Exclusion Algorithm (1962)

code simultaneously. If all is well, this variable can never be assigned a value greater than one or less than zero. An assertion in the code can check if this is indeed the case.

We use a local variable, i of type pid, to record the instantiation numbers of the running process. Each process must also know the *pid* of its competitor, and since we only have two processes here, predictably with *pid* numbers zero and one, each process can obtain the *pid* of its peer by subtracting its own *pid* from one.

The attempt to gain access to the critical section in the code starts by setting an element of boolean array flag to *true*. This is followed by a loop that cannot be exited until the competing process disavows interest in entering the critical section by turning its element in array `flag` to *false*. The real problem to be solved is of course when both processes set their element in the `flag` array to *true* simultaneously. The global variable `turn` will in that case be the tie breaker. For some measure of fairness,[2] upon exit from the critical section each process sets the value of `turn` to favor its competitor, should a similar tie occur again.

When a process is forced, by the current value of `turn`, to yield to the other process, it turns its element of `flag` to *false* and then waits for the other process to exit the critical section. It waits at the condition statement:

```
(turn != j) ->
```

In most languages it would be meaningless to write a condition all by itself, that is, outside a selection or iteration construct. In fact, in C it would not make a difference whether the expression would evaluate to *true* or *false*; execution of the program would continue immediately in both cases. A unique feature of PROMELA is that *every* type of statement can act as a guard in *any* context, even when used stand-alone as here. For each statement, the semantic rules of PROMELA define the precise conditions under which the statement is "executable" and what its effect is when it is executed. For most types of statements these rules are fairly standard. A `printf` statement, for instance, is always executable and its effect is to print output during simulation runs. An assignment like `turn=j` is also unconditionally executable, and its effect is to assign the current value of the expression on the right-hand side of the `=` sign to the variable that is on the left-hand side. A stand-alone expression (exp) is "executable" if and only if the expression evaluates to *true*. The statement blocks the process that attempts to "execute" the expression when it evaluates to *false*. Fortunately, and not coincidentally, all expressions in PROMELA are guaranteed to be free of side effects when they evaluate to *false*, so it does not matter how often we may have to evaluate the executability of a statement before it turns *true*: there can be no side effects on the system state as a result of these evaluations.

We can simulate the execution of Dekker's algorithm as before. No output is generated in this case, and fortunately no assertion violations either. To prove that assertion violations are indeed impossible, and that Dekker's algorithm correctly solves the mutual exclusion problem for two processes, we need SPIN's verification mode. The verification takes a fraction of a second, and quickly confirms that assertion violations are indeed impossible.

---

2. The term *fairness* is used informally here. We discuss a more formal notion of process scheduling fairness in Chapter 4.

```
$ spin -a mutex.pml
$ cc -o pan pan.c
$ ./pan
(Spin Version 4.0.7 -- 1 August 2003)
        + Partial Order Reduction

Full statespace search for:
        never claim            - (none specified)
        assertion violations   +
        acceptance   cycles    - (not selected)
        invalid end states     +

State-vector 36 byte, depth reached 65, errors: 0
     190 states, stored
     173 states, matched
     363 transitions (= stored+matched)
       0 atomic steps
hash conflicts: 0 (resolved)
(max size 2^18 states)

1.573   memory usage (Mbyte)

unreached in proctype mutex
        line 38, state 23, "-end-"
        (1 of 23 states)
```

The one line of real interest in the output that SPIN produces here is the error count: zero. The remainder of the ouput spells out more details of the run that was completed, but we can safely ignore all that for the time being.

Though verification can settle the issue of correctness, Dekker's algorithm has been a rich source of inspiration for many years. One thought that immediately comes to mind is whether the algorithm could not be simplified or generalized in some way. For instance, is the outer do-loop really necessary, or could it be turned into an if-selection? This observation was first made in Doran and Thomas [1980], and at the time it required very careful thought and proof to determine its accuracy. Today, a verification run with SPIN can produce a definitive verdict virtually instantaneously: confirming that the observation is indeed correct. The change does not alter the number of reachable states, and fully preserves the correctness of the algorithm.

If the do-loop is dispensable, could not the whole nested structure be dispensed with as well? None of these issues are easy to settle by pen and paper arguments. The number if incorrect mutual exclusion algorithms that have been dreamt up over the years, often supported by long and persuasive correctness arguments, is considerably larger than the number of correct ones. Figure 2.4, for instance, shows a version, converted into PROMELA, that was recommended by a major computer manufacturer in the not too distant past.

A tool like SPIN has not much trouble exposing the flaw in this algorithm.

```
byte cnt;
byte x, y, z;

active [2] proctype user()
{    byte me = _pid + 1;      /* me is 1 or 2 */

again:
    x = me;
    if
    :: (y == 0 || y == me) -> skip
    :: else -> goto again
    fi;

    z = me;
    if
    :: (x == me) -> skip
    :: else    -> goto again
    fi;

    y = me;
    if
    :: (z == me) -> skip
    :: else -> goto again
    fi;

    /* enter critical section */
    cnt++;
    assert(cnt == 1);
    cnt--;
    goto again
}
```

Figure 2.4 Faulty Mutual Exclusion Algorithm

SPIN's verdict on this model is obtained as follows:

```
$ spin -a mutex_flaw.pml
$ cc -o pan pan.c
$ ./pan
pan: assertion violated (cnt==1) (at depth 53)
pan: wrote mutex_flaw.pml.trail
...
```

The verifier halts execution the moment it has established the possibility of an assertion violation, and it writes the execution sequence into a trail file.[3] The trail file contains codes that can be understood by the SPIN simulator to recreate that execution path in as much, or in as little, detail as we can now choose. We can tell SPIN to use the trail file in a simulation (which is now a *guided* simulation run) by using the option letter -t. Before we do so, though, we note from the output above that the error trail is 53 steps long. We could wonder if there isn't a shorter execution trace that can lead to the same assertion violation. Given that we already know that we do not have to search deeper than 53 steps, we can set up such a search as follows:

```
$ cc -DREACH -o pan pan.c       # compile differently
$ ./pan -i -m53                 # extra run-time options
```

The compile-time directive -DREACH arranges for the verifier to use a different storage discipline that allows it to keep track of the depth at which each reachable state is found. The run-time option -i instructs the verifier to iteratively home in on the shortest error trace it can find, by using the extra information that is now available. A description of the algorithm that is used for this is given in Chapter 8 (see p. 171).

In this case we also give the verifier a preset maximum search depth of 53, since we already know that there is an error sequence of that number of steps, but this is of course not required.

The new output that is produced by the verifier is as follows:

```
$ ./pan -i -m53
error: max search depth too small
pan: assertion violated (cnt==1) (at depth 45)
pan: wrote mutex_flaw.pml.trail
pan: reducing search depth to 45
...

pan: reducing search depth to 15
pan: wrote mutex_flaw.pml.trail
pan: reducing search depth to 14
pan: wrote mutex_flaw.pml.trail
pan: reducing search depth to 14
(Spin Version 4.0.7 -- 1 August 2003)
        + Partial Order Reduction
...
```

In the first line of output, the verifier duly informs us that there do exist longer executions than the depth limit (i.e., the maximum search depth) of fifty-three steps allows us to peruse this time. Then, it finds the first error trace at a depth of forty-five steps, and starts looking for an even shorter example by trimming the search depth to that new limit. Eventually, the shortest trace that the verifier can find turns out to be fourteen steps long.

An easy alternative to this procedure is to compile the verifier to use an

---

3. On some systems a filename can only have one period. In that case Spin will strip the extension .pml, if present, before adding the suffix .trail. Similarly, if only a three-letter file extension is allowed, Spin will use the suffix .tra instead of .trail.

alternative search mode: using a breadth-first search, instead of the default depth-first search, discipline. In that case we find the shortest path immediately:

```
$ cc -DBFS -o pan pan.c
$ ./pan
pan: assertion violated (cnt==1) (at depth 14)
pan: wrote mutex_flaw.pml.trail
...
```

We will see later in which cases the breadth-first search mode can be used, and in which cases it cannot.

We can now ask SPIN to perform a guided simulation for this last version of the error trace that was written into the trail file, by giving the command:

```
$ spin -p -t mutex_flaw.pml
   1:     proc  1 (user) line   5 ... [x = me]
   2:     proc  1 (user) line   8 ... [(((y==0)||(y==me)))]
   3:     proc  1 (user) line  10 ... [z = me]
   4:     proc  1 (user) line  13 ... [((x==me))]
   5:     proc  0 (user) line   5 ... [x = me]

   6:     proc  0 (user) line   8 ... [(((y==0)||(y==me)))]
   7:     proc  1 (user) line  15 ... [y = me]
   8:     proc  1 (user) line  18 ... [((z==me))]
   9:     proc  1 (user) line  22 ... [cnt = (cnt+1)]
  10:     proc  0 (user) line  10 ... [z = me]
  11:     proc  0 (user) line  13 ... [((x==me))]
  12:     proc  0 (user) line  15 ... [y = me]
  13:     proc  0 (user) line  18 ... [((z==me))]
  14:     proc  0 (user) line  22 ... [cnt = (cnt+1)]
spin: line  23 "mutex_flaw.pml", Error: assertion violated
spin: text of failed assertion: assert((cnt==1))
  15:     proc  0 (user) line  23 ... [assert((cnt==1))]
spin: trail ends after 15 steps
#processes: 2
                     cnt = 2
                     x = 1
                     y = 1
                     z = 1
  15:     proc  1 (user) line  23 "mutex_flaw.pml" (state 20)
  15:     proc  0 (user) line  24 "mutex_flaw.pml" (state 21)
2 processes created
```

We have abbreviated the output slightly here for layout purposes. It is clear, though, that the executions of the two user processes are interleaved in such a way here that the variable in ends up being incremented twice, once at step nine and once at step fourteen, which leads immediately to the assertion violation.

Curiously, there exists a much simpler solution to the mutual exclusion

```
bool    turn, flag[2];
byte    cnt;

active [2] proctype P1()
{   pid i, j;

    i = _pid;
    j = 1 - _pid;

again:
    flag[i] = true;
    turn = i;
    (flag[j] == false || turn != i) -> /* wait until true */

    cnt++;
    assert(cnt == 1);
    cnt--;

    flag[i] = false;
    goto again
}
```

Figure 2.5 Peterson´s Mutual Exclusion Algorithm (1981)

problem, but it took more than fifteen years before it was discovered. In 1981 G.L. Peterson published the solution shown in Figure 2.5, which SPIN quickly proves correct.

Much of the algorithm looks familiar, apart from the wonderful simplicity of the solution. Now we can again wonder, would it not be possible to simplify this algorithm still a little bit further? We may, for instance, consider if the wait condition could not be simplified to merely (flag[j]==false). SPIN quickly shows that if this is done a deadlock can result when both processes reach the wait condition simultaneously, with both elements of array flag set to *false*. At this point both processes are caught waiting for the other, a problem that is avoided in Peterson's version of the algorithm.

MESSAGE PASSING

So far we have not shown any example of the use of message passing between asynchronous processes. We will remedy that now. The following example illustrates the basic mechanism. The specification in Figure 2.6 models a protocol that was proposed in 1981 at Bell Labs for use in a new data switch.

The first line of the specification contains a declaration of symbolic names for seven different types of messages, using an mtype declaration as before. Next, we see a new data type called chan. On two subsequent lines, two

```
mtype = { ini, ack, dreq, data, shutup, quiet, dead };

chan M = [1] of { mtype };
chan W = [1] of { mtype };

active proctype Mproc()
{
    W!ini;                      /* connection        */
    M?ack;                      /* handshake         */

    timeout ->                  /* wait              */
    if                          /* two options:      */
    :: W!shutup                 /* start shutdown    */
    :: W!dreq;                  /* or request data   */
        M?data ->               /* receive data      */
        do
        :: W!data               /* send data         */
        :: W!shutup;            /* or shutdown       */
            break
        od
    fi;

    M?shutup;                   /* shutdown handshake */
    W!quiet;
    M?dead
}


active proctype Wproc()
{
    W?ini;                      /* wait for ini      */
    M!ack;                      /* acknowledge       */

    do                          /* 3 options:        */
    :: W?dreq ->                /* data requested    */
        M!data                  /* send data         */
    :: W?data ->                /* receive data      */
        skip                    /* no response       */
    :: W?shutup ->              /* start shutdown    */
        M!shutup;
        break
    od;

    W?quiet;
    M!dead
}
```

Figure 2.6 Data Transfer Protocol

buffered message channels are declared, each with a capacity to store one message. The messages themselves that can be stored in these channels are in both cases declared to be of type `mtype` (i.e., one of the values from the `mtype` declaration on the first line). In general, there can be any number of message fields, of arbitrary types, which could be specified in a comma-separated list in the spot where we now find only the one `mtype` keyword.

Two types of processes are declared and instantiated, as stipulated by the prefix `active`. The first process, of type `Mproc`, receives messages via channel `M` and sends them to its peer via channel `W`. The second process, of type `Wproc`, does the reverse.

The first process initiates a connection with its peer by sending the message `ini`. It then waits for a response, which is expected to be the message `ack`. The syntax for specifying a message transmission resembles that of Hoare's CSP language here: the send operator is represented by an exclamation mark and the receive operator is represented by a question mark.

Both operators have two (sets of) operands: one operand is always written to the left of the mark and identifies the message channel that is addressed by the operation. The remaining operands follow to the right of the mark, and specify the details of the message to be transmitted or received. In this case we declared message channels with just one field for each message, so in this example just one right-hand side operand suffices in all message passing operations.

After the first message exchange is completed, the system comes to a halt. The second process waits for the first process to send it one of three possible message types. The first process, however, does nothing until it times out. The PROMELA semantics state that the predefined boolean variable `timeout` is *true* if and only if no other statement[4] in the entire system is executable; otherwise it is *false*.

Once the `timeout` condition evaluates to *true*, the process of type `Mproc` has two options for execution. It can either send a message of type `dreq` to request a data transmission from its peer, or it can choose to close down the connection with a message of type `shutup`.

Can this protocol ever deadlock the two processes? We can get an impression of the feasible executions by running some simulations as before. We might see, for instance, the following output, which confirms that correct execution is at least possible. We use the `-c` option to SPIN in this case, to get a conveniently columnated output of just the message exchanges.

---

4. Notice that in this respect the semantics of the PROMELA `timeout` condition resemble that of the `else`. The difference is that `else` provides an escape clause at the process level, while `timeout` does so at the system level.

```
$ spin -c protocol
proc 0 = Mproc
proc 1 = Wproc
q\p    0    1
   1   W!ini
   1   .    W?ini
   2   .    M!ack
   2   M?ack
timeout
   1   W!shutup
   1   .    W?shutup
   2   .    M!shutup

   2   M?shutup
   1   W!quiet
   1   .    W?quiet
   2   .    M!dead
   2   M?dead
   . . .
```

To show also that *incorrect* execution is *not* possible, we will need the verifier.
In verification mode, SPIN quickly homes in on the following sample execution that does lead into a deadly embrace. We will skip the incantations of
SPIN to obtain a short error trace, which proceeds in the same way as in the
last example, and go straight to the guided simulation run that replays the fatal
sequence of steps that SPIN finds. It looks as follows:

```
$ spin -c -t protocol
proc 0 = Mproc
proc 1 = Wproc
q\p    0    1
   1   W!ini
   1   .    W?ini
   2   .    M!ack
   2   M?ack
   1   W!dreq
   1   .    W?dreq
   2   .    M!data
   2   M?data
   1   W!data
   1   .    W?data
[deadlock state]
-------------
final state:
-------------
#processes: 2
                queue 2 (M):
                queue 1 (W):
  12:    proc 1 (Wproc) line  31 "protocol" (state 10)
  12:    proc 0 (Mproc) line  12 "protocol" (state 10)
2 processes created
```

After the initial connection setup, the two parties successfully exchange one data item, but then get stuck. The error is in the encoding of the inner loop inside `proctype Mproc`. It can be solved by adding an additional timeout option in this loop, which gives the process an alternate route to the shutdown procedure.

IN SUMMARY

In this chapter we have taken a first look at some small examples of PROMELA verification models. The examples are not meant to give an exhaustive overview of the PROMELA language, but they are meant to give an idea of its main focus, which is to model the behavior of interacting asynchronous processes in distributed systems. The aim of the SPIN verifier is not to verify the computational aspects of an application; it is to reliably identify problems that are caused by process interaction. This means that we are interested in the quirky problems of process coordination, and not in the properties of local, sequential, or deterministic computations.

At this point, two types of criticism of the language we have discussed may legitimately be raised. The first is that the language is too permissive, making it too easy to encode dubious constructs, such as arbitrary `goto` jumps, and unrestricted access to global variables or message channels. Another valid criticism can be that the language is too restrictive, lacking many of the more salient features of implementation languages such as C.

To counter the first criticism, it suffices to note that the purpose of this modeling language is not to *prevent* the construction of dubious constructs, but to allow the user to investigate them thoroughly with the help of formal verification. The language allows us to *expose* dubious constructs not by argument but by verification, especially in cases where the designer never suspected that there could possibly be a problem.

So if the language is not too permissive, is it too restrictive? Why, for instance, not use full C as the specification language for SPIN? The sobering answer is that we would quickly find that virtually all properties of interest would become undecidable. We can only obtain an effectively useful verification system by imposing some reasonable limits on what can be specified. There is no possibility, for instance, to define an infinite buffer in basic PROMELA, or to describe systems that would require the creation of an infinite number data objects or processes to execute. Attempts to do so are pedantically flagged as errors by the SPIN verifier. Fortunately, we will see that it is not hard to live within the self-imposed limits. With some experience in model construction, we can prove or disprove critical correctness properties of even very substantial systems. The parsimony of PROMELA has another benefit, which is that compared to more elaborate implementation or specification languages, it takes most users relatively little time to learn the main concepts well enough to start writing models with confidence.

Curiously, in this context, one of the more interesting recent extensions of the PROMELA language has broken with the strict enforcement of the rule of parsimony by allowing the inclusion of embedded fragments of C code into SPIN models. This extension allows us to come very close to the modeling of implementation level code, especially when we use automated model extraction tools. With the additional power come additional dangers. As Brian Kernighan and Rob Pike once put it: "C is a razor-sharp tool, with which one can create an elegant and efficient program or a bloody mess."

We discuss model extraction techniques and the extensions that allow the use of embedded C code in SPIN models in Chapters 10 and 17.

BIBLIOGRAPHIC NOTES

The quote about C from the last section appeared first on page 71 of Kernighan and Pike [1999].

The producer-consumer problem is one of the many intriguing problems in concurrent systems design that were first introduced and solved by Edsger Dijkstra. The example first appeared in a series of lecture notes that Dijkstra wrote in early 1965, and made available to friends and colleagues as EWD123. A revised version of the report was later distributed more broadly as Dijkstra [1968].

The mutual exclusion problem that we referred to in this chapter also has a long and colorful history. The problem was first clearly articulated in Dijkstra [1965], and has triggered a long series of papers and books that continues to this day. We will not attempt to summarize the debate about mutual exclusion here. A good starting point for a study can be Raynal [1986], or Lamport [1986].

A start with the design of the PROMELA language was made in 1979 to support the specification of verification models for SPIN's earliest predecessor PAN,[5] as described in Holzmann [1981]. There was no firm name for the language at first, although for brief moments we used the terms PSL, short for *Process Specification Language*, PROTO, short for *Proto*-typing language, and even the non-acronym "Argos" in Holzmann [1987].

The language was influenced in important ways by Dijkstra [1975]. Dijkstra's proposal for a non-deterministic guarded command language, though, did not contain primitives for message passing. The syntax for the notation that was adopted in PROMELA was taken from Hoare's CSP language, as documented in Hoare [1978].

---

5. PAN was originally the name of a stand-alone tool, and was short for *Protocol Analyzer*. Many years later, we reused the name for the verifiers that can be generated by SPIN. The name is now more comfortably understood as an acronym for *Process Analyzer*.

A third influence on the design of PROMELA that is often mentioned is the programming language C, as first described in Kernighan and Ritchie [1978]. This influence is also mostly restricted to syntax. Though PROMELA was influenced by several other languages, there are important differences that we will discuss in more detail in Chapter 3. The differences are motivated by the unique purpose that PROMELA has. PROMELA models are not meant to be analyzed manually, and they are not meant to be used as implementations. The purpose of a PROMELA model is solely to support the effective, automated verification of problems in distributed systems design.

AN OVERVIEW OF PROMELA **3**

"What we see depends on mainly what we look for."
(Sir John Lubbock, 1834–1913)

In the last chapter we saw that the emphasis in PROMELA models is placed on the coordination and synchronization aspects of a distributed system, and not on its computational aspects. There are some good reasons for this choice. First, the design and verification of correct coordination structures for distributed systems software tends to be much harder in practice than the design of a non-interactive sequential computation, such as the computation of compound interest or square roots. Second, the curious situation exists that the logical *verification* of the interaction in a distributed system, though often computationally expensive, can be done more thoroughly and more reliably today than the verification of even the simplest computational procedure. The specification language we use for systems verification is therefore deliberately designed to encourage the user to abstract from the purely computational aspects of a design, and to focus on the specification of process interaction at the system level.

As a result of this specialization, PROMELA contains many features that are not found in mainstream programming languages. These features are intended to facilitate the construction of high-level models of distributed systems, The language supports, for instance, the specification non-deterministic control structures; it includes primitives for process creation, and a fairly rich set of primitives for interprocess communication. The other side of the coin is that the language also lacks some features that are found in most programming languages, such as functions that return values, expressions with side effects, data and functions pointers, etc. The reason is simple: PROMELA is not a programming language. PROMELA is a language for building verification models.

A verification model differs in at least two important ways from a program written in a mainstream programming language such as Java or C.

- A verification model represents an *abstraction* of a design that contains only those aspects of a system that are relevant to the properties one wants to verify.
- A verification model often contains things that are typically not part of an implementation. It can, for instance, include worst-case assumptions about the behavior of the *environment* that may interact with the modeled system, and, most importantly, it either explicitly or implicitly contains a specification of *correctness properties.*

Even though it can be attractive to have a single specification that can serve as both a verification model and as an implementation of a system design — verification and implementation have some fundamentally different objectives. A verification model is comparable in its purpose to the prototype or design model that a civil engineer might construct: it serves to prove that the design principles are sound. Design models are normally not expected to be part of the final implementation of a system.

A full system implementation typically contains more information, and far more detail, than a design model. This means that it can be difficult to find automatic procedures for converting design models into system implementations. The reverse, however, is not necessarily true. In Chapter 10 we will explore means for mechanically extracting the main elements of a verification model directly from an implementation, guided by abstraction techniques. Similarly, in Chapter 17 we will discuss the specific constructs that are available in PROMELA to facilitate model extraction tools. These topics, though, should be considered advanced use of the model checker, so we will conveniently ignore them for now.

In the last chapter we gave a bird's-eye view of the language, briefly touching on some of the main language constructs that are available to build verification models. In this chapter we cover the language more thoroughly. We will try to cover all main language features in a systematic way, starting with the most general constructs, and slowly descending into more of the specifics. We restrict ourselves here to the mechanisms that are at our disposal for describing process behavior and process interaction. In the next chapter we will continue the discussion with a description of the various means we have to define correctness claims. After we have covered these basics, we move on in Chapter 5 to discuss methods for exploiting design abstraction techniques as an aid in the control of verification complexity.

First then, our overview of the basic language for specifying the behavior of concurrently executing, and potentially interacting, processes in a distributed system.

TYPES OF OBJECTS

PROMELA derives many of its notational conventions from the C programming language. This includes, for instance, the syntax for boolean and arithmetic operators, for assignment (a single equals) and equality (a double equals), for variable and parameter declarations, variable initialization and comments, and the use of curly braces to indicate the beginning and end of program blocks. But there are also important differences, prompted by the focus in PROMELA on the construction of high-level models of the interactions in distributed systems.

A PROMELA model is constructed from three basic types of objects:

- Processes
- Data objects
- Message channels

Processes are instantiations of `proctypes`, and are used to define behavior. There must be at least one `proctype` declaration in a model, and for the model to be of much use there will normally also be at least one process instantiation.

A `proctype` body consists of zero or more data declarations, and one or more statements. The semantics of statement execution is somewhat special in PROMELA, since it also doubles as the primary mechanism for enforcing process synchronizations. We have seen some of this in the last chapter, and we will return to it in more detail in the section on *executability* (p. 51).

Process types are always declared globally. Data objects and message channels can be declared either globally, that is, outside all process type declarations, or locally, that is, within a process type declaration. Accordingly, there are only two levels of scope in PROMELA: global and process local. It is, for instance, not possible to restrict the scope of a global object to only a subset of the processes, or to restrict the scope of a local object to only part of a `proctype` body.

The next three sections contain a more detailed discussion of each of the three basic types of objects in PROMELA. This is followed by a discussion of PROMELA's rules for executability, and a more comprehensive overview of the primitives in PROMELA for defining flow of control.

PROCESSES

In the last chapter we saw that we can declare and instantiate processes by prefixing a `proctype` declaration with the keyword `active`. There are several ways to instantiate processes in PROMELA. We can create multiple instantiations of a given `proctype` by adding the desired number in square brackets to the `active` prefix, for instance as follows:

```
active [2] proctype you_run()
{
        printf("my pid is: %d\n", _pid)
}
```

Each running process has a unique process instantiation number. These instantiation numbers are always non-negative, and are assigned in order of creation, starting at zero for the first created process. Each process can refer to its own instantiation number via the predefined local variable _pid. Simulating the example above, for instance, produces the following output:

```
$ spin you_run.pml
my pid is: 0
        my pid is: 1
2 processes created
```

The two processes that are instantiated here each print the value of their process instantiation number and then terminate. The two lines of output happen to come out in numeric order here, but since process execution is asynchronous, it could just as well have been the opposite. By default, during simulation runs, SPIN arranges for the output of each active process to appear in a different column: the *pid* number is used to set the number of tab stops used to indent each new line of output that is produced by a process.[1]

There is also another way to instantiate new PROMELA processes. Any running process can start other processes by using a predefined operator called run. For instance, we could rewrite the last example as follows:

```
proctype you_run(byte x)
{
        printf("x = %d, pid = %d\n", x, _pid)
}

init {
        run you_run(0);
        run you_run(1)
}
```

A disadvantage of this solution is that it often creates one process more than strictly necessary (i.e., the init process). For simulation or implementation, the extra process would not matter too much, but in system verification we usually take every possible precaution to keep the system descriptions at a minimum: avoiding all unnecessary elements.

A simulation run of the last model produces the following result:

---

1. We can now see that the string *hello world* in the last chapter was printed left justified by a happy coincidence. It was because the process executing the statement had *pid* zero. We can suppress the default indentations by invoking spin with option -T (see p. 513).

```
$ spin you_run2.pml
                x = 1, pid = 2
        x = 0, pid = 1
3 processes created
```

In this version of the `proctype` `you_run`, we added a parameter of type `byte`. This formal parameter is initialized in the `run` statement, which appears here in the `init` process. This means that when the "execution" of a `run` statement results in the creation of a new process, all formal parameters from the target `proctype` declaration are initialized to the values of the corresponding actual parameters that are provided in the `run` statement (i.e., parameter passing is by value).

Parameter values, of course, cannot be passed to the `init` process, or to processes that are instantiated as `active proctypes`. If processes created through the use of an `active` prefix have formal parameters, they are treated as if they were local variables, and they are initialized to zero. This initialization rule matches the rule for all data objects in PROMELA: if no explicit initialization is present, an object is always initialized to zero.

A newly created process may, *but need not*, start executing immediately after it is instantiated. Similarly, the new process may, but need not and generally will not, terminate before the process that created it moves on to its next statement. That is: processes do not behave like functions. Each process, no matter how it is created, defines an asynchronous thread of execution that can interleave its statement executions in arbitrary ways with other processes.

We mentioned in passing that `run` is really an *operator*, and therefore technically what so far we have casually referred to as a `run` "statement" is really an *expression*. Technically again, the expression is not "executed" but evaluated. The `run` expression is the only type of expression that can have a side effect when it evaluates to non-zero, but not when it evaluates to zero (i.e., when it fails to instantiate a new process). A run expression is also special in the sense that it can contain only one `run` operator and cannot be combined with any other conditionals.

The value of a `run` expression evaluates to zero if no process can be instantiated, otherwise it evaluates to a non-zero value which equals the process instantiation number of the newly created process. Note that the *pid* returned upon successful process instantiation can never itself be zero, because there must be at least one process running to evaluate the expression. Evaluating a `run` expression, then, produces a value of type `pid` (cf. p. 16, 36).

Because `run` is an operator, we can also change the definition of `init` in the last example into the following version, where the process instantiation numbers are stored in local variables.

```
init {   pid p0, p1;

         p0 = run you_run(0);
         p1 = run you_run(1);
         printf("pids: %d and %d\n", p0, p1)
}
```

Simulating the execution of this model produces:

```
$ spin you_run2.pml
        x = 1, pid = 2
pids: 1 and 2
              x = 0, pid = 1
3 processes created
```

Note that the output from the three processes can again appear in any order because of the concurrent nature of the executions.

Finiteness: Why would evaluating a run expression ever *fail* to instantiate a new process, and return zero? The reason lies in the fact that a PROMELA model can only define finite systems. Enforcing that restriction helps to guarantee that any correctness property that can be stated in PROMELA is decidable. It is impossible to define a PROMELA model for which the total number of reachable system states can grow to infinity. Data objects can only have a finite range of possible values; there can be only finitely many active processes, finitely many message channels, and every such channel can have only finite capacity. The language does not prescribe a precise bound for all these quantities, other than that there is such a bound and that it is finite. For all currently existing versions of SPIN, the bound on the number of active processes and the bound on the number of message channels is put at 255.

An attempt to ignore these bounds will necessarily fail. For instance, we could try to define the following model:

```
active proctype splurge(int n)
{       pid p;
        printf("%d\n", n);
        p = run splurge(n+1)
}
```

Simulating the execution of this model with SPIN, using the -T option to disable the default indentation of printf output, produces the following result:

```
$ spin -T splurge.pml
0
1
2
3
...
```

```
252
253
254
spin: too many processes (255 max)
255 processes created
```

The creation of the 256th process fails (note that the process numbering start at zero) and ends the simulation run. But there are more interesting things to discover here, not just about how processes are instantiated, but also about how they can terminate and die. Process termination and process death are two distinct events in PROMELA.

- A process "terminates" when it reaches the end of its code, that is, the closing curly brace at the end of the proctype body from which it was instantiated.
- A process can only "die" and be removed as an active process if all processes that were instantiated later than this process have died first.

Processes can *terminate* in any order, but they can only *die* in the reverse order of their creation. When a process reaches the end of its code this only signifies process *termination*, but not process *death*. When a process has terminated, this means that it can no longer execute statements, but will still be counted as an active process in the system. Specifically, the process *pid* number remains associated with this process and cannot be reused for a new process. When a process dies, it is removed from the system and its *pid* can be reused for another process.

This means that each instantiation of the proctype splurge in the last example *terminates* immediately after it creates the next process, but none of these processes can *die* until the process creation fails for the first time on the 255th attempt. That last process is the first process that can die and be removed from the system, since it is the most recently created process in the system. Once this happens, its immediate predecessor can die, followed by its predecessor, and all the way back to the first created process in stack order, until the number of active processes drops to zero, and the simulation ends.

PROVIDED CLAUSES
Process execution is normally only guided by the rules of synchronization captured in the statement semantics of proctype specifications. It is possible, though, to define additional global constraints on process executions. This can be done with the help of the keyword provided which can follow the parameter list of a proctype declaration, as illustrated in the following example:

```
bool    toggle = true;         /* global variables   */
short   cnt;                   /* visible to A and B */

active proctype A() provided (toggle == true)
{
L:      cnt++;              /* means: cnt = cnt+1 */
        printf("A: cnt=%d\n", cnt);
        toggle = false; /* yield control to B */
        goto L              /* do it again */
}

active proctype B() provided (toggle == false)
{
L:      cnt--;              /* means: cnt = cnt-1 */
        printf("B: cnt=%d\n", cnt);
        toggle = true;  /* yield control to A */
        goto L
}
```

The `provided` clauses used in this example force the process executions to alternate, producing an infinite stream of output:

```
$ spin toggle.pml | more
A: cnt=1
        B: cnt=0
A: cnt=1
        B: cnt=0
A: cnt=1
        B: cnt=0
A: cnt=1
...
```

A process cannot take any step unless its `provided` clause evaluates to *true*. An absent `provided` clause defaults to the expression *true*, imposing no additional constraints on process execution.

Provided clauses can be used to implement non-standard process scheduling algorithms. This feature can carry a price-tag in system verification, though. The use of `provided` clauses can disable some of SPIN's most powerful search optimization algorithms (cf. Chapter 9).

DATA OBJECTS

There are only two levels of scope in PROMELA models: global and process local. Naturally, within each level of scope, all objects must be declared before they can first be referenced. Because there are no intermediate levels of scope, the scope of a global variable cannot be restricted to just a subset of processes, and the scope of a process local variable cannot be restricted to specific blocks of statements. A local variable can be referenced from its point of declaration to the end of the `proctype` body in which it appears,

Table 3.1 Basic Data Types

Type	Typical Range
bit	0,1
bool	*false,true*
byte	0..255
chan	1..255
mtype	1..255
pid	0..255
short	$-2^{15} .. 2^{15} - 1$
int	$-2^{31} .. 2^{31} - 1$
unsigned	$0 .. 2^n - 1$

even when it appears in a nested block (i.e., a piece of code enclosed in curly braces). This is illustrated by the following example:

```
init {
        /* x declared in outer block */
        int x;
        {       /* y declared in inner block */
                int y;
                printf("x = %d, y = %d\n", x, y);
                x++;
                y++;
        }
        /* y remains in scope */
        printf("x = %d, y = %d\n", x, y);
}
```

When simulated this model produces the output:

```
$ spin scope.pml
x = 0, y = 0
x = 1, y = 1
1 process created
```

Table 3.1 summarizes the basic data types in PROMELA, and the typical range of values that corresponds to each type on most machines.

The data type unsigned, like its counterpart in the C programming language, can be used to declare a quantity that is stored in a user-defined number of bits n, with $1 \leq n \leq 32$. With just two exceptions, these data types can store only unsigned values. The two exceptions are short and int, which can hold either positive or negative values. The precise value ranges of the various types is implementation dependent. For short, int, and unsigned, the effective range matches those of the same types in C programs when compiled on the same hardware. For `byte`, `chan`, `mtype`, and `pid`, the range matches that of the type `unsigned char` in C programs. The value ranges for `bit` and `bool` are always restricted to two values.

Typical declarations of variables of these basic types include:

```
bit   x, y;             /* two single bits, initially 0    */
bool turn = true;       /* boolean value, initially true   */
byte a[12];             /* all elements initialized to 0    */
chan m;                 /* uninitialized message channel    */
mtype n;                /* uninitialized mtype variable     */
short b[4] = 89;        /* all elements initialized to 89   */
int   cnt = 67;         /* integer scalar, initially 67     */
unsigned v : 5;         /* unsigned stored in 5 bits        */
unsigned w : 3 = 5;     /* value range 0..7, initially 5    */
```

Only one-dimensional arrays of variables are supported, although there are indirect ways of defining multidimensional arrays through the use of structure definitions, as we will see shortly. All variables, including arrays, are by default initialized to zero, independent of whether they are global or local to a process.

Variables always have a strictly bounded range of possible values. The variable `w` in the last example, for instance, can only contain values that can be stored in three bits of memory: from zero to seven. A variable of type `short`, similarly, can only contain values that can be stored in sixteen bits of memory (cf. Table 3.1). In general, if a value is assigned to a variable that lies outside its declared domain, the assigned value is automatically truncated. For instance, the assignment

```
byte a = 300;
```

results in the assignment of the value 44 (300%256). When such an assignment is performed during random or guided simulations, SPIN prints an error message to alert the user to the truncation. The warning is not generated during verification runs, to avoid generating large volumes of repetitive output.

As usual, multiple variables of the same type can be grouped behind a single type name, as in:

```
byte a, b[3] = 1, c = 4;
```

In this case, the variable named `a` is, by default, initialized to zero; all elements of array `b` are initialized to one, and variable `c` is initialized to the value four.

Variables of type `mtype` can hold symbolic values that must be introduced with one or more `mtype` declarations. An `mtype` declaration is typically placed at the start of the specification, and merely enumerates the names, for instance, as follows:

```
mtype = { appel, pear, orange, banana };
mtype = { fruit, vegetables, cardboard };

init {
        mtype n = pear; /* initialize n to pear */

        printf("the value of n is ");
        printm(n);
        printf("\n")
}
```

Of course, none of the names specified in an `mtype` declaration can match reserved words from PROMELA, such as `init`, or `short`.

As shown here, there is a special predefined print routine `printm` that can be used to print the symbolic name of an `mtype` variable. There can be multiple `mtype` declarations in a model, but distinct declarations do not declare distinct types. The last model, for instance, is indistinguishable to SPIN from a model with a single `mtype` declaration, containing the concatenation (in reverse order) of the two lists, as in:

```
mtype = { fruit, vegetables, cardboard,
          appel, pear, orange, banana };
```

Because of the restricted value range of the underlying type, no more than 255 symbolic names can be declared in all `mtype` declarations combined. The SPIN parser flags an error if this limit is exceeded.

DATA STRUCTURES

PROMELA has a simple mechanism for introducing new types of record structures of variables. The following example declares two such structures, and uses them to pass a set of data from one process to another in a single, indivisible operation:

```
typedef Field {
        short f = 3;
        byte  g
};

typedef Record {
        byte a[3];
        int fld1;
        Field fld2;
        chan p[3];
        bit b
};

proctype me(Field z) {
        z.g = 12
}
```

```
init {
        Record goo;
        Field  foo;

        run me(foo)
}
```

We have defined two new data types named `Field` and `Record`, respectively. The local variable `goo` in the `init` process is declared to be of type `Record`. As before, all fields in the new data types that are not explicitly initialized (e.g., all fields except `f` in variables of type `Field`) are by default initialized to zero. References to the elements of a structure are written in a dot notation, as in for instance:

```
goo.a[2] = goo.fld2.f + 12
```

A variable of a user-defined type can be passed as a single argument to a new process in `run` statements, as shown in the example, provided that it contains no arrays. So in this case it is valid to pass the variable named `foo` as a parameter to the `run` operator, but using `goo` would trigger an error message from SPIN about the hidden arrays. In the next section we shall see that these structure type names can also be used as a field declarator in channel declarations.

The mechanism for introducing user-defined types allows for an indirect way of declaring multidimensional arrays, even though PROMELA supports only one-dimensional arrays as first class objects. A two-dimensional array can be created, for instance, as follows:

```
typedef Array {
        byte el[4]
};

Array a[4];
```

This creates a data structure of sixteen elements, that can now be referenced as `a[i].el[j]`.

As in C, the indices of an array of `N` elements range from zero to `N-1`.

MESSAGE CHANNELS

Message channels are used to model the exchange of data between processes. They are declared either locally or globally. In the declaration

```
chan qname = [16] of { short, byte, bool }
```

the typename `chan` introduces a channel declaration. In this case, the channel is named `qname`, and it is declared to be capable of storing up to sixteen messages. There can be any finite number of fields per message. In the example, each message is said to consist of three fields: the first is declared to be of type `short`, the second is of type `byte`, and the last is of type `bool`. Each field must be either a user-defined type, such as `Field` from the last section, or a predefined type from Table 3.1. In particular, it is not possible to use an array as a type declarator in a message field. An indirect way of achieving this effect is again to embed the array into a user-defined type, and to use the type name as the type declarator for the message field. Note also that since the type `chan` appears in Table 3.1, it is always valid to use `chan` itself as a field declarator. We can make good use of this capability to pass channel identifiers from one process to another.

The statement

```
qname!expr1,expr2,expr3
```

sends a message with the values of the three expressions listed to the channel that we just created. The value of each expression is cast to the type of the message field that corresponds with its relative position in the list of message parameters. By default[2] the send statement is only executable if the target channel is not yet full, and otherwise it blocks.

The statement

```
qname?var1,var2,var3
```

retrieves a message from the head of the same buffer and stores the values from the three fields into the corresponding variables.

The receive statement is executable only if the source channel is non-empty.

It is an error to send or receive either more or fewer message fields than were declared for the message channel that is addressed.

An alternative, and equivalent, notation for the send and receive operations is to use the first message field as a message type indication, and to enclose the remaining fields in parentheses, for instance, as follows:

```
qname!expr1(expr2,expr3)
qname?var1(var2,var3)
```

Some or all of the parameters to a receive operation can be given as constants (e.g., `mtype` symbolic constants) instead of variables:

```
qname?cons1,var2,cons2
```

In this case, an extra condition on the executability of the receive operation is that the value of all message fields specified as constants match the value of the corresponding fields in the message that is to be received. If we want to use the current value of a variable for this purpose, that is, to constrain the

---

2. This default can be changed with SPIN option -m into one where the send statement is always executable, but the message will be lost when an attempt is made to send a message to a full channel.

receive operation to messages that have a matching field, we can use the pre-defined function `eval`, for instance, as follows:

```
qname?eval(var1),var2,var3
```

In this case, the variable `var1` is evaluated, and its value is used as a constraint on incoming messages, just like a constant. The receive operation is now executable only if a message is available that has a first field with a value that matches the current value of `var1`. If so, the values of `var2` and `var3` are set to the values of the corresponding fields in that message, and the message is removed from channel `qname`.

A simple example of the mechanisms discussed so far is as follows:

```
mtype = { msg0, msg1, ack0, ack1 };

chan    to_sndr = [2] of { mtype };
chan    to_rcvr = [2] of { mtype };

active proctype Sender()
{
again:   to_rcvr!msg1;
         to_sndr?ack1;
         to_rcvr!msg0;
         to_sndr?ack0;
         goto again
}

active proctype Receiver()
{
again:   to_rcvr?msg1;
         to_sndr!ack1;
         to_rcvr?msg0;
         to_sndr!ack0;
         goto again
}
```

The model shown here is a simplified version of the alternating bit protocol as defined by Bartlett, Scantlebury, and Wilkinson [1969]. We will extend it into a more complete version shortly, after we have covered a little bit more of the language.

The declaration

```
mtype = { msg0, msg1, ack0, ack1 };
```

introduces the four types of messages we will consider as symbolic constants.

We have used a label, named `again` in each `proctype` and a `goto` statement, with the usual semantics. We talk in more detail about control-flow constructs towards the end of this chapter. The first ten steps of a simulation run with the model above generate the following output.

```
$ spin -c -u10 alternatingbit.pml
proc 0 = Sender
proc 1 = Receiver
q    0    1
   1    to_rcvr!msg1
   1    .    to_rcvr?msg1
   2    .    to_sndr!ack1
   2    to_sndr?ack1
   1    to_rcvr!msg0
   1    .    to_rcvr?msg0
   2    .    to_sndr!ack0
   2    to_sndr?ack0
- - - - - - - - - - - - -
depth-limit (-u10 steps) reached
- - - - - - - - - - - - -
. . .
```

We have used the SPIN option -c to generate a columnated display of just the send and receive operations, which in many cases gives us just the right type of information about process interaction patterns. Every channel and every process is assigned an identifying instantiation number. Each column in the display above corresponds to a process number as before. Each row (line) of output also contains the instantiation number of the channel that is addressed in the left margin.

We have also used the SPIN option -u10 to limit the maximum number of steps that will be executed in the simulation to ten.

There are many more operations in PROMELA that may be performed on message channels. We will review the most important operations here.

The predefined function len(qname) returns the number of messages that is currently stored in channel qname. Some shorthands for the most common uses of this function are: empty(qname), nempty(qname), full(qname), and nfull(qname) with the obvious connotations.

In some cases we may want to test whether a send or receive operation would be executable, without actually executing the operation. To do so, we can transform each of the channel operations into a side effect free expression. It is, for instance, not valid to say:

```
(a > b && qname?msg0)              /* not valid */
```

or

```
(len(qname) == 0 && qname!msg0)   /* not valid */
```

because these expressions cannot be evaluated without side effects, or more to the point, because send and receive operations do not qualify as expressions (they are i/o statements).

To state a condition that should evaluate to *true* when both (a > b) and the first message in channel qname is of type msg0, we can, however, write in

PROMELA:

```
(a > b && qname?[msg0])                /* valid */
```

The expression qname?[msg0] is *true* precisely when the receive statement qname?msg0 would be executable at the same point in the execution, but the actual receive is not executed, only its precondition is evaluated. Any receive statement can be turned into a side effect free expression in a similar way, by placing square brackets around the list of message parameters. The channel contents remain undisturbed by the evaluation of such expressions.

CHANNEL POLL OPERATIONS

It is also possible to limit the effect of a receive statement to just the copying of parameter values from message fields, without removing the message from the channel. These operations are called *channel poll* operations. Any receive statement can be turned into a poll operation by placing angle brackets around its list of parameters. For instance, assuming that we have declared a channel q with two message fields of type int, the receive statement

```
q?<eval(y),x>
```

where x and y are variables, is executable only if channel q contains at least one message *and* if the first field in that message has a value that is equal to the current value of variable y. When the statement is executed the value of the second field in the incoming message is copied into variable x, but the message itself is not removed from the channel.

SORTED SEND AND RANDOM RECEIVE

Two other types of send and receive statements are used less frequently: sorted send and random receive. A sorted send operation is written with two, instead of one, exclamation marks, as follows:

```
qname!!msg0
```

A sorted send operation inserts a message into the channel's buffer in numerical, rather than in FIFO, order. For instance, if a process sends the numbers from one to ten into a channel in random order, but using the sorted send operation, the channel automatically sorts them, and stores them in numerical order.

When a sorted send operation is executed, the existing contents of the target channel is scanned from the first message towards the last, and the new message is inserted immediately before the first message that follows it in numerical order. To determine the numerical order, all message fields are taken into account and are interpreted as integer values.

The counterpart of the sorted send operation is the random receive. It is written with two, instead of one, question marks:

```
qname??msg0
```

A random receive operation is executable if it is executable for *any* message that is currently buffered in a message channel (instead of being restricted to a match on the first message in the channel). In effect, the random receive operation as implemented in SPIN will always return the *first* message in the channel buffer that matches, so the term "random receive" is a bit of a misnomer.

Normal send and receive operations can freely be combined with sorted send and random receive operations. As a small example, if we consider the channel with the sorted list of integers from one to ten, a normal receive operation can only retrieve the first message, which will be the smallest value one. A random receive operation on the same channel would succeed for any of the values from one to ten: the message need not be at the head of the queue. Of course, a random receive operation only makes sense if at least one of the parameters is a constant, and not a variable. (Note that the value of a variable is not evaluated to a constant unless forced with an `eval` function.)

RENDEZVOUS COMMUNICATION

So far we have talked about asynchronous communication between processes via message channels that are declared for instance as

```
chan qname = [N] of { byte }
```

where N is a positive constant that defines the maximum number of messages that can be stored in the channel. A logical extension is to allow for the declaration

```
chan port = [0] of { byte }
```

to define a rendezvous port. The channel capacity is now zero, that is, the channel `port` can pass, but cannot store messages. Message interactions via such rendezvous ports are by definition synchronous. Consider the following example:

```
mtype = { msgtype };

chan name = [0] of { mtype, byte };

active proctype A()
{       name!msgtype(124);
        name!msgtype(121)
}

active proctype B()
{       byte state;
        name?msgtype(state)
}
```

Channel `name` is a rendezvous port. The two processes synchronously execute their first statement: a handshake on message `msgtype` and a transfer of the value 124 from process A into local variable `state` in process B. The second statement in process A is unexecutable (it blocks), because there is no matching receive operation for it in process B.

If the channel `name` is defined with a non-zero buffer capacity, the behavior is different. If the buffer size is at least two, the process of type A can complete its execution, before its peer even starts. If the buffer size is one, the sequence of events is as follows. The process of type A can complete its first send action, but it blocks on the second, because the channel is now filled to capacity. The process of type B can then retrieve the first message and terminate. At this point A becomes executable again and also terminates, leaving its second message as a residual in the channel.

Rendezvous communication is binary: only two processes, a sender and a receiver, can meet in a rendezvous handshake.

Message parameters are always passed by value in PROMELA. This still leaves open the possibility to pass the *value* of a locally declared and instantiated message channel from one process to another. The value stored in a variable of type `chan` is nothing other than the channel identity that is needed to address the channel in send and receive operations. Even though we cannot send the name of the variable in which a channel identity is stored, we can send the identity itself as a value, and thereby make even a local channel accessible to other processes. When the process that declares and instantiates a channel dies, though, the corresponding channel object disappears, and any attempt to access it from another process fails (causing an error that can be caught in verification mode).

As an example, consider the following model:

```
mtype = { msgtype };

chan glob = [0] of { chan };

active proctype A()
{       chan loc = [0] of { mtype, byte };
        glob!loc;
        loc?msgtype(121)
}

active proctype B()
{       chan who;
        glob?who;
        who!msgtype(121)
}
```

There are two channels in this model, declared and instantiated in two different levels of scope. The channel named `glob` is initially visible to both processes. The channel named `loc` is initially only visible to the process that contains its declaration. Process A sends the value of its local channel variable to process B via the global channel, and thereby makes it available to that process for further communications. Process B now transmits a message of the proper type via a rendezvous handshake on that channel and both processes can terminate. When process A dies, channel loc is destroyed and any further attempts to use it will cause an error.

RULES FOR EXECUTABILITY

The definition of PROMELA centers on its semantics of *executability*, which provides the basic means in the language for modeling process synchronizations. Depending on the system state, any statement in a SPIN model is either *executable* or *blocked*. We have already seen four basic types of statements in PROMELA: print statements, assignments, i/o statements, and expression statements. A curiosity in PROMELA is indeed that expressions can be used as if they were statements in any context. They are "executable" (i.e., passable) if and only if they evaluate to the boolean value *true*, or equivalently to a non-zero integer value. The semantics rules of PROMELA further state that print statements and assignments are always unconditionally executable. If a process reaches a point in its code where it has no executable statements left to execute, it simply blocks.

For instance, instead of writing a busy wait loop

```
while (a != b)   /* while is not a keyword in Promela  */
        skip;    /* do nothing, while waiting for a==b */
```

we achieve the same effect in PROMELA with the single statement

```
(a == b);        /* block until a equals b */
```

The same effect could be obtained in PROMELA with constructions such as

```
L:        /* dubious */
          if
          :: (a == b) -> skip
          :: else -> goto L
          fi
```

or

```
do      /* also dubious */
:: (a == b) -> break
:: else -> skip
od
```

but this is always less efficient, and is frowned upon by PROMELA natives. (We will cover selection and repetition structures in more detail starting at p. 56.)

We saw earlier that expressions in PROMELA must be side effect free. The reason will be clear: a blocking expression statement may have to be evaluated many times over before it becomes executable, and if each evaluation could have a side effect, chaos would result. There is one exception to the rule. An expression that contains the `run` operator we discussed earlier can have a side effect, and it is therefore subject to some syntactic restrictions. The main restriction is that there can be only one `run` operator in an expression, and if it appears it cannot be combined with any other operators. This, of course, still allows us to use a `run` statement as a potentially blocking expression. We can indicate this effect more explicitly if instead of writing

```
run you_run(0);          /* potentially blocking */
```

without change of meaning, we write

```
(run you_run(0)) ->      /* potentially blocking */
```

Consider, for instance, what the effect is if we use such a `run` expression in the following model, as a variation on the model we saw on p. 39.

```
active proctype new_splurge(int n)
{
        printf("%d\n", n);
        run new_splurge(n+1)
}
```

As before, because of the bound on the number of processes that can be running simultanesously, the 255th attempt to instantiate a new process will fail. The failure causes the `run` expression to evaluate to zero, and thereby it permanently blocks the process. The blocked process can now not reach the end of its code and it therefore cannot terminate or die. As a result, none of its predecessors can die either. The system of 255 processes comes to a grinding halt with 254 processes terminated but blocked in their attempt to die, and one process blocked in its attempt to start a new process.

If the evaluation of the `run` expression returns zero, execution blocks, but no side effects have occurred, so there is again no danger of repeated side effects in consecutive tests for executability. If the evaluation returns non-zero, there is a side effect as the execution of the statement completes, but the statement as a whole cannot block now. It would decidedly be dubious if compound conditions could be built with `run` operators. For instance,

```
run you_run(0) && run you_run(1)        /* not valid */
```

would block if both processes could not be instantiated, but it would not reveal whether one process was created or none at all. Similarly,

```
run you_run(0) || run you_run(1)        /* not valid */
```

would block if both attempts to instantiate a process fail, but if successful would not reveal which of the two processes was created.

ASSIGNMENTS AND EXPRESSIONS
As in C, the assignments

```
    c = c + 1; c = c - 1      /* valid */
```

can be abbreviated to

```
    c++; c--                  /* valid */
```

but, unlike in C,

```
    b = c++
```

is not a valid assignment in PROMELA, because the right-hand side operand is not a side effect free expression. There is no equivalent to the shorthands

```
    --c; ++c                  /* not valid */
```

in PROMELA, because assignment statements such as

```
    c = c-1; c = c+1          /* valid */
```

when taken as a unit are not equivalent to expressions in PROMELA. With these constraints, a statement such as `--c` is always indistinguishable from `c--`, which is supported.

In assignments such as

```
    variable = expression
```

the values of all operands used in the expression on the right-hand side of the assignment operator are first cast to signed integers, before any of the operands are applied. The operator precedence rules from C determine the order of evaluation, as reproduced in Table 3.2. After the evaluation of the right-hand side expression completes, and before the assignment takes place, the value produced is cast to the type of the target variable. If the right-hand side yields a value outside the range of the target type, truncation of the assigned value can result. In simulation mode SPIN issues a warning when this occurs; in verification mode, however, this type of truncation is not intercepted.

It is also possible to use C-style conditional expressions in any context where expressions are allowed. The syntax, however, is slightly different from the one used in C. Where in C one would write

```
    expr1 ? expr2 : expr3          /* not valid */
```

one writes in PROMELA

```
    (expr1 -> expr2 : expr3)        /* valid */
```

The arrow symbol is used here to avoid possible confusion with the question mark from PROMELA receive operations. The value of the conditional expression is equal to the value of `expr2` if and only if `expr1` evaluates to *true* and otherwise it equals the value of `expr3`. PROMELA conditional expressions must be surrounded by parentheses (round braces) to avoid misinterpretation of the arrow as a statement separator.

Table 3.2 Operator Precedence, High to Low

Operators	Associativity	Comment
() [] .	left to right	parentheses, array brackets
! ˜ ++ --	right to left	negation, complement, increment, decrement
* / %	left to right	multiplication, division, modulo
+ -	left to right	addition, subtraction
<< >>	left to right	left and right shift
< <= > >=	left to right	relational operators
== !=	left to right	equal, unequal
&	left to right	bitwise and
ˆ	left to right	bitwise exclusive or
|	left to right	bitwise or
&&	left to right	logical and
||	left to right	logical or
-> :	right to left	conditional expression operators
=	right to left	assignment (lowest precedence)

CONTROL FLOW: COMPOUND STATEMENTS

So far, we have mainly focused on the basic statements of PROMELA, and the way in which they can be combined to model process behavior. The main types of statements we have mentioned so far are: print and assignment statements, expressions, and send and receive statements.

We saw that `run` is an operator, which makes a statement such as `run sender()` an expression. Similarly, `skip` is not a statement but an expression: it is equivalent to `(1)` or *true*.

There are five types of compound statements in PROMELA:
- Atomic sequences
- Deterministic steps
- Selections
- Repetitions
- Escape sequences

Another control flow structuring mechanism is available through the definition of macros and PROMELA inline functions. We discuss these constructs in the remaining subsections of this chapter.

ATOMIC SEQUENCES

The simplest compound statement is the atomic sequence. A simple example of an atomic sequence is, for instance:

```
atomic {              /* swap the values of a and b */
        tmp = b;
        b = a;
        a = tmp
}
```

In the example, the values of two variables a and b are swapped in a sequence of statement executions that is defined to be uninterruptable. That is, in the interleaving of process executions, no other process can execute statements from the moment that the first statement of this sequence begins to execute until the last one has completed.

It is often useful to use `atomic` sequences to initialize a series of processes in such a way that none of them can start executing statements until the initialization of all of them has been completed:

```
init {
        atomic {
                run A(1,2);
                run B(2,3)
}         }
```

Atomic sequences may be non-deterministic. If, however, any statement inside an atomic sequence is found to be unexecutable (i.e., blocks the execution), the atomic chain is broken and another process can take over control. When the blocking statement becomes executable later, control can non-deterministically return to the process, and the atomic execution of the sequence resumes as if it had not been interrupted.

Note carefully that without atomic sequences, in two subsequent statements such as

```
nfull(qname)  -> qname!msg0
```

or

```
qname?[msg0]  -> qname?msg0
```

the second statement is not necessarily executable after the first one is executed. There may be race conditions when access to the channels is shared between several processes. In the first example, another process can send a message to the channel just after this process determined that it was not full. In the second example, another process can steal away the message just after our process determined its presence. On the other, it would be redundant to write

```
atomic { qname?[msg0]  -> qname?msg0 }
```

since this is equivalent to the single statement

```
qname?msg0
```

DETERMINISTIC STEPS

Another way to define an indivisible sequence of actions is to use the `d_step` statement. In the above case, for instance, we could also have written:

```
d_step {   /* swap the values of a and b */
        tmp = b;
        b = a;
        a = tmp
}
```

Unlike an atomic sequence, a `d_step` sequence is always executed as if it were a single statement: it is intended to provide a means for defining new types of primitive statements in PROMELA. This restricts the use of `d_step` sequences in several ways, compared to atomic sequences:

- The execution of a `d_step` sequence is always deterministic. If non-determinism is encountered in a `d_step` sequence, it is resolved in a fixed way, for example, by executing the first true guard in each non-deterministic selection or repetition structure. The precise way in which the non-determinism inside `d_step` sequences is resolved is undefined.
- No `goto` jumps into or out of `d_step` sequences are permitted: they will be flagged as errors by the SPIN parser.
- The execution of a `d_step` sequence may not be interrupted by blocking statements. It is an error if any statement other than the first one (the *guard* statement) in a `d_step` sequence is found to be unexecutable.

None of the above three restrictions apply to atomic sequences. This means that the keyword `d_step` can always be replaced with the keyword `atomic`, but not vice versa. It is safe to embed `d_step` sequences inside atomic sequences, but the reverse is not allowed.

SELECTION

Using the relative values of two variables `a` and `b` we can define a choice between the execution of two different options with a selection structure, as follows:

```
if
:: (a != b) -> option1
:: (a == b) -> option2
fi
```

The selection structure above contains two execution sequences, each preceded by a double colon. Only one sequence from the list will be executed. A sequence can be selected only if its first statement, that is, the first statement that follows the double colon, is executable. The first statement is therefore called the *guard* of the option sequence.

In the last example the guards are mutually exclusive, but they need not be. If more than one guard is executable, one of the corresponding sequences is selected nondeterministically. If all guards are unexecutable the process will block until at least one of them can be selected. There is no restriction on the type of statements that can be used as a guard: it may include sends or receives, assignments, `printf`, `skip`, etc. The rules of executability determine in each case what the semantics of the complete selection structure will be. The following example, for instance, illustrates the use of send statements as guards in a selection.

```
mtype = { a, b };

chan ch = [1] of { mtype };

active proctype A() { ch?a }

active proctype B() { ch?b }

active proctype C()
{       if
        :: ch!a
        :: ch!b
        fi
}
```

The example defines three processes and one channel. The first option in the selection structure of the process of type `C` is executable if channel `ch` is non-full, a condition that is satisfied in the initial state. Since both guards are executable, the process of type `C` can arbitrarily pick one, and execute it, depositing a message in channel `ch`. The process of type `A` can execute its sole statement if the message sent was an a, where a is a symbolic constant defined in the `mtype` declaration at the start of the model. Its peer process of type `B` can execute its sole statement if the message is of type b, where, similarly, b is a symbolic constant.

If we switch all send statements for receive statements, and vice versa, we also get a valid PROMELA model. This time, the choice in `C` is forced by the message that gets sent into the channel, which in turn depends on the unknown relative speeds of execution of the processes of type `A` and `B`. In both versions of the model, one of the three running processes hangs at the end of system execution, and will fail to terminate.

A process of the following type either increments or decrements the value of variable `count`. Because assignments are always executable, the choice made here is truly a non-deterministic one that is independent of the initial value of the variable `count`.

```
byte count;        /* initial value defaults to zero */

active proctype counter()
{
        if
        :: count++
        :: count--
        fi
}
```

REPETITION

We can modify the last model to obtain a cyclic program that randomly changes the value of the variable up or down by replacing the selection structure with a repetition.

```
byte count;

active proctype counter()
{
        do
        :: count++
        :: count--
        :: (count == 0)  -> break
        od
}
```

As before, only one option can be selected for execution at a time. After the option completes, the execution of the repetition structure is repeated. The normal way to terminate the repetition structure is with a `break` statement. In the example, the loop can be broken only when the count reaches zero. Note, however, that it need not terminate since the other two options always remain executable. To force termination we could modify the program as follows:

```
active proctype counter()
{
        do
        :: (count != 0)  ->
                if
                :: count++
                :: count--
                fi
        :: (count == 0) -> break
        od
}
```

A special type of statement that is useful in selection and repetition structures is the `else` statement. An `else` statement becomes executable only if no other statement within the same process, at the same control-flow point, is executable. We could try to use it in two places in the example, as follows:

```
active proctype counter()
{
        do
        :: (count != 0) ->
                if
                :: count++
                :: count--
                :: else
                fi
        :: else -> break
        od
}
```

The first `else`, inside the nested selection structure, can never become executable though, and is therefore redundant (both alternative guards of the selection are assignments, which are always executable). The second use of the `else`, however, becomes executable exactly when `!(count != 0)` or `(count == 0)`, and therefore preserves the option to break from the loop.

There is also an alternative way to exit the do-loop, without using a `break` statement: the infamous `goto`. This is illustrated in the following PROMELA implementation of Euclid's algorithm for finding the greatest common divisor of two non-zero, positive numbers.

```
proctype Euclid(int x, y)
{
        do
        :: (x >  y) -> x = x - y
        :: (x <  y) -> y = y - x
        :: (x == y) -> goto done
        od;

done:
        printf("answer: %d\n", x)
}

init { run Euclid(36, 12) }
```

Simulating the execution of this model, with the numbers given, yields:

```
$ spin euclid.pml
        answer: 12
2 processes created
```

The `goto` in this example jumps to a label named `done`. Multiple labels may be used to label the same statement, but at least one statement is required. If, for instance, we wanted to omit the `printf` statement behind the label, we must replace it with a dummy `skip`. Like a `skip`, a `goto` statement is always executable and has no other effect than to change the control-flow point of the process that executes it.

With these extra constructs, we can now also define a slightly more complete description of the alternating bit protocol (cf. p. 46).

```
mtype = { msg, ack };

chan    to_sndr = [2] of { mtype, bit };
chan    to_rcvr = [2] of { mtype, bit };

active proctype Sender()
{       bool seq_out, seq_in;
        do
        :: to_rcvr!msg(seq_out) ->
                to_sndr?ack(seq_in);
                if
                :: seq_in == seq_out ->
                        seq_out = 1 - seq_out;
                :: else
                fi
        od
}

active proctype Receiver()
{       bool seq_in;
        do
        :: to_rcvr?msg(seq_in) ->
                to_sndr!ack(seq_in)
        :: timeout ->    /* recover from msg loss */
                to_sndr!ack(seq_in)
        od
}
```

The sender transmits messages of type msg to the receiver, and then waits for an acknowledgement of type ack with a matching sequence number. If an acknowledgement with the wrong sequence number comes back, the sender retransmits the message. The receiver can timeout while waiting for a new message to arrive, and will then retransmit its last acknowledgement.

The semantics of PROMELA's timeout statement is very similar to that of the else statement we saw earlier. A timeout is defined at the system level, though, and an else statement is defined at the process level. timeout is a predefined global variable that becomes *true* if and only if there are no executable statements at all in any of the currently running processes. The primary purpose of timeout is to allow us to model recovery actions from potential deadlock states. Note carefully that timeout is a predefined variable and not a function: it takes no parameters, and in particular it is not possible to specify a numeric argument with a specific timebound after which the timeout should become executable. The reason is that the types of properties we would like to prove for PROMELA models must be fully independent of all absolute and relative timing considerations. The relative speeds of processes is a fundamentally unknown and unknowable quantity in an asynchronous system.

ESCAPE SEQUENCES

The last type of compound structure to be discussed is the `unless` statement. This type of statement is used less frequently, but it requires a little more explanation. It is safe to skip this section on a first reading.

The syntax of an escape sequence is as follows:

```
{ P } unless { E }
```

where the letters `P` and `E` represent arbitrary PROMELA fragments. Execution of the `unless` statement begins with the execution of statements from `P`. Before each statement execution in `P` the executability of the first statement of `E` is checked, using the normal PROMELA semantics of executability. Execution of statements from `P` proceeds only while the first statement of `E` remains unexecutable. The first time that this 'guard of the escape sequence' is found to be executable, control changes to it, and execution continues as defined for `E`. Individual statement executions remain indivisible, so control can only change from inside `P` to the start of `E` in between individual statement executions. If the guard of the escape sequence does not become executable during the execution of `P`, then it is skipped entirely when `P` terminates.

An example of the use of escape sequences is:

```
A;
do
:: b1 -> B1
:: b2 -> B2
. . .
od  unless  { c -> C };
D
```

As shown in the example, the curly braces around the main sequence (or the escape sequence) can be deleted if there can be no confusion about which statements belong to those sequences. In the example, condition `c` acts as a watchdog on the repetition construct from the main sequence. Note that this is not necessarily equivalent to the construct

```
A;
do
:: b1 -> B1
:: b2 -> B2
. . .
:: c -> break
od; C; D
```

if `B1` or `B2` are non-empty. In the first version of the example, execution of the iteration can be interrupted at *any* point inside each option sequence. In the second version, execution can only be interrupted at the start of the option sequences.

An example application of an escape sequence is shown in Figure 3.1. Shown here is a somewhat naive model of the behavior of a *pots* (*p*lain *o*ld *t*elephone *s*ervice) system (cf. Chapter 14, p. 299).

There are two processes in this system, a subscriber and the *pots* server. The subscriber process follows a strict regimen. After going offhook it always waits for a dial tone, and it always sends a number to be connected to when the dial tone message is received. After that it waits to receive either a busy or a ring tone. On seeing a busy tone, our idealized subscriber process hangs up and tries the call again. On seeing a ring tone, it either waits for the signal that the call is connected, or it impatiently hangs up. When connected, it waits for notification from the *pots* server that the remote party has disconnected the call, but if this does not come, it can timeout and terminate the call anyway.

The model of the subscriber behavior is fairly standard, requiring no unusual control-flow constructs. We can be more creative in modeling the *pots* server. The server process starts in its *idle* state by waiting for a subscriber to send an offhook signal together with the channel via which it wants to communicate with the server for this session. The server always complies by sending a dial tone, and then waits for the number to be dialed. Once the number has been received, either a busy tone or a ring tone is chosen, matching the subscriber's expectations at this point in the call. A ring tone is followed by a connected signal, and after this the server process proceeds to the *zombie* state where it waits for the subscriber to hangup the phone, possibly, but not necessarily sending a `hungup` message first. Note that the `skip` and the `goto zombie` statements lead to the same next state in this case (meaning that the `goto` is really redundant here).

Note that we have not included any treatment for a subscriber `hangup` message in this main flow of the *pots* behavior. The reason is that we would like to model the fact that the behavior of the *pots* server can be interrupted at *any* point in this flow if a `hangup` message should unexpectedly arrive. Similarly, if the *pots* server gets stuck at any point in its flow, it should be possible to define a timeout option, without spelling out that very same option at any point in the main flow where the server could possibly get stuck. The escape clause of the `unless` construct spells out the two conditions under which the main flow should be aborted, and gives the actions that must be taken in each case. After a `hangup`, the server simply returns to its *idle* state, since it knows that the subscriber is back onhook. After a *timeout*, it moves to the *zombie* state.

A fragment of the output for a SPIN simulation run for this system follows. The run can in principle be continued *ad infinitum*, so it is prudent to filter the output from SPIN through a utility like `more`. The first two full executions, starting and ending with both processes in their *idle* state, look as follows:

```
mtype = { offhook, dialtone, number, ringing,
          busy, connected, hangup, hungup };

chan line = [0] of { mtype, chan };

active proctype pots()
{       chan who;
idle:   line?offhook,who;
        {       who!dialtone;
                who?number;
                if
                :: who!busy; goto zombie
                :: who!ringing ->
                        who!connected;
                        if
                        :: who!hungup; goto zombie
                        :: skip
                        fi
                fi
        } unless
        {       if
                :: who?hangup -> goto idle
                :: timeout -> goto zombie
                fi
        }
zombie: who?hangup; goto idle
}

active proctype subscriber()
{       chan me = [0] of { mtype };
idle:   line!offhook,me;
        me?dialtone;
        me!number;
        if
        :: me?busy
        :: me?ringing ->
                if
                :: me?connected;
                        if
                        :: me?hungup
                        :: timeout
                        fi
                :: skip
                fi
        fi;
        me!hangup; goto idle
}
```

Figure 3.1 Simple Model of a Telephone System

```
$ spin -c pots.pml | more
proc 0 = pots
proc 1 = subscriber
q\p    0    1
  2    .    line!offhook,1
  2    line?offhook,1
  1    who!dialtone
  1    .    me?dialtone
  1    .    me!number
  1    who?number
  1    who!ringing
  1    .    me?ringing
  1    who!connected
  1    .    me?connected
timeout
  1    .    me!hangup
  1    who?hangup
  2    .    line!offhook,1
  2    line?offhook,1
  1    who!dialtone
  1    .    me?dialtone
  1    .    me!number

  1    who?number
  1    who!ringing
  1    .    me?ringing
  1    .    me!hangup
  1    who?hangup
```

There are no surprises here. The model, though, cannot properly be called a verification model just yet. For that, we would have to add some statement of the requirements or properties that we would like this model to satisfy. We may well ask, for instance, if it is possible for the server to get stuck permanently in the *zombie* state. Only a verification run can give the answer to such questions.

INLINE DEFINITIONS

Some motivation for and examples of the use of PROMELA inline's was already given in the last chapter. The PROMELA inline is meant to provide some of the structuring mechanism of a traditional procedure call, without introducing any overhead during the verification process. The PROMELA parser replaces each point of invocation of an inline with the text of the inline body. If any parameters are used, their actual values from the call will textually replace the formal place holders that are used inside the definition of the inline body. That is, there is no concept of value passing with inline's. The parameter names used inside the definition are mere stand ins for the names provided at the place of call. A small example can clarify the working and intent of this mechanism, as follows:

```
inline example(x, y) {
        y = a;
        x = b;
        assert(x)
}
init {
        int a, b;

        example(a,b)
}
```

In this example we have defined an `inline` named `example` and we gave it two parameters. The parameters do not have a type associated with them. They could in fact be replaced in a call with variables of any type that matches the use of the names inside the `inline` body.

At the point of invocation the names of two variables are provided as actual parameters. The parser treats this code as if we had written the following specification instead:

```
init {
        int a, b;

        b = a;
        a = b;
        assert(a)
}
```

This version of the model is obtained by inserting the body of the `inline` at the point of call, while textually replacing every occurrence of the name x with the name a and every occurrence of y with b, as stipulated by the parameter list at the point of invocation.

We could have achieved the same effect by defining a C-style macro, as follows:

```
#define example(x, y) \
        y = a;  \
        x = b;  \
        assert(x)

init {
        int a, b;

        example(a,b)
}
```

For a small `inline` function the difference is not that remarkable, but for larger pieces of code the macro method can quickly become unwieldy. There is one other benefit to the use of an `inline` compared to a macro definition. When we simulate (or verify) the version of the example using the `inline` definition of `example`, we see the following output:

```
$ spin inline.pml
spin: line    4 "inline", Error: assertion violated
spin: text of failed assertion: assert(a)
#processes: 1
   3:    proc  0 (:init:) line   4 "inline" (state 3)
1 process created
```

Not surprisingly, the assertion is violated. The line number pointed at by SPIN is the location of the `assert` statement inside the `inline` body, as one would expect. If, however, we try to do the same with the version using a macro, we see this result:

```
$ spin macro.pml
spin: line    9 "macro", Error: assertion violated
spin: text of failed assertion: assert(a)
#processes: 1
   3:    proc  0 (:init:) line   9 "macro" (state 3)
1 process created
```

The same assertion violation is reported, but the line number reference now gives the point of invocation of the macro, rather than the location of the failing assertion. Finding the source of an error by searching through possibly complex macro definitions can be challenging, which makes the use of PROMELA `inline`s preferable in most cases.

To help find out what really happens with parameter substitution in `inline` functions and preprocessing macros, option `-I` causes SPIN to generate a version of the source text that shows the result of all macro-processing and inlining on `proctype` bodies. It can be an invaluable source of information in determining the cause of subtle problems with preprocessing. The two versions of our sample program, the first using an `inline` definition and the second using a macro, produce the following results:

```
$ spin -I inline.pml
proctype :init:()
{
    {
      b = a;
      a = b;
      assert(a);
    };
}

$ spin -I macro.pml
proctype :init:()
{
    b = a;
    a = b;
    assert(a);
}
```

Note that the version of the model that is generated with the `-I` option is not itself a complete model. No variable declarations are included, and some of the names used for `proctypes` and labels are the internally assigned names used by SPIN (using, for instance, `:init:` instead of `init`). The `proctype` body text, though, shows the result of all preprocessing.

There is not much difference in the output for the two versions, except that the use of the `inline` function creates a non-atomic sequence (the part enclosed in curly braces), where the macro definition does not. There is no difference in behavior.

When using `inline` definitions, it is good to keep the scope rules of PROMELA in mind. Because PROMELA only knows two levels of scope for variables, global and process local, there is no subscope for `inline` bodies. This means that an attempt to declare a local scratch variable, such as this:

```
inline thisworks (x)  {
        int y;

        y = x;
        printf ("%d\n", y)
}

init {
        int a;
        a = 34;
        thisworks (a)
}
```

produces the following, after inlining is performed:

```
init {
        int a;
        a = 34;

        int y;
        y = a;
        printf ("%d\n", y)
}
```

This works because variable declarations can appear anywhere in a PROMELA model, with their scope extending from the point of declaration to the closing curly brace of the surrounding `proctype` or `init` body. This means that the variable y remains in scope, also after the point of invocation of the `inline`. It would therefore be valid, though certainly confusing, to write

```
inline thisworks2 (x) {
        int y;

        y = x;
        printf ("%d\n", y)
}
```

```
init {
        int a;
        a = 34;
        thisworks(a);
        y = 0
}
```

that is, to access the variable y outside the inline body in which it was declared.

READING INPUT

On an initial introduction to PROMELA it may strike one as odd that there is a generic output statement to communicate information to the user in the form of the printf, but there is no matching scanf statement to read information from the input. The reason is that we want verification models to be *closed* to their environment. A model must always contain *all* the information that could possibly be required to verify its properties. It would be rather clumsy, for instance, if the model checker would have to be stopped dead in its tracks each time it needed to read information from the user's keyboard.

Outputs, like printf, are harmless in this context, since they generate no new information that can affect future behavior of the executing process, but the executing of an input statement like scanf can cause the modification of variable values that can impact future behavior. If input is required, its source must always be represented in the model. The input can then be captured with the available primitives in PROMELA, such as sends and receives.

In one minor instance we deviate from this rather strict standard. When SPIN is used in *simulation mode*, there is a way to read characters interactively from a user-defined input. To enable this feature, it suffices to declare a channel of the reserved type STDIN in a PROMELA model. There is only one message field available on this predefined channel, and it is of type int. The model in Figure 3.2 shows a simple word count program as an example.

We can simulate the execution of this model (but not verify it) by invoking SPIN as follows, feeding the source text for the model itself as input.

```
$ spin wc.pml < wc.pml
27      85      699
1 process created
```

PROMELA supports a small number of other special purpose keywords that can be used to fine-tune verification models for optimal performance of the verifiers that can be generated by SPIN. We mention the most important of these here. (This section can safely be skipped on a first reading.)

SPECIAL FEATURES

The verifiers that can be generated by SPIN by default apply a partial order reduction algorithm that tries to minimize the amount of work done to prove

```
chan STDIN;
int c, nl, nw, nc;

init {
        bool inword = false;

        do
        :: STDIN?c ->
                if
                :: c == -1 ->
                        break    /* EOF */
                :: c == '\n' ->
                        nc++;
                        nl++
                :: else ->
                        nc++
                fi;
                if
                :: c == ' '
                || c == '\t'
                || c == '\n' ->
                        inword = false
                :: else ->
                        if
                        :: !inword ->
                                nw++;
                                inword = true
                        :: else /* do nothing */
                        fi
                fi
        od;
        assert(nc >= nl);
        printf("%d\t%d\t%d\n", nl, nw, nc)
}
```

Figure 3.2 Word Count Program Using STDIN Feature

system properties. The performance of this algorithm can be improved, some-times very substantially, if the user provides some hints about the usage of data objects. For instance, if it is known that some of the message channels are only used to receive messages from a single source process, the user can record this knowledge in a channel assertion.

In the example shown in Figure 3.3, for instance, the number of states that has to be searched by the verifier is reduced by 16 percent if the lines containing the keywords xr and xs are included. (The two keywords are acronyms for *exclusive read* access and *exclusive write* access, respectively.) These

```
mtype = { msg, ack, nak };

chan q = [2] of { mtype, byte };
chan r = [2] of { mtype };

active proctype S()
{       byte s = 1;

        xs q;   /* assert that only S sends to chan q */
        xr r;   /* and only S receives from chan r */

        do
        :: q!msg(s);
                if
                :: r?ack; s++
                :: r?nak
                fi
        od
}
active proctype R()
{       byte ns, s;

        xs r;   /* only R sends messages to chan r */
        xr q;   /* only R retrieves messages from chan q */

        do
        :: q?msg(ns);
                if
                :: (ns == s+1) -> s = ns; r!ack
                :: else -> r!nak
                fi
        od

}
```

Figure 3.3 Using Channel Assertions

statements are called *channel assertions*.

The statements are called assertions because the validity of the claims they make about channel usage can, and will, be checked during verifications. If, for instance, it is possible for a process to send messages to a channel that was claimed to be non-shared by another process, then the verifier can always detect this and it can flag a channel assertion violation. The violation of a channel assertion in effect means that the additional reduction that is based on its presence is invalid. The correct counter-measure is to then remove the channel assertion.

The reduction method used in SPIN (more fully explained in Chapter 9) can also take advantage of the fact that the access to local variables cannot be shared between processes. If, however, the verification model contains a globally declared variable that the user knows to be non-shared, the keyword `local` can be used as a prefix to the variable declaration. For instance, in the last example we could have declared the variable ns from `proctype R` as a global variable, without incurring a penalty for this change from the partial order reduction algorithm, by declaring it globally as:

```
local byte ns;
```

The use of this prefix allows the verifier to treat all access to this variable as if it were access to a process local variable. Other than for channel assertions, though, the verifier does not check if the use of the prefix is unwarranted.

Another case that one occasionally runs into is when a variable is used only as a scratch variable, for temporary use, say, deep inside a `d_step` or an `atomic` sequence. In that case, it can be beneficial to tell the verifier that the variable has no permanent state information and should not be stored as part of the global state-descriptor for the modeled system. We can do so by using the prefix `hidden`. The variable must again be declared globally, for instance, as:

```
hidden int t;
```

In the following PROMELA fragment the variable t is used as a temporary variable that stores no relevant information that must be preserved outside the `d_step` sequence in which it is used:

```
d_step {            /* swap the values of a an b */
        t = a;
        a = b;
        b = t
}
```

As with the use of the `local` prefix, the verifier takes the information on good faith and does not check if the use of the `hidden` keyword is unwarranted. If a hidden variable does contain relevant state information, the search performed by the verifier will be incomplete and the results of the search become unreliable.

There is a third, and last, type of prefix that can be used with variable declarations in special cases. The use of the prefix `show` on a variable declaration, as in

```
show byte cnt;
```

tells SPIN's graphical user interface XSPIN that any value changes of this variable should be visualized in the message sequence charts that it can generate. We will discuss this interface in more detail in Chapter 12.

The `show` prefix can be used on both global and local variable declarations.

FINDING OUT MORE

This concludes our overview of the main features of the PROMELA specification language. A few more seldomly used constructs were only mentioned in passing here, but are discussed in greater detail in the manual pages that are included in Chapters 16 and 17. More examples of PROMELA models are included in Chapters 14 and 15. A definition of the operational semantics for PROMELA can be found in Chapter 7.

Alternate introductions to the language can be found in, for instance, Ruys [2001] and Holzmann [1991]. Several other tutorial-style introductions to the language can also be found on the SPIN Web site (see Appendix D).

DEFINING
CORRECTNESS CLAIMS **4**

If the odds are a million to one against something
occurring, chances are fifty-fifty that it will.
(Folklore wisdom)

The goal of system verification is to establish what is possible and what is not. Often, this assessment of what is logically possible will be subject to some set of assumptions about the context in which a system executes, such as the possible behavior of external components that the system will be interacting with. When performing logical verification we are especially interested in determining whether design requirements could *possibly* be violated, not necessarily in how likely or unlikely such violations might be. Dramatic system failures are almost always the result of seemingly unlikely sequences of events: that is precisely why these sequences of events are often overlooked in the design phase. Once we understand how a requirement may be violated, we can reconsider the original design decisions made, and devise alternate strategies that can prevent the error from occurring. Logical correctness, then, is concerned primarily with *possibilities*, not with *probabilities*.

STRONGER PROOF
This restriction to the possible, rather than the probable, has two implications. For one, it can strengthen the proofs of correctness we can achieve with system verification. If the verifier tells us that there is no possible violation of a given requirement, this is a significantly stronger result than the verdict that violating executions have a low probability of occurrence. Secondly, the restriction makes it possible to perform verification more efficiently than if we attempted to consider also the probability of execution scenarios. The results of probability estimates are further undermined by the difficulty one would face in deriving accurate metrics for the probabilities of execution of specific

statements in the system. Any errors of judgment made here are magnified in the verification process, limiting the value of the final results.

We should be able to prove the essential logical correctness properties of a distributed system independently of *any* assumption about the relative speeds of execution of processes, the time it takes to execute specific instructions, or the probability of occurrence of particular types of events, such as the loss of messages on a transmission channel or the failure of external devices.

The proof of correctness of an algorithm is ideally also implementation independent. Specifically, the correctness of the algorithm should not depend on whether it is implemented on a fast machine or on a slow machine. In the verification process, therefore, we should not rely on such assumptions. It is even desirable that we cannot make such statements at all. Not surprisingly, PROMELA effectively makes it impossible to state any correctness requirement that would violate these rules.

The rules we follow here are specific to our area of interest: the verification of distributed systems software. Different rules apply in, for instance, hardware verification. The correctness of a chip may well depend critically, and unavoidably, on signal propagation delays and the speed of individual circuit elements. Signal propagation times and the layout of circuit elements are part of a chip's design and functionality: they cannot be changed independently from it. The correctness of a data communications protocol or a distributed operating system, on the other hand, should never depend on such issues. The speed of execution of a software system is almost guaranteed to change dramatically over the lifetime of the design.

BASIC TYPES OF CLAIMS

In distributed systems design it is standard to make a distinction between two types of correctness requirements: safety and liveness. Safety is usually defined as the set of properties that the system may not violate, while liveness is defined as the set of properties that the system must satisfy. Safety, then, defines the *bad* things that should be avoided, and liveness defines the *good* things that capture the required functionality of a system. The function of a verification system, however, is not as lofty. It need not, and indeed cannot, determine what is good or bad; it can only help the designer to determine what is *possible* and what is not.

From the point of view of the verifier there are also two types of correctness claims: claims about reachable or unreachable states and claims about feasible or infeasible executions (i.e., sequences of states). The former are sometimes called *state properties* and the latter *path properties*. Paths, or executions, can be either finite or infinite (e.g., cyclic).

A simple type of state property is a *system invariant* that should hold in every reachable state of the system. A slightly weaker version is a *process assertion* that should hold only in specific reachable states. State properties can be combined to build path properties. An example of a path property is, for instance, that every visit to a state with property P must eventually be followed by a visit to a state with property Q, without in the interim visiting any state with property R. The verifier SPIN can check both state and path properties, and both can be expressed in the specification language PROMELA.

Some types of properties are so basic that they need not be stated explicitly. SPIN checks them by default. One such property is, for instance, the absence of reachable *system deadlock* states. The user can, however, modify the semantics of also the built-in checks through a simple form of statement labeling. A deadlock, for instance, is by default considered to be an unintended end state of the system. We can tell the verifier that certain specific end states are intended by placing end-state labels, as we shall see shortly.

Correctness properties are formalized in PROMELA through the use of the following constructs:

- Basic assertions
- End-state labels
- Progress-state labels
- Accept-state labels
- `Never` claims
- Trace assertions

`Never` claims can be written by hand, or they can (often more easily) be automatically generated from *logic formulae* or from *timeline property* descriptions. We will discuss each of these constructs in more detail below.

BASIC ASSERTIONS
Statements of the form

```
assert(expression)
```

are called *basic assertions* in PROMELA to distinguish them from *trace assertions* that we will discuss later. The usefulness of assertions of this type was recognized very early on. A mention of it can even be found in the work of John von Neumann (1903-1957). It reads as follows. Of course, the letter C that is used here does not refer to programming language that would be created some 30 years later:

> It may be true, that whenever C actually reaches a certain point in the flow diagram, one or more bound variables will necessarily possess certain specified values, or possess certain properties, or satisfy certain relations with each other. Furthermore, we may, at such a point, indicate the validity of these limitations. For this reason we will denote each area in which the validity of such limitations is being asserted, by a special box, which we call an 'assertion box.'
>
> Goldstein and von Neumann, 1947

PROMELA basic assertions are always executable, much like assignments, and print or `skip` statements. The execution of this type of statement has no effect provided that the expression that is specified evaluates to the boolean value *true*, or alternatively to a non-zero integer value. The implied correctness property is that it is never possible for the expression to evaluate to *false* (or zero). A failing assertion will trigger an error message.

As also noted in Chapter 2 (p. 18), the trivial model:

```
init { assert(false) }
```

results in the following output when executed:

```
$ spin false.pml
spin: line    1 "false.pml", Error: assertion violated
#processes: 1
  1:    proc  0 (:init:) line    1 "false.pml" (state 1)
1 process created
```

Here SPIN is used in simulation mode. Execution stops at the point in the model where the assertion failure was detected. When the simulation stops, the executing process, with *pid* zero, is at the internal state numbered one. The simulator will always list the precise state at which execution stops for all processes that have been initiated but that have not yet died. If we change the expression used in the assertion to *true*, no output of note will appear, because there are no running processes left when the execution stops with the death of the only process.

```
$ spin true.pml
1 process created
```

An assertion statement is the only type of correctness property in PROMELA that can be checked during simulation runs with SPIN. All other properties discussed in this chapter require SPIN to be run in verification mode to be checked. If SPIN fails to find an assertion violation in any number of simulation runs, this does not mean that the assertions that are embedded in the model that is simulated cannot be violated. Only a verification run with SPIN can establish that result.

META LABELS

Labels in a PROMELA specification ordinarily serve merely as targets for unconditional `goto` jumps. There are three types of labels, though, that have a special meaning when SPIN is run in verification mode. The labels are used to identify:

- End states
- Progress states
- Accept states

END STATES: When a PROMELA model is checked for reachable deadlock states, using SPIN in verification mode, the verifier must be able to distinguish

```
mtype { p, v };

chan sema = [0] of { mtype };

active proctype Dijkstra()
{       byte count = 1;

end:    do
        :: (count == 1) ->
                sema!p; count = 0
        :: (count == 0) ->
                sema?v; count = 1
        od
}

active [3] proctype user()
{       do
        :: sema?p;              /* enter */
critical:   skip;              /* leave */
            sema!v;
        od
}
```

Figure 4.1 Labeling End States

valid system `end` states from invalid ones. By default, the only valid end states, or termination points, are those in which every PROMELA process that was instantiated has reached the end of its code (i.e., the closing curly brace in the corresponding `proctype` body). Not all PROMELA processes, however, are meant to reach the end of their code. Some may very well linger in a known wait state, or they may sit patiently in a loop ready to spring back to action when new input arrives.

To make it clear to the verifier that these alternate end states are also valid, we can define special labels, called `end`-state labels. We have done so, for instance, in Figure 4.1 in process type `Dijkstra`, which models a semaphore with the help of a rendezvous port `sema`. The semaphore guarantees that only one of three user processes can enter its critical section at a time. The `end` label defines that it is not an error if, at the end of an execution sequence, the process has not reached its closing curly brace, but waits at the label. Of course, such a state could still be part of a deadlock state, but if so, it is not caused by this particular process.

There can be any number of end-state labels per PROMELA model, provided that all labels that occur within the same `proctype` body remain unique.

To allow the use of more than one end-state label within the same `proctype`
body, PROMELA uses the rule that every label name that starts with the
three-letter prefix `end` defines an end-state label. The following label names,
therefore, are all counted as valid end-state labels: `endme`, `end0`,
`end_of_this_part`.

In verification mode, SPIN checks for invalid end states by default, so no special precautions need to be made to intercept these types of errors. If, on the
other hand, the user is *not* interested in hearing about these types of errors, the
run-time flag `-E` can be used to suppress these reports. In a similar way, using
the run-time flag `-A` we can disable the reporting of assertion violations (e.g.,
if we are hunting for other types of errors that may appear only later in a verification run). To disable both types of reports for the sample model in Figure
4.1, we would proceed as follows:

```
$ spin -a dijkstra.pml
$ cc -o pan pan.c
$ ./pan -E -A   # add two restrictions
(Spin Version 4.0.7 -- 1 August 2003)
        + Partial Order Reduction

Full statespace search for:
        never claim            - (none specified)
        assertion violations   - (disabled by -A flag)
        acceptance   cycles    - (not selected)
        invalid end states     - (disabled by -E flag)

State-vector 36 byte, depth reached 8, errors: 0
        15 states, stored
         4 states, matched
        19 transitions (= stored+matched)
         0 atomic steps
hash conflicts: 0 (resolved)
(max size 2^18 states)

1.573   memory usage (Mbyte)

unreached in proctype Dijkstra
        line 14, state 10, "-end-"
        (1 of 10 states)
unreached in proctype user
        line 22, state 7, "-end-"
        (1 of 7 states)
```

The output is virtually identical to the one we would get if we had not used
either the `-A` or the `-E` option, since there are neither invalid end states nor
assertion violations in this model. As a reminder of the restrictions used,
though, the verifier duly notes in its output that it has in fact disabled both
types of reports.

A SPIN generated verifier can also be asked to impose a stricter requirement on

end states than the defaults sketched above. If the additional run-time option
-q is used with the compiled verifier, all processes must have reached a valid
end state and all message channels must be empty for a system state to be
considered valid. In the normal case, that is without the -q option, the
requirement on the emptiness of message channels is omitted.

PROGRESS STATES: Similar syntax conventions apply to the use of
PROMELA progress labels. We can use progress labels to mark statements in
a PROMELA model that accomplish something desirable, signifying that the
executing process is making effective progress, rather than just idling or waiting for other processes to make progress. We can use the verification mode of
SPIN to verify that every potentially infinite execution cycle that is permitted
by a model passes through at least one of the progress labels in that model. If
cycles can be found that do not have this property, the verifier can declare the
existence of a non-progress loop, corresponding to possible starvation.

We can, for instance, place a progress label in the Dijkstra example from
Figure 4.1, as follows:

```
active proctype Dijkstra()
{        byte count = 1;

end:     do
         :: (count == 1) ->
progress:        sema!p; count = 0
         :: (count == 0) ->
                sema?v; count = 1
         od
}
```

We interpret the successful passing of a semaphore test as progress here and
ask the verifier to make sure that in all infinite executions the semaphore process reach the progress label infinitely often.

To run a check for the absence of non-progress cycles we have to compile the
verifier with a special option that adds the right type of temporal claim to the
model (we will show the details of that claim on p. 93). The check then proceeds as follows:

```
$ spin -a dijkstra_progress.pml
$ cc -DNP -o pan pan.c   # enable non-progress checking
$ ./pan -l               # search for non-progress cycles
(Spin Version 4.0.7 -- 1 August 2003)
        + Partial Order Reduction

Full statespace search for:
        never claim             +
        assertion violations    + (if within scope of claim)
        non-progress cycles     + (fairness disabled)
        invalid end states      - (disabled by never claim)
```

```
State-vector 40 byte, depth reached 18, errors: 0
      27 states, stored (39 visited)
      27 states, matched
      66 transitions (= visited+matched)
       0 atomic steps
hash conflicts: 0 (resolved)
(max size 2^18 states)

1.573    memory usage (Mbyte)

unreached in proctype Dijkstra
        line 14, state 10, "-end-"
        (1 of 10 states)

unreached in proctype user
        line 22, state 7, "-end-"
        (1 of 7 states)
```

At the start of the output we see that the search for non-progress cycles was enabled, and that a `never` claim was used. The latter may be surprising, since our model did not contain such a claim. `Never` claims are usually user-defined, or derived from logic formulae. A claim can also be generated by SPIN internally, though, to support a predefined check. In this case, the claim was generated by SPIN and automatically inserted into the model to define a check for the non-progress property. The insertion of the claim was triggered by the use of compiler directive `-DNP`. We will cover the purpose and use of user-defined `never` claims in more detail later in this chapter.

The output from the verifier also tells us that a check for both assertion violations and for non-progress cycles was performed. The error count is zero, which means that no assertion violations or non-progress cycles were found. We can conclude that the model from Figure 4.1 permits no infinite executions that do not contain infinitely many semaphore P operations.

By enabling the search for non-progress properties (a liveness property), we automatically disabled the search for invalid end states (a safety property). It is also worth noting that, compared to our last check, the number of reachable states has almost doubled. When we discuss the search algorithms that are used in SPIN for checking the various types of properties (Chapter 8, p. 167) we will see what the cause is.

If more than one state carries a progress label, variations with a common prefix are again valid, such as `progress0`, or `progression`.

As a very simple example of what a non-progress cycle might look like, consider the following contrived model with two processes.[1]

---

1. Note that the two `proctype` bodies are equal. We could, therefore, also have defined the same behavior with two instantiations of a single `proctype`.

```
byte x = 2;

active proctype A()
{       do
        :: x = 3 - x
        od
}

active proctype B()
{       do
        :: x = 3 - x
        od
}
```

Clearly, the two processes will cause the value of the global variable x to alternate between 2 and 1, *ad infinitum*. No progress labels were used, so every cycle is guaranteed to be a non-progress cycle.

We perform the check for non-progress cycles as before:

```
$ spin -a fair.pml
$ cc -DNP -o pan pan.c   # enable non-progress checking
$ ./pan -l               # search for non-progress cycles
pan: non-progress cycle (at depth 2)
pan: wrote fair.pml.trail
(Spin Version 4.0.7 -- 1 August 2003)
Warning: Search not completed
        + Partial Order Reduction

Full statespace search for:
        never claim            +
        assertion violations   + (if within scope of claim)
        non-progress cycles    + (fairness disabled)
        invalid end states     - (disabled by never claim)

State-vector 24 byte, depth reached 7, errors: 1
        3 states, stored (5 visited)
        4 states, matched
        9 transitions (= visited+matched)
        0 atomic steps
hash conflicts: 0 (resolved)
(max size 2^18 states)

1.573   memory usage (Mbyte)
```

As expected, a non-progress cycle is found. Recall that when the verifier finds an error it writes a complete trace fpr the error execution into a file called pan.trail. Using that file, we can reproduce the error trail with the help of SPIN's guided simulation option, for instance, as follows:

```
$ spin -t -p fair.pml
spin: couldn't find claim (ignored)
   2:   proc   1 (B) line   12 "fair.pml" (state 1) [x = (3-x)]
   4:   proc   1 (B) line   12 "fair.pml" (state 1) [x = (3-x)]
   <<<<<START OF CYCLE>>>>>
   6:   proc   1 (B) line   12 "fair.pml" (state 1) [x = (3-x)]
   8:   proc   1 (B) line   12 "fair.pml" (state 1) [x = (3-x)]
spin: trail ends after 8 steps
#processes: 2
                    x = 2
   8:   proc   1 (B) line   11 "fair.pml" (state 2)
   8:   proc   0 (A) line    5 "fair.pml" (state 2)
2 processes created
```

The warning that SPIN could not locate the claim for this error trail is inno-
cent: the claim we used to state that non-progress cycles cannot exist was predefined. (This claim turns out to be false for this model.) The steps that do
not appear in the numbered output (steps 1, 3, 5, and 7) are the steps that were
executed by the hidden claim automaton.

FAIR CYCLES

The counterexample shows an infinite execution of the process of type B
alone, without participation of any other process in the system. Given the fact
that SPIN does not allow us to make *any* assumptions about the relative speeds
of execution of processes, the special-case where the process of type A pauses
indefinitely is allowed, and so the counterexample is valid. Still, there may
well be cases where we would be interested in the existence of property violations under more realistic fairness assumptions. One such assumption is the
finite progress assumption. It says that any process than *can* execute a statement will eventually proceed with that execution.

There are two variations of this assumption. The stricter version states that if
a process reaches a point where it has an executable statement, and the
executability of that statement never changes, it will eventually proceed by
executing the statement. A more general version states that if the process
reaches a point where it has a statement that becomes executable infinitely
often, it will eventually proceed by executing the statement. The first version
is commonly referred to as *weak fairness* and the second as *strong fairness*.
In our example enforcing *weak fairness* in the search for non-progress cycles
would rule out the counterexample that is reported in the default search. We
can enforce the weak fairness rule as follows during the verification:

```
$ ./pan -l -f
pan: non-progress cycle (at depth 8)
pan: wrote fair.pml.trail
(Spin Version 4.0.7 -- 1 August 2003)
Warning: Search not completed
        + Partial Order Reduction
```

```
Full statespace search for:
        never claim                   +
        assertion violations          + (if within scope of claim)
        non-progress cycles           + (fairness enabled)
        invalid end states            - (disabled by never claim)

State-vector 24 byte, depth reached 15, errors: 1
        4 states, stored (12 visited)
        9 states, matched
       21 transitions (= visited+matched)
        0 atomic steps
hash conflicts: 0 (resolved)
(max size 2^18 states)

1.573   memory usage (Mbyte)
```

The new cycle that is reported here should now be consistent with the weak fairness finite progress assumption. A quick look at the new counterexample can confirm this.

```
$ spin -t -p fair.pml
spin: couldn't find claim (ignored)
  2:   proc  1 (B) line  12 "fair.pml" (state 1) [x = (3-x)]
  4:   proc  1 (B) line  12 "fair.pml" (state 1) [x = (3-x)]
  6:   proc  1 (B) line  12 "fair.pml" (state 1) [x = (3-x)]
  8:   proc  0 (A) line   6 "fair.pml" (state 1) [x = (3-x)]
  <<<<<START OF CYCLE>>>>>
 10:   proc  1 (B) line  12 "fair.pml" (state 1) [x = (3-x)]
 12:   proc  1 (B) line  12 "fair.pml" (state 1) [x = (3-x)]
 14:   proc  1 (B) line  12 "fair.pml" (state 1) [x = (3-x)]

 16:   proc  0 (A) line   6 "fair.pml" (state 1) [x = (3-x)]
spin: trail ends after 16 steps
#processes: 2
                 x = 2
 16:   proc  1 (B) line  11 "fair.pml" (state 2)
 16:   proc  0 (A) line   5 "fair.pml" (state 2)
2 processes created
```

As another experiment, we could now add a progress label into one (but not both) of the two proctypes, for instance, as follows:

```
active proctype B()
{
        do
        :: x = 3 - x; progress: skip
        od
}
```

The process of type B will now alternate between a progress state and a non-progress state, and in principle it could pause forever in its non-progress state at the start of the loop. Think for a moment what you would expect the verifier to find now with the different options we have discussed for finding non-progress cycles, with and without the weak fairness option. Perform the experiment and see if it matches your understanding.[2]

Of course, the enforcement of the additional fairness constraint adds to the computational complexity of the verification problem. It is not very noticeable in this small example, but in general, the amount of work that the verifier has to do can increase by a factor N, where N is the number of active processes. The cost would be even higher for enforcing a *strong fairness* assumption (increasing to a factor of N^2). In practice, this type of overhead would limit the use of a strong fairness option to only the simplest of test cases. Where needed, arbitrary variations of finite progress and fairness assumptions can always be expressed with the help of temporal logic formula, or directly as ω-regular properties with the help of PROMELA `never` claims.

Note also that the notion of fairness that is used in SPIN applies to process scheduling decisions only: it does not apply to the resolution of non-deterministic choices inside processes. Where needed, other types of fairness can be defined with logic formula. We will return to this in Chapter 6.

We will talk more about the implementation of the weak fairness option in SPIN in Chapter 8 (p. 182).

ACCEPT STATES: The last type of label, the accept-state label, is normally reserved for use in `never` claims, which are often mechanically generated from logic formulae. We discuss `never` claims in the next section. Although this is rarely done, accept-state labels can also be used elsewhere in a PROMELA model, and do not require the presence of a `never` claim.

By marking a state with any label that starts with the prefix `accept` we can ask the verifier to find all cycles that *do* pass through at least one of those labels.

Like progress-state labels, accept-state labels have no meaning in simulation runs: they are only interpreted when SPIN is used in verification mode.

The implicit correctness claim that is expressed by the presence of an accept-state label is that there should not exist any executions that can pass through an accept-state label infinitely often.

To allow for the use of more than one accept-state label in a single `proctype` or `never` claim, the name can again be extended. For instance, the following variants are all valid: `accept`, `acceptance`, `accepting`.

The observations we made above about the use of fairness assumptions apply equally to non-progress cycles and acceptance cycles. Try, for instance, to

---

2. If all is well, you should be able to confirm with this experiment that only non-fair non-progress cycles exist.

replace the progress label in the last example with an accept label, and confirm that the verifier can find both fair and non-fair acceptance cycles in the resulting model. The verification steps to be performed are as follows:

```
$ spin -a fair_accept.pml
$ cc -o pan pan.c          # note: no -DNP is used
$ ./pan -a                 # all acceptance cycles
...
$ ./pan -a -f              # fair acceptance cycles only
...
```

NEVER CLAIMS

Up to this point we have talked about the specification of correctness criteria with assertion statements and with meta labels. Powerful types of correctness criteria can already be expressed with these tools, yet so far our only option is to add them into the individual proctype declarations. We cannot easily express the claim, "every system state in which property p is *true* eventually leads to a system state in which property q is *true*." The reason we cannot check this property with the mechanisms we have described so far is that we have no way yet of defining a check that would be performed at *every single execution step* of the system. Note that we cannot make assumptions about the relative speeds of processes, which means that in between any two statement executions any standard PROMELA process can pause for an arbitrary number of steps taken by other system processes. PROMELA never claims are meant to give us the needed capability for defining more precise checks.

In a nutshell: a never claim is normally used to specify either finite or infinite system behavior that should *never* occur.

HOW A NEVER CLAIM WORKS

Consider the following execution of the little *pots* model from the Chapter 3 (p. 64).

```
$ spin -c pots.pml | more
proc 0 = pots
proc 1 = subscriber
q   0   1
  2   .   line!offhook,1
  2   line?offhook,1
  1   who!dialtone
  1   .   me?dialtone
  1   .   me!number
  1   who?number
  1   who!ringing
  1   .   me?ringing
  1   who!connected
```

```
      1   .     me?connected
timeout
      1   .     me!hangup
      1   who?hangup
      2   .      line!offhook,1
      2   line?offhook,1
      1   who!dialtone
      1   .     me?dialtone
      1   .     me!number
      1   who?number
      1   who!ringing
      1   .     me?ringing
      1   .     me!hangup
      1   who?hangup
```

There are twenty-four system execution steps here. Eleven statements were executed by the *pots* server and thirteen were executed by the *subscriber* process. Because this is a distributed system, not only the specific sequence of statements executed in each process, is important, but also the way in which these statement executions are interleaved in time to form a *system* execution.

A never claim gives us the capability to check system properties just before and just after each statement execution, no matter which process performs them. A never claim can define precisely which properties we would like to check at each step. The simplest type of claim would be to check a single property p at each and every step, to make sure that it *never* fails. It is easy to check system invariants in this way.

A claim to check such an invariant property could be written in several ways. Originally, a never claim was only meant to match behavior that should *never* occur. That is, the verification system could flag it as an error if the full behavior specified in the claim could be matched by any feasible system execution. The simplest way to write a never claim that checks for the invariance of the system property p then would be as follows:

```
never {
        do
        :: !p -> break
        :: else
        od
}
```

The claim process is executed at each step of the system. As soon as property p is found to be *false*, the claim process breaks from its loop and terminates, thereby indicating that the error behavior occurred. As long as p remains *true*, though, the claim remains in its initial state, and all is well.

It is easy to abuse the properties of a never claim a little by writing more intuitive versions of the checker. For instance, we accomplish the same effect with the following version of the never claim:

```
never {
        do
        :: assert(p)
        od
}
```

The loop now contains the relevant assertion that the property p is always *true*. The assertion statement is executed over and over. It is executed for the first time in the initial system state. After that point it is executed again immediately following each system execution step that can be performed. If the property is violated in the initial system state, the claim exits immediately, reporting the error before any system step was taken. Clearly, both the expression statement !p and the assertion assert(p) are always side effect free, so neither version of the claim can enable system behavior that would not be possible in the claim's absence.

For the property we are considering, a simple system invariant, we could also get away with an alternative specification without using never claims. We could, for instance, express the property also by adding an extra PROMELA process that acts as a monitor on system executions, as follows:

```
active proctype monitor()
{
        atomic { !p -> assert(false) }
}
```

The monitor *could* initiate the execution of the atomic sequence at *any* point in the system execution where p is found to be *false*. This means that if there exists any reachable system state where the invariant property p is violated, the monitor *could* execute in precisely that state and flag a violation. If the behavior is *possible* this means that the verifier *will* find it and report it, so in this case the monitor process could solve the problem. This is not necessarily the case once we move to slightly more complex temporal properties.

Consider, for instance, the property:

> *Every system state in which* p *is true eventually leads to a system state in which* q *is true, and in the interim* p *remains true.*

In SPIN verifications, we are not interested in system executions that *satisfy* this property, but in the executions that can *violate* it. This means that we want to know if it is possible for first p to become *true* in an execution and thereafter q either to remain *false* forever, or p to become *false* before q becomes *true*. This behavior should *never* happen.

Note that a violation of the property where q remains *false* forever can only be demonstrated with an infinite execution. Since we are dealing with finite state spaces, every infinite execution is necessarily a cyclic execution. We cannot use simple process assertions to capture such (liveness) errors. We can capture precisely the right type of check, though, with the following never claim.

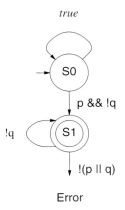

true

!q

p && !q

!(p || q)

Error

Figure 4.2 Control Flow Structure for LTL Property $\neg \Box (p \rightarrow (p \,U\, q))$
(LTL, or Linear Temporal Logic, is discussed in Chapter 6)

```
never {
S0:       do
          :: p && !q -> break
          :: true
          od;
S1:
accept:
          do
          :: !q
          :: !(p || q) -> break
          od
}
```

This type of claim is most easily written as a formula in Linear Temporal
Logic (LTL), as illustrated in Figure 4.2.[3] We will explore the link with LTL
in more detail in the next section, and we will explore the use of LTL itself in
greater detail in Chapter 6.

Claims like this are only interpreted when SPIN is run in verification mode.
They are ignored in SPIN simulation runs. The first thing that will happen in a
verification is a claim step, to make sure that the never claim can perform its
first check on the initial system state itself.

---

3. We follow the usual conventions by indicating the initial state of every automaton with a
short arrow, and by marking the accepting states with a double circle (more details on this will
follow in Chapter 6).

Execution of the claim starts at the statement labeled `S0`, which contains a loop with two options for execution. The second option has just a single statement, the expression statement *true*. Clearly, this option is always executable and has no effect when executed. It leaves the claim in its initial state. The first option is only executable when expression p evaluates to *true* and expression q evaluates to *false*. If this is the case, we have found a match for the antecedent of the property: the truth of p but not yet the truth of also q. Execution will continue at the statement labeled `accept`. As can also be seen in Figure 4.2, the interpretation of a `break` statement, like a `goto` statement, does not really take up an execution step. It merely acts as a special type of statement separator that overrides the default allocation of a successor state. The `break` that appears here defines which statement is to be executed after the second guard in the first cycle is successfully passed.

> *(Can be skipped on a first reading.)* In principle, the order in which options are placed in a selection or repetition structure is irrelevant: it does not change the semantics of the model. The verifier will consider all possible executions of the model. Although this is strictly seen immaterial, when it has a choice, the verifier will try the various options for execution in the order in which they are listed in the specification. The fact that we have placed the option that can jump to the accept state first in the list of options for state `S0` is therefore no accident: it can help the verifier to find the accepting runs faster.

Clearly, the claim cannot get stuck in its first state, since it always has at least the *true* guard to execute. Executing the *true* guard in effect amounts to the claim ignoring the system for one step, deferring any checks until later.

In the `accept` state of the claim there are again two options for execution. The only way for the claim to remain in this state is for expression q to remain *false* forever. If this is possible, it would constitute a violation of our property. For this reason we have marked the state with an `accept` label. The violation can now be caught by the verifier as an acceptance cycle. The only other possible way in which the property can be violated is when p becomes *false* before q becomes *true*. This type of violation is caught by forcing the termination of the `never` claim. Termination of the claim is interpreted as a full match of the behavior specified; behavior that is *never* supposed to happen.

What happens when both p and q are found to be *true* while the claim executes in its `accept` state? Neither of the two options for continued execution are executable: the claim gets stuck. Curiously, this is not an error but a desirable condition. If the claim cannot match the system execution in its next step, then this means that the undesirable behavior that is captured in the `never` claim cannot fully be matched in a system execution. All is well; the claim stops tracking the system along this execution path and no error is reported. For the verifier to be of use here, we should be able to guarantee that the verifier effectively matches the behavior expressed by the claim against not just one but *all* possible system executions, so that if any such execution can match, it will be found. Clearly, in simulation mode SPIN cannot give any such guarantee, but in verification mode it can, and it does.

There is one other important observation to be made about the sample `never` claim above. Note that when p is *true* and q is *false* in state S0, the claim has two possible options for execution: both guards in the loop are executable. This form of non-determinism is critically important here. If the guard that is now expressed as *true* would be replaced with *else*, the claim would require only that the *first* time in a system execution that expression p becomes *true* should lead to a state where q is also *true*. It would not place any requirements on any future events that would make p *true* after the requirement is met the first time. The non-determinism makes it possible to make a far stronger statement: *every* time that p becomes *true* should lead to a state where also q is *true*.

In the sample `never` claims we have given here, the statements we used were always side effect free. In fact, apart from general control-flow constructs, we have used only two types of statements: condition statements and assertions. This is of course no accident. A `never` claim is meant to *monitor* or *track* system behavior and not to contribute to it. The declaration or the manipulation of variables or message channels, or generally the execution of any statement that could have a side effect on the state of data objects used in the system, is therefore never allowed inside `never` claims.

A nice property of `never` claims is that they can be used not just to define correctness properties, but also to *restrict* the search of the verifier to a user-defined subset, or slice, of the system. The verifier in effect always eliminates all behavior that cannot be matched by the claim. This is safe to do in verification because the claim is used to specify only invalid behavior, which means that behavior that is eliminated is by definition (of the claim) behavior that is irrelevant to the verification attempt. As a very simple example of this, note that a very simple claim such as

```
never { do :: p od }
```

can be used to restrict a verification run to all states where the condition p evaluates to *true*. If p is in fact a system invariant, this results in no reduction of work, but otherwise the state space that is searched is reduced by this claim. Of course, if condition p turns out to be *false* in the initial system state, the state space will be completely empty, which is unlikely to be useful.

THE LINK WITH LTL

`Never` claims provide a powerful mechanism for expressing properties of distributed systems. Admittedly, though, it can be hard to come up with correct formalizations of system properties by directly encoding them into `never` claims. Fortunately, there are easier ways to do this. One such method is to use SPIN's built-in translator from formulae in linear temporal logic (LTL) to never claims. The last claim, for instance, corresponds to the LTL formula

```
![](p -> (p U q))
```

We can generate the never claim from this formula with the command:

```
$ spin -f '![](p -> (p U q))'
never {      /* ![](p-> (p U q)) */
T0_init:
        if
        :: (! ((q)) && (p)) -> goto accept_S4
        :: (1) -> goto T0_init
        fi;
accept_S4:
        if
        :: (! ((q))) -> goto accept_S4
        :: (! ((p)) && ! ((q))) -> goto accept_all
        fi;
accept_all:
        skip
}
```

Another method is to use a little graphical tool, called the *timeline editor*, to convert timeline descriptions into never claims. In many cases, temporal logic formulae are simpler to understand and use than never claims, but they are also strictly less expressive. Timeline properties, in turn, are simpler to understand and use than temporal logic formulae, but again less expressive than these. Fortunately, almost all properties of interest can be expressed as either timeline properties or temporal logic formulae. We will discuss temporal logic in more detail in Chapter 6, and the various methods to generate never claims mechanically from either formulae or timelines in, respectively, Chapter 6 (p. 127) and Chapter 13 (p. 283).

TRACE ASSERTIONS

Like never claims, a trace assertion does not specify new behavior, but instead expresses a correctness requirement on existing behavior in the remainder of the system. A trace assertion expresses properties of message channels, and in particular it formalizes statements about valid or invalid sequences of operations that processes can perform on message channels.

All channel names referenced in a trace assertion must be globally declared, and all message fields must be globally known constants or mtype symbolic constants. A simple example of a trace assertion is as follows:

```
trace {
        do
        :: q1!a; q2?b
        od
}
```

In this example, the assertion specifies the correctness requirement that send operations on channel q1 alternate with receive operations on channel q2, and furthermore that all send operations on q1 are exclusively messages of type a, and all receive operations on channel q2 are exclusively messages of type b.

Trace assertions apply only to send and receive operations on message channels. They can be used to specify a specific relative order in which these types of operations must always be performed. Only the channel names that are specified in the assertion are considered to be within the scope of the check. All send and receive operations on other channels are ignored. The trace assertion trivially defines an automaton that can step through a finite number of control states while it monitors a system execution. The automaton only changes state when a send or a receive operation is executed that is within its scope. If an operation is executed that is within scope, but that cannot be matched by a transition of the trace automaton, the verifier will immediately report an error.

If at least one send (receive) operation on a channel appears in a trace assertion, then all send (receive) operations on that channel are subject to the check.

As with never claims, there are some restrictions on the types of statements that can appear in a trace assertion. Apart from control-flow constructs, a trace assertion may contain only simple send and receive operations. It cannot contain variations such as random receive, sorted send, or channel poll operations. No data objects can be declared or referred to inside a trace assertion.

If a message field must be matched in a send or receive operation that appears inside a trace assertion, it must be specified with a standard mtype name or with a constant value. Don't care values for specific message fields can be specified with the predefined write-only variable _ (i.e., the underscore symbol).

Sends and receives that appear in an event trace are called monitored events. These events do not generate new behavior, but they are required to match send or receive events on the same channels in the model, with matching message parameters. A send or receive event occurs when a send or a receive statement is executed in the system, that is, an event that occurs during a state transition.

On rendezvous channels, a rendezvous handshake consists of an offer (the send half of the handshake) and an accept (the receive half of the handshake). Even traces can only capture the occurrence of the receive part of a handshake, not of the send part. The reason is that the send (the offer) can be made many times before it results in a successful accept.

A trace assertion can contain *end-state*, *progress-state*, and *accept-state*

labels with the usual interpretation. There are, however, a few important differences between `trace` assertions and `never` claims:
- Unlike `never` claims, `trace` assertions must always be deterministic.
- A `trace` assertion can match event occurrences that occur in the transitions between system states, whereas a `never` claim matches propositional values on system states only.
- A `trace` assertion monitors only a subset of the events in a system: only those of the types that are mentioned in the `trace` (i.e., the monitored events). A `never` claim, on the other hand, looks at all global system states that are reached, and must be able to match the state assignments in the system for every state reached.

A `trace` assertion, just like a `never` claim, has a current state, but it only executes transitions if a monitored event occurs in the system. Unlike `never` claims, `trace` assertions do not execute synchronously with the system; they only execute when events of interest occur.

Note that receive events on rendezvous channels can be monitored with `trace` assertions, but not with `never` claims.

NOTRACE
Sometimes it is desirable to specify precisely the opposite of a `trace` assertion: a sequence of events that should not occur in an execution. For this purpose the keyword `notrace` is also supported, though it is only rarely used. A `notrace` assertion is violated if the event sequence that is specified, subject to the same rules as `trace` assertions, is matched completely. The assertion is considered to be matched completely when either an *end-state* label is reached inside the `notrace` sequence, or the closing curly brace of that sequence is reached.

PREDEFINED VARIABLES AND FUNCTIONS
Some predefined variables and functions can be especially useful in `trace` assertions and `never` claims.

There are only four predefined variables in PROMELA. They are:

```
_
np_
_pid
_last
```

We have discussed the `_pid` variable before (p. 16, 36), as well as the global write-only variable `_` (p. 92). These two variables can be used freely in any `proctype` declaration.

But we have not encountered the two variables `np_` and `_last` before. These two variables are meant to be used *only* inside `trace` assertions or `never` claims.

The predefined variable np_ holds the boolean value *false* in all system states
where at least one running process is currently at a control-flow state that was
marked with a progress label. That is, the value of variable np_ tells
whether the system is currently in a progress or a non-progress state. We can
use this variable easily to build a never claim that can detect the existence of
non-progress cycles, for instance, as follows:

```
never { /* non-progress cycle detector */
        do
        :: true
        :: np_ -> break
        od;
accept:
        do
        :: np_
        od
}
```

After a finite prefix of arbitrary length, optionally passing through any finite
number of non-progress states, the claim automaton moves from its initial
state to the final accepting state, where it can only remain if there exists at
least one infinitely long execution sequence that never traverses any more
progress states.

The true purpose of the np_ variable is not in the definition of this claim,
since this precise claim is used automatically when SPIN's default search for
non-progress cycles is invoked. The availability of the variable makes it possible to include the non-progress property into other more complex types of
temporal properties. A standard application, for instance, would be to search
for non-progress cycles while at the same time enforcing non-standard fairness constraints.

The predefined global variable _last holds the instantiation number of the
process that performed the *last* step in a system execution sequence. Its value
is not part of the system state unless it is explicitly used in a specification. Its
initial value is zero.

The use of the following three predefined functions is restricted to never
claims:

```
pc_value(pid)
enabled(pid)
procname[pid]@label
```

The first of these functions,

```
pc_value(pid)
```

returns the current control state of the process with instantiation number pid
or zero if no such process exists. The number returned is always a

non-negative integer and it corresponds to the internal state number that SPIN tracks as the equivalent of a program-counter in a running process.

In the following example, one process will print out its internal state number for three consecutive steps, and a second blocks until the first process reaches at least a state that is numbered higher than two.

```
active proctype A()
{
        printf("%d\n", pc_value(_pid));
        printf("%d\n", pc_value(_pid));
        printf("%d\n", pc_value(_pid));
}

active proctype B()
{
        (pc_value(0) > 2);
        printf("ok\n")
}
```

If we simulate the execution of this model, the following is one of two possible runs:

```
$ spin pcval.pml
spin: Warning, using pc_value() outside never claim
        1
        2
            ok
        3
2 processes created
```

SPIN's warning reminds us that the use of this predefined function is intended to be restricted to never claims.

The function

```
        enabled(pid)
```

tells whether the process with instantiation number pid has at least one statement that is *executable* in its current state. The following example illustrates the use of _last and enabled():

```
/* It is not possible for the process with pid 1
 * to remain enabled without ever executing.
 */
never {
accept:
        do
        :: _last != 1 && enabled(1)
        od
}
```

The last predefined function

```
procname[pid]@label
```

returns a nonzero value only if the next statement that can be executed in the process with instantiation number `pid` is the statement that was marked with label `label` in `proctype procname`. It is an error if the process referred to with the `pid` number is not an instantiation of the specified `proctype`.

The following example shows how one might employ this type of remote referencing inside a `never` claim:

```
/*
 * Processes 1 and 2 cannot enter their
 * critical sections at the same time.
 */
never {
        do
        :: user[1]@critical && user[2]@critical ->
                break   /* implicitly accepting */
        :: else /* repeat */
        od
}
```

If there is only one instantiation of a given `proctype` in the system, the process identify is really superfluous, and (in SPIN version 4.0 and higher) the reference from the last example can in that case be given as

```
user@critical.
```

If, nonetheless, there turns out to be more than one instantiation of the `proc-type`, this type of reference selects an arbitrary one of them. The SPIN simulator issues a warning if it encounters a case like this; the verifier does not.

REMOTE REFERENCING

In SPIN version 4.0 and higher (cf. Chapters 10 and 17), another type of reference is also supported. The additional type of reference bypasses the standard scope rules of PROMELA by making it possible for any process, and also the `never` claim, to refer to the current value of local variables from other processes. This capability should be used with caution, since it conflicts with the assumptions about scope rules that are made in SPIN's partial order reduction strategy (see Chapter 9).

The syntax is the same as for remote label references, with the replacement of the "@" symbol for a single colon ":". For instance, if we wanted to refer to the variable `count` in the process of type `Dijkstra` in the example on page 77, we could do so with the syntax

```
Dijkstra[0]:count.
```

If there is only one instantiation of `proctype Dijkstra`, we can again use the shorter version

```
Dijkstra:count,
```

following the same rules as before.

PATH QUANTIFICATION

We will discuss the verification algorithms used in SPIN in more detail in later chapters, but we can already note a few important features of the approach taken. All correctness properties that can be verified with the SPIN system can be interpreted as formal claims that certain types of behavior are, or are not, possible.

- An assertion statement formalizes the claim that it is impossible for the given expression to evaluate to *false*.
- An end label states that it is impossible for the system to terminate without all active processes having either terminated or stopped at one of the specially labeled end states.
- A progress label states that it is impossible for the system to execute forever without also passing through at least one of the specially labeled progress states infinitely often.
- An accept label states that it is impossible for the system to execute forever while also passing through at least one of the specially labeled accept states infinitely often.
- A `never` claim states that it is impossible for the system to exhibit, either infinite or finite, behavior that completely matches the behavior that is formalized by the claim.
- A trace assertion, finally, states that it is impossible for the system to deviate from the behavior that is formalized.

In all cases, the verification performed by SPIN is designed to prove the user wrong: SPIN will try its best to find a counterexample to at least one of the formal claims that is stated. So, in a way SPIN never tries to prove the *correctness* of a specification. It tries to do the opposite.

Hunting for counterexamples, rather than direct proof, has advantages. Specifically, it can allow the verifier to employ a more efficient search procedure. If, for instance, the error behavior is formalized in a `never` claim, SPIN can restrict its search for counterexamples to the behaviors that match the claim. `never` claims, then, in a way act as a restriction on the search space. If the error behavior is indeed impossible, as the user claims, the verifier may have very little work to do. If the error behavior is *almost* impossible, it may have to do a little more work, but still not necessarily as much as when it has to search the entire space of all possible behaviors. This only happens in the worst case.

FORMALITIES

Let E be the complete set of all possible ω-runs of the system. Given a correctness property ϕ formalized as an LTL property, we say that the system satisfies ϕ if and only if all runs in E do. We can express this as

$$(E \models \phi) \leftrightarrow \forall \sigma, (\sigma \in E \rightarrow \sigma \models \phi). \qquad [4.1]$$

Spin, however, does not attempt to prove this directly. We can only use Spin in an attempt to *disprove* the claim by trying to find a counterexample that shows that $\neg \phi$ is satisfied for at least one run. That is, instead of proving [4.1] directly, Spin tries to show the opposite

$$\neg (E \models \phi) \leftrightarrow \exists \sigma, (\sigma \in E \wedge \neg (\sigma \models \phi)) \qquad [4.2]$$

where of course $\neg (\sigma \models \phi)$ means that $(\sigma \models \neg \phi)$.

If the attempt to show that the right-hand side of [4.2] holds *succeeds*, we have shown that $\neg (E \models \phi)$, and therefore that the left-hand side of [4.1] does *not* hold: the system does not satisfy the property.

If the attempt to find a counterexample *fails*, we have shown that the left-hand side of [4.2] does not hold, and therefore that the left-hand side of [4.1] must hold: the system satisfies the property.

This all looks fairly straightforward, but note carefully that the step from [4.1] to [4.2] cannot be achieved by the mere negation of property ϕ. If, for instance, instead of property ϕ we try to prove with the same procedure that $\neg \phi$ is satisfied, then [4.1] becomes

$$(E \models \neg \phi) \leftrightarrow \forall \sigma, (\sigma \in E \rightarrow (\sigma \models \neg \phi)). \qquad [4.3]$$

which is the same as

$$(E \models \neg \phi) \leftrightarrow \forall \sigma, (\sigma \in E \rightarrow \neg (\sigma \models \phi)). \qquad [4.4]$$

Note that the right-hand sides of [4.2] and [4.4] differ. The logical negation of the right-hand side of [4.1] is the right-hand side of [4.2], and not the right-hand side of [4.4]. In other words, $(E \models \neg \phi)$ is *not* the same as $\neg (E \models \phi)$. The first equation does logically imply the second, but the reverse is not necessarily true:

$$(E \models \neg \phi) \rightarrow \neg (E \models \phi). \qquad [4.5]$$

It is not too hard to come up with examples where we have simultaneously:

$$\neg (E \models \neg \phi) \wedge \neg (E \models \phi). \qquad [4.6]$$

For instance, if ϕ is the property that some variable x is never equal to zero, then $\neg \phi$ states that x is zero at least once. It is quite possible to construct a model that has at least one run where variable x eventually becomes zero (providing a counterexample to ϕ), and also at least one run where x never becomes zero (providing a counterexample to $\neg \phi$).

The following simple system has precisely that property.

```
byte x = 1;

init {
        do
        :: x = 0
        :: x = 2
        od
}

#define p       (x != 0)

#ifdef PHI

never {    /* []p */
accept:
        do
        :: (p)
        od
}

#else

never {    /* ![]p */
        do
        :: !p -> break
        :: true
        od
}

#endif
```

Both the property []p and its negation ![]p will produce counterexamples for this model, as is quickly demonstrated by SPIN:

```
$ spin -DPHI -a prop.pml
$ cc -o pan pan.c
$ ./pan -a
pan: acceptance cycle (at depth 2)
pan: wrote prop.pml.trail
...
```

We can replay this first error trail with the guided simulation option, as before.

```
$ spin -t -p -v -DPHI prop.pml
1: proc - (:never:) line 18 "prop.pml" (state 1) [(x!=0)]
Never claim moves to line 18  [(x!=0)]
2: proc  0 (:init:) line  7 "prop.pml" (state 2) [x = 2]
  <<<<<START OF CYCLE>>>>>
```

```
3: proc - (:never:) line 18 "prop.pml" (state 1) [(x!=0)]
4: proc 0 (:init:)  line  7 "prop.pml" (state 2) [x = 2]
5: proc - (:never:) line 18 "prop.pml" (state 1) [(x!=0)]
spin: trail ends after 5 steps
. . .
```

And, for the negated version of the claim:

```
$ spin -DNOTPHI -a prop.pml
$ cc -o pan pan.c
$ ./pan
pan: claim violated! (at depth 3)
pan: wrote prop.pml.trail
. . .
$ spin -t -p -v -DNOTPHI prop.pml
1: proc - (:never:) line 27 "prop.pml" (state 3) [(1)]
Never claim moves to line 27   [(1)]
2: proc 0 (:init:) line   6 "prop.pml" (state 1) [x = 0]
3: proc - (:never:) line 26 "prop.pml" (state 1) [!(x!=0)]
Never claim moves to line 26   [!(x!=0)]
spin: trail ends after 3 steps
. . .
```

Specifically, therefore, if a SPIN verification run shows that a given system S fails to satisfy property ϕ, we cannot conclude that the same system S will satisfy the inverse property $\neg\phi$.

FINDING OUT MORE

This concludes our overview of the various ways for expressing correctness requirements that are supported in PROMELA. More information about the derivation of never claims from Linear Temporal Logic formulae can be found in Chapter 6. More about the specification of requirements for a SPIN verification in a more intuitive, graphical format can be found in Chapter 13 where we discuss the timeline editing tool.

We have seen in this chapter that there are many different ways in which correctness requirements can be expressed. Be reassured, though, that the most easily understood mechanism for this purpose is also the most commonly used: the simple use of assertions.

The terms *safety* and *liveness* were first systematically discussed by Leslie Lamport, cf. Lamport [1983], and see also Alpern and Schneider [1985,1987]. An excellent introduction to the formalization of correctness properties for distributed systems can be found in Manna and Pnueli [1995]. Many other textbooks contain excellent introductions to this material; see, for instance, Berard et al. [2001], Clarke et al. [2000], or Huth and Ryan [2000].

A more detailed treatment of the differences between various ways of specifying, for instance, system invariants in PROMELA can be found in Ruys [2001].

USING DESIGN ABSTRACTION 5

> *"Seek simplicity, and distrust it."*
> *(Alfred North Whitehead, 1861–1947)*

System design is a process of discovery. By exploring possible solutions, a designer discovers the initially unknown constraints, and weeds out the designs that seemed plausible at first, but that do not survive closer scrutiny. In the process, the designer determines not only what is right and what is wrong, but also what is relevant and what is irrelevant to the basic design premises.

For a design *tool* to be effective in this context, it needs to be able to assist the designer in the creation and the analysis of intuitive high-level abstractions without requiring the resolution of implementation-level detail. The tool should be able to warn when the design premises are logically flawed, for instance, when the design is ambiguous, incomplete, or inconsistent, or when it does not exhibit the properties it was designed to have. To use such a tool well, the designer should be comfortable building and checking design abstractions. This task is sufficiently different from the task of building design implementations that it is worth a closer look.

WHAT MAKES A GOOD DESIGN ABSTRACTION?

The purpose of a design model is to free a designer from having to resolve implementation-level details before the main design premises can be checked. SPIN not only supports design abstractions, it requires them. At first sight, SPIN's input language may look like an imperative programming language, but it intentionally excludes a number of features that would be critical to an implementation language. It is not directly possible, for instance, to express floating point arithmetic, process scheduling, or memory management operations. Although all of these things can be important in an implementation, they can and should be abstracted from a high-level design model. Note that in much the same vein, most of today's higher-level programming languages make it impossible to express decisions on register allocation, or the management of instruction caches. These issues, though important, are best resolved and checked at a different level of abstraction.

So, what makes a good design abstraction in concurrent systems design? The focus on concurrent systems has important implications. In a sequential application, the best abstraction is typically data-oriented. In a concurrent application the preferred abstraction is control-oriented.

DATA AND CONTROL

A large sequential program is typically divided into smaller modules, each performing a well-defined computational function. The interfaces between these modules are kept as small as possible, reducing the number of assumptions that one module must make about the others. The interface definitions in this case are data-oriented, not control-oriented. The modules in a sequential application typically do not maintain internal state information independently from the rest of the program.

This is different in distributed systems design. In a distributed system, the module structure is typically determined by an externally imposed system architecture (e.g., determined by a physical separation of the main components of the system). Each module then has its own independent thread of control, which necessarily carries state information. In this case control, not data, is the primary concern in the definition of module interfaces.

In a SPIN verification model the focus is on the control aspects of a distributed application, not on the computational aspects. PROMELA allows us to express the assumptions that are made within each module about the interactions with other modules. The language discourages the specification of detailed assumptions about process-internal computations.

To make sure that the models we can specify in PROMELA always have effectively verifiable properties, we impose two requirements:

- the model can only specify finite systems, even if the underlying application is potentially infinite, and
- the model must be fully specified, that is, it must be closed to its environment.

The second requirement says that the behavior that is defined in a verification model may not depend on any hidden assumptions or components. All input sources must be part of the model, at least in abstract form.

For arbitrary software applications these two requirements are not automatically satisfied. To achieve verifiability, we have to apply abstraction.

A program that allows unrestricted recursion, or that contains unbounded buffers, for instance, is not finite-state. A program that reads input from a file-descriptor or an input-stream, similarly, is not closed to its environment. These programs cannot be verified with automatic techniques unless some abstractions are made.

The need for abstraction, or modeling, is often seen as a hurdle instead of a feature in model checking applications. Choosing the right level of abstraction, though, can mean the difference between a tractable model with provable properties and an intractable model that is only amenable to simulation, testing, or manual review. Sometimes we have to choose between proving simple properties of a complex model, formalized at a low-level abstraction, and proving more complex properties of a simpler model, formalized at a higher-level abstraction.

The importance of abstraction places demands on the design of the input language of a model checking tool. If the input language is too detailed, it discourages abstractions, which in the end obstructs the verification process. We have to be careful, therefore, in choosing which features are supported in a verification system. In SPIN, for instance, a number of otherwise desirable language features have been left out of the specification language. Among them are support for memory management, floating point calculations, and numerical analysis. Other verification systems are even more restrictive, and exclude also structured data types, message passing, and process creation. Still other systems are more permissive, and, at the price of increased complexity, include support for: real-time verification, probabilities, and procedures. All other things being equal, we should expect the most permissive system to be the easiest to build models for, but the least efficient to verify them. SPIN attempts to find a balance between ease of use and model checking efficiency.

The recommended way to develop a verification model is as follows:

- First decide which aspects of the design are important and require verification. Express these in a set of system requirements. Requirements, to be of use in the verification process, must be *testable*. It should be possible to state clearly under which precise conditions a requirement is violated. It should further not be possible for the system to fail without violating at least one of the requirements. The collection of an adequate set of requirements is in itself a process of discovery. What at first may be thought to be an insignificant requirement may become the dominant design issue over time. Other design requirements or design constraints may at first be completely unknown, until an initial analysis reveals their relevance.
- Next, consider the essence of the design itself, specifically those aspects that are meant to secure the behavior of interest, and that help the system meet its requirements.
- Only then construct an executable abstraction in PROMELA for the

design. The abstraction should be detailed enough to capture the essence of the solution, and no more. What we are looking for is the *smallest sufficient model* that allows us to perform a verification.

It is sometimes helpful to think of a verification model as a system of process modules and interfaces. Each process module represents an asynchronous entity in a distributed system. Each process is only detailed enough to capture the minimal set of assumptions that this module must make its peers. These assumptions take the form of interface definitions. The purpose of the verification is to check that all interface definitions, formalizing the assumptions that processes in the system make about each other, are logically consistent. We can perform such checks without having to detail each module's precise implementation. The modules remain, as it were, black boxes.

Phrased differently, the purpose of design verification is to find logical flaws in the reasoning that produced a design. The goal is not to find computational errors or coding errors.

The verification model must allow us to make refutable statements about a design. As Imre Lakatos once phrased it

> *"The purpose of analysis is not to compel belief but rather to suggest doubt."*

Elements of a model that cannot contribute to its refutability can and should be deleted in the interest of enhancing the model's verifiability.

In the last two decades verification tools have evolved from simple reachability analyzers, run on relatively small machines, into powerful model checking systems, that can be run on machines that are orders of magnitude faster and larger. One thing has not changed though: computational complexity remains the single most important issue in this area. There is just one powerful weapon that can reliably defeat the dragon of computational complexity, and that weapon is abstraction.

New users of SPIN often attempt to build verification models that remain relatively close to the implementation level of an application, making only syntactic changes to accommodate the whims of the input language. These users often only seriously consider abstraction when a concept or feature is encountered that cannot be represented at all in the language of the model checker. At this point, the user is often frustrated, and frustration is a poor motivator in the search for good design abstractions. Much of the detail included in verification models that are produced in this way is functionally irrelevant to the properties to be checked, yet all this detail can seriously limit the thoroughness of a possible check.

THE SMALLEST SUFFICIENT MODEL

It is sometimes easy to lose sight of the one real purpose of using a model checking system: it is to verify system properties that cannot be verified adequately by other means. If verification is our objective, computational complexity is our foe. The effort of finding a suitable design abstraction is therefore the effort of finding the smallest model that is sufficient to verify the properties that we are interested in. No more, and no less. A one-to-one translation of an implementation into a verification modeling language such as PROMELA may pass the standard of sufficiency, but it is certainly not the smallest such model and may cause unnecessary complexity in verification, or even render the verification intractable. To reduce verification complexity we may sometimes choose to generalize a problem, and sometimes we may choose to specialize it.

As the difference between a verification model and an implementation artifact becomes larger, one may well question if the facts that we are proving still have relevance. We take a very pragmatic view of this here. For our purposes, two models are equivalent if they have the same properties. This means that we can always simplify a verification model if its properties of interest are unaffected by the simplifications. A verification system, for that matter, is effective if it can be used to uncover real defects in real systems. There is little doubt that the verification methodology we are discussing here can do precisely that.

AVOIDING REDUNDANCY

The success of the model checking process for larger applications relies on our skill in finding and applying abstractions. For smaller applications this skill amounts mostly to avoiding simple cases of redundancy. It should be noted, for instance, that paradigms that are commonly used in simulation or testing can be counterproductive when used in verification. A few examples will suffice to make this point.

COUNTERS

In the construction of a simulation model it is often convenient to add counters, for instance, to keep track of the number of steps performed. The counter is basically a write-only variable, used only in print statements.

The example in Figure 5.1 illustrates a typical use. The variable cnt is used here as if it were a natural number with infinite range. No check for overflow, which will inevitably occur, is made. The implicit assumption that in practical cases overflow is not likely to be a concern may be valid in program testing or simulation; it is false in verifications where *all* possible behaviors must be taken into account.

It should be noted carefully that it is not necessarily a problem that the variable cnt may take up to 32 bits of storage to maintain its value. The real problem is that this variable can reach 2^{32} distinct values (over four billion). The complexity of the verification problem may be increased by that same amount. Phrased differently: Removing a redundant counter can reduce the complexity of a naive verification model by about nine orders of magnitude.

```
active proctype counter()
{    int cnt = 1;

     do
     :: can_proceed ->
        /* perform a step */
        cnt++;
        printf("step: %d\n", cnt)
     od
}
```

Figure 5.1 Counter Example

SINKS, SOURCES, AND FILTERS

Another avoidable source of complexity is the definition of processes that act solely as a source, a filter, or a sink for a message stream. Such processes often add no refutation power to a verification model, and are almost always better avoided.[1]

- A *sink* process, for instance, merely receives and then discards messages. Since the messages are discarded in the model, they should probably not even be sent within the model. Having them sent but not processed would indicate an incomplete abstraction.
- A *source* process generates a set of possible messages that is then forwarded to a given destination. If the sole function of the source process is to provide the choice of messages, this choice can possibly be moved beneficially into the destination process, avoiding the sending of these messages altogether.
- A *filter* process passes messages from one process to another, possibly making small changes in the stream by dropping, duplicating, inserting, or altering messages. Again, if the desired effect is to generate a stream with a particular mix of messages, it is often possible to generate just such a stream directly.

Figure 5.2 shows a simple example of each of these three types of processes. To see how much can be saved by removing the sink process, for instance, consider the number of reachable states that is contributed by the storage of messages in the channel named q. The channel can hold between zero and eight distinct messages, and each of these is one of three possible types. This

---

1. The exception would be if a given correctness property directly depends on the process being present in the model. This should be rare.

```
mtype = { one, two, three };

chan q = [8] of { mtype };
chan c = [8] of { mtype };

active proctype sink()
{
    do
    :: q?one
    :: q?two
    :: q?three
    od
}

active proctype filter()
{        mtype m;
         do
         :: c?m -> q!m
         od
}

active proctype source()
{
    do
    :: c!one
    :: c!two
    :: c!three
    od
}
```

Figure 5.2 A Sink, a Source, and a Filter Process

gives a total number of states equal to:

$$\sum_{i=0}^{8} 3^i = 9,841$$

This means that removing the process and the associated channel can decrease the complexity of the model by almost four orders of magnitude. The refutation power of the model is increased accordingly.

The temptation to include a dummy process is often given by a desire to model all existing parts of a system. The application being modeled may, for instance, contain a process or a task that performs a function that ends up being of only peripheral interest to the verification. There is an understandable uneasiness in the user to discard such processes, until it is reinforced that one is constructing a verification *model*, not the duplicate of an implementation. The difference in complexity can again be orders of magnitude.

SIMPLE REFUTATION MODELS

Is it realistic to expect that we can build models that are of practical significance and that remain computationally tractable? To answer this, we discuss two remarkably simple models that have this property. The first model counts just twelve reachable states, which could be sketched on a napkin. The second model is not much larger, with fifty-one reachable states, yet it too has undeniable practical significance. A naive model for either of these examples could easily defeat the capabilities of the most powerful model checking system. By finding the right abstraction, though, we can demonstrate that the design represented by the first model contains a design flaw, and we can prove the other to be a reliable template for the implementation of device drivers in an operating systems kernel.

The two abstractions discussed here require less computational power to be verified than what is available on an average wristwatch today. To be sure, it is often harder to find a simple model than it is to build a complex one, but the effort to find the simplest possible expression of a design idea can provide considerably greater benefits.

PATHFINDER

NASA's Pathfinder landed on the surface of Mars on July 4th, 1997, releasing a small rover to roam the surface. The mechanical and physical problems that had to be overcome to make this mission possible are phenomenal. Designing the software to control the craft may in this context seem to have been one of the simpler tasks, but designing any system that involves concurrency is challenging and requires the best minds and tools. Specifically, in this case, it was no easier to design the software than the rest of the spacecraft. And, as it turned out, it was only the control software that occasionally failed during the Pathfinder mission. A design fault caused the craft to lose contact with earth at unpredictable moments, causing valuable time to be lost in the transfer of data.

It took the designers a few days to identify the origin of the bug. To do so required an attempt to reproduce an unknown, non-deterministic execution sequence with only the tools from a standard system test environment, which can be very time-consuming.

The flaw turned out to be a conflict between a mutual exclusion rule and a priority rule used in the real-time task scheduling algorithm. The essence of the problem can be modeled in a SPIN verification model in just a few lines of code, as illustrated in Figure 5.3.

Two priority levels are modeled here as `active proctypes`. Both processes

```
mtype = { free, busy, idle, waiting, running };

mtype H_state = idle;
mtype L_state = idle;
mtype mutex = free;

active proctype high_priority()
{
end:
    do
    :: H_state = waiting;
        atomic { mutex == free -> mutex = busy };
        H_state = running;

        /* produce data */

        atomic { H_state = idle; mutex = free }
    od
}

active proctype low_priority() provided (H_state == idle)
{
end:
    do
    :: L_state = waiting;
        atomic { mutex == free -> mutex = busy };
        L_state = running;

        /* consume data */

        atomic { L_state = idle; mutex = free }
    od
}
```

Figure 5.3 Small Model for the Pathfinder Problem

need access to a critical region for transferring data from one process to the other, which is protected by a mutual exclusion lock. If by chance the high priority process starts running while the low priority process holds the lock, neither process can proceed: the high priority process is locked out by the mutex rule, and the low priority process is locked out by the priority rule, which is modeled by a provided clause on the low priority process.

The model shown here captures the essence of this problem in as few lines as possible. A verification of this model is a routine exercise with SPIN. The verifier is generated and compiled for exhaustive search as follows:

```
$ spin -a pathfinder.pml
$ cc -o pan pan.c
```

Next, the verification run is performed:

```
$ ./pan
pan: invalid end state (at depth 4)
pan: wrote pathfinder.pml.trail
(Spin Version 4.0.7 -- 1 August 2003)
Warning: Search not completed
        + Partial Order Reduction

Full statespace search for:
        never claim             - (none specified)
        assertion violations    +
        acceptance    cycles    - (not selected)
        invalid end states      +

State-vector 20 byte, depth reached 4, errors: 1
        5 states, stored
        1 states, matched
        6 transitions (= stored+matched)
        0 atomic steps
hash conflicts: 0 (resolved)
(max size 2^18 states)

1.493    memory usage (Mbyte)
```

The verifier finds an error after exploring only five system states. The full state space counts no more than twelve reachable system states, as illustrated in Figure 5.4, which should be compared to the many billions of possible states of the real memory-module in the Pathfinder controller that must be searched in exhaustive tests of the non-abstracted system. (All states can be generated by the verifier if we use option -c0, cf. Chapter 19, p. 536.)

The complete reachability graph for this system is readily built, even by a human model checker without computerized assistance. In Figure 5.4 we have marked the reachable system states with a triple. The first two elements of the triple identify the local state of each of the two processes: i for idle, w for waiting, and r for running. The third element of the triple records the state of the shared mutual exclusion lock variable: f for free, and b for busy.

Clearly, with two processes and one boolean lock, this level of abstraction gives rise to a maximum of eighteen system states (3x3x2), only twelve of which are effectively reachable from the initial system state. A verifier such as SPIN can efficiently build and analyze reachability graphs with billions of reachable system states, so a problem of this size is hardly challenging.

In this case, it is also not difficult to identify the two possible deadlock trajectories in the reachability graph, even by hand. The two system deadlock states in the graph are the states without any outgoing arrows. There is no possible

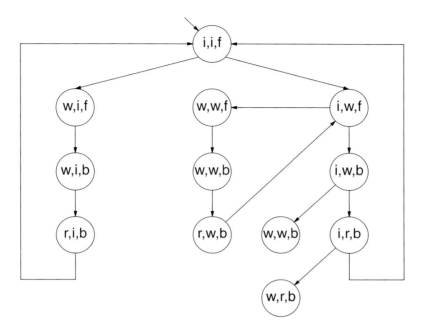

Figure 5.4 Reachability Graph for Pathfinder Problem

Process states: i = idle, w = waiting, r = running
Mutex lock states: f == free, b = busy
System states (x,y,z): x = high priority process, y = low priority process, z = mutex lock
Reachable Deadlock states: (w,w,b) and (w,r,b)
Starvation Cycles: {(i,i,f),(w,i,f),(w,i,b),(r,i,b)} and {(i,w,f),(w.w.f),(w,w,b),(r,w,b)}

exit from either state (w,w,b) or state (w,r,b) because in both cases the low priority process holds the lock and thereby blocks the high priority process, but the process holding the lock cannot proceed because of the priority rule that blocks it when the high priority process is not idle.

To analyze the behavior of this model we can look for paths leading into deadlock states. The verifier found the first such path, ending in state (w,r,b) (some information is elided for layout purposes):

```
$ spin -t -p pathfinder.pml
1: proc 1 (low)   line   40 ...   [l_state = waiting]
2: proc 1 (low)   line   41 ...   [((mutex==free))]
2: proc 1 (low)   line   41 ...   [mutex = busy]
```

```
3: proc 1 (low)  line  42 ... [l_state = running]
4: proc 0 (high) line  27 ... [h_state = waiting]
spin: trail ends after 4 steps
#processes: 2
          h_state = waiting
          l_state = running
          mutex = busy
4: proc 1 (low)  line  46 "pathfinder.pml" (state 8)
4: proc 0 (high) line  28 "pathfinder.pml" (state 4)
2 processes created
```

We can also use the verifier to look for more subtle types of properties. We may ask, for instance, if there is any way for one process to delay the execution of the other process indefinitely. Of course, because of the priority rule, there is such a possibility here. The use of the term *indefinitely* means that we are looking for possibly infinite executions with a special property.

The only type of infinite execution that can be performed in a finite reachability graph is, of course, a cyclic one. It is not hard to identify three basic cycles in the graph from Figure 5.4 with the property that only one of the processes repeatedly gets to its running state, while the other remains in its idle, or waiting state.

There is only effective denial of service if a process is indefinitely waiting to execute, that is, if the denied process has at least reached its waiting state. This rules out one of the three cycles, but leaves the other two as candidates for further inspection. As we shall see in more detail in Chapters 8 and 9, SPIN can reveal the existence of executions like this in even very large reachability graphs. One way to do so, in this case, is to mark the running state of either process as a progress state, and then ask SPIN to report on the existence of non-progress cycles in the reachability graph.

We will mark the running state in the low priority process as a progress state, as follows:

```
progress:      l_state = running;
```

The check for the absence of non-progress cycles is now performed as follows:

```
$ spin -a pathfinder.pml
$ cc -DNP -o pan pan.c  # enable NP algorithm
$ ./pan -l -f   # search for fair non-progress cycles
pan: non-progress cycle (at depth 24)
pan: wrote pathfinder.pml.trail
(Spin Version 4.0.7 -- 1 August 2003)
Warning: Search not completed
        + Partial Order Reduction
```

```
Full statespace search for:
        never claim            +
        assertion violations   + (if within scope of claim)
        non-progress cycles    + (fairness enabled)
        invalid end states     - (disabled by never claim)

State-vector 24 byte, depth reached 31, errors: 1
      11 states, stored (23 visited)
       4 states, matched
      27 transitions (= visited+matched)
       0 atomic steps
hash conflicts: 0 (resolved)
(max size 2^18 states)

1.493    memory usage (Mbyte)
```

Inspecting the error trail reveals the path leading into a potentially infinite cycle where the high priority process starves its low priority counterpart:

```
$ spin -t -p pathfinder.pml
 2: proc  1 (low)  line  40 ... [l_state = waiting]
 4: proc  1 (low)  line  41 ... [((mutex==free))]
 4: proc  1 (low)  line  41 ... [mutex = busy]
 6: proc  1 (low)  line  42 ... [l_state = running]
 8: proc  1 (low)  line  46 ... [l_state = idle]
 8: proc  1 (low)  line  46 ... [mutex = free]
10: proc  1 (low)  line  40 ... [l_state = waiting]
12: proc  0 (high) line  27 ... [h_state = waiting]
14: proc  0 (high) line  28 ... [((mutex==free))]
14: proc  0 (high) line  28 ... [mutex = busy]
16: proc  0 (high) line  29 ... [h_state = running]
18: proc  0 (high) line  33 ... [h_state = idle]
18: proc  0 (high) line  33 ... [mutex = free]
20: proc  0 (high) line  27 ... [h_state = waiting]
22: proc  0 (high) line  28 ... [((mutex==free))]
22: proc  0 (high) line  28 ... [mutex = busy]
24: proc  0 (high) line  29 ... [h_state = running]
 <<<<<START OF CYCLE>>>>>
26: proc  0 (high) line  33 ... [h_state = idle]
26: proc  0 (high) line  33 ... [mutex = free]
28: proc  0 (high) line  27 ... [h_state = waiting]
30: proc  0 (high) line  28 ... [((mutex==free))]
30: proc  0 (high) line  28 ... [mutex = busy]
32: proc  0 (high) line  29 ... [h_state = running]
spin: trail ends after 32 steps
#processes: 2
                h_state = running
                l_state = waiting
                mutex = busy
32: proc  1 (low) line  41 "pathfinder.pml" (state 4)
32: proc  0 (high) line  33 "pathfinder.pml" (state 8)
2 processes created
```

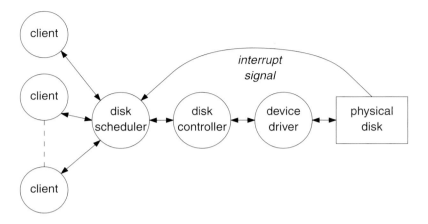

Figure 5.5 Disk Scheduler Context

Although the sample verification model for the Pathfinder problem is trivial to analyze, it should be added here that if a model of the mutual exclusion and priority scheduling rules had been constructed before the launch of the mission, before the design flaw manifested itself, the verification model would likely have contained more detail. In the real system, for instance, a third intermediate priority level was responsible for keeping the low priority process from releasing the lock, which prevented the high priority process from completing its task. Similarly, there were also other tasks in the system that manipulated the mutual exclusion locks that would likely have been included into the model and thereby increased the complexity of the verification beyond mere napkin size. The verification itself, though, should also in these cases have been able to reveal the problem.

A DISK-HEAD SCHEDULER

The next example illustrates how an abstract model can be constructed, again in just a few lines of high-level code, to confirm that a design has the properties it is intended to have. The example is a standard problem in operating system design: scheduling access of multiple client processes to a single server, which in this case is a disk scheduler. Only one client request is served by the disk-scheduler at a time. If multiple requests arrive, they are to be queued and served in order of arrival.

In a first attempt to build a verification model for this problem, it is natural to introduce separate processes to model the disk scheduler, the disk controller,

```
proctype Contr(chan req, signal)
{
    do
    :: req?IO ->
        /* perform IO operations */
        signal!Interrupt
    od
}
```

Figure 5.6 Minimal Device Driver Interface Model

the disk device driver, and the individual client processes that submit requests. To initiate a disk operation, a client process submits a request to the scheduler, where it may get queued. When it is ready to be serviced, the scheduler sends a start command to the controller, which then initiates the requested operation through the device driver. Completion of the operation is signaled by a hardware interrupt, which is intercepted by the scheduler. This basic architecture is illustrated in Figure 5.5.

Our objective is to check the basic design of the interaction between the disk scheduler and its clients. This means that the internal details of the device driver (e.g., mapping disk blocks to cylinders, sending commands to move the disk heads, etc.) are not directly relevant to this aspect of the design. To focus the verification model on the area of primary interest, we can and should abstract from the internals of the device driver process and the physical disk. The possible interactions between the device driver and the scheduler are, for instance, already captured in the device driver model from Figure 5.6.

The only assumption we are making here about the behavior of the device driver is that it will respond to every IO request with an interrupt signal within a finite, but otherwise arbitrary, amount of time. The relevant behavior of a client process can be modeled very similarly. It suffices to assume that each client can submit one request at a time, and that it will then wait for the matching response from the scheduler.

Before looking at the remainder of the verification model, though, we can already see that these initial models for the device driver and the client have all the characteristics of filter processes. The same is true for a minimal model of the disk controller. This is not too surprising, since we deliberately placed the focus on the verification of request queuing at the disk scheduler, not on the surrounding processes.

The temptation is to include the extra processes in the abstract model anyway, simply because they represent artifacts in the application. For the actual verification job, however, their presence serves no purpose and will increase the

```
#define Nclients        3

inline disk_io() {
    activeproc = curproc;
    assert(Interrupt_set == false);
    Interrupt_set = true;
}

inline Serve_client(x) {
    client_busy[x] = true;
    curproc = x+1;
    if     /* check disk status */
    :: activeproc == 0 -> disk_io()
    :: else /* Busy */ -> req_q!curproc
    fi
}

inline Handle() {
    Interrupt_set = false;
    client_busy[activeproc-1] = false;
    if
    :: req_q?curproc -> disk_io()
    :: empty(req_q) -> activeproc = 0
    fi
}

active proctype disk_sched()
{   chan req_q = [Nclients] of { byte };
    bool client_busy[Nclients] = false;
    bool Interrupt_set = false;
    byte activeproc, curproc;

    do
    :: !client_busy[0] -> progress_0: Serve_client(0)
    :: !client_busy[1] -> progress_1: Serve_client(1)
    :: !client_busy[2] -> progress_2: Serve_client(2)
    :: Interrupt_set == true -> Handle()
    od
}
```

Figure 5.7 Disk Scheduler Model

complexity of the model. These types of processes can be removed readily by applying the relatively simple abstractions of the type we have discussed. Doing so leads to the model shown in Figure 5.7.

A client process should be unable to submit a new request until the last one was completed. In the model from Figure 5.7, the client's busy status is recorded in a boolean array (rather than recorded as a process state, as in the equivalent of Figure 5.6).

We have added two correctness properties to this model. The first property is an assertion, claiming that no new interrupt can be generated before the last one was handled. The second property is expressed with a `progress` label which appears at the point in the code where a new client request is submitted. SPIN can check that neither assertion violations nor non-progress cycles are possible for this design. The validity of the second property implies that there cannot be any infinite execution without infinite progress for at least some client.

With two clients, the reachability graph for the model in Figure 5.7 has no more than 35 states. With three clients, as shown, the number of states increases to 142. In both cases this poses no challenge to any verifier.

For a complete verification, we will have to do two separate verification runs: one run to prove absence of assertion violations and deadlock states (safety properties), and a second run to prove the absence of non-progress cycles (a liveness property). The first check, for assertion violations and deadlock states proceeds as follows:

```
$ spin -a diskhead.pml
$ cc -o pan pan.c
$ ./pan
(Spin Version 4.0.7 -- 1 August 2003)
        + Partial Order Reduction

Full statespace search for:
        never claim             - (none specified)
        assertion violations    +
        acceptance   cycles     - (not selected)
        invalid end states      +

State-vector 25 byte, depth reached 67, errors: 0
      142 states, stored
       27 states, matched
      169 transitions (= stored+matched)
        0 atomic steps
hash conflicts: 0 (resolved)
(max size 2^18 states)

1.493   memory usage (Mbyte)

unreached in proctype disk_sched
        line 41, state 56, "-end-"
        (1 of 56 states)
```

The run shows that assertion violations or deadlocks (invalid end states) are not possible, and that all local process states in the disk_sched process are effectively reachable.

To check for the presence of non-progress cycles requires a slightly larger search, where each state can be visited up to two times. The run confirms that also non-progress cycles are not possible in this model:

```
$ spin -a diskhead.pml
$ cc -DNP -o pan pan.c
$ ./pan -l
(Spin Version 4.0.7 -- 1 August 2003)
        + Partial Order Reduction

Full statespace search for:
        never claim              +
        assertion violations     + (if within scope of claim)
        non-progress cycles       + (fairness disabled)
        invalid end states        - (disabled by never claim)

State-vector 29 byte, depth reached 146, errors: 0
     268 states, stored (391 visited)
     252 states, matched
     643 transitions (= visited+matched)
       0 atomic steps
hash conflicts: 0 (resolved)
(max size 2^18 states)


1.493    memory usage (Mbyte)

unreached in proctype disk_sched
        line 41, state 56, "-end-"
        (1 of 56 states)
```

But are three clients also sufficient to prove the required properties for an arbitrary number of clients? Every increase in the number of clients naturally increases the number of reachable states to be inspected due in large part to the increased number of permutations of distinct client requests in the request queue. Since all clients behave the same, it should suffice to prove each client-specific property for one arbitrarily chosen client.

We can do this by showing that a client-specific property holds no matter at what point in the disk scheduler's operation the client's request may arrive. Assuming that the request queue is large enough to hold the maximum number of simultaneous requests from clients, there are just three boolean conditions that together completely determine the scheduler's state and its actions upon accepting a new client request. They are:

- `empty(req_q)`
- `(activeproc == 0)`
- `Interrupt_set == true`

This gives us maximally eight relevant combinations (i.e., local scheduler states). With just one client process the truth assignment to the three conditions necessarily defaults to true, true, and false when a new request is initiated, so this definitely does not suffice to produce all eight combinations. With two clients we reach more, but we still cannot have both `Inter-rupt_set` and `empty(req_q)` be true at the same time. Three clients are the minimum needed to cover all eight combinations. Adding more client processes can increase the complexity of the verification further, but it cannot cover more cases or reveal anything new about this model. Admittedly, this is a very simple example of a system where processes communicate exclusively through message passing and do not access any globally shared data. Nonetheless, the original model of this system was successfully used as a guideline for the correct design and implementation of device driver modules in a commercial operating system, so even simple verification models can have realistic practical significance.

In practice, the need to produce simple verification models is not as strict as what may be suggested by the examples from this chapter. Spin can analyze models at a rate of 10,000 to 100,000 states per second, depending on the size of the state descriptors, and the speed of the CPU. This much power should in most cases suffice to tackle even the most challenging design problems.

CONTROLLING COMPLEXITY

We will see in Chapter 8 that the worst-case computational expense of verifying any type of correctness property with a model checker increases with the number of reachable system states R of a model. By reducing the size of R, therefore, we can try to reduce the complexity of a verification. Abstraction is the key tool we can use to keep the size of R small, but there are also other factors that we could exploit in model building.

Let n be the number of concurrent components, and let m be the total number of data objects they access. If we represent the number of control states of the i-th component by T_i, and the number of possible values for the j-th data object by D_j, then in the worst case the size of R could be the product of all values T_1 to T_n and all values D_1 to $\times D_m$. That is, the value of R itself may well be exponential in the number of concurrent components and the number of data objects. As a general rule, therefore, it is always good to search for a model with the fewest number of components (processes, channels, data objects), that is, to construct the smallest sufficient model.

EXAMPLE

Let us consider the complexity that can be introduced by a single useful type of abstract data object that is commonly used in distributed systems: a message channel or buffer. Let q be the number of buffers we have, let s be the maximum number of messages we can store in each buffer, and let m be the number of different message types that can be used. In how many different states can this set of data objects be? Each buffer can hold between zero and s messages, with each message being a choice of one out of m, therefore, the number of states R_Q is:

$$R_Q = \left(\sum_{i=0}^{s} m^i \right)^q .$$

Figure 5.8 shows how the number of states varies for different choices of the parameters q, s, and m. In the top-left graph of Figure 5.8, the parameters s and q are fixed to a value of 2, and the number of message types is varied from 1 to 10. There is a geometric increase in the number of states, but clearly not an exponential one. In the top-right graph, the parameters m and q are fixed to a value of 2, and the number of queue slots s is varied. This time there is an exponential increase in the number of states. Similarly, in the bottom-left graph, the parameters m and s are fixed, and the number of queues is varied. Again, we see an exponential increase in the number of states. Worse still, in the bottom-right graph of the figure, only the number of message types is fixed and the parameters s and q are equal and varied from 1 to 10. As can be expected, the increase is now doubly exponential. The number of possible states quickly reaches astronomical values.

Exponential effects work both ways. They can quickly make simple correctness properties of an uncarefully constructed model computationally intractable, but they can also help the model builder to prove subtle properties of complex systems by controlling just a few carefully chosen parameters.

The size of the available memory on a computer unavoidably restricts the size of the largest problems we can verify. We can try clever encoding and storage options for state space information, but at some point either the machine will run out of available memory or the user will run out of time, waiting for a verification run to complete. If the system is too complex to be analyzed exhaustively, we have no choice but to model it with a system that has fewer states. The tools that are used to accomplish this are: reduction, abstraction, modularity, and structure.

The existence of the state explosion phenomenon we have sketched above should never be used to excuse a designer from proving that a concurrent system fulfills its correctness requirements. It may well be considered to be the very objective of design verification to construct a tractable model and to formalize its properties. After all, since the final verification is a purely mechanical task, model building is the only real problem that the human designer must tackle.

A FORMAL BASIS FOR REDUCTION

The SPIN verification algorithms work by detecting the presence of a counterexample to a correctness claim. If we want to prove that p holds, we can use SPIN to try to find a counterexample where *the negation of* p holds. For

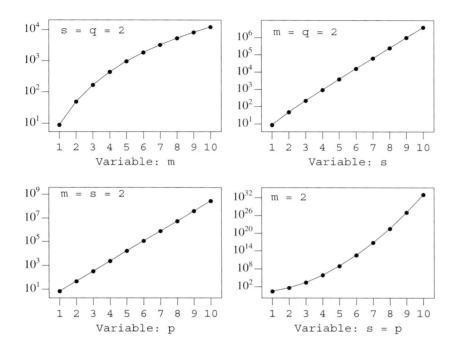

Figure 5.8 Number of Possible States for q Message Buffers
with s Buffer Slots and m Message Types

temporal logic formulae the same principle is applied. Instead of proving that there exist behaviors for which a given temporal logic formula is valid, SPIN tries to do the opposite: it attempts to find at least one behavior for which the negation of the formula is satisfied. If no counterexample can be found in an exhaustive verification, the formula is proven valid for *all* possible behaviors.

Call E the set of all possible runs of a system. The verification algorithms we have discussed demonstrate that either E does not contain any runs that violate a correctness requirement, or they provide positive proof that at least one such run exists. The verifier need not search for all possible runs in which the correctness requirement is *satisfied*, and indeed it often cannot do so.

This means that it is possible to *add* runs to E without affecting the validity of the proof, provided of course that we do not remove or alter any of the existing runs in E. We will use an example to demonstrate a number of strategies that can be used to reduce the complexity of a verification task by adding runs to E, such that in all cases $E \subseteq E'$. This principle is formalized in the following property.[2]

---

2. The formal definitions for the terms "finite state automaton," "run," and "correctness property" are given in Chapter 6.

Property 5.1 (Reduction Property)

Given two finite state automata T and T′, with sets of runs E and E′, respectively. If E⊆E′ then any correctness property proven for T′ necessarily also holds for T.

Proof: The violation of a correctness property for T is not possible without the existence of a run in E that demonstrates it. If no such run exists in E′ then no such run can exist in E either, since E′ includes E. □

We will see that abstractions of this type can dramatically reduce the number of reachable states of a system. Note that we can generalize a problem by removing constraints from it. The behavior of a model that is less specific often can be represented with fewer states. The least specific model would be one that imposes no constraints whatsoever on, for instance, the messages it can send. It can be represented by a one-state demon that randomly generates messages within its vocabulary, one by one, in an infinite sequence.

EXAMPLE – A FILE SERVER

Assume our task is to verify the correctness of a transfer protocol that is used to access a remote file server. Our first obligation is to determine precisely which correctness properties the transfer protocol must have, and what may be assumed about the behavior of the file server and of the transmission channel.

Consider first the transmission channel. Assume the channel is an optical fiber link. The protocol verifier's job is *not* to reproduce the behavior of the fiber link at the finest level of detail. The quality of a verification does *not* improve with a more detailed model of the link. Just the opposite is the case. This is worth stating explicitly:

A *less detailed* verification model is often more tractable, and allows for more general, and thus *stronger*, proofs.

A verification model should represent only those behaviors that are relevant to the verification task at hand. It need not contain information about the causes of those behaviors. If, in the file server example, the fiber link has a non-zero probability of errors, then the possibility of errors must be present in our model, but little more. The types of errors modeled could include disconnection, message-loss, duplication, insertion, or distortion. If all these types of errors are present, and relevant to the verification task at hand, it should suffice to model the link as a one-state demon that can randomly disconnect, lose, duplicate, insert, or distort messages.

A fully detailed model of the link could require several thousand states, representing, for instance, the clustering of errors, or the nature of distortions. For a design verification of the transfer protocol, however, it not only suffices to represent the link by a one-state demon: doing so guarantees a stronger verification result that is *independent* of clustering or distortion effects. Clearly, a model that randomly produces *all* relevant events that can be part of the real link behavior satisfies the requirements of Property 5.1. Of course, the random model of a link can contribute artificial behaviors where specific types of errors are repeated without bound. Our verification algorithms, however, provide the means to prune out the uninteresting subsets of these behaviors. If, for instance, we mark message loss as a pseudo *progress event* and start a search for non-progress cycles, we can secure that every cyclic execution that is reported by the verifier contains only finitely many message loss events.

Next, consider the file server. It can receive requests to create and delete, open and close, or read and write distinct files. Each such request can either succeed or fail. A read request on a closed file, for instance, will fail. Similarly, a create or write request will fail if the file server runs out of space. Again, for the verification of the interactions with the file server, we need not model in detail under what circumstances each request may succeed or fail. Our model of the server could again be a simple one-state demon that randomly accepts or rejects requests for service, without even looking at the specifics of the request.

Our one-state server would be able to exhibit behaviors that the real system would not allow, for instance, by rejecting valid requests.[3] All behaviors of the real server, however, are represented in the abstract model. If the transfer protocol can be proven correct, despite the fact that our model server may behave worse than the real one, the result is stronger than it would have been if we had represented the server in more detail. By generalizing the model of the file server, we separate, or shield, the correctness of the transfer protocol from the correctness requirements of the server. Again, the model that randomly produces *all* relevant events satisfies the requirements of Property 5.1.

Finally, let us consider the number of message types and message buffers that are needed to represent the interaction of user processes with the remote file server. If no single user can ever have more than one request outstanding, we need minimally three distinct types of messages, independent of how many distinct services the remote system actually offers. The three message types are **request, accept,** and **reject.**

If there are q users and only one server, the server must of course know which response corresponds to which request. Suppose that we use a single buffer for incoming requests at the server, and mark each request with a parameter that identifies the user. This gives q distinct types of messages that could arrive at the server. If $q \times s$ is the total number of slots in that buffer, the number of distinct states will be:

---

3. Remember that it is not the file server's behavior we are verifying, but the behavior of the transfer protocol. If the file server would have been the target of our verification, we would try to model it in more detail and generalize the transfer protocol that accesses it.

$$\sum_{i=0}^{q \times s} q^i.$$

What if we replaced the single buffer with q distinct buffers, each of s slots, one for each user? Now we need only one type of request, and the number of buffer states is now $(s + 1)^q$. Which is better?

Note that every feasible state of the multiple buffers can be mapped to a specific state of the single buffer, for instance, by simply concatenating all s slots of all q buffers, in numerical order, into the $q \times s$ slots of the single buffer. But the single buffer has many more states, that is, all those states that correspond to arbitrary interleavings of the contents of the multiple buffers. With these parameters, then, it can make a large difference in complexity if we replace a single buffer with a set of buffers.

To get an idea of the difference, assume $s = 5$ and $q = 3$; then the total number of states of all multiple buffers combined is $(s + 1)^q = 6^3 = 216$, and the total number of states of the single buffer is

$$\sum_{i=0}^{q \times s} q^i = \sum_{i=0}^{15} 3^i = 21,523,360$$

or about five orders of magnitude larger. Of course, in all these cases it remains the responsibility of the model builder to make certain that only abstractions are made that are independent of the property to be proven, and that satisfy the requirements of Property 5.1.

Assuming that we have the smallest possible model that still captures the essential features of a system, is there anything more we can do to reduce the complexity of the verification task still further? Fortunately, the answer is yes. In the next two sections, we will discuss two such techniques. The first technique modifies the verification algorithms we have developed in the previous chapter in such a way that redundant work can be avoided without diminishing the accuracy or the validity of the verification itself. The second technique is meant for cases where all the other reduction methods have failed, and we are faced with a verification problem that is still too complex to handle within the confines of available computational resources. This technique attempts to maximize the accuracy of a verification for those cases where no exact proofs are possible.

IN SUMMARY

The goal of this chapter is to show that applying model checking tools in a focused and targeted manner can be far more effective than blindly applying them as brute force reachability analyzers.

In a nutshell, the application of model checking in a design project typically consists of the following four steps:

- First, the designer chooses the properties (the correctness requirements) that are critical to the design.

- Second, the correctness properties are used as a guideline in the construction of a verification model. Following the principle of the smallest sufficient model, the verification model is designed to capture everything that is relevant to the properties to be verified, and little else. The power of the model checking approach comes in large part from our ability to define and use abstractions. Much of that power may be lost if we allow the verification model to come too close to the specifics of an implementation.

- Third, the model and the properties are used to select the appropriate verification method. If the model is very large, this could mean the choice between a precise verification of basic system properties (such as a check for absence of deadlock and the correctness of all process and system assertions), or a more approximate check of more complex logical and temporal properties.

- Fourth, the result of the verification is used to refine the verification model and the correctness requirements until all correctness concerns are adequately satisfied.

In the construction of a verifiable model it is good to be aware of the main causes of combinatorial complexity: the number and size of buffered channels, and the number of asynchronously executing processes. We can often bring the complexity of a verification task under control by carefully monitoring and adjusting these few parameters.

We return to the topic of abstraction in Chapter 10, where we consider it in the context of automated model extraction methods from implementation level code.

BIBLIOGRAPHIC NOTES

The solution to the disk scheduler problem discussed in this chapter is based on Villiers [1979].

The importance of abstraction in verification is generally recognized and features prominently in many papers in this area. Foundational work goes back to the early work of Patrick and Radhia Cousot on abstract interpretation, e.g., Cousot and Cousot [1976].

A detailed discussion of the theoretical background for abstraction is well beyond the scope of this book, but a good starting point for such a discussion can be found in, for instance, the work of Abadi and Lamport [1991], Kurshan [1993], Clarke, Grumberg, and Long [1994], Graf and Saidi [1997], Dams [1996], Dams, Gerth, and Grumberg [1997], Kesten and Pnueli [1998], Das, Dill, and Park [1999], and in Chechik and Ding [2002]. A good overview can also be found in Shankar [2002]. A general discussion of the role of abstraction in applications of SPIN is also given in Holzmann [1998b], from which we have also derived some of the examples that were used in this chapter.

An interesting discussion of the use of abstraction techniques that exploit symmetry in systems models to achieve a reduction in the complexity of verifications can be found in Ip and Dill [1996].

AUTOMATA AND LOGIC **6**

*"Obstacles are those frightful things you
see when you take your eyes off your goal."*
(Henry Ford, 1863–1947)

The model checking method that we will describe in the next few chapters is based on a variation of the classic theory of finite automata. This variation is known as the theory of ω-automata. The main difference with standard finite automata theory is that the acceptance conditions for ω-automata cover not just finite but also infinite executions.

Logical correctness properties are formalized in this theory as ω-regular properties. We will see shortly that ω-automata have just the right type of expressive power to model both process behavior in distributed systems and a broad range of correctness properties that we may be interested in proving about such systems.

AUTOMATA

To develop the theory, we begin with a few basic definitions.

Definition 6.1 (FSA)

A *finite state automaton* is a tuple (S, s_0, L, T, F), where

S	is a finite set of *states*,
s_0	is a distinguished initial state, $s_0 \in S$,
L	is a finite set of *labels*,
T	is a set of *transitions*, $T \subseteq (S \times L \times S)$, and
F	is a set of *final* states, $F \subseteq S$.

We will refer to state set S of finite state automaton A with a dot notation: $A.S$. Similarly, the initial state of A is referred to as $A.s_0$, etc.

In the simplest case, an automaton is deterministic, with the successor state of each transition uniquely defined by the source state and the transition label. Determinism is defined more formally as follows.

Definition 6.2 (Determinism)

A finite state automaton (S, s_0, L, T, F) is *deterministic* if, and only if,

$$\forall s \forall l, ((s, l, s') \in T \land (s, l, s'') \in T) \rightarrow s' \equiv s''.$$

Many of the automata we will use do not have this property, that is, they will be used to specify non-deterministic behaviors. As we shall see, there is nothing in the theory that would make the handling of non-deterministic automata particularly troublesome.

Definition 6.3 (Runs)

A *run* of a finite state automaton (S, s_0, L, T, F) is an ordered, possibly infinite, set of transitions (a sequence)

$$\{(s_0, l_0, s_1), (s_1, l_1, s_2), (s_2, l_2, s_3), \ldots \}$$

such that

$$\forall i, (i \geq 0) \rightarrow (s_i, l_i, s_{i+1}) \in T.$$

Occasionally we will want to talk about specific aspects of a given run, such as the sequence of states that is traversed, or the sequence of transition labels that it defines. Note that for non-deterministic automata the sequence of states traversed cannot necessarily be derived from the sequence of transition labels, and vice versa.

Definition 6.4 (Standard acceptance)

An *accepting run* of finite state automaton (S, s_0, L, T, F) is a *finite* run in which the final transition (s_{n-1}, l_{n-1}, s_n) has the property that $s_n \in F$.

The run is considered *accepted* if and only if it terminates in a final state of the automaton.

Figure 6.1 shows a simple finite state automaton with five states. It is defined as follows:

```
S = { s₀, s₁, s₂, s₃, s₄ },
L = { α₀, α₁, α₂, α₃, α₄, α₅ },
F = { s₄ }, and
T = { (s₀ , α₀ , s₁) , (s₁ , α₁ , s₂) ,
      (s₂ , α₂ , s₁) , (s₂ , α₃ , s₃) ,
      (s₃ , α₄ , s₂) , (s₂ , α₅ , s₄) } .
```

The initial state s_0 is traditionally marked with a short arrow, and the elements of set F are marked with a double circle in graphical representations, as we have done in Figure 6.1.

The labels on the transitions in a finite state automaton do not themselves have any inherent semantics. For the purpose of the definitions, they are just symbols or uninterpreted text strings. We can freely choose to interpret some of these labels as inputs or outputs or, where appropriate, as conditions or actions. The sample automaton from Figure 6.1, for instance, could be interpreted as modeling the life of a user process in a time-sharing system,

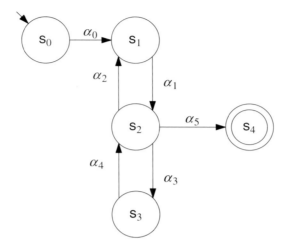

Figure 6.1 A Simple Finite State Automaton

controlled by a process scheduler, as illustrated in Figure 6.2. State s_0 then represents the 'Initial' state where the process is being instantiated, state s_1 is the 'Ready' state, s_2 is the 'Run' state, s_3 is the 'Blocked' state, for example, where the process may be waiting for a system call to complete, and s_4 is the 'End' state, reached if and when the process terminates.

One possible accepting run of this system is represented by the sequence

$$(s_0, \alpha_0, s_1) , \quad (s_1, \alpha_1, s_2) , \quad (s_2, \alpha_5, s_4) ,$$

which, under our chosen interpretation, corresponds to the sequence of scheduler actions: start, run, stop.

OMEGA ACCEPTANCE

With the definition of a finite state automaton given here, we can model terminating executions, but we still cannot decide on acceptance or non-acceptance of ongoing, potentially infinite, executions. Looking at Figure 6.2, for instance, if we were to model the underlying scheduler, rather than the processes being scheduled, the termination of the scheduler itself would not necessarily be a desirable result. The same is true for many other interesting systems, such as the control software for a nuclear power plant, a telephone switch, an ATM machine, or a traffic light.

An infinite run is often called an ω-run (pronounced: "*omega run*"). Acceptance properties for ω-runs can be defined in a number of different ways. The

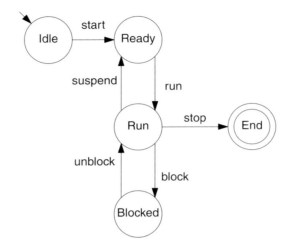

Figure 6.2 A Possible Interpretation of the Automaton in Figure 6.1

one we will adopt here was introduced by J.R. Büchi [1960].

If σ is an infinite run, let the symbol σ^ω represent the set of states that appear infinitely often within σ's set of transitions, and σ^+ the set of states that appear only finitely many times. The notion of Büchi acceptance is defined as follows.

Definition 6.5 (Büchi acceptance)

An *accepting ω-run* of finite state automaton (S, s_0, L, T, F) is any *infinite run* σ such that $\exists s_f, s_f \in F \wedge s_f \in \sigma^\omega$.

That is, an infinite run is accepted if and only if some state in F is visited infinitely often in the run. Without further precautions then, in the automaton from Figure 6.1 we could only see an accepting run under the definition of Büchi acceptance if at least one of the states s_1, s_2, or s_3 were members of final set F, since only these states can be visited infinitely often in a run.

With these definitions it is also easy to formalize the notion of non-progress that we discussed before. Let $P \subseteq S$ be the set of progress states. An ω-run σ then corresponds to a non-progress cycle if: $\forall s_f, s_f \in \sigma^\omega \rightarrow s_f \notin P$.

THE STUTTER EXTENSION RULE

The given formalization of acceptance applies only to infinite runs. It would clearly be convenient if we could somehow find a way to extend it so that the classic notion of acceptance for finite runs (cf. Definition 6.4) would be included as a special case. This can be done with the adoption of a stuttering rule. To apply the rule, we must extend our label sets with a fixed predefined null-label ε, representing a no-op operation that is always executable and has no effect (much like PROMELA's skip statement). The *stutter* extension of a finite run can now be defined as follows.

Definition 6.6 (Stutter Extension)

The *stutter extension* of finite run σ with final state s_n is the ω-run $\sigma, (s_n, \varepsilon, s_n)^\omega$.

The final state of the run, then, is thought to persist forever by infinitely repeating the null action ε. It follows that such a run would satisfy the rules for Büchi acceptance if, and only if, the original final state s_n is in the set of accepting states F, which means that it indeed generalizes the classical definition of finite acceptance.

A couple of abbreviations are so frequently used that it is good to summarize them here. The set of runs that is accepted by an automaton is often referred to as the *language* of the automaton. An automaton with acceptance conditions that are defined over infinite runs is often called an ω-automaton.

Accepting ω-runs of a finite state automaton can always be written in the form of an expression, using a dot to represent concatenation and the superfix ω to represent infinite repetition:

$$\bigcup_{i=1}^{N} U_i \cdot V_i^\omega$$

with U_i and V_i regular expressions over transitions in the automaton. That is, each such run consists of a finite prefix U, corresponding to an initial part of the run that is executed just once, and a finite suffix V, corresponding to a part of the run that is repeated *ad infinitum*. These expressions are called ω-regular expressions, and the class of properties that they express are called ω-regular properties. As a final bit of terminology, it is common to refer to automata with Büchi acceptance conditions simply as *Büchi Automata*.

FINITE STATES, INFINITE RUNS

It is clear that also an automaton with only finitely many states can have runs that are infinitely long, as already illustrated by Figure 6.1. With some reflection, it will also be clear that a finite automaton can have infinitely many distinct infinite runs.

To see this, imagine a simple automaton with eleven states, ten states named s_0 to s_9, and one final (accepting) state s_{10}. Define a transition relation for this automaton that connects every state to every other state, and also include a transition from each state back to itself (a self-loop). Label the transition from state s_i to s_j with the PROMELA print statement printf("%d\n", i). Use this labeling rule for all transitions *except* the self-loop on the one final state s_{10}, which is labeled skip. That is, if the transition from s_i to s_j is taken, the index number of the source transition will be printed, with as the single exception the transition from s_{10} back to s_{10}, which produces no output.

Every accepting run of this automaton will cause a number to be printed. This automaton has precisely one accepting run for every imaginable non-negative integer number, and there are infinitely many distinct numbers of this type.

OTHER TYPES OF ACCEPTANCE

There are of course many other ways to formalize the acceptance conditions of ω-automata. Most of these methods are named after the authors that first proposed them.

- Define F to be a set of subsets from state set S, that is, $F \subseteq 2^S$. We can require that the set of all states that are visited infinitely often in run σ equals one of the subsets in F:

$$\exists f, \ f \in F \ \wedge \ \sigma^\omega \equiv f .$$

  This notion of acceptance is called Muller acceptance, and the corresponding automata are called *Muller Automata*.

- We can also define a finite set of n pairs, where for each pair (L_i, U_i) we have $L_i \subseteq S$ and $U_i \subseteq S$. We can now require that there is at least one pair i in the set for which none of the states in L_i appear infinitely often in σ, but at least one state in U_i does:

$$\exists i, (1 \leq i \leq n), \ \forall s, \ (s \in L_i \rightarrow s \notin \sigma^\omega) \ \wedge \ \exists t, (t \in U_i \wedge t \in \sigma^\omega).$$

  This notion of acceptance is called Rabin acceptance, and the corresponding automata are called *Rabin Automata*.

- Using the same definition of pairs of sets states, we can also define the opposite condition that for all pairs in the set either none of the states in U_i appear infinitely often in σ, or at least one state in L_i does:

$$\forall i, (1 \leq i \leq n), \ \exists s, (s \in L_i \wedge s \in \sigma^\omega) \ \vee \ \forall t, (t \in U_i \rightarrow t \notin \sigma^\omega).$$

  This notion of acceptance is called Streett acceptance, and the corresponding automata are called *Streett Automata*.

All these types of acceptance are equally expressive and define the same class of ω-regular properties as Büchi Automata.

Many interesting properties of Büchi automata have been shown to be decidable. Most importantly, this applies to checks for language *emptiness* (i.e., deciding whether the set of accepting runs of a given Büchi automaton is empty), and language *intersection* (i.e., generating a single Büchi automaton that accepts precisely those ω-runs that are accepted by *all* members of a given set of Büchi automata). We shall see in Chapter 8 that the verification

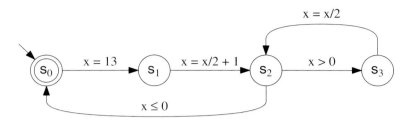

Figure 6.3 Model of a Simple Computation

problem for SPIN models is equivalent to an emptiness test for an intersection product of Büchi automata.

LOGIC

Automata models offer a good formalism for the analysis of distributed system models. As noted in earlier chapters, though, a complete verification model contains not just the specification of system behavior but also a formalization of the *correctness requirements* that apply to the system. We will now show how higher-level requirements can be expressed in a special type of logic that has a direct connection to the formalism of Büchi Automata.

A *run* of an automaton captures the notion of system execution. Through the definition of acceptance conditions we can already distinguish the runs that satisfy a given set of requirements from those that violate it. It can be a daunting task, though, to express correctness requirements at this relatively low level of abstraction. We need a more convenient method.

Consider the automaton from Figure 6.3 with initial and final state s_0. The formulation of a correctness property for this automaton requires the ability to *interpret* its runs, minimally to distinguish the good runs from the bad ones. To do so, we can define a semantics on the labels that are used. We will use the semantics interpretation of PROMELA. An integer variable named x is assigned values, and is tested in conditionals.

The sequence of states traversed during a run of this (deterministic) automaton is:

$$s_0, s_1, s_2, s_3, s_2, s_3, s_2, s_3, s_2, s_0, \cdots.$$

Of course, not every accepting run of the automaton will automatically be consistent with our chosen semantics interpretation of the labels. Given an initial value for x, we can write down the new value for x that is consistent with the PROMELA assignment statements from the labels. A run is only consistent with the semantics interpretation if all condition labels that appear in the run, such as $x > 0$ and $x \leq 0$, evaluate to *true*.

Given the initial value zero of x, we can annotate each state in the run above with the corresponding value for x, as follows:

$(s_0, 0), (s_1, 13), (s_2, 7), (s_3, 7), (s_2, 3), (s_3, 3), (s_2, 1), (s_3, 1),$
$(s_2, 0), (s_0, 0), \cdots.$

Jointly, the state number s_i and the value of variable x define an extended *system state*. We can derive a pure (non-extended) finite state automaton from the one that is specified in Figure 6.3 by expanding the set of states. State s_2, for instance, would generate four copies in such an unfolding. For values 7, 3, 1, and 0 of x, and state s_3 would generate three copies, one for each of the values 7, 3, and 1. The resulting expanded finite state automaton has nine states, all of which appear in the annotated state sequence.

We can formulate properties of runs of the expanded automaton. The most interesting properties would deal with the achievable and non-achievable values of x during a run. Consider, for instance, the properties

    p: *"the value of x is odd"*
    q: *"the value of x is 13"*

We can deduce a truth value for p and for q at each extended system state. These types of properties are formally called *state formulae*, to distinguish them from the *temporal formulae* we will discuss next. The sequence of truth values for p and q then are:

    p: *false, true, true, true, true, true, true, true, false, false,* ...
    q: *false, true, false, false, false, false, false, false, false, false,* ...

To pursue this idea one step further still, we can make statements about possible and impossible sequences of boolean values for p and q throughout a run, as in:

- p is invariantly *true*,
- p eventually becomes invariantly *false*,
- p always eventually becomes *false* at least once more,
- q always implies ¬p,
- p always implies eventually q.

Note that the latter types of statements can only be fully evaluated for complete runs of the system, not just for individual system states in isolation. It is clear that the first two properties above do not hold for the (single) accepting run of our extended finite state automaton. The third and the fifth properties both hold, but the fourth does not.

There are two questions that remain to be answered: can we formalize the properties of the type we have just discussed in terms of a simple logic, and can we express the properties in terms of Büchi acceptance conditions? The next two sections provide the answers to these two questions.

TEMPORAL LOGIC

The branch of logic that allows one to reason about both causal and temporal relations of properties is called *temporal logic*. Temporal logic was first studied in the late sixties and early seventies, but primarily as a tool in philosophical arguments that involved the passage of time. A first paper proposing the application of this type of logic for the analysis of distributed system was authored by Amir Pnueli in 1977. It took more than a decade, though, for the fundamental importance of these ideas to be more generally accepted.

Temporal logic allows us to formalize the properties of a run unambiguously and concisely with the help of a small number of special temporal operators. Most relevant to the verification of asynchronous process systems is a specific branch of temporal logic that is known as *linear* temporal logic, commonly abbreviated as LTL. The semantics of LTL is defined over infinite runs. With the help of the stutter extension rule, however, it applies equally to finite runs, as we shall see in more detail shortly.

A well-formed temporal formula is built from state formulae and temporal operators, using the following two basic rules:

Definition 6.7 (Well-Formed Temporal Formulae)

- All state formulae, including `true` and `false`, are *well-formed temporal formulae.*
- If α is a unary temporal operator, β is a binary temporal operator, and p and q are well-formed temporal formulae, than so are α p, p β q, (p), and !p ($\neg$ p).

The first temporal operator we will discuss is the binary operator *until*, which we will represent by the symbol U. The truth of a formula such as pUq can be evaluated for any given ω-run σ. The symbols p and q can be replaced with arbitrary state formulae or with temporal sub-formulae. If a temporal formula f holds for ω-run σ, we write:

$$\sigma \models f.$$

In the definitions that follow, we use the notational convention that σ_i represents the i-th element of the run σ, and $\sigma[i]$ represents the suffix of σ that starts at the i-th element. Trivially $\sigma \equiv \sigma[1] \equiv \sigma_1\sigma[2]$.

There are two variations of the until operator that are distinguished by the adjective *weak* and *strong*. The definition of the weak until operator is:

Definition 6.8 (Weak Until)

$$\sigma[i] \models (p\ U\ q) \quad \Leftrightarrow \quad \sigma_i \models q \quad \vee \quad (\sigma_i \models p \wedge \sigma[i+1] \models (p\ U\ q)).$$

Notice that this definition does not require that the sub-formula q ever become *true*. The second variant of the operator, called strong until and written U, adds that requirement.

Definition 6.9 (Strong Until)

$\sigma[i] \models (p\ U\ q) \iff \sigma[i] \models (p\ U\ q) \land \exists j, j \geq i, \sigma_j \models q.$

There are two special cases of these two definitions that prove to be especially useful in practice. The first is a formula of the type p U *false*. Note that the truth of this formula only depends on the value of sub-formula p. We introduce a special operator to capture this:

Definition 6.10 (Always)

$\sigma \models \Box\ p \iff \sigma \models (p\ U\ false).$

The formula $\Box$ p captures the notion that the property p remains invariantly *true* throughout a run. The operator $\Box$ is therefore pronounced *always* or *box*.

The second special case is a formula of the type *true* U q, which again reduces the number of operands from two to one. The case is important enough to warrant the introduction of another shorthand.

Definition 6.11 (Eventually)

$\sigma \models \Diamond\ q \iff \sigma \models (true\ U\ q).$

The formula $\Diamond$ p captures the notion that the property p is guaranteed to eventually become *true* at least once in a run. The operator $\Diamond$ is therefore pronounced *eventually*, or *diamond*. It conveniently captures the notion of liveness.

There is just one other temporal operator that we have to discuss here to complete the basic temporal logic framework. This is the unary *next* operator which is represented by the symbol X. The semantics of the X operator can be defined as follows.

Definition 6.12 (Next)

$\sigma[i] \models X\ p \iff \sigma_{i+1} \models p.$

The formula X p then simply states that property p is *true* in the immediately following state of the run.

RECURRENCE AND STABILITY

There are many standard types of correctness properties that can be expressed with the temporal operators we have defined. Two important types are defined next.

Definition 6.13

A *recurrence property* is any temporal formula that can be written in the form $\Box\Diamond p$, where p is a state formula.

The recurrence property $\Box\Diamond p$ states that if p happens to be false at any given point in a run, it is always guaranteed to become true again if the run is continued.

Table 6.1 Frequently Used LTL Formulae

Formula	Pronounced	Type/Template
□ p	always p	*invariance*
◊ p	eventually p	*guarantee*
p → ◊ q	p implies eventually q	*response*
p → q U r	p implies q until r	*precedence*
□ ◊ p	always eventually p	*recurrence (progress)*
◊ □ p	eventually always p	*stability (non-progress)*
◊ p → ◊ q	eventually p implies eventually q	*correlation*

Definition 6.14
   A *stability property* is any temporal formula that can be written in the form ◊□p, where p is a state formula.

The stability property ◊□p states that there is always a point in a run where p will become invariantly true for the remainder of the run.

Recurrence and stability are in many ways dual properties that reflect a similar duality between the two earlier canonical correctness requirements we discussed: absence of non-progress cycles and absence of acceptance cycles.

There are other interesting types of duality. For instance, if '!' denotes logical negation, it is not hard to prove that in any context:

$$!□p \quad\quad \Leftrightarrow \quad ◊!p \quad\quad\quad [1]$$
$$!◊p \quad\quad \Leftrightarrow \quad □!p \quad\quad\quad [2]$$

Which also implies, for instance, □p ⇔ !◊!p and ◊p ⇔ !□!p. We will refer to the above two standard equivalence rules by number in the remainder of this chapter. Some other commonly used rules are:

$$!(p\ U\ q) \quad \Leftrightarrow \quad (!q)U(!p \wedge !q)$$
$$!(p\ U\ q) \quad \Leftrightarrow \quad (!q)U(!p \wedge !q)$$
$$□(p \wedge q) \quad \Leftrightarrow \quad □p \wedge □q$$
$$◊(p \vee q) \quad \Leftrightarrow \quad ◊p \vee ◊q$$
$$p\ U\ (q \vee r) \quad \Leftrightarrow \quad (p\ U\ q) \vee (p\ U\ r)$$
$$(p \wedge q)\ U\ r \quad \Leftrightarrow \quad (p\ U\ r) \wedge (q\ U\ r)$$
$$p\ U\ (q \vee r) \quad \Leftrightarrow \quad (p\ U\ q) \vee (p\ U\ r)$$
$$(p \wedge q)\ U\ r \quad \Leftrightarrow \quad (p\ U\ r) \wedge (q\ U\ r)$$
$$□◊(p \vee q) \quad \Leftrightarrow \quad □◊p \vee □◊q$$
$$◊□(p \wedge q) \quad \Leftrightarrow \quad ◊□p \wedge ◊□q$$

Many types of temporal logic formula are used so frequently that they have special names. One can consider such formulae *templates* for expressing common types of properties. Table 6.1 lists the most popular of these templates. We use the symbols → and ↔ for logical implication and equivalence,

Table 6.2 Formalization of Properties

Formula	English
□ p	p is invariantly *true*,
◊ □ !p	p eventually becomes invariantly *false*
□ ◊ !p	p always eventually becomes *false* at least once more
□ (q → !p)	q always implies !p
□ (p → ◊ q)	p always implies eventually q

defined as follows.

Definition 6.15 (Implication)

    p → q $\models$ (!p) ∨ q.

Definition 6.16 (Equivalence)

    p ↔ q $\models$ (p → q) ∧ (q → p).

Armed with this logic, we can now revisit the earlier examples of temporal properties that we wanted to be able to express (p. 134), as shown in Table 6.2.

USING TEMPORAL LOGIC

The logic looks straightforward enough, and it is not difficult to develop an intuition for the meaning of the operators. Still, it can sometimes be difficult to find the right formalization in temporal logic of informally stated requirements. As an example, consider the informal system requirement that p implies q. The formalization that first comes to mind is

    p → q

which is almost certainly wrong. Note that as a formula in temporal logic this property must hold for every run of the system. There are no temporal operators used here, just logical implication. This means that it holds if and only if

    $\sigma \models$ (!p) ∨ q

which holds if in the first state of the run either p is *false* or q is *true*. It says nothing about the remaining steps in $\sigma[2]$. To make the property apply to all steps in the run we would have to change it into

    □ (p → q)

but also that is most likely not what is meant, because this expresses merely a logical implication between p and q, not a temporal implication. If a temporal implication was meant, the formula should be written as follows:

    □ (p → ◊ q)

This still leaves some room for doubt, since it allows for the case where q becomes *true* in precisely the same state as where p becomes *true*. It would be hard to argue that this accurately captures the notion that the truth of q is somehow caused by the truth of p. To capture this, we need to modify the formula again, for instance, by adding a next operator.

$$\Box\ (p \rightarrow X\ (\Diamond\ q))$$

After all this work, this formula may still prove to be misleading. If the antecedent p is invariantly *false* throughout each run, for instance, the property will be satisfied. In this case, we call the property *vacuously true*. It is almost surely not what we meant when we formalized the property. This brings us to the final revision of the formula by adding the statement that we expect p to become *true* at some point. This produces the final form

$$\Box\ (p \rightarrow X\ (\Diamond\ q)) \wedge \Diamond\ p$$

which is quite different from the initial guess of $(p \rightarrow q)$.

VALUATION SEQUENCES

Let P be the set of all state formulae that are used in a given temporal logic formula. Each such state formula is typically represented by a lower-case propositional symbol (say p or q). Let, further, V represent the set of all the possible boolean truth assignments to the propositional symbols in P (i.e., set V has $2^{|P|}$ elements, where $|P|$ is the number of elements of set P). We call V the set of *valuations* of P. With each run σ of a system we can now associate a sequence of valuations from V, denoting the specific boolean values that all propositional symbols take, as we illustrated earlier for the system in Figure 6.3. We will refer to that sequence as $V(\sigma)$.

STUTTER INVARIANCE

The next operator, X, can be useful to express complex system requirements, but it should be used with caution. Note first that in a distributed system the very notion of a "next" state is somewhat ambiguous. It is usually unknown and unknowable how the executions of asynchronously execution processes are going to be interleaved in time. It can therefore usually not be determined with certainty how a given current system state relates to the one that happens to follow it after one more step in a run. We can assume that every process will make finite progress, unless it becomes permanently blocked, but it is usually not justified to make more specific assumptions about the precise rate of progress, relative to other processes, since this may depend on uncontrollable and often unobservable aspects of a distributed system, such as the relative speeds of processors or subtle details of process scheduling.

These somewhat vague notions about what can and what cannot safely be stated about the runs of a distributed system can be made more precise with the help of the notion of *stutter invariance*.

Consider a run σ and its valuation $\phi = V(\sigma)$. Remember that ϕ is a sequence of truth assignments to the elements of a finite set of boolean propositions P used in a given temporal formula. Two subsequent elements of this sequence are either equal or they differ. We will replace series of equal consecutive elements in a valuation with a single symbol with the number of repetitions recorded in a superfix.

Let N be a sequence of positive numbers N_1, N_2, $\cdots$. Each valuation ϕ of a run can then be written in the form

$$\phi_1^{N_1}, \phi_2^{N_2}, \cdots$$

with an appropriate choice for N. Given such a sequence ϕ, we can derive a *stutter-free* variant of ϕ by setting all elements of N to one: $N = 1, 1, \cdots$. We can also derive a set of variants of ϕ that includes all possible choices for N. Such a set is called the *stutter extension* of ϕ and written as $\mathsf{E}(\phi)$.

For temporal logic formula f to be satisfied on some run σ, the valuation $\mathsf{V}(\sigma)$ must satisfy the formula, that is, we must have $\mathsf{V}(\sigma) \models f$. We are now ready to define stutter invariance.

Definition 6.17 (Stutter invariance)

A temporal logic formula f is stutter invariant if and only if
$$\mathsf{V}(\sigma) \models f \to \forall \phi, \phi \in \mathsf{E}(\sigma), \mathsf{V}(\phi) \models f.$$

This means that the property is stutter invariant if it is insensitive to the number of steps that individual valuations of the boolean propositions remain in effect.

We argued earlier that it would be dangerous for the correctness of a system to depend on execution speed, so this nicely captures our intuition about well-formed formulae in temporal logic: such formulae should be stutter invariant.

It can be shown that if we bar the next operator, X, from temporal logic, the temporal formulae that we write will be guaranteed to be stutter invariant. Moreover, it can also be shown that without the next operator we can precisely express *all* stutter invariant properties. This does not mean that a temporal logic formula that includes a X operator is necessarily not stutter invariant: it may well be so, but it is not guaranteed.

In a later chapter we will see another reason why we will want to be cautious with the use of X: properties that are known to be stutter invariant can be verified more efficiently than properties that do not have this property.

FAIRNESS

One of the attractive features of LTL is that it can be used to express a fairly broad range of fairness assumptions. SPIN itself supports only a limited notion of fairness that applies only to the specific way in which process-level non-determinism is resolved (i.e., it applies only to process scheduling decisions). In some cases, we may want to express that also non-deterministic choices within a process are resolved conform some user-specified notion a fairness. These types of fairness conditions are readily expressed in LTL. If, for instance, our correctness claim is ϕ, we can add the fairness constraint that if a process of type P visits a state labeled U infinitely often, it must also visit a state labeled L infinitely often, by adding a conjunct to the property:

$$\phi \ \wedge ((\Box \Diamond \, P@U) \to (\Box \Diamond \, P@L)).$$

FROM LOGIC TO AUTOMATA

It was shown in the mid eighties that for every temporal logic formula there exists a Büchi automaton that accepts precisely those runs that satisfy the formula. There are algorithms that can mechanically convert any temporal logic formulae into the equivalent Büchi automaton. One such algorithm is built into SPIN.

Strictly speaking, the system description language PROMELA does not include syntax for the specification of temporal logic formulae, but SPIN does have a separate parser for such formulae and it can mechanically translate them into PROMELA syntax, so that LTL can effectively become part of the language that is accepted by SPIN. LTL, however, can only be used for specifying correctness requirements on PROMELA verification models. The models themselves cannot be specified in LTL. SPIN's conversion algorithm translates LTL formulae into `never` claims, and it automatically places accept labels within the claim to capture the semantics of the ω-regular property that is expressed in LTL.

To make it easier to type LTL formulae, the box (always) operator is written as a combination of the two symbols [], and the diamond operator (eventually) is written as the two symbols <>. SPIN only supports the *strong* version of the until operator, represented by the capital letter U. To avoid confusion, state properties are always written with lower-case symbols such as p and q.

We can, for instance, invoke SPIN as follows:

```
$ spin -f '<>[] p'
never {      /* <>[]p */
T0_init:
        if
        :: (p) -> goto accept_S4
        :: (1) -> goto T0_init
        fi;
accept_S4:
        if
        :: (p) -> goto accept_S4
        fi
}
```

Note carefully that in a UNIX environment the temporal logic formula must be quoted to avoid misinterpretation of the angle symbols by the command interpreter, and to secure that the formula is seen as a single argument even if it contains spaces.[1] SPIN places braces around all expressions to make sure that there can be no surprises in the enforcement of precedence rules in their evaluation. Note also that the guard condition (1) is equivalent to the boolean value *true*.

> *A note on syntax:* SPIN accepts LTL formulae that consist of propositional symbols (including the predefined terms true and false), unary and binary temporal operators, and the three logical operators ! (logical negation), ∧ (logical and), and ∨ (logical or). The logical and operator can also be written in C style as &&, and the logical or operator can also be written as ||. Also supported are the abbreviations -> for logical implication and <-> for logical equivalence (see Definitions 6.15 and 6.16). Arithmetic operators (e.g., +, -, *, /) and relational operators (e.g., >, >=, <, <=, ==, !=) cannot appear directly in LTL formulae.

For example, the following attempt to convert a formula fails:

```
$ spin -f '([] p -> <> (a+b <= c))'
tl_spin: expected ')', saw '+'
tl_spin: ([] p -> <> (a+b <= c))
----------------------^
```

To succesfully convert this formula, we must introduce a new propositional symbol to hide the arithmetic and relational operators, as follows:

```
#define q        (a+b <= c)
```

We can now invoke SPIN's converter on the new formula:

```
$ spin -f '([] p -> <> q)'
```

Also be aware of operator precedence rules. The formula above is quite different, for instance, from:

```
$ spin -f '([] (p -> <> q))'
```

(Hint: try the conversions with SPIN to see the difference).

The automaton for the formula ◊ □ p is shown in Figure 6.4. The automaton has two states, one initial state s_0, which corresponds to the never claim state T0_init, and one accepting state s_1, which corresponds to never claim state accept_S4.

Note that the automaton contains no transitions labelled (!p), in state accept_S4 or s_1. The reason is that when p becomes *false* after we have reach this state, the continuation of the run can no longer lead to acceptance. The automaton needs to monitor only those runs that may still produce a counterexample if continued sufficiently far. All other runs are irrelevant to

---

1. On some, but not all, UNIX systems, the argument with the formula can also be enclosed in double quotes.

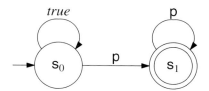

Figure 6.4 Automaton for ◊ □ p

the verification procedure and can summarily be rejected. A direct benefit of leaving the automaton incomplete in this sense is therefore that the verifier will have to inspect fewer runs, which makes it more efficient.

The `never` claim that is generated by SPIN can be included into a PROMELA model to check if the behavior defined by the temporal logic formula can occur in the model, provided that the propositional symbols that are used (here only p) are defined. Typically, the definitions are done with macros, for instance, as follows:

```
#define p        (x > 0 && x <= 100)
```

SPIN will flag it as an error if an accepting run can be found that matched the behavior expressed. That is, SPIN will find those runs that *satisfy* the LTL formula that was used to generate the `never` claim. To show that a property such as ◊ □ p should not be *violated*, we can simply negate the formula before the claim is generated, for instance, as follows:

```
$ spin -f '!<>[]p'
never {      /* !<>[]p */
T0_init:
        if
        :: (!(p)) -> goto accept_S9
        :: (1) -> goto T0_init
        fi;
accept_S9:
        if
        :: (1) -> goto T0_init
        fi;
}
```

The corresponding automaton is shown in Figure 6.5.

Because of the known equivalences we can deduce that !<>□p is equivalent to □!□p which in turn is equivalent to □◊!p. This means that if we ask SPIN to convert the formula □◊!p we should get the same result as for !<>□p. This is readily confirmed by a little experiment:

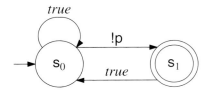

Figure 6.5 Automaton for $\neg\Diamond\,\Box\,p = \Box\,\Diamond\,\neg p$

```
$ spin -f '[]<>!p'
never {    /* []<>!p */
T0_init:
        if
        :: (!(p)) -> goto accept_S9
        :: (1) -> goto T0_init
        fi;
accept_S9:
        if
        :: (1) -> goto T0_init
        fi;
}
```

It should be carefully noted that the automaton for neither the original nor the negated version of this formula can accept finite runs (cf. p. 130), and neither version necessarily matches all possible system behaviors. The claim is meant to capture only those accepting runs that satisfy the temporal formula; no more and no less.

The automata that are produced by most conversion algorithms are not always the smallest possible. It can be useful to understand how never claims work, so that in special cases, when performance is at a premium, the claim automaton can be edited to remove unnecessary states or transitions. A detailed explanation of the working of never claims can be found in Chapter 4, p. 85.

In some cases, also, it can be difficult, or risky, to manually change a Spin generated claim. It can then be useful to compare the Spin generated claims with those produced by alternate converters. As an example, consider the following suboptimal claim for the requirement $\Box(p \rightarrow \Diamond q)$:

```
$ spin -f '[] (p -> <> q)'
never {    /* [] (p -> <> q) */
T0_init:
        if
        :: ((! (p)) || (q)) -> goto accept_S20
        :: (1) -> goto T0_S27
        fi;
```

```
accept_S20:
        if
        :: ((! (p)) || (q)) -> goto T0_init
        :: (1) -> goto T0_S27
        fi;

accept_S27:
        if
        :: (q) -> goto T0_init
        :: (1) -> goto T0_S27
        fi;

T0_S27:
        if
        :: (q) -> goto accept_S20
        :: (1) -> goto T0_S27
        :: (q) -> goto accept_S27
        fi;
}
```

An alternative **converter**,[2] called ltl2ba, written by Paul Gastin and Denis Oddoux, produces a smaller claim:

```
$ ltl2ba -f '[] (p -> <> q)'
never { /* [] (p -> <> q) */
accept_init:
        if
        :: (!p) || (q) -> goto accept_init
        :: (1) -> goto T0_S2
        fi;
T0_S2:
        if
        :: (1) -> goto T0_S2
        :: (q) -> goto accept_init
        fi;
}
```

The corresponding automaton structure is shown in Figure 6.6.

The logical negation of this last requirement is also interesting. It can be derived as follows:

$$
\begin{array}{lll}
!\Box(p \to \Diamond q) & \Leftrightarrow & \text{(by the definition of } \to) \\
!\Box(!p \lor \Diamond q) & \Leftrightarrow & \text{(by equivalence rule [1], p. 137)} \\
\Diamond!(!p \lor \Diamond q) & \Leftrightarrow & \text{(by De Morgan's Laws)} \\
\Diamond(p \land !\Diamond q) & \Leftrightarrow & \text{(by equivalence rule [2])} \\
\Diamond(p \land \Box!q).
\end{array}
$$

2. Gastin and Oddoux's converter is available as part of the standard SPIN distribution. See Appendix D.

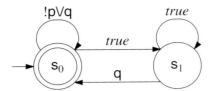

Figure 6.6 Automaton for $\square(p \rightarrow \lozenge q)$

The corresponding `never` claim is shown in Figure 6.7.

We can of course also let SPIN do the derivation of the negated formula. The `never` claim that matches Figure 6.7 is generated as follows:

```
$ spin -f '![] (p -> <> q)'
never {    /* ![] (p -> <> q) */
T0_init:
        if
        :: (! ((q)) && (p)) -> goto accept_S4
        :: (1) -> goto T0_init
        fi;
accept_S4:
        if
        :: (! ((q))) -> goto accept_S4
        fi;
}
```

This time the built-in algorithm from SPIN does much better in generating a small automaton. Note carefully that using `else` instead of `(1)` (i.e., `true`) in the first selection construct would imply a check for just the *first* occurrence of expression `(!(q)&&(p))` becoming *true* in the run. The claim as generated checks for *all* such occurrences, anywhere in a run.

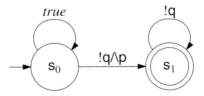

Figure 6.7 Never Automaton for $\lozenge(p \wedge \square!q)$

As a slightly more complicated variation on the previous example, consider the requirement $\square (p \rightarrow (r U q))$. The corresponding automaton is shown in

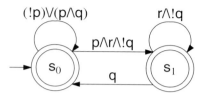

Figure 6.8 Automaton for □(p → (rUq))

Figure 6.8. In this case, all possible (infinite) runs of the automaton are accepting. But not all runs are possible. Runs in which, for instance, r becomes *false* before q becomes *true* in state s_1 are not accepted. The negation of the property can be derived as follows.

!□(p → (rUq))	⇔	(by the definition of →)
!□(!p∨(rUq))	⇔	(by equivalence rule [1], p. 137)
◊!(!p∨(rUq))	⇔	(by De Morgan's Laws)
◊(p∧!(rUq)).		

Of course, it is typically easier to let SPIN handle the negation and do the conversion than to work out the negations manually. The automaton that corresponds to either the LTL formula ◊(p∧!(rUq)) or the formula !□(p → (rUq)) is shown in Figure 6.9.

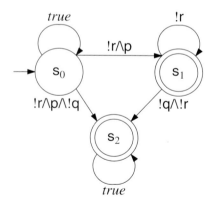

Figure 6.9 Automaton for ◊(p∧!(rUq))

This three-state ω-automaton can be generated in SPIN's never claim format as follows:

```
$ spin -f '![] (p -> (q U r))'
never {     /* ![] (p -> (q U r)) */
T0_init:
        if
        :: (!(r) && (p)) -> goto accept_S4
        :: (!(r) && (p) && (!(q))) -> goto accept_all
        :: (1) -> goto T0_init
        fi;
accept_S4:
        if
        :: (!(r)) -> goto accept_S4
        :: (!(q)) && (!(r)) -> goto accept_all
        fi;
accept_all:     /* instant violation */
        skip
}
```

Note again the use of (1) (or equivalently true) instead of else to allow us to initiate the check anywhere in an infinite run.

Not all properties of interest can be specified in LTL, so in some cases we can build a stronger property by hand-writing a never claim directly, instead of deriving one from an LTL formula. Technically, the properties that can be express in LTL are a subset of the set of ω-regular properties. PROMELA never claims can express all ω-regular properties, and are therefore somewhat more expressive than LTL alone.

AN EXAMPLE

Consider the following model:

```
int x = 100;

active proctype A()
{
        do
        :: x%2 -> x = 3*x+1
        od
}

active proctype B()
{
        do
        :: !(x%2) -> x = x/2
        od
}
```

What can the range of values of x be? We may want to prove that x can never become negative or, more interestingly, that it can never exceed its initial value of one hundred. We can try to express this in the following formula:

```
$ spin -f '[] (x > 0 && x <= 100)'          # wrong
tl_spin: expected ')', saw '>'
tl_spin: [] (x > 0 && x <= 100)
----------------^
```

But this is not right for two reasons. The first is indicated by the syntax error that SPIN flags. For SPIN to be able to translate a temporal formula it may contain only logical and temporal operators and propositional symbols: it cannot directly include arithmetic or relational expressions. We therefore have to introduce a propositional symbol to represent the expression (x > 0 && x <= 100), and write

```
$ spin -f '[] p'          # better, but still wrong
never {       /* []p */
accept_init:
T0_init:
        if
        :: p -> goto T0_init
        fi;
}
```

Elsewhere in the model itself we can now define p as:

```
#define p          (x > 0 && x <= 100)
```

To see that this is still incorrect, notice that we have used SPIN to generate a never claim: expressing behavior that should *never* happen. We can use SPIN only to check for *violations* of requirements. So what we really meant to state was that the following property, the violation of the first, cannot be satisfied:

```
$ spin -f '![] p'          # correct
never {       /* ![]p */
T0_init:
        if
        :: (!(p)) -> goto accept_all
        :: (1) -> goto T0_init
        fi;
accept_all:
        true
}
```

This automaton exits, signifying a violation, when the condition p ever becomes *false*, which is what we intended to express. SPIN can readily prove that violations are not possible, proving that with the given initialization the value of x is indeed bounded.

Another property we can try to prove is that the value of x eventually always returns to one. Again, to check that this is true we must check that the opposite cannot happen. First we introduce a new propositional symbol q.

```
#define q          (x == 1)
```

Using q, the negated property is written as follows:

149

```
$ spin -f '![]<>q'
never {     /* ![]<>q */
T0_init:
        if
        :: (!(q)) -> goto accept_S4
        :: (1) -> goto T0_init
        fi;
accept_S4:
        if
        :: (!(q)) -> goto accept_S4
        fi;
}
```

Also in this case SPIN readily proves the truth of the property.

Note also that to make these claims about the possible values of the integer variable x, the scope of the variable must include the never claim. This means that we can only make these claims about global variables. A local variable is never within the scope of a PROMELA never claim.

OMEGA-REGULAR PROPERTIES

PROMELA never claims can express a broader range of properties that can be expressed in temporal logic, even when the next operator is allowed. Formally, a never claim can express any ω-regular property. To capture a property that is not expressible in temporal logic we can try to encode it directly into a never claim, but this is an error-prone process. There is an alternative, first proposed by Kousha Etessami. The alternative is to extend the formalism of temporal logic. A sufficient extension is to allow each temporal logic formula to be prefixed by an existential quantifier that is applied to one of the propositional symbols in the formula. Etessami proved that this single extension suffices to extend the power of temporal logic to cover all ω-regular properties.

Consider the case where we want to prove that it is impossible for p to hold only in even steps in a run, but never at odd steps. The temporal logic property [] X p would be too strong for this, since it would require p to hold on *all* even steps. This property can be expressed with existential quantification over some pseudo variable t as follows.

```
{E t} t && [](t -> X !t) && [](!t -> X t) && [](p -> !t)
```

This property states that there exists a propositional symbol t that is initially *true* and forever alternates between *true* and *false*, much like a clock. The formula further states that the truth of the p that we are interested in always logically implies the falseness of the alternating t. The automaton that corresponds to this formula is as follows.

```
$ eqltl -f '{E t} t && [] (t -> X !t) && \
        [] (!t -> X t) && [] (p -> !t)'
never {
accept0:
        if
        :: (!(p)) -> goto accept1
        fi;
accept1:
        if
        :: (1) -> goto accept0
        fi
}
```

In the first step, and every subsequent odd step in the run, p is not allowed to be *true*. No check on the value of p is in effect during the even steps.

The eqltl program was developed by Kousha Etessami.

OTHER LOGICS
The branch of temporal logic that we have described here, and that is supported by the SPIN system, is known as *linear* time temporal logic. The prefix *linear* is due to the fact that these formulae are evaluated over single sequential runs of the system. With the exception of the small extension that we discussed in the previous section, no quantifiers are used. Linear temporal logic is the dominant formalism in software verification. In applications of model checking to hardware verification another version of temporal logic is frequently used. This logic is known as *branching time* temporal logic, with as the best known example CTL (an acronym for *computation tree logic*), which was developed at Carnegie Mellon University. CTL includes both universal and existential quantification, and this additional power means that CTL formulae are evaluated over sets of executions (trees), rather than over individual linear execution paths. There has been much debate in the literature about the relative merits of branching and linear time logics, a debate that has never culminated in any clear conclusions. Despite many claims to the contrary, there is no definitive advantage to the use of either formalism with regard to the complexity of verification. This complexity is dominated by the size of the verification model itself, not by the type of logic used to verify it. This issue, and some other frequently debated issues in model checking, is explored in greater detail in Appendix B.

BIBLIOGRAPHIC NOTES
The basic theory of finite automata was developed in the fifties. A good summary of the early work can be found in Perrin [1990]. The theory of ω-automata dates back almost as far, starting with the work of Büchi [1960]. An excellent survey of this work, including definitions of the various types of acceptance conditions, can be found in Thomas [1990].

Amir Pnueli's influential paper, first proposing the use of temporal logic in the analysis of distributed systems, is Pnueli [1977]. The main notions used in the definition of temporal logic were derived from earlier work on tense logics. Curiously, this work, including the definition of some of the key operators from temporal logic, did not originate in computer science but in philosophy, see, for instance, Prior [1957,1967], and Rescher and Urquhart [1971]. An excellent overview of temporal logic can be found in Emerson [1990].

The correspondence between linear temporal logic formulae and Büchi automata was first described in Wolper, Vardi, and Sistla [1983]. An efficient conversion procedure, which forms the basis for the implementation used in SPIN, was given in Gerth, Peled, Vardi, and Wolper [1995]. The SPIN implementation uses some further optimizations of this basic procedure that are described in Etessami and Holzmann [2000].

There are several other implementations of the LTL conversion procedure, many of which can outperform the procedure that is currently built into SPIN. A good example is the procedure outlined in Gastin and Oddoux [2001]. Their converter, called ltl2ba, is available as part of the SPIN distribution.

The notion of stuttering is due to Lamport [1983], see also Peled, Wilke, and Wolper [1996] and Peled and Wilke [1997]. Etessami's conversion routine for handling LTL formulae with existential quantification is described in Etessami, Wilke, and Schuller [2001].

PROMELA SEMANTICS 7

"The whole is often more than the sum of its parts."
(Aristotle, Metaphysica, 10f–1045a, ca. 330 B.C.)

As we have seen in the earlier chapters, a SPIN model can be used to specify the behavior of collections of asynchronously executing processes in a distributed system. By simulating the execution of a SPIN model we can in principle generate a large directed graph of all reachable system states. Each node in that graph represents a possible state of the model, and each edge represents a single possible execution step by one of the processes. PROMELA is defined in such a way that we know up-front that this graph will always be finite. There can, for instance, be no more than a finite number of processes and message channels, there is a preset bound on the number of messages that can be stored in each channel, and each variable has a preset and finite range of possible values that it can attain during an execution. So, in principle, the complete graph can always be built and analyzed in a finite amount of time.

Basic correctness claims in PROMELA can be interpreted as statements about the presence or absence of specific types of nodes or edges in the global reachability graph. More sophisticated temporal logic properties can be interpreted to express claims about the presence or absence of certain types of subgraphs, or paths, in the reachability graph. The global reachability graph can itself also be interpreted as a formal object: a finite automaton, as defined in Appendix A (p. 553).

The structure of the reachability graph is determined by the semantics of PROMELA. In effect, the PROMELA semantics rules define how the global reachability graph for any given PROMELA model is to be generated. In this chapter we give operational semantics of PROMELA in precisely those terms. The operational semantics definitions should allow us to derive in detail what the structure of the global reachability graph is for any given SPIN model.

```
active proctype not_euclid(int x, y)
{
        if
        :: (x >  y) -> L: x = x - y
        :: (x <  y) -> y = y - x
        :: (x == y) -> assert(x!=y); goto L
        fi;
        printf("%d\n", x)
}
```

Figure 7.1 Sample PROMELA Model

TRANSITION RELATION

Every PROMELA proctype defines a finite state automaton, (S, s_0, L, T, F), as defined in Chapter 6. The set of states of this automaton S corresponds to the possible points of control within the proctype. Transition relation T defines the flow of control. The transition label set L links each transition in T with a specific basic statement that defines the executability and the effect of that transition. The set of final states F, finally, is defined with the help of PROMELA end-state, accept-state, and progress-state labels. A precise description of how set F is defined for safety and for liveness properties can be found in Appendix A.

Conveniently, the set of basic statements in PROMELA is very small. It contains just six elements: assignments, assertions, print statements, send or receive statements, and PROMELA's expression statement (cf. p. 51). *All* other language elements of PROMELA serve only to specify the possible flow of control in a process execution, that is, they help to specify the details of transition relation T. As one small example, note that goto is not a basic statement in PROMELA. The goto statement, much like the semicolon, merely defines control-flow.

As a small example of how PROMELA definitions translate into automata structures, consider the PROMELA model shown in Figure 7.1, which corresponds to the automaton structure shown in Figure 7.2. The presence of the goto achieves that the execution of the assertion statement leads to control state s_2, instead of s_4. Thereby it changes the target state of a transition, but it does not in itself *add* any transitions. In other words, the goto effects a change in transition relation T, but it does not, and cannot, appear in label set L.

Two points are especially worth noting here. First, language elements such as if, goto, the statement separators semicolon and arrow, and similarly also do, break, unless, atomic, and d_step, cannot appear as labels on transitions: only the six basic types of statements in PROMELA can appear in set L.

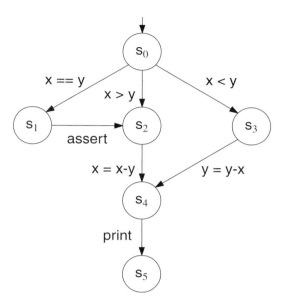

Figure 7.2 Transition Relation for the Model in Figure 7.1

Second, note that expression statements do appear as first-class transition labels in the automaton, and they are from that point of view indistinguishable from the other types of basic statements. In PROMELA *every* basic statement has a precondition that defines when it is executable, and an effect that defines what happens when it is executed. We explore many of these issues in more detail in the remainder of this chapter.

OPERATIONAL MODEL

Our operation model centers on the specification of a *semantics engine* which determines how a given PROMELA model defines system executions, including the rules that apply to the interleaved execution of process actions. The semantics engine operates on abstract objects that correspond to asynchronous processes, variables, and message channels. We give formal definitions of these abstract objects first. We also define the concept of a global system state and a state transition, corresponding, respectively, to nodes and edges in a global reachability graph. We skip the definition of more basic terms, such as *sets*, *identifiers*, *integers*, and *booleans*.

Definition 7.1 (Variable)

A *variable* is a tuple (name, scope, domain, inival, curval) where name is an *identifier* that is unique within the given scope,

scope is either *global* or local to a specific *process*.
domain is a finite set of *integers*.
inival, the initial value, is an *integer* from the given domain, and
curval, the current value, is also an *integer* from the given domain.

We will refer to the elements of a tuple with a dot notation. For instance, if v is a variable, then v.scope is its scope.

The scope of a variable is either *global*, including all processes, or it is restricted to one specific *process* (to be defined below). The type of a variable trivially determines its domain. For instance, a variable of type bit has domain {0,1}.

Definition 7.2 (Message)

A *message* is an ordered set of *variables* (Def. 7.1).

Definition 7.3 (Message Channel)

A *channel* is a tuple (ch_id,nslots,contents) where
ch_id is a positive *integer* that uniquely identifies the channel,
nslots is an *integer*, and
contents is an ordered set of *messages* (Def. 7.2) with maximum cardinality nslots.

Note that the definition of a channel does not contain a scope, like the definition of a variable. A PROMELA channel always has *global* scope. It can be created either globally or locally, by an active process, but its method of creation does not affect its scope. Every channel is in principle accessible to every active process, by knowledge of channel instantiation number ch_id. The variable that holds this channel instantiation number can have a local scope, but not the channel itself.

Definition 7.4 (Process)

A *process* is a tuple
(pid,lvars,lstates,initial,curstate,trans) where
pid is a positive *integer* that uniquely identifies the process,
lvars is a finite set of local *variables* (Def. 7.1), each with a scope that is restricted to the process with instantiation number pid.
lstates is a finite set of *integers* (see below),
initial and curstate are elements of set lstates, and
trans is a finite set of *transitions* (Def. 7.5) on lstates.

The pid value is the process instantiation number which uniquely identifies a running process within the system. In the initial state of a newly created process curstate=initial, and all elements of lvars have curval=inival.

We refer to the elements of set lstates as the *local states* of a process. The integer values serve to uniquely identify each state within the set, but hold no more information.

Definition 7.5 (Transition)

A *transition* in process P is defined by a tuple
(tr_id, source, target, cond, effect, prty, rv) where
   tr_id is a non-negative *integer*,
   source and target are elements from set P.lstates (i.e., *integers*),
   cond is a boolean condition on the global *system state* (Def. 7.6),
   effect is a function that modifies the global *system state* (Def. 7.6),
   prty and rv are *integers*.

As we shall see later, the integers prty and rv are used inside cond and effect definitions to enforce the semantics of unless constructs and rendezvous operations, respectively.

Definition 7.6 (System State)

A global *system state* is a tuple of the form
(gvars, procs, chans, exclusive, handshake, timeout, else, stutter) where
   gvars is a finite set of *variables* (Def. 7.1) with *global* scope,
   procs is a finite set of *processes* (Def. 7.4),
   chans is a finite set of *message channels* (Def. 7.3),
   exclusive, and handshake are *integers*,
   timeout, else, and stutter are *boolean*s.

In the initial system state all processes (Def. 7.4) are in their initial state, all global variables (Def. 7.1) have curval=inival, all message channels (Def. 7.3) have contents={} (i.e., empty), exclusive and handshake are zero, and the *boolean*s timeout and else and stutter all have the initial value *false*.

Definitions 7.1 to 7.6 capture the minimal information that is needed to define the semantics of the PROMELA language in terms of an operational model, with processes defined as transition systems (i.e., automata). A small number of predefined integer "system variables" that are manipulated by the semantics engine appear in these definitions:

- prty, which is used to enforce the semantics of the unless construct,
- rv and handshake, to enforce the semantics of rendezvous operations,
- exclusive, to enforce the semantics of atomic and d_step sequences,
- stutter, to enforce the stutter extension rule (cf. p. 130), and
  timeout and else, to enforce the semantics of the matching PROMELA statements.

In the next section we define the semantics engine. With the help of this definition it should be possible to resolve any question about the interpretation of PROMELA constructs independently from the implementation of SPIN.

OPERATIONAL MODEL, SEMANTICS ENGINE

The semantics engine executes a SPIN model in a step by step manner. In each step, one *executable* basic statement is selected. To determine if a statement is executable or not, one of the conditions that must be evaluated is the corresponding *executability* clause, as described in the PROMELA manual pages that start on p. 363. If more than one statement is executable, any one of them can be selected. The semantics definitions deliberately do not specify (or restrict) how the selection of a statement from a set of simultaneously executable statements should be done. The selection could, for instance, be random. By leaving this decision open, we in effect specify that the correctness of every SPIN model should be independent of the selection criterion that is used.

For the selected statement, the *effect* clause from the statement is applied, as described in the PROMELA manual pages for that statement, and the control state of the process that executes the statement is updated. The semantics engine continues executing statements until no executable statements remain, which happens if either the number of processes drops to zero, or when the remaining processes reach a system deadlock state.

The semantics engine executes the system, at least conceptually, in a stepwise manner: selecting and executing one basic statement at a time. At the highest level of abstraction, the behavior of this engine can be defined as follows:

Let E be a set of pairs (p,t), with p a process, and t a transition. Let `executable(s)` be a function, yet to be defined, that returns a set of such pairs, one for each executable transition in system state s. The semantics engine then performs as shown in Figure 7.3.

As long as there are executable transitions (corresponding to the basic statements of PROMELA), the semantics engine repeatedly selects one of them at random and executes it.

The function `apply()` applies the *effect* of the selected transition to the system state, possibly modifying system and local variables, the contents of channels, or even the values of the reserved variables `exclusive` and `handshake`, as defined in the *effect* clauses from `atomic` or rendezvous `send` operations, respectively. If no rendezvous offer was made (line 6), the global state change takes effect by an update of the system state (line 7), and the current state of the process that executed the transition is updated (line 8).

If a rendezvous offer was made in the last transition, it cannot result in a global state change unless the offer can also be accepted. On line 11 the transitions that have now become executable are selected. The definition of the function `executable()` below guarantees that this set can only contain accepting transitions for the given offer. If there are none, the global state change is declined, and execution proceeds with the selection of a new executable candidate transition from the original set E. If the offer can be matched, the global state change takes effect (line 15). In both processes, the

```
 1 while ((E = executable(s)) != {})
 2 {
 3       for some (p,t) from E
 4       {    s' = apply(t.effect, s)
 5
 6            if (handshake == 0)
 7            {   s = s'
 8                p.curstate = t.target
 9            } else
10            {    /* try to complete rv handshake */
11                E' = executable(s')
12                /* if E' is {}, s is unchanged  */
13
14                for some (p',t') from E'
15                {    s = apply(t'.effect, s')
16                     p.curstate  = t.target
17                     p'.curstate = t'.target
18                }
19                handshake = 0
20       }       }
21 }
22 while (stutter) { s = s }   /* 'stutter' extension */
```

Figure 7.3 PROMELA Semantics Engine

current control state is now updated from source to target state (lines 16 and 17).

To verify liveness properties with SPIN, we must be able to treat finite executions as special cases of infinite executions. The standard way of doing so is to define a *stutter extension* of finite executions, where the final state is repeated *ad infinitum*. The engine in Figure 7.3 uses the system variable **stutter** to determine if the stuttering rule is in effect (line 22). Only the verification system can change this variable.

Changes in the value of this particular system variable are not covered by the semantics of PROMELA proper, but they are determined by the verification algorithms that are used for checking, for instance, ω-regular properties of PROMELA models. Note that the **stutter** variable is only used to render a formal *judgment* on the semantics of a given model; it is not part of the semantics definition itself. More specific notes on the verification of PROMELA models follow at the end of this chapter.

A key part of the semantics is in the definition of what precisely constitutes an *executable* transition. One part will be clear: for transition t to be executable in the current system state, its executability clause t.cond must be satisfied. But there is more, as illustrated by the specification of function executable() in Figure 7.4. To avoid confusion, the reserved state variables timeout, else, and exclusive are set in bold in the figure. These variables are the only ones that can be modified within this function as part of the selection process.

For a transition to be added to the set of executable transitions it has to pass a number of tests.

- The test on line 10-11 checks the value of the reserved system variable exclusive. By default it is zero, and the semantics engine itself never changes the value to non-zero. Any transition that is part of an atomic sequence sets exclusive to the value of p.pid, to make sure that the sequence is not interrupted by other processes, unless the sequence itself blocks. In the latter case the semantics engine restores the defaults (line 32).
- The test on line 16 checks the priority level, set on line 12. Within each process, the semantics engine selects the highest priority transitions that are executable. Note that priorities can affect the selection of transitions within a process, not *between* processes. Priorities are defined in PROMELA with the unless construct.
- The test on line 15 matches the source state of the transition in the labeled transition system with the current state of the process, selected on line 9.
- The test on lines 17-18 makes sure that either no rendezvous offer is outstanding, or, if one is, that the transition being considered can accept the offer on the corresponding rendezvous port.
- The test on line 19, finally, checks whether the *executability* condition for the transition itself is satisfied.

If no transitions are found to be executable with the default value *false* for system variable else, the transitions of the current process are checked again, this time with else equal to *true* (lines 26-27). If no transitions are executable in any process, the value of system variable timeout is changed to *true* and the entire selection process is repeated (lines 32-35). The new value of timeout sticks for just one step (line 7), but it can cause any number of transitions in any number of processes to become executable in the current global system state. The syntax of PROMELA prohibits the use of both else and timeout within a single condition statement.

Note again that the semantics engine does not establish the validity or invalidity of correctness requirements, as the judgement of what is correct system behavior is formally outside the definition of PROMELA semantics proper.

INTERPRETING PROMELA MODELS

The basic objects that are manipulated by the semantics engine are, of course, intended to correspond to the basic objects of a PROMELA model. Much of the language merely provides a convenient mechanism for dealing with the underlying objects. In the PROMELA reference manual in Chapter 16, some language constructs are defined as meta-terms, syntactic sugar that is translated into

```
 1 Set
 2 executable(State s)
 3 {     new Set E
 4       new Set e
 5
 6       E = {}
 7       timeout = false
 8 AllProcs:
 9       for each active process p
10       {   if (exclusive == 0
11           or  exclusive == p.pid)
12           {   for u from high to low   /* priority */
13               {   e = {}; else = false
14 OneProc:          for each transition t in p.trans
15                   {   if (t.source == p.curstate
16                       and t.prty == u
17                       and (handshake == 0
18                       or  handshake == t.rv)
19                       and  eval(t.cond) == true)
20                       {     add (p,t) to set e
21                   }   }
22                   if (e != {})
23                   {   add all elements of e to E
24                       break   /* on to next process */
25                   } else if (else == false)
26                   {   else = true
27                       goto OneProc
28                   } /* or else lower the priority */
29       }   }   }
30
31       if (E == {} and exclusive != 0)
32       {   exclusive = 0
33           goto AllProcs
34       }
35       if (E == {} and timeout == false)
36       {   timeout = true
37           goto AllProcs
38       }
39
40       return E    /* executable transitions */
41 }
```

Figure 7.4 Specification of Procedure `executable()`

PROMELA proper by SPIN's preprocessor. Other language elements deal with the mechanism for declaring and instantiating variables, processes, and message channels. The control-flow constructs, finally, provide a convenient high-level means for defining transition relations on processes. An if statement, for instance, defines how multiple transitions can exit from the same local process state. The semantics engine does not have to know anything about control-flow constructs such as if, do, break, and goto; as shown, it merely deals with local states and transitions.

Some PROMELA constructs, such as assignments and message passing operations, cannot be translated away. The semantics model is defined in such a way that these primitive constructs correspond directly to the transitions of the underlying state machines. We call these PROMELA constructs *basic statements*, and there are surprisingly few of them in the language. The language reference manual defines the transition elements for each *basic statement* that is part of the language.

THREE EXAMPLES
Consider the following PROMELA model.

```
chan x = [0] of { bit };
chan y = [0] of { bit };
active proctype A() { x?0 unless y!0 }
active proctype B() { y?0 unless x!0 }
```

Only one of two possible rendezvous handshakes can take place. Do the semantics rules tell us which one? If so, can the same rules also resolve the following, very similar, situation?

```
chan x = [0] of { bit };
chan y = [0] of { bit };
active proctype A() { x!0 unless y!0 }
active proctype B() { y?0 unless x?0 }
```

And, finally, what should we expect to happen in the following case?

```
chan x = [0] of { bit };
chan y = [0] of { bit };
active proctype A() { x!0 unless y?0 }
active proctype B() { y!0 unless x?0 }
```

Each of these cases can be hard to resolve without guidance from a semantics definition. The semantics rules for handling rendezvous communication and for handling unless statements seem to conflict here. This is what we know.

- The definition of unless states that the statement that precedes the unless keyword has a lower execution priority than the statement that follows it. These priorities must be used to resolve executability conflicts between the two transitions within each process.

- Rendezvous handshakes occur in two parts: the send statement constitutes a rendezvous offer, which can succeed if it is matched by a receive operation on the same channel in the immediately following execution step by the other process. To make the offer, the send statement must be executable by the rules of the semantics engine, and to accept the offer the matching receive operation must be executable.

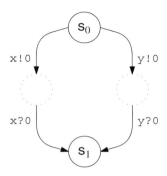

Figure 7.5 State Space Structure for First and Third Example

- The *effect* clause of the rendezvous send operation states that the value of reserved variable `handshake` is set to the value of the channel instantiation number `ch_id` for the channel used. Lines 17-18 in Figure 7.4 then imply that no statement can now be executed, unless it has the `rv` parameter on that transition set to the same value, which is only the case for receive operations that target the same channel. A global state transition in the main execution loop of the semantics engine can only take place for rendezvous operations if the offer can be accepted.

We are now ready to resolve the semantics questions.

In the *first example*, according to the priority rule enforced by the `unless` operator, two statements are executable in the initial state: `x!0` and `y!0`. Either one could be selected for execution. If the first is executed, we enter a rendezvous offer, with `handshake` set to the `ch_id` of channel x. In the intermediate global state s′ then reached, only one statement can be added to set E′, namely `x?0`. The final successor state has `handshake == 0` with both processes in their final state. Alternatively, `y!0` could be selected for execution, with an analogous result. The resulting state space structure is illustrated in Figure 7.5. For convenience, we have included the intermediate states where rendezvous offers are in progress. If a rendezvous offer cannot be accepted, the search algorithm will not actually store the intermediate state in the state space. Similarly, if the offer is accepted, the transition from state s_0 to s_1 is equivalent to an atomic step.

In the *second example*, only one statement is executable in the initial system state: `y!0`, and only the corresponding handshake can take place. The resulting state space structure is illustrated in Figure 7.6.

In the *third example*, the first two statements considered, at the highest

Figure 7.6 State Space Structure for Second Example

priority (line 12, Figure 7.3), are both unexecutable. One priority level lower, though, two statements become executable: x!0 and y!0, and the resulting two system executions are again analogous to those from the first example, as illustrated in Figure 7.5.

A few quick checks with SPIN can confirm that indeed the basic executions we derived here are the only ones that can occur.

VERIFICATION

The addition of a verification option does not affect the semantics of a PROMELA model as it is defined here. Note, for instance, that the semantics engine does not include any special mention or interpretation of valid end states, accepting states, non-progress states, or assertions, and it does not include a definition for the semantics of never claims or trace assertions. The reason is that these language elements have no formal semantics *within* the model: they cannot be used to define any part of the behavior of a model.

Assertion statements, special labels, never claims, and trace assertions are used for making meta statements *about* the semantics of a model. How such meta statements are to be interpreted is defined in a verifier, as part of the verification algorithm.

When a verifier checks for safety properties it is interested, for instance, in cases where an assert statement can fail, or in the presence of executions that violate the requirements for proper termination (e.g., with all processes in a valid end state, and all message channels empty). In this case, the predefined system variable stutter, used in the definition of the semantics engine on line 22 in Figure 7.3, is set to *false*, and any mechanism can be in principle used to generate the executions of the system, in search of the violations.

```
 1 while ((E = executable(s)) != {})
*2 {    if (check_fails()) Stop;
 3      for some (p,t) from E
   . . .
21 }
*22 while (stutter) { s = s; if (check_fails()) Stop; }
```

Figure 7.7 Claim Stutter

When the verifier checks for liveness properties, it is interested in the presence of infinite executions that either contain finitely many traversals of user-defined progress states, or infinitely many traversals of user-defined accept states. The predefined system variable stutter is set to *true* in this case, and, again, any mechanism can be used to generate the infinite executions, as long as it conforms to the semantics as defined before. We discuss the algorithms that SPIN uses to solve these problems in Chapters 8 and 9. The definition of final states in product automata is further detailed in Appendix A.

THE NEVER CLAIM

For purposes of verification, it is not necessary that indeed *all* finite or infinite executions that comply with the formal semantics are inspected by the verifier. In fact, the verifiers that are generated by SPIN make every effort to avoid inspecting all possible executions. Instead, they try to concentrate their efforts on a small set of executions that suffices to produce possible counterexamples to the correctness properties. The use of never claims plays an important role here. A never claim does not define new semantics, but is used to *identify* which part of the existing semantics can violate an independently stated correctness criterion.

The interpretation of a never claim by the verifier in the context of the semantics engine is as follows. Note that the purpose of the claim is to *suppress* the inspection of executions that could not possibly lead to a counterexample. To accomplish this, the verifier tries to reject some valid executions as soon as possible. The decision whether an execution should be rejected or continued can happen in two places: at line 2 of the semantics engine, and at line 22 (Figure 7.3), as illustrated in Figure 7.7.

SPIN implements the decision from line 22 by checking at the end of a finite execution if the never claim automaton can execute at least one more transition. Repeated stutter steps can then still lead to a counterexample. When the claim is generated from an LTL formula, all its transitions are condition statements, formalizing atomic propositions on the global system state. Only infinite executions that are consistent with the formal semantics of the model *and* with the constraint expressed by the `never` claim can now be generated.

With or without a constraint provided by a `never` claim, a verifier hunting for violations of liveness properties can check infinite executions for the presence of counterexamples to a correctness property. The method that the verifier uses to find and report those infinite executions is discussed in Chapter 8.

SEARCH ALGORITHMS **8**

> *"If I had eight hours to chop down a tree,*
> *I'd spend six hours sharpening my axe."*
> *(Abraham Lincoln, 1809–1865)*

In this chapter we will discuss the basic algorithms that SPIN uses to verify correctness properties of PROMELA models. The basic algorithms are fairly simple and can quickly be explained. But, if we are interested in applying a verifier to problems of practical size, the mere basics do not always suffice. There are many ways in which the memory use and the run-time requirements of the basic algorithms can be optimized. Perhaps SPIN's main strength lies in the range of options it offers to perform such optimizations, so that even very large problem sizes can be handled efficiently. To structure the discussion somewhat, we will discuss the main optimization methods that SPIN uses separately, in the next chapter. In this chapter we restrict ourselves to a discussion of the essential elements of the search method that SPIN employs.

We start with the definition of a depth-first search algorithm, which we can then extend to perform the types of functions we need for systems verification.

DEPTH-FIRST SEARCH

Consider a finite state automaton $A = (S, s_0, L, T, F)$ as defined in Chapter 6 (p. 127). This automaton could, for instance, be the type of automaton that is generated by the PROMELA semantics engine from Chapter 7, capturing the joint behavior of a number of asynchronously executing processes. Every state in such an automaton then represents a global system state. For the discussion that follows, though, it is immaterial how the automaton was constructed or what it represents precisely.

The algorithm shown in Figure 8.1 performs a depth-first search to visit every

```
Stack D = {}
Statespace V = {}

Start()
{
        Add_Statespace(V, A.s₀)
        Push_Stack(D, A.s₀)
        Search()
}

Search()
{
        s = Top_Stack(D)
        for each (s,l,s') ∈ A.T
                if In_Statespace(V, s') == false
                {       Add_Statespace(V, s')
                        Push_Stack(D, s')
                        Search()
                }
        Pop_Stack(D)
}
```

Figure 8.1 Basic Depth-First Search Algorithm

state in set A. S that is reachable from the initial state A. s_0. The algorithm uses two data structures: a stack D and a state space V.

A *state space* is an unordered set of states. As a side effect of the execution of the algorithm in Figure 8.1, some of the contents of set A. S is reproduced in state space V, using the definition of initial state A. s_0 and of transition relation A. T. Not all elements of A. S will necessarily appear in set V, because not all these elements may effectively be reachable from the given initial state.

The algorithm uses just two routines to update the contents of the state space:

*   Add_Statespace(V, s) adds state s as an element to state space V
*   In_Statespace(V, s) returns *true* if s is an element of V, otherwise it returns *false*

A *stack* is an *ordered* set of states. If the symbols < and > indicate the ordering relation, we have for any stack D:

$$\forall s_1, s_2 \in D: (s_1 \neq s_2 \rightarrow s_1 < s_2 \lor s_1 > s_2)$$
$$\forall s_1, s_2, s_3 \in D: (s_1 < s_2 < s_3 \rightarrow s_1 < s_3)$$

Because of the ordering relation, a stack also has a unique top and bottom element. If the stack is non-empty, the top is the most recently added element and the bottom is the least recently added element.

The algorithm in Figure 8.1 uses three routines to access stack D:

- `Push_Stack(D,s)` adds state `s` as an element to stack `D`
- `Top_Stack(D)` returns the top element from `D`, if `D` is non-empty, and otherwise returns nil
- `Pop_Stack(D)` removes the top element from `D`, if `D` is non-empty, and otherwise returns nil

It is not hard to show that this algorithm secures that state space V will contain no duplicates and can grow no larger than A. S.

The algorithm deliberately stores only states in set V, and no transitions. In this case complete information about all possible transitions is of course already available in relation A. T, but we may not always have this information available in precomputed form. When SPIN executes algorithm 8.1, for instance, it constructs both state set A. S and transition relation A. T *on-the-fly*, as an interleaving product of smaller automata, each one of which represents an independent thread of control, as explained in more detail in Appendix A.

To modify the algorithm from Figure 8.1 for on-the-fly verification is straightforward. The modified algorithm starts from a global initial system state, which is now specified as a composite of component states: { $A_1.s_0$, $A_2.s_0$, $\cdots$, $A_n.s_0$ }. All other system states in A. S are unknown at this point. Instead of relying on a precomputed definition of A. T, the successor states of any given system state { $A_1.s_i$, $A_2.s_j$, $\cdots$, $A_n.s_k$ } are now computed on the fly from the transition relations of the individual components { $A_1.T_1$, $A_2.T_2$, $\cdots$, $A_n.T_n$ }, subject to the semantics rules from Chapter 7.

By avoiding the storage of transitions in the state space, we can gain a substantial savings in the memory requirements during verification. We will see shortly that to perform safety and liveness checks we only need the information that is collected in the two data-structures that are maintained by the algorithm from Figure 8.1: state space V and stack D.

The algorithm in Figure 8.1 has the following important property:

Property 8.1
The algorithm from Figure 8.1 always terminates within a finite number of steps.

Proof:
Before each new recursive call to routine `Search()`, at least one state from A. S that is not yet contained in V must be added to V. Because set A. S is finite, this can only happen a finite number of times. □

CHECKING SAFETY PROPERTIES
The depth-first search algorithm systematically visits every reachable state, so it is relatively straightforward to extend the algorithm with an evaluation routine that can check arbitrary state or safety properties. The extension of the search algorithm that we will use is shown in Figure 8.2. It uses a generic

```
Stack D = {}
Statespace V = {}

Start()
{
        Add_Statespace(V, A.s₀)
        Push_Stack(D, A.s₀)
        Search()
}

Search()
{
        s = Top_Stack(D)
*       if !Safety(s)
*       {       Print_Stack(D)
*       }
        for each (s,l,s') ∈ A.T
                if In_Statespace(V, s') == false
                {       Add_Statespace(V, s')
                        Push_Stack(D, s')
                        Search()
                }
        Pop_Stack(D)
}
```

Figure 8.2 Extension of Figure 8.1 for Checking Safety Properties

routine for checking the state properties for any given state s, called Safety(s).

This routine could, for instance, flag the presence of a deadlock state by checking if state s has any successors, but it can also flag the violation of process assertions or system invariants that should hold at s. Since the algorithm visits *all* reachable states, it has the desirable property that it can reliably identify *all* possible deadlocks and assertion violations.

The only real issue to resolve is what precisely the algorithm should do when it finds that a state property is violated. It could, of course, merely print a message, saying, for instance:

```
dfs: line 322, assertion (a > b) can be violated, aborting.
```

There are two things wrong with this approach. First and foremost, this solution would leave it to the user to determine just how and why the assertion could be violated. Just knowing that a state property *can* be violated does not help us to understand *how* this could happen. Secondly, it is not necessary to abort a verification run after a single violation was found. The search for other violations can continue.

To solve the first problem, we would like our algorithm to provide the user with some more information about the sequence of steps that can lead to the property violation. Fortunately, all the information to do so is readily available. Our algorithm can produce a complete execution trace that demonstrates how the state property was violated. The trace can start in the initial system state, and end at the property violation itself. That information is contained in stack D. For this purpose, the algorithm in Figure 8.2 makes use of a new stack routine `Print_Stack(D)`:

> `Print_Stack(D)` prints out the elements of stack D in order, from the bottom element up to and including the top element.

When SPIN uses this algorithm, it prints out not just each state that is reached along the execution path that leads from the initial state to the state where a property violation was discovered, it also adds some details on the transitions from set A. T that generated each new state in the path. To allow SPIN to do so, all that is needed is to save an integer index into a lookup table of local process transitions with each element in stack D.

Note that the counterexamples that are produced with this algorithm are not necessarily the shortest possible counterexamples. This is unpleasant, but not fatal: it often suffices to look at just the last few steps in an execution sequence to understand the nature of a property violation.

DEPTH-LIMITED SEARCH

We can adapt the depth-first search algorithm fairly easily into a depth-limited search that guarantees coverage up to a given depth bound. Such an algorithm is given in Figure 8.4. One change is the addition of an integer variable depth to maintain a running count of the size of stack D. Before growing the stack, the algorithm now checks the value of variable Depth against upper-bound BOUND. If the upper-bound is exceeded, routine Search() does not descend the search tree any further, but returns to the previous expansion step.

This change by itself is not sufficient to guarantee that all safety violations that could occur within BOUND steps will always be found. Assume, for instance, an upper-bound value of three for the size of D. Now consider a state s_2 that is reachable from the initial state via two paths: one path of two steps and one path of one step. If s_2 has an error state e among its successors (i.e., a state exhibiting a property violation) that error state is reachable via either a path of three steps or via a path of two steps. The first path exceeds our presumed bound of three, but the second does not. If the depth-first search starts by traversing the first path, it will have added states s_0, s_1, and s_2 to state space V when it runs into the depth bound of three. It will then return, first to state s_1 and next to state s_0 to explore the remaining successor states. One such successor state of s_0 is s_2. This state, however, is at this point already in V and therefore not reconsidered. (It will not be added to the

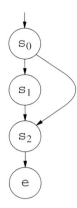

Figure 8.3 Example for Depth-Limited Search

stack again.) The second path to the error state e will therefore not be
explored completely, and the reachability of the error state within three steps
will go unreported. The situation is illustrated in Figure 8.3.

We can avoid this type of incompleteness by storing the value of variable
Depth together with each state in state space V. The algorithm from Figure
8.4 uses this information in a slightly modified version of the two state space
access routines, as follows:

- Add_Statespace(V,s,d) adds the pair (s,d) to state space V, where s
  is a state and d the value of Depth, that is, the current size of the stack
- In_Statespace(V,s,d) returns *true* if there exists a pair (s′,d′) in V
  such that s′ ≡ s and d′ ≤ d. Otherwise it returns *false*

Compared to the simpler algorithm from Figure 8.2, this version of the
depth-first search is clearly more expensive. In the worst case, if R is the
number of reachable states that is explored, we may have to explore each state
up to R times. This means that in this worst case there can be a quadratic
increase in the run-time requirements of the algorithm, while the memory
requirements increase only linearly with R to accommodate the depth field in
V.

The algorithm from Figure 8.4 is implemented as an option in SPIN. To invoke
it, the verifier is compiled with a special compiler directive -DREACH. If the
verifier is compiled in this way, the run-time option -i can be used to iteratively search for the shortest error trail. This only works for safety properties
though. An alternative algorithm to use in this case is a breadth-first search,
which we will discuss shortly (see Figure 8.6).

```
Stack D = {}
Statespace V = {}
int Depth = 0

Start()
{
        Add_Statespace(V, A.s₀, 0)
        Push_Stack(D, A.s₀)
        Search()
}

Search()
{
*       if Depth >= BOUND
*       {       return
*       }
*       Depth++
        s = Top_Stack(D)
        if !Safety(s)
        {       Print_Stack(D)
        }
        for each (s,l,s') ∈ A.T
*               if In_Statespace(V, s', Depth) == false
*               {       Add_Statespace(V, s', Depth)
                        Push_Stack(D, s')
                        Search()
                }
        Pop_Stack(D)
*       Depth--
}
```

Figure 8.4 Depth-Limited Search

The example from Figure 8.3 could be expressed in PROMELA as follows:

```
init {  /* Figure 8.3 */

        byte x;
S0:     if
        :: x = 1; goto S1
        :: x = 2; goto S2
        fi;
S1:     x++;
S2:     x++;
E:      assert(false)
}
```

We can confirm that the default search with a depth-limit of three fails to find the assertion violation.

```
$ spin -a example.pml
$ cc -o pan pan.c
$ ./pan -m3
error: max search depth too small
(Spin Version 4.0.7 -- 1 August 2003)
        + Partial Order Reduction

Full statespace search for:
        never claim              - (none specified)
        assertion violations     +
        acceptance   cycles      - (not selected)
        invalid end states       +

State-vector 12 byte, depth reached 2, errors: 0
        3 states, stored
        2 states, matched
        5 transitions (= stored+matched)
        0 atomic steps
hash conflicts: 0 (resolved)
(max size 2^18 states)

1.253   memory usage (Mbyte)

unreached in proctype :init:
        line 10, state 10, "-end-"
        (1 of 10 states)
```

If we switch to the depth-bounded search algorithm from Figure 8.4, and repeat the search with the same depth bound, the assertion violation is correctly reported:

```
$ spin -a example.pml
$ cc -DREACH -o pan pan.c
$ ./pan -m3
error: max search depth too small
pan: assertion violated 0 (at depth 2)
pan: wrote example.pml.trail
...
```

The search algorithm can also be extended to allow the verifier to iteratively home in on the shortest possible path to an error state, but adjusting the depth bound to the length of the last error path that was reported and allowing the search to continue after each new error, until the entire graph has been searched. In this case, we would replace the part of the code in Figure 8.4 that does the error check with the following fragment:

```
        if !Safety(s)
        {       Print_Stack(D)
*               if (iterative)
*                       BOUND = Depth
        }
```

Each new error path is now guaranteed to be shorter than all earlier paths, which means that the last reported path will also be the shortest. A run of the verifier that uses this option looks as follows:

```
$ ./pan -i        # iterative search for shortest error
pan: assertion violated 0 (at depth 3)
pan: wrote example.pml.trail
pan: reducing search depth to 3
pan: wrote example.pml.trail
pan: reducing search depth to 2
(Spin Version 4.0.7 -- 1 August 2003)
        + Partial Order Reduction

Full statespace search for:
        never claim             - (none specified)
        assertion violations    +
        acceptance   cycles     - (not selected)
        invalid end states      +

State-vector 12 byte, depth reached 3, errors: 2
        4 states, stored
        2 states, matched
        6 transitions (= stored+matched)
        0 atomic steps
hash conflicts: 0 (resolved)
(max size 2^18 states)

1.573    memory usage (Mbyte)
```

The first error path reported in this run is of length three. The new depth bound is then set to three and the search continues. Next, the shorter path of two steps is found and reported, which is also the shortest such path. Even though the worst case behavior of this algorithm is disconcerting, to say the least, this worst case behavior is rarely observed in practice. The typical use of the iterative search option is to find a shorter equivalent to an error path, only *after* the existence of an error path was demonstrated with a regular search. The length of that error path can then be used as an initial upper-bound for the iterative search.

TRADE-OFFS

The computational requirements for the depth-first search algorithm are linear in the number of reachable states in A. S. If A. S is itself computed from asynchronous components, which is the typical case in applications of SPIN, the size of this state set is in the worst case equal to the size of the Cartesian product of all component state sets $A_i. S$ (cf. Appendix A). The size of this set can increase exponentially with the number of component systems. Although in practice the number of reachable states is no more than a small fraction of this upper bound, a small fraction of a potentially astronomically large number can still be very large.

```
Stack D = {}

Start()
{
*       Push_Stack(D, A.s₀)
        Search()
}

Search()
{
        s = Top_Stack(D)
        if !Safety(s)
        {       Print_Stack(D)
                if (iterative)
                        BOUND = Depth
        }
        for each (s,l,s') ∈ A.T
*               if In_Stack(D, s') == false
*               {       Push_Stack(D, s')
                        Search()
                }
        Pop_Stack(D)
}
```

Figure 8.5 Stateless Search

One of the advantages of on-the-fly verification is that it allows us to trade memory requirements for run-time requirements when needed. One way to do this would be to randomly erase part of the state space when the algorithm runs out of memory, provided that the part erased contains no states that are still on the stack. Note carefully that the state space access routines (*not* the stack routines) serve only to prevent the multiple exploration of states. These routines do not affect the actual coverage of the search.

If we omit the call on routine Add_Statespace(), and replace the routine In_Statespace() with a new stack routine In_Stack(), we still have a correct algorithm that is guaranteed to terminate within a finite number of steps. The routine In_Stack(D,s) can be defined to return *true* if state s is currently contained in stack D, and *false* in all other cases.

The real purpose of the state space access routines is to improve the efficiency of the search by avoiding the repetition of work. If we completely eliminate the state space routines, as illustrated in Figure 8.5, the efficiency of the search could deteriorate dramatically. This change may cause each state to be revisited once from every other state in the state space, which means a worst-case increase in complexity from $O(R)$ to $O(R^R)$ steps, where R is the total number of reachable states.

```
Queue D = {}
Statespace V = {}

Start()
{
        Add_Statespace(V, A.s₀)
        Add_Queue(D, A.s₀)
        Search()
}

Search()
{
        s = Del_Queue(D)
        for each (s, l, s') ∈ A.T
                if In_Statespace(V, s') == false
                {       Add_Statespace(V, s')
                        Add_Queue(D, s')
                        Search()
                }
}
```

Figure 8.6 Breadth-First Search Algorithm

Intermediate solutions are possible, for example, by changing the state space V from an exhaustive set into a cache of randomly selected previously visited states, but it is hard to avoid cases of seriously degraded performance. SPIN therefore does not use caching strategies to reduce memory use. The optimization strategies implemented in SPIN are all meant to have a more predictable effect on performance. We discuss these strategies in Chapter 9.

BREADTH-FIRST SEARCH

The implementation of a breadth-first search discipline looks very similar to that of the depth-first search. Instead of a search stack, though, we now use a standard queue. Successor states are added to the tail of the queue during the search, and they are removed from the head. A queue is just an ordered set of states. We use two new functions to access it.

- Add_Queue(D, s) adds state s to the tail of queue D,
- Del_Queue(D) deletes the element from the head of D and returns it.

This search procedure is illustrated in Figure 8.6.

Despite the similarities of depth-first and breadth-first searches, the two algorithms have quite different properties. For one, the depth-first search can easily be extended to detect cycles in graphs; the breadth-first search cannot. With the depth-first search algorithm, we also saw that it suffices to print out the contents of the stack to reconstruct an error path. If we want to do something similar with a breadth-first search, we have to store more information. One simple method is to store a link at state in state space V that points to one of the predecessors of each state. These links can then be followed to trace a path back from an error state to the initial system state when an error is encountered. It is then easy to use the breadth-first search algorithm for the detection of safety violations, for instance with the following extension that can be placed immediately after the point where a new state s is retrieved from queue D.

```
if !Safety(s)
{       Find_Path(s)
}
```

We have introduced a new procedure Find_Path(s) here that traces back and reproduces the required error path. SPIN has an implementation of this procedure that is enabled by compiling the verifier source text with the optional compiler directive -DBFS. For the example specification, for instance, this gives us the shortest error path immediately.

```
$ spin -a example.pml
$ cc -DBFS -o pan pan.c
$ ./pan
pan: assertion violated 0 (at depth 2)
pan: wrote example.pml.trail
. . .
```

The clear advantage of this method is that, if the memory requirements are manageable, it will guarantee that the shortest possible safety errors will be found first. The main disadvantages of the method are that it can sometimes substantially increase the memory requirements of the search, and that it cannot easily be extended beyond safety properties, unlike the depth-first search method.

CHECKING LIVENESS PROPERTIES

We will show how the basic algorithm from Figure 8.1 can be extended for the detection of liveness properties, as expressible in linear temporal logic. Liveness deals with infinite runs, ω-runs. Clearly, we can only have an infinite run in a finite system if the run is *cyclic*: it reaches at least some of the states in the system infinitely often. We are particularly interested in cases where the set of states that are reached infinitely often contains one or more accepting states, since these runs correspond to ω-accepting runs. We have seen in Chapter 6 how we can arrange things in such a way that accepting runs correspond precisely to the violation of linear temporal logic formulae.

An acceptance cycle in the reachability graph of automaton A exists if and only if two conditions are met. First, at least one accepting state is reachable from the initial state of the automaton A. s_0. Second, at least one of those accepting states is reachable from itself.

The algorithm that is used in SPIN to detect reachable accepting states that are also reachable from themselves is shown in Figure 8.7. The state space and stack structures now store pairs of elements: a state and a boolean value `toggle`, for reasons we will see shortly.

When the algorithm determines that an accepting state has been reached, and all successors of that state have also been explored, it starts a nested search to see if the state is reachable from itself. It does so by storing a copy of the accepting state in a global called `seed`. If this `seed` state can be reached again in the second search, the accepting state was shown to be reachable from itself, and an accepting ω-run can be reported.

The check for a revisit to the `seed` state contains one alternative condition that is equivalent to a match on the `seed` state itself. If a successor state `s'` appears on the stack of the first search (that lead us to the `seed` state), then we know immediately that there also exists a path from `s'` back to the `seed` state. That path is contained in stack D, starting at the state that is matched here and ending at the first visit to the `seed` state, from which the nested search was started.

Property 8.2

The algorithm from Figure 8.7 will detect *at least one* acceptance cycle if at least one such cycle exists.

Proof

For an acceptance cycle to exist there must be at least one accepting state that is both reachable from the initial system state and reachable from itself. Consider the very first such state that is encountered in post-order during the depth-first search; call it z_a. This need not be the first accepting state encountered as such, since there may well be accepting states that are *not* reachable from themselves that were encountered earlier in the search.

After all states that are reachable from z_a have been explored with a `toggle` attribute *false*, `seed` is set to z_a. The value of `toggle` is now set to *true*, and a new search (the nested search) is initiated starting from `seed`.

At this point there can only be states in the state space with a `toggle` attribute equal to *true* if they are either accepting states that were reached earlier in the *first* depth-first search, or if they are states that are reachable from those accepting states.

There is only one case in which the nested depth-first search starting at z_a can fail to generate a full path back to z_a. This case occurs if that path contains a state that is already present in the state space with a *true* `toggle` attribute. Call that earlier state z_e, and call the earlier accepting state from which it was reached z_n. Note that the nested depth-first search truncates when reaching state z_e for the second time.

Now, even though state z_a is reachable from an earlier accepting state z_n in the *nested* search, z_a could not have been reached from z_n in the *first*

```
Stack D = {}
Statespace V = {}
State seed = nil
Boolean toggle = false

Start()
{
        Add_Statespace(V, A.s₀, toggle)
        Push_Stack(D, A.s₀, toggle)
        Search()
}

Search()
{
        (s,toggle) = Top_Stack(D)
        for each (s,l,s') ∈ A.T
        {
                /* check if seed is reachable from itself */
                if s' == seed V On_Stack(D,s',false)
                {       PrintStack(D)
                        PopStack(D)
                        return
                }

                if In_Statespace(V, s', toggle) == false
                {       Add_Statespace(V, s', toggle)
                        Push_Stack(D, s', toggle)
                        Search()
                }
        }

        if s ∈ A.F && toggle == false
        {       seed = s        /* reachable accepting state */
                toggle = true
                Push_Stack(D, s, toggle)
                Search()        /* start 2nd search */
                Pop_Stack(D)
                seed = nil
                toggle = false
        }

        Pop_Stack(D)
}
```

Figure 8.7 Nested Depth-First Search for Checking Liveness Properties

search, because in that case the nested search for z_a would have been initiated *before* the nested search for z_n. (Due to the post-order search discipline.) This necessarily means that the path that leads from z_e to z_a must intersect the depth-first search stack in the first search somewhere *above* state z_n. But if that is the case, the earlier accepting state z_n is necessarily also reachable from itself, through the path that is on the stack. This contradicts the assumption that z_a is the *first* accepting state encountered that is reachable from itself.□

When, therefore, the *first* accepting state that is reachable from itself is generated the state space cannot contain any previously visited states with a *true* `toggle` attribute from which this state is reachable, and thus the self-loop is necessarily constructed.

The property we have proven above does not necessarily hold for any accepting state after the first one that is encountered that is reachable from itself. Therefore, this algorithm can only guarantee that if one or more acceptance cycles exist, *at least one* of them will be found. That property suffices to perform formal verification. After all, only one counterexample is needed to disprove a correctness claim.

As in Figure 8.1, we have defined the algorithm in Figure 8.7 for a single given automaton A. In the context of SPIN, the automaton A is not given but has to be computed. If, for instance, we want to verify an LTL property f for a given system automaton S, then we first convert $\neg f$ into a `never` claim (a Büchi automaton) B. The desired automaton A is then computed as the *synchronous* product of S and B. System automaton S may have to be computed as the *asynchronous* product of n components $\{S_1, S_2, \cdots S_n\}$ as well. The definitions of synchronous and asynchronous products can be found in Appendix A.

ADDING FAIRNESS

LTL is rich enough to express many fairness constraints directly, for example, in properties of the form ($\square$ `trigger` $\rightarrow$ $\lozenge$ `response`). Specific types of fairness can also be predefined and built into the search algorithm. Recall that the asynchronous product of finite automata that is the ultimate subject of LTL model checking is built as an interleaving of transitions from smaller automata, $A = A_1 \times A_2 \cdots A_k$ (cf. Appendix A). Each of the automata $A_1 \times A_2 \cdots A_k$ contributes transitions to the runs of A. Component automaton A_i is said to be `enabled` at state s of the global automaton A if s has at least one valid outgoing transition from A_i. We can now define two standard notions of fairness.

Definition 8.1 (Strong Fairness)

An ω-run σ satisfies the ***strong fairness*** requirement if it contains infinitely many transitions from every component automaton that is enabled *infinitely often* in σ.

Definition 8.2 (Weak Fairness)

An ω-run σ satisfies the *weak fairness* requirement if it contains infinitely many transitions from every component automaton that is enabled *infinitely long* in σ.

The two definitions differ just in the use of the terms *infinitely often* and *infinitely long*, yet the computational overhead that is required to check these two requirements is vastly different. As we shall see shortly, the check for weak fairness increases the run-time expense of a verification run by a factor that is linear in the number of component automata (i.e., the number of running processes in a SPIN model). To check strong fairness within a system like SPIN, however, would increase the run time of a basic verification by a factor that is quadratic in the number of component automata, which for all practical purposes puts it beyond our reach. Not surprisingly, therefore, SPIN only includes support for weak fairness, and not for strong fairness.

SPIN's implementation of the weak fairness requirement is based on Choueka's flag construction method (see the Bibliographic Notes at the end of this chapter). Although the details of the implementation in SPIN are complex, it is not hard to describe the intuition behind the algorithm.

The depth-first search algorithm from Figure 8.1 explores the global reachability graph for an automaton A. Assume again that A itself is computed as the product of k component automata $A_1, \cdots, A_k$. We will now create $(k + 2)$ copies of the global reachability graph that is computed by the algorithm from Figure 8.1. We preserve the acceptance labels from all accepting states only in the *first* copy of the state graph, that for convenience we will call the *0-th* copy. We remove the accepting labels from all states in the remaining $(k + 1)$ copies. Next, we make some changes in the transition relation to connect all copies of the state graph, without really removing or adding any behavior.

We change the destination states for all outgoing transitions of accepting states in the *0-th* copy of the state space, so that they point to the same states in the next copy of the state space, with copy number one.

In the i-th copy of the state graph, with $1 \le i \le k$, we change the destination state of each transition that was contributed by component automaton A_i (i.e., the i-th *process*) to the same state in the $(i + 1)$-th copy of the state graph. For the last copy of the state space, numbered $(k + 1)$, we change *all* transitions such that their destination state is now in the *0-th* copy of the state graph.

The unfolding effect is illustrated in Figure 8.8, which is based on a similar figure in Bosnacki [2001].

These changes do not add or remove behavior, but it should be clear that any accepting ω-run in the $(k + 2)$ times unfolded state space now necessarily includes transitions from *all* k component automata. Note particularly that there can be no accepting cycles that are contained within the *0-th* copy of the state graph, since all transitions that emerge from accepting states lead out of

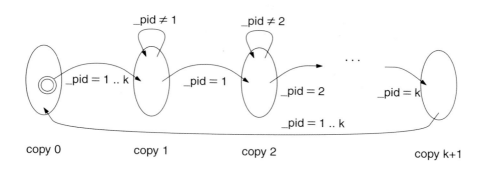

Figure 8.8 (k+2) Times Unfolded State Space for Weak Fairness

that graph. This means that we can use the nested depth-first search procedure from Figure 8.7 on the unfolded state graph to detect all fair accepting
runs in the original graph.

We have to make one final adjustment to this procedure to account for the fact
that, according to Definition 8.2, a component automaton that has no enabled
transitions in a given state need not participate in an infinite run that traverses
that state. To account for this we can add a null transition from every state s
in the i-th copy of the state graph, $1 \le i \le k$, to the *same* state s in the
$(i + 1)$-th copy whenever automaton component i has no enabled transitions
in s. Without that null transition a complete cycle through all $(k + 2)$ copies
would of course not always be possible.

The algorithm thus modified can enforce weak fairness, but not strong fairness. Consider, for instance, the case where a component automaton is inter-
mittently blocked and enabled. With the procedure we have outlined we cannot detect whether this automaton should or should not be included in an
accepting ω-run.

Drawing the unfolded state space for even small examples can create rather
complex graphs. A trivial example is shown in Figure 8.9, where we have
drawn a two-state state space, which we assume to be generated by the joint
execution of two asynchronous processes. The process numbered one contributes one single transition, from state s_1 to state s_2, and the process numbered two contributes one single transition back from state s_2 to state s_1.
State s_2 is assumed to be accepting. Clearly, in this case there is just one
behavior, and this one behavior corresponds to a fair acceptance cycle. With
k equal to two, the unfolded state space, shown in Figure 8.10, contains four
copies of the state space, each with two states. Only five of the eight states in
the unfolded state space are reachable, though. The acceptance cycle is

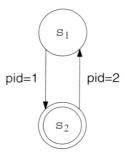

Figure 8.9 A Two-State Global State Space Example

indicated with the bold arrows in Figure 8.10. Note also that as a side effect of the state space unfolding the length of the counterexample that will be generated by SPIN can be longer than strictly necessary. The path contains four steps in this case. The shortest possible counterexample would contain just two steps.

As another, only slightly more realistic, example, consider the following PROMELA model with two processes:

```
active proctype A()
{       bit i;

accept:
        do
        :: i = 1-i
        od
}

active proctype B()
{       bit i;

        do
        :: i = 1-i
        od
}
```

The verifier is generated and compiled as usual.

```
$ spin -a fairness.pml
$ cc -o pan pan.c
```

The default search for acceptance cycles then quickly succeeds.

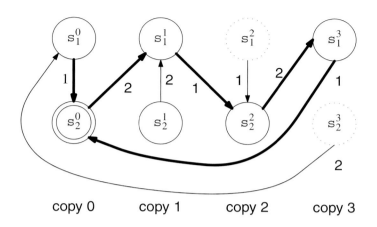

copy 0   copy 1   copy 2   copy 3

Figure 8.10 Unfolded State Space for Example in Figure 8.9

```
$ ./pan -a
pan: acceptance cycle (at depth 2)
pan: wrote fairness.pml.trail
(Spin Version 4.0.7 -- 1 August 2003)
Warning: Search not completed
        + Partial Order Reduction
Full statespace search for:
        never claim            - (none specified)
        assertion violations   +
        acceptance    cycles   + (fairness disabled)
        invalid end states     +

State-vector 16 byte, depth reached 3, errors: 1
       3 states, stored (5 visited)
       5 states, matched
      10 transitions (= visited+matched)
       0 atomic steps
...
```

This cycle, however, is restricted to just executions of the process of type B, which is not very interesting (and violates a reasonable assumption of *finite progress* that we could make for both processes in this system).

```
$ spin -t -p fairness.pml
  1: proc 1 (B) line 13 "fairness.pml" (state 1) [i=(1-i)]
  2: proc 0 (A) line  6 "fairness.pml" (state 1) [i=(1-i)]
  <<<<<START OF CYCLE>>>>>
  3: proc 1 (B) line 13 "fairness.pml" (state 1) [i=(1-i)]
```

```
   4: proc 1 (B) line 13 "fairness.pml" (state 1) [i=(1-i)]
spin: trail ends after 4 steps
#processes: 2
   4: proc 1 (B) line 12 "fairness.pml" (state 2)
   4: proc 0 (A) line  5 "fairness.pml" (state 2)
2 processes created
```

The problem is resolved if we enforce weak fairness. We repeat the search as follows:

```
$ ./pan -a -f
pan: acceptance cycle (at depth 4)
pan: wrote fairness.pml.trail
(Spin Version 4.0.7 -- 1 August 2003)
Warning: Search not completed
        + Partial Order Reduction

Full statespace search for:
        never claim            - (none specified)
        assertion violations   +
        acceptance   cycles    + (fairness enabled)
        invalid end states     +

State-vector 16 byte, depth reached 11, errors: 1
        3 states, stored (15 visited)
       10 states, matched
       25 transitions (= visited+matched)
        0 atomic steps
...
```

Note that a little more work was done in the search, reflected by an increase in the number of states that were visited and the number of transitions that were executed. The number of states stored, however, does not increase. The new cycle that is found now looks as follows:

```
$ spin -t -p fairness.pml
   1: proc 1 (B) line 13 "fairness.pml" (state 1) [i=(1-i)]
   2: proc 1 (B) line 13 "fairness.pml" (state 1) [i=(1-i)]
   3: proc 0 (A) line  6 "fairness.pml" (state 1) [i=(1-i)]
   4: proc 1 (B) line 13 "fairness.pml" (state 1) [i=(1-i)]
   <<<<<START OF CYCLE>>>>>
   5: proc 1 (B) line 13 "fairness.pml" (state 1) [i=(1-i)]
   6: proc 1 (B) line 13 "fairness.pml" (state 1) [i=(1-i)]
   7: proc 0 (A) line  6 "fairness.pml" (state 1) [i=(1-i)]
   8: proc 1 (B) line 13 "fairness.pml" (state 1) [i=(1-i)]
   9: proc 1 (B) line 13 "fairness.pml" (state 1) [i=(1-i)]
  10: proc 1 (B) line 13 "fairness.pml" (state 1) [i=(1-i)]
  11: proc 0 (A) line  6 "fairness.pml" (state 1) [i=(1-i)]
  12: proc 1 (B) line 13 "fairness.pml" (state 1) [i=(1-i)]
```

```
spin: trail ends after 12 steps
#processes: 2
 12:   proc 1 (B) line 12 "fairness.pml" (state 2)
 12:   proc 0 (A) line  5 "fairness.pml" (state 2)
2 processes created
```

This time the trace includes actions from both processes. The trace is of course not the shortest possible one. At a risk of increasing the complexity of the search, we can try to find a shorter variant by proceeding as follows:

```
$ cc -DREACH -o pan pan.c
$ ./pan -a -f -i
pan: acceptance cycle (at depth 4)
pan: wrote fairness.pml.trail
pan: reducing search depth to 12
pan: wrote fairness.pml.trail
pan: reducing search depth to 11
(Spin Version 4.0.7 -- 1 August 2003)
        + Partial Order Reduction

Full statespace search for:
        never claim             - (none specified)
        assertion violations    +
        acceptance   cycles     + (fairness enabled)
        invalid end states      +

State-vector 16 byte, depth reached 11, errors: 2
        4 states, stored (19 visited)
       16 states, matched
       35 transitions (= visited+matched)
        0 atomic steps
 . . .
```

Although the verifier did find a shorter variant of the cycle in this case, in general this is not guaranteed to be the case. Note that the -DREACH variant of the search is designed for the detection of safety errors, using a *single* depth-first search. It can lose its essential properties in a nested search. This can mean, for instance, that an interative search for cycles *without* the -DREACH option could in principle find a shorter variant of a cycle than a search performed with the option, though not in this case. So, for liveness properties, it can be worth trying both approaches to see which one produces the shortest trail. When the -DREACH option was used, the verifier had to do a little more work to build the state space, and it could run out of memory sooner than the variant without the option.

The shorter acceptance cycle that was found looks as follows:

```
$ spin -t -p fairness.pml
  1: proc 1 (B) line 13 "fairness.pml" (state 1) [i=(1-i)]
  2: proc 1 (B) line 13 "fairness.pml" (state 1) [i=(1-i)]
```

```
 3: proc 0 (A) line  6 "fairness.pml" (state 1) [i=(1-i)]
 4: proc 1 (B) line 13 "fairness.pml" (state 1) [i=(1-i)]
 5: proc 1 (B) line 13 "fairness.pml" (state 1) [i=(1-i)]
 6: proc 1 (B) line 13 "fairness.pml" (state 1) [i=(1-i)]
 7: proc 0 (A) line  6 "fairness.pml" (state 1) [i=(1-i)]
 <<<<<START OF CYCLE>>>>>
 8: proc 1 (B) line 13 "fairness.pml" (state 1) [i=(1-i)]
 9: proc 0 (A) line  6 "fairness.pml" (state 1) [i=(1-i)]
10: proc 1 (B) line 13 "fairness.pml" (state 1) [i=(1-i)]
11: proc 0 (A) line  6 "fairness.pml" (state 1) [i=(1-i)]
12: proc 0 (A) line  6 "fairness.pml" (state 1) [i=(1-i)]
spin: trail ends after 12 steps
#processes: 2
12:    proc 1 (B) line 12 "fairness.pml" (state 2)
12:    proc 0 (A) line  5 "fairness.pml" (state 2)
2 processes created
```

THE SPIN IMPLEMENTATION

(Can be skipped on a first reading.) SPIN's implementation of the weak fairness algorithm differs on minor points from the description we have given. The modifications are meant to reduce the memory and run-time requirements of the search.

A first difference is that the SPIN implementation does not actually store $(k + 2)$ full copies of each reachable state. Doing so would dramatically increase the memory requirements for the weak fairness option. It suffices to store just one copy of each state plus $(k + 2)$ *bits* of overhead. The additional bits record in which copy of the state graph each state was visited: the i-th bit is set when the state is encountered in the i-th copy of the state graph. Creating one extra copy of the state graph now requires just one extra bit per state. If the reachable state space contains R states, each of B bits, the memory requirements for the algorithm can thus be reduced from $(R \times B) \times (k + 2)$ to $(R \times B) + (k + 2)$ bits.

Another small difference is that the nested depth-first search for cycles is not initiated from an acceptance state in the *0-th* copy of the state graph, but from the *last* copy of the state graph. Note that whenever this last copy is reached we can be certain of two things:

- A reachable accepting state exists.
- A (weakly) fair execution is possible starting from that accepting state.

Each state in the last copy of the state graph now serves as the seed state for a run of the nested depth-first search algorithm, in an effort to find a cycle. As before, all transitions from the last copy of the state graph move the system unconditionally back to the *0-th* copy of the state graph, and therefore the only way to revisit the seed state is to pass an accepting state and close the cycle with a fair sequence of transitions.

COMPLEXITY REVISITED

In the worst case, the algorithm from Figure 8.7 for checking liveness properties uses twice as much run time as the algorithm from Figure 8.2, which sufficed only for checking safety properties. Clearly, in the algorithm from Figure 8.7 each state can now appear in the state space twice: once with the a *true*
`toggle` and once with a *false* `toggle` attribute. The algorithm can, however,
be implemented with almost no memory overhead. As we noted earlier in the
discussion of weak fairness, each state needs only be stored once, and not
twice, with the right bookkeeping information. The bookkeeping information
in this case requires just two bits per state. The first bit is set to one when the
state is visited with a `toggle` value *false*; the second bit is set to one if the
state is visited with a `toggle` value *true* (i.e., in the nested part of the search).
Clearly, the combination (0,0) for these two bits will never be seen in practice,
but each of the three remaining combinations can appear and the two bits
together suffice to accurately identify all reached states separately in each of
the two (virtual) state graphs.

The algorithm from Figure 8.2 incurs a computational expense that is linear in
the number of reachable states for a given system model, that is, there is a
largely fixed amount of work (computation time and memory space) associated with each reachable system state. Adding cycle detection increases the
run-time expenses by a factor of maximally two, but does not impact the
memory requirements noticeably. Adding a property automaton (e.g., a
`never` claim generated from an LTL requirement) of N states increases the
expense of a straight reachability by another factor of maximally N. The size
N of the property automaton itself, though, can increase exponentially with the
number of temporal operators used in an LTL formula. This exponential
effect, though, is rarely, if ever, seen in practice.

Adding the weak fairness constraint causes an unfolding of the reachable state
space by a factor of $(k + 2)$, where k is the number of active processes in the
system. In the implementation, the memory cost of the unfolding is reduced
significantly by storing each copy of a reachable state not $(k + 2)$ times but
once, and annotating it with $(k + 2)$ bits to record in which copies of the state
graph the state has been encountered. If we use the nested depth-first search
cycle detection method, the memory overhead per reachable state then
remains limited to $2(k + 2)$ bits per reached state. In the worst case, though,
the run-time requirements can increase by a factor of $2(k + 2)$, although in
practice it is rare to see an increase greater than two.

Clearly, automated verification can be done most efficiently for pure safety
properties: basic assertions, system invariants, absence of deadlock, etc. Next
in efficiency is the verification of liveness properties: proving the absence of
non-progress cycles or the presence of acceptance cycles. Next in complexity
comes the verification of LTL properties. The more complex the temporal
formula, the more states there can be in the corresponding property

automaton, and the greater the computational expense of the verification can be. This is a worst-case assessment only, though. In many cases, there is a tight coupling between transitions in a property automaton that is generated from an LTL formula and the reachable states of a system, which means that often the computational expense is only modestly affected by the size of the property automaton or the size of the underlying LTL formula.

BIBLIOGRAPHIC NOTES

The best known alternative method to detect acceptance cycles in a finite graph is based on the construction of all the maximal strongly connected components in the graph. If at least one component contains at least one accepting state, then an accepting ω-run can be constructed. The strongly connected components in a graph can be constructed with time and space that is linear in the size of the graph with a depth-first search, Tarjan [1972]. Tarjan's procedure requires the use of two integers to annotate each state (the depth-first number and the low-link number), while the nested depth-first search procedure from Figure 8.7 requires the addition of just two bits of information. Tarjan's procedure, though, can identify *all* accepting ω-runs in a graph. The nested depth-first search procedure can always identify at least one such run, but not necessarily all. The nested depth-first search procedure is compatible with all lossless and lossy memory compression algorithms that we will explore in the next chapter, while Tarjan's procedure is not.

State space caching methods were described in Holzmann, Godefroid, and Pirottin [1992], and in Godefroid, Holzmann, and Pirottin [1995].

The nested depth-first search procedure was first described in Courcoubetis, Vardi, Wolper, and Yannakakis [1990], and its application to SPIN is described in Godefroid and Holzmann [1993]. A similar procedure for the detection of non-progress cycles can also be found in Holzmann [1991], and is discussed in more detail in Holzmann [2000]. A modification of the nested depth-first search procedure to secure compatibility with partial order reduction methods is described in Holzmann, Peled, and Yannakakis [1996].

Choueka's flag construction method was first described in Choueka [1974]. Its potential use for the enforcement of fairness with a nested depth-first search was mentioned in Courcoubetis et al. [1990]. An alternative, detailed description of SPIN's implementation of the weak fairness algorithm can be found in Chapters 3 and 7 of Bosnacki [2001].

SEARCH OPTIMIZATION 9

The basic algorithms for performing explicit state verification, as implemented in SPIN, are not very complicated. The hard problem in the construction of a verification system is therefore not so much in the implementation of these algorithms, but in finding effective ways to scale them to handle large to very large verification problems. In this chapter we discuss the methods that were implemented in SPIN to address this issue.

The optimization techniques we will review here have one of two possible aims: to reduce the number of reachable system states that must be searched to verify properties, or to reduce the amount of memory that is needed to store each state.

SPIN's partial order reduction strategy and statement merging technique fall into the first of these two categories. In the second category we find techniques that are based on either lossless or lossy compression methods. The former preserve the capability to perform exhaustive verifications, though often trading reductions in memory use for increases in run time. The lossy compression methods can be more aggressive in saving memory use without incurring run-time penalties, by trading reductions in both memory use and speed for a potential loss of coverage. The bitstate hashing method, for which SPIN is perhaps best known, falls into the latter category. A range of lossless compression methods is also supported in SPIN. We will briefly discuss the principle of operation of the hash-compact method, collapse compression, and the minimized automaton representation. We begin with a discussion of partial order reduction.

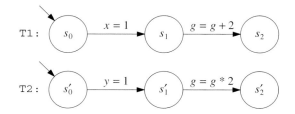

Figure 9.1 The Finite State Automata $T1$ and $T2$

PARTIAL ORDER REDUCTION

Consider the two finite state automata $T1$ and $T2$ shown in Figure 9.1. If we interpret the labels on the transitions, we can see that the execution of each system is meant to have a side effect on three data objects. The automata share access to an integer data object named g, and they each have access to a private data object, named x and y, respectively. Assume that the initial value of all data objects is zero, and the range of possible values is 0...4.

The expanded asynchronous product of $T1$ and $T2$ (cf. Appendix A) is illustrated in Figure 9.2. We have used the state labels in Figure 9.2 to record the values of the data objects in the order: x, y, g.

The paths through the graph from Figure 9.2 represent all possible interleavings of the combined execution of the four statements from automata $T1$ and $T2$. Clearly, the two possible interleavings of the statements $x = 1$ and $y = 1$ both lead to the same result, where both x and y have value 1. The two possible interleavings of the statements $g = g + 2$ and $g = g * 2$, on the other hand, lead to two different values for g. The underlying notion of data independence and data dependence can be exploited to define an equivalence relation on runs.

The system is small enough that we can exhaustively write down all finite runs. There are only six:

$$\sigma_1 = \{(0,0,0),(1,0,0),(1,0,2),(1,1,2),(1,1,4)\}$$
$$\sigma_2 = \{(0,0,0),(1,0,0),(1,1,0),(1,1,2),(1,1,4)\}$$
$$\sigma_3 = \{(0,0,0),(1,0,0),(1,1,0),(1,1,0),(1,1,2)\}$$
$$\sigma_4 = \{(0,0,0),(0,1,0),(0,1,0),(1,1,0),(1,1,2)\}$$
$$\sigma_5 = \{(0,0,0),(0,1,0),(1,1,0),(1,1,0),(1,1,2)\}$$
$$\sigma_6 = \{(0,0,0),(0,1,0),(1,1,0),(1,1,2),(1,1,4)\}$$

The sequence of statement executions that correspond to these six runs can be written as follows:

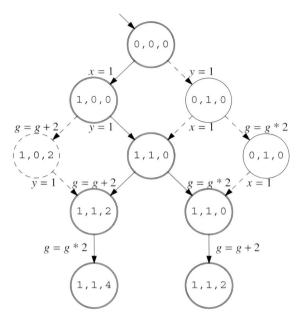

Figure 9.2 Expanded Asynchronous Product of $T1$ and $T2$

1:     x = 1; g = g+2; y = 1; g = g*2;
2:     x = 1; y = 1; g = g+2; g = g*2;
3:     x = 1; y = 1; g = g*2; g = g+2;
4:     y = 1; g = g*2; x = 1; g = g+2;
5:     y = 1; x = 1; g = g*2; g = g+2;
6:     y = 1; x = 1; g = g+2; g = g*2;

The first two runs differ only in the relative order of execution of the two transitions y = 1 and g = g+2, which are independent operations. Similarly, runs σ_4 and σ_5 differ only in the relative order of execution of the independent operations x = 1 and g = g*2, By a process of elimination, we can reduce the number of distinct runs to just two, for instance to:

2:     x = 1; y = 1; g = g+2; g = g*2;
3:     x = 1; y = 1; g = g*2; g = g+2;

The four other runs can be obtained from these two by the permutation of adjacent independent operations. We have the following mutual dependencies in this set of transitions:

g = g*2 and g = g+2   because they touch the same data object
x = 1   and g = g+2   because they are both part of automaton $T1$
y = 1   and g = g*2   because they are both part of automaton $T2$

The following operations are mutually independent:

x = 1 and y = 1
x = 1 and g = g*2
y = 1 and g = g+2

Using this classification of dependent and independent operations, we can partition the runs of the system into two equivalence classes: $\{\sigma_1,\sigma_2,\sigma_6\}$ and $\{\sigma_3,\sigma_4,\sigma_5\}$. Within each class, each run can be obtained from the other runs by one or more permutations of adjacent independent transitions. The eventual outcome of a computation remains unchanged under such permutations. For verification, it therefore would suffice to consider just one run from each equivalence class.

For the system from Figure 9.2 it would suffice, for instance, to consider only runs σ_2 and σ_3. In effect this restriction amounts to a reduction of the graph in Figure 9.2 to the portion that is spanned by the *solid* arrows, including only the states that are indicated in *bold*. There are three states fewer in this graph and only half the number of transitions, yet it would suffice to accurately prove LTL formulae such as:

$\square\,(g \equiv 0 \vee g > x)$
$\lozenge\,(g \geq 2)$
$(g \equiv 0)\ \boldsymbol{U}\,(x \equiv 1)$

VISIBILITY

Would it be possible to formulate LTL properties for which a verification could return different results for the reduced graph and the full graph? To answer this question, consider the LTL formula

$\square\,(x \geq y).$

This formula indeed has the unfortunate property that it holds in the reduced graph but can be violated in the full graph.

What happened? The formula secretly introduces a data dependence that was assumed not to exist: it relates the values of the data objects x and y, while we earlier used the assumption that operations on these two data objects were always independent. The dependence of operations, therefore, does not just depend on automata structure and access to data, but also on the logical properties that we are interested in proving about a system. If we remove the pair $x = 1$ and $y = 1$ from the set of mutually independent operations, the number of equivalence classes of runs that we can deduce increases to four, and the reduced graph gains one extra state and two extra transitions.

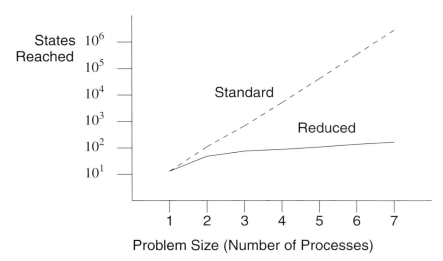

Figure 9.3 Effect of Partial Order Reduction
Increase in Number of States as a Function of Problem Size
(Sample of Best Case Performance for Leader Election Protocol)

The new graph will now correctly expose the last LTL formula as invalid, in both the full and in the reduced graph.

The potential benefits of partial order reduction are illustrated in Figure 9.3. Shown is the reduction in the number of states in the product graph that needs to be explored to perform model checking when partial order reduction is either enabled (solid line) or disabled (dashed line). In this case, the improvement increases exponentially with the problem size. It is not hard to construct cases where partial order reduction cannot contribute any improvement (e.g., if all operations are dependent). The challenge in implementing this strategy in a model checker is therefore to secure that in the worst case the graph construction will not suffer any noticeable overhead. This was done in the SPIN model checker with a *static reduction method*. In this case, the dependency relations are computed offline, before a model checking run is initiated, so that no noticeable run-time overhead is incurred.

The partial order reduction strategy is enabled by default for all SPIN verification runs. There are a small number of language constructions that are not compatible with the enforcement of a partial order reduction strategy. They are listed in Chapter 16. In these cases, and for experimental purposes, the partial order reduction strategy can be disabled by compiling the verification code that is generated by SPIN with the compiler directive -DNOREDUCE.

STATEMENT MERGING

A special case of partial order reduction is a technique that tries to combine sequences of transitions within the same process into a single step, thus avoiding the creation of intermediate system states after each separate transition. The merging operation can be performed, for instance, for sequences of operations that touch only local data. In effect, this technique automatically adds d_steps into a specification, wherever this can safely be done.

To see the potential effect of statement merging, consider the following example:

```
#ifdef GLOBAL
        byte c;
#endif

active proctype merging()
{
#ifndef GLOBAL
        byte c;
#endif
        if
        :: c = 0
        :: c = 1
        :: c = 2
        fi;
        do
        :: c < 2 -> c++
        :: c > 0 -> c--
        od
}
```

If we make the declaration for variable c global, none of the operations on this variable can be considered safe under the partial order reduction rules, and the statement merging technique cannot be applied.

Note that proctype merging has five control states, and variable c can take three different values, so there can be no more than fifteen system states.

There is one control state before, and one after the if statement. Then there is also one control state at each of the two arrow symbols. The fifth control control state is the termination state of the process: immediately following the do construct.

It turns out that only eight of these fifteen states can be reached, as confirmed by this first run:

```
$ spin -DGLOBAL -a merging.pml
$ cc -o pan pan.c
$ ./pan
(Spin Version 4.0.7 -- 1 August 2003)
        + Partial Order Reduction
```

```
Full statespace search for:
        never claim             - (none specified)
        assertion violations    +
        acceptance    cycles    - (not selected)
        invalid end states      +

State-vector 16 byte, depth reached 6, errors: 0
        8 states, stored
        4 states, matched
       12 transitions (= stored+matched)
        0 atomic steps
 . . .
```

If we now turn c from a global into a local variable, all operations on this variable become local to the one process in this system, which means that the SPIN parser can recognize the corresponding transitions as necessarily independent from any other statement execution in the system. The statement merging technique can now combine the two option-sequences inside the do loop into a single step each, and thereby removes two of the control states. The result should be a reduction in the number of states that is reached in a verification. If we perform this experiment, we can see this effect confirmed:

```
$ spin -a merging.pml
$ cc -o pan pan.c
$ ./pan
(Spin Version 4.0.7 -- 1 August 2003)
        + Partial Order Reduction

Full statespace search for:
        never claim             - (none specified)
        assertion violations    +
        acceptance    cycles    - (not selected)
        invalid end states      +

State-vector 16 byte, depth reached 3, errors: 0
        4 states, stored
        4 states, matched
        8 transitions (= stored+matched)
        0 atomic steps
 . . .
```

There is only one downside to the statement merging technique: it can make it harder to understand the automaton structure that is used in the verification process. Statement merging can be disabled with an extra command-line option in SPIN. For instance, if we generate the verifier as follows:

```
$ spin -a -o3 merging.pml
```

statement merging is surpressed, and the system will again create eight system states during a verification.

STATE COMPRESSION

The aim of the partial order reduction strategy is to reduce the number of system states that needs to be visited and stored in the state space to solve the model checking problem. An orthogonal strategy is to reduce the amount of memory that is required to store each system state. This is the domain of memory compression techniques.

SPIN supports options for both lossless and lossy compression: the first type of compression reduces the memory requirements of an exhaustive search by increasing the run-time requirements. The second offers a range of *proof approximation* techniques that can work with very little memory, but without guarantees of exhaustive coverage.

We first consider lossless state compression. SPIN has two different algorithms of this type. The COLLAPSE compression mode exploits a hierarchical indexing method to achieve compression. The MA, or minimized automaton, compression mode reduces memory by building and updating a minimized finite state recognizer for state descriptors.

COLLAPSE COMPRESSION

At first sight, it may strike us as somewhat curious that the number of distinct system states that the verifier can encounter during a search can become so large so quickly, despite the fact that each process and each data object can typically reach only a small number of distinct states (i.e., values). The explosion in the number of reachable system states is only caused by the relatively large number of ways in which the local states of individual system components, such as processes and data objects, can be *combined*. Replicating a complete description of all local components of the system state in each global state that is stored is therefore an inherently wasteful technique, although it can be implemented very efficiently.

SPIN's collapse compression mode tries to exploit this observation by storing smaller state components separately while assigning small unique index numbers to each one. The unique index numbers for the smaller components are now combined to form the global state descriptor.

There are now several choices that can be made about how precisely to break down a global system state into separate components, ideally with as little correlation as possible between components. SPIN assigns components as illustrated in Figure 9.4.

- A first component is formed by the set of all global data objects in the model, including the contents of all message channels, irrespective of whether they were declared locally or globally. This component also includes a length field that records the original length of the state vector (i.e., the state descriptor) before compression.
- Next, there is one component for each active process, recording its control

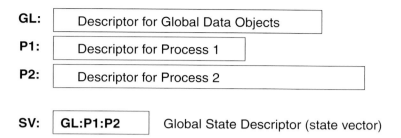

Figure 9.4 State Components for COLLAPSE Compression

state together with the state of all its local variables, but excluding the contents of locally declared channels.

Because the number of component states cannot be known in advance, the method should be able to adjust the number of bits it uses to record index values. The SPIN implementation does this by adding an extra two bits to each component index to record how many bytes are used for the corresponding index field. In this way, the compressor can use up to four bytes per index, which suffices for up to 2^{32} possible separate component states. The table of index widths is added to the global variables component. The width of the index for the global variables component itself is stored in a fixed separate byte of the compressed state descriptor.

To make sure no false partial matches can occur, the length of each separately stored component is also always stored with the component data.

The collapse compression method is invoked by compiling the verifier source text that is generated by SPIN with the extra compile-time directive -DCOL-LAPSE. For instance:

```
$ spin -a model
$ cc -DCOLLAPSE -o pan pan.c
$ ./pan
...
```

There should be no change in the results delivered by the verifier, other than that run time may increase while the memory requirements decrease.

To see the effect of the COLLAPSE algorithm, consider the example PROMELA model of the leader election protocol that is part of the standard SPIN distribution. We will set the number of processes to seven (changing it from the default value in the distributed version of five) and will disable the partial order reduction method to increase the state space size to a more interesting value. We proceed as follows:

```
$ spin -a leader.pml
$ cc -DNOREDUCE -DMEMLIM=200 pan.c
$ time ./pan
(Spin Version 4.0.7 -- 1 August 2003)

Full statespace search for:
        never claim              - (none specified)
        assertion violations     +
        acceptance   cycles      - (not selected)
        invalid end states       +

State-vector 276 byte, depth reached 148, errors: 0
  723053 states, stored
3.00211e+006 states, matched
3.72517e+006 transitions (= stored+matched)
      16 atomic steps
hash conflicts: 2.70635e+006 (resolved)
(max size 2^18 states)

Stats on memory usage (in Megabytes):
205.347 equivalent memory usage for states (...)
174.346 actual memory usage for states (compression: 84.90%)
        State-vector as stored = 233 byte + 8 byte overhead
1.049   memory used for hash table (-w18)
0.240   memory used for DFS stack (-m10000)
175.266 total actual memory usage

unreached in proctype node
        line 53, state 28, "out!two,nr"
        (1 of 49 states)
unreached in proctype :init:
        (0 of 11 states)

real    0m16.657s
user    0m0.015s
sys     0m0.015s
```

Running on a 2.5 GHz PC, the search took 16.7 seconds, and it consumed 175.2 Mbytes of memory. A statistic is also printed for the "equivalent memory usage," which is obtained by multiplying the number of stored states with the size of each state descriptor, plus the overhead of the lookup table. The default search does a little better than this by always using a simple byte masking technique that omits some redundant information from the state descriptors before they are stored (e.g, padded bytes that are inserted to secure proper alignment of components inside the state descriptor).

Next, we recompile the model checker with COLLAPSE compression enabled and repeat the search.

```
$ cc -DMEMLIM=200 -DNOREDUCE -DCOLLAPSE pan.c
$ time ./pan
(Spin Version 4.0.7 -- 1 August 2003)
        + Compression

Full statespace search for:
        never claim            - (none specified)
        assertion violations   +
        acceptance    cycles   - (not selected)
        invalid end states     +

State-vector 276 byte, depth reached 148, errors: 0
  723053 states, stored
3.00211e+006 states, matched
3.72517e+006 transitions (= stored+matched)
      16 atomic steps
hash conflicts: 3.23779e+006 (resolved)
(max size 2^18 states)

Stats on memory usage (in Megabytes):
208.239 equivalent memory usage for states (...)
23.547  actual memory usage for states (compression: 11.31%)
        State-vector as stored = 21 byte + 12 byte overhead
1.049   memory used for hash table (-w18)
0.240   memory used for DFS stack (-m10000)
24.738  total actual memory usage

nr of templates: [ globals chans procs ]
collapse counts: [ 2765 129 2 ]
unreached in proctype node
        line 53, state 28, "out!two,nr"
        (1 of 49 states)
unreached in proctype :init:
        (0 of 11 states)

real    0m20.104s
user    0m0.015s
sys     0m0.015s
```

As expected, the same number of states was reached, but this time the search took 20.1 seconds (about 20% more than the first run) and the memory usage dropped to 24.7 Mbytes (a decrease of about 85%). The use of COLLAPSE is well rewarded in this case.

At the end of the run, a few additional statistics are printed to give some impression of how many components of each basic type were seen. The components are called *templates* in this list, and the maximum number of entries made in the lookup table for each basic type (global variables, message channels, and processes) is given here as 2,765, 129, and 2.

Although the effect of the reduction looks impressive, if we repeat this search

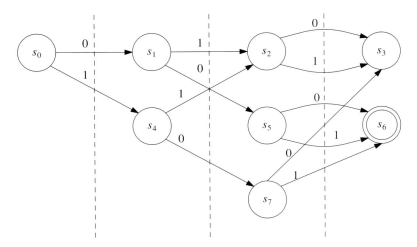

Figure 9.5 Minimized Automaton Structure After Storing {000, 001, 101}

with the standard partial order reduction strategy enabled, the state space size reduces to just 133 states in this case. As a result, the run time drops to a fraction of a second, and the memory requirements to about 1.5 Mbytes. Clearly, state compression is not an alternative to partial order reduction, but can be combined with it very fruitfully.

MINIMIZED AUTOMATON REPRESENTATION

A second lossless compression method that is supported in SPIN optionally stores the set of reachable system states not in a conventional lookup table, but instead performs state matching by building and maintaining a minimal deterministic finite state automaton that acts as a recognizer for sets of state descriptors. The automaton, represented as a finite graph, is interrogated for every system state encountered during the search, and updated immediately if a new state descriptor is seen. The savings in memory use with this method can be very large, sometimes allowing the verifier to use exponentially smaller amounts of memory than required for the standard search methods. The run-time penalty, though, can be very significant.

Figure 9.5 shows the minimized automaton structure for a state descriptor of three bits, after the first three state descriptors have been stored. All paths in the automaton that lead from node s_0 to the accepting state s_6 are part of the state space, all paths from node s_0 to the non-accepting terminal state s_3 are not part of the state space. The dashed lines separate the subsequent layers in the automaton. The edges between the node in the first (left-most) layer and

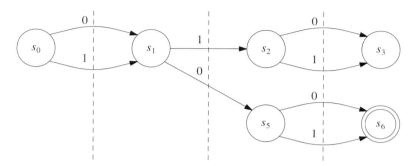

Figure 9.6 Automaton Structure After Storing $\{000, 001, 101, 100\}$

the second layer represent the possible values of the first bit in the state descriptor, those between the second and the third layer represent possible values of the second bit, and so on.

Figure 9.6 shows how this structure is updated when one more state descriptor is added, again restoring the minimized form. There is a close resemblance between this minimized automaton structure and OBDDs (ordered binary decision diagrams). In our implementation of this storage method, each node in the graph does not represent a single bit but a byte of information, and each node therefore can have up to 255 outgoing edges. Edges are merged into ranges wherever possible to speed up the lookup and update procedures.

In principle, the minimized automaton has the same expected complexity as the standard search based on the storage of system states in a hashed lookup table. In both cases, an update of the state space has expected complexity $O(S)$, with S the maximum length of the state descriptor for a system state. The constant factors in both procedures are very different, though, which means that the minimized automaton procedure can consume considerably more time than the other optimization algorithms that are implemented in SPIN. Nonetheless, when memory is at a premium, it can well be worth the extra wait to use the more aggressive reduction technique.

To enable the minimized automaton procedure, the user should provide an initial estimate of the maximal depth of the graph that is constructed for the minimized automaton representation. The estimate is not hard to obtain: the size of the state vector that the verifier prints at the end of a normal run can serve as the initial estimate. The number can be used as an initial value for the compile-time directive that enables the minimized automaton procedure. For instance, if we take the last run for the leader election protocol as a starting point. The state vector size reported there was 276 bytes. The size needed for the minimized automaton structure is typically a little smaller, so we make an initial guess of 270 bytes and recompile and run the verifier as follows:

```
$ cc -DMEMLIM=200 -DNOREDUCE -DMA=270 pan.c
$ time ./pan
(Spin Version 4.0.7 -- 1 August 2003)
        + Graph Encoding (-DMA=270)

Full statespace search for:
        never claim              - (none specified)
        assertion violations     +
        acceptance    cycles     - (not selected)
        invalid end states       +

State-vector 276 byte, depth reached 148, errors: 0
MA stats: -DMA=234 is sufficient
Minimized Automaton:     161769 nodes and 397920 edges
  723053 states, stored
3.00211e+006 states, matched
3.72517e+006 transitions (= stored+matched)
       16 atomic steps
hash conflicts: 0 (resolved)
(max size 2^18 states)

Stats on memory usage (in Megabytes):
202.455 equivalent memory usage for states (...)
7.235    actual memory usage for states (compression: 3.57%)
0.200    memory used for DFS stack (-m10000)
7.338    total actual memory usage

unreached in proctype node
        line 53, state 28, "out!two,nr"
        (1 of 49 states)
unreached in proctype :init:
        (0 of 11 states)

real    1m11.428s
user    0m0.015s
sys     0m0.015s
```

Again, the same number of states was reached, but note that the memory requirements dropped to just 7.338 Mbytes, compared to 175 Mbytes for the default search without compression, giving an average of just 10 bytes used per state stored. This impressive reduction comes at a price, though. While the memory requirements were reduced, the run-time requirements increased from 16.7 seconds to about 71.4 seconds: a very noticeable penalty.

At the end of the run, the verifier also tells us that instead of our estimate of 270 bytes, a smaller value of 234 bytes would have sufficed. Using that value could reduce the memory and run-time requirements somewhat. In this case, the run time would reduce to 133 seconds and the memory requirements to

7.301 Mbytes, giving a small additional benefit.

It is safe to combine the minimized automaton compression method with the COLLAPSE compression method to achieve additional reductions. If we do this for the leader election protocol (while still suppressing the partial order reduction algorithm to create a large state space), we obtain the following result:

```
$ cc -DMEMLIM=200 -DNOREDUCE -DMA=21 -DCOLLAPSE pan.c
$ ./pan
(Spin Version 4.0.7 -- 1 August 2003)
        + Compression
        + Graph Encoding (-DMA=21)

Full statespace search for:
        never claim             - (none specified)
        assertion violations    +
        acceptance    cycles    - (not selected)
        invalid end states      +

State-vector 276 byte, depth reached 148, errors: 0
Minimized Automaton:       5499 nodes and   25262 edges
  723053 states, stored
3.00211e+006 states, matched
3.72517e+006 transitions (= stored+matched)
       16 atomic steps
hash conflicts: 0 (resolved)
(max size 2^18 states)

Stats on memory usage (in Megabytes):
208.239 equivalent memory usage for states (...)
0.892   actual memory usage for states (compression: 0.43%)
1.049   memory used for hash table (-w18)
0.200   memory used for DFS stack (-m10000)
2.068   total actual memory usage

nr of templates: [ globals chans procs ]
collapse counts: [ 2765 129 2 ]
unreached in proctype node
        line 53, state 28, "out!two,nr"
        (1 of 49 states)
unreached in proctype :init:
        (0 of 11 states)

real    0m44.214s
user    0m0.015s
sys     0m0.015s
```

After one iteration, we could determine that the value for compiler directive MA that suffices now reduces to just 21, and with this value the memory requirements drop to a remarkable 2.068 Mbyte, while the search stores the same number of reachable states as before. The run-time requirements are now also slightly less, reducing to 44.2 seconds, thanks to the smaller, collapsed state descriptors that are now handled by the minimized automaton recognizer. This favorable effect is not always observed, but an experiment like this is often worth trying.

Note carefully that even though this last search consumed only 2.7 bytes for each state stored, the search was still completely exhaustive, and the result of the verification is 100% accurate. This is due to the fact that both the COL-LAPSE and the MA compression methods are lossless. If we give up the requirement of guaranteed exhaustive coverage, a number of other interesting search techniques become possible. Some of these techniques can succeed in analyzing very large problem sizes with very minimal run-time requirements. We will consider two of the techniques that are implemented in SPIN: bitstate hashing and hash-compact.

> *"An approximate answer to the right question*
> *is worth a great deal more than*
> *a precise answer to the wrong question."*
> *(John Tukey, 1915–2000)*

BITSTATE HASHING

The standard depth-first search algorithm constructs a set of states. Each state that is explored in the verification process is stored in a *state space*. Since the model checking problem for all practical purposes is reduced to the solution of a reachability problem (cf. Chapter 8), all the model checker does is construct states and check whether they were previously visited or new. The performance of a model checker is determined by how fast it can do this.

The state space structure serves to prevent the re-exploration of previously visited states during the search: it turns what would otherwise be an exponential algorithm into a linear one, that visits every reachable state in the graph at most once. To enable fast lookup of states, the states are normally stored in a hash table, as illustrated in Figure 9.7.

Assume we have a hash table with h slots. Each slot contains a list of zero or more states. To determine in which list we store a new state s, we compute a hash-value $hash(s)$, unique to s and randomly chosen in the range $0..h\text{-}1$. We check the states stored in the list in hash table slot $hash(s)$ for a possible match with s. If a match is found, the state was previously visited and need not be explored again. If no match is found, state s is added to the list, and the search continues.

Each state is represented in memory as a sequence of S bits. A simple (but very slow) hashing method would be to consider the array of bits as one large unsigned integer, and to calculate the remainder of its division by h,

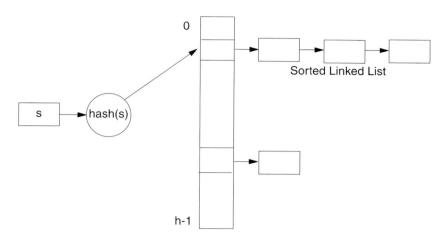

Figure 9.7 Standard Hash Table Lookup

with h a prime number. A more efficient method, and one of the methods implemented in SPIN, is to use a *checksum polynomial* to compute the hash values. We now choose h as a power of 2 and use the polynomial to compute a checksum of $log(h)$ bits. This checksum is then used as the hash value.

The default hashing method that is currently implemented in SPIN is based on a method known as Jenkins' hash. It is slightly slower than the checksum polynomial method, but it can be shown to give notably better coverage.

Let r be the number of states stored in the hash table and h the number of slots in that table. When $h \gg r$, each state can be stored in a different slot, provided that the hash function is of sufficiently good quality. The lists stored in each slot of the hash table will either be empty or contain one single state. State storage has only a constant overhead in this case, carrying virtually no time penalty.

When $h < r$, there will be cases for which the hash function computes the same hash value for different states. These *hash collisions* are resolved by placing all states that hash to the same value in a linked list at the corresponding slot in the hash table. In this case we may have to do multiple state comparisons for each new state that is checked against the hash table: towards the end of the search on average r/h comparisons will be required per state. The overhead incurred increases linearly with growing r/h, once the number of stored states r exceeds h.

Clearly, we would like to be in the situation where $h \gg r$. In this case, a hash value uniquely identifies a state, with low probability of collision. The only information that is contained in the hash table is now primarily whether or not the state that corresponds to the hash value has been visited. This is one single bit of information. A rash proposal is now to indeed store only this one bit of information, instead of the S bits of the state itself. This leads to the following trade-offs.

Assume that we have m bits of memory to store the hash table, S bits of data in each state descriptor, r reachable states, and a hash table with h slots. Clearly, fewer than m/S states will fit in memory, since the hash table itself will also take some memory. If $r > m/S$, the search will exhaust the available resources (and stop) after exploring a fraction of $m/(r \cdot S)$ of the state space. Typical values for these parameters are: $m = 10^9$, $S = 10^3$, and $r = 10^7$, which gives a ratio $m/(r \cdot S) = 10^{-2}$, or a coverage of the problem size of only 1%.

If we configure the hash table as an array of $8m$ bits, using it as a hash table with $h = 8m$ 1-bit slots, we now have $h \gg r$, since $8 \cdot 10^9 \gg 10^7$, which should give us an expected coverage close to 100%. When, with low probability, a hash collision happens, our model checking algorithm will conclude incorrectly that a state was visited before, and it will skip it. It may now miss other states that can only be reached via a path in the reachability graph that passes through this state. This, therefore, would lead to loss of coverage, but it cannot lead to false error reports. We will see shortly that in almost all cases where this method is used (i.e., when normal state storage is impossible due to limited resources available), coverage increases far more due to the increased capacity to store states than it is reduced due to hash collisions.

This storage discipline was referred to in Morris [1968] as follows:

> "A curious possible use of virtual scatter tables arises when a hash address can be computed with more than about three times as many bits as are actually needed for a calculated address. The possibility that two different keys have the same virtual hash address becomes so remote that the keys might not need to be examined at all. If a new key has the same virtual hash address as an existing entry, then the keys could be assumed to be the same. Then, of course, there is no longer any need to keep the keys in the entry; unless they are needed for some other purpose, they can just be thrown away. Typically, years could go by without encountering two keys in the same program with the same virtual address. Of course, one would have to be quite certain that the hash addresses were uniformly spread over the available addresses.
>
> No one, to the author's knowledge, has ever implemented this idea, and if anyone has, he might well not admit it."

To reduce the probability of collision, we can use multiple independent hash functions, and set more than one bit per state. Using more bits can increase the precision but reduce the number of available slots in the bit hash-table. The trade-offs are delicate and deserve a more careful study.

BLOOM FILTERS

Let m again be the size of the hash table in bits, r is the number of states stored, and k the number of hash functions used. That is, we store k bits for each state stored, with each of the k bit-positions computed with an independent hash function that uses the S bits of the state descriptor as the key.

Initially, all bits in the hash table are zero. When r states have been stored, the probability that any one specific bit is still zero is:

$$\left(1 - \frac{1}{m}\right)^k \cdot r$$

The probability of a hash collision on the $(r + 1)$st state entered is then

$$\left(1 - \left(1 - \frac{1}{m}\right)^k \cdot r\right)^k \approx \left(1 - e^{-k \cdot r/m}\right)^k$$

which gives us an upper-bound for the probability of hash collisions on the first r states entered. (The probability of a hash collision is trivially zero for the first state entered.) The probability of hash collisions is minimal when $k = log(2) \cdot m/r$, which gives

$$\left(\frac{1}{2}\right)^k = 0.6185^{m/r}$$

For $m = 10^9$ and $r = 10^7$ this gives us an upper-bound on the probability of collision in the order 10^{-21}, for a value of $k = 89.315$. Figure 9.8 illustrates these dependencies.

In practice, k must be an integer (e.g., 90). In a well-tuned model checker, the run-time requirements of the search depend linearly on k: computing hash values is the single most expensive operation that the model checker must perform. The larger the value of k, therefore, the longer the search for errors will take. In the model checker SPIN, for instance, a run with $k = 90$ would take approximately 45 times longer than a run with $k = 2$. Although time is a more flexible commodity than memory, the difference is significant. The question is then how much quality we sacrifice if we select a smaller than optimal value of k. The trade-off is illustrated in Figure 9.8.

For the suboptimal value $k = 2$, the value used in SPIN, the upper-bound on the collision probability becomes $4 \cdot 10^{-4}$, which reduces the expected coverage of the search from 100% to near 99%, still two orders of magnitude greater than realized by a hash table lookup method for this case. We can also see in Figure 9.8 that the hashing method starts getting very reliable for m/r ratios over 100. To be compatible with traditional storage methods, this means that for state descriptors of less than 100 bits (about 12 bytes), this method is not competitive. In practice, state descriptors exceed this lower-bound by a significant margin (one or two orders of magnitude).

The bitstate hashing method is invoked by compiling the verifier source with the additional compiler directive -DBITSTATE, for instance, as follows:

```
$ spin -a model
$ cc -DBITSTATE -o pan pan.c
$ ./pan
...
```

A straight bitstate run for the leader election protocol example, for instance, produces this result:

```
$ spin -a leader.pml
$ cc -DNOREDUCE -DMEMLIM -DBITSTATE -o pan pan.c
$ time ./pan
(Spin Version 4.0.7 -- 1 August 2003)

Bit statespace search for:
        never claim             - (none specified)
        assertion violations    +
        acceptance   cycles     - (not selected)
        invalid end states      +

State-vector 276 byte, depth reached 148, errors: 0
  700457 states, stored
2.9073e+006 states, matched
3.60775e+006 transitions (= stored+matched)
      16 atomic steps
hash factor: 5.98795 (best coverage if >100)
(max size 2^22 states)

Stats on memory usage (in Megabytes):
198.930 equivalent memory usage for states (...)
0.524   memory used for hash array (-w22)
2.097   memory used for bit stack
0.240   memory used for DFS stack (-m10000)
3.066   total actual memory usage

unreached in proctype node
        line 53, state 28, "out!two,nr"
        (1 of 49 states)
unreached in proctype :init:
        (0 of 11 states)

real    0m28.550s
user    0m0.015s
sys     0m0.015s
```

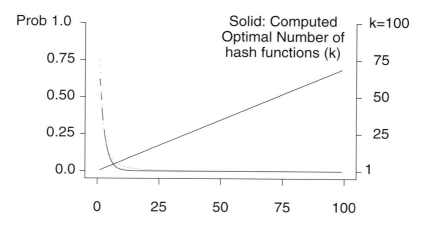

Memory bits divided by Number of States (m/r)

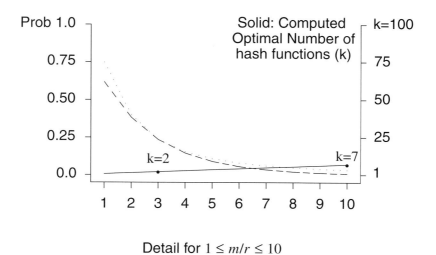

Detail for $1 \leq m/r \leq 10$

Figure 9.8 Optimal Number of Hash Functions and Probability of Hash Collision
The dashed line plots the probabilitie for optimal k
The dotted line plots the probabilities for fixed k=2
The solid line plots the optimal value for k, $1 \leq k < 100$

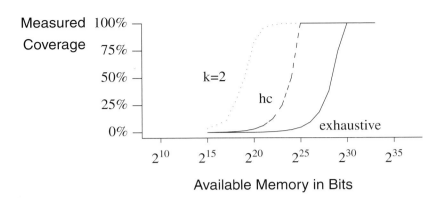

Figure 9.9 Measured Coverage of Double Bitstate Hashing (k=2)
Compared with Hash-Compact (hc), and Exhaustive Search
Problem size: 427567 reachable states, state descriptor 1376 bits

The number of states explored is a little short of the real number of reachable states that we can measure in an exhaustive run. Still, the run reached 96.7% of all reachable states, while the memory requirements dropped from 175 to 3 Mbytes, and the run-time requirements remained relatively low at 28.5 seconds.

HASH-COMPACT

An interesting variant of this strategy is the *hash-compact* method, first proposed for use in verification by Pierre Wolper. In this case we try to increase the size of m far beyond what would be available on an average machine, for instance to 2^{64} bits. We now compute a single hash value within the range $0..(2^{64}-1)$ as a 64-bit number, and store this number, instead of the full state s, in a regular hash table. We have one hash function, so $k = 1$, and we simulate a memory size of $m = 2^{64} \approx 10^{19}$ bits. For the value of $r = 10^7$, we then get a probability of collision near 10^{-57}, giving an expected coverage of 100%. To store 10^7 64-bit numbers takes less than $m = 10^9$ bits. Instead of storing 64 bits at a time, we can also store a smaller or larger number of bits. The maximum number of bits that could be accommodated is trivially m/r. The 64-bit version of hash-compact, then, should be expected to perform best when $r.64 \leq m \leq r.S$. Unfortunately, although m and S are often known *a priori*, in most cases r is usually not known before an exhaustive verification is completed, and therefore the optimal ration m/r is also typically unknown.

A measurement of the performance of the hash-compact method and double-bit hashing (i.e., with two independent hash functions) for a fixed problem size r and available memory m varying from 0 to $m > r$. S is shown in Figure 9.9, which is taken from Holzmann [1998].

When sufficient memory is available, traditional exhaustive state storage is preferred, since it gives full coverage with certainty. For the problem shown in Figure 9.9 this is the area of the graph with $m > 2^{29}$. Barring this, if sufficient memory is available for the hash-compact method, then this is the preferred method. This is the area of the graph where $2^{23} < m < 2^{29}$. Below that, in Figure 9.9 for all values $m < 2^{23}$, the double-bit hashing method is superior. The latter method, for instance, still achieves a problem coverage here of 50% when only 0.1% of the memory resources required for an traditional exhaustive search are available.

The hash-compact method can be enabled by compiling a SPIN-generated verifier with the compiler directive HC4, for instance as follows (see also Chapter 19, p. 530):

```
$ spin -a model
$ cc -DHC4 -o pan pan.c
$ ./pan
...
```

Applying the hash-compact to the leader election protocol from before, using four bytes per state, produces this result:

```
$ cc -DNOREDUCE -DMEMLIM=200 -DHC4 -o pan pan.c
$ time ./pan
(Spin Version 4.0.7 -- 1 August 2003)

Hash-Compact 4 search for:
        never claim             - (none specified)
        assertion violations    +
        acceptance   cycles     - (not selected)
        invalid end states      +

State-vector 276 byte, depth reached 148, errors: 0
  723053 states, stored
3.00211e+006 states, matched
3.72517e+006 transitions (= stored+matched)
      16 atomic steps
hash conflicts: 2.41742e+006 (resolved)
(max size 2^18 states)

Stats on memory usage (in Megabytes):
205.347 equivalent memory usage for states (...)
11.770  actual memory usage for states (compression: 5.73%)
        State-vector as stored = 8 byte + 8 byte overhead
```

```
1.049    memory used for hash table (-w18)
0.240    memory used for DFS stack (-m10000)

12.962   total actual memory usage

unreached in proctype node
        line 53, state 28, "out!two,nr"
        (1 of 49 states)
unreached in proctype :init:
        (0 of 11 states)

real     0m15.522s
user     0m0.031s
sys      0m0.000s
```

No states are missed. The memory requirements dropped to 12.9 Megabytes, and the run-time requirements remained largely unchanged from an exhaustive search.

The coverage of both the hash-compact and the double-bit hashing method can be increased by performing multiple searches, each time with an independent set of hash functions. If each search misses a fraction p of the state space, t independent searches could reduce this to p^t. Though potentially expensive in run time, this gives us a capability to increase the quality of a verification under adverse constraints.

Which of all these storage methods is best? There is, alas, no single answer to this question. The behavior of each algorithm can depend to some extent on unpredictable particulars of an application. All compression methods can be expected to bring some improvement, but the maximal improvement is not always achieved with the same technique for all applications. If there is enough memory to complete an exhaustive search, the problem of search optimization need not even be considered. When the problem is too large to be verified exhaustively with the default search method, two experiments that can be performed relatively quickly and without much thought are collapse compression and hash-compact. To go beyond what is achieved with these methods, more thought, and perhaps more search time, may be needed. As a last resort, but only for very large problem sizes, the bitstate hashing method is often hard to defeat, and will likely give the best results.

BIBLIOGRAPHIC NOTES

A formal treatments of the notions of dependence of actions (transitions) and the equivalence of ω-runs can be found in, for instance, Mazurkiewicz [1986], and Kwiatkowska [1989]. The application of these notions to model checking is described in Peled [1994], and Holzmann and Peled [1994], with a small, but important, adjustment that is explained in Holzmann, Peled, and Yannakakis [1996].

A formal proof of correctness of the partial order reduction algorithm implemented in SPIN is given in Chou and Peled [1999], and is also discussed in Clarke, Grumberg, and Peled [2000].

The statement merging technique that is implemented in SPIN was first proposed in Schoot and Ural [1996]. The SPIN implementation is discussed in Holzmann [1999].

The `COLLAPSE` compression method is described in detail in Holzmann [1997]. The design and implementation of the minimized automaton storage method is detailed in Holzmann and Puri [1999]. There are several interesting similarities, but also significant differences, between the minimized automaton procedure and methods based on the use of BDDs (binary decision diagrams) that are commonly used in model checking tools for hardware circuit verification. A discussion of these and other points can be found in Holzmann and Puri [1999].

The application of the hash-compact method to verification was described in Wolper and Leroy [1993], and also independently in Stern and Dill [1995]. An earlier theoretical treatment of this storage method can also be found in Carter at al. [1978].

Bitstate hashing, sometimes called *supertrace*, was introduced in Holzmann [1988] and studied in more detail in Holzmann [1998]. The first explicit description of the notion of bitstate hashing, though not the term, appeared in Morris [1968], in a paper on "scatter storage" techniques. In Bob Morris's original paper, the technique was mentioned mostly as a theoretical curiosity, unlikely to have serious applications. Dennis Ritchie and Doug McIlroy found an application of this storage technique in 1979 to speed up the UNIX spelling checking program, as later described in McIlroy [1982].

The original implementation of `spell` was done by Steve Johnson. The new, faster version was written by Dennis Ritchie, and was distributed as part of the 7th Edition version of UNIX. The mathematics McIlroy used in his 1982 paper to explain the working of the method is similar to the elegant exposition from Bloom [1970]. Bloom's 1970 paper, in turn, was written in response to Morris [1968], but was rediscovered only recently. Bob Morris, Dennis Ritchie, Doug McIlroy, and Steve Johnson all worked in the UNIX group at Bell Labs at the time.

The code used in the 1979 version of `spell` for table lookup differs significantly from the version that is used in the SPIN implementation for bitstate hashing, given the differences in target use. The first hash function that was implemented in SPIN for default state storage during verification was based on the computation of 32-bit cyclic redundancy checksum polynomials, and was implemented in close collaboration with (then) Bell Labs researchers Jim Reeds, Ken Thompson, and Rob Pike.

The current hashing code used in SPIN is based on Jenkins [1997]. Jenkins' hash function is slightly slower than the original code, but it incurs fewer col-lissions. The original hash functions are reinstated when the `pan.c` source code is compiled with directive `-DOHASH`.

NOTES ON
MODEL EXTRACTION **10**

Arguably, the most powerful tool we have in our arsenal for the verification of software applications is logical abstraction. By capturing the essence of a design in a mathematical model, we can often demonstrate conclusively that the design has certain inevitable properties. The purpose of a verification model, then, is to *enable* proof. If it fails to do so, within the resource limits that are available to the verification system, the model should be considered inadequate.

THE ROLE OF ABSTRACTION

The type of abstraction that is appropriate for a given application depends both on the type of logical properties that we are interested in proving *and* on the resource limits of the verification system. This situation is quite familiar: it is no different from the one that applies in standard mathematics. When we reason about the correctness of a system without the benefit of a mechanized prover, using straight logic and pen and paper mathematics, we must also use our judgement in deciding which parts of a system are relevant, and which are not, with respect to the properties to be proven. Similarly, we must be aware of resource limitations in this situation as well. If only a very limited amount of time, or a very limited amount of mathematical talent, is available for rendering the proof, perhaps a coarser proof would have to be used. If unlimited time and talent is available, a more detailed proof may be possible. Whether we choose a mechanized process or a manual one, we have to recognize that some really difficult types of problems may remain beyond our reach. It is the skill of the verifier to solve as much of a problem as is feasible, within given resource limits.

For the best choice of an abstraction method in the construction of a verification model, we unavoidably have to rely on human judgement. Which parts of the system should we look at? What properties should apply? These types of decisions would be hard to automate. But even though there will unavoidably be a human element in the setup of a verification process, once the basic decisions about abstractions are made and recorded, it should in principle be possible to mechanize the remainder of the verification process.

Given the source text of an application and the properties of interest, we would like to generate a verification model automatically from the source text, where the model extraction process is guided by a user-defined abstraction function. In this chapter we discuss how we can do so.

FROM ANSI-C TO PROMELA

To get an impression of what it takes to mechanically convert a C program into a PROMELA model, consider the following program. The program is one of the first examples used in Kernighan and Ritchie's introduction to the C programming language, with a slightly more interesting control structure than the infamous *hello world* example.

```
#include <stdio.h>

int
main(void)
{       int lower, upper, step;
        float fahr, celsius;

        lower = 0;
        upper = 300;
        step = 20;

        fahr = lower;
        while (fahr <= upper) {
                celsius = (5.0/9.0) * (fahr - 32.0);
                printf("%4.0f %6.1f\n", fahr, celsius);
                fahr = fahr + step;
        }
}
```

The program defines a function called main, declares five local variables, and does some standard manipulations to compute a conversion table from temperature measured in degrees Fahrenheit to the equivalent expressed in degrees Celsius. Suppose we wanted to convert this little program into a PROMELA model. The first problem we would run into is that PROMELA does not support the C data-type float, and has no keyword while. The control-structure that is used in the program, though, could easily be expressed in PROMELA. If we ignore the data-types for the moment, and pretend that they

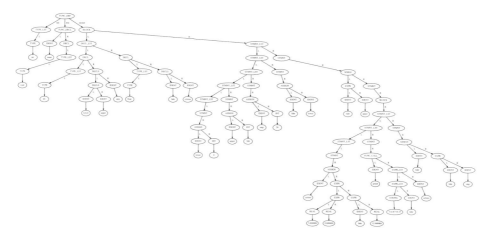

Figure 10.1 The Complete Parse Tree for fahr.c

are integers, the `while` loop could be expressed like this:

```
fahr = lower;
do
:: (fahr <= upper) ->
        celsius = (5/9) * (fahr-32);
        printf("%d %d\n", fahr, celsius);
        fahr = fahr + step;
:: else -> break
od
```

It is not hard to see almost all control-flow structures that can be defined in C can be replicated in PROMELA. (There are some exceptions, though, that we will consider shortly.) The control structure can be derived, for instance, from the standard parse-tree representation of a program that is constructed by a C compiler. Figure 10.1 shows a parse tree for the example temperature conversion program.

The complete tree is large, even for this small program, including nodes for the main program, but also for all default global declarations that are retrieved from the included `stdio.h` file. The interesting part of the tree is on the lower right, which is reproduced in a little more detail in Figure 10.2. It contains the top of the parse-tree structure for the `while` loop.

The node at the top of Figure 10.2 has two successors. The left child (reached via the transition marked `L` defines the loop condition, and the right child defines the code fragment for the loop body as a sequence of statements that are further detailed in the subtree below it.

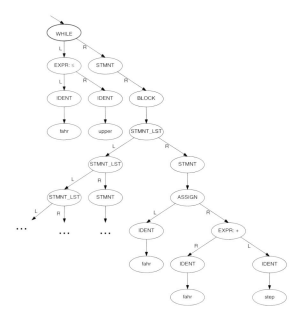

Figure 10.2 Part of Parse Tree Structure for the While Loop

A parse tree is acyclic. To convert it into a control-flow graph we have to interpret the semantics of keywords such as `if`, `for`, `while`, and `goto`. The control flow graph representation shown in Figure 10.3 can be derived automatically from the parse tree structure in this way, and is already much closer to the final automaton representation that we would like to generate.

So, although there can be some thorny issues that we will sidestep for now, it should be clear that most of the control flow from a C program can be reproduced in a PROMELA model without too many difficulties. But what about C declarations and basic C statements that manipulate the values of data objects that have no direct equivalent in PROMELA? To make a conversion work, we must also find a method to bridge this gap. One way to handle this would be to rely solely on abstraction methods, for instance, to map values of type `float`, which are not defined in PROMELA, to values of type `int`, or perhaps even `bool`. This may not always be possible, or convenient, though. It should, in principle, also be possible to use only minimal abstractions, and to build a verification model that behaves as closely as possible to the real application, including the use of variables of type `float`, for instance, if that is most convenient.

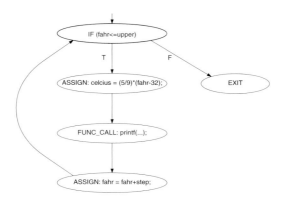

Figure 10.3 Control-Flow Graph for While Construct from Figure 10.2

The key to the solution of this problem lies in the observation that SPIN already generates C code from PROMELA models when it generates the pan.c code for a verification run. To do this, SPIN must generate a fragment of C code for every basic PROMELA statement that can appear in the model. This mechanism gives us a good way to use C as a host language for other parts of a model specification. Rather than write the complete model in PROMELA, we can devise means to write parts of it directly in C code, in such a way that these C code fragments can be embedded directly into the verifiers that are generated by SPIN.

In SPIN version 4.0 and later, trusted fragments of C code can be embedded into a SPIN model as basic statements. For this purpose, PROMELA uses a new type of primitive statement, called c_code. An embedded C code statement for the manipulation of the two variables of type float in the example program, for instance, could be written in PROMELA as follows:

```
c_code { celsius = (5/9) * (fahr-32); };
```

Similarly, the model can contain trusted declarations for embedded data declarations of C data objects that are included into the model, and become an integral part of the state descriptor. The embedded statements and declarations are *trusted*, because they fall outside the PROMELA language definition and their syntax or semantics cannot be checked by the SPIN parser.

The extensions allow us to bypass the PROMELA parser to include native C data objects into the state vector of the model checker, and the matching state transformers that are written as embedded fragments of native C code. To declare the foreign data objects fahr and celsius as C data-types, we can use the declarator `c_state`, as follows:

```
c_state "float fahr" "Local main"
c_state "float celsius" "Local main"
```

The first of these two declarations states that the declaration `float fahr` is to be inserted into the `proctype` declaration called `main` as a local data object. Similarly, the second declaration introduces `celsius` as another data object of type `float`. The first argument to `c_state` remains uninterpreted. To SPIN it is merely a string that is inserted at the appropriate point into the source text of the model checker as a data declaration. If the declaration is in error, for instance, if it used the data type `floatt` instead of `float`, SPIN would not be able to detect it. The error would show up only when we compile the generated model checking code: the embedded fragments are trusted blindly by SPIN.

With these declarations, we have to modify our embedded C code fragment a little bit, to inform the C compiler that the two `float` variables are not regular C variables, but imported local variables that will appear in the state descriptor. This is done by prefixing the variable names, for instance, as follows:

```
c_code { Pmain->celsius = (5/9) * (Pmain->fahr-32); };
```

A detailed explanation of the rules for accessing local or global variables, and the extensions to PROMELA that support the use of embedded declarations and C code fragments, is given in Chapter 17. For the purpose of this chapter, it suffices to know the basic mechanism that can be exploited. Since the embedded code fragments bypass the checks that SPIN can normally make, the intent of the PROMELA extensions is primarily, perhaps exclusively, to support automated model extraction tools that can replicate trusted portions of application software in a PROMELA verification model.

The complete model for the Fahrenheit conversion program, generated automatically by the model extraction tool MODEX,[1] is shown in Figure 10.4.

The model extractor makes sure that all declared state variables are accessed with the proper prefixes. The `Printf` function is a predefined function within SPIN that makes sure that calls to `printf` are suppressed during the depth-first search process, but enabled when an error trail is played back.

Although we have not specified any properties to be verified for this model, we can let the verifier check how many reachable system states there are.

```
$ spin -a fahr.pml
$ cc -o pan pan.c
```

---

1. See Appendix D for downloading the MODEX software.

```
c_state "float fahr" "Local main"
c_state "float celsius" "Local main"

active proctype main()
{    int lower;
     int upper;
     int step;

     c_code { Pmain->lower=0; };
     c_code { Pmain->upper=300; };
     c_code { Pmain->step=20; };
     c_code { Pmain->fahr=Pmain->lower; };

     do
     :: c_expr { (Pmain->fahr <= Pmain->upper) };
        c_code { Pmain->celsius =
                    ((5.0/9.0)*(Pmain->fahr-32.0)); };
        c_code { Printf("%4.0f %6.1f\n",
                    Pmain->fahr, Pmain->celsius); };
        c_code { Pmain->fahr = (Pmain->fahr+Pmain->step); };
     :: else -> break
     od
}
```

Figure 10.4 MODEX Generated SPIN model

```
$ ./pan
(Spin Version 4.0.7 -- 1 August 2003)
        + Partial Order Reduction

Full statespace search for:
        never claim             - (none specified)
        assertion violations    +
        acceptance   cycles     - (not selected)
        invalid end states      +

State-vector 32 byte, depth reached 70, errors: 0
      71 states, stored
       0 states, matched
      71 transitions (= stored+matched)
       0 atomic steps
hash conflicts: 0 (resolved)
(max size 2^18 states)

1.573   memory usage (Mbyte)
```

```
unreached in proctype main
        (0 of 13 states)
```

The four statements in the loop are executed a total of sixteen times, once for each of the values of `fahr` between 0 and 300 inclusive (in increments of 20). That loop traversal should generate a total of 4x16 = 64 distinct system states. Then there are a total of four initialization statements for the various local variables, increasing the total to 68, plus the initial state for the system, and two terminal states: one where the process reaches the closing curly brace and terminates, and another state that is reached after the process has died and been removed from the state descriptor altogether. This gives us a sum total of 71 reachable states, which matches the number that is reported by the verifier.

There is nothing very remarkable about the run, other than the fact that the statements executed manipulate data objects and use operations that are not part of the PROMELA language. Note, for instance, that using the same principles we can analyze code that contains C pointers and arbitrary types of data structures, provided that we make sure that all data objects that contain state information are registered with the model checker so that it can be included in the state descriptors.

If we wanted to get a sample error trace from the model, it would be simple enough to add an `assert(false)` as the last statement in the model. If we repeat the verification, we now find the assertion violation after 70 steps.

Basically, what we have defined here is that the only possible execution of the model, which is the computation and printing of the conversion table, is erroneous. If we reproduce the error trail in non-verbose mode, using the executable `pan`, the computation and generation of the conversion table is reproduced precisely:

```
$ ./pan -r -n    # replay error trail in non-verbose mode
    0   -17.8
   20    -6.7
   40     4.4
   60    15.6
   80    26.7
  100    37.8
  120    48.9
  140    60.0
  160    71.1
  180    82.2
  200    93.3
  220   104.4
  240   115.6
  260   126.7
  280   137.8
  300   148.9
```

```
pan: assertion violated 0 (at depth 70)
spin: trail ends after 70 steps
#processes 1:
  70:    proc 0 (main)  line  28 (state 14)
                  assert(0)
global vars:
local vars proc 0 (main):
          int    lower:    0
          int    upper:    300
          int    step:     20
```

If we were to use the standard guided simulation option of SPIN to reproduce the trail, the best that SPIN can do is to reproduce the text of every C code fragment, but it cannot execute it.

```
$ spin -t fahr.pml
c_code1:  {  Pmain->lower=0;  }
c_code2:  {  Pmain->upper=300;  }
c_code3:  {  Pmain->step=20;  }
c_code4:  {  Pmain->fahr=Pmain->lower;  }
c_code5:  (Pmain->fahr <= Pmain->upper)
c_code6:  {  Pmain->celsius =
                  ((5.0/9.0)*(Pmain->fahr-32.0));  }
c_code7:  {  Printf("%4.0f %6.1f\n",
                  Pmain->fahr, Pmain->celsius);  }
c_code8:  {  Pmain->fahr = (Pmain->fahr+Pmain->step);  }
...
spin: line  28 "fahr.pml", Error: assertion violated
spin: text of failed assertion: assert(0)
spin: trail ends after 70 steps
#processes: 1
  70:    proc  0 (main) line  30 "fahr.pml" (state 15)
1 process created
```

In order for SPIN to be able to also execute the embedded C code fragments in simulation mode, it would need to have access to a built-in interpreter for the complete C language. The alternative that has been adopted is, instead of using SPIN's existing simulation mode, to reproduce all error trails that contain embedded C code with the executable program pan, which of course already contains the compiled code for all embedded C code fragments.

EMBEDDED ASSERTIONS

Because SPIN lacks a parser for the C language, it has to treat all embedded C code fragments as trusted code that is passed through to the model checker as user-defined text strings. The intent is that the C code fragments are generated by a model extraction program, but even then the possibility still exists that the code thus generated may contain subtle bugs that cannot be intercepted by the model checker either, and that could cause the program to crash without producing any useful results. A mild remedy is to allow the user, or model extractor, to annotate every c_expr and c_code statement with a precondition that, if it evaluates to true, can guarantee that the statement can be executed correctly.

The preconditions act as embedded assertions. We can write, for instance

```
c_state "int *ptr;" "Local main"
...
c_code [Pmain->ptr != NULL] { *(Pmain->ptr) = 5; };
```

to state that the integer pointer variable `ptr` must have a non-zero value for the pointer dereference operation that follows in the code fragment to be safely executable. If a case is found where `ptr` evaluates to `NULL` (i.e., the precondition evaluates to false), then an assertion violation is reported and an error trail can be generated. Without the optional precondition, the model checker would try to execute the dereference operation without checks, and an unhelpful crash of the program would result.

We can use this feature to intercept at least some very common causes of program failures: nil-pointer dereferencing, illegal memory access operations, and out of bound array indexing operations. Consider the following example. For simplicity, we will ignore standard prefixing on state variables for a moment, and illustrate the concept here with access to non-state variables only.

```
c_code {
        int *ptr;
        int x[256];
        int j;
};
...
c_code { ptr = x; };
if
:: c_expr [j >= 0 && j < 256] { x[j] != 25 } ->
        c_code [ptr >= x && ptr < &(x[256])] { *ptr = 25; }
:: else
fi
```

If the variable `j` is not initialized, more than likely it would cause an out of bound array index in the `c_expr` statement. The precondition checks for the bounds, so that such an occurrence can be intercepted as a failure to satisfy the precondition of the statement. Similarly, the correctness of indirect access to array locations via pointer `ptr` can be secured with the use of a precondition.

A FRAMEWORK FOR ABSTRACTION

Let us take another look at the temperature conversion example. We have noted that we can distinguish the problem of converting the control flow structure of the program cleanly from the problem of converting the actions that are performed: the basic statements. Converting the control flow structure is the easier of the two problems, although there can be some thorny issues there that we will consider more closely later.

We will now consider how we can apply user-defined abstractions systematically to the statements that appear in a program. It is important to note that the control flow aspect of a program is only of secondary importance in this regard. Once some of the basic statements in a program have been replaced with abstracted versions, it may well be that also the control flow structure of the program can be simplified. The latter is only done, though, if it does not change the meaning of the program. We will see some examples of this notion shortly. The abstractions we will consider here are applied exclusively to the basic statements that appear in a program, and to the data objects that they access.

Given an ANSI-C program, like the Fahrenheit to Celcius conversion example, the model extractor MODEX can generate a default translation of each procedure that appears in the program into a PROMELA proctype, using embedded C code fragments to reproduce those statements that have no equivalent in PROMELA itself. The translation can be specified as a MODEX lookup table, using a simple two column format with the source text on the left and the text for the corresponding abstraction to be used in the verification model on the right. For instance, a lookup table that describes the defaults used in MODEX (i.e., without user-defined abstraction) for the Fahrenheit program would map the nine entries:

```
(fahr<=upper)
!(fahr<=upper)
lower=0
upper=300
step=20
fahr=lower
fahr=(fahr+step)
celsius=((5/9)*(fahr-32))
printf("%4.0f %6.1f\n",fahr,celsius)
```

to the following nine results:

```
c_expr { (Pmain->fahr<=Pmain->upper) }
else
c_code { Pmain->lower=0; }
c_code { Pmain->upper=300; }
c_code { Pmain->step=20; }
c_code { Pmain->fahr=Pmain->lower; }
c_code { Pmain->fahr=(Pmain->fahr+Pmain->step); }
c_code { Pmain->celsius=((5.0/9.0)*(Pmain->fahr-32.0)); }
c_code { Printf("%4.0f %6.1f\n", \
                 Pmain->fahr, Pmain->celsius); }
```

The first entry in the table is the conditional from the while statement in the C version of the code. The negation of that statement, corresponding to the exit condition from the loop, appears as a separate entry in the table, to make it possible to define a different translation for it. It would, for instance, be possible to replace the target code for both the loop condition and the loop exit condition with the boolean value *true* to create a non-deterministic control structure in the model. (In this case, of course, this would not be helpful.) The default conversion for the remaining statements simply embeds the original code within a PROMELA c_code statement, and prefixes every variable reference as required for local variables that appear in the model.

The default treatment in MODEX for variable declarations is to embed them into the model with the help of PROMELA c_state statements. All the defaults, though, can be overridden, for instance, to enforce abstraction.

As a small illustration of the mechanism that can be invoked here to enforce abstraction, let us assume we wanted to generate a pure PROMELA model from the C code, using integer variables and integer computations to approximate the results of the Fahrenheit to Celsius conversions. The mechanism for doing so that is supported in MODEX is the lookup table.

First, we replace the default embedded data declarations with an integer version. We do so by including the following five lines in the user-defined version of the lookup table that will be used to override MODEX's defaults.

```
Declare int     fahr     main
Declare int     celsius  main
Declare int     upper    main
Declare int     lower    main
Declare int     step     main
```

The keyword Declare is followed by three tab-separated fields. The first field specifies the name of a data type, the second the name of a variable, and the third specifies the scope of the variable. In this case, the scope is local and indicated by the name of the target proctype, "main." If global, the last field would contain the MODEX keyword Global.

Now that we have integer data, the C statements from the original program can be interpreted directly as PROMELA statements, rather than as embedded C code fragments. We can specify this by using the MODEX keyword keep as the target for the corresponding entries in the lookup table. This can be done for seven of the nine entries, as follows:

```
(fahr<=upper)                       keep
!(fahr<=upper)                      else
lower=0                             keep
upper=300                          keep
step=20                           keep
fahr=lower                        keep
fahr=(fahr+step)                   keep
```

The computation of the conversion values for the variable celcius will have to be done a little more carefully. Note that the sub-expression (5/9) would evaluate to zero in integer arithmetic, resulting in all computed values being approximated as zero. With the following translations, we avoid this by making sure that the division by nine happens last, not first. Next, the print statement needs a slightly different format to print integer instead of floating point values. Because the integer data types are recognized by PROMELA directly, these statements need not be embedded in C code fragments, but can also be generated directly as PROMELA code, as follows:

```
celsius=((5/9)*(fahr-32))   celsius = ((fahr-32)*5)/9
printf(...                  printf("%d  %d\n",fahr,celsius)
```

The model extractor checks for an entry in user-supplied lookup tables, based on a textual match on entries in the left-hand side column, and uses the user-defined translation when given, or else the default translation. Simple abbreviations, such as the ellipses (the three dots at the end of the print statement) in the second entry above, are also supported. In this case every statement that starts with the character string "printf(" is matched and translated to the fixed target translation on right-hand side of this table entry.

From the new explicit lookup table, the following model can now be generated mechanically by the MODEX tool:

```
active proctype main()
{    int step;
     int lower;
     int upper;
     int celsius;
     int fahr;

     lower = 0;
     upper = 300;
     step = 20;
     fahr = lower;

     do
     :: (fahr<=upper);
         celsius = ((fahr-32)*5)/9;
         printf("%d  %d\n", fahr, celsius);
         fahr=(fahr+step)
     :: else -> break
     od
}
```

The new model uses no embedded C code, so we can use it to generate the approximate integer values for the temperature conversions with a standard SPIN simulation run, as follows:

```
$ spin fahr2.pml
     0   -17
    20   -6
```

```
      40    4
      60    15
      80    26
      100   37
      120   48
      140   60
      160   71
      180   82
      200   93
      220   104
      240   115
      260   126
      280   137
      300   148
  1 process created
```

A model extractor, used in combination with user-defined mapping tables, can generate almost any transformation of a given program, being restricted only to the fixed control flow structure that is specified in the original program. This can be considered to be both a strength and a weakness of the method. It clearly gives the model extractor all the power it needs to support arbitrary abstraction methods in applications of software verification. But the method can also easily be abused to generate meaningless or nonsensical abstractions. By itself, the model extractor is only a tool that can be used to define abstractions: it cannot determine what proper abstractions are or how they should be derived. For that we need different mechanisms that we discuss next.

SOUND AND COMPLETE ABSTRACTION

One critical issue that we have not yet discussed is how we can define abstractions and how we can make sure that they are meaningful. The best abstraction to be used in a given application will depend on the types of correctness properties that we are interested in proving. The properties alone determine which aspects of the application are relevant to the verification attempt, and which are not.

Let P be the original program, and let L be a logical property we want to prove about P. Let further α be an abstraction function.

Let us begin by considering the case where abstraction α is defined as a MODEX lookup table. We will denote by $\alpha(P)$ the abstract model that is derived by MODEX from program P for abstraction α. That is, $\alpha(P)$ is the model in which every basic statement in P is replaced with its target from the MODEX lookup table, but with the same control flow structure which is reproduced in the syntax of PROMELA.

Under a given abstraction α, the original property L will generally need to be modified to be usable as a property of the abstract model $\alpha(P)$. Property L may, for instance, refer to program locations in P or refer to data objects that were deleted or renamed by α. L may also refer to data objects for which the type was changed, for instance, from integer to boolean. We will denote this abstraction of L by $\alpha(L)$.

The inverse of abstraction α can be called a *concretization*, which we will denote by $\bar{\alpha}$. A concretization can be used to translate, or *lift*, abstract statements from the model back into the concrete domain of the original program. In general, because of the nature of abstraction, any given abstract statement can map to one or more possible concrete statements. This means that for a given statements S, $\alpha(S)$ defines a single abstract statement, but concretization $\bar{\alpha}(\alpha(S))$ defines a set of possible concrete statements, such that

$$\forall S, S \in \bar{\alpha}(\alpha(S)).$$

Similarly, for every abstract execution sequence ϕ in model $\alpha(P)$ we can derive a set of concrete execution sequences, denoted by $\bar{\alpha}(\phi)$, in the original program. Given that an abstraction will almost always remove some information from a program, it is not necessarily the case that for every feasible execution ϕ of the abstract program there also exists a corresponding feasible execution within $\bar{\alpha}(\phi)$ of the concrete program. This brings us to the definition of two useful types of requirements that we can impose on abstractions: logical soundness and completeness.

Definition 10.1 (Logical Soundness)

Abstraction α is logically sound with respect to program P and property L if for any concrete execution ϕ of P that violates L there exists a corresponding abstract execution of $\alpha(P)$ in $\alpha(\phi)$ that violates $\alpha(L)$.

Informally, this means that an abstraction is logically sound if it excludes the possibility of *false positives*. The correctness of the model always implies the correctness of the program.

Definition 10.2 (Logical Completeness)

Abstraction α is logically complete with respect to program P and property L if, for any abstract execution ϕ of $\alpha(P)$ that violates $\alpha(L)$, there exists a corresponding concrete execution of P in $\bar{\alpha}(\phi)$ that violates L.

Informally, this means that an abstraction is logically complete if it excludes the possibility of *false negatives*. The incorrectness of the model always implies the incorrectness of the program.

SELECTIVE DATA HIDING

An example of a fairly conservative and simple abstraction method that guarantees logical soundness and completeness with respect to any property that can be defined in LTL is *selective data hiding*. To use this method we must be able to identify a set of data objects that is provably irrelevant to the correctness properties that we are interested in proving about a model, and that can therefore be removed from the model, together with all associated operations.

This abstraction method can be automated by applying a fairly simple version of a program slicing algorithm. One such algorithm is built into SPIN. This algorithm computes, based on the given properties, which statements can be omitted from the model without affecting the soundness and completeness of the verification of those properties. The algorithm works as follows. First, a set of *slice criteria* is constructed, initially including only those data objects that are referred to explicitly in one or more correctness properties (e.g., in basic assertions or in an LTL formula). Through data and control dependency analysis, the algorithm then determines on which larger set of data objects the slice criteria depend for their values. All data objects that are independent of the slice criteria, and not contained in the set of slice criteria themselves, can then be considered irrelevant to the verification and can be removed from the model, together with all associated operations.

The data hiding operation can be implemented trivially with the help of a MODEX lookup table, by arranging for all irrelevant data manipulations to be mapped to either `true` (for condition statements) or to `skip` (for other statements). Note that under this transformation the basic control flow structure of the model is still retained, which means that no execution cycles can be added to or removed from the model, which is important to the preservation of liveness properties.

Although this method can be shown to preserve both logical soundness and logical completeness of the correctness properties that are used in deriving the abstraction, it does not necessarily have these desirable properties for some other types of correctness requirements that cannot be expressed in assertions or in LTL formulae. An example of such a property is *absence of deadlock*. Note that the introduction of extra behavior in a model can result in the disappearance of system deadlocks.

EXAMPLE

To illustrate the use of selective data hiding, consider the model of a word count program shown in Figure 10.5. The program receives characters, encoded as integers, over the channel `stdin`, and counts the number of newlines, characters, and white-space separated words, up to an end-of-file marker which is encoded as the number `-1`.

The assertion checks that at the end of each execution the number of characters counted must always be larger than or equal to the number of newlines. We want to find a simpler version of the model that would allow us to check this specific property more efficiently. Variables `nc` and `nl` are clearly relevant to this verification, since they appear explicitly in the assertions. So clearly the statements in which these variables appear cannot be removed from the model. But which other statements can safely be removed?

When we invoke SPIN's built-in slicing algorithm it tells us:

```
 1 chan STDIN;
 2 int c, nl, nw, nc;
 3
 4 init {
 5     bool inword = false;
 6
 7     do
 8     :: STDIN?c ->
 9         if
10         :: c == -1 ->    break        /* EOF */
11         :: c == '\n' -> nc++; nl++
12         :: else ->       nc++
13         fi;
14         if
15         :: c == ' ' || c == '\t' || c == '\n' ->
16             inword = false
17         :: else ->
18             if
19             :: !inword ->
20                 nw++; inword = true
21             :: else /* do nothing */
22             fi
23         fi
24     od;
25     assert(nc >= nl);
26     printf("%d\t%d\t%d\n", nl, nw, nc)
27 }
```

Figure 10.5 Word Count Model

```
$ spin -A wc.pml
spin: redundant in proctype :init: (for given property):
 line  19 ... [(!(inword))]
 line  20 ... [nw = (nw+1)]
 line  20 ... [inword = true]
 line  15 ... [((((c==' ')||(c=='\t'))||(c=='\n)))]
 line  16 ... [inword = false]

spin: redundant vars (for given property):
   int    nw      0      <:global:>   <variable>
   bit    inword  0      <:init:>     <variable>
spin: consider using predicate abstraction to replace:
   int    c       0      <:global:>   <variable>
```

From this output we can conclude that the program fragment between lines 14
to 23 is irrelevant, and similarly variables nw and inword. SPIN also suggests
that the declaration of variable c could be improved: it is declared as an integer variable, but within the model only three or four value ranges of this

```
 1 chan STDIN;
 2 int c, nl, nc;
 3
 4 init {
 5
 6
 7     do
 8     :: STDIN?c ->
 9         if
10         :: c == -1 ->    break   /* EOF */
11         :: c == '\n' -> nc++; nl++
12         :: else ->       nc++
13         fi;
14         if
15         :: true ->
16             skip
17         :: true ->
18             if
19             :: true ->
20                 skip; skip
21             :: true
22             fi
23         fi
24     od;
25     assert(nc >= nl);
26     printf("%d\t%d\n", nl, nc)
27 }
```

Figure 10.6 Abstracted Word Count Model

variable are really relevant. We could do better by using four symbolic values for those ranges, and declaring c as an mtype variable. This suggestion, though, is independent of the data hiding abstraction that we can now apply. If we preserve the entire control-flow structure of the original, the abstraction based on data hiding could now be constructed (manually) as shown in Figure 10.6.

We can simplify this model without adding or deleting any control-flow cycles, by collapsing sequences of consecutive true and skip statements. It is important that we do not add or omit cycles from the model in simplifications of this type, because this can directly affect the proof of liveness properties. A cycle, for instance, could only safely be added to or omitted from the model if we separately prove that the cycle always terminates within a finite number of traversals. The simplified model looks as shown in Figure 10.7.

Because the abstraction we have applied is sound and complete, any possible execution that would lead to an assertion violation in this simplified model

```
 1 chan STDIN;
 2 int c, nl, nc;
 3
 4 init {
 5
 6     do
 7     :: STDIN?c ->
 8         if
 9         :: c == -1 ->     break   /* EOF */
10         :: c == '\n' -> nc++; nl++
11         :: else ->        nc++
12         fi
13     od;
14     assert(nc >= nl);
15     printf("%d\t%d\n", nl, nc)
16 }
```

Figure 10.7 Simplified Model

implies immediately that a similar violating execution must exist in the original concrete model. Perhaps surprisingly, there is indeed such an execution. An assertion violation can occur when the value of variable nc wraps around its maximal value of $2^{32} - 1$ before the value of variable nl does, which can happen for a sufficiently large number of input characters.

BOLDER ABSTRACTIONS
Logically sound and complete abstractions are not always sufficient to render large verification problems tractable. In those cases, one has to resort to abstraction strategies that lack either one or both of these qualities. These abstraction strategies are often based on human judgement of what the most interesting, or most suspect, system behaviors might be, and can therefore usually not be automated. Using these strategies also puts a greater burden on the user to rule out the possibility of false negatives or positives with additional, and often manual, analyses.

We will discuss two examples of abstraction methods in this class:
- Selective restriction
- Data type abstraction

The first method is neither sound nor complete. The second method is complete, but not necessarily sound.

Selective restriction is commonly used in applications of model checking tools to limit the scope of a verification to a subset of the original problem. We can do so, for instance, by limiting the maximum capacity of message buffers below what would be needed for a full verification, or by limiting the maximum number of active processes. This method is indubitably useful in an exploratory phase of a verification, to study problem variants with an often significantly lower computational complexity than the full problem that is to be solved. This type of abstraction, though, is to be used with care since it can introduce both false negatives and false positives into the verification process. An example of this type of selective restriction is, for instance, the verification model of a leader election algorithm that can be found in the standard SPIN distribution. To make finite state model checking possible, the number of processes that participate in the leader election procedure must be fixed, although clearly the full problem would require us to perform a verification for every conceivable number of processes. As another example from the same set of verification models in the SPIN distribution, consider the PROMELA model of a file transfer protocol named `pftp`. For exhaustive verification, each channel size should be set to a bound larger than the largest number of messages that can ever be stored in the channel. By lowering the bound, partial verifications can be done at a lower cost, though without any guarantee of soundness or completeness.

Data type abstraction aims to reduce the value range of selected data objects. An example of this type of abstraction could be to reduce a variable of type integer to an enumeration variable with just three values. The three values can then be used to represent three ranges of values in the integer domain (e.g., negative, zero, and positive). The change can be justified if the correctness properties of a model do not depend on detailed values, but only on the chosen value ranges.

A data type abstraction applied to one variable will generally also affect other variables within the same model. The type of, and operations on, all variables that depend on the modified variables, either directly or indirectly, may have to be adjusted. A data and control dependency analysis can again serve to identify the set of data objects that is affected in this operation, and can be used to deduce the required changes.

Denote by V the set of concrete values of an object and by A the associated set of abstract values under type abstraction α. To guarantee logical completeness, a data type abstraction must satisfy the following relation, known as the *Galois connection*:[2]

$$\forall v \in V,\ v \in \bar{\alpha}(\alpha(v))\ \wedge\ \forall w \in A, \forall x \in \bar{\alpha}(w),\ w \equiv \alpha(x).$$

Consider, for instance, the property

$$\Box((x < 0) \rightarrow \Diamond(x \geq 0))$$

---

2. Note that concretization function $\bar{\alpha}$ defines a set.

Table 10.1 Example of Type Abstraction

Statement	Abstraction
$(x > 5)$ $x = 0$ $x + +$	$(!neg\_x)$ $neg\_x = false$ *if* $:: neg\_x$ -> *if* /* *non-deterministic choice* */ $:: neg\_x = true$ $:: neg\_x = false$ *fi* $:: else$ -> *skip* *fi*

The property depends only on the sign of variable x, but not on its absolute value. With a data type abstraction we can try to replace every occurrence of x in the model with a new variable that captures only its sign, and not its value. For example, if the model contains assignment and condition statements such as

```
(x > 5); x = 0; x++;
```

we can replace all occurrences of x in these statements with a new boolean variable neg_x. The property then becomes:

$$\Box((neg\_x) \rightarrow \Diamond(\neg neg\_x))$$

The assignments and conditions are now mapped as shown in Table 10.1. Under this abstraction, precise information about the value of the integer variable x can be replaced with non-deterministic guesses about the possible new values of the boolean variable neg_x. Note, for instance, that when neg_x is *true*, and the value of x is incremented, the new value of x could be either positive or remain negative. This is reflected in a non-deterministic choice in the assignment of either *true* or *false* to neg_x. If, however, x is known to be non-negative, it will remain so after the increment, and the value of neg_x remains *false*. The condition $(x > 5)$ can clearly only be true when x is non-negative, but beyond that we cannot guess. The Galois connection holds for these abstractions.

DEALING WITH FALSE NEGATIVES

The occurrence of false negatives as a result of a logically unsound abstraction is not as harmful as it might at first sight seem to be. By analyzing concretizations of counterexample executions it can often quickly be determined what piece of information was lost in the abstraction that permitted the generation of the false negative. The counterexample in effect proves to the user that the information that was assumed irrelevant is in fact relevant. Guided by the counterexample, the abstraction can now be refined to eliminate the false negatives one by one, until either valid counterexamples are generated, or a proof of correctness is obtained. It is generally much harder to accurately analyze a false positive result of a model checker, for instance, if selective restrictions were applied: *caveat emptor*.

THORNY ISSUES WITH EMBEDDED C CODE

The support in SPIN for embedded C code significantly extends the range of applications that can be verified, but it is also fraught with danger. Like a good set of knifes, this extension can be powerful when used well, but also disastrous when used badly. As one simple example, it is readily possible to divide a floating pointer number by zero in an embedded C code fragment, or to dereference a nil-pointer. Since SPIN deliberately does not look inside embedded C code fragments, it cannot offer any help in diagnosing problems that are caused in this way. To SPIN, embedded C code fragments are trusted pieces of foreign code that define state transitions and become part of the model checker. In effect, the PROMELA extensions allow the user to redefine parts of the PROMELA language. It is ultimately the user's responsibility to make sure that these language extensions make sense.

We can place our trust in a model extraction tool such as MODEX to generate embedded C code that is (automatically) guarded with embedded assertions, but there are certainly still cases where also that protection can prove to be insufficient. Note, for instance, that it is readily possible within embedded C code fragments to unwittingly modify relevant state information that is beyond the purview of the model checker. External state information could, for instance, be read from external files, the contents of which can clearly not be tracked by the model checker. Hidden data could also be created and manipulated with calls to a memory allocator, or even by directly communicating with external processes through real network connections.

In cases where the model checker is set to work on a model with relevant state information that is not represented in the internal state vectors, false negatives and positives become possible. False negatives can again more easily be dealt with than false positives. Inspecting a counterexample can usually quickly reveal what state information was missed. False positives are also here the more dangerous flaw of an extended SPIN model. It will often be possible to incorporate hidden state information explicitly in a PROMELA model. Calls to a memory allocator such as `malloc`, for instance, can be replaced with calls to a specially constructed PROMELA model of the allocator, with all state information explicitly represented in the model. Similarly, information read from files or from network connections can be replaced with information retrieved from internal PROMELA processes, again making sure that all relevant state information becomes an explicit part of the verification model.

There can also be delicate issues in the framework we have sketched for model extraction from ANSI C source code. While it is true that most of the control-flow structures of a C program can be reproduced faithfully in a PROMELA verification model, there are some notable exceptions. The invocation of a function via a function pointer in C, for instance, could be preserved within an embedded C code fragment in PROMELA, but it would be very hard to intercept such calls and turn them into PROMELA process instantiations. In this case, too, we have to accept that there are limits to our verification technology. We can occasionally move the limits, but as these examples show, we cannot altogether remove them. Although much of the verification process can be automated, some barriers remain that can only be scaled with the help of human skill and judgement.

THE MODEL EXTRACTION PROCESS

Using MODEX and SPIN, we can now approach software verification problems with the following general methodology.

- The first step is to decide what precisely the critical correctness properties of the application are. The properties of special interest are those that are non-computational in nature. Model checkers are especially strong in verifying concurrency-related problems.
- Next, we identify those parts of the system that contribute most critically to the behavior of primary interest. The effort here is again to find the smallest sufficient portion of the system to prove that the properties of interest are satisfied.
- The first two decisions can now guide us in the construction of an abstraction table that suppresses irrelevant detail and highlights the important aspects of the system. In many cases, no special user decisions will be needed and we can rely on the model extractor to use appropriate default translations. A model extractor like MODEX can also guide the user in the construction of the abstraction tables to make sure that no cases are missed.
- Verification can now begin. Inevitably, there will be things that need adjusting: mistranslations, or missed cases. The attempt itself to perform verification helps to identify these cases. If the model with its embedded C code is incomplete, for instance, either SPIN or the C compiler will reject it, in both cases with detailed explanations of the underlying reasons.
- Once we have a working verifier, we can start seeing counterexamples. Again, there will be a learning cycle, where false negatives will need to be weeded out and the abstraction tables adjusted based on everything that is learned in this phase.
- Eventually, either we find a valid counterexample, or a clean bill of

health from the model checker. A valid counterexample is in this sense the desired outcome. A clean bill of health (i.e., the absence of counterexamples) should be treated with suspicion. Were the properties correctly formalized? Are they not vacuously true? Did the abstraction preserve enough information to prove or disprove them? A few experiments with properties that are known to be valid or invalid can be very illuminating in this phase, and can help build confidence in the accuracy of the results.

The process as it is sketched here still seems far removed from our ideal of developing a fully automated framework for thoroughly checking large and complex software packages. At the same time, though, it is encouraging that the approach we have described here offers an unprecedented level of thoroughness in software testing. As yet, there is no other method known that can verify distributed systems software at the level of accuracy that model extraction tools allow. The combination of model extraction and model checking enables us to eliminate the two main issues that hamper traditional testing by providing a reliable mechanism for both controllability and observability of all the essential elements of a distributed system.

To close the gap between the current user-driven methodology and a fully automated framework still requires some work to be done. Given the importance of this problem, and the number of people that are focusing on it today, we can be fairly confident that this gap can successfully be closed in the not too distant future.

THE HALTING PROBLEM REVISITED
In the days when C was still just a letter in the alphabet, and C++ a typo, it was already well established that it would be folly to search for a computer program that could decide mechanically if some arbitrary other computer program had an arbitrary given property. Turing's formal proof for the unsolvability of the halting problem was illustrated in 1965 by Strachey with the following basic argument. Suppose we had a program mc(P) that could decide in bounded time if some other program P would eventually terminate (i.e., halt); we could then write a new program nmc(P) that again inspects some other program P (e.g., after reading it), and uses mc(P) in the background. We now write nmc(P) in such a way that it terminates if P does not terminate, and vice-versa. All is well until we decide to run nmc(nmc) to see if nmc itself is guaranteed to terminate. After all, nmc is just another program, so this would be fair game.

Strachey's construction is similar to Betrand Russell's famous class paradox, which makes it somewhat dubious to use as a basis for a logical argument. In fairness, Strachey's construction does not really prove the unsolvability of the halting problem, but it does prove that it is in general impossible to write a program that can establish arbitrary properties of *itself*. This, of course, does not mean that no programs could be written that can establish *specific* properties of themselves. A word-count program, for instance, can trivially determine its own length, and a C-compiler can confirm its own syntactic correctness, and even recompile itself.

Clearly we cannot write a program that could ever prove its own logical correctness. Note, for instance, that such a program could easily report its own correctness erroneously.

So far, this debate about *arbitrary* programs and *arbitrary* properties is purely academic, as it has been for pretty much the last 100 years. Curiously, though, the extensions to SPIN with embedded C code have made it possible to actually write a very real version of Strachey's construction. First, we write a little script that returns *true* if SPIN determines that a given model has at least one invalid end state, and *false* if it does not.

```
#!/bin/sh
### filename: halts

echo -n "testing $1: "

spin -a $1                  # generate model
cc -DSAFETY -o pan pan.c    # compile it
./pan | grep "errors: 0"    # run it and grep stats
if $?                       # test exit status of grep
then
     echo "halts"
else
     echo "does not halt"
fi
```

We can try this on some little examples to make sure that it does the right thing. For instance, if we apply our script to the hello world example from Chapter 2, we get reassuringly:

```
$ ./halts hello.pml
halts
```

If we add a blocking statement to this model

```
active proctype main()
{
        printf("hello world0);
        false    /* block the execution */
}
```

and run the script again, we get

```
$ ./halts hello_blocking.pml
does not halt
```

We can now try to invoke this program in a c_expr statement with SPIN version 4, in the devious manner that was envisioned by Strachey.

```
init {   /* filename: strachey */
        do
        :: c_expr { system("halts strachey") } /* loop */
        :: else -> break
        od;
        false    /* block the execution */
}
```

What would happen if we now execute

```
$ ./halts strachey
. . . . .
```

The `halts` program ends up going into an infinite descent. Each time the verifier gets to the point where it needs to establish the executability of the `c_expr`, it needs to invoke the `halts` script once more and restart itself. The behavior of the model is defined in terms of itself, which puts it outside the scope of systems that can be verified with finitary methods. It would be hard to maintain that the infinite recursion is caused by the method that we used to implement the `halts` script. Note that if the `halts` script only needed to read the program before rendering its verdict, and did not need to execute it, the same infinite descent would still occur.

Curiously, the fact that the `halts` program loops on some inputs could in principle be detected by a higher-level program. But, as soon as we extend our framework again to give that new program the capability to reason about itself, we inevitably recreate the problem.

The example aptly illustrates that by allowing embedded C code inside SPIN models the modeling language becomes Turing complete, and we lose formal decidability. As yet another corollary of Kurt Gödel's famous incompleteness theorem: any system that is expressive enough to describe itself cannot be powerful enough to prove every true property within its domain.

BIBLIOGRAPHIC NOTES

Alan Turing's seminal paper on computable and uncomputable functions appeared in 1936, Turing [1936]. Christopher Strachey's elegant construction to illustrate the unsolvability of the halting problem first appeared in Strachey [1965]. In this very short note, Strachey refers to an informal conversation he had with Turing many years earlier about a different version of the proof.

The class paradox was first described in Russell [1903]. A fascinating glimpse of the correspondence between Russell and Frege about the discovery of this paradox in 1902 can be found in Heijenoort [2000]. Gödel's original paper is Gödel [1931].

General references to abstraction techniques can be found in the Bibliographic Notes to Chapter 5. Here we focus more on abstraction techniques that are used specifically for application in model extraction and model checking.

Data type abstractions can in some cases be computed mechanically for restricted types of statements and conditions, for instance, when operations are restricted to Pressburger arithmetic. In these cases, one can use a mechanized decision procedure for the necessary computations (see, for instance, Levitt [1998]). A description of an automated tool for computing program or model slices based on selective data hiding can be found in Dams, Hesse, and Holzmann [2002].

In the literature, logical completeness is often defined only for abstraction *methods*, not for abstract *models* as we have done in this chapter. For a more standard discussion of soundness and completeness, see, for instance, Kesten, Pnueli, and Vardi [2001].

An excellent overview of general program slicing techniques can be found in Tip [1995].

The first attempts to extract verification models mechanically from implementation level code targeted the conversion of Java source code into PROMELA models. Among the first to pursue this, starting in late 1997, were Klaus Havelund from the NASA Ames Research Center, and Matt Dwyer and John Hatcliff from Kansas State University, as described in Havelund and Pressburger [2000], Brat, Havelund, Park, and Visser [2000], and Corbett, Dwyer, Hatcliff, et al. [2000].

The work at Ames led to the Pathfinder verification tool. The first version of this tool, written by Havelund, converted Java to PROMELA, using a one-to-one mapping. The current version, called Java Pathfinder-2, was written at Ames by Willem Visser as a stand-alone model checker, that uses an instrumented virtual machine to perform the verification.

The work at Kansas State on the Bandera tool suite targets the conversion from Java to PROMELA, and it includes direct support for data type abstraction and program slicing. The Bandera tool supports a number of other model checking tools as alternative verifiers, in addition to the SPIN tool.

The work at Bell Labs, starting in 1998, was the first attempt to convert ANSI C source code into abstract PROMELA verification models. It is described in, for instance, Holzmann and Smith [1999,2000,2002], and Holzmann [2000]. The code for the model extractor MODEX and for the extended version of SPIN is generally available today (see Appendix D). A more detailed description of the use of this tool, and the recommended way to develop a test harness definition, can be found in the online user guide for MODEX.

A related attempt to systematically extract abstract verification models from sequential C source code is pursued at Microsoft Research in the SLAM project, see Ball, Majumdar, Millstein, and Rajamani [2001]. The Bebop tool being developed in this project is based on the systematic application of predicate and data type abstractions.

The problem of detecting whether or not a property is vacuously satisfied was dealt with in the FeaVer system by implementing an automated check on the number of states that was reached in the `never` claim automata, see Holzmann and Smith [2000,2002]. A high fraction of unreachable states was found to correlate well with vacuously true properties. A more thorough method of vacuity checking is described in Kupferman and Vardi [1999].

USING SPIN **11**

*"The difference between theory and practice
is a lot bigger in practice than in theory."*
(Peter van der Linden, Expert C Programming, p. 134)

Although SPIN verifications are often performed most conveniently with the help of the graphical interface XSPIN, we will postpone a discussion of that tool for one more chapter and concentrate here on a bare bones use of SPIN itself. It can be very useful to know how to run short verification jobs manually through SPIN's command line interface, especially when trying to troubleshoot unexpected results.

The number of industrial applications of SPIN is steadily increasing. The core intended use of the tool, though, has always been to support both research and teaching of formal verification. One clear advantage of this primary focus is that the sources to SPIN remain freely available, also for commercial use.[1] The large number of users of the tool mean that any flaws that occasionally slip into the software are typically reported and fixed much more rapidly than would be possible for a commercial tool. A possible disadvantage is that the tool continues to evolve, which means that whatever version of the software you happen to be using, there is likely to be a more recent and better version available by the time you figure out how to use it. The basic use of the tool, though, does not change much from version to version, and it is this basic use that we will discuss in this chapter.

SPIN STRUCTURE

The basic structure of SPIN is illustrated in Figure 11.1. The workflow starts with the specification of a high-level verification model of a concurrent

---

1. Downloading instructions for SPIN can be found in Appendix D (p. 579).

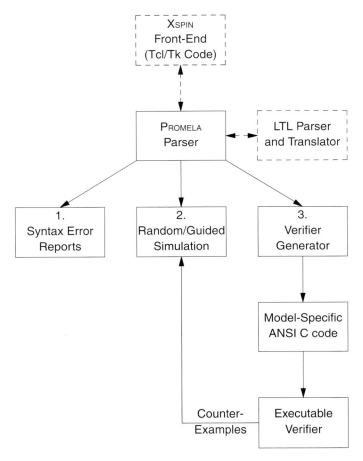

Figure 11.1 The Structure of SPIN

system, or distributed algorithm, optionally using SPIN's graphical front-end XSPIN. After fixing syntax errors, interactive simulation is performed until the user gains the basic confidence that the model has the intended properties. Optionally, a PROMELA correctness claim can be generated from an logic formula specified in linear temporal logic (LTL). Then, in the third main step, SPIN is used to generate an optimized on-the-fly verification program from the high-level specification. This verification program is compiled, with possible compile-time choices for the types of reduction algorithms that are to be used, and it is then executed to perform the verification itself. If any counterexamples to the correctness claims are detected, these can be fed back into the SPIN simulator. The simulation trail can then be inspected in detail to determine the cause of the correctness violation.[2]

In the remainder of this chapter we give some more detailed guideliness of how each of the main steps of specification, simulation, and verification can be performed.

ROADMAP

A verification is often performed in an iterative process with increasingly detailed models. Each new model can be verified under different types of assumptions about the environment and for different types of correctness properties. If a property is not valid under a given set of assumptions, SPIN can produce a counterexample that shows explicitly how the property may be violated. The model can then be modified to prevent the property violation.

Once a property has been shown to hold, it is often possible to then reduce the complexity of that model by using the now trusted property as a simplifying assumption. The simpler model may then be used to prove other properties.

A more detailed sequence of steps that the (human) verifier can take in tackling a systems verification problem is as follows. We will assume that an initial verification model, saved in a file called `model`, has been built, including an initial formalization of all relevant correctness properties.

1. The first step is to perform a sanity check of the PROMELA code by executing the command:[3]

   ```
   $ spin -A model          # perform thorough syntax check
   ```

   The output from SPIN will include warnings about syntax errors, possibly dubious constructs that were used, as well as suggestions on possible improvements of the model. A second, more basic check of the model can be performed by attempting to generate the source code for a verifier from the model with the command:

   ```
   $ spin -a model          # generate verifier
   ```

2. Once the first sanity checks are completed, and any flaws that were found have been repaired, a good insight into the behavior that is captured can be obtained with a series of either random or interactive simulation runs. If enough information can be gleaned from just the execution of print statements that are contained within the model, it may suffice to say simply:

   ```
   $ spin model             # non-verbose simulation
   ```

---

2. When embedded C code is used, the trail can only be reproduced by the verifier itself. See Chapter 17 for details.

3. In the command line examples that follow, the # symbol indicates the start of a comment.

However, especially for the first few runs, or when it is known that the simulation could continue *ad infinitum*, it is wise to add a more verbose output option, and to limit the maximum number of steps that may be executed, for instance, by executing the command:

```
$ spin -p -u200 model   # more verbose simulation
```

With these parameters every single step that is executed will produce at least some visible output. Also, the simulation will reliably stop after at most 200 steps were made, protecting against a runaway execution.

If the model contains message passing operations, the best information is often obtained from the following type of run:

```
$ spin -c -u200 model   # bounded simulation
```

To obtain better insight into seemingly obscure behavior, it is often very useful to add some extra print statements or assertions to the model. User-defined print statements can provide additional information about the evolving state of the model that may not be available from predefined simulation options.

Unfortunately, if the model contains embedded C code, a direct simulation of the model with SPIN as suggested above cannot reveal too much information about an execution. In that case we will have to gain insight into the model's execution from the verifier, as outlined in the next few steps.

3. Once all small modeling errors have been fixed, a more thorough verification process can begin by generating, compiling, and executing the model-specific verifier. In its most basic mode, this is done as follows:

```
$ spin -a model        # generate verifier
$ cc -o pan pan.c      # compile verifier
$ ./pan                # perform verification
```

The verifier can be generated and compiled in several different ways, depending on the type of verification that is desired, as more fully explained later in this chapter, and also in Chapter 18 (p. 513).

4. If a counterexample to a correctness property is generated by the verifier, it can be explored in detail with SPIN's guided simulation options. For models without embedded C code, this is done by executing, for instance:

```
$ spin -t -p model     # replay error trail
```

All options that are available for random and interactive simulations are again available to determine the precise cause of the property violation that was discovered. For instance, we can skip the first 200 steps in a long simulation trail by executing:

```
$ spin -t -p -j200 model       # skip first 200 steps
```

or we can revert to the mode where message passing details are shown:

```
$ spin -t -c model      # simulation with io details
```

If the model contains embedded C code, a guided simulation run with SPIN will only be able to print but not execute the embedded code fragments. In this case we can execute the error trail with an additional option in the verifier itself, for instance, as follows:

```
$ ./pan -C      # replay a trail with embedded C code
```

These options are more fully explained in Chapter 17 (p. 495). By analyzing the counterexample, we can conclude that either the model or the correctness properties were at fault, and the appropriate remedy can be taken.

5. There is a range of options available in the SPIN verifiers to control the complexity of a large verification run, or to perform various types of approximate verification runs. The details can be found later in this chapter and also in Chapters 9, 18, and 19 (pgs. 191, 513, and 527, respectively). If, nonetheless, a verification cannot be completed exhaustively, or if an approximate verification run cannot be completed with sufficient coverage, it is time to reconsider the PROMELA model itself and remove any potential causes of computational complexity that can be identified. This approach is discussed in more detail in Chapter 5 (p. 101).

The main steps in the verification process sketched above are reviewed in a little more detail in the remainder of this chapter. As a general hint, if you are ever unsure which options SPIN supports, typing

```
$ spin --      # list available command-line options
```

will produce a list, with a brief explanation of each option. The command

```
$ spin -V      # print version number and exit
```

prints the number and date of the specific version of SPIN that you are using. The same principle holds for the verifiers generated by SPIN. Typing

```
$ ./pan --      # list available run-time options
```

lists all available run-time options, and

```
$ ./pan -V      # print version number and exit
```

prints the number of the version of SPIN that was used to generate the verifier, and lists the precise set of compile-time directives that was used to compile the pan executable.

SIMULATION

We will now take a closer look at the main options for performing random, interactive, and guided simulations with SPIN.

RANDOM SIMULATION

Given a model in PROMELA, say, stored in a file called `model`, the easiest mode of operation is to perform a random simulation. For instance,

```
$ spin -p model
```

tells SPIN to perform a random simulation while printing the process moves selected for execution at each step. If invoked without any options, SPIN prints no output other than what is explicitly produced by the model itself with print statements. Sometimes, simulation runs can go on indefinitely, and the output can quickly become overwhelming. One simple way of controlling the flow of output would be to pipe the output into a UNIX paging tool, for instance

```
$ spin -p model | more
```

This does not work on all PCs though.[4] We can restrict the output to the first N steps by using the `-u`N option. Similarly, it is also possible to skip over an initial sequence of N steps with the `-j`N option. The two options can be used in combination, for instance, to see only the detailed output for one hundred execution steps starting at the 100th statement execution; one would say:

```
$ spin -p -j100 -u200 model      # print steps 100 to 200
```

This type of simulation is random, which means that every new simulation run may produce a different type of execution. By default, the current time is used to seed the random number generator that SPIN uses in random simulation mode. To fix a user-defined seed value instead, and to make the simulation run completely reproducible, we can say, for instance

```
$ spin -p -j100 -u200 -n123 model        # fix seed
```

which initializes the random number generator with a user-defined seed of 123 in this case.

A range of options exists to make the results of a simulation more verbose, for example, by adding printouts of local variables (add option `-l`), global variables (option `-g`), send statements (option `-s`), or receive statements (option `-r`).

Options can be combined in arbitrary order, as in:

```
$ spin -p -l -g -r -s -n1 -j10 -u20 model
```

which can look quite baffling at first, but quickly starts to make sense.

A quick inspection of the available options with the command

```
$ spin --
```

---

4. A recommended way to make this work on a PC is to install the (free) `cygwin` toolset from `www.cygwin.com`, which approximates a very usable UNIX environment on Windows PCs.

usually suffices to select the right parameters for a simulation run of this type.

INTERACTIVE SIMULATION

It is not always desirable to have SPIN automatically resolve all non-deterministic choices in the model with calls on a random number generator. For these cases, there is an interactive simulation mode of SPIN that is selected through command-line option -i. For instance, when we type:

```
$ spin -i -p model
```

a menu with choices is offered each time that the execution can proceed in more than one way. For instance, for the leader election model from the standard SPIN distribution, we might see:[5]

```
$ spin -i -p leader
0: proc - (:root:) creates proc  0 (:init:)
1: proc  0 (:init:) ... (state 10) [proc = 1]
2: proc  0 (:init:) ... (state 8)  [.(goto)]
Select stmnt (proc  0 (:init:) )
    choice 1: ((proc<=5))
Select [0-2]: 1
3: proc  0 (:init:) ... (state 7)  [((proc<=5))]
4: proc  0 (:init:) creates proc  1 (node)
4: proc  0 (:init:) ... (state 3)  [(run node(...)]
5: proc  0 (:init:) ... (state 4)  [proc = (proc+1)]
6: proc  0 (:init:) ... (state 8)  [.(goto)]
Select stmnt (proc  0 (:init:) )
    choice 0: other process
    choice 1: ((proc<=5))
Select [0-2]: 0
Selet a statement
    choice 1: proc  1 (node) ... (state 1) [printf(...)]
    choice 2: proc  0 (:init:) ... (state 7) [((proc<=5))]
Select [1-3]: q
$
```

Everything typed by the user after SPIN starts executing in response to a `Select` request from the tool is indicated in bold. The user is asked to make a choice from one or more non-deterministic alternatives for execution by typing a number within the range that is indicated by the `Select` request. In most cases, if there is only one choice, SPIN will immediately select that option without asking the user for guidance, but this is not always the case, as illustrated by the first query that the tool issues in the preceding example. The simulation can be stopped at any point by typing the letter q (for 'quit') at a selection menu.

If initial steps in the execution are skipped with a -jN option, then SPIN will

---

5. We have deleted line numbers and source file references from the output for layout purposes.

resolve the non-determinism for those steps internally with the random number generator, and yield control to the user at the desired point. Again, it is wise to fix a seed to SPIN's random number generator in this case to make sure that the intial part of the simulation run proceeds in a reproducible way. An upper limit, specified with option -uN, will stop the simulation after N steps have been executed.

Simulations, of course, are intended primarily for the debugging of a model. Only basic assertions are checked in this mode, but even if none of these assertions are violated in a large battery of random simulation runs, we cannot conclude that such violations are impossible. To do so requires verification.

GUIDED SIMULATION

SPIN can also be run in guided simulation mode. To do so, though, requires the existence of a specially encoded trail file to guide the search. These trail files are generated only in verification mode, when the verifier discovers a correctness violation. The execution sequence leading up to the error is stored in the trail file, allowing SPIN to replay the scenario in a guided simulation, with access to all user-defined options that were discussed earlier for random simulation. We will return to this option on page 258.

VERIFICATION

Perhaps the most important feature of SPIN is that it can generate optimized verifiers from a user-defined PROMELA model. SPIN does not attempt to verify properties of a model directly, with any generic built-in code. By generating a verifier that can be compiled and run separately a significant gain in performance can be realized.

GENERATING A VERIFIER

When done debugging, we can use SPIN option -a to produce the source code for a model specific verifier, for instance, as follows:

```
$ spin -a model
```

There are actually two different semantic models that may be used to generate the verifier at this point. The alternative semantic model is obtained with the command:

```
$ spin -a -m model
```

By default, send operations are considered to be unexecutable when the channel to which the message is sent is full. With option -m, this semantic changes into one where send operations are always executable, but messages sent to full channels are lost. The standard semantics of PROMELA correspond to the default model, where option -m is not used.

The verifier is generated as a C program that is stored in a number of files with a fixed set of names, all starting with the three-letter prefix[6] pan. For instance, we may see this result:

```
$ spin -a leader
$ ls -l pan.?
-rw-r--r--   1 gerard    user      2633 Aug 18 12:33 pan.b
-rw-r--r--   1 gerard    user    147964 Aug 18 12:33 pan.c
-rw-r--r--   1 gerard    user      9865 Aug 18 12:33 pan.h
-rw-r--r--   1 gerard    user     13280 Aug 18 12:33 pan.m
-rw-r--r--   1 gerard    user     18851 Aug 18 12:33 pan.t
$
```

The file named pan.h is a generic header file for the verifier that contains, for instance, the translated declarations of all global variables, all channels, and all process types. File pan.m defines the executability rules for all PROMELA statements used in the model, and the effect they have on the system state when successfully executed. File pan.b defines how the effect of each statement from pan.m can be undone when the direction of the depth-first search is reversed. File pan.t contains the transition matrix that encodes the labeled transition system for each process type. Finally, file pan.c contains the algorithms for the computation of the asynchronous and synchronous products of the labeled transition systems, and the state space maintenance and cycle detection algorithms, encoding optimized versions of either a depth-first or a breadth-first search.

COMPILING THE VERIFIER

The best performance of the SPIN-generated verifiers can be obtained if the physical limitations of the computer system that will be used to run the verifications are known. If it is known, for instance, how much physical (not virtual) memory the system has available, the verifier can take advantage of that. Initially, the verifier can simply be compiled for a straight exhaustive verification, which can also deliver the strongest possible verification result, provided that there is sufficient memory to complete the run. Compile as follows:

```
$ cc -o pan pan.c   # compile for exhaustive search
```

The pan.c file includes all other files that are generated by SPIN, so the name of only this file needs to be provided to the compiler. If this compilation attempt fails, make sure that you have an ANSI compatible C compiler. Almost all C compilers today conform to this standard. In case of doubt, though, the generally available Gnu C compilers have the right properties. They are often available as gcc, rather than cc. The result of the compilation on UNIX systems will be an executable file called pan.

---

6. The prefix pan is short for *protocol an*alyzer, and a reference to SPIN's earliest predecessor from 1980.

On a Windows PC system with the Microsoft Visual C++ compiler installed, the compilation would be done as follows:

```
$ cl pan.c
```

which if all is well also produces an executable verifier named pan.exe.

If a memory bound is known at the time of compilation, it should be compiled into the verifier so that any paging behavior can be avoided. If, for instance, the system is known to have no more than 512 Megabytes of physical RAM memory, the compiler-directive to add would be:

```
$ cc -DMEMLIM=512 -o pan pan.c
```

If the verifier runs out of memory before completing its task, the bound could be increased to see if this brings relief, but a better strategy is to try some of SPIN's memory compression options. For instance, a good first attempt could be to compile with the memory collapse option, which retains all the benefits of an exhaustive verification, but uses less memory:

```
$ cc -DCOLLAPSE -o pan pan.c    # collapse compression
```

If the verifier still runs out of memory before it can complete the search, a good strategy is to attempt the hash-compact option, which uses less memory, at a small risk of incompleteness of the search:

```
$ cc -DHC4 -o pan pan.c         # hash-compact strategy
```

If that also fails, the recommended strategy is to use a series of bitstate verification runs to get a better impression of the complexity of the problem that is being tackled. Although the bitstate verification mode cannot guarantee exhaustive coverage, it is often very successful in identifying correctness violations.

```
$ cc -DBITSTATE -o pan pan.c    # bitstate compression
```

Whichever type of compilation was selected, an executable version of the verifier should be created in a file called either pan (on UNIX systems) or pan.exe (on PCs), and we can proceed to the actual verification step.

TUNING A VERIFICATION RUN
A few decisions can be made at this point that can improve the performance of the verifier. It is, for instance, useful, though not strictly required, if we can provide the verifier with an estimate of the likely number of reachable states, and the maximum number of unique steps that could be performed along any single non-cyclic execution path (defining the maximum depth of the execution tree). We will explain in the next few sections how those estimates can be provided. If no estimates are available, the verifier will use default settings that will be adequate in most cases. The feedback from the verifier after a first trial run usually provides enough clues to pick better values for these two

parameters, if the defaults do not work well.

Next, we must choose whether we want the verifier to search for violations of *safety* properties (assertion violations, deadlocks, etc.) or for *liveness* properties (e.g., to show the absence of non-progress cycles or acceptance cycles). The two types of searches cannot be combined.

A search for safety properties is the default. This default is changed into a search for acceptance cycles if run-time option -a is used. To perform a search for non-progress cycles, we have to compile the pan.c source with the compile-time directive -DNP, and use run-time option -l, instead of -a. We will return to some of these choices on page 257.

THE NUMBER OF REACHABLE STATES

The verifier stores all reachable states in a lookup table. In exhaustive search mode, that table is a conventional hash table, with a default size of 2^{18} slots. This state storage method works optimally if the table has at least as many slots as there are reachable states that will have to be stored in it, although nothing disastrous will happen if there are less or more states than slots in the lookup table. Strictly speaking, if the table has too many slots, the verifier wastes memory. If the table has too few slots, the verifier wastes CPU cycles. In neither case is the correctness of the verification process itself in peril.

The built-in default for the size of the hash table can be changed with run-time option -wN. For instance,

```
$  ./pan -w23
```

changes the size of the lookup table in exhaustive search mode from 2^{18} to 2^{23} slots.

The hash table lookup idea works basically the same when the verifier is compiled for bitstate verification, instead of for the default exhaustive search. For a bitstate run, the size of the hash table in effect equals the number of bits in the entire memory arena that is available to the verifier. If the verifier is compiled for bitstate verification, the default size of the hash array is 2^{22} bits, that is, 2^{19} bytes. We can override the built-in default by specifying, for instance,

```
$  ./pan -w28
```

to use a hash array of 2^{28} bits or 2^{25} bytes. The optimal value to be used depends primarily on the amount of physical memory that is available to run the verification. For instance, use -w23 if you expect 8 million reachable states and have access to at least 1 Megabyte of memory (2^{20} bytes). A bitstate run with too small of a setting for the hash array will get less coverage than possible, but it will also run faster. Sometimes increased speed is desired, and sometimes greater coverage.

One way to exploit the greater speed obtained with the small hash arrays is, for instance, to apply an iterative refinement method. If at least 64 Megabytes of physical memory are available, such an iterative search method could be performed as follows, assuming a UNIX system running the standard Bourne shell:

```
$ spin -a model
$ cc -DBITSTATE -DMEMLIM=80 -o pan pan.c
$ for i in 20 21 22 23 24 25 26 27 28 29
  do
        ./pan -w$i
        if [ -f model.trail ]
        then
                exit
        fi
  done
$
```

The search starts with a hash array of just 2^{20} bits (128 Kbytes), which should not take more than a fraction of a second on most systems. If an error is found, the search stops at this point. If no error is found, the hash array doubles in size and the search is repeated. This continues until either an error is found or the maximal amount of memory has been used for the hash array. In this case, that would be with a hash array of 2^{29} bits (64 Megabytes). The verifier source is compiled with a limit of 80 Megabytes in this case, to allow some room for other data structures in the verifier, so that also the last step can be run to completion.

SEARCH DEPTH

By default, the verifiers generated by SPIN have a search depth restriction of 10,000 steps. If this isn't enough, the search will truncate at 9,999 steps (watch for this telltale number in the printout at the end of a run). A different search depth of N steps can be defined by using run-time option -mN, for instance, by typing

```
$ ./pan -m1000000
```

to increase the maximum search depth to 1,000,000 steps. A deeper search depth requires more memory for the search; memory that cannot be used to store reachable states, so it is best not to overestimate here. If this limit is also exceeded, it is probably good to take some time to consider if the model defines finite behavior. Check, for instance, if attempts are made to create an unbounded number of processes, or to increment integer variables without bound. If the model is finite, increase the search depth at least as far as is required to avoid truncation of the search.

In the rare case that there is not enough memory to allocate a search stack for very deep searches, an alternative is to use SPIN's stack-cycling algorithm that arranges for the verifier to swap parts of the search stack to disk during a verification run, retaining only a small portion in memory. Such a search can be set up and executed, for instance, as follows:

```
$ spin -a model
$ cc -DSC -o pan pan.c  # use stack-cycling
$ ./pan -m100000
```

In this case, the value specified with the -m option defines the size of the search stack that will reside in memory. There is *no* preset maximum search depth in this mode: the search can go arbitrarily deep, or at least it will proceed until also the diskspace that is available to store the temporary stack files is exhausted.

If a particularly nasty error is found that takes a relatively large number of steps to hit, you can try to find a shorter error trail by forcing a shorter depth-limit with the -m parameter. If the error disappears with a lower depth-limit, increase it in steps until it reappears.

Another, and often more reliable, way to find the shortest possible error sequence is to compile and run the verifier for iterative depth adjustment. For instance, if we already know that there exists an error sequence of 1,000 steps, we can try to find a shorter equivalent, as follows:

```
$ spin -a model
$ cc -DREACH -o pan pan.c
$ ./pan -i -m1000    # iteratively find shortest error
```

Be warned, though, that the use of -DREACH can cause an increase in run time and does not work for bitstate searches, that is, it cannot be combined with -DBITSTATE.

Finally, if the property of interest is a safety property (i.e., it does not require a search for cyclic executions), we can consider compiling the verifier for a breadth-first, instead of the standard depth-first, search:

```
$ cc -DBFS -o pan pan.c
$ ./pan
```

This type of search tends to be a little slower than the default search mode, and it can consume more memory, but if these limitations do not prevent it, it is guaranteed to find the shortest path to an error. Combinations with state compression methods are again possible here. Reasonable attempts to control excessive memory use can, for instance, be to compile the verifier with the hash-compact option, using the additional compiler directive -DHC4.

CYCLE DETECTION

The most important decision to be made in setting up a verification run is to decide if we want to perform a check for safety or for liveness properties. There are optimized algorithms in the verifier for both types of verification, but only one type of search can be performed at a time. The three main types of search, with the corresponding compilation modes, are as follows:

```
$ spin -a model
$ cc -DSAFETY -o pan pan.c   # compilation for safety
$ ./pan                      # find safety violations
$ cc -o pan pan.c            # default compilation
$ ./pan -a                   # find acceptance cycles
$ cc -DNP -o pan pan.c       # non-progress cycle detection
$ ./pan -l                   # find non-progress cycles
```

By default, that is in the absence of option -l and -a, only safety properties are checked: assertion violations, absence of unreachable code, absence of race conditions, etc. The use of the directive -DSAFETY is optional when a search for safety properties is performed. But, when the directive is used, the search for safety violations can be performed somewhat more efficiently.

If accept labels are present in the model, for instance, as part of a never claim, then a complete verification will require the use of the -a option. Typically, when a never claim is generated from an LTL formula, it will contain accept labels.

Adding run-time option -f restricts a search for liveness properties further by enforcing a *weak fairness* constraint:

```
pan -f -l      # search for fair non-progress cycles
pan -f -a      # search for fair acceptance cycles
```

With this constraint, a non-progress cycle or an acceptance cycle is only reported if every running process either executes an infinite number of steps or is blocked at an unexecutable statement at least once in the execution cycle. Adding the fairness constraint multiplies the time requirements of a verification by a factor that is linear in the number of running processes.

By default, the verifier will always report every statement that is found to be unreachable in the verification model. This reachability report can be suppressed with run-time option -n, as, for instance, in:

```
$ ./pan -n -f -a
```

The order in which the options such as these are listed is always irrelevant.

INSPECTING ERROR TRACES

If the verification run reports an error, SPIN dumps an error trail into a file named model.trail, where model is the name of the PROMELA specification. To inspect the trail, and to determine the cause of the error, SPIN's guided simulation option can be used (assuming that the model does not contain embedded C code fragments, cf. p. 495). The basic use is the command

```
$ spin -t -p model
```

with as many extra or different options as are needed to pin down the error. For instance,

```
$ spin -t -r -s -l -g model
```

The verifier normally stops when a first violation has been found. If the first violation is not particularly interesting, run-time option `-cN` can be used to identify others. For instance,

```
$ ./pan -c3
```

ignores the first two violations and reports only the third one, assuming of course that at least three errors can be found.

To eliminate entire classes of errors, two special purpose options may be useful. A search with

```
$ ./pan -A
```

will ignore all violations of basic assertion statements in the model, and a search with

```
$ ./pan -E
```

will ignore all invalid end-state errors. For example, to search *only* acceptance cycles, the search could be initiated as:

```
$ ./pan -a -A -E
```

To merely count the number of all violations, without generating error trails, use

```
$ ./pan -c0
```

To do the same while also generating an error trail for each violation found, use

```
$ ./pan -c0 -e
```

The error trails now carry a sequence number as part of the file names. To replay a specific numbered trail, say, the Nth copy, provide the sequence number in the `-t` parameter, for instance,

```
$ spin -t3 model
```

performs a guided simulation for the third error trail found, using the file `model3.trail`.

INTERNAL STATE NUMBERS

Internally, the verifiers produced by SPIN deal with a formalization of a PROMELA model in terms of finite automata. SPIN therefore assigns state and transition numbers to all control flow points and statements in the model. The automata state numbers are listed in all the relevant outputs to make it unambiguous (source line references unfortunately do not always have that property). To reveal the internal state assignments, run-time option `-d` can be used. For instance,

```
$ ./pan -d
```

prints a table with all internal state and transition assignments used by the verifier for each distinct `proctype` in the model. The output does not clearly show merged transition sequences. To obtain that output it is best to disable the transition merging algorithm that is used in SPIN. To do so, proceed as follows:

```
$ spin -o3 model
$ cc -o pan pan.c
$ ./pan -d
```

To see the unoptimized versions of the internal state assignments, every repetition of the `-d` argument will arrange for an earlier version of the internal state tables to be printed, up to the original version that is exported by the SPIN parser. Try, for instance, the following command for your favorite model:

```
$ ./pan -d -d -d
```

and compare it with the output that is obtained with a single `-d` argument.

SPECIAL CASES

We conclude this chapter with a discussion of some special cases that may arise in the verification of PROMELA models with SPIN. In special circumstances, the user may, for instance, want to disable the partial order reduction algorithm. Alternatively, the user may want to spend some extra time to boost the performance of the partial order reduction by adding some additional declarations that SPIN can exploit. Finally, in most serious applications of automated verification tools, the user will sooner or later run into complexity bottlenecks. Although it is not possible to say specifically how complexity can be reduced in each specific case, it is possible to make some general recommendations.

DISABLING PARTIAL ORDER REDUCTION

Partial order reduction is enabled by default in the SPIN generated verifiers. In special cases, for instance, when the verifier warns the user that constructions are used that are not compatible with the partial order reduction strategy, the reduction method can be disabled by compiling the verifier's source code with an extra directive:

```
$ spin -a model
$ cc -DNOREDUCE -o pan pan.c # disable p.o. reduction
```

BOOSTING PERFORMANCE

The performance of the default partial order reduction algorithm can also be boosted substantially if the verifier can be provided with some extra information about possible and impossible access patterns of processes to message channels. For this purpose, there are two special types of assertions in PROMELA that allow one to assert that specific channels are used exclusively by specific processes. For example, the channel assertions

```
xr q1;
xs q2;
```

claim that the process that executes them is the *only* process that will receive messages from channel q1, and the *only* process that will send messages to channel q2.

If an exclusive usage assertion turns out to be invalid, the verifier will always be able to detect this and report it as a violation of an implicit correctness requirement.

Note that every type of access to a message channel can introduce dependencies that may affect the exclusive usage assertions. If, for instance, a process uses the len(qname) function to check the number of messages stored in a channel named qname, this counts as a read access to qname, which can invalidate an exclusive access pattern.

There are two special operators that can be used to poll the size of a channel in a way that is always compatible with the reduction strategy:

```
nfull(qname)
```

returns *true* if channel qname is not full, and

```
nempty(qname)
```

returns *true* if channel qname contains at least one message. The SPIN parser will reject attempts to bypass the protection offered by these primitives with expressions like

```
!full(qname),
!empty(qname),
!nfull(qname), or
!nempty(qname).
```

In special cases, the user may want to claim that the particular type of access to message channels that is specified in xr and xs assertions need not be checked. The checks can then be suppressed by compiling the verifier with the extra directive -DXUSAFE, for instance, as in:

```
$ cc -DXUSAFE -o pan pan.c
```

SEPARATE COMPILATION

Often, a verification model is checked for a range of logic properties, and not just a single property. If properties are specified in LTL, or with the Timeline Editor, we can build a library of properties, each of which must be checked against the model. The easiest way to do this is to first generate all property automata from the formulae, or from the visual time line specifications, and store each one in a separately named file. Next we can set up a verification script that invokes SPIN on the basic model, but for each run picking up a different property automaton file, for instance with SPIN's run-time option -N.

If the main verification model is stored in a file called `model.pml` and the property automata are all stored in file names with the three-letter extension `.prp`, we can build a minimal verification script, using the UNIX Bourne shell, for instance, as follows:

```
#!/bin/sh

for i in *.prp
do
        echo "property: $i"
        if spin -N $i -a model.pml
        then    ;
        else    echo "parsing error"
                exit 1
        fi
        if cc -o pan pan.c
        then    ;
        else    echo "compilation error"
                exit 1
        fi
        ./pan -a
od
exit 0
```

In most cases, the time that is required to parse the model, to generate the verifier source text and to compile the verifier, is small compared to the time that is required to run the actual verification. But, this is not always the case.

As the model text becomes larger, the time that is needed to compile the verifier source text will also increase. If the compilation process starts to take a noticeable amount of time, and there is a substantial library of properties that need to be checked, we may want to optimize this process.

We can assume that if the compilation time starts to become noticeable, this is typically do to the large size of the basic verification model itself, not the size of the property. In SPIN model checking it would be very rare for a property automaton to exceed a size of perhaps ten to twenty control states. A system model, though, can easily produce an automaton description that spans many thousands of process states. Compiling the automata descriptions for the main verification model, then, can sometimes require significantly more time than compiling the source code that is associated with the implementation of a property automaton.

SPIN supports a method to generate the source code for the model and for the property separately, so that these two separate parts of the source code can also be compiled separately. The idea is that we only need to generate and compile the source code for the main system model once (the slow part), and we can repeat the generation and compilation of the much smaller source code fragments for the property automata separately.

If we revise the verification script from our first example to exploit this separate compilation option, it would look like this:

```
#!/bin/sh

if spin -S1 model.pml    # model, without properties
then    ;
else    echo "parsing error in main model"
        exit 1
fi

if cc -c pan_s.c        # compile main part once
then    ;
else    echo "compilation error in main model"
fi

for i in *.prp
do
        echo "property: $i"
        if spin -N $i -S2 model.pml
        then    ;
        else    echo "parsing error in property"
                exit 1
        fi
        # next, compile only the code for the
        # property and link it to the previously
        # compiled module
        if cc -c pan_t.c                # property code
        then    ;
        else    echo "compilation error in property"
                exit 1
        fi
        if cc -o pan pan_s.o pan_t.o    # link
        then    ;
        else    echo "link error"
                exit 1
        fi
        ./pan -a
od
exit 0
```

To get an idea of how much time the separate compilation strategy can save us, assume that we have a library of one hundred properties. If the compilation of the complete model code takes seventy-two seconds, and compilation of just the property related code takes seven seconds, then the first verification script would take

```
100 * 72 = 7,200 seconds = 2 hours
```

The second verification script, using separate compilation, would take:

```
72 + 100 * 7 = 772 seconds = 11 minutes, 12 seconds
```

The time to run each verification would be the same in both scenarios.

In some cases, when the property automata refer to data that is external to the module that contains the property related source code, it can be necessary to add some code into the source file. This can be done via the addition at compile-time of so-called *provisioning* information, as follows:

```
$ cc -DPROV=\"extra.c\" -c pan_t.c
$ cc -o pan pan_s.o pan_t.o
```

The provisioning information (such as declarations for external variables) is provided in a separate file that is prepared by the user. It can contain declarations for external variables, and also initialization for selected global variables.

LOWERING VERIFICATION COMPLEXITY

If none of SPIN's built-in features for managing the complexity of a verification run seem to be adequate, consider the following suggestions to lower the inherent complexity of the verification model itself:

- Make the model more general; more abstract. Remove everything from the model that is not directly related to the correctness property that you are trying to prove. Remove all redundant computations and redundant data. Use the output from SPIN option -A as a starting point.

- Avoid using variables with large value ranges, such as integer counters, clocks, or sequence numbers.

- Try to split channels that receive messages from multiple senders into separate channels, one for each source of messages. Similarly, try to split channels that are read by multiple processes into separate channels, one for each receiver. The interleaving of independent message streams in a single channel can be a huge source of avoidable complexity.

- Reduce the number of slots in asynchronous channels to as small a number as seems reasonable. See Chapter 5, p. 101, on the effect that channel sizes can have on search complexity.

- Group all local computations into `atomic` sequences, and wherever possible into `d_step` sequences.

- Avoid leaving scratch data around in local or global variables. The number of reachable system states can often be reduced by resetting local variables that are used only inside `atomic` or `d_step` sequences to zero at the end of those sequences.

There is a special keyword in the language that can be used to hide a scratch variable from the verifier completely. It is mentioned only in passing here, since the mechanism is easily misused. Nonetheless, if you declare a global variable, of arbitrary type, as in:

```
hidden byte var;
```

then the variable, named `var` here, is not considered part of the state descriptor. Clearly, values that are stored in `hidden` variables cannot be assumed to persist. A typical use could be to flush the contents of a channel, for instance, as follows:

```
do
:: nempty(q) -> q?var
:: else -> break
od
```

If the variable `var` were not hidden, each new value stored in it would cause the creation of a new global state. In this case this could needlessly increase the size of the reachable state space. Use with caution. An alternative method is to use the predefined hidden variable named _ (underscore). This write-only variable need not be declared and is always available to store scratch values. The last example can therefore also be written as:

```
do
:: q?_
:: empty(q) -> break
od
```

- Try to avoid the use of global variables. SPIN's partial order reduction technique can take advantage of the fact that a local variable can only be accessed by a single process.

- Where possible, add the channel assertions `xr` and `xs` (see p. 261 in this chapter).

- Always use the predefined functions `nempty(q)` and `nfull(q)` instead of the equivalent expressions `len(q)>0` and `len(q)<MAX`, respectively; the partial order reduction algorithm can take advantage of the special cases where these expressions are needed.

- Where possible, combine the behavior of multiple processes in a single one. The larger the number of asynchronously executing processes, the greater the potential search complexity will be. The principle to be used here is to *generalize* the behavior that is captured in a verification model. Focus on properly defining the interfaces *between* processes, rather than the computation performed inside processes.

In any case: Don't give up. A model checker is a powerful tool that can assist us in proving interesting facts of distributed systems. But, in the end, it is still only a tool. Our own powers of abstraction in formulating problems that the model checker can effectively solve will always outstrip the power of the model checker itself. Fortunately, the ability to predict what types of models can be verified most efficiently grows with experience: you will get better at it each time you use the tool.

> *"The road to wisdom is plain and simple to express:*
> *Err and err and err again, but less and less and less."*
> *(Piet Hein, 1905–1996)*

NOTES ON XSPIN   **12**

> *"The ability to simplify means to eliminate*
> *the unnecessary so that the necessary may speak."*
> *(Hans Hofmann, 1880–1966)*

XSPIN is the graphical interface to SPIN that for many users is the first introduction to the tool. It can be a considerable benefit, though, if the user is
familiar with the basic operation of SPIN before switching to XSPIN, especially
when more subtle design problems are encountered.

The interface operates independently from SPIN itself. It synthesizes and
executes SPIN commands in the background, in response to user selections and
button clicks. Nonetheless, this front-end tool supplies a significant added
value by providing graphical displays of, for instance, message flows and time
sequence diagrams. XSPIN also provides a clean overview of the many options
in SPIN that are available for performing simulations and verifications.

To run XSPIN, you first of all need to be able to run SPIN itself, which means
that you minimally will need access to an ANSI compatible C preprocessor
and compiler. XSPIN is written in Tcl/Tk, so if you have a local installation of
the Tcl/Tk toolset,[1] you can run it directly from its source. You do not need to
install Tcl/Tk to run the tool, though. It is also available as a stand-alone
binary executable that is available as part of the standard SPIN distribution (see
Appendix D).

This chapter gives a brief overview of the main options that are available
through XSPIN. The interface is intuitive enough that most questions can be
answered by simply running the tool and by exploring its options and help
menus interactively.

---

1. Tcl/Tk can be downloaded free of charge from www.tcl.tk.

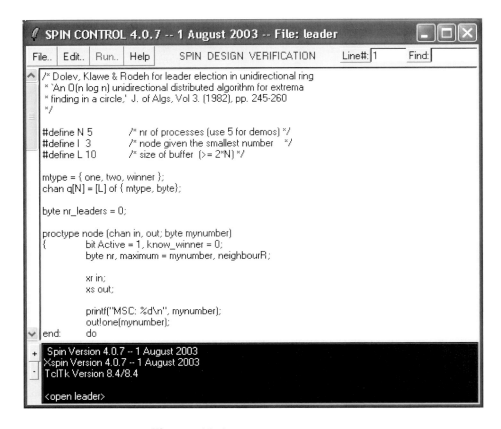

Figure 12.1 XSPIN Main Window

STARTING A SESSION WITH XSPIN

Assuming all the software has been installed properly, XSPIN can be started on both UNIX systems and Windows PC systems from the shell command line with the name of a file containing a PROMELA specification as an argument, for instance, as follows:

```
$ xspin leader
```

On a Windows system the program can also be selected from the start menu, or by double-clicking the source file named xspin.tcl.

When XSPIN starts, it first checks that good versions of SPIN and Tcl/Tk are available. It prints the version numbers in a command-log window, and optionally opens and loads an initial PROMELA file.

Throughout the use of XSPIN, a log of all actions performed is maintained in a special command-log window that appears at the bottom of the XSPIN display. Syntax errors, unexpected events, time-consuming actions such as background compilations and verification runs, can be tracked in the log.

The main display of XSPIN is a text window that displays the file being used, just like a graphical text editor would do. The file name, if any, is shown in the title bar. The view in the text window can be changed in four different ways:

- With the scroll bar on the left-hand side of the text window.
- By typing a line number (followed by a <return>) in the box in the title bar marked `Line#:`.
- By typing a regular expression pattern (followed by a <return>) in the box marked `Find:`.
- By moving a three-button mouse with the middle mouse button down, or a two-button mouse with both buttons down.

Moving around in the text with the mouse buttons down (the last method above) is the most convenient, and it works in most of the text displays that are provided by XSPIN.

There are four other buttons in the title bar of the XSPIN display: `File..`, `Edit..`, `Run..`, and `Help`, as shown in Figure 12.1. We will discuss each of these separately in the following sections.

THE FILE MENU

The file menu gives a choice of seven actions: `New`, `UnSelect`, `ReOpen`, `Open`, `Save As`, `Save`, and `Quit`.

`New` clears the contents of the main window, but does not reset the file name or affect any other parameter.

`UnSelect` removes any selection highlights that the user or a background program may have placed in the main window.

`ReOpen` reloads the contents of the current file in the main text window, discarding any changes made since the last `Save` operation.

`Open` prompts the user with a standard file dialogue, listing all files in the current directory. Double-clicking any of the files will cause XSPIN to open it and place it in its text window. Of course, this only makes sense for PROMELA specifications. Double-clicking a directory name will cause the browse window to descend into that directory and display the files listed there. Double-clicking the up-arrow icon will cause the browse window to move up to the parent directory, and display the files listed there.

`Save As..` provides a file browse dialogue, allowing the user to select a file name in which the current contents of the text window should be saved. During each session, XSPIN always maintains a private copy of the current contents of the text window in a file called `pan_in` to avoid unintentional changes in the original source of the PROMELA specification. The source file itself is only (re)written with an explicit `Save` command.

`Quit` terminates the session of XSPIN, removing any temporary files that were created during simulation or verification runs. No warning is issued if the file being edited was changed since the last time it was saved.

THE EDIT MENU

The edit menu contains the three standard entries for performing `Cut`, `Copy`, and `Paste` operations on selected text in the main window. Text can be selected as usual, by sweeping with the left mouse button down, or by double-clicking text strings. Cut, copy, and paste operations are also available with control-key combinations: control-X for cut, control-C for copy, and control-V for paste. Be careful though, there is no undo operation implemented in XSPIN.

THE HELP MENU

The help menu gives a quick online review of the main usage options of SPIN and XSPIN, and contains an explanation of the proper setting of the main parameters for verification and simulation runs. The menu also provide hints for reducing search complexity. The entries in this menu will be self-explanatory.

THE RUN MENU

The run menu has eight entries for performing syntax checks, property-based slicing, setting simulation or verification parameters, running simulations or verifications, and viewing the internal automata structures computed by SPIN. We discuss each of these menu choices next.

SYNTAX CHECK

XSPIN runs a syntax check by asking SPIN to execute the command:

```
$ spin -a -v pan_in
```

in the background, using its private file copy of the PROMELA text in the main window. Results, if any, are displayed in the standard command log window and in a separate popup window that can be closed again with a mouse-click on its `Ok` button. Wherever possible, error text is highlighted in the main XSPIN window for ease of reference.

PROPERTY-BASED SLICING

To run the slicing algorithm, which also provides a thorough syntax check of the PROMELA source, XSPIN executes the following command:

```
$ spin -A pan_in
```

The slicing algorithm tries to locate all logical properties that are part of the model, for instance, as expressed in assertions and in a never claim, and it uses this information to identify those parts of the model that cannot possibly affect the correctness or incorrectness of those properties. In the absence of properties, the algorithm can still do useful things, by identifying portions of the model that are redundant no matter which properties are specified.

The results that are produced are displayed both in the command log window and in a separate popup window. Included in the output are also any warnings about potentially wasteful constructs, such as variables that were declared as integers but that assume only boolean values. If no redundancies can be found in the model, SPIN will report this as well, so this option is also generally useful as a somewhat more thorough check of the model.

SET SIMULATION PARAMETERS

The simulation options panel allows the user to select the types of displays that will be generated during simulation runs. In the upper right-hand corner of the panel the choice between random, guided, and interactive simulation can be made. When XSPIN is used, random simulation is by default done with a predefined seed value of one. This seed value can be changed freely to obtain different types of runs, but once the seed value is fixed, all experiments are fully reproducible. If the entry box for the seed value is left blank, the current system time is used as a seed value, which of course does not guarantee reproducibility. The guided simulation option requires the presence of a file named pan.trail, which is normally produced in a verification run when SPIN finds a counterexample to a correctness property. The number of steps that should be skipped before the display of the sequence is initiated can be specified, the default value being zero.

Two further options are selectable in the right-hand side column of the simulation options panel. For send statements, the user has a choice of semantics. Either a send operation that targets a full message channel (queue) blocks, or can be defined to be non-blocking. If non-blocking, messages sent to a full channel are lost. Up to three channel numbers (queue numbers) can be specified in the three entry boxes at the bottom of the right-hand column. If channel numbers are entered, send and receive operations that target the corresponding channels will *not* be displayed in graphical MSC (message sequence chart) displays.

On the left-hand side of the panel four types of outputs can be requested. By default, only two of these will be selected. A most useful type of display is the MSC (message sequence chart) panel. Normally, the execution steps in this display are tagged with identifying numbers. By moving the mouse cursor over one of the steps, the source text will show and the main text window will scroll to the corresponding statement. Alternatively, the user can also choose to have the source text shown for each step in the display. For very long runs, the message sequence chart can be compacted somewhat by selecting the condensed spacing option.

Normally, the message sequence chart will display only send and receive actions, connecting matching pairs with arrows. The output from print statements can be added to a message sequence chart by starting any newline terminated string to be printed with the prefix "MSC:" followed by a space, for instance, as in:

```
printf("MSC: this will appear in the MSC\n");
```

The default background color for text boxes that are created in this manner is *yellow*. The color of the box can also be changed by starting the text string to be printed with a special two-character control sequence. For instance,

```
printf("MSC: ~W uses a white box\n");
printf("MSC: ~G uses a green box\n");
printf("MSC: ~R uses a red box\n");
printf("MSC: ~B uses a blue box\n");
```

The prefix MSC: and an optional two-character control codes for setting colors do not appear in the output itself.

As a special feature of print statements, if the statement

```
printf("MSC: BREAK\n");
```

causes XSPIN to suspend the simulation run temporarily, simulating a breakpoint in the run. The run can be restarted from the main simulation output panel.

The *time-sequence* panel can show verbose output of the simulation run. Normally, the output is shown in the interleaving order from the execution, but it can also be split out into separate windows so that a separate trace for each executing process can be obtained. If the number of running processes is large, this option can require a lot of real estate on the screen, so it is not always helpful. The main window can also be replicated, by selecting the "One Trace per Process" option, so that each text window can track the execution of one specific process. There are actually two ways to track individual process executions: as an basic listing of all steps performed, and with a moving highlight in the source text that moves from step to step. The latter mode is selected with the "One Window per Process" option.

The data values panel shows the most recently assigned values for variables in the model. By default, only global variable values are shown. The output for local variable values can be added by selecting the corresponding box on the options panel. Note that only variables that change value appear here, not variables that still retain their initial value from a declaration. If the amount

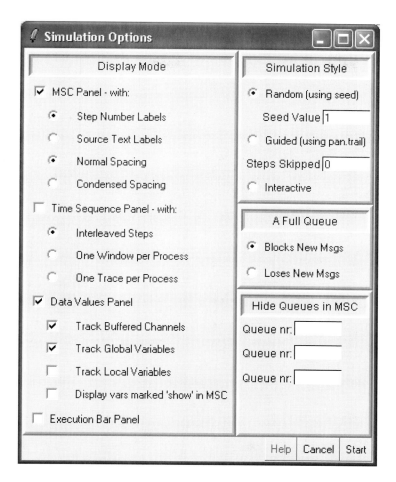

Figure 12.2 The Simulations Options Panel

of output produced for larger models becomes too large, an alternative option is available to display only the values of selected variables. To select such variables, the keyword `show` can be added in the PROMELA model before the variable declaration, for instance, as in:

```
show byte nr_leaders = 0;
```

By selecting the box marked `Display vars marked 'show'`, the output in the Message Sequence Chart panel will now include an entry for each value change of (only) these specially marked variables.

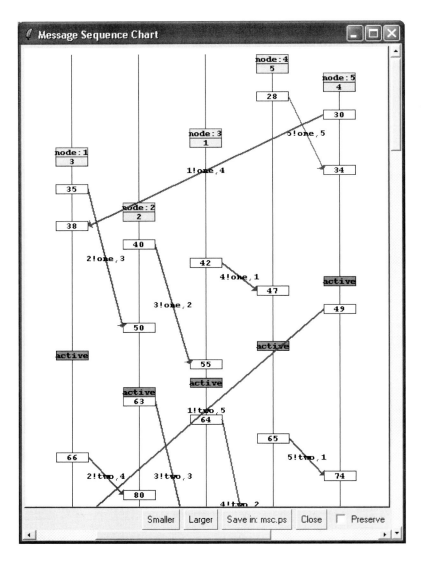

Figure 12.3 Message Sequence Chart Display (portion)

The *execution bar* panel, selectable at the bottom of the left-hand column in the simulation options panel (see Figure 12.2), gives a dynamically updated bar-chart of the number of statement executions in each running process.

Selecting the `Start` button will bring up the initial contents of the display

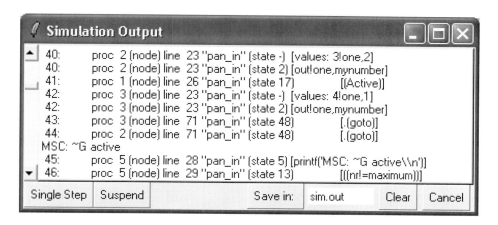

Figure 12.4 Main Simulation Output Panel

panels that were selected, such as the message sequence chart display shown in Figure 12.3, and executes a first single step in the simulation. By selecting Single Step we can now step through a simulation, one statement execution at a time. By selecting Run, SPIN will take over and run the simulation. The label on this button then changes to Suspend as shown in Figure 12.4. The button toggles back and forth between these two modes each time it is clicked.

(RE)RUN SIMULATION
When the simulation parameters have been set once, they persist for the remainder of the session, or until the setting is changed. New simulation runs can now be initiated directly with these settings by selecting this menu option from the Run menu. The option is grayed out, and remains unselectable, until the simulation parameters panel has been displayed at least once.

SET VERIFICATION PARAMETERS
The verification parameters panel gives visual control over most of the options that SPIN provides for performing automated verifications. The initial settings of all parameters are chosen in such a way that they provide a reasonable starting point for most applications. A first verification run, therefore, can in most cases safely be performed by hitting the Run button in the lower right corner of the panel, without altering the default settings.

When a verification run completes, XSPIN attempts to provide hints about ways to proceed, based on the results obtained. No hints are provided when a clean run is performed, that is, a complete exhaustive search that did not

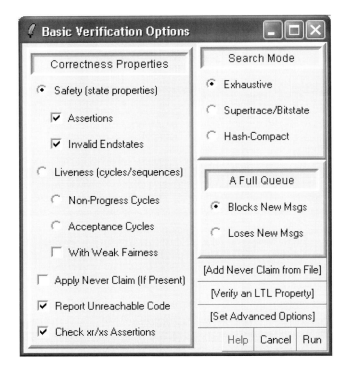

Figure 12.5 Basic Verification Options

reveal any errors. The default hint in cases like these would be to consider whether or not the properties that were proven are the correct ones, and whether or not other properties still remain to be proven.

The default settings define a search for safety properties only. Proving liveness properties (properties of infinite behaviors as manifested by execution cycles) requires a separate verification run with the appropriate options selected in the Correctness Properties section of the verification parameters panel, shown in Figure 12.5.

Note that if the PROMELA specification contains syntax errors, these errors will show up in the XSPIN log when the Run button is selected. The run itself is canceled in that case. It is useful to keep an eye on such error reports, and to be aware of the types of things that XSPIN or SPIN perform in the background.

Three main search modes are selectable in the upper right-hand corner of the panel: exhaustive verification, bitstate approximation, or hash-compact. Some of the more rarely used settings for performing verifications are delegated to a

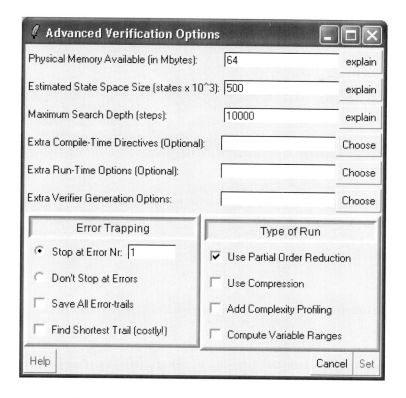

Figure 12.6 Advanced Verification Options

special `Advanced Options` panel, shown in Figure 12.6, that can be selected in the lower right-hand corner of the basic verification options panel. Especially in the beginning, this panel can safely be ignored.

Also selectable via the basic verification options panel is the LTL Property panel, which we will discuss in more detail shortly. Finally, if a `never` claim is present in a file, but not already included within the PROMELA model itself, it can be picked up by the verifier for a single verification run by selecting the `Add Never Claim from File` option. This option is, for instance, the simplest method for including `never` claims that are generated with the Time-line editing tool that is discussed in Chapter 13 (p. 283).

(RE)RUN VERIFICATION

When the verification parameters panel has been displayed at least once, this menu entry becomes selectable. It will initiate a new verification run, preserving all parameter settings that were chosen earlier. This can be useful, for instance, when small changes in the PROMELA model are made to remedy problems uncovered in earlier verification runs.

LTL PROPERTY MANAGER

Selecting this entry from the Run menu brings up a panel for entering an LTL formula to be used in a verification attempt, shown in Figure 12.7. By clicking on the button labeled Generate, or by typing a return character in the formula entry box, the formula is converted into a never claim. Both this claim and the main PROMELA specification are now submitted to SPIN when the Run Verification button is selected.

Templates of standard forms of LTL formulae can be loaded into the LTL property window with the Load option in the upper right corner of the display. Four templates are predefined for invariance properties, response properties, precedence properties, and objective properties. They have the following general form:

```
[] p                 # invariance
p -> <> q            # response
p -> (q U r)         # precendence
p -> <> (q || r)     # objective
```

Each of these generic types of properties can (and will generally have to) be prefixed by temporal operators such as [], <>, []<>, or <>[]. The property type named objective can be read to mean that p (a state property) is an enabling condition that determines when the requirement becomes applicable. Once enabled, the truth of state property q can signify the fullfillment of the requirement, while the truth of r can be treated as a discharging condition that voids the requirement.

LTL properties consist of temporal and logical operators and user-defined propositional symbols. For propositional symbols any name that starts with a lowercase character can be used. It is customary to use single character names, such as the p, q, and r that we used in the template formulae.

The LTL property can be cast as either a positive (desired) or a negative (undesired) property of the model by selecting the corresponding field below the formula entry box.

A positive property is negated by the convertor to convert it into a never claim. A negative property is not negated.

Each propositional symbol that is used in the formula must be defined as a boolean expression in the Symbol Definitions panel.

These definitions will be remembered as part of the property definition, together with any annotations and verification results if the formula is saved as a template with the Save As option in the lower right-hand corner of the display. Always make sure to enclose symbol definitions in round braces to

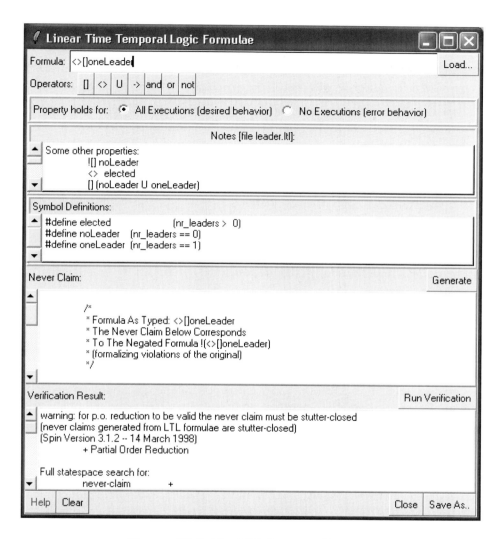

Figure 12.7 The LTL Property Manager

secure a proper interpretation of operator precedence rules. For instance:

```
#define p       (a > b)
#define q       (len(q) < 5)
```

where a and b are global variables in the PROMELA model, and q is a global channel.

Valid temporal operators are:

```
[]   always (with no space between [ and ])
<>   eventually (no space between < and >)
U    (strong) until, and
V    the dual of the until operator: (p V q) == !(!p U !q)
```

All operators are left-associative, including U and V. The V operator is rarely used in user-defined formulae, but it is often used internally by SPIN when it normalizes formulae.

Boolean operators can also be used inside LTL formulae, using standard PROMELA syntax.

```
&&   logical and
!    logical negation
||   logical or
```

Arithmetic operators are not allowed within an LTL formula, but can be used within the macro definitions of the propositional symbols.

Two shorthands are available for defining logical implication and equivalence.

```
->   logical implication
<->  logical equivalence
```

The formula (p -> q) is short for (!p || q) and (p <-> q) is short for (p -> q) && (q -> p).

Recall that logical implication and logical equivalence are boolean and not temporal operators, and that therefore no passage of time is implied by the use of a subformula such as (p -> q). (On this point, see also the section on Using Temporal Logic in Chapter 6.)

The names of operands in an LTL formula must be alphanumeric names, always beginning with a lowercase letter. The preferred style is to use only single-character names, such as p, q, and r. Prudence, further, dictates that the right-hand side of each of the corresponding symbol definitions is enclosed in round braces, to protect against unintended effects of operator precedence rules. For instance, instead of defining

```
#define p       a < b
```

the preferred style us to use

```
#define p       (a < b)
```

Remote reference operations can also only be used indirectly, via a symbol definition, which again are normally enclosed in round braces for security, as in, for instance:

```
#define q       (main[5]@label)
```

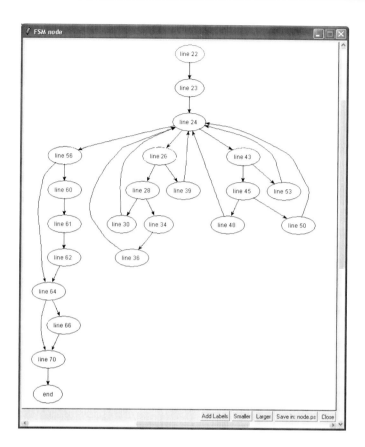

Figure 12.8 The Automata View

THE AUTOMATON VIEW OPTION

The automaton view option, finally, allows for the selection of one of the
proctypes that are part of the PROMELA specification, so that it can be displayed in automaton form.

When this option is selected, XSPIN first generates and compiles an executable
verifier. It then use the output from PAN's run-time option -d to synthesize
the automaton view. It is highly recommended to have a copy of the graph
layout tool dot installed on the system.[2] If it is present, XSPIN will use it to
compute the layout for the automaton graph, as illustrated in Figure 12.8. If
absent, a cruder approximation of the layout will be used.

2. Dot can be downloaded from http://www.research.att.com/sw/tools/graphviz/.

The view in Figure 12.8 shows all states in `proctype node` from the leader election protocol example. For simplicity, we have turned off the display of the statement labels in this display. They can be restored by selecting the button labeled `Add Labels` at the bottom of the display.

Each state in the graph by default shows the line number in the source file that correspond to that state. Moving the cursor over a state causes the corresponding line to be highlighted in the main text window, and changes the line number text for the internally assigned state number. The display of the line number is restored when the cursor is moved away from the state. The graphical display that is generated is for information only; it cannot be edited.

IN SUMMARY

XSPIN synthesizes commands that are issued to the SPIN model checker based on user selections and preferences. For each run performed by SPIN in the background, XSPIN also intercepts the output and presents it in a slightly more pleasing visual way through its graphical interface.

An arbitrary number of assertions, `progress`, `accept`, and `end` state labels can be defined in a model, but at all times there can be only one `never` claim. If `never` claims are derived from LTL formulae, the LTL property manager makes it easy to build a library of formulae, each of which can be stored in a separate file and checked against the model. The results of each run are stored automatically in the file that contains the corresponding LTL property. These files have the default extension `.ltl`.

THE TIMELINE EDITOR **13**

A design without requirements cannot be incorrect.
It can only be surprising.
(Willem L. van der Poel, 1926–)

Although SPIN provides direct support for the formalization of correctness requirements in terms of linear temporal logic formulae, the use of this logic is not always as intuitive as one would like. The precise meaning of a temporal logic formula is sometimes counterintuitive, and can confound even the experts.

An alternative method, that we will explore in this chapter, is to express properties visually, with the help of a graphical tool. The tool we discuss here is called the *timeline editor*, created by Margaret Smith at Bell Labs. The inspiration for this tool came directly from lengthy discussions on the semantics of temporal logic, which led us to draw many small pictures of timelines on the whiteboard to illustrate sample execution sequences that were either intended to satisfy or to violate a given property. The timeline pictures were so useful that we decided to provide direct tool support for them. The tool was originally envisioned to generate only linear temporal logic formula as its output, but we later found it more effective to generate `never` claim automata in PROMELA syntax that can be used directly by SPIN in verifications.

Technically, the types of properties that can be expressed with the timeline editor tool do not cover everything that can be verified by SPIN, that is, they cover only a small subset of the set of all ω-regular properties. The tool is not even expressive enough to let us specify everything that can be expressed with linear temporal logic, which itself also covers only a subset of the ω-regular properties. Yet, the types of properties that can be expressed seems rich enough to specify many of the types of properties that one needs in system verification in practice. Users of model checking tools often tend to shy away

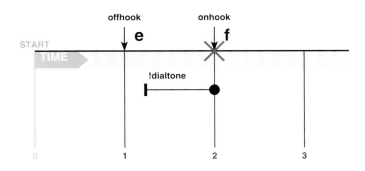

Figure 13.1 Simple Example of a Timeline Specification

from the use of truly complex temporal properties and restrict themselves wisely to a smaller subset of formulae for which it is easier to develop an accurate intuition. The timeline tool appears to capture just that subset and not much more.

The timeline tool allows us to define a causal relation on the events that can occur in a distributed system. It also allows us to restrict the set of sequences that contain the specified events to smaller sets that satisfy additional constraints on specific, user-defined intervals on the timeline. That is, the timeline allows us to select the set of execution sequences that is of interest to us, and then define some correctness criteria for them. The correctness criteria are expressed in the form of events that either must or may not be present at specific points in the execution.

AN EXAMPLE

A first example of a timeline specification is shown in Figure 13.1. It defines two events and one constraint on a system execution. At the top of the drawing canvas is a grey horizontal bar that represents the timeline. Time progresses from left to right along the bar. At regular intervals, there are vertical blue lines, called marks, that intersect the timeline. The first mark, numbered 0, is colored grey and for reference only. The remaining marks indicate points on the timeline where events and constraints can be attached. Marks do *not* represent clock ticks, but are simply used to indicate points of interest during a possibly long system execution. In between two marks any number of execution steps could pass.

Events are attached directly to marks, and placed on the timeline itself. In Figure 13.1 there are two events: *offhook* and *onhook*. Constraints are placed underneath the timeline, spanning intervals between marks. One constraint, named *!dialtone*, is also shown. During verification the model checker attempts to match each system execution to the events that are placed on the timeline, provided that all corresponding constraints are satisfied. In Figure 13.1, no constraint applies to the occurrence of the first event, *offhook*, but as soon as it has occurred (immediately in the next state), the constraint *!dialtone* must be satisfied for the execution sequence to continue to match the timeline. If eventually, with the constraint still satisfied, the event *onhook* is seen, the timeline is completely matched. Reaching the end of a timeline by itself does not constitute an error condition. In this case, though, an error can be reported because the final event matched on the timeline is a *fail* event.

The requirement specified with the timeline in Figure 13.1 states that it is an error if an *offhook* event can be followed by an *onhook* event without a *dialtone* event occurring first.

For the purposes of property specification, the term *event* is somewhat of a misnomer. Both events and constraints are really conditions (state properties) that must be satisfied (i.e., that must hold) at specific points in an execution. In a PROMELA model, a state property is simply a boolean condition on global state variables that is said to be satisfied when it evaluates to *true*. This means that within the context of SPIN, an event occurrence is not necessarily an instantaneous phenomenon, but can persist for any amount of time. As a simple, though contrived, example, we could define the meaning of event *offhook* in Figure 13.1 to be *true*. This would mean that the event can be detected in any system state, and the event occurrence, as it were, persists forever. If the event persists forever, this merely means that it can be matched at any time during a system execution, so wherever we would place such an event on the timeline, it could always be matched. An event defined as *false*, on the other hand, could never be matched. If we define *onhook* as *false* in Figure 13.1, for instance, then the timeline specification could never be violated, not even if we also define the constraint *!dialtone* as *true*.

TYPES OF EVENTS
There are three different types of events that can be placed on a timeline.

- Regular events are labeled with the letter **e**. If a regular event occurs at a point in a system execution where its occurrence is specified, the execution matches the timeline. If it does not occur, the execution does not match. This does not mean that the execution is in error; it only means that the timeline property does not apply to the non-matching execution.
- Required events are labeled with the letter **r**. A required event can be matched in a system execution just like a regular event. This time, though, it is considered an error if the required event does not appear in the system execution at the point where it is specified, assuming of

course that all earlier events on the timeline were matched, and all applicable constraints are satisfied.

- Failure events are labeled with the letter **f**. Failure events record conditions that should never be true at the point in a system execution where they are specified. It is considered to be an error if a failure event is matched. It is not an error if a failure event does not occur (i.e., is skipped).

Constraints are specified underneath a timeline. Each constraint persists over specific intervals of the timeline. Constraints are denoted by horizontal lines below the main timeline. The start and the end point of each constraint is always associated with a specific timeline mark. Optionally, the constraint can include or exclude the events that are attached to the begin and end marks on the timeline.

There can be any number of events and any number of constraints in a timeline specification, but only one event can be attached to any single timeline mark.

DEFINING EVENTS

Events and constraints are represented by user-defined names on the timeline. The name can contain special characters, such as the negation symbols that we used in the name of the constraint in Figure 13.1. The names can be used directly to generate PROMELA `never` claims, but more typically one will want to define them more precisely to reflect the exact, perhaps more complex, conditions that must be satisfied for the corresponding event or constraint to apply. For the example in Figure 13.1, we can provide definitions for the events *offhook*, *onhook*, and *!dialtone*. The details of these definitions depend on the specifics of the verification model that is used to verify the timeline property. The timeline properties themselves are intended to be definable in a format that is largely model independent. For the final version of the model of a phone system that we develop in Chapter 14, the definitions of the events and the constraint used in Figure 13.1 could be as follows:

```
#define offhook        (last_sent == offhook)
#define onhook         (last_sent == onhook)
#define !dialtone      !(session_ss7@Dial)
```

where the dialtone constraint is specified with the help of a remote reference to the process of type `session_ss7`. There is no real difference in the way that events or constraints are defined. Both events and constraints define state properties: boolean conditions on the system state that can be evaluated to *true* or *false* in any reachable system state of the model. Only their relative placement on a timeline determine their precise semantics, that is, whether they are used to act as events to guide the matching of system executions, or as constraints to restrict the types of executions that can match.

MATCHING A TIMELINE

The verification of a timeline proceeds as follows. In the initial system state, the first mark on the timeline is designated as the *current mark*. At each execution step of the system, the verifier evaluates the event condition attached to the current mark on the timeline, and it evaluates all constraint conditions attached to intervals that intersect the blue vertical line for this mark. If the next event to be matched is a failure event, then the event that follows it on the timeline, if any, will also be evaluated. If a condition evaluates to *true*, the corresponding event or constraint is said to be *matched*; otherwise, it is not matched. The context now determines what happens next. There are several possibilities.

- The current execution sequence no longer matches the timeline specification because a constraint condition is now violated. The verification attempt for this sequence can be abandoned.
- If all constraint conditions are satisfied and the event condition at the current mark is matched and that event is a failure event, an error can be reported.

  If under the same conditions the event at the current mark is not a failure event, the current mark is advanced to the next mark on the timeline, and the verification is repeated after the next system execution step is performed.
- If all constraint conditions are matched, but the event condition is not matched and the current event is not a failure event, then the current mark remains where it is, and the verification is repeated after the next system execution step is performed.

  If under the same conditions the current event is a failure event, and the next event on the timeline, if any, is matched, the current mark moves to the event that follows that next event, and the verification is repeated after the next system execution step is performed. The timeline tool does not permit two adjacent failure events on a timeline, so an event that follows a failure event is either a regular or a required event.
- If the end of an execution sequence is reached, but the end of the timeline has not been reached *and* the event at the current mark of the timeline is a required event, an error can be reported for this execution sequence.

If the end of a timeline is reached before the end of an execution, the verification effort can also be abandoned, since no further errors are possible.

AUTOMATA DEFINITIONS

The Büchi automaton that corresponds to the timeline specification from Figure 13.1 is shown in Figure 13.2. The automaton has three states, one of which, state s_2, is accepting. The initial state of the automaton is s_0.

The automaton can be generated automatically by the timeline editor either in graphical form, as shown in Figure 13.2, or in PROMELA syntax as a never

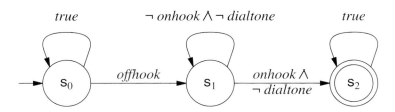

Figure 13.2 Büchi Automaton for the Timeline in Figure 13.1

---

claim. The PROMELA version of the automaton is shown in Figure 13.3.

The second state of the automaton can only be reached if an *offhook* event occurs, which is followed by an interval in which *dialtone* remains *false* and no *onhook* event is detected. Then the transition to the accepting can be made if an *onhook* event occurs, still in the absence of a *dialtone* event. Once the accepting state is reached, the remainder of the run is automatically accepted due to the self-loop on *true* in state s_2: the violation has already occured and can no longer be undone by any future event.

```
#define p1 (last_sent == offhook)      /* offhook */
#define p2 (last_sent == onhook)       /* onhook */
#define p3 !(session_ss7@Dial)         /* !dialtone */

never {
S0:     do
        :: p1 -> goto S1
        :: true
        od;
acceptF0:
        assert(0);
        0;
S1:     do
        :: p2 && p3 -> goto acceptF0
        :: !p2 && p3
        od;
}
```

Figure 13.3 Never Claim for the Timeline in Figure 13.1

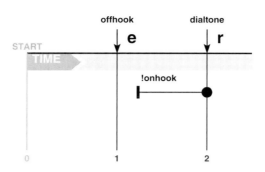

Figure 13.4 Variation on the Timeline from Figure 13.1

CONSTRAINTS

A constraint interval always has one of four possible forms, depending on whether the start and the end points of the interval are included or excluded from the constraint. By adding constraints, we never really modify the structure of the Büchi automaton, or of the PROMELA never claim, that corresponds to a timeline. Added constraints can only restrict the number of sequences that can be matched at each step of the timeline, by adding conditionals to the transitions of an existing automaton structure.

VARIATIONS ON A THEME

We have not said much about the rationale for the property that is expressed by the timeline specification from Figure 13.1. Informally, the property states that it would be an error if there can exist execution sequences in which an *offhook* event can be followed by an *onhook* event, without *dialtone* being generated in the interim. It may of course be possible for a telephone subscriber to generate a fast *offhook–onhook* sequence, but we may want to use the timeline specification to inspect precisely what happens under these circumstances by generating the matching execution scenarios.

We can also attempt to express this property in a different way. There can be small differences in semantics, depending on whether conditions are used as events or as constraints. As a small example, consider the variant of this property that is shown in Figure 13.4. We have switched the roles of *dialtone* and *onhook* as event and constraint here, compared to Figure 13.1.

At first blush, this timeline appears to express the same property, this time labeling the appearance of *dialtone* after an *offhook* as a required event, and the absence of *onhook* as a constraint.

We can see more clearly what is required to match this timeline by inspecting

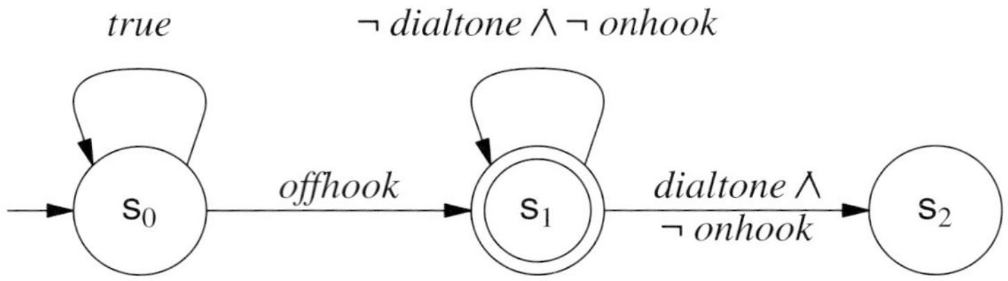

Figure 13.5 Büchi Automaton for the Timeline in Figure 13.4

the corresponding automaton structure, as shown in Figure 13.5.

This time, state s_1 is the Büchi accepting state. The only way for an execution sequence to trigger an error would be if it contained an *offhook* event that is never followed by either an *onhook* or a *dialtone* event. When state s_2 is reached instead, the requirement expressed by the timeline specification is satisfied, and no further errors can result. This means that, technically, state s_2, and the transition that leads to it, is redundant and could be omitted from the automaton without changing its meaning.

Assume now that there were an execution of the switch system we intended to verify that would occasionally fail to give *dialtone* after an *offhook*. Very likely, both in a verification model and in real life, the unlucky subscriber who encounters this behavior will not remain *offhook* forever, but eventually return the phone *onhook*. This means that the error, if present, would not be caught by this specific variant of the specification, unless we explicitly model behavior where the subscriber can permanently keep the phone off-hook.

In reality, the dialtone property for a telephone switch has both a functional and a real-time performance requirement. Dialtone should not only be generated after an *offhook* event, but on average also follow that event in 0.6 seconds. In 98.5% of the cases, further, dialtone should appear within 3 seconds after an *offhook*. Since timelines and SPIN models target the verification of only functional system requirements, the real-time performance aspects of requirements cannot be captured or checked in this way.

TIMELINES WITH ONE EVENT
There are only two useful types of timelines that contain one single event. A timeline with a single regular event is not of use, since it does not express any requirement on an execution. That is, the timeline might match an execution that contains the event that is specified, but no matching execution can ever be flagged as erroneous in this way. The two smallest timelines of interest are the ones that contain either a single required or a single fail event, as

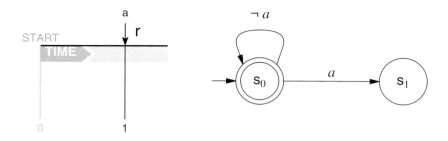

Figure 13.6 Timeline and Automaton for a Single Required Event

illustrated in Figures 13.6 and 13.7.

The timeline specification from Figure 13.6 traps a system execution error in the same cases as the LTL formula that we would use to express the violation of a system invariant property

$$\Box\neg\, a \;=\; \neg\, \Diamond\, a.$$

The timeline specification in Figure 13.7, similarly, traps a system execution error in the same cases as the property

$$\Diamond\, a.$$

These first two properties can be seen as duals: one requires the absence of an event, and the other requires at least one occurrence.

TIMELINES WITH MULTIPLE EVENTS

With two events, we can form five different types of timelines. Each of the two events can be one of three different types, but clearly four of the nine possible combinations are not meaningful. A timeline with two regular events, for instance, cannot fail any system execution to which it is applied. Further, if the last event of the timeline is a regular event, then that event would always be redundant. And, finally, a timeline with two fail events that are placed on adjacent marks has no reasonable semantics, and is therefore rejected by the timeline tool. (In this case the conditions for the two fail events should probably be combined into a single condition.)

One of the five remaining meaningful combinations of two events is reproduced, with the corresponding automaton, in Figure 13.8.

The timeline property from Figure 13.8 is similar, though not identical, to the LTL response property:

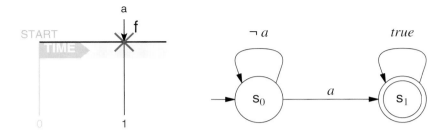

Figure 13.7 Timeline and Automaton for a Single Fail Event

$$\neg(a \rightarrow \lozenge b).$$

Note that the LTL property requires condition a to hold at the start of each sequence, since it is not preceded by a temporal operator. The timeline specification does not have that requirement. The LTL formula that precisely captures the timeline property from Figure 13.8 is somewhat more complex, namely:

$$\neg (\square (a \rightarrow X(\lozenge b))).$$

The example timeline in Figure 13.9 contains three of the five possible combinations of two events.

We have labeled the four events on this timeline with letters from a to d, and added a constraint named z. A specification of this type could be used to check one of the requirements for the implementation of call waiting on telephone lines. Event a could then represent the occurrence of an incoming call on a line that is currently involved in a stable two-party call. The requirements state that with the call waiting feature in effect, the subscriber should at this point receive a call waiting alert tone, which would correspond to event b. Provided that none of the parties involved abandon their call attempts, or take any other action (which can be captured in constraint z), the first alert tone must be followed by a second such tone, but there may not be more than these two alerts. So, events b, c, and d would in this application of the timeline all represent the appearance of a call waiting alert tone, which is required twice, but erroneous if issued three or more times. The Büchi automaton that corresponds to the timeline from Figure 13.9 is shown in Figure 13.10. There are three accepting states corresponding to the three different ways in which this timeline specification could be violated: either one of the two required events

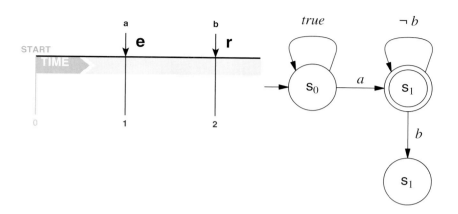

Figure 13.8 Timeline and Automaton for a Regular and a Required Event

could fail to show up, or the failure event could appear when it should not.

Another type of timeline, with the remaining two possible event combinations, is shown in Figure 13.11. This time, a failure event precedes a required event, indicating that after the optional occurrence of the event named a, the occurrence of c is required, and the occurrence of b forbidden.

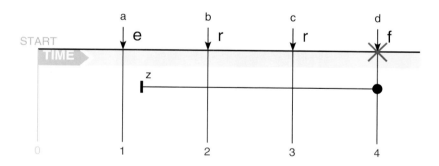

Figure 13.9 A More Complex Timeline Specification

A timeline specification of this type may be used to check the property that *offhook* and *onhook* events must always alternate. We can achieve this by

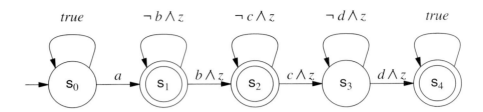

Figure 13.10 Büchi Automaton for the Timeline in Figure 13.9

defining events a and b both as *offhook* events, and event c as an *onhook* event. Constraint z then can restrict the executions that are considered for compliance with this requirement to those where no *onhook* event appears in the interval between a and b.

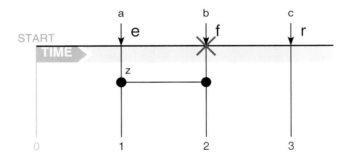

Figure 13.11 Timeline Specification with Three Events

The Büchi automaton corresponding to the timeline from Figure 13.11 is shown in Figure 13.12. The automaton has four states, two of which are accepting. Note again that the automaton is not necessarily completely speci-fied. There is, for instance, no transition out of state s_1 if simultaneously ($\neg z \wedge \neg c$). In this case, we have just passed the first step of the timeline, and wait for either c or b to occur while z remains *true*. If neither event c nor event b occurs in a given run and constraint z is no longer satisfied, the automaton can stop tracking the run, since no violation matching the timeline is possible in the remainder of this execution.

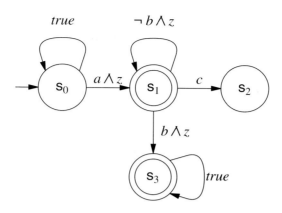

Figure 13.12 Büchi Automaton for the Timeline in Figure 13.11

THE LINK WITH LTL

It is not hard to show that for every timeline specification there exists a formalization in LTL, but the reverse is not necessarily true. Timelines are strictly less expressive than linear temporal logic, and therefore they are also less expressive than ω-automata (which includes PROMELA never claims).

Consider, for instance, the LTL formula: $!(a \ \mathbf{U} \ b)$. The positive version of this requirement would match any run in which a remains *true* at least until the first moment that b becomes *true*. If b is already *true* in the initial state, the requirement is immediately satisfied. The negation of the requirement matches any run where the positive version is violated. This means that in such a run b cannot be *true* in the initial state, and a must become *false* before b becomes *true*.

This seems like a requirement that we should be able to express in a timeline specification. The timeline we may draw to capture it is shown, together with the corresponding Büchi automaton, in Figure 13.13. We are slightly pushing the paradigm of timeline events here, by putting a negation sign before the name of a timeline event. Doing so, we exploit the fact that at least in the context of SPIN an event is really a state property that can be evaluated to *true* or *false* in every reachable system state.

Unfortunately, the automaton that is generated does not precisely capture the LTL semantics. The correct Büchi automaton, generated with SPIN's built-in LTL converter, is shown in Figure 13.14. It closely resembles the timeline automaton from Figure 13.13, but it is not identical. In the correct version, the self-loop on state s_0 requires only b to be false, but makes no requirement on the value of a.

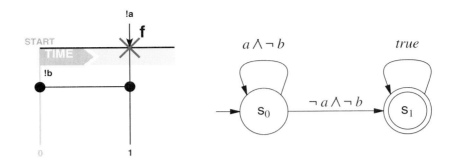

Figure 13.13 Attempt to Express the LTL property !(a **U** b)

In the timeline from Figure 13.13 we used a negation sign in front of an event symbol, in an attempt to capture the semantics of the LTL until property. If we go a little further and use arbitrary boolean expressions as place holders for events, we can create many more types of timelines. As just one example, consider the timeline that is shown in Figure 13.15. Although it looks very different from the timeline from Figure 13.13, it turns out to define precisely the same property.

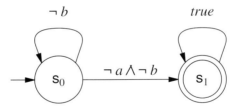

Figure 13.14 The Correct Büchi Automaton for LTL property !(a **U** b)

Fortunately it is not hard to check and compare the semantics of timeline descriptions by using the timeline editing tool to generate the corresponding Büchi automata. The automaton that corresponds to the timeline from Figure 13.15, for instance, is identical to the one shown in Figure 13.13. It can be very hard, though, to reason backwards, and to find the proper timeline speci-fication for a given Büchi automaton, such as the one from Figure 13.14, assuming, of course, that one exists.

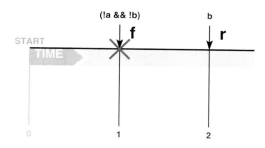

Figure 13.15 A Variant of the Timeline in Figure 13.13

Timelines can easily be used to express system safety properties, but they can only express a small class of liveness properties. The only mechanism from timeline specification that we can use to express liveness properties is the notation for a required event. The relatively simple visual formalism from a timeline specification, though, appears to suffice for handeling most cases of practical interest in systems verification.

An often heard criticism of LTL is, for instance, that the true meaning of formulae with more than two or three temporal operators can be very difficult to understand, even by experts. Similarly, accurately capturing the correct semantics of a complex temporal property in an LTL formula can be a daunting task. Some interpret this to mean that we should shy away from the complex formulae in systems verification. In this respect, the lack of expressiveness of the timeline editing tool may well be regarded a strength.

> *"Mathematicians are like Frenchmen: whenever you say*
> *something to them they translate it into their own language,*
> *and at once it is something entirely different."*
> *J.W. von Goethe (1749–1832)*

BIBLIOGRAPHIC NOTES

Several other visual formalisms for specifying systems and properties have been proposed over the years. The best known such proposals include Harel [1987] for systems specifications, and Schlor and Damm [1993] or Dillon, Kutty, Moser, et al. [1994] for property specication.

An alternative method to make it easier to capture complex logic properties as formulae in temporal logic is pursued by Matt Dwyer and colleagues at Kansas State University. Dwyer, Avrunin, and Corbett [1999] describe the design and construction of a comprehensive patterns database with formula templates for the most commonly occuring types of correctness properties.

Information for downloading the timeline editor, which is freely available from Bell Labs, can be found in Appendix D.

A VERIFICATION MODEL
OF A TELEPHONE SWITCH **14**

"For when the actual facts show a thing to be impossible
we are instantly convinced that it is so."
(Polybius, The Histories, Book XII)

When faced with a software verification problem, it is often tempting to build
a model that is as close to reality as possible. If an implementation exists, the
temptation is to duplicate its functionality as faithfully as possible within the
language of the model checker used. If only a design exists, the attempt can
be to build a trial implementation for verification purposes. The purpose of
this chapter is to show that this is not the best approach. The proper management of computational complexity is a key issue in all but the simplest applications of formal verification, and more often than not determines the success
or failure of the attempt.

GENERAL APPROACH
The intuitive approach to software verification sketched here should be con-
trasted with the standard approach that one routinely takes in physics or mathematics. When one wants to analyze, say, the structural integrity of a bridge
or a building, one does not start with a description of the structure that is as
close to reality as possible. The best approach is to start with the simplest
possible description of the structure that can capture the essential characteristics that must be analyzed. The reason is proper management of complexity.
Even when mathematics is sufficiently expressive to describe reality in its
minutest details, doing so would not only be a laborious task, it would not
help in the least to simplify analytical chores. Computations on highly
detailed descriptions, by man or by machine, can become so complex and
time-consuming that the end results, if obtainable at all, become subject to
doubt.

KEEP IT SIMPLE

The purpose of a model checking exercise is not to build and analyze verification models that are as detailed as possible: it is the opposite. The best we can do is to find and build the *smallest sufficient model* to describe the essential elements of a system design. To construct that model, we attempt to simplify the problem, eliminating elements that have no direct bearing on the characteristics we want to verify. There is no universal recipe for how this can be accomplished. What works best is almost always problem dependent. Sometimes the smallest sufficient model can be constructed by generalizing a problem, and sometimes it requires specializing a problem.

The hardest problem of a verification project is to get started. The best advice that can be given here is to make a deliberate effort to start *simple*, perhaps even with a coarser abstraction than may seem justified. Then slowly evolve the verification model, and the corresponding correctness requirements, until sufficient confidence in the correctness of the design has been established. It is only reasonable to invest considerable resources into a verification at the very last phase of a project—to perform a final and thorough check to make sure that nothing of importance was missed in the earlier steps.

Throughout most of a verification effort, a tool like SPIN should be used in a mode where one can get instantaneous feedback about relatively simple descriptions of the design problem. Slowly, the description can become more refined, and as our confidence in its accuracy grows, our willingness to spend a little more time on each verification task can grow.

MANAGING COMPLEXITY

On a reasonably modern machine SPIN verifications should not consume more than a few seconds during the initial development of a verification model, and no more than a few minutes during the latter stages of verification. In very rare cases it may be necessary to spend up to a portion of an hour on a thorough verification in a *final check*, but this should be a very rare exception indeed.

To summarize this approach:[1]

- Start simple. Try to find the smallest sufficient model that can express something interesting about the problem you are trying to solve.
  Check the initial model thoroughly. More often than not you will be surprised that what you believed to be trivially true in the simplified world is not true at all. The typical reasons are small misjudgements in the development of the model, or subtle misunderstanding in the formulation of the properties checked for.

---

1. This approach to verification was first articulated by Prof. Jay Strother Moore from the University of Texas at Austin, when describing the proper use of interactive theorem provers.

- Evolve the model and, if possible, its correctness properties step by step. Keep each incremental step small, and repeat the checks at each step. Stop when the complexity grows too rapidly and rethink the last change made. Try to find alternatives that can reduce the complexity. The numbers of asynchronously executing processes and the size of message buffers are the two most important sources of complexity in SPIN models, so try to keep these as small as possible at first.
- Keep the verification tool on a short leash. Do not spend more than a few seconds on initial verifications until you have developed sufficient confidence that what you ask the tool to verify is actually what you are interested in.

To illustrate this approach, we will discuss the development of a SPIN verification model for a significant fragment of an important and very well-known type of distributed system: a telephone switch. The problem context is familiar enough that many have attempted to build models like the ones we will discuss. Many of these attempts have ended in either a lost battle with the fundamental complexity of the underlying problem, or the adoption of simplifying but rather unrealistic assumptions about how a phone system actually works. We will try to do better here.

MODELING A SWITCH

The telephone system is so familiar to us that few of us realize that the underlying behavior can be phenomenally complex. Much of this complexity is due to the addition of feature behavior. Features such as three-way calling, call waiting, and call forwarding can interact in often unforeseen ways. Making sure that all such possible interactions comply with the relevant standards is a non-trivial task, even for experts. The problem is still quite non-trivial if we trim it down to its bare essence: providing support for only basic POTS (Plain Old Telephone Service) calls.

The normal dialogue for a POTS call looks simple. After taking the receiver off-hook, the subscriber hears a dial tone. This is the signal for the subscriber to dial a number. If that number is valid, the subscriber can expect to hear either a ring tone or a busy tone. If the number is invalid, an error tone or a busy tone will be the result. After a while, a ring tone can disappear when the call is answered, or it can turn into a busy tone when the maximum ring-time is exceeded. At any time during this sequence, the subscriber can abort the call and return the phone on-hook. This scenario is illustrated in Figure 14.1.

Before reading on, put this book aside and attempt to build a small SPIN model that captures the interactions between a subscriber and a switch, as just sketched, restricting to outgoing calls for simplicity. Then do some verifications with SPIN to discover all the things that can go wrong with your model.

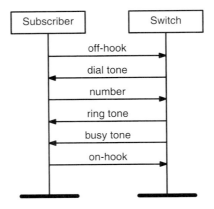

Figure 14.1 Typical Scenario for a POTS Call

SUBSCRIBER MODEL

To develop a model that can reproduce the behavior from Figure 14.1, we will minimally have to model two entities: subscribers and switches. Because our focus will be on verifying properties of switch behavior, we should try to keep the number of assumptions we make about the behavior of subscribers as small as possible. We do not need to know, for instance, when or why subscribers place calls, why they hang up or why they sometimes fail to hang up. All we need to know about subscribers is what they can do that is *visible to the switch*. The set of things that a subscriber can do that is visible to the switch is blissfully small: the subscriber can lift the receiver off-hook, or return it on-hook. In between those two actions the subscriber can dial digits and flash the hook[2], and that is all we need to know.

Let us first consider the sample subscriber model from Figure 14.2. It tries to capture the behavior of a fairly reasonable subscriber, responding to the tones that may be generated by the switch. Some of these tones are generated in response to subscriber actions and some can be generated seemingly spontaneously by the switch, for instance, to alert the subscriber to incoming calls.

It is important to realize at this point that the subscriber model from Figure 14.2, though quite persuasive, is inadequate for our verification task. For our current purpose, the subscriber model is meant to capture the *minimal* set of

---

2. A flash-hook signal can have special significance for certain call features, such as, for instance, three-way calling. We will discuss this feature later in the chapter.

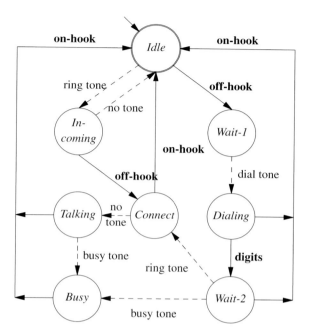

Figure 14.2 Initial Behavior Model of a POTS Subscriber
(Solid arrows refer to events triggered by the subscriber, and
dashed arrows refer to signals that are generated by the switch.)

assumptions that the switch can make about subscriber actions. In this context, then, it is unnecessary and even unwarranted to assume that the subscriber will always behave reasonably. Fortunately, many potentially unreasonable behaviors of the subscriber are in fact physically impossible. The subscriber cannot, for instance, generate two off-hook signals in a row without an intervening on-hook, and the subscriber cannot dial digits with the phone on-hook. There is, however, no reason to assume that the subscriber will always wait for a dial tone before aborting a call attempt, as Figure 14.2 seems to indicate. In fact, a subscriber may well ignore all tones from the switch in deciding what to do next.

We can modify the model from Figure 14.2 to reflect these assumptions by combining all states that are connected by transitions that correspond to the generation of audible tones in the switch (i.e., all dashed arrows). This produces the three-state model shown on the left in Figure 14.3.

The subscriber can either go off-hook without dialing digits (e.g., to accept an incoming call), or the subscriber can go off-hook with the intent to dial digits

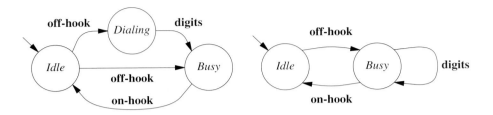

Figure 14.3 Two Alternative Subscriber Models

(e.g., to initiate an outgoing call). But in the new model the difference between incoming and outgoing calls is no longer visible. We can therefore go one step further and combine also the two states that can be reached by the subscriber going off-hook into one single state. This leads to the two-state model shown on the right in Figure 14.3.

This last model clearly admits more behaviors than the earlier two models. It allows, for instance, for the scenario in which the subscriber keeps dialing digits while off-hook, as indeed a real subscriber might do. In the first two models this behavior was not represented, as a result of the assumptions about reasonable behavior that was made in the creation of the first model in Figure 14.2. There are several other such assumptions in Figure 14.2 that are not present in the two-state model from Figure 14.3.

We will use the two-state subscriber model as the simplest sufficient model of subscriber behavior. This model is readily expressed in PROMELA. To do so, however, we need to decide how to model the exchange of signals between subscriber and switch. In the simple model, the information flows only from the subscriber to the switch in the form of off-hook, on-hook, and digit signals. The telephone switch is designed to be much faster than a human subscriber, so it is safe to assume that the switch will always be ready to receive any signal sent by its subscribers. The simplest way to formalize this in PROMELA is with the use of a global rendezvous port. We will call the port over which a subscriber can reach the switch *tpc*, as a shorthand for *t*he *p*hone *c*ompany. This resulting subscriber model expressed in PROMELA is shown in Figure 14.4.

In constructing the model we will initially restrict our attention to modeling the interactions of a single subscriber with a single local switch. At this stage, nothing of interest is gained by adding multiple subscribers into the model: the switch looks at each subscriber line independently. We can significantly reduce the complexity of verification by representing the possible interactions

```
mtype = { offhook, digits, onhook };

chan tpc = [0] of { mtype };

active proctype subscriber()
{
Idle:      tpc!offhook;

Busy:      if
           :: tpc!digits -> goto Busy
           :: tpc!onhook -> goto Idle
           fi
}
```

Figure 14.4 Two-State Model of Subscriber

of subscribers in a slightly more abstract way. An outgoing call attempt of our subscriber of interest may succeed or fail, for instance, depending on the state of the network and the state of other subscribers. All we are interested in is the effects of success or failure, not in the precise circumstances of success or failure. We will illustrate these notions in more detail shortly.

SWITCH MODEL

The real complexity inevitably comes in the definition of the switch behavior, so it is again important to keep things as simple as possible at first. We will develop a switch model here for the handling of outgoing calls only, reducing the number of issues that we will have to confront somewhat. The interplay of incoming and outgoing calls can be subtle, but it can be studied separately once we have confidence in the basic model we are developing here.

A first-cut model of the switch behavior can then be formalized in PROMELA, in a simple state-oriented format, as shown in Figure 14.5. Because the audible tones are generated more for information than to restrict the subscriber actions, they appear in this model as print statements only. In particular, these signals need not be recorded in state variables.

In this model, the success or failure of an outgoing call is represented as a non-deterministic choice between the generation of a ring tone or a busy tone signal in state named *Wait*. The state named *Connect* represents the situation where call setup is completed. The call can now end either by the remote subscriber (which is not explicitly present in the model here) hanging up first, or the local subscriber hanging up first. In the first case, a busy tone will be generated; in the latter case no tone is generated. The two possibilities are again formalized with the help of a non-deterministic choice, indicating that both

```
active proctype switch()    /* outgoing calls only */
{
Idle:
        if
        :: tpc?offhook ->
                printf("dial tone\n"); goto Dial
        fi;
Dial:
        if
        :: tpc?digits ->
                printf("no tone\n"); goto Wait
        :: tpc?onhook ->
                printf("no tone\n"); goto Idle
        fi;
Wait:
        if
        :: printf("ring tone\n") -> goto Connect;
        :: printf("busy tone\n") -> goto Busy
        fi;
Connect:
        if
        :: printf("busy tone\n") -> goto Busy
        :: printf("no tone\n")    -> goto Busy
        fi;
Busy:
        if
        :: tpc?onhook ->
                printf("no tone\n"); goto Idle
        fi
}
```

Figure 14.5 Simple Switch Model for Outgoing Calls

scenarios are possible.

There is no interaction with remote switches in the network represented in this model just yet. We will add that shortly, after we can convince ourselves that the simpler model is on track. As a first check, we can perform some short simulation runs, limiting the run to twenty steps. Such simulations show sensible call scenarios for this model, for instance, as follows:

```
$ spin -c -u20 version1
proc 0 = subscriber
proc 1 = switch
q\p    0    1
  1    tpc!offhook
  1    .    tpc?offhook
```

```
                dialtone
    1    tpc!digits
    1    .    tpc?digits
                notone
                ringtone
                notone
    1    tpc!onhook
    1    .    tpc?onhook
                notone
    1    tpc!offhook
    1    .    tpc?offhook
                dialtone
    1    tpc!digits
    1    .    tpc?digits
                notone
                ringtone
-------------
depth-limit (-u20 steps) reached
-------------
final state:
-------------
#processes: 2
 20:    proc  1 (switch) line  29 "version1" (state 12)
 20:    proc  0 (subscriber) line  11 "version1" (state 6)
2 processes created
```

Next, we perform a verification. The verification run confirms that there are no major problems and that the behavior is still exceedingly simple, with just nine reachable, and no unreachable states. The results are as follows:

```
$ spin -a version1
$ cc -o pan pan.c
$ ./pan
(Spin Version 4.0.7 -- 1 August 2003)
        + Partial Order Reduction

Full statespace search for:
        never claim             - (none specified)
        assertion violations    +
        acceptance    cycles    - (not selected)
        invalid end states      +

State-vector 24 byte, depth reached 11, errors: 0
       9 states, stored
       6 states, matched
      15 transitions (= stored+matched)
       0 atomic steps
hash conflicts: 0 (resolved)
(max size 2^18 states)

1.573   memory usage (Mbyte)
```

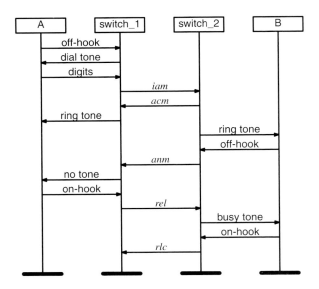

Figure 14.6 SS7 Scenario for Call Setup

```
unreached in proctype subscriber
        line 15, state 8, "-end-"
        (1 of 8 states)
unreached in proctype switch
        line 40, state 29, "-end-"
        (1 of 29 states)
```

This puts us in a good position to extend our first model to a slightly more realistic one by adding the possible interactions with remote switches.

REMOTE SWITCHES
So far, our switch model decides internally whether or not a call attempt failed or succeeded by making a non-deterministic decision on the generation of either a ring tone or a busy tone. We will now add a little more of the dialogue that can actually take place inside the switch during the setup of an outgoing call. In most cases the switch will have to interact with remote switches in the network to determine if the called number and the network resources that are needed to connect to it are available. The protocol for that is known as Signaling System 7, SS7 for short. A typical SS7 dialogue is shown in Figure 14.6.

The first message sent by the local switch to a remote switch is called the initial address message, *iam*. The message triggers an address complete message, *acm*, in response. When the call is answered, an answer message, *anm*, follows. The teardown phase is started with a release, *rel*, request, which is acknowledged with a release confirmation, *rlc*.

To model this interaction we have to add a model of a remote switch. Note that we do not need to model the behavior of remote subscribers directly, because their behavior is not directly visible to the local switch. The remote subscribers are hidden behind remote switches and all negotiations about the setup and teardown of calls happen only through the intermediation of the remote switches. Also note that even though every switch acts both as a local switch to its local subscribers and as a remote switch to the rest of the network, it would be overkill to clone the local switch behavior to derive remote switch behavior. Doing so has the unintended consequence of making the detailed internal behavior of remote switches and remote subscribers visible to the verifier, which can significantly increase verification complexity.

Let us first extend the model of the local switch with the new SS7 message exchanges. This leads to the extended switch model shown in Figure 14.7.

We have introduced two new states, called *Zombie1* and *Zombie2*, to represent different intermediate phases of a call teardown which now requires interaction with the remote switch.

The next step is to add a matching model for a remote switch, handling incoming request for connections. The switch can reject calls by immediately sending the *rel* message in response to the initial *iam* message, to signify that it is busy or otherwise unable to handle the request. The *rel* message is always acknowledged with an *rlc* confirmation.

An outline for the behavior of a remote switch is shown in Figure 14.8. Message names in bold indicate incoming messages; the remaining messages are the responses. Note that there can be a race between the two subscribers for the teardown of the call. Messages between local and remote switches travel over the network and will generally incur some latency, so rather than a rendezvous port we have used a buffered message channel, though with a very small buffer capacity of one message to keep things simple.

The outline from Figure 14.8 is represented in PROMELA in Figure 14.9.

The verifier is content with these extensions, reporting the following result:

```
$ spin -a version2
$ cc -o pan.c
$ ./pan
(Spin Version 4.0.7 -- 1 August 2003)
      + Partial Order Reduction
```

```
mtype = { iam, acm, anm, rel, rlc }; /* ss7 messages */

chan rms = [1] of { mtype }; /* channel to remote switch */

active proctype switch_ss7()
{
Idle:
    if
    :: tpc?offhook -> printf("dial tone\n"); goto Dial
    fi;
Dial:
    if
    :: tpc?digits -> printf("no tone\n"); rms!iam;
                     goto Wait
    :: tpc?onhook -> printf("no tone\n"); goto Idle
    fi;
Wait:
    if
    :: tpc?acm -> printf("ring tone\n"); goto Wait
    :: tpc?anm -> printf("no tone\n"); goto Connect
    :: tpc?rel -> rms!rlc; printf("busy tone\n");
                  goto Busy
    :: tpc?onhook -> rms!rel; goto Zombie1
    fi;
Connect:
    if
    :: tpc?rel -> rms!rlc; printf("busy tone\n"); goto Busy
    :: tpc?onhook -> rms!rel; goto Zombie1
    fi;
Busy:           /* off-hook, waiting for on-hook */
    if
    :: tpc?onhook -> printf("no tone\n"); goto Idle
    fi;

Zombie1:        /* on-hook, waiting for rlc */
    if
    :: tpc?rel -> rms!rlc; goto Zombie1
    :: tpc?rlc -> goto Idle
    :: tpc?offhook -> goto Zombie2
    fi;
Zombie2:        /* off-hook, waiting for rlc */
    if
    :: tpc?rel -> rms!rlc; goto Zombie2
    :: tpc?rlc -> goto Busy
    :: tpc?onhook -> goto Zombie1
    fi
}
```

Figure 14.7 Extended Local Switch Model

```
Full statespace search for:
        never claim                    - (none specified)

        assertion violations      +
        acceptance    cycles      - (not selected)
        invalid end states        +

State-vector 32 byte, depth reached 30, errors: 0
        52 states, stored
        36 states, matched
        88 transitions (= stored+matched)
         0 atomic steps
hash conflicts: 0 (resolved)
(max size 2^18 states)


1.573   memory usage (Mbyte)


unreached in proctype subscriber
        line 15, state 8, "-end-"
        (1 of 8 states)
unreached in proctype switch_ss7
        line 87, state 62, "-end-"
        (1 of 62 states)
unreached in proctype remote_ss7
        line 125, state 41, "-end-"
        (1 of 41 states)
```

The number of reachable states has increased, but we have succeeded in keeping the model small. We may also be curious to see what the effect is of a more generous allotment of buffer capacity in the message channel between local and remote switches. If we change the number of slots in the buffer from one to two, the number of reachable system states increases to 60, implying that this change does indeed allow for some new behaviors. A further increase to three slots increases the number of states to 64, which remains unaffected by any further increases.

ADDING FEATURES

At this point we can improve the model by adding a treatment for incoming calls that originate at remote switches. We could also consider extending the model to handle multiple subscribers or end-to-end connections. Instead, we will try extend the switch behavior in a slightly more interesting way—by adding a call processing feature.

THREE-WAY CALLING

We would like to add the capability for a subscriber to flash the hook after a call has been set up (i.e., quickly going on-hook and back off-hook) to place the currently connected party on hold and get a new dial tone. The subscriber should then be able to dial a new call, and establish a three-way connection by

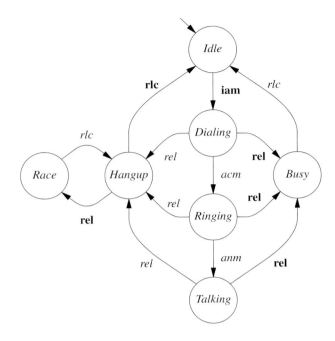

Figure 14.8 POTS Interface Model for a Remote Switch

flashing the hook a second time. A third flash of the hook should terminate the three-way connection by dropping the last dialed party. We will assume that an on-hook from the originating subscriber during the call terminates all connections, independent of the current state of the call.

The addition of feature behavior like this to an existing call model often introduces unexpected types of interaction between the existing, trusted behavior and the newly added behavior. Being able to check these types of extensions with small verification models can therefore be of considerable value.

The switch must now be able to manage two connections for the same subscriber, so we will need to extend the model to have at least two instantiations of the model for a remote switch. We want to keep the control of the different connections separate, to make sure that we do not unnecessarily complicate the behavior of the switch. We can accomplish this by introducing a subscriber line session manager process that can interact with multiple session handlers. The manager keeps track of which session is active and shuttles the messages between sessions and subscriber. The various sessions are unaware of each other's existence and can behave just like in the single connection model from before.

```
active proctype remote_ss7()
{
Idle:
        if
        :: rms?iam -> goto Dialing
        fi;
Dialing:
        if
        :: tpc!acm -> goto Ringing
        :: tpc!rel -> goto Hangup
        :: rms?rel -> goto Busy
        fi;
Ringing:
        if
        :: tpc!anm -> goto Talking
        :: tpc!rel -> goto Hangup
        :: rms?rel -> goto Busy
        fi;
Talking:
        if
        :: tpc!rel -> goto Hangup
        :: rms?rel -> goto Busy
        fi;
Hangup:
        if
        :: rms?rlc -> goto Idle
        :: rms?rel -> goto Race
        fi;
Busy:
        if
        :: rms?rlc -> goto Idle
        fi;

Race:   if
        :: tpc!rlc -> goto Busy
        fi
}
```

Figure 14.9 PROMELA Model of Visible Behavior of Remote Switch

A first change that we have to make to accomplish all this in the last model is
to change the role of the switch process into that of a session manager. Before
making any other changes to support the three-way calling feature directly, we
will make and check this change. Figure 14.10 shows the new version of the
switch process.

In this version of the switch process we have used a slightly different
approach to the representation of the call states. Instead of using labeled

```
chan sess = [0] of { mtype };

mtype = { idle, busy }; /* call states */
mtype s_state = idle;

active proctype switch()
{        mtype x;

         atomic
         {       run session_ss7(sess, rms);
                 run remote_ss7(rms, sess)
         };
end:     do
         :: tpc?x ->
                 if
                 :: x == offhook ->
                         assert(s_state == idle);
                         s_state = busy
                 :: x == onhook ->
                         assert(s_state == busy);
                         s_state = idle
                 :: else
                 fi;
                 sess!x  /* forward message */
         od
}
```

Figure 14.10 Switch Session Management Structure

control-flow points (as in Figure 14.9), we use `mtype` variables to store the state information.

The switch process now creates instantiations for a single session handler process and a remote switch, passing the proper message channels for input and output as parameters to these processes. We have added a channel named *sess* to be used by the switch process to pass call control messages from the subscriber to the local session handler. Since this is a local interaction within the switch, we can safely make this a rendezvous port again. We have also added a global variable *s_state* to record the call state of the session process, in so far as it is known by the session manager.

The remote switch process remains as it was in Figure 14.9, except that it is now instantiated dynamically by the switch process and sends to and receives from message channels that are passed to it by the switch process via parameters. Similarly, the session handler process remains as it was in Figure 14.7, except for the the name change from *switch* to *session_ss7* and the use of message channels that are passed via parameters.

In checking this version of the model, we would expect the number of reachable states to increase somewhat, because of the addition of the session management process, but there should be no change in functionality. Some initial simulation runs appear to confirm the latter. Running the verification produces the following result:

```
$ spin -a version3
$ cc -o pan pan.c
$ ./pan
pan: invalid end state (at depth 41)
pan: wrote version3.trail
(Spin Version 4.0.7 -- 1 August 2003)
Warning: Search not completed
        + Partial Order Reduction

Full statespace search for:
        never claim             - (none specified)
        assertion violations    +
        acceptance   cycles     - (not selected)
        invalid end states      +

State-vector 52 byte, depth reached 42, errors: 1
        30 states, stored
         0 states, matched
        30 transitions (= stored+matched)
         1 atomic steps
hash conflicts: 0 (resolved)
(max size 2^18 states)

1.573   memory usage (Mbyte)
```

The error reported here reveals one of a series of problems with the new model. Seven of these problems are cases of incompleteness. We find that in the new session handler, based on the version in Figure 14.7, the *digits* message can be received in states *Wait*, *Connect*, *Busy*, and *Zombie2*, where the message is currently not expected. Similarly, the *acm* and *anm* messages can arrive in state *Zombie1*. Further, we now also detect an incompleteness in the remote switch process, which we based on Figure 14.9. Here the message *rlc* can now arrive in the *Race* state.

The sample executions that are generated by SPIN leave little room for doubt that these errors are real and must be corrected. Why is it that these errors did not show up before we introduced the session manager process? The reason is simple, but only in retrospect. In the earlier version of the model, there was a direct communication channel between switch and subscriber, based on rendezvous. The subscriber could offer to perform a rendezvous handshake on a *digits* message while the switch process was in state *Wait*, but because the switch process had no matching receive operation at that state, the offer could be declined without causing an error. In the new model the communication is in two steps, introducing an asynchronous decoupling of behaviors. Offers from the subscriber on any messages are now always accepted by the session management process, independent of the session state, and they must now be passed on successfully to the new session handler. We could have found the same problems in the earlier model if we switched from rendezvous communication to a buffered communication channel between subscriber and switch.

If we repair the newly found omissions in the session handler process we obtain the new model in Figure 14.11. Similarly, the corrected model for the remote switch is shown in Figure 14.12.

If we repeat the verification with this model, all error reports disappear. As expected, the number of reachable states increases a little further, to 263 states, due to the addition of the session management process. We are now set to add support for handling an extra call session to support the three-way calling feature. First, we add the *flash* message, and some extra call states, with the following declarations:

```
/* Revised Declarations for Three-Way Calling */

#define NS      2           /* nr of sessions in 3way call */

mtype = { offhook, digits, flash, onhook }
mtype = { iam, acm, anm, rel, rlc };
mtype = { idle, busy, setup, threeway };

chan tpc      = [0] of { mtype };
chan rms[NS]  = [1] of { mtype };        /* added */
chan sess[NS] = [0] of { mtype };        /* added */

mtype s_state = idle;
```

The new switch process is shown in Figure 14.13. It has to handle the additional scenarios, but it is still fairly close to the last version.

The handling of the messages arriving at the session manager now depends on the state of the call, in a fairly straightforward way. Running a verification of this extended model produces the following result:

```
$ spin -a version4
$ cc -o pan pan.c
$ ./pan
(Spin Version 4.0.7 -- 1 August 2003)
        + Partial Order Reduction

Full statespace search for:
        never claim             - (none specified)
        assertion violations    +
```

```
proctype session_ss7(chan inp; chan out)
{
Idle:
    if
    :: inp?offhook -> printf("dial tone\n"); goto Dial
    fi;
Dial:
    if
    :: inp?digits -> printf("no tone\n");
                        out!iam; goto Wait
    :: inp?onhook -> printf("no tone\n"); goto Idle
    fi;
Wait:
    if
    :: inp?acm -> printf("ring tone\n"); goto Wait
    :: inp?anm -> printf("no tone\n"); goto Connect
    :: inp?rel -> out!rlc; printf("busy tone\n"); goto Busy
    :: inp?onhook -> out!rel; goto Zombie1
    :: inp?digits -> goto Wait /* added */
    fi;
Connect:
    if
    :: inp?rel -> out!rlc; printf("busy tone\n"); goto Busy
    :: inp?onhook -> out!rel; goto Zombie1
    :: inp?digits -> goto Connect /* added */
    fi;
Busy:            /* off-hook, waiting for on-hook */
    if
    :: inp?onhook -> printf("no tone\n"); goto Idle
    :: inp?digits -> goto Busy /* added */
    fi;
Zombie1:         /* on-hook, waiting for rlc */
    if
    :: inp?rel -> out!rlc; goto Zombie1
    :: inp?rlc -> goto Idle
    :: inp?offhook -> goto Zombie2
    :: inp?acm -> goto Zombie1 /* added */
    :: inp?anm -> goto Zombie1 /* added */
    fi;
Zombie2:         /* off-hook, waiting for rlc */
    if
    :: inp?rel -> out!rlc; goto Zombie2
    :: inp?rlc -> goto Busy
    :: inp?onhook -> goto Zombie1
    :: inp?digits -> goto Zombie2 /* added */
    fi
}
```

Figure 14.11 New Model for the Session Handler

317

```
              acceptance    cycles     - (not selected)
              invalid end states        +

State-vector 80 byte, depth reached 5531, errors: 0
   30479 states, stored
   55947 states, matched
   86426 transitions (= stored+matched)
       3 atomic steps
hash conflicts: 1836 (resolved)
(max size 2^18 states)

Stats on memory usage (in Megabytes):
2.682    equivalent memory usage for states ...
1.827    actual memory usage for states (compression: 68.13%)
         State-vector as stored = 52 byte + 8 byte overhead
1.049    memory used for hash table (-w18)
0.320    memory used for DFS stack (-m10000)
3.109    total actual memory usage

unreached in proctype subscriber
        line 22, state 10, "-end-"
        (1 of 10 states)
unreached in proctype session_ss7
        line 106, state 74, "-end-"
        (1 of 74 states)
unreached in proctype switch
        line 156, state 46, "-end-"
        (1 of 46 states)
unreached in proctype remote_ss7
        line 196, state 44, "-end-"
        (1 of 44 states)
```

The number of reachable states has now increased from 263 to 30,479, but no new errors, and no unreachable states, are reported.

A THREE-WAY CALLING SCENARIO

Did we actually succeed in reproducing the three-way calling behavior we had in mind? We can make sure of this by formalizing and checking some properties that can together establish compliance with the required feature behavior. As one of those checks, we can check that the intended three-way calling behavior is at least possible, simply by claiming that it cannot occur and allowing SPIN to generate a counterexample. We can, for instance, check the behavior that results if the subscriber generates the sequence of off-hook, digit, and flash signals that corresponds to the correct setup of a three-way call. The problem we have to solve now is to detect the occurrence of these events with a system state property. The interaction between subscriber and the switch currently takes place via a rendezvous port, which cannot be polled for the presence of messages. We can get around this problem in two different ways. The more obvious method is perhaps to change the rendezvous port

```
proctype remote_ss7(chan inp; chan out)
{
Idle:
        if
        :: inp?iam -> goto Dialing
        fi;
Dialing:
        if
        :: out!acm -> goto Ringing
        :: out!rel -> goto Hangup
        :: inp?rel -> goto Busy
        fi;
Ringing:
        if
        :: out!anm -> goto Talking
        :: out!rel -> goto Hangup
        :: inp?rel -> goto Busy
        fi;
Talking:
        if
        :: out!rel -> goto Hangup
        :: inp?rel -> goto Busy
        fi;
Hangup:
        if
        :: inp?rlc -> goto Idle
        :: inp?rel -> goto Race
        fi;
Busy:
        if
        :: inp?rlc -> goto Idle
        fi;

Race:   if
        :: out!rlc -> goto Busy
        :: inp?rlc ->   /* added */
                out!rlc; goto Idle
        fi
}
```

Figure 14.12 New Model for the Remote Switch

named *tpc* into a one-slot buffered message channel, so that the contents of the single slot can be polled. This change is effective, but it also increases the complexity of the verification, and it may introduce new behaviors. A quick check with SPIN tells us that the number of system states roughly triples (reaching 97,791 states), but no error behaviors are introduced.

```
active proctype switch()
{       mtype x;

        atomic
        {       run session_ss7(sess[0], rms[0]);
                run session_ss7(sess[1], rms[1]);
                run remote_ss7(rms[0], sess[0]);
                run remote_ss7(rms[1], sess[1])
        };
end:    do
        :: tpc?x ->
                if
                :: x == offhook ->
                        assert(s_state == idle);
                        s_state = busy;
                        sess[0]!x
                :: x == onhook ->
                        assert(s_state != idle);
                        if
                        :: s_state == busy ->
                                sess[0]!x
                        :: else ->
                                sess[0]!x; sess[1]!x
                        fi;
                        s_state = idle
                :: x == flash ->
                        assert(s_state != idle);
                        if
                        :: s_state == busy ->
                                sess[1]!offhook;
                                s_state = setup
                        :: s_state == setup ->
                                s_state = threeway
                        :: s_state == threeway ->
                                sess[1]!onhook;
                                s_state = busy
                        fi
                :: else ->
                        if
                        :: s_state == idle
                                /* ignored */
                        :: s_state == busy ->
                                sess[0]!x
                        :: else ->
                                sess[1]!x
                        fi
                fi
        od
}
```

Figure 14.13 New Version of the Session Manager

```
mtype last_sent;

active proctype subscriber()
{
Idle:     tpc!offhook;
          last_sent = offhook;

Busy:     if
          :: atomic { tpc!digits ->
                  last_sent = digits;
                  goto Busy
               }
          :: atomic { tpc!flash ->
                  last_sent = flash;
                  goto Busy
               }
          :: atomic { tpc!onhook ->
                  last_sent = onhook;
                  goto Idle
               }
          fi
}
```

Figure 14.14 Revised Subscriber Process

Another method, which in this case incurs lower overhead, is to add a global state variable called *last_sent*, and to change the subscriber process in such a way that it always assigns the value of the last sent message to that variable, where it can be checked with a simple state property. The updated version of the subscriber process would then look as shown in Figure 14.14.

With this change, the number of reachable states increases from 30,479 to 35,449 system states, a far smaller penalty.

The claim we are interested in can be formalized as shown in Figure 14.15. In this claim, we need to refer to the process instantiation numbers of the processes of type `remote_ss7` and `session_ss7`. A simple way to find out what these `pid` numbers are is to print them in a verbose simulation run of the system.

A sample three-way calling scenario is now quickly generated. We first compile and run the model checker in a mode that allows us to generate the shortest possible scenario that matches the claim. Because the claim expresses a safety property (there are no accept-state or progress-state labels), we can find such a scenario with a breadth-first search.

```
#define Final \
        subscriber@Idle && switch@end \
        && remote_ss7[4]@Idle && remote_ss7[5]@Idle \
        && session_ss7[2]@Idle && session_ss7[3]@Idle

#define Event(x) \
        do \
        :: last_sent == x -> break \
        :: else \
        od

never { /* sample of a 3way call: */
        Event(offhook);
        Event(digits);
        Event(flash);
        Event(digits);
        Event(flash);
        Event(digits);
        Event(flash);
        Event(onhook);
        do
        :: Final -> break
        :: else
        od
}
```

Figure 14.15 Never Claim to Trigger Three-Way Calling Scenario

```
$ spin -a version6
$ cc -DBFS -o pan pan.c
$ ./pan
...
pan: claim violated! (at depth 79)
pan: wrote version6.trail
...
```

We can reproduce the scenario with SPIN's guided simulation option, as follows. Because the claim successfully matched the scenario we are interested in, we do not need to scrutinize it too much further. If, however, no matching execution would have been found, we would have had to consider more carefully if, for instance, the claim structure is compatible with the requirements of SPIN's partial order reduction algorithm, i.e., that it expresses a stutter-invariant property (it does), and if not, we would have repeated the check with partial order reduction disabled.

```
$ spin -t -c version6
```

```
proc 0 = subscriber
proc 1 = switch
proc 2 = session_ss7
proc 3 = session_ss7
proc 4 = remote_ss7
proc 5 = remote_ss7
q\p   0    1    2    3    4    5
   5  tpc!offhook
   5  .    tpc?offhook
   1  .    sess[0]!offhook
   1  .    .    .    inp?offhook
                    MSC: dial tone
   5  tpc!digits
   5  .    tpc?digits
   1  .    sess[0]!digits
   1  .    .    .    inp?digits
                    MSC: no tone
   3  .    .    .    out!iam
   3  .    .    .    .    .    inp?iam
   1  .    .    .    .    .    out!rel
   1  .    .    .    inp?rel
   3  .    .    .    out!rlc
                    MSC: busy tone
   3  .    .    .    .    .    inp?rlc
   5  tpc!flash
   5  .    tpc?flash
   2  .    sess[1]!offhook
   2  .    .    .    inp?offhook
                    MSC: dial tone
   5  tpc!digits
   5  .    tpc?digits
   2  .    sess[1]!digits
   2  .    .    .    inp?digits
                    MSC: no tone
   4  .    .    .    .    out!iam
   4  .    .    .    .    .    .    inp?iam
   2  .    .    .    .    .    .    out!rel
   2  .    .    .    .    inp?rel
   4  .    .    .    .    out!rlc
                    MSC: busy tone
   4  .    .    .    .    .    .    inp?rlc
   5  tpc!flash
   5  .    tpc?flash
   5  tpc!digits
   5  .    tpc?digits
   2  .    sess[1]!digits
   2  .    .    .    inp?digits
   5  tpc!flash
   5  .    tpc?flash
   2  .    sess[1]!onhook
```

```
    2    .    .    .    .    inp?onhook
                        MSC: no tone
    5    tpc!onhook
    5    .    tpc?onhook
    1    .    sess[0]!onhook
    1    .    .    .    inp?onhook
                        MSC: no tone
spin: trail ends after 79 steps
- - - - - - - - - - - - -
final state:
- - - - - - - - - - - - -
#processes: 7
                    queue 3 (rms[0]):
                    queue 4 (rms[1]):
                    s_state = idle
                    last_sent = onhook
   79:    proc  5 (remote_ss7) line 172 "vertsion6" (state 3)
   79:    proc  4 (remote_ss7) line 172 "vertsion6" (state 3)
   79:    proc  3 (session_ss7) line  38 "vertsion6" (state 4)
   79:    proc  2 (session_ss7) line  38 "vertsion6" (state 4)
   79:    proc  1 (switch) line 128 "vertsion6" (state 43) ...
   79:    proc  0 (subscriber) line  16 "vertsion6" (state 1)
   79:    proc  - (:never:) line 227 "vertsion6" (state 52)
   7 processes created
```

IN SUMMARY

In this chapter we have developed a relatively simple model of a telephone switch that represents an interesting fragment of its behavior for handling outgoing calls.

By starting with a very simple model that was revised in small and easily understood increments, we can catch errors at an early stage and avoid large blowups in the complexity of verification. After each small incremental step, we can check our intuition about the behavior of the model with short simulation and verification runs. Despite a few obvious limitations (e.g., the absence of a treatment for incoming calls), the model already includes some feature behavior that can be very challenging to implement correctly. The hard part of an exercise like this is to keep the model and its state space small, so that we can continue to verify it rigorously. This is an exercise in restriction and judicious abstraction. The target of this exercise is always to find the smallest sufficient model that allows us to verify all properties of interest.

Perhaps one of the nicer things about the use of a model checker such as SPIN is that the tool does not expect us to get things right on the first attempt. The tool can help us find both sources of complexity and sources of error. A model checking tool is often conveniently used as an exploratory tool: allowing the user to answer quick what-if questions about possible directions that might be taken to solve complex software design problems.

SAMPLE SPIN MODELS   **15**

> *"Few things are harder to put up with than*
> *the annoyance of a good example."*
> *(Mark Twain, 1835–1910)*

In this chapter we will discuss a few small PROMELA models that exploit some interesting and possibly useful features of the specification language. We will focus mostly on language and modeling issues here. More examples of PROMELA models can be found in the standard SPIN distribution.

ERATOSTHENES

Our first example is a PROMELA version of an ancient algorithm for finding primes by counting off numbers and systematically intercepting the non-primes among them. The algorithm, a favorite programming exercise today, is due to the Greek philosopher and mathematician Eratosthenes of Cyrene (a city in modern day Libya which is today called Shahhat). Figure 15.1 shows a version in PROMELA that makes use of the fact that we can use dynamic process creation and pass channel identifiers between running processes.

Because a PROMELA model must always be finite, we have to place an upper-bound on the largest integer value that we will test for primality. SPIN is not designed to handle computational problems, so do not expect to get away with a very large bound here. The bound is defined in Figure 15.1 in a macro definition named MAX. We have used the value 25. Only two types of messages are used, defined in an mtype declaration, and named number and eof. The latter type of message is used to trigger an orderly termination of the system of processes when the test for primality of the number with the maximal value allowed has been completed.

```
 1  /*
 2      The Sieve of Eratosthenes (c. 276-196 BC)
 3      Prints all prime numbers up to MAX
 4  */
 5  #define MAX 25
 6
 7  mtype = { number, eof };
 8
 9  chan root = [0] of { mtype, int };
10
11  proctype sieve(chan c; int prime)
12  {    chan child = [0] of { mtype, int };
13       bool haschild;
14       int n;
15
16       printf("MSC: %d is prime\n", prime);
17  end: do
18       :: c?number(n) ->
19          if
20          :: (n%prime) == 0 ->
21             printf("MSC: %d = %d*%d\n", n, prime, n/prime)
22          :: else ->
23             if
24             :: !haschild -> /* new prime */
25                     haschild = true;
26                     run sieve(child, n);
27             :: else ->
28                     child!number(n)
29             fi;
30           fi
31       :: c?eof(0) ->
32          break
33       od;
34       if
35       :: haschild ->
36          child!eof(0)
37       :: else
38       fi
39  }
40
41  init
42  {    int n = 2;
43
44       run sieve(root, n);
45       do
46       :: (n <  MAX) -> n++; root!number(n)
47       :: (n >= MAX) -> root!eof(0); break
48       od
49  }
```

Figure 15.1 The Sieve of Eratosthenes

Our system of processes starts off with just a single running process: init. The principle of operation of the algorithm is that we test integer numbers one by one, in ascending order. We will start off assuming that we know only that two is a prime. Clearly, for any higher number to be prime, it should minimally not be divisible by two, so the first thing that the initial process will do is to start up a tester for that value. The initial process does so by creating a first process of type sieve, and passing it in an argument the value two as a first prime number to use in the tests. Also passed is an argument is the name of the channel that the initial process will use to communicate further information to the sieve process. For the first process this is a globally declared rendezvous channel named root.

Once the first test process is set up, the initial process will simply pass all integer numbers greater than two, up to the preset maximum, to its newly created child. It is the child's job now to figure out if the numbers passed to it are prime, and it is free to create its own children to help do the job.

When a process of type sieve starts up, the first thing it will do is to acknowledge the fact that it was passed, what it trusts is, a prime number as an argument. It does so by printing the number (line 16 in Figure 15.1), using the prefix MSC: to make sure that this line of output will be picked up in the message sequence charts that can be created by XSPIN. Next, it stops and waits for input to arrive on the channel that was passed to it by its parent.

One of only two types of messages can arrive, as shown on line 18 and line 31 in Figure 15.1.

A message of type number carries an integer number that is to be tested for primality. Every single instantiation of the sieve process will test if the number is divisible by the prime number it was passed by its parent. If divisible, the number is not prime, and that fact is printed. Otherwise, the number is passed to the next process to test for possibly more known primes. If no next process exists yet, the value of local boolean variable haschild will still be *false* (the default initial value). The sieve process will now clone itself and start up a new copy of sieve, passing the newly discovered prime number as an argument, as well as the name of the local channel child that it will use to pass new numbers.

If a child process already exists, that means that more tests for primality have yet to be done before this new number can be declared prime. The number is simply sent to the child process over the local channel, and the test process is repeated.

Meanwhile, the initial process can be sending a new number into the pipeline of primality testers, and in principle all processes can be active simultaneously, each testing the divisibility of a different number against the prime number they each hold. A simulation run might proceed as follows:

```
$ spin eratosthenes
      MSC: 2 is prime
        MSC: 3 is prime
      MSC: 4 = 2*2
            MSC: 5 is prime
      MSC: 6 = 2*3
      MSC: 8 = 2*4
        MSC: 9 = 3*3
                 MSC: 7 is prime
      MSC: 10 = 2*5
      MSC: 12 = 2*6
      MSC: 14 = 2*7
                   MSC: 11 is prime
      MSC: 16 = 2*8
        MSC: 15 = 3*5
                     MSC: 13 is prime
      MSC: 18 = 2*9
      MSC: 20 = 2*10
        MSC: 21 = 3*7
                       MSC: 17 is prime
      MSC: 22 = 2*11
      MSC: 24 = 2*12
          MSC: 25 = 5*5
                         MSC: 19 is prime
                          MSC: 23 is prime

  10 processes created
```

Although the algorithm itself is deterministic, the process scheduling is not, and in different runs this can cause print statements to appear in slightly different orders. Ten processes were created, one of which is the initial process. This means that the algorithm accurately found the nine prime numbers between one and 25. When the maximal number is reached, the eof messages is passed down the chain all the way from the initial process to the most recently created sieve process, and all processes will make an orderly exit.

A verification run with the model as specified is uneventful:

```
(Spin Version 4.0.7 -- 1 August 2003)
      + Partial Order Reduction

Full statespace search for:
      never claim              - (none specified)
      assertion violations     +
      acceptance   cycles      - (not selected)
      invalid end states       +

State-vector 284 byte, depth reached 288, errors: 0
   2093 states, stored
    478 states, matched
   2571 transitions (= stored+matched)
```

```
        0 atomic steps
hash conflicts: 1 (resolved)
(max size 2^18 states)

Stats on memory usage (in Megabytes):
0.611   equivalent memory usage for states ...
0.508   actual memory usage for states (compression: 83.13%)
        State-vector as stored = 235 byte + 8 byte overhead
1.049   memory used for hash table (-w18)
0.240   memory used for DFS stack (-m10000)
1.698   total actual memory usage

unreached in proctype sieve
        (0 of 25 states)
unreached in proctype :init:
        (0 of 11 states)
```

There are no deadlocks and there is no unreachable code, as we would expect. The partial order reduction algorithm could in principle work better, though, if we can provide some extra information about the way that the initial and the sieve processes access the message channels. In principle, this is not too hard in this case. On line 15, for instance, we can try to add the channel assertions

```
15      xr c; xs child;
```

because the sieve process is guaranteed to be the only process to read from the channel that was passed to it as an argument, and the only one to send messages to the channel it will use to communicate with a possible child process. Similarly, the assertion

```
43      xs root;
```

could be included on line 43 in the init process to assert that the initial process is the only process to send messages to channel root. If we do so, however, the verifier will warn us sternly that channel assertions are not allowed on rendezvous channels.

```
$ spin -a eratosthenes
$ cc -o pan pan.c
$ ./pan
chan root (0), sndr proc :init: (0)
pan: xs chans cannot be used for rv (at depth 0)
pan: wrote eratosthenes.trail
...
```

We can correct this by turning the two rendezvous channels declared on lines 9 and 12 in Figure 15.1 into buffered message channels with the minimum storage capacity of one message. Line 9 in Figure 15.1 then becomes:

```
9 chan root = [1] of { mtype, int };
```

Similarly, line 12 is now written:

```
12 {    chan child = [1] of { mtype, int };
```

This of course in itself will increase the number of potentially reachable states, since it decouples the process executions a little more. Repeating the verification confirms this. If the channel assertions are *not* included, the number of reachable states now increases tenfold (to 24,548). With the channel assertions, however, the size of the state space *decreases* tenfold to a mere 289 reachable states, which provides a compelling illustration of the effectiveness of channel assertions.

In this first model we are using one process for each prime number that is found. Because there cannot be more than 255 running processes in a SPIN model, we cannot use this model to find more than only the first 254 prime numbers greater than one. This means that a value for MAX greater than 1,609 (the 254th prime) would be of little use, unless we can somehow rearrange the code to avoid the dynamic creation of processes. This is not too hard, as shown in Figure 15.2, though the resulting model is not quite as elegant.

This time we store prime numbers in a channel, and retrieve them from there for primality testing. We have set the capacity of the channel generously to the value of MAX, although a much smaller value would also suffice. Only a number that is not divisible by any of the previously discovered primes is itself prime and can then be added into the channel. In this version of the sieve process we have left the macro MAX undefined, which means that we can now pass a value in via a command-line argument to SPIN. We can now surpass the old limit of 254 primes easily, for instance, as follows:

```
$ spin -DMAX=10000 eratosthenes2
      MSC: 2 is prime
      MSC: 3 is prime nr 2
      ...
      MSC: 9941 is prime nr 1226
      MSC: 9949 is prime nr 1227
      MSC: 9967 is prime nr 1228
      MSC: 9973 is prime nr 1229
1 process created
```

If we repeat the verification attempt for the alternative model, using the same value for MAX as before, we see that the number of states has increased a little compared to the best attempt from before using channel assertions.

```
$ spin -DMAX=25 -a eratosthenes2
$ cc -o pan pan.c
$ ./pan
(Spin Version 4.0.7 -- 1 August 2003)
        + Partial Order Reduction

Full statespace search for:
```

```
 1 mtype = { number, eof };
 2
 3 chan found = [MAX] of { int };
 4
 5 active proctype sieve()
 6 {   int n = 3;
 7     int prime = 2;
 8     int i;
 9
10     found!prime;
11     printf("MSC: %d is prime\n", prime);
12     do
13     :: n < MAX ->
14         i = len(found);
15         assert(i > 0);
16         do
17         :: i > 0 ->
18             found?prime;
19             found!prime; /* put back at end */
20             if
21             :: (n%prime) == 0 ->
22             /*  printf("MSC: %d = %d*%d\n",
23                         n, prime, n/prime); */
24                 break
25             :: else ->
26                 i--
27             fi
28         :: else ->
29             break
30         od;
31         if
32         :: i == 0 ->
33             found!n;
34             printf("MSC: %d is prime number %d\n",
35                         n, len(found))
36         :: else
37         fi;
38         n++
39     :: else ->
40         break
41     od
42 }
```

Figure 15.2 Alternative Structure for Sieve

```
        never claim                - (none specified)
        assertion violations       +
        acceptance    cycles       - (not selected)
        invalid end states         +

State-vector 132 byte, depth reached 479, errors: 0
      480 states, stored
        0 states, matched
      480 transitions (= stored+matched)
        0 atomic steps
hash conflicts: 0 (resolved)
(max size 2^18 states)

1.493   memory usage (Mbyte)

unreached in proctype sieve
        (0 of 32 states)
```

However, we can also note that the size of the state vector has decreased from 284 bytes in the first model, which increases with MAX, to a fixed size of just 132 bytes in the new model. This means that the 289 states from before will actually take up more memory than the 480 states from the new model. The simpler model usually wins in a battle for complexity control.

PROCESS SCHEDULING

The next problem concerns the design of a reasonably efficient method for scheduling process execution in a multiprocessor system. The processes compete for access to shared resources, and they may have to be suspended when a resource is temporarily unavailable. The process suspension is done with a system call named sleep, which also records the particular resource that the process is waiting to access. When a process releases a resource, it calls the routine wakeup, which checks if any processes are currently suspended, waiting for the resource being released, and if so resumes execution of those processes. The data structures that record the state of the resource, and the data structures that record the state of the processes, are themselves also shared resources in the system, and access to them has to be protected with locks. In a uniprocessor system simply masking interrupts can suffice to lock out competing processes while operations on shared data structures are performed, but in a multiprocessor system this is not sufficient and we need to rely on higher-level locks.

In most systems, the availability of a global, indivisible test and set instruction can be assumed to solve this problem. If, for instance, we have a lock variable named lk, the indivisible test and set instruction, which is called spinlock in the UTS system, can be modeled in PROMELA as

```
    #define spinlock(lk)    atomic { (lk == 0) -> lk = 1 }
```

and the matching lock release operation as

```
#define freelock(lk)      lk = 0
```

The scheduling problem is easy to solve if we would allow a process to simply set the `spinlock` for the duration of all access to the resource: it would effectively lock out all other processes. Such a solution would be very inefficient, though, forcing other processes to continue executing while competing to set the lock variable. The real challenge is to minimize the use of global locks, suspending process executions where possible, while securing that no process can accidentally be suspended forever. The latter problem is called a "missed wakeup."

The algorithm that was adopted for the Plan9 operating system was discussed in Pike et al. [1991], including a verification with and early version of SPIN. Another solution was proposed in Ruane [1990] for use in Amdahl's UNIX time sharing system, UTS®. We will consider Ruane's method here. An earlier discussion of this method appeared in Holzmann [1997b] with a commentary, exposing some flaws in that discussion, appearing in Bang [2001].

For our current purpose it is sufficient to restrict the number of shared resources in the system to just one single resource. This resource can be represented in the C implementation by a data structure of the following type:

```
typedef struct R {
        int lock;          /* locks access to resource */
        int wanted;        /* processes waiting  */
        ...                /* other fields */
} R;

R *r;   /* pointer to resource structure */
```

A process that gains access to the resource will set the `lock` field in the resource data structure to record that the resource is in use. If a process finds the resource locked, it suspends itself after setting the `wanted` flag to one, to record that at least one process is waiting for the resource to be released. A process that releases the resource first checks the `wanted` flag to see if any processes are waiting, and if so it will restart those processes one by one. Each such process then retests the resource `lock` field to try again to gain access to the resource.

In the UTS solution, a process can be suspended while holding the global lock variable with a variant of the `sleep` routine, called `sleepl`. The implementation of `sleepl` then has to make sure that the global lock is released while the process is suspended and reacquired when it is resumed.

To acquire access to the resource, the code that was used would first set the spinlock on `lk`, and then test the value of the `lock` variable from the resource, as follows:

```
spinlock(&lk);
while (r->lock) {
        r->wanted = 1;
        sleepl(r, &lk);
}
r->lock = 1;
freelock(&lk);
```

As a minor detail, note that in the C code a pointer to lock variable lk is passed to the routines spinlock and freelock, where in the PROMELA version we passed the variable name itself.

To release the resource, a process executes the following piece of code:

```
r->lock = 0;
waitlock(&lk);
if (r->wanted) {
        r->wanted = 0;
        wakeup(r);
}
```

If the wanted flag indicates that at least one process is waiting to access the resource, the waiting processes are restarted through a call to the wakeup routine. A waitlock is used here instead of a spinlock. The waitlock primitive can be modeled in PROMELA as follows:

```
#define waitlock(lk)      (lk == 0)
```

Ruane reported that some time after these routines had been implemented a race condition was discovered that could lead to a process being suspended without ever being resumed. After analyzing the problem, the designers of the code proposed a change in the wakeup routine that looked as follows:

```
r->lock = 0;
waitlock(&lk);
if (r->wanted) {
        r->wanted = 0;
        waitlock(&lk);
        wakeup(r);
}
```

For a while, no further problems were detected, but the designers had a lingering doubt about the adequacy of their fix. They asked two specific questions:

- Could a SPIN verification have found the problem?
- Is the modified version free from other race conditions?

To answer these questions, we will build a basic SPIN model without resort to embedded C code. This means that we cannot use pointers, and we will have to make some changes in the way that the resource flags are specified. All changes are relatively minor.

We begin by modeling the effect of the system routines sleepl and wakeup with two `inline` definitions. To do so, we have to decide how to represent the process states. We use a one-dimensional array to record process states, indexed by the process instantiation numbers, as follows:

```
mtype = { Wakeme, Running };      /* process states  */
mtype pstate[N] = Running;
```

The initial state of each process is `Running`. Access to the process states has to be protected by a special lock, which we call `sq`. The `wakeup` routine, shown in Figure 15.3, acquires this lock and checks if any processes are suspended on access to the resource. If it finds any, it moves them back into the `Running` state.

The `sleepl` routine changes the process state, again under protection of the `sq` lock, and it releases the global lock. The lock is reacquired when the process is moved back into the `Running` state. The first argument to `sleepl`, which points to the resource data structure in the original code, can be ignored here since we consider access to only a single resource.

In the verification model from Figure 15.4, a user process alternately tries to gain access to the resource and then release it, following the proposed UTS code for the calls on `sleepl` and `wakeup`.

The proposed fix can be included into, or excluded from, the model by defining or undefining the preprocessor directive named `FIX`. The original C code is placed next to the PROMELA code in comments to show the correspondence. Apart from syntax, there is a fairly close match.

To verify the model we must now formulate a correctness property. To show that there can be no missed wakeups, we should be able to show, for instance, that it is impossible for any process to remain in the `Wakeme` state forever. If we define the propositional symbol p as:

```
#define p        (pstate[0] == Wakeme)
```

it should be impossible for p to remain *true* infinitely long in an execution of the system. The corresponding LTL formula is `<>[]p`. The claim that can now be appended to the model is generated with SPIN as follows:

```
$ spin -f '<>[]p'
never {    /* <>[]p */
T0_init:
        if
        :: ((p)) -> goto accept_S4
        :: (1) -> goto T0_init
        fi;
accept_S4:
        if
        :: ((p)) -> goto accept_S4
        fi;
}
```

```
 1 #define N    3                    /* nr of processes */
 2
 3 mtype = { Wakeme, Running };   /* process states  */
 4
 5 mtype pstate[N] = Running;
 6
 7 bit r_lock;
 8 bit r_wanted;                      /* resource state */
 9 bit lk, sq;                        /* locks */
10
11 #define freelock(x) x = 0
12 #define waitlock(x) (x == 0)
13 #define spinlock(x) atomic { waitlock(x) -> x = 1 }
14
15 inline wakeup(x) {
16     spinlock(sq);
17     i = 0;
18     do :: i < N ->
19             if
20             :: pstate[i] == Wakeme ->
21                     pstate[i] = Running
22             :: else -> i++
23             fi
24        :: else -> break
25     od;
26     freelock(sq)
27 }
28 inline sleepl(y, x) {
29     spinlock(sq);
30     freelock(x);
31     pstate[_pid] = Wakeme;
32     freelock(sq);
33     (pstate[_pid] == Running);
34     spinlock(x)
35 }
36
```

Figure 15.3 Sleep-Wakeup Routines

The process instantiation numbers are 0, 1, and 2 in this model. Because the system is symmetrical, it should not matter which process we select for the check in property p.

The verifier is now first generated and compiled without enabling the fix, as follows:

```
$ spin -a uts_model              # no FIX
$ cc -o pan pan.c
```

The verifier quickly finds a counterexample. We can produce a relatively

```
37 active [N] proctype user()
38 {  pid i;
39    do :: spinlock(lk);        /* spinlock(&lk);      */
40       do :: r_lock ->          /* while (r->lock) {  */
41             r_wanted = 1;      /*   r->wanted = 1;   */
42             sleep1(_, lk)      /*   sleep1(r, &lk);  */
43          :: else -> break
44       od;                      /* }                  */
45       r_lock = 1;              /* r->lock = 1;       */
46       freelock(lk);            /* freelock(&lk);     */
47
48 R:    /* use resource r */
49
50       r_lock = 0;              /* r->lock = 0;       */
51       waitlock(lk);            /* waitlock(&lk);     */
52       if
53       :: r_wanted ->           /* if (r->wanted) {   */
54          r_wanted = 0;         /*   r->wanted = 0;   */
55 #ifdef FIX
56          waitlock(lk);         /*   waitlock(&lk);   */
57 #endif
58          wakeup(_);            /*   wakeup(r);       */
59       :: else
60       fi                       /* }                  */
61    od
62 }
```

Figure 15.4 Remainder of Verification Model for UTS

short error trail by restricting the search depth to 60 steps.

```
$ ./pan -a -m60
...
pan: acceptance cycle (at depth 42)
pan: wrote uts_model.trail
...
```

The error sequence can be reproduced with SPIN's guided simulation option, for instance, as in:

```
$ spin -t -p uts_model
...
```

For clarity, we will edit the output a little here to indicate the sequence of steps taken by each of the three processes, using macro and inline names from the model to shorten the trail some more. We list the actions of the user processes in three columns, in the order of their process instantiation numbers. The first step is taken by the user process with pid number 2, which appears in the third column.

```
                              /* pid 2 */
    1                         spinlock(lk)
    2                         else
    3                         r_lock = 1
    4                         freelock(lk)
    5                         /* use resource */
    6                         r_lock = 0
                    /* pid 1 */
    7               spinlock(lk)
    8               else
    9               rlock = 1
   10               freelock(lk)
   11               /* use resource */
                              /* pid 2 */
   12                         waitlock(lk)
          /* pid 0 */
   13 spinlock(lk)
   14 (r_lock)
   15 r_wanted = 1
                              /* pid 2 */
   16                         (r_wanted)
   17                         r_wanted = 0
          /* pid 0 */
   18 sleepl(r,lk)
                              /* pid 2 */
   19                         waitlock(lk)
   20                         wakeup(r)
                    /* pid 1 */
   21               <<<CYCLE>>>
   22               r_lock = 0
   23               waitlock(lk)
   24               else
   25               spinlock(lk)
   26               else
   27               r_lock = 1
   28               freelock(lk)
   29               /* use resource */
```

In this scenario, the user process with pid 0, executing at steps 13, 14, 15, and 18, is indeed indefinitely held in its Wakeme state, but the scenario also shows that the processes with pid 2 is assumed to be delayed indefinitely in its call of the wakeup routine, trying to acquire the spinlock inside this call in step 20.

The spinlock on lk is repeatedly set and released by the remaining process in steps 25 and 28.

This is a valid but not an interesting counterexample because it assumes unfair process scheduling decisions. To home in on the more interesting cases, we have to add fairness constraints to the property. Our verification model already contains the label R at the point where access to the resource is obtained. We can extend the property to state that it should be impossible for one of the processes to remain in its Wakeme state, only while the other two processes continue to access the resource. The system is symmetrical, so it should not matter which process we pick for the check. The new property can be expressed in LTL formula

```
<>[]p && []<>q && []<>r
```

with the propositional symbol definitions:

```
#define p        (pstate[0] == Wakeme)
#define q        (user[1]@R)
#define r        (user[2]@R)
```

If we repeat the verification, again for the model without the fix enabled, we can obtain another error scenario, now slightly longer. The essence of this scenario can be summarized in the following steps:

```
 1        spinlock(lk)
 2        else
 3        r_lock = 1
 4        /* use resource */
 5        freelock(lk)
 6        r_lock = 0
 7        waitlock(lk)

 8                    spinlock(lk)
 9                    else
10                    r_lock = 1
11                    freelock(lk)
12                    /* use resource */

13 spinlock(lk)
14 (r_lock)

15                    r_lock = 0

16 r_wanted = 1

17        (r_wanted)
18        r_wanted = 0
19        wakeup(_)

20 sleepl(_,lk)
```

The process with pid 1 accesses the resource and releases the resource lock in step 6. It is about to check, in step 17, if any processes are suspended, waiting to access the resource. Meanwhile, the process with pid 2 acquires access in steps 8-12, and causes the process with pid 1 to prepare for a call on sleepl, after finding the lock set, in step 14. The process sets the wanted flag, which is immediately detected and cleared by the process with pid 1. This process now proceeds with the execution of the wakeup routine, but process 0 has not actually been suspended yet. As a result, when process 0 finally suspends itself, the wanted flag is zero, which means that it can no longer be detected.

The process can now remain suspended indefinitely, while the other processes continue to acquire and release the resource.

We can now repeat the verification with the proposed fix enabled. The relevant part of the output is as follows:

```
$ spin -a -DFIX uts_model        # include the FIX
$ cc -o pan pan.c
$ ./pan -a
(Spin Version 4.0.7 -- 1 August 2003)
        + Partial Order Reduction

Full statespace search for:
        never claim             +
        assertion violations    + (if within scope of claim)
        acceptance   cycles     + (fairness disabled)
        invalid end states      - (disabled by never claim)

State-vector 44 byte, depth reached 5619, errors: 0
   47835 states, stored (49399 visited)
   56388 states, matched
  105787 transitions (= visited+matched)
       0 atomic steps
```

The state space for this three-process model is still relatively small, with under 50,000 reachable states. The verification run shows that the fix does indeed secure that the correctness property can no longer be violated.

Out of curiosity, we can also repeat the last run, but this time leave out the LTL property, to see how much complexity the verification of the claim added above the complexity of a basic reachability analysis for safety properties. We proceed as follows.

```
$ cc -DNOCLAIM -o pan pan.c
$ ./pan
(Spin Version 4.0.7 -- 1 August 2003)
        + Partial Order Reduction

Full statespace search for:
        never claim             - (not selected)
        assertion violations    +
        acceptance   cycles     - (not selected)
        invalid end states      +

State-vector 40 byte, depth reached 2809, errors: 0
   42983 states, stored
   43494 states, matched

   86477 transitions (= stored+matched)
       0 atomic steps
```

Note that the inclusion of the LTL property increased the state space by just

4,852 reachable states, or just under 11.3%. Note also that the use of the nested depth-first search algorithm causes the depth reached in the state space to double in this case.

A CLIENT-SERVER MODEL

It is relatively simple to create SPIN models with a dynamically changing number of active processes. Each newly created process can declare and instantiate its own set of local variables, so through the creation of a new process we can also create additional message channels. It may be somewhat confusing at first that message channel identifiers can have a process local scope, if declared within a `proctype` body , but that the message channels themselves are always global objects. The decision to define channels in this way makes it possible to restrict the access to a message channel to only specifically identified processes: message channels can be passed from one process to another. We will use this feature in the design of a simple, and fairly generic client-server model.

We will design a system with a single, fixed server that can receive requests from clients over a known global channel. When the server accepts a request for service, it assigns that request to an agent and provides a private channel name to the client that the client can use to communicate with the agent. The remainder of the transaction can now place between agent and client, communicating across a private channel without further requiring the intermediacy of the server process. Once the transaction is complete, the agent returns the identifier for the private channel to the server and exits.

Figure 15.5 shows the design of the agent and server processes. The fixed global channel on which the server process listens is declared as a rendezvous port called `server`. The server process has a private, locally declared, set of instantiated channels in reserve. We have given the server process a separate local channel, named `pool`, in which it can queue the channels that have not yet been assigned to an agent. The first few lines in the server process declaration fill up this queue with all available channels.

A client sending a request to the server attaches the name of the channel where it will listen for responses from the server or the server's agent. If the channel pool is empty at this point, the server has no choice but to deny the request immediately. If a channel is available, an agent process is started and the name of the new private channel is passed to that agent, together with the channel through which the client can be reached. The server now goes back to its main loop, waiting for new client requests. Eventually, when the client transaction is complete, the server's agent will return the now freed up private channel, so that the server can add it back into its pool of free channels.

We have set up the agent to randomly decide to either grant or deny a request, or to inform the client that the request is on hold. (Think of a library system, where a user can request books. In some cases a book can be on loan, and the

```
#define N        2

mtype = { request, deny, hold, grant, return };

chan server = [0] of { mtype, chan };

proctype Agent(chan listen, talk)
{
        do
        :: talk!hold(listen)
        :: talk!deny(listen) -> break
        :: talk!grant(listen) ->
wait:            listen?return; break
        od;
        server!return(listen)
}

active proctype Server()
{       chan agents[N] = [0] of { mtype };
        chan pool = [N] of { chan };
        chan client, agent;
        byte i;

        do
        :: i < N -> pool!agents[i]; i++
        :: else -> break
        od;

end:    do
        :: server?request(client) ->
                if
                :: empty(pool) ->
                        client!deny(0)
                :: nempty(pool) ->
                        pool?agent;
                        run Agent(agent,client)
                fi
        :: server?return(agent) ->
                pool!agent
        od
}
```

Figure 15.5 Agent and Server Processes

```
#define M          2

active [M] proctype Client()
{          chan me = [0] of { mtype, chan };
           chan agent;

end:       do
           :: timeout ->
                   server!request(me);
                   do
                   :: me?hold(agent)
                   :: me?deny(agent) ->
                           break
                   :: me?grant(agent) ->
                           agent!return;
                           break
                   od
           od
}
```

Figure 15.6 The Client Processes

user may be informed that the book was placed on hold.) If the request is granted, the agent will move to a wait state where it expects the client to eventually send a return response, signifying that the transaction is now complete. The agent process will now notify the server that the private channel can be freed up again, and it terminates.

Figure 15.6 shows the structure of the client process for this system. The client has its own private channel that it reserves for communications with the server. It initiates the communication, after a timeout in this case, by sending a first request to the server on the known global channel, with its own channel identifier attached. It will now wait for the response from either the server or the server's agent. A denial from the server brings the client back to its initial state, where it can repeat the attempt to get a request granted. A hold message is simply ignored by this client, although in an extended model we could consider giving the client the option of canceling its request in this case. When the request is granted, the client will faithfully respond with a return message, to allow the server's agent to conclude the transaction.

In this model, we have both dynamic process creation and the passing of channel identifiers from one process to the next. Dynamic process creation in a model such as this one can sometimes hold some surprises, so it will be worth our while to try some basic verification runs with this model. Clearly, the complexity of the model will depend on the number of client processes and the maximum number of agents that the server can employ. We will start simple, with just two client processes and maximally two agents. The verification then proceeds as follows:

```
$ spin -a client_server.pml
$ cc -o pan pan.c
$ ./pan
(Spin Version 4.0.7 -- 1 August 2003)
        + Partial Order Reduction

Full statespace search for:
        never claim              - (none specified)
        assertion violations     +
        acceptance    cycles     - (not selected)
        invalid end states       +

State-vector 72 byte, depth reached 124, errors: 0
     190 states, stored
      74 states, matched
     264 transitions (= stored+matched)
       0 atomic steps
hash conflicts: 0 (resolved)
(max size 2^18 states)


1.573    memory usage (Mbyte)

unreached in proctype Agent
        (0 of 11 states)
unreached in proctype Server
        line 33, state 11, "client!deny,0"
        line 41, state 22, "-end-"
        (2 of 22 states)
unreached in proctype Client
        line 61, state 15, "-end-"
        (1 of 15 states)
```

Perhaps the one surprising detail in this result is that the statement on line 33, where the server summarily has to deny the request because its pool of available private channels is found to be empty, is not reachable. Given that the number of private channels in the server was defined to be equal to the number of clients, this result is easily understood. We can try to confirm our initial understanding of this phenomenon by increasing the number of client processes to three, without changing the number of channels declared in the server. Our expectation is now that the one unreachable statement in the server should disappear. This is the result:

```
$ spin -a client_server3.pml
$ cc -o pan pan.c
$ ./pan
```

```
(Spin Version 4.0.7 -- 1 August 2003)
        + Partial Order Reduction

Full statespace search for:
        never claim              - (none specified)
        assertion violations     +
        acceptance    cycles     - (not selected)
        invalid end states       +

State-vector 84 byte, depth reached 331, errors: 0
     935 states, stored
     393 states, matched
    1328 transitions (= stored+matched)
       0 atomic steps
hash conflicts: 0 (resolved)
(max size 2^18 states)


1.573    memory usage (Mbyte)

unreached in proctype Agent
        (0 of 11 states)
unreached in proctype Server
        line 33, state 11, "client!deny,0"
        line 41, state 22, "-end-"
        (2 of 22 states)
unreached in proctype Client
        line 62, state 15, "-end-"
        (1 of 15 states)
```

We can see that the number of reachable states increased, as expected given that we have more processes running in this system. But the statement on line 33 is still unreachable. What is going on?

Now we look more closely at the way in which we have defined the client processes. Note that a client process can only initiate a new request when time-out is *true*. This only happens if no other process in the entire system can make a step. This means that effectively only one of the three client processes will be executing in this system at a time. (Exercise: try to find a way to prove by model checking that this is true.) The three clients have different process identifiers, so each of the clients generates a different set of system states when it executes. The symmetry in this system is not automatically exploited by SPIN.

As an experiment, we can replace the timeout condition with true, and see if this helps to exercise the rogue statement. This is most easily done by adding a macro definition to the model, for instance, as follows:

```
#define timeout true
```

Repeating the verification run now produces the following surprising result:

```
$ ./pan
error: max search depth too small
pan: out of memory
        2.68428e+008 bytes used
        102400 bytes more needed
        2.68435e+008 bytes limit
hint: to reduce memory, recompile with
  -DCOLLAPSE # good, fast compression, or
  -DMA=652   # better/slower compression, or
  -DHC # hash-compaction, approximation
  -DBITSTATE # supertrace, approximation
(Spin Version 4.0.7 -- 1 August 2003)
Warning: Search not completed
...
```

The search ran out of memory. What happened?

By making it possible for the client processes to initiate requests at any time, we made it possible for a client to resubmit a request for service before the agent process that handled its last request has terminated. Consider, for instance, a request that was granted. After the client concludes the transaction by sending its return message, the agent process still has a number of steps to take before it can terminate. It must, for instance, first return the identifier of the now freed up private channel back to the server. If the client is fast enough, it can initiate a new transaction before the agent has completed the handling of its last transaction. This means that the process identificatio number of the last agent process cannot be recycled and reassigned for the new tranaction: the number of running agent processes can increase arbitrarily far. Most of these agent processes will eventually reach their termination state, where they *could* die. Because process death can only happen in stack order, the newly created agent processes now prevent the older processes from dying.

Though annoying, this potentially infinite increase in resource consumption does reflect a real hazard scenario that could also happen in a real system execution, so it is not without value. Our job as system designers is to find a way to make sure that this scenario cannot happen, by modifying the system design.

The best way to prevent the potential for runaway resource consumption is at the source: in the client processes. Sadly, there is no general rule for how this is best done: it will depend on the specifics of the model that one is using. In this case, we can easily make sure that no new client request can be submitted until the agent process for prior requests have terminated by replacing the timeout with a slightly more restrictive condition than true. The condition we will use in this model is as follows:

```
#define timeout (_nr_pr <= N+M)
```

The variable _nr_pr is a predefined system variable (see the manual pages) that gives the precise number of active processes in the model. How many processes should we maximally have in this model? There are M client processes, one server process, and maximally N agent processes. This gives an upper limit of (N+M+1) active processes. When a client is about to submit a new request, though, it should have no active agent process associated with itself anymore, so the maximum number of active processes in the system at the time that a new request is made should not be larger than (N+M).

If we add this condition to the model and repeat the verification we see the following result:

```
$ ./pan -m30000
(Spin Version 4.0.7 -- 1 August 2003)
        + Partial Order Reduction

Full statespace search for:
        never claim            - (none specified)
        assertion violations   +
        acceptance   cycles    - (not selected)
        invalid end states     +

State-vector 108 byte, depth reached 26939, errors: 0
   133932 states, stored
   306997 states, matched
   440929 transitions (= stored+matched)
        0 atomic steps
hash conflicts: 47515 (resolved)
(max size 2^18 states)


Stats on memory usage (in Megabytes):
15.536   equivalent memory usage for states
7.194    actual memory usage for states (compression: 46.30%)
         State-vector as stored = 46 byte + 8 byte overhead
1.049    memory used for hash table (-w18)
0.960    memory used for DFS stack (-m30000)
9.177    total actual memory usage

unreached in proctype Agent
        (0 of 11 states)
unreached in proctype Server
        line 41, state 22, "-end-"
        (1 of 22 states)
unreached in proctype Client
        line 63, state 15, "-end-"
        (1 of 15 states)
```

This is the result we were expecting when we tried to change timeout into true: all statements in the model, including the pesky statement on line 33, are now reachable, though at the expense of a considerable increase of the reachable state space.

As a general rule, when you see apparently infinite growth of the state space, signified by an apparently uncontrollable growth of either the state vector or the search depth, it is worth looking carefully at all the run statements in the model, to see if a scenario like the one we have discussed here is possible.

SQUARE ROOTS?

We began our introduction to PROMELA in Chapter 2 almost inevitably with the PROMELA version of *hello world*. In retrospect, we can see that this example stretches the meaning of the term *verification model*. It defines only one single process, so clearly not much process interaction or synchronization could be happening. A model checker may be used to demonstrate that this little system cannot deadlock or get entangled into non-progress cycles, but the results that are obtained from such experiments will not be much of a revelation. Of course, PROMELA does not prevent us from writing such models, although it does try to deprive us from the tools we would need to put too much emphasis on non-concurrency aspects. This shows up specifically in the rudimentary support in the language for specifying pure computations. There are, for instance, no data types for float, double, or real in PROMELA. There is also no direct support for function calls or for recursion. These omissions are not accidental. It is deliberately hard to specify anything other than rudimentary computations in PROMELA, and deliberately easy to specify the infrastructure and the mutual dependency of concurrently executing processes.

This is not to say that no computation whatsoever can be done in PROMELA. It can. As a small example, consider the following PROMELA program that computes the integer square root of a given integer number.[1]

```
proctype sqroot(int N)
{       int x, y;

        y = 1<<15;
        do
        :: y > 0 ->
                x = x^y;            /* set bit   */
                if
                :: x*x > N ->       /* too large */
                        x = x^y     /* clear bit */
                :: else             /* leave set */
                fi;
                y = y>>1            /* next bit  */
        :: else ->
                break               /* done      */
        od;
        printf("integer sqrt(%d) = %d\n", N, x)
}
```

A few constructs are used here that will look familiar to C programmers. The proctype named sqroot is declared non-active, which means that no

---

1. The algorithm is due to Mark Borgerding. It appeared first at http://www.azillion-monkeys.com/qed/sqroot.html.

instance of it is assumed to be started by default. An instance can be initiated by another process, and at the same time that process can then pass an integer parameter, N, to the newly instantiated process, specifying the number for which the integer square root is to be computed. That instantiation can look, for instance, as follows:

```
active proctype main()
{
        run sqroot(3601)
}
```

which uses the second mechanism in PROMELA to instantiate processes: through the use of the run operator.

Another, perhaps more convenient, way of defining the instantiation would be with a parameter, as in:

```
active proctype main()
{
        run sqroot(NR)
}
```

This allows us to experiment more easily with different inputs by invoking SPIN as follows:

```
$ spin -DNR=1024 sqroot.pml
integer sqrt(3601) = 55
2 processes created
```

SPIN reminds us that it created two process instances to execute this model: one called main and the other sqroot.

The body of proctype sqroot begins with the declaration of two integers. Since we do not have a floating point data type, using integers is the best we can do here. Unlike in C, the default initial value of *all* variables is zero in PROMELA, so both variables have a known initial value at this point. The variable y is assigned the value of an expression with one operator and two operands. The operator is the left-shift operator from C. This is a bit-operator that left-shifts the bit-pattern of the left operand the number of positions indicated by the right operand. If the left operand is one, as in this case, this amounts to computing the value of the expression 2^n, where n is the value of the right operand.

The next statement in the program is a loop. If the variable y is larger than zero, which upon first entry to the loop it will be, the first option sequence is executed. Once y reaches zero, the second option sequence will break from the loop, which causes the execution of the printf statement.

After the expression y>0, we see an assignment to variable x. The assignment computes the binary *exclusive or* of x and y and assigns it to x. The desired effect in this case is to set the bit position given by variable y (initially bit position 15, corresponding to a power of two).

The algorithm attempts to compute the value of the square root of N in variable x. It approaches the value from below, first looking for the highest power of two that can be included, without exceeding the target value. If the target value is exceeded, the bit position indicated by y is cleared again, by repeating the *exclusive or* operation; otherwise nothing needs to be done. The latter happens when the else in the selection statement becomes executable. Since nothing needs to be done, no statements need to be listed here. Some SPIN users feel uncomfortable about this, and would prefer to write the selection statements as follows, inserting a dummy skip statement after the lonely else, but it is not required.

```
if
:: x*x > N ->              /* too large */
        x = x^y            /* clear bit */
:: else ->                 /* leave set */
        skip
fi;
```

After the selection statement, the single bit in variable y is right-shifted by one position to derive the next lower power of two to be tested. When y reaches zero, the algorithm terminates and prints the computed integer value of the square root of N, as desired.

Because the entire computation is deterministic, there are many optimizations we could make in this little program to help SPIN execute it faster (e.g., by embedding the entire computation within an atomic or d_step statement), but we will leave well enough alone. The same observation that we made in the *hello world* example holds for this one, though: it would be a stretch to call this specification a verification model, since it defines no system design properties that could be verified with a model checker.

ADDING INTERACTION

The main objection we can levy against the last example is that it really defines only sequential, not concurrent, behavior, with no synchronizations or interactions. With a few small changes we can turn the example into a slightly more interesting, though still rather minimal, distributed system model. We will set up the integer square root routine as a little square root server process that can perform its computations at the request of client processes. We will rearrange the code somewhat to accomplish this.

The first thing that we need to do is to declare a message channel for communication between clients and server, for instance, as follows:

```
#define NC       4

chan server = [NC] of { chan, int };
```

The first line defines a constant named NC. The constant is used in the declaration to set the capacity of the channel named server. The messages that can be passed through this channel are declared to have two fields: one of type chan that can hold a channel identifier, and one of type int that can hold an integer value.

Next, we rewrite the square root server process, so that it will read requests from this channel and respond to the client with the computed value, via a channel that the client provides in the request. The new version looks as follows:

```
active proctype sqroot()
{        chan who;
         int val, n;

         do
         :: server?who,n ->
                 compute(n, val);
                 who!val
         od
}
```

First, the server process declares a channel identifier named who, which this time is not initialized in the declaration. It also declares an integer variable n. These two variables are used to store the parameter values for the communication with a client, as provided by that client. A second integer variable val will be used to retrieve the result value that is to be communicated back to the client. The body of the square root server consists of a do loop with just one option, guarded by a message receive operation.

We have moved the actual computation into an inline definition, named compute. The variable name n, recording the value received from the client, is passed to the inline, as is the name of the variable val in which the result is to be computed.

After the call to compute completes, the value is returned to the client process in a send operation.

Before we fill in the details of the inline call, recall that an inline is merely a structured piece of macro text where the names of variables that are passed in as parameters textually substitute their placeholders inside the inline definition. Therefore, inlines are not the same as procedures: they cannot return results, and they do not have their own variable scope. All variables that are visible at the point of call of an inline are also visible inside the inline body, and, perhaps more noteworthy, all variables declared inside the inline are also visible outside it, after the point of call.

The inlined code for compute can now be written as follows:

```
inline compute(N, x)
{       int y;

        y = 1<<15;
        do
        :: y > 0 ->
                x = x^y;                /* set bit   */
                if
                :: x*x > N ->           /* too large */
                        x = x^y         /* clear bit */
                :: else                 /* leave set */
                fi;
                y = y>>1                /* next bit  */
        :: else ->
                break                   /* done      */
        od;
}
```

All we need to complete the model is the code for the client process(es). The following declaration instantiates four distinct processes. Each has its own copy of a channel through which it can be reached by the server process.

```
active [NC] proctype client()
{       chan me = [0] of { int };
        int val;

        server!me,10*_pid ->
        me?val;
        printf("integer sqrt(%d) = %d\n", 10*_pid, val)
}
```

Each process multiplies its own process identifier, available in the predefined variable _pid, by ten and asks the square root server to compute the square root of the resulting number. It does so by sending this value, together with the value of the channel variable over which it can be reached through a send operation. Again, the types of the variables that make up the message sent must match the corresponding fields in the channel declaration for the channel addressed. In this case, it is a channel type, followed by an integer. The send operation is executable when the channel is non-full.

The private channel of the client process is declared in a slightly different way from the global channel named server. First, it has only one field, of type int. Next, the number of slots in this channel is declared to be zero to identify the channel as a rendezvous port that can pass messages in an atomic operation but cannot store or buffer messages. The receive operation on the client's rendezvous port is executable only if and when the server process reaches the send statement in its code. The client is blocked until this happens, but once it happens the client can print the value and terminate.

The complete model we have discussed is shown in Figure 15.7. Executing this model, using SPIN's default simulation mode, produces the following output:

```
$ spin sqroot_server
                            integer sqrt(30) = 5
          integer sqrt(10) = 3
                                   integer sqrt(40) = 6
                  integer sqrt(20) = 4
timeout
#processes: 1
                  queue 5 (server):
481:     proc  0 (sqroot) line  27 "srs" (state 19)
5 processes created
```

The output is somewhat more interesting this time. Each of the four client processes prints one line of output. To make it easier to keep track of consecutive output from individual processes, SPIN arranges for the output from each process to appear in a different column. Next, the system execution comes to a halt without all processes having been terminated. SPIN tries in this case to enable a timeout mechanism that can trigger further actions from the halted processes (we will see later how this is done). In this case, the `timeout` event triggers no further executions, and to wrap up the simulation SPIN reports for each non-terminated process at which line number and internal state is blocked. Only the square root server process is blocked, patiently waiting for further requests from clients, which in this model can no longer come.

If we wanted the server process to exit when the system comes to a halt, we could give it a timeout option as follows:

```
active proctype sqroot()
{       chan who;
        int n, val;

        do
        :: server?who,n ->
                compute(n,val);
                who!x
        :: timeout ->
                break
        od
}
```

With this extension, the final wrapup of the execution will reduce to just the note about the number of processes that was executed.

To see the communication inside this little process model, we can use some other SPIN options, for instance, as follows:

```
$ spin -b -c sqroot_server
proc 0 = sqroot
proc 1-4 = client
```

```
#define NC      4

chan server = [NC] of { chan, int };

inline compute(N, x)
{       int y;

        y = 1<<15;
        x = 0;                          /* reset x    */
        do
        :: y > 0 ->
                x = x^y;            /* set bit    */
                if
                :: x*x > N ->       /* too large  */
                        x = x^y     /* clear bit  */
                :: else             /* leave set  */
                fi;
                y = y>>1            /* next bit   */
        :: else ->
                break               /* done       */
        od;
}

active proctype sqroot()
{       chan who;
        int n, val;

        do
        :: server?who,n ->
                compute(n,val);
                who!val
        od
}

active [NC] proctype client()
{       chan me = [0] of { int };
        int val;

        server!me(10*_pid) ->
        me?val;
        printf("integer sqrt(%d) = %d\n", 10*_pid, val)
}
```

Figure 15.7 Square Root Server Model

```
q\p   0    1    2    3    4
   5   .    .    .    server!3,30
   5   server?3,30
   5   .    .    server!2,20
   5   .    server!1,10
   5   .    .    .    .    server!4,40
   3   who!5
   3   .    .    .    me?5
   5   server?2,20
   2   who!4
   2   .    .    me?4
   5   server?1,10
   1   who!3
   1   .    me?3
   5   server?4,40
   4   who!6
   4   .    .    .    .    me?6
 5 processes created
```

The left hand column prints the channel number on which communication takes place, if any, and the top row gives the process pid numbers. Still more verbose output is also possible, for instance, by printing every single statement executed, or only specific types of statements. We will review the full range of simulation and verification options later in the book.

ADDING ASSERTIONS

In the last version of the model we captured the behavior of a system of at least a few concurrent processes, and there was some interaction to boot. It is still not quite a verification model, though. The only thing we could prove about this system, for instance, is that it cannot deadlock and has no unreachable code segments. SPIN does not allow us to prove any mathematical properties of this (or any) square root algorithm. The reason is that SPIN was designed to prove properties of process interactions in a distributed system, not of process of computations.

To prove some minor additional facts about the process behaviors in this example, we can nonetheless consider adding some assertions. We may, for instance, want to show that on the specific execution of the square root computations that we execute, the result will be in the expected range. We could do so in the client processes, for instance, by modifying the code as follows:

```
active [NC] proctype client()
{       chan me = [0] of { int };
        int v;

        server!me(10*_pid) -> me?v;
        assert(v*v <= 10*_pid && (v+1)*(v+1) > 10*_pid)
}
```

Another thing we can do is to select a more interesting set of values on which to run the computation. A good choice would be to select a value in the middle of the range of integer values, and a few more that try to probe boundary cases. Since we cannot directly prove the mathematical properties of the code, the best we can do is to use one approach that resembles testing here. To illustrate this, we now change the client processes into a single tester process that is defined as follows:

```
active proctype tester()
{       chan me = [0] of { int };
        int n, v;

        if
        :: n = -1       /* fails */
        :: n = 0        /* ok */
        :: n = 1023     /* ok */
        :: n = 1<<29    /* ok */
        :: n = 1<<30    /* fails */
        fi;
        server!me(n) -> me?v;
        assert(v*v <= n && (v+1)*(v+1) > n)
}
```

Executing this model in SPIN's simulation mode as before may now succeed or fail, depending on the specific value for n that is chosen in the non-deterministic selection at the start of the tester. Along the way, it is worth observing that the five option sequences in this selection structure all consist of a single guard, and the guards are all assignments, not conditional expressions. The PROMELA semantics state that assignments are always executable, independent of the value that is assigned. If we execute the little model often enough, for example, five or more times, we will likely see all possible behaviors.

Not surprisingly, the algorithm is not equipped to handle negative numbers as input; the choice of -1 leads to an assertion failure. All other values, except for the last, work fine. When the value 1<<30 is chosen, though, the result is:

```
$ spin -c sqroot_tester
proc 0 = sqroot
proc 1 = tester
q    0    1
  2    .    server!1,1073741824
  2    server?1,1073741824
  1    who!65535
  1    .    me?65535
spin: line  45 "srs2", Error: assertion violated
spin: text of failed assertion:
        assert((((v*v)<=n)&&((((v+1)*(v+1))>n))))
-------------
final state:
-------------
```

```
#processes: 2
                  queue 2 (server):
108:    proc  1 (tester) line  45 "srs2" (state 9)
108:    proc  0 (sqroot) line  27 "srs2" (state 19)
2 processes created
```

It would be erroneous to conclude anything about the correctness of the algorithm other than for the specific values used here. For instance, it would *not* be safe to conclude that the algorithm would work correctly for all positive values up to `(1<<30)-1`.

Executing the simulation repeatedly by hand, until all cases in non-deterministic selection structures were hit, would of course be a tiresome procedure. The errors will come out more easily by simply running the verifier, for instance, as follows:

```
$ spin -a sqroot_tester
$ cl -DPC pan.c
$ pan
(Spin Version 4.0.7 -- 1 August 2003)
Warning: Search not completed
        + Partial Order Reduction

Full statespace search for:
        never claim             - (none specified)
        assertion violations    +
        acceptance   cycles     - (not selected)
        invalid end states      +

State-vector 92 byte, depth reached 39, errors: 1
        39 states, stored
         0 states, matched
        39 transitions (= stored+matched)
         0 atomic steps
hash conflicts: 0 (resolved)
(max size 2^18 states)

1.573   memory usage (Mbyte)
```

The trail reveals the cause of the error. It is generated as follows:

```
$ spin -t -c sqroot_tester
proc 0 = sqroot
proc 1 = tester
q   0   1
   2    .     server!1,-1
   2    server?1,-1
   1    who!0
   1    .     me?0
spin: line  72 "sqroot_tester", Error: assertion violated
spin: trail ends after 40 steps
```

```
    -------------
    final state:
    -------------
    #processes: 2
                       queue 2 (server):
      40:      proc  1 (tester) line  73 "sqroot_tester" (state 11)
      40:      proc  0 (sqroot) line  28 "sqroot_tester" (state 21)
    2 processes created
```

A COMMENT FILTER

In Chapter 3 (p. 69) we briefly discussed a seldom used feature in PROMELA that allows us to read input from the user terminal in simulation experiments. The use of STDIN immediately implies that we are not dealing with a closed system, which makes verification impossible. Still, the feature makes for nice demos, and we will use it in this last example to illustrate the use of PROMELA inlines.

The problem we will use as an excuse to write this model is to strip C-style comments from text files. Figure 15.8 shows the general outline of a deterministic automaton for stripping comment strings from C programs. According to the rules of C, the character pair /* starts a comment and the first subsequent occurrence of the pair */ ends it. There are some exceptions to this rule though. If the combination /* appears inside a quoted string, for instance, it does not start a comment, so the automaton must be able to recognize not just comments but also quoted strings. To make things more interesting still, the quote character that starts or ends a string can itself be quoted (as in '"') or escaped with a backslash (as in "\""). In the automaton from Figure 15.8, states s_1 and s_2 deal with strings, and states s_6, s_7, and s_8 deal with quoted characters.

The transition labels that we have used in Figure 15.8 represent classes of input characters that must be matched for the transition to be executable. The meaning is as follows. A transition label that consists of a single symbol, represents a match in the input stream of the corresponding ASCII character. A dot symbol, for example, on the transition from s_2 to s_1, represents a match of *any* single character in the input stream. The symbol ¬ (pronounced *not*) represents a match on any character other than *all* those that are listed behind the ¬ symbol in the transition label. This symbol is not itself an ASCII character, so there can be no confusion about its meaning. The label ¬ * on the transition from s_3 to s_4, for instance, represents the match of any character other than *, and the label ¬ /" on the self-loop at state s_0 means any character other than the forward slash character / or the quote character ".

If the input sequence provided to this automaton conforms to the C comment conventions that are captured here, the automaton should terminate in its initial (and final) state s_0.

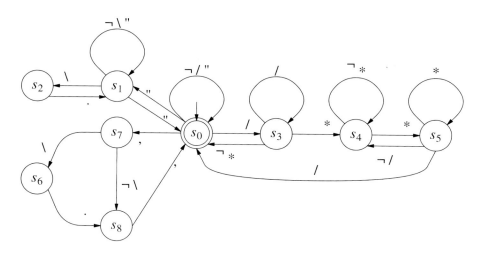

Figure 15.8 A Sample Automaton to Check C-Style Comment Conventions

Part of the complexity of this automaton comes from the fact that characters can be escaped with backslashes, and can appear inside single or double quote marks. The comment delimiters could also appear inside text strings, making it hard to accurately recognize where a comment begins and ends in cases such as these:

```
/* the comment begins here
 * printf("but it doesn't end */ here yet\n");
 */
if (s == '"') /* not the start of a string */
        printf("/* not a comment */\n");
```

To simplify things a little, and to allow us to concentrate on the use of `inlines` in the example, we will cheat and not implement the full automaton but just a portion of it that implements the most basic functionality.

The basic model shown in Figure 15.9 can strip standard comments from text files, but does not make any exceptions for quoted or escaped characters, and it does not skip over text that is embedded in strings, as it formally should.

As a quick test, if we run this program on itself, it nicely reproduces its own code, but without the comments. To avoid automatic indentation of the output, we can use SPIN's option `-T`. The command we execute is then:

```
$ spin -T strip < strip
```

which, in part, produces as output:

```
 1 /* strip C-style comments -- simple version */
 2
 3 chan STDIN;
 4
 5 #define FlipState in_comment = (in_comment -> false : true)
 6
 7 inline Print() {
 8     if
 9     :: !in_comment -> printf("%c", c)
10     :: else /* inside a comment string */
11     fi;
12 }
13 inline Getc(prev) {
14     do
15     :: STDIN?c ->
16             if
17             :: c == -1 -> goto done
18             :: c != prev -> break
19             :: c == prev -> Print()
20             fi
21     od
22 }
23 inline Handle(have, expect) {
24     oc = have;
25     Getc(have);
26     nc = c;
27     if
28     :: c == expect -> FlipState; goto again
29     :: else -> c = oc; Print(); c = nc
30     fi
31 }
32 init {
33     int c, oc, nc;
34     bool in_comment;
35
36 again:      do
37     :: Getc(0) ->
38             if
39             :: !in_comment && c == '/' ->
40                     Handle('/', '*')
41             :: in_comment && c == '*' ->
42                     Handle('*', '/')
43             :: else
44             fi;
45             Print()
46     od;
47 done:       skip    /* saw the -1 end-of-file marker */
48 }
```

Figure 15.9 A Simple C-Style Comment Filter

```
chan STDIN;

#define FlipState in_comment = (in_comment -> false : true)

inline Print() {
        if
        :: !in_comment -> printf("%c", c)
        :: else
        fi;
}

...

init {
        int c, oc, nc;
        bool in_comment;

again:  do
        :: Getc(0) ->
                if
                :: !in_comment && c == '/' ->
                        Handle('/', '*')
                :: in_comment && c == '*' ->
                        Handle('*', '/')
                :: else
                fi;
                Print()
        od;
done:   skip
}
1 process created
$
```

We use SPIN's -T option here to make sure that the printed characters are produced without indentation.

The main execution loop of the `strip` model appears in the `init` process. The boolean variable `in_comment` is initially *false*. It changes its value each time that the macro `FlipState` is called, which uses PROMELA's syntax for a conditional expression to do so. An equally effective method would be to use the following definition:

```
#define FlipState      in_comment = 1 - in_comment
```

but this relies perhaps a bit too much on the fact the SPIN normally does very little type checking.

The main execution loop in the initial process starts with an an `inline` call, using the parameter value zero. The inline reads a character from the magic STDIN channel, and checks whether it equals the predefined value for end-of-file: -1. Note that for this reason it is important to read the value into a signed integer here: using an unsigned `byte` variable would not work. If not the end-of-file marker, the value is compared with the parameter value that was passed in and if it does not match it, the read loop ends. In this case, the value read cannot be zero, so the loop will end on its first termination, leaving the value read in the integer variable c.

The next thing to do is to check for either the start or the end of a comment string, depending on the current state of variable in_comment. The one tricky part here is to correctly recognize the comment string in cases such as the following:

```
c//**** a strange comment ***/c
```

which, after stripping the embedded comment, should produce:

```
c/c
```

The inline function Handle checks for the expected character, but also passes the current character to Getc where it can now check for repetitions. Once the expected value is seen, the state of in_comment can change. If the character sequence turns out *not* to be a comment delimiter, though, we must be able to reproduce the actual text that was seen. For this reason, the Handle function uses the local variables oc and nc. Note that even though these two variables are only used inside the Handle function, the scope of all local variables is the same, no matter where in a process the declaration appears. Also, since the Handle function is called twice, we want to avoid inserting the declaration of these two variables twice into the body of the proctype init, which would happen if we moved the declaration into the Handle function itself.

The calls to inline function Print can appear up to three levels deep in an inlining sequence. For instance, Handle calls Getc, which can call Print. The calling sequence is valid, as long as it is not cyclic, since that would cause an infinite regression of inlining attempts. The SPIN parser can readily reject attempts to create a cyclic inlining sequences, as it requires that every inline function is declared before it is used.

We leave the extension of the model from Figure 15.9 to match the complete automaton structure from Figure 15.8 as an exercise.

PROMELA LANGUAGE REFERENCE 16

"The infinite multitude of things
is incomprehensible, and more than a
man may be able to contemplate."
(Giambattista della Porta, 1535–1615, Natural Magick)

The PROMELA manual pages that are included in this book can be grouped into seven main sections. The first five of these sections, plus the grammar description given here, describe the language proper. The entries from the sixth section cover those things that are deliberately not in the language, and contain a brief explanation of why they were left out. The entries from the seventh and last section cover the more recent extensions to the PROMELA language to support the use of embedded C code statements and data declarations. The main sections are:

1. Meta Terms (translated by preprocessors into vanilla PROMELA)
2. Declarators (for defining process, channel, and data objects)
3. Control Flow Constructors (separators, compound statements, jumps, labels, etc.)
4. Basic Statements (such as send, receive, assignment, etc.)
5. Predefined Functions and Operators (such as len, run, nempty, etc.)
6. Omissions (such as floating point, probabilities, etc.)
7. Extensions (for embedded C code)

This chapter contains the manual pages for the first six of these sections, listed in alphabetical order with the section name indicated at the top of each page. Chapter 17 separately introduces the extensions for embedded C code and contains the corresponding manual pages from the last section in our list.

In the tradition of the classic UNIX manuals, each manual page contains some or all of the following eight defining elements.

NAME

A one sentence synopsis of the language construct and its main purpose.

SYNTAX

The syntax rules for the language construct. Optional terms are enclosed in (non-quoted) square brackets. The Kleene star * is used to indicate zero or more repetitions of an optional term. When the special symbols ' [', '] ', or ' * ', appear as literals, they are quoted. For instance, in

chan *name* = '[' *const* ']' of { *typename* [, *typename*] * }

the first two square brackets are literals, and the last two enclose an optional part of the definition that can be repeated zero or more times.

The terms set in italic, such as *name*, *const*, and *typename*, refer to the grammar rules that follow.

EXECUTABILITY

Defines all conditions that must be satisfied for a basic statement from the fourth section to be eligible for execution. Some standard parts of these conditions are assumed and not repeated throughout. One such implied condition is, for instance, that the executing process has reached the point in its code where the basic statement is defined. Implied conditions of this type are defined in the description of PROMELA semantics in Chapter 7. If the executability clause is described as *true*, no conditions other than the implied conditions apply.

EFFECT

Defines the effect that the execution of a basic statement from the fourth section will cause on the system state. One standard part of the effect is again always implied and not repeated everywhere: the execution of the statement may change the local state of the executing process. If the effect clause is described as none, no effect other than the implicit change in local state is defined. See also the PROMELA semantics description in Chapter 7.

DESCRIPTION

Describes in informal terms the purpose and use of the language construct that is defined.

EXAMPLES

Gives some typical applications of the construct.

NOTES

Adds some additional notes about special circumstances or cautions.

SEE ALSO

Gives references to other manual pages that may provide additional explanations.

GRAMMAR RULES

The following list defines the basic grammar of PROMELA. Choices are separated by vertical bars; optional parts are included in square brackets; a Kleene star indicates zero or more repetitions of the immediately preceding grammar fragment; literals are enclosed in single quotes; uppercase names are keywords; lowercase names refer to the grammar rules from this list. The name any_ascii_char appears once, and is used to refer to any printable ASCII character except ' " '. PROMELA keywords are spelled like the token-names in the grammar, but in lowercase instead of uppercase.

The statement separator used in this list is the semicolon ';'. In all cases, the semicolon can be replaced with the two-character arrow symbol: '−>' without change of meaning.

We will not attempt to include a full grammar description for the language C, as it can appear inside the embedded C code statements. Where it appears, we have abbreviated this as ... C ... in the grammar rules that follow.

```
spec      : module [ module ] *

module    : utype       /* user defined types   */
          | mtype       /* mtype declaration    */
          | decl_lst    /* global vars, chans   */
          | proctype    /* proctype declaration */
          | init        /* init process - max 1 per model */
          | never       /* never claim  - max 1 per model */
          | trace       /* event trace  - max 1 per model */
          | c_code '{' ... C ... '}'
          | c_decl '{' ... C ... '}'
          | c_state string string [ string ]
          | c_track string string

proctype: [ active ] PROCTYPE name '(' [ decl_lst ]')'
          [ priority ] [ enabler ] '{' sequence '}'

init      : INIT [ priority ] '{' sequence '}'

never     : NEVER '{' sequence '}'

trace     : TRACE '{' sequence '}'
          | NOTRACE '{' sequence '}'

utype     : TYPEDEF name '{' decl_lst '}'

mtype     : MTYPE [ '=' ] '{' name [ ',' name ] * '}'

decl_lst: one_decl [ ';' one_decl ] *
```

```
one_decl: [ visible ] typename  ivar [',' ivar ] *

typename: BIT    | BOOL | BYTE   | PID
          | SHORT | INT  | MTYPE | CHAN
          | uname /* user defined typenames (see utype)  */

active  : ACTIVE [ '[' const ']' ]  /* instantiation   */

priority: PRIORITY const              /* simulation only */

enabler : PROVIDED '(' expr ')'      /* constraint      */

visible : HIDDEN
          | SHOW

sequence: step [ ';' step ] *

step    : decl_lst
          | stmnt [ UNLESS stmnt ]
          | XR varref [',' varref ] *
          | XS varref [',' varref ] *

ivar    : name [ '[' const ']' ]
                [ '=' any_expr | '=' ch_init ]

ch_init : '[' const ']' OF
                '{' typename [ ',' typename ] * '}'

varref  : name [ '[' any_expr ']' ] [ '.' varref ]

send    : varref '!' send_args         /* fifo send   */
          | varref '!' '!' send_args       /* sorted send */

receive : varref '?' recv_args         /* fifo receive   */
          | varref '?' '?' recv_args       /* random receive */
          | varref '?' '<' recv_args '>'  /* poll */
          | varref '?' '?' '<' recv_args '>'

recv_poll: varref '?' '[' recv_args ']' /* test */
          | varref '?' '?' '[' recv_args ']'

send_args: arg_lst
          | any_expr '(' arg_lst ')'

arg_lst : any_expr [ ',' any_expr ] *

recv_args: recv_arg [ ',' recv_arg ] *
          | recv_arg '(' recv_args ')'
```

```
recv_arg : varref
         | EVAL '(' varref ')'
         | [ '-' ] const

assign   : varref '=' any_expr      /* assignment */
         | varref '+' '+'           /* increment  */
         | varref '-' '-'           /* decrement  */

stmnt    : IF options FI            /* selection  */
         | DO options OD            /* iteration  */
         | ATOMIC '{' sequence '}'
         | D_STEP '{' sequence '}'
         | '{' sequence '}'
         | send
         | receive
         | assign
         | ELSE                     /* guard statement    */
         | BREAK                    /* only inside loops */
         | GOTO name                /* anywhere          */
         | name ':' stmnt           /* labeled statement */
         | PRINT '(' string [ ',' arg_lst ] ')'
         | ASSERT expr
         | expr                     /* condition */
         | c_code [ c_assert ] '{' ... C ... '}'
         | c_expr [ c_assert ] '{' ... C ... '}'

c_assert: '[' ... C ... ']'        /* see p. 505 */

options : ':' ':' sequence [ ':' ':' sequence ] *

andor   : '&' '&' | '|' '|'

binarop : '+' | '-' | '*' | '/' | '%' | '&' | '^' | '|'
        | '>' | '<' | '>' '=' | '<' '=' | '=' '=' | '!' '='
        | '<' '<' | '>' '>' | andor

unarop  : '~' | '-' | '!'

any_expr: '(' any_expr ')'
        | any_expr binarop any_expr
        | unarop any_expr
        | '(' any_expr '-' '>' any_expr ':' any_expr ')'
        | LEN '(' varref ')'    /* nr of messages in chan */
        | recv_poll
        | varref
        | const
        | TIMEOUT          /* hang system state */
        | NP_              /* non-progress system state */
```

```
                  |  ENABLED '(' any_expr ')'
                  |  PC_VALUE '(' any_expr ')'
                  |  name '[' any_expr ']' '@' name
                  |  RUN name '(' [ arg_lst ] ')' [ priority ]

      expr      :  any_expr
                  |  '(' expr ')'
                  |  expr andor expr
                  |  chanop '(' varref ')'

      chanop    :  FULL  |  EMPTY  |  NFULL  |  NEMPTY

      string    :  '"' [ any_ascii_char ] * '"'

      uname     :  name

      name      :  alpha [ alpha | const | '_' ] *

      const     :  TRUE  |  FALSE  |  SKIP  |  number [ number ] *

      alpha     :  'a'  |  'b'  |  'c'  |  'd'  |  'e'  |  'f'
                  |  'g'  |  'h'  |  'i'  |  'j'  |  'k'  |  'l'
                  |  'm'  |  'n'  |  'o'  |  'p'  |  'q'  |  'r'
                  |  's'  |  't'  |  'u'  |  'v'  |  'w'  |  'x'
                  |  'y'  |  'z'
                  |  'A'  |  'B'  |  'C'  |  'D'  |  'E'  |  'F'
                  |  'G'  |  'H'  |  'I'  |  'J'  |  'K'  |  'L'
                  |  'M'  |  'N'  |  'O'  |  'P'  |  'Q'  |  'R'
                  |  'S'  |  'T'  |  'U'  |  'V'  |  'W'  |  'X'
                  |  'Y'  |  'Z'

      number    :  '0'  |  '1'  |  '2'  |  '3'  |  '4'  |  '5'
                  |  '6'  |  '7'  |  '8'  |  '9'
```

MAIN SECTIONS

The manual pages that follow are in alphabetical order, with the section name
indicated. The pages can be grouped per section as follows:

META TERMS

comments (p. 396), false (p. 416), inline (p. 428), ltl (p. 434), macros (p.
436), skip (p. 478), true (p. 486).

DECLARATORS

accept (p. 379), active (p. 381), arrays (p. 383), bit (p. 403), bool (p. 403),
byte (p. 403), chan (p. 394), D_proctype (p. 458), datatypes (p. 403), end
(p. 413), hidden (p. 422), init (p. 426), int (p. 403), local (p. 433), mtype

(p. 438), never (p. 441), notrace (p. 483), pid (p. 403), priority (p. 453), proctype (p. 458), progress (p. 459), provided (p. 461), short (p. 403), show (p. 477), trace (p. 483), typedef (p. 487), unsigned (p. 403), xr (p. 493), xs (p. 493).

CONTROL FLOW

atomic (p. 390), break (p. 393), d_step (p. 401), do (p. 406), fi (p. 424), goto (p. 420), if (p. 424), labels (p. 430), od (p. 406), separators (p. 475), sequence (p. 476), unless (p. 490).

BASIC STATEMENTS

assert (p. 385), assign (p. 388), condition (p. 400), printf (p. 451), printm (p. 451), receive (p. 466), send (p. 473).

PREDEFINED

_ (p. 373), _last (p. 373last), _nr_pr (p. 373nr_pr), _pid (p. 377), cond_expr (p. 398), else (p. 408), empty (p. 410), enabled (p. 412), eval (p. 415), full (p. 419), len (p. 432), nempty (p. 440), nfull (p. 446), np_ (p. 447), pc_value (p. 448), poll (p. 450), remoterefs (p. 468), run (p. 470), STDIN (p. 480), timeout (p. 481).

EMBEDDED C CODE

c_expr (p. 511), c_code (p. 505), c_decl (p. 508), c_state (p. 508), c_track (p. 508).

OMISSIONS

float (p. 417), hierarchy (p. 423), pointers (p. 449), probabilities (p. 454), procedures (p. 455), rand (p. 462), realtime (p. 464), scanf (p. 472).

REFERENCE

Table 16.1 gives an overview of all the manual pages that describe the PROMELA language, together with the corresponding page numbers. Five of the primitives are discussed in Chapter 17, with the corresponding manual pages following on pages 505 to 511.

SPECIAL CASES

Several language features apply only in special cases. Two types of special cases include those features that only affect the specific way in which either a simulation or a verification run is performed. Other types of special case include features that are either incompatible with the enforcement of SPIN's partial order reduction method or with the breadth-first search option, and features that are mutually incompatible. We summarize all these special cases next.

Table 16.1 Index of All Manual Pages

Name	Page	Name	Page	Name	Page	Name	Page
_	373	condition	400	len	432	provided	461
_last	374	D_proctype	458	local	433	rand	462
_nr_pr	376	d_step	401	ltl	434	realtime	464
_pid	377	datatypes	403	macros	436	receive	466
accept	379	do	406	mtype	438	remoterefs	468
active	381	else	408	nempty	440	run	470
arrays	383	empty	410	never	441	scanf	472
assert	385	enabled	412	nfull	446	send	473
assign	388	end	413	notrace	483	separators	475
atomic	390	eval	415	np_	447	sequence	476
bit	403	false	416	od	406	short	403
bool	403	fi	424	pc_value	448	show	477
break	393	float	417	pid	403	skip	478
byte	403	full	419	pointers	449	STDIN	480
c_code	505	goto	420	poll	450	timeout	481
c_decl	508	hidden	422	printf	451	trace	483
c_expr	511	hierarchy	423	printm	451	true	486
c_state	508	if	424	priority	453	typedef	487
c_track	508	init	426	probabilities	454	unless	490
chan	394	inline	428	procedures	455	unsigned	403
comments	396	int	403	proctype	458	xr	493
cond_expr	398	labels	430	progress	459	xs	493

SIMULATION ONLY

A small number of language features apply *only* to simulations, and are ignored in verification runs. They are:

priority (p. 453), show (p. 477), and STDIN (p. 480).

The use of some special keywords inside print statements, such as MSC: and BREAK are only interpreted by the graphical user interface XSPIN. An explanation of these special keywords can be found in the manpage for the print statement on p. 451, and in Chapter 12 on p.272.

VERIFICATION ONLY

Some language features apply *only* to verifications, and are ignored in simulation runs. They include the special labels:

accept (p. 379), progress (p. 459), and end (p. 413),

as well as the verification related features:

ltl (434), never (p. 441), trace (p. 483), notrace (p, 483), xr (p. 493), and xs (p. 493).

PARTIAL ORDER REDUCTION

Two PROMELA language features are incompatible with the enforcement of SPIN's partial order reduction algorithm. They are:
_last (p. 374), enabled (p. 412), and provided (p. 461).

This means that if these constructs appear in a verification model, the use of the partial order reduction algorithm cannot be considered safe and may cause an incompleteness of the search. If an error is found, the error report remains valid, but if no error is found this no longer implies that errors are impossible. The verifier will issue a warning when it detects the presence of one or both of the above two constructs, and the user did not disable the partial order reduction algorithm. To avoid the warning, and the problem, it suffices to compile the pan.c source with the extra directive -DNOREDUCE. As a result, the time and memory requirements may increase, but the accuracy of the search process will be secure.

Rendezvous: Rendezvous communication is incompatible with partial order reduction in a small number of cases. The partial order reduction algorithm can produce an invalid reduction when rendezvous send operations can appear in the guard of an escape clause of a PROMELA unless statement. When the verifier detects that a model contains both unless statements and rendezvous message passing operations, it will therefore always issue a warning, recommending the use of directive -DNOREDUCE to disable partial order reduction. If the warning is ignored and an error trace is found, it will nonetheless be accurate, so this mode of search may still be of some use.

Breadth-First Search: The situation is less favorable when a breadth-first search is performed for the same type of model. In this case false error reports would become possible, even in the absence of partial order reduction. If, therefore, the verifier detects the use of a rendezvous send operation as the guard statement of the escape clause of an unless statement, the verifier will abort the run in breadth-first search mode with an error message. The use of a rendezvous receive operation in the escape clause of an unless statement can be considered safe in both cases.

The LTL Next Operator: If SPIN is compiled from its sources with the additional compiler directive -DNXT, the use of the LTL 'next' operator, which is written X, is enabled. The use of this operator can conflict with SPIN's partial order reduction if the LTL formula that is specified is not stutter invariant. If you are not sure about stutter invariance, it is always best to disable partial order reduction whenever the X operator is used.

Fairness: In models that use rendezvous message passing, the weak fairness option is also not compatible with the use of partial order reduction. If this case is detected, the verifier will issue a warning. To suppress it, either omit the weak fairness option, or disable partial order reduction with compile-time directive -DNOREDUCE.

Remote References: Partial order reduction is incompatible with the use of remote referencing operations. The verifier will issue a warning if this is detected.

There are a few other types of incompatibility.

Channel Assertions and Buffered Channels: The channel assertions xr and xs can only be applied to buffered message channels; they cannot be used on rendezvous ports (i.e., on channels with a zero capacity).

Breadth-First Search and Rendezvous: The breadth-first search algorithm cannot be used on models that contain rendezvous statements in the escape clause of an unless statement. The verifier will issue a warning when it encounters this case.

Breadth-First Search and _last: Breadth-first search, finally, is incompatible with the use of the predefined variable _last. The verifier will issue a warning also in this case.

NAME

_ – a predefined, global, write-only, integer variable.

SYNTAX

_

DESCRIPTION

The underscore symbol _ refers to a global, predefined, write-only, integer variable that can be used to store scratch values. It is an error to attempt to use or reference the value of this variable in any context.

EXAMPLES

The following example uses a do-loop to flush the contents of a channel with two message fields of arbitrary type, while ignoring the values of the retrieved messages:

```
do
:: q?_,_
:: empty(q) -> break
od
```

SEE ALSO

_nr_pr, **_last**, **_pid**, **np_**, **hidden**

NAME

`_last` – a predefined, global, read-only variable of type `pid`.

SYNTAX

`_last`

DESCRIPTION

`_last` is a predefined, global, read-only variable of type `pid` that holds the instantiation number of the process that performed the last step in the current execution sequence. The initial value of `_last` is zero.

The `_last` variable can only be used inside `never` claims. It is an error to assign a value to this variable in any context.

EXAMPLES

The following sample `never` claim attempts to match an infinite run in which the process with process initialization number one executes every other step, once it starts executing.

```
never {
        do
        :: (_last != 1)
        :: else -> break
        od;
accept:
        do
        :: (_last != 1) -> (_last == 1)
        od
}
```

Because the initial value of variable `_last` is zero, the first guard in the first `do` loop is always *true* in the initial state. This first loop is designed to allow the claim automaton to execute dummy steps (passing through its `else` clause) until the process with instantiation number one executes its first step, and the value of `_last` becomes one. Immediately after this happens, the claim automaton moves from into its second state, which is accepting. The remainder of the run can only be accepted, and reported through SPIN's acceptance cycle detection method, if the process with instantiation number one continues to execute every other step. The system as a whole may very well allow other executions, of course. The `never` claim is designed, though, to intercept just those runs that match the property of interest.

NOTES

During verifications, this variable is not part of the state descriptor unless it is referred to at least once. The additional state information that is recorded in this variable will generally cause an increase of the number of reachable states. The most serious side effect of the use of the variable _last in a model is, though, that it prevents the use of both partial order reduction and of the breadth-first search option.

SEE ALSO
_, _nr_pr, _pid, never, np_

NAME

_nr_pr – a predefined, global, read-only, integer variable.

SYNTAX

_nr_pr

DESCRIPTION

The predefined, global, read-only variable _nr_pr records the number of processes that are currently running (i.e., active processes). It is an error to attempt to assign a value to this variable in any context.

EXAMPLES

The variable can be used to delay a parent process until all of the child processes that it created have terminated. The following example illustrates this type of use:

```
proctype child()
{
        printf("child %d\n", _pid)
}

active proctype parent()
{
        do
        :: (_nr_pr == 1) ->
                run child()
        od
}
```

The use of the precondition on the creation of a new child process in the parent process guarantees that each child process will have process instantiation number one: one higher than the parent process. There can never be more than two processes running simultaneously in this system. Without the condition, a new child process could be created before the last one terminates and dies. This means that, in principle, an infinite number of processes could result. The verifier puts the limit on the number of processes that can effectively be created at 256, so in practice, if this was attempted, the 256th attempt to create a child process would fail, and the run statement from this example would then block.

SEE ALSO

_, **_last**, **_pid**, **active**, **procedures**, **run**

NAME

_pid – a predefined, local, read-only variable of type pid that stores the instantiation number of the executing process.

SYNTAX

_pid

DESCRIPTION

Process instantiation numbers begin at zero for the first process created and count up for every new process added. The first process, with instantiation number zero, is always created by the system. Processes are created in order of declaration in the model. In the initial system state only process are created for active proctype declarations, and for an init declaration, if present. There must be at least one active proctype or init declaration in the model.

When a process terminates, it can only die and make its _pid number available for the creation of another process, if and when it has the highest _pid number in the system. This means that processes can only die in the reverse order of their creation (in stack order).

The value of the process instantiation number for a process that is created with the run operator is returned by that operator.

Instantiation numbers can be referred to locally by the executing process, through the predefined local _pid variable, and globally in never claims through remote references.

It is an error to attempt to assign a new value to this variable.

EXAMPLES

The following example shows a way to discover the _pid number of a process, and gives a possible use for a process instantiation number in a remote reference inside a never claim.

```
active [3] proctype A()
{
        printf("this is process: %d\n", _pid);
L:      printf("it terminates after two steps\n")
}

never {
        do
        :: A[0]@L -> break
        od
}
```

The remote reference in the claim automaton checks whether the process with instantiation number zero has reached the statement that was marked with the label L. As soon as it does, the claim automaton reaches its end state by executing the break statement, and reports a match. The three processes that are instantiated in the active proctype declaration can execute in any order, so it is quite possible for the processes with instantiation numbers one and two to terminate before the first process reaches label L.

NOTES

A never claim, if present, is internally also represented by the verifier as a running process. This claim process has no visible instantiation number, and therefore cannot be referred to from within the model. From the user's point of view, the process instantiation numbers are independent of the use of a never claim.

SEE ALSO

_, _last, _nr_pr, active, init, never, proctype, remoterefs, run

NAME

accept – label-name prefix used for specifying liveness properties.

SYNTAX

accept[a-zA-Z0-9_]*: *stmnt*

DESCRIPTION

An accept label is any label name that starts with the six-character sequence accept. It can appear anywhere a label can appear as a prefix to a PROMELA statement.

Accept labels are used to formalize Büchi acceptance conditions. They are most often used inside never claims, but their special meaning is also recognized when they are used inside trace assertions, or in the body of a proctype declaration. There can be any number of accept labels in a model, subject to the naming restrictions that apply to all labels (i.e., a given label name cannot appear more than once within the same defining scope).

A local process statement that is marked with an accept label can also mark a set of global system states. This set includes all states where the marked statement has been reached in the process considered, but where the statement has not yet been executed. The SPIN generated verifiers can prove either the absence or presence of infinite runs that traverse at least one accept state in the global system state space infinitely often. The mechanism can be used, for instance, to prove LTL liveness properties.

EXAMPLES

The following proctype declaration translates into an automaton with precisely three local states: the initial state, the state in between the send and the receive, and the (unreachable) final state at the closing curly brace of the declaration.

The accept label in this model formalizes the requirement that the second state cannot persist forever, and cannot be revisited infinitely often either. In the given program this would imply that the execution should eventually always stop at the initial state, just before the execution of sema!p.

```
active proctype dijkstra()
{        do
         :: sema!p ->
accept:           sema?v
         od
}
```

NOTES

When a `never` claim is generated from an LTL formula, it already includes all required accept labels. As an example, consider the following SPIN generated `never` claim:

```
dell: spin -f '[]<>(p U q)'
never {      /* []<>(p U q) */
T0_init:
        if
        :: (q) -> goto accept_S9
        :: (1) -> goto T0_init
        fi;
accept_S9:
        if
        :: (1) -> goto T0_init
        fi;
}
```

In this example, the second state of the claim automaton was marked as an accepting state.

Since in most cases the `accept` labels are automatically generated from LTL formula, it should rarely be needed to manually add additional labels of this type elswhere in a verification model.

SEE ALSO

end, labels, ltl, never, progress, trace

NAME

`active` – prefix for `proctype` declarations to instantiate an initial set of processes.

SYNTAX

`active proctype` *name* ([*decl_lst*]   )   { *sequence* }

`active` ' [' *const* '] ' `proctype` *name* ([*decl_lst*]   )   { *sequence* }

DESCRIPTION

The keyword `active` can be prefixed to any `proctype` declaration to define a set of processes that are required to be active (i.e., running) in the initial system state. At least one active process must always exist in the initial system state. Such a process can also be declared with the help of the keyword `init`.

Multiple instantiations of the same `proctype` can be specified with an optional array suffix of the `active` prefix. The instantiation of a `proctype` requires the allocation of a process state and the instantiation of all associated local variables. At the time of instantiation, a unique process instantiation number is assigned. The maximum number of simultaneously running processes is 255. Specifying a constant greater than 255 in the suffix of an `active` keyword would result in a warning from the SPIN parser, and the creation of only the first 255 processes.

Processes that are instantiated through an `active` prefix cannot be passed arguments. It is, nonetheless, legal to declare a list of formal parameters for such processes to allow for argument passing in additional instantiations with a `run` operator. In this case, copies of the processes instantiated through the `active` prefix have all formal parameters initialized to zero. Each active process is guaranteed to have a unique `_pid` within the system.

EXAMPLES

```
active proctype A(int a) { ... }
active [4] proctype B() { run A(_pid) }
```

One instance of `proctype` A is created in the initial system state with a parameter value for a of zero. In this case, the variable a is indistinguishable from a locally declared variable. Four instances of `proctype` B are also created. Each of these four instances will create one additional copy of `proctype` A, and each of these has a parameter value equal to the process instantiation number of the executing process of type B. If the process of type A is assigned `_pid` zero, then the four process of type B will be assigned `_pid` numbers one to three. All five processes that are declared through the use of the two `active` prefixes are guaranteed to be created and instantiated before any of these processes starts executing.

NOTES

In many PROMELA models, the `init` process is used exclusively to initialize other processes with the `run` operator. By using `active` prefixes instead, the `init` process becomes superfluous and can be omitted, which reduces the amount of memory needed to store global states.

If the total number of active processes specified with `active` prefixes is larger than 255, only the first 255 processes (in the order of declaration) will be created.

SEE ALSO

_pid, init, proctype, remoterefs, run

NAME

arrays – syntax for declaring and initializing a one-dimensional array of variables.

SYNTAX

typename name ' [' *const* '] ' [= *any_expr*]

DESCRIPTION

An object of any predefined or user-defined datatype can be declared either as a scalar or as an array. The array elements are distinguished from one another by their array index. As in the C language, the first element in an array always has index zero. The number of elements in an array must be specified in the array declaration with an integer constant (i.e., it cannot be specified with an expression). If an initializer is present, the initializing expression is evaluated once, and all array elements are initialized to the same resulting value.

In the absence of an explicit initializer, all array elements are initialized to zero.

Data initialization for global variables happens in the initial system state. All process local variables are initialized at process instantiation. The moment of creation and initialization of a local variable is independent of the precise place within the `proctype` body where the variable declaration is placed.

EXAMPLES

The declaration

```
byte state[N]
```

with N a constant declares an array of N bytes, all initialized to zero by default. The array elements can be assigned to and referred to in statements such as

```
state[0] = state[3] + 5 * state[3*2/n]
```

where n is a constant or a variable declared elsewhere. An array index in a variable reference can be any valid (i.e., side-effect free) PROMELA expression. The valid range of indices for the array state, as declared here, is 0..N-1.

NOTES

Scalar objects are treated as shorthands for array objects with just one element. This means that references to scalar objects can always be suffixed with [0] without triggering a complaint from the SPIN parser. Be warned, therefore, that if two arrays are declared as

```
byte a[N], b[N];
```

then the assignment

```
a = b;
```

will have the same effect as

```
a[0] = b[0];
```

and will not copy all the elements of the arrays.

An array of `bit` or `bool` variables is stored by the verifier as an array of `unsigned char` variable, and therefore saves no memory over a `byte` array. It can be better, therefore, to use integers in combination with bit-masking operations to simulate operations on a bit-array when memory is tight. The same rules apply here as would apply for the use of bit-arrays in C programs.

Multidimensional arrays can be constructed indirectly with the use of `typedef` definitions.

The use of an array index value outside the declared range triggers a run-time error in SPIN. This default array-index bound checking can be turned off during verifications, if desired, for increased performance. This can be done by compiling the `pan.c` source with the additional directive `-DNOBOUNDCHECK`.

SEE ALSO
chan, datatypes, mtype, typedef

NAME

`assert` – for stating simple safety properties.

SYNTAX

`assert(` *expr* `)`

EXECUTABILITY

true

EFFECT

`none`

DESCRIPTION

An `assert` statement is similar to `skip` in the sense that it is always executable and has no other effect on the state of the system than to change the local control state of the process that executes it. A very desirable side effect of the execution of this statement is, however, that it can trap violations of simple safety properties during verification and simulation runs with SPIN.

The `assert` statement takes any valid PROMELA expression as its argument. The expression is evaluated each time the statement is executed. If the expression evaluates to *false* (or, equivalently, to the integer value zero), an assertion violation is reported.

Assertion violations can be ignored in a verification run, by invoking the SPIN generated verifier with run-time option `-A`, as in:

```
$ ./pan -A
```

EXAMPLES

The most common type of assertion statement is one that contains just a simple boolean expression on global or local variable values, for instance, as in:

```
assert(a > b)
```

A second common use of the assertion is to mark locations in a `proctype` body that are required, or assumed, to be unreachable, as in:

```
assert(false)
```

If the statement is reached nonetheless, it will be reported as an assertion violation. A statement of this type is comparable to the infamous

```
printf("this cannot happen\n");
```

from C programs.

If more than one such assertion is needed, tracking can be made easier by using slight variations of expressions that necessarily will evaluate to `false`, such as:

```
assert(1+1 != 2)
assert(1>2)
assert(2>3)
```

The `assert` statement can also be used to formalize general system invariants, that is, boolean conditions that are required to be invariantly *true* in all reachable system states. To express this, we can place the system invariant in an independently executed process, as in:

```
active proctype monitor()
{
        assert(invariant)
}
```

where the name of the proctype is immaterial. Since the process instance is executed independently from the rest of the system, the assertion may be evaluated at any time: immediately after process instantiation in the initial system state, or at any time later in the system execution.

Several observations can be made about this example. First note that the process of type `monitor` has two states, and that the transition from the first to the second state is always unconditionally executable. This means that during verifications the addition of this specific form of the monitor process will double the size of the reachable state space. We can avoid this doubling by restricting the execution of the assertion to only those cases where it could actually lead to the detection of an assertion violation, for instance, as follows:

```
active proctype monitor()
{
        atomic { !invariant -> assert(false) }
}
```

This also solves another problem with the first version. Note that if our model contains a timeout condition, then the first monitor process would always be forced to execute the assertion before the system variable `timeout` variable could be set to *true*. This would mean that the assertion could never be checked beyond the first firing of a `timeout`. The second version of the monitor does not have this problem.

NOTES

A simulation, instead of a verification, will not necessarily prove that a safety property expressed with an `assert` statement is valid, because it will check its validity on just a randomly chosen execution. Note that placing a system invariant assertion inside a loop, as in

```
active proctype wrong()
{
        do
        :: assert(invariant)
        od
}
```

still cannot guarantee that a simulation would check the assertion at every step. Recall that the fact that a statement *can* be executed at every step does not guarantee that it also *will* be executed in that way. One way to accomplish a tighter connection between program steps and assertion checks is to use a one-state never claim, for instance, as in:

```
never {
        do
        :: assert(invariant)
        od
}
```

This is an acceptable alternative in verifications, but since never claims are ignored in simulation runs, it would make it impossible to detect the assertion violation during simulations.

SEE ALSO
ltl, never, timeout, trace

NAME
assignment – for assigning a new value to a variable.

SYNTAX
varref = *any_expr*
varref ++   as shorthand for *varref* = *varref* +1
varref - -   as shorthand for *varref* = *varref* -1

EXECUTABILITY
true

EFFECT
Replaces the value of *varref* with the value of *any_expr*, where necessary truncating the latter value to the range of the datatype of *varref*.

DESCRIPTION
The assignment statement has the standard semantics from most programming languages: replacing the value stored in a data object with the value returned by the evaluation of an expression. Other than in the C language, the assignment as a whole returns no value and can therefore itself not be part of an expression.

The variable reference that appears on the left-hand side of the assignment operator can be a scalar variable, an array element, or a structure element.

EXAMPLES
```
a = 12                    /* scalar */
r.b[a] = a * 4 + 7        /* array element in structure */
```

Note that it is not valid to write:

```
a = b++
```

because the right-hand side of this assignment is not a side effect free expression in PROMELA, but it is shorthand for another assignment statement. The effect of this statement can be obtained, though, by writing:

```
atomic { a = b; b++ }
```

or even more efficiently:

```
d_step { a = b; b++ }
```

Similarly, there are no shorthands for other C shorthands, such as ++b, --b, b *= 2, b += a, etc. Where needed, their effect can be reproduced by using the non-shortened equivalents, or in some cases with atomic or d_step sequences.

NOTES

There are no compound assignments in PROMELA, e.g., assignments of structures to structures or arrays to arrays in a single operation. If x and y are structures, though, the effect of a compound assignment could be approximated by passing the structure through a message channel, for instance as in:

```
typedef D {
        short f;
        byte  g
};

chan m = [1] of { D };

init {
        D x, y;

        m!x;    /* send structure x to channel m      */
        m?y     /* receive and assign to structure y */
}
```

All variables must be declared before they can be referenced or assigned to. The default initial value of all variables is zero.

SEE ALSO

arrays, condition, datatypes, typedef

NAME

atomic – for defining a fragment of code that is to be executed indivisibly.

SYNTAX

atomic { *sequence* }

EFFECT

Within the semantics model, as defined in Chapter 7, a side effect of the execution of any statement, except the last, from an atomic sequence is to set global system variable exclusive to the instantiation number of the executing process, thus preserving the exclusive privilige to execute.

DESCRIPTION

If a sequence of statements is enclosed in parentheses and prefixed with the keyword atomic, this indicates that the sequence is to be executed as one indivisible unit, non-interleaved with other processes. In the interleaving of process executions, no other process can execute statements from the moment that the first statement of an atomic sequence is executed until the last one has completed. The sequence can contain arbitrary PROMELA statements, and may be non-deterministic.

If any statement within the atomic sequence blocks, atomicity is lost, and other processes are then allowed to start executing statements. When the blocked statement becomes executable again, the execution of the atomic sequence can be resumed at any time, but not necessarily immediately. Before the process can resume the atomic execution of the remainder of the sequence, the process must first compete with all other active processes in the system to regain control, that is, it must first be scheduled for execution.

If an atomic sequence contains a rendezvous send statement, control passes from sender to receiver when the rendezvous handshake completes. Control can return to the sender at a later time, under the normal rules of nondeterministic process interleaving, to allow it to continue the atomic execution of the remainder of the sequence. In the special case where the recepient of the rendezvous handshake is also inside an atomic sequence, atomicity will be passed through the rendezvous handshake from sender to receiver and is not interrupted (except that another process now holds the exclusive privilige to execute).

An atomic sequence can be used wherever a PROMELA statement can be used. The first statement of the sequence is called its *guard*, because it determines when the sequence can be started. It is allowed, though not good style, to jump into the middle of an atomic sequence with a goto statement, or to jump out of it in the same way. After jumping into the sequence, atomic execution may begin when the process gains control, provided that the statement jumped to is executable. After jumping out of an atomic sequence, atomicity is lost, unless the target of the jump is also contained in an atomic sequence.

EXAMPLES

```
atomic {              /* swap the values of a and b */
        tmp = b;
        b = a;
        a = tmp
}
```

In the example, the values of two variables a and b are swapped in an uninterruptable sequence of statement executions. The execution of this sequence cannot be blocked, since all the statements it contains are always unconditionally executable.

An example of a non-deterministic atomic sequence is the following:

```
atomic {
        if
        :: a = 1
        :: a = 2
        fi;
        if
        :: b = 1
        :: b = 2
        fi
}
```

In this example, the variables a and b are assigned a single value, with no possible intervening statement from any other process. There are four possible ways to execute this atomic sequence.

It is possible to create a global atomic chain of executions, with two or more processes alternately executing, by passing control back and forth with rendezvous operations.

```
chan q = [0] of { bool };
active proctype X() { atomic { A; q!0; B } }
active proctype Y() { atomic { q?0 -> C } }
```

In this example, for instance, execution could start in process X with the program block named A. When the rendezvous handshake is executed, atomicity would pass to process Y, which now starts executing the block named C. When it terminates, control can pass back to X, which can then atomically execute the block named B.

It is often useful to use atomic sequences to start a series of processes in such a way that none of them can start executing statements until all of them have been initialized:

```
atomic {
        run A(1,2);
        run B(2,3);
        run C(3,1)
}
```

NOTES

Atomic sequences can be used to reduce the complexity of a verification.

If an infinite loop is accidentily included in an atomic sequence, the verifier cannot always recognize the cycle. In the default depth-first search mode, the occurrence of such an infinite cycle will ultimately lead to the depth limit being exceeded, which will truncate the loop. In breadth-first search mode, though, this type of an infinite cycle will be detected. Note that it is an error if an infinite cycle appears inside an atomic sequence, since in that case the atomic sequence could not possibly be executed atomically in any real implementation.

PROMELA d_step sequences can be executed significantly more efficiently by the verifier than atomic sequences, but do not allow non-determinism.

SEE ALSO

d_step, goto, receive, send

NAME

break – jump to the end of the innermostn do loop.

SYNTAX

break

DESCRIPTION

The keyword break does not indicate an executable statement, but it instead acts like a special type of semicolon: merely indicating the next statement to be executed. The search for the next statement to execute continues at the point that immediately follows the innermost do loop.

When the keyword break does not follow a statement, but appears as a guard in an option of a selection structure or do loop, then the execution of this statement takes one execution step to reach the target state, as if it were a skip. In all other cases, the execution of a break statement requires no separate step; the move to the target state then occurs after the execution of the preceding statement is completed.

If the repetition structure in which the break statement occurs is the last statement in a proctype body or never claim, then the target state for the break is the process's or claim's normal termination state, where the process or claim remains until it dies and is removed from the system.

EXAMPLES

```
L1: do
    :: t1 -> t2
    :: t3 -> break
    :: break
    od;
L2: ...
```

In this example, control reaches the label L1 immediately after statement t2 is executed. Control can also reach label L2 immediately after statement t3 is executed, and optionally, in one execution step, control can also move from label L1 to label L2.

NOTES

It is an error to place a break statement where there is no surrounding repetition structure. The effect of a break statement can always be replicated with the use of a goto statement and a label.

SEE ALSO

do, goto, if, labels, skip

NAME

chan – syntax for declaring and initializing message passing channels.

SYNTAX

chan *name*
chan *name* = ' [' *const* ']' of { *typename* [, *typename*] * }

DESCRIPTION

Channels are used to transfer messages between active processes. Channels are declared using the keyword chan, either locally or globally, much like integer variables. Channels by default store messages in first-in first-out order (but see also the sorted send option in the manual page for send and the random receive option in the manual page for receive).

The keyword chan can be followed by one or more names, in a comma-separated list, each optionally followed by a channel initializer. The syntax

```
chan a, b, c[3]
```

declares the names a, b, and c as uninitialized channels, the last one as an array of three elements.

A channel variable must be initialized before it can be used to transfer messages. It is rare to declare just a channel name without initialization, but it occurs in, for instance, proctype parameter lists, where the initialized version of a channel is not passed to the process until a process is instantiated with a run operator.

The channel initializer specifies a channel capacity, as a constant, and the structure of the messages that can be stored in the channel, as a comma-separated list of type names. If the channel capacity is larger than zero, a *buffered* channel is initialized, with the given number of slots to store messages. If the capacity is specified to be zero, a *rendezvous* port, also called a *synchronous* channel, is created. Rendezvous ports can pass messages only through synchronous handshakes between sender and receiver, but they cannot store messages.

All data types can be used inside a channel initializer, including type-def structure names, but *not* including the typename unsigned.

EXAMPLES

The following channel declaration contains an initializer:

```
chan a = [16] of { short }
```

The initializer says that channel a can store up to 16 messages. Each message is defined to have only one single field, which must be of type `short`. Similarly,

```
chan c[3] = [0] of { mtype }
```

initializes an array of three rendezvous channels for messages that contain just one message field, of type `mtype`.

The following is an example of the declaration of a channel that can pass messages with multiple field:

```
chan qname = [8] of { mtype, int, chan, byte }
```

This time the channel can store up to eight messages, each consisting of four fields of the types listed. The `chan` field can be used to pass a channel identifier from one process to another. In this way, a channel that is declared locally within one process, can be made accessible to other processes. A locally declared and instantiated channel disappears, though, when the process that contain the declaration dies.

NOTES

The first field in a channel type declaration is conventionally of type `mtype`, and is used to store a message type indicator in symbolic form.

In verification, buffered channels contribute significantly to verification complexity. For an initial verification run, choose a small channel capacity, of, say, two or three slots. If the verification completes swiftly, consider increasing the capacity to a larger size.

SEE ALSO

arrays, **datatypes**, **empty**, **full**, **len**, **mtype**, **nempty**, **nfull**, **poll**, **receive**, **send**

NAME

comments – default preprocessing rules for comments.

SYNTAX

/'*' [*any_ascii_char*]* '*'/

DESCRIPTION

A comment starts with the two character sequence /* and ends at the first occurrence of the two character sequence */. In between these two delimiters, any text, including newlines and control characters, is allowed. None of the text has semantic meaning in PROMELA.

A comment can be placed at any point in a verification model where white space (spaces, tabs, newlines) can appear.

EXAMPLES

```
/* comment */ init /* comment */ {
        int /* an integer */ v /* variable */;

        v /* this / * is * / okay */ ++;
}
```

This PROMELA fragment is indistinguishable to the parser to the following PROMELA text, written without comments:

```
init {
        int v;
        v++;
}
```

NOTES

Comments are removed from the PROMELA source before any other operation is performed. The comments are removed by invoking the standard C preprocessor cpp (or any equivalent program, such as gcc -E), which then runs as an external program in the background. This means that the precise rules for comments are determined by the specific C preprocessor that is used. Some preprocessors, for instance, accept the C++ commenting style, where comments can start with two forward slashes and end at the first newline. The specific preprocessor that is used can be set by the user. For more details on this, see the manual page for macros.

With the default preprocessor, conform ANSI-C conventions, comments do not nest. Be careful, therefore, that if a closing comment delimiter is accidently deleted, all text up to and including the end of the next comment may be stripped.

On a PC, SPIN first tries to use a small, built-in macro preprocessor.

When this fails, for instance, when macros with multiple parameters are used or when additional preprocessor directives are provided on the command line, the standard external C preprocessor is called. The use of the built-in preprocessor can, with older PC operating systems, avoid the the awkward brief appearance of an external shell window in the parsing phase.

SEE ALSO

macros

NAME

conditional expression – shorthand for a conditional evaluation.

SYNTAX

(*any_expr* -> *any_expr* : *any_expr*)

DESCRIPTION

The conditional expression in PROMELA is based on the version from the C programming language. To avoid parsing conflicts, though, the syntax differs slightly from C. Where in C one would write

```
p?q:r
```

the corresponding expression in PROMELA is

```
(p -> q : r)
```

The question mark from the C version is replaced with an arrow symbol, to avoid confusion with the PROMELA receive operator. The round braces around the conditional expression are required, in this case to avoid the misinterpretation of the arrow symbol as a statement separator.

When the first expression (p in the example) evaluates to non-zero, the conditional expression as a whole obtains the value of the second expression (q), and else it obtains the value of the last expression (r).

EXAMPLES

The following example shows a simple way to implement conditional rendezvous operations.

```
chan q[3] = [0] of { mtype };

sender:    q[(P -> 1 : 2)]!msg -> ...

receiver:  q[(Q -> 1 : 0)]?msg -> ...
```

Two dummy rendezvous channels (q[0] and q[2]) are used here to deflect handshake attempts that should fail. The handshake can only successfully complete (on channel q[1]) if both the boolean expression P at the receiver side and the boolean expression Q at the sender side evaluate to *true* simultaneously. The dummy rendezvous channels q[0] and q[2] that are used here do not contribute any measurable overhead in a verification, since rendezvous channels take up no memory in the state vector.

An alternative way of specifying a conditional rendezvous operation is to add an extra message field to the channel and to use the predefined eval function in the receive statement, as follows.

```
global:        chan port = [0] of { mtype, byte, byte };

sender:        port!mesg(12, (P -> 1 : 0))
receiver:      port?mesg(data, eval(Q -> 1 : 2))
```

The handshake can again only happen if both P and Q evaluate to *true*. Unfortunately, the message field cannot be declared as a boolean, since we need a third value to make sure no match occurs when both P and Q evaluate to *false*.

SEE ALSO
condition, do, eval, if, unless

NAME
condition statement – for conditional execution and synchronization.

SYNTAX
expr

EXECUTABILITY
(*expr* != 0)

EFFECT
none

DESCRIPTION
In PROMELA, a standalone expression is a valid statement. A condition statement is often used as a guard at the start of an option sequence in a selection or repetition structure. Execution of a condition statement is blocked until the expression evaluates to a non-zero value (or, equivalently, to the boolean value *true*). All PROMELA expressions are required to be side effect free.

EXAMPLES
```
(1)          /* always executable                 */
(0)          /* never executable                  */
skip         /* always executable, same as (1)    */
true         /* always executable, same as skip   */
false        /* always blocks, same as (0)         */
a == b       /* executable only when a equals b   */
```

A condition statement can only be executed (passed) if it holds. This means that the statement from the first example can always be passed, the second can never be passed, and the last cannot be passed as long as the values of variables a and b differ. If the variables a and b are local, the result of the evaluation cannot be influenced by other processes, and this statement will work as either `true` or `false`, depending on the values of the variables. If at least one of the variables is global, the statement can act as a synchronizer between processes.

SEE ALSO
do, else, false, if, skip, true, timeout, unless

NAME

d_step – introduces a deterministic code fragment that is executed indivisibly.

SYNTAX

d_step { *sequence* }

DESCRIPTION

A d_step sequence is executed as if it were one single indivisible statement. It is comparable to an atomic sequence, but it differs from such sequences on the following three points:

- No goto jumps into or out of a d_step sequence are allowed.
- The sequence is executed *deterministically*. If non-determinism is present, it is resolved in a fixed and deterministic way, for instance, by always selecting the first true guard in every selection and repetition structure.
- It is an error if the execution of any statement inside the sequence can block. This means, for instance, that in most cases send and receive statements cannot be used inside d_step sequences.

EXAMPLES

The following example uses a d_step sequence to swap the value of all elements in two arrays:

```
#define N        16

byte a[N], B[N];

init {
        d_step {              /* swap elements */
                byte i, tmp;

                i = 0;
                do
                :: i < N ->
                        tmp = b[i];
                        b[i] = a[i];
                        a[i] = tmp; i++
                :: else ->
                        break
                od;
                skip    /* add target for break */
        }
        ...
}
```

A number of points should be noted in this example. First, the scope of variables i and tmp is independent of the precise point of declaration within the `init` body. In particular, by placing the declaration inside the `d_step` sequence we do not limit the scope of these variables to the `d_step` sequence: they remain visible also after the sequence.

Second, we have to be careful that the loop that is contained within this `d_step` sequence terminates. No system states are saved, restored, or checked during the execution of a `d_step` sequence. If an infinite loop is accidentily included in such a sequence, it can cause the verifier to hang.

Third and last, because one cannot jump into or out of a `d_step` sequence, a `break` from a `do` loop which appears as the last construct in a `d_step` sequence will trigger a parse error from SPIN. Note that this type of `break` statement creates an hidden jump out of the `d_step`, to the statement that immediately follows the `do` loop, which is outside the `d_step` itself in this case. The problem can be avoided by inserting a dummy `skip` after the loop, as shown in the example. There is no run-time penalty for this `skip` statement.

NOTES

A `d_step` sequence can be executed much more efficiently during verifications than an `atomic` sequence. The difference in performance can be significant, especially in large-scale verifications.

The `d_step` sequence also provides a mechanism in PROMELA to add new types of statements to the language, translating into new types of transitions in the underlying automata. A `c_code` statement has similar properties.

SEE ALSO
atomic, **c_code**, **goto**, **sequence**

NAME

bit, bool, byte, pid, short, int, unsigned – predefined data types.

SYNTAX

typename name [= *anyexpr*]
unsigned *name* : constant [= *anyexpr*]

DESCRIPTION

There are seven predefined integer data types: bit, bool, byte, pid, short, int, and unsigned. There are also constructors for user-defined data types (see the manual pages for mtype, and typedef), and there is a separate predefined data type for message passing channels (see the manual page for chan).

Variables of the predefined types can be declared in C-like style, with a declaration that consists of a *typename* followed by a comma-separated list of one or more identifiers. Each variable can optionally be followed by an initializer. Each variable can also optionally be declared as an array, rather than as a scalar (see the manual page for arrays).

The predefined data types differ only in the domain of integer values that they provide. The precise domain may be system dependent in the same way that the corresponding data types in the C language can be system dependent.

Variables of type bit and bool are stored in a single bit of memory, which means that they can hold only binary, or boolean values.

ISO compliant implementations of C define the domains of all integer data types in a system header file named limits.h, which is accessible by the C compiler. Table 16.2 summarizes these definitions for a typical system.

Variables of type unsigned are stored in the number of bits that is specified in the (required) constant field from the declaration. For instance,

```
unsigned x : 5 = 15;
```

declares a variable named x that is stored in five bits of memory. This declaration also states that the variable is to be initialized to the value 15. As with all variable declarations, an explicit initialization field is optional. The default initial value for all variables is zero. This applies both to scalar variables and to array variables, and it applies to both global and to local variables.

If an attempt is made to assign a value outside the domain of the variable type, the actual value assigned is obtained by a type cast operation that truncates the value to the domain. Information is lost if such a truncation is applied. SPIN will warn if this happens only during random or guided

Table 16.2 Typical Data Ranges

Type	C-Equivalent	limits.h	Typical Range
bit	bit-field	–	0..1
bool	bit-field	–	0..1
byte	unsigned char	CHAR_BIT	0..255
pid	unsigned char	CHAR_BIT	0..255
short	short int	SHRT_MIN..SHRT_MAX	$-2^{15}..2^{15} - 1$
int	int	INT_MIN..INT_MAX	$-2^{31}..2^{31} - 1$

simulation runs.

Scope: The scope of a variable declaration is global if it appears outside all proctype or init declarations. The scope of a local variable includes the complete body of a proctype. The declaration itself can be placed anywhere within the proctype or init declaration, provided only that it appears before the first use of the variable. Each separate process has a private copy of all variables that are declared locally within the corresponding proctype or init declaration.

The formal parameters of a proctype are indistinguishable from local variables. These formal parameters are initialized to the values that are specified in a run statement, or they are initialized to zero when the process is instantiated through an active prefix on a proctype declaration.

EXAMPLES

The code fragment

```
byte a, b = 2; short c[3] = 3;
```

declares the names a and b as variables of type byte, and c as an array of three variables of type short. Variable a has the default initial value zero. Variable b is initialized to the value 2, and all three elements of array c are initialized to 3.

A variable may also be initialized with an expression, but this is generally not recommended. Note that if global variables are referenced in such initializations, the precise value of such globals may be uncertain. If local variables from the same proctype declaration are referenced in one of the variable declarations, there are some additional dangers that can be caused by the fact the variable declarations can physically appear anywhere in a proctype declaration, but functionally they always act as if they are all moved to the start of the proctype body.

In the following model fragment, for instance, the value that is assigned to variable b in the declaration is 2, and not 4, as might be expected.

```
init {
        byte a = 2;

        a = 4;

        byte b = a;

        printf("b: %d\n", b)
}
```

When a process is instantiated, SPIN first collects all variable declarations from the corresponding `proctype` declaration, and it then creates and initializes each of these variables, in order of declaration in the `proctype`, but otherwise before the process itself starts executing. The example code above, therefore, is evaluated as if the declaration of variable b was moved to the start of the `proctype` declaration, immediately following that of a. Use with caution.

NOTES

Each process has a predefined local variable _pid of type `pid` that holds the process instantiation number. Each model also has a predefined, write-only, global variable _ (underscore) of type `int` that can be used as a scratch variable, and predefined, read-only, global variables _nr_pr (of type `int`) and _last (of type `pid`). See the corresponding manual pages for further details on these variables.

An array of `bit`, `bool`, or `unsigned` variables is stored internally as an array of `byte` variables. This may affect the behavior of the model if, for instance, the user relies on automatic truncation effects during a verification (an unwise strategy). When the verifier source is generated in verbose mode, SPIN will warn if it encounters such cases.

In the C language, the keywords `short` and `unsigned` can be used as a prefix of `int`. This is not valid in PROMELA.

SEE ALSO

_, _last, _pid, arrays, chan, mtype, run, typedef

NAME

do – repetition construct.

SYNTAX

do :: *sequence* [:: *sequence*] * od

DESCRIPTION

The repetition construct, like all other control-flow constructs, is strictly seen not a statement, but a convenient method to define the *structure* of the underlying automaton.

A repetition construct has a single start and stop state. Each option sequence within the construct defines outgoing transitions for the start state. The end of each option sequence transfers control back to the start state of the construct, allowing for repeated execution. The stop state of the construct is only reachable via a break statement from within one of its option sequences.

There must be at least one option sequence in each repetition construct. Each option sequence starts with a double-colon. The first statement in each sequence is called its *guard*. An option can be selected for execution only when its guard statement is executable. If more than one guard statement is executable, one of them will be selected non-deterministically. If none of the guards are executable, the repetition construct as a whole blocks.

A repetition construct as a whole is executable if and only if at least one of its guards is executable.

EXAMPLES

The following example defines a cyclic process that non-deterministically increments or decrements a variable named count:

```
byte count;

active proctype counter()
{
        do
        :: count++
        :: count--
        :: (count == 0) ->
                break
        od
}
```

In this example the loop can be broken only when count reaches zero. It need not terminate, though, because the other two options always remain unconditionally executable. To force termination, we can modify the program as follows:

```
active proctype counter()
{
        do
        :: count != 0 ->
                if
                :: count++
                :: count--
                fi
        :: else ->
                break
        od
}
```

NOTES

The semantics of a PROMELA repetition construct differ from a similar control flow construct tha was included in Dijkstra's seminal proposal for a non-deterministic guarded command language. In Dijkstra's language, the repetition construct is aborted when none of the guards are executable; in PROMELA, execution is merely blocked in this case. In PROMELA, executability is used as the basic mechanism for enforcing process synchronization, and it is not considered to be an error if statements occasionally block. The PROMELA repetition construct also differs from a similar control flow construct in Hoare's classic language CSP. In CSP, send and receive statements cannot appear as guards of an option sequence. In PROMELA, there is no such restriction.

The guard statements in option sequences cannot individually be prefixed by a label, since all option sequences start from the same state (the start state of the construct). If a label is required, it should be placed before the keyword do.

SEE ALSO

break, **else**, **goto**, **if**, **timeout**, **unless**

NAME

`else` – a system defined condition statement.

SYNTAX

`else`

DESCRIPTION

The predefined condition statement `else` is intended to be used as a guard (i.e., the first statement) of an option sequence inside selection or repetition constructs.

An `else` condition statement is executable if and only if no other statement within the same process is executable at the same local control state (i.e., process state).

It is an error to define control flow constructs in which more than one `else` may need to be evaluated in a single process state.

EXAMPLES

In the first example, the condition statement `else` is equivalent to the regular expression statement `(a < b)`.

```
if
:: a > b -> ...
:: a == b -> ...
:: else -> ...   /* evaluates to: a < b */
fi
```

Note also that round braces are optional around expression statements.

In this example:

```
A: do
   :: if
      :: x > 0 -> x--
      :: else  -> break
      fi
   :: else -> x = 10
   od
```

both `else` statements apply to the same control state, which is marked with the label A here. To show the ambiguity more clearly, we can rewrite this example also as:

```
A: do
   :: x > 0 -> x--
   :: else -> break
   :: else -> x = 10
   od
```

It is unclear what should happen when `(x < 0)`, and therefore the SPIN parser will reject constructs such as these.

Another construction that the parser will reject is the use of an `else` in combination with an operation on a channel, for instance, as follows:

```
A: if
   :: q?a -> ...
   :: else -> ...
   fi
```

Note that a race condition is built-in to this type of code. How long should the process wait, for instance, before deciding that the message receive operation will not be executable? The problem can be avoided by using message poll operations, for instance, as follows:

```
A: if
   :: atomic { q?[a] -> q?a }
   :: else -> ...
   fi
```

Now the meaning is clear, if the message `a` is present in channel `q` when control reaches the statement that was marked with the label `A`, then that message will be retrieved, otherwise the `else` clause will be selected.

NOTES

The semantics as given would in principle also allow for an `else` to be used outside selection or repetition constructs, in a non-branching sequence of statements. The `else` would then be equivalent to a `skip` statement, since it would have no alternatives within the local context. The PROMELA parser, however, will flag such use as an error.

The executability of the `else` statement depends only on local context within a process. The PROMELA semantics for `timeout` can be seen as a global version of `else`. A `timeout` is executable only when no alternative statement within the global context of the system is executable. A `timeout` may not be combined with an `else` in the same selection construct.

SEE ALSO

condition, do, false, if, skip, true, timeout, unless

NAME

empty – predefined, boolean function to test emptiness of a buffered channel.

SYNTAX

empty(*name*)

DESCRIPTION

Empty is a predefined function that takes the name of a channel as an argument and returns *true* if the number of messages that it currently holds is zero; otherwise it returns *false*. The expression

```
empty(q)
```

where q is a channel name, is equivalent to the expression

```
(len(q) == 0)
```

EXAMPLES

```
chan q = [8] of { mtype };

d_step {
        do
        :: q?_
        :: empty(q) -> break
        od;
        skip
}
```

This example shows how the contents of a message channel can be flushed in one indivisible step, without knowing, or storing, the detailed contents of the channel. Note that execution of this code is deterministic. The reason for the skip statement at the end is explained in the manual page for d_step.

NOTES

A call on empty can be used as a guard, or it can be used in combination with other conditionals in a boolean expression. The expression in which it appears, though, may not be negated. (The SPIN parser will intercept this.) Another predefined function, nempty, can be used when the negated version is needed. The reason for the use of empty and nempty is to assist SPIN's partial order reduction strategy during verification.

If predefined functions such as empty and nempty are used in the symbol definitions of an LTL formula, they may unintentionally appear under a negation sign in the generated automaton, which can then trigger a surprising syntax error from SPIN. The easiest way to remedy such a problem, if it occurs, is to revise the generated `never` claim automaton directly, and replace every occurrence of `!empty()` with `nempty()` and every occurrence of `!nempty()` with `empty()`.

SEE ALSO
_, condition, full, ltl len, nempty, nfull

NAME

enabled – predefined boolean function for testing the enabledness of a process from within a never claim.

SYNTAX

enabled(*any_expr*)

DESCRIPTION

This predefined function can only be used inside a never claim, or equivalently in the symbol definition for an LTL formula.

Given the instantiation number of an active process, the function returns *true* if the process has at least one executable statement in its current control state, and *false* otherwise. When given the instantiation number of a non-existing process, the function always returns *false*.

In every global state where enabled(p) returns *true*, the process with instantiation number p has at least one executable statement. Of course, the executability status of that process can change after the next execution step is taken in the system, which may or may not be from process p.

EXAMPLES

The following never claim attempts to match executions in which the process with instantiation number one remains enabled infinitely long without ever executing.

```
never {
accept:
        do
        :: _last != 1 && enabled(1)
        od
}
```

NOTES

The use of this function is incompatible with SPIN's partial order reduction strategy, and can therefore increase the computational requirements of a verification.

SEE ALSO

_last, **_pid**, **ltl**, **never**, **pc_value**, **run**

NAME

end – label-name prefix for marking valid termination states.

SYNTAX

end[a-zA-Z0-9_]*: *stmnt*

DESCRIPTION

An end-state label is any label name that starts with the three-character sequence end. End-state labels can be used in proctype, trace, and notrace declarations.

When used in a proctype declaration, the end-state label marks a local control state that is acceptable as a valid termination point for all instantiations of that proctype.

If used in an event trace definition, the end-state label marks a global control state that corresponds to a valid termination point for the system as a whole.

If used in an event notrace definition, though, the normal meaning reverses: the event trace is now considered to have been completely matched when the end state is reached, thus signifying an error condition, rather than normal system termination.

End-state labels have no special meaning when used in never claims.

EXAMPLES

In the following example the end-state label defines that the expected termination point of the process is at the start of the loop.

```
active proctype dijkstra()
{
end:    do
        :: sema!p -> sema?v
        od
}
```

It will now be flagged as an invalid end-state error if the system that contains this proctype declaration can terminate in a state where the process of type dijkstra remains at the control state that exists just after the arrow symbol.

NOTES

It is considered an invalid end-state error if a system can terminate in a state where not all active processes are either at the end of their code (i.e., at the closing curly brace of their proctype declarations) or at a local state that is marked with and end-state label.

If the run-time option -q is used with the compiled verifier, an additional constraint is applied for a state to be considered a valid `end` state: all message channels must then also be empty.

SEE ALSO
accept, **labels**, **notrace**, **progress**, **trace**

NAME

`eval` – predefined unary function to turn an expression into a constant.

SYNTAX

`eval` (*any_expr*)

DESCRIPTION

The intended use of `eval` is in `receive` statements to force a match of a message field with the current value of a local or global variable. Normally, such a match can only be forced by specifying a constant. If a variable name is used directly, without the `eval` function, the variable would be assigned the value from the corresponding message field, instead of serving as a match of values.

EXAMPLES

In the following example the two receive operations are only executable if the precise values specified were sent to channel q: first an `ack` and then a `msg`.

```
mtype = { msg, ack, other };
chan q = [4] of { mtype };

mtype x;

x = ack; q?eval(x)        /* same as: q?ack */
x = msg; q?eval(x)        /* same as: q?msg */
```

Without the `eval` function, writing simply

```
q?x
```

would mean that whatever value was sent to the channel (e.g., the value `other`) would be assigned to x when the receive operation is executed.

NOTES

Any expression can be used as an argument to the `eval` function. The result of the evaluation of the expression is then used as if it were a constant value.

This mechanism can also be used to specify a conditional rendezvous operation, for instance by using the value *true* in the sender and using a conditional expression with an `eval` function at the receiver; see also the manual page for conditional expressions.

SEE ALSO

cond_expr, condition, poll, receive

NAME
`false` – predefined boolean constant.

SYNTAX
`false`

DESCRIPTION
The keyword `false` is a synonym of the constant value zero (0), and can be used in any context. If it is used as a stand-alone condition statement, it will block system execution as if it were a *halt* instruction.

NOTES
Because they are intercepted in the lexical analyzer as meta terms, `false`, `true`, and `skip` do not show up as such in error traces. They will appear as their numeric equivalents `(0)` or `(1)`.

SEE
condition, **skip**, **true**

NAME

`float` – floating point numbers.

DESCRIPTION

There are no floating point numbers in basic PROMELA because the purpose the language is to encourage abstraction from the computational aspects of a distributed application while focusing on the verification of process interaction, synchronization, and coordination.

Consider, for instance, the verification of a sequential C procedure that computes square roots. Exhaustive state-based verification would not be the best approach to verify this procedure. In a verification model, it often suffices to abstract this type of procedure into a simple two-state demon that non-deterministically decides to give either a correct or incorrect answer. The following example illustrates this approach.

```
mtype = { number, correct, incorrect };
chan sqrt = [0] of { mtype, chan };

active proctype sqrt_server()
{
        do
        :: sqrt?number(answer) ->
                /* abstract from local computations */
                if
                :: answer!correct
                :: answer!incorrect
                fi
        od
}

active proctype user()
{       chan me = [0] of { mtype };

        do
        :: sqrt!number(me);
                if
                :: me?correct -> break
                :: me?incorrect ->
                        . . .
                fi;
        od;
        . . .
}
```

The predefined data types from PROMELA are a compromise between notational convenience and modest constraints that can facilitate the construction of tractable verification models. The largest numeric quantity that can be manipulated is, for instance, a 32-bit integer number. The number of different values that even one single integer variable can record, for instance, when used as a simple counter, is already well beyond the scope of a state-based model checker. Even integer quantities, therefore, are to be treated with some suspicion in verification models, and can very often be replaced advantageously with `byte` or `bit` variables.

NOTES

In the newer versions of SPIN, there is an indirect way to use external data types, such as `float`, via embedded code and embedded declarations. The burden on the user to find abstractions can thus be lightened, in return for a potential increase in verification complexity. When using embedded C code, the user can decide separately if some or all of the embedded data objects should be treated as part of the state descriptor in the verification model, with the use of `c_state` or `c_track` declarators. See Chapter 17 for a detailed description.

SEE ALSO

c_code, **c_decl**, **c_expr**, **datatypes**

NAME

full – predefined, boolean function to test fullness of a channel.

SYNTAX

full (*varref*)

DESCRIPTION

Full is a predefined function that takes the name of a channel as an argument and returns *true* if that channel currently contains its maximum number of messages, and otherwise it returns *false*. It is equivalent to the expression

```
(len(q) == QSZ)
```

where q is the channel name, and QSZ is the message capacity of the channel.

This function can only be applied to buffered channels. The value returned for rendezvous channels would always be *false*, since a rendezvous channel cannot store messages.

EXAMPLES

```
chan q = [8] of { byte };
byte one_more = 0;

do
:: q!one_more; one_more++        /* send messages */
:: full(q) -> break              /* until full    */
od;
assert(len(q) == 8)
```

NOTES

Full can be used as a guard, by itself, or it can be used as a general boolean function in expressions. It can, however, not be negated (for an explanation see also the manual page for empty).

If predefined functions such as full, or nfull are used in the symbol definitions of an LTL formula, they may unintentionally appear under a negation sign in the generated automaton, which can then trigger a surprising syntax error from SPIN.

SEE ALSO

condition, empty, len, ltl, nempty, nfull

NAME

goto – unconditional jump to a labeled statement.

SYNTAX

goto *name*

DESCRIPTION

The goto is normally not executed, but is used by the parser to determine the target control state for the immediately preceding statement; see also the manual page for break. The target state is identified by the label *name* and must be unique within the surrounding proctype declaration or never claim.

In cases where there is no immediately preceding statement, for instance, when the goto appears as a guard in an option of a selection or repetition structure, the goto is executed as if it were a skip, taking one execution step to reach the labeled state.

EXAMPLES

The following program fragment defines two control states, labeled by L1 and L2:

```
L1:     if
        :: a != b -> goto L1
        :: a == b -> goto L2
        fi;
L2:     ...
```

If the values of variables a and b are equal, control moves from L1 to L2 *immediately* following the execution of condition statement a == b. If the values are unequal, control returns to L1 *immediately* following the execution (evaluation) of a != b. The statement is therefore equivalent to

```
L1:     do
        :: a != b
        :: a == b -> break
        od;
L2:
```

and could also be written more efficiently in PROMELA as simply:

```
L1:     a == b;
L2:
```

Note that the last version makes use of the capability of PROMELA to synchronize on a standalone condition statement.

NOTES

It is an error if no target for the `goto` is defined within the surrounding `proctype` or `never` claim declaration.

SEE ALSO

break, condition, labels

NAME

hidden – for excluding data from the state descriptor during verification.

SYNTAX

hidden *typename ivar*

DESCRIPTION

The keyword hidden can be used to prefix the declaration of any variable to exclude the value of that variable from the definition of the global system state. The addition of this prefix can affect only the verification process, by potentially changing the outcome of state matching operations.

EXAMPLES

```
hidden byte a;
hidden short p[3];
```

NOTES

The prefix should only be used for write-only scratch variables. Alternatively, the predefined write-only scratch variable _ (underscore) can always be used instead of a hidden integer variable.

It is safe to use hidden variables as pseudo-local variables inside d_step sequences, provided that they are not referenced anywhere outside that sequence.

SEE ALSO

_, **datatypes**, **local**, **show**

NAME

`hierarchy` – for defining layered systems.

DESCRIPTION

There is no mechanism for defining a hierarchically layered system in PROMELA, nor is there a good excuse to justify this omission. At present, the only structuring principles supported in PROMELA are `proctypes`, `inlines`, and `macros`.

SEE ALSO

inline, **macros**, **proctype**, **procedures**

NAME

`if` – selection construct.

SYNTAX

`if` :: *sequence* [:: *sequence*]* `fi`

DESCRIPTION

The selection construct, like all other control-flow constructs, is strictly seen not a statement, but a convenient method to define the *structure* of the underlying automaton. Each selection construct has a unique start and stop state. Each option sequence within the construct defines outgoing transitions for the start state, leading to the stop state. There can be one or more option sequences. By default, the end of each option sequence leads to the control state that follows the construct.

There must be at least one option sequence in each selection construct. Each option sequence starts with a double-colon. The first statement in each sequence is called its *guard*. An option can be selected for execution only when its guard statement is executable. If more than one guard statement is executable, one of them will be selected non-deterministically. If none of the guards are executable, the selection construct as a whole blocks.

The selection construct as a whole is executable if and only if at least one of its guards is executable.

EXAMPLES

Using the relative values of two variables a and b to choose between two options, we can write

```
if
:: (a != b) -> ...
:: (a == b) -> ...
fi
```

This selection structure contains two option sequences, each preceded by a double colon. Only one sequence from the list will be executed. A sequence can be selected only if its guard statement is executable (the first statement). In the example the two guards are mutually exclusive, but this is not required.

The guards from a selection structure cannot be prefixed by labels individually. These guards really define the outgoing transitions of a *single* control state, and therefore any label on one guard is really a label on the source state for *all* guards belonging on the selection construct itself (cf. label L0 in the next example). It is tempting to circumvent this rule and try to label a guard by inserting a `skip` in front of it, for instance, as follows:

```
L0:      if
         :: skip;
L1:               (a != b) -> ...
         :: (a == b) -> ...
         fi;
```

But note that this modification alters the meaning of the selection from a choice between (a != b) and (a == b), to a choice between skip (which is the same as (1) or true) and (a == b). The addition of the skip statement also adds an extra intermediate state, immediately followin the skip statement itself.

NOTES

The semantics of a PROMELA selection construct differ from similar control flow constructs in Hoare's language CSP, and in Dijkstra's earlier definition of a non-deterministic guarded command language. In Dijkstra's definition, the selection construct is aborted when none of the guards is executable. In PROMELA, execution blocks in this case. In PROMELA, executability is used as the basic means to enforce process synchronization, and it is not considered to be an error if statements block temporarily. Another difference with CSP is that in PROMELA there is no restriction on the type of statement that can be used as a guard of an option sequence. Any type of statement can be used as a guard, including assignments, and send or receive operations.

SEE ALSO
do, **else**, **goto**, **timeout**

NAME

init – for declaring an initial process.

SYNTAX

init { *sequence* }

DESCRIPTION

The init keyword is used to declare the behavior of a process that is active in the initial system state.

An init process has no parameters, and no additional copies of the process can be created (that is, the keyword cannot be used as an argument to the run operator).

Active processes can be differentiated from each other by the value of their process instantiation number, which is available in the predefined local variable _pid. Active processes are always instantiated in the order in which they appear in the model, so that the first such process (whether it is declared as an active process or as an init process) will receive the lowest instantiation number, which is zero.

EXAMPLES

The smallest possible PROMELA model is:

```
init { skip }
```

where skip is PROMELA's null statement, or perhaps more usefully

```
init { printf("hello world\n") }
```

The init process is most commonly used to initialize global variables, and to instantiate other processes, through the use of the run operator, before system execution starts. Any process, not just the init process, can do so, though.

It is convention to instantiate groups of processes within atomic sequences, to make sure that their execution begins at the same instant. For instance, in the leader election example, included as a test case in the SPIN distribution, the initial process is used to start up N copies of the proctype node. Each new instance of the proctype is given different parameters, which in this case consist of two channel names and an indentifying number. The node proctype is then of the form:

```
proctype node(chan in, chan out, byte mynumber)
{          ...
}
```

and the init process is structured as follows.

```
init {
   byte proc;
   atomic {
     proc = 1;
     do
     :: proc <= N ->
        run node (q[proc-1],q[proc%N],(N+I-proc)%N+1);
        proc++
     :: proc > N ->
        break
     od
   }
}
```

After the instantiation, the initial process terminates.

A process in PROMELA, however, cannot die and be removed from the system until all its children have died first. That is, PROMELA processes can only die in reverse order of creation (in stack order). This means that if an init process is used to create all other processes in the system, the init process itself will continue to exist, and take up memory, as long as the system exists. Systems in which all processes can be instantiated with active prefixes, instead of through the intermediacy of an init process, can therefore often be verified more efficiently. The following code fragment illustrates an alternative initialization for the leader election protocol, avoiding the use of an init process:

```
active [N] proctype node ()
{       chan in  = q[_pid];
        chan out = q[(_pid+1)%N];
        byte mynumber = (N+I-(_pid+1))%N+1;
        . . .
}
```

Because no parameter values can be passed to an active process declaration, the parameters are now replaced with local variables.

NOTES

The init keyword has become largely redundant with the addition of the active prefix for proctype declarations.

SEE ALSO

_pid, active, proctype, run, skip

NAME

`inline` – a stylized version of a macro.

SYNTAX

`inline` *name* ([*arg_lst*]) { *sequence* }

DESCRIPTION

An `inline` definition must appear before its first use, and must always be defined globally, that is, at the same level as a `proctype` declaration. An `inline` definition works much like a preprocessor macro, in the sense that it just defines a replacement text for a symbolic name, possibly with parameters. It does not define a new variable scope. The body of an `inline` is directly pasted into the body of a `proctype` at each point of invocation. An invocation (an `inline` call) is performed with a syntax that is similar to a procedure call in C, but, like a macro, a PROMELA `inline` cannot return a value to the caller.

An `inline` call may appear anywhere a stand-alone PROMELA statement can appear. This means that, unlike a macro call, an `inline` call cannot appear in a parameter list of the `run` operator, and it cannot be used as an operand in an expression. It also cannot be used on the left- or right-hand side of an assignment statement.

The parameters to an `inline` definition are typically names of variables.

An `inline` definition may itself contain other `inline` calls, but it may not call itself recursively.

EXAMPLES

The following example illustrates the use of `inline` definitions in a version of the alternating bit protocol.

```
mtype = { msg0, msg1, ack0, ack1 };

chan sender = [1] of { mtype };
chan receiver = [1] of { mtype };

inline recv(cur_msg, cur_ack, lst_msg, lst_ack)
{
        do
        :: receiver?cur_msg ->
                sender!cur_ack; break /* accept */
        :: receiver?lst_msg ->
                sender!lst_ack
        od;
}
```

```
inline phase(msg, good_ack, bad_ack)
{
        do
        :: sender?good_ack -> break
        :: sender?bad_ack
        :: timeout ->
                if
                :: receiver!msg;
                :: skip /* lose message */
                fi;
        od
}

active proctype Sender()
{
        do
        :: phase(msg1, ack1, ack0);
           phase(msg0, ack0, ack1)
        od
}

active proctype Receiver()
{
        do
        :: recv(msg1, ack1, msg0, ack0);
           recv(msg0, ack0, msg1, ack1)
        od
}
```

In simulations, line number references are preserved and will point to the source line inside the `inline` definition where possible. In some cases, in the example for instance at the start of the `Sender` and the `Receiver` process, the control point is inside the `proctype` body and not yet inside the `inline`.

NOTES

The PROMELA scope rules for variables are not affected by `inline` definitions. If, for instance, the body of an `inline` contains variable declarations, their scope would be the same as if they were declared outside the `inline`, at the point of invocation. The scope of such variables is the entire body of the `proctype` in which the invocation appears. If such an `inline` would be invoked in two different places within the same `proctype`, the declaration would also appear twice, and a syntax error would result.

SEE ALSO
comments, **macros**

NAME

label – to identify a unique control state in a proctype declaration.

SYNTAX

name : *stmnt*

DESCRIPTION

Any statement or control-flow construct can be preceded by a label. The label can, but need not, be used as a destination of a goto or can be used in a remote reference inside a never claim. Label names must be unique within the surrounding proctype, trace, notrace, or never claim declaration.

A label always prefixes a statement, and thereby uniquely identifies a control state in a transition system, that is, the source state of the transition that corresponds to the labeled statement.

Any number of labels can be attached to a single statement.

EXAMPLES

The following proctype declaration translates into a transition system with precisely three local process states: initial state S1, state S2 in between the send and the receive, and the (unreachable) final state S3, immediately following the repetition construct.

```
active proctype dijkstra()
{
S0:
S1:      do
         :: q!p ->
S2:              q?v
         :: true
         od
/* S3 */
}
```

The first state has two labels: S0 and S1. This state has two outgoing transitions: one corresponding to the send statement q!p, and one corresponding to the condition statement true. Observe carefully that there is no separate control state at the start of each guard in a selection or repetition construct. Both guards share the same start state S1.

NOTES

A label name can be any alphanumeric character string, with the exception that the first character in the label name may not be a digit or an underscore symbol.

The guard statement in a selection or repetition construct cannot be prefixed by a label individually; see the manual page for `if` and `do` for details.

There are three types of labels with special meaning, see the manual pages named `accept`, `end`, and `progress`.

SEE ALSO
accept, do, end, if, goto, progress, remoterefs

NAME

len – predefined, integer function to determine the number of messages that is stored in a buffered channel.

SYNTAX

len (*varref*)

DESCRIPTION

A predefined function that takes the name of a channel as an argument and returns the number of messages that it currently holds.

EXAMPLES

```
#define QSZ      4

chan q = [QSZ] of { mtype, short };

len(q) >  0      /* same as nempty(q) */
len(q) == 0      /* same as empty(q) */
len(q) == QSZ    /* same as full(q) */
len(q) <  QSZ    /* same as nfull(q) */
```

NOTES

When possible, it is always better to use the predefined, boolean functions empty, nempty, full, and nfull, since these define special cases that can be exploited in SPIN's partial order reduction algorithm during verification.

If len is used stand-alone as a condition statement, it will block execution until the channel is non-empty.

SEE ALSO

chan, **condition**, **empty**, **full**, **nempty**, **nfull**, **xr**, **xs**

NAME

local – prefix on global variable declarations to assert exclusive use by a single process.

SYNTAX

local *typename ivar*

DESCRIPTION

The keyword local can be used to prefix the declaration of any global variable. It persuades the partial order reduction algorithm in the model checker to treat the variable as if it were declared local to a single process, yet by being declared global it can freely be used in LTL formulae and in never claims.

The addition of this prefix can increase the effect of partial order reduction during verification, and lower verification complexity.

EXAMPLES

```
local byte a;
local short p[3];
```

NOTES

If a variable marked as local is in fact accessed by more than one process, the partial order reduction may become invalid and the result of a verification incomplete. Such violations are not detected by the verifier.

SEE ALSO

_, **datatypes**, **hidden**, **ltl**, **never**, **show**

NAME

ltl – linear time temporal logic formulae for specifying correctness requirements.

SYNTAX

Grammar:

ltl ::= **opd** | (ltl) | ltl **binop** ltl | **unop** ltl

Operands (**opd**):

true, false, and user-defined names starting with a lower-case letter

Unary Operators (**unop**):

[]   (the temporal operator *always*)
< >   (the temporal operator *eventually*)
!   (the boolean operator for *negation*)

Binary Operators (**binop**):

U   (the temporal operator *strong until*)
V   (the dual of U): (p V q) means !(!p U !q))
&&   (the boolean operator for *logical and*)
| | (the boolean operator for *logical or*)
/\   (alternative form of &&)
\/   (alternative form of | |)
- >   (the boolean operator for *logical implication*)
< - >   (the boolean operator for *logical equivalence*)

DESCRIPTION

SPIN can translate LTL formulae into PROMELA never claims with command line option -f. The never claim that is generated encodes the Büchi acceptance conditions from the LTL formula. Formally, any ω-run that satisfies the LTL formula is guaranteed to correspond to an accepting run of the never claim.

The operands of an LTL formula are often one-character symbols, such as p, q, r, but they can also be symbolic names, provided that they start with a lowercase character, to avoid confusion with some of the temporal operators which are in uppercase. The names or symbols must be defined to represent boolean expressions on global variables from the model. The names or symbols are normally defined with macro definitions.

All binary operators are left-associative. Parentheses can be used to override this default. Note that implication and equivalence are not temporal but logical operators (see Chapter 6).

EXAMPLES

Some examples of valid LTL formulae follow, as they would be passed in command-line arguments to SPIN for translation into `never` claims. Each formula passed to SPIN has to be quoted. We use single quotes in all examples in this book, which will work correctly on most systems (including UNIX systems and Windows systems with the `cygwin` toolset). On some systems double quotes can also be used.

```
spin -f '[] p'
spin -f '!( <> !q )'
spin -f 'p U q'
spin -f 'p U ([] (q U r))'
```

The conditions p, q, and r can be defined with macros, for instance as:

```
#define p        (a > b)
#define q        (len(q) < 5)
#define r        (root@Label)
```

elsewhere in the PROMELA model. It is prudent to always enclose these macro definitions in round braces to avoid misinterpretation of the precedence rules on any operators in the context where the names end up being used in the final `never` claim. The variables a and b, the channel name q, and the `proctype` name `root` from the preceding example, must be globally declared.

NOTES

If the SPIN sources are compiled with the preprocessor directive -DNXT, the set of temporal operators is extended with one additional unary operator: X (next). The X operator asserts the truth of the subformula that follows it for the *next* system state that is reached. The use of this operator can void the validity of the partial order reduction algorithm that is used in SPIN, if it changes the stutter invariance of an LTL formula. For the partial order reduction strategy to be valid, only LTL properties that are stutter invariant can be used. Every LTL property that does not contain the X operator is guaranteed to satisfy the required property. A property that is not stutter invariant can still be checked, but only without the application of partial order reduction.

An alternative converter for LTL formulae, that can often produce smaller automata, is the tool `ltl2ba`, see p. 145.

SEE ALSO

condition, macros, never, notrace, remoterefs, trace

NAME

macros and include files – preprocessing support.

SYNTAX

```
#define name token-string
#define name(arg, ..., arg)   token-string
#ifdef name
#ifndef name
#if constant-expression
#else
#endif
#undef name
#include "filename"
```

DESCRIPTION

PROMELA source text is always processed by the C preprocessor, conventionally named cpp, before being parsed by SPIN. When properly compiled, SPIN has a link to the C preprocessor built-in, so that this first processing step becomes invisible to the user. If a problem arises, though, or if a different preprocessor should be used, SPIN recognizes an option -Pxxx that allows one to define a full pathname for an alternative preprocessor. The only requirement is that this preprocessor should read standard input and write its result on standard output.

EXAMPLES

```
#include "promela_model"

#define p       (a>b)

never { /* <>!p */
        do
        :: !p -> assert(false)
        :: else /* else ignore */
        od
}
```

It is always wise to put braces around the replacement text in the macro-definitions to make sure the precedence of operator evaluation is preserved when a macro name is used in a different context, for example, within a composite boolean expression.

NOTES

The details of the working of the preprocessor can be system dependent. For the specifics, consult the manual pages for cpp that came with the C compiler that is installed on your system.

On PCs, if no macros with more than one parameter appear in the model, and no extra compiler directives are defined on the command line, Spin will use a simple built-in version of the C preprocessor to bypass the call on the external program. When needed, this call can be suppressed by adding a dummy compiler directive to the command line, as in:

```
$ spin -DDUMMY -a model
```

The call could also be suppressed by adding a dummy macro definition with more than one parameter to the model itself, as in:

```
#define dummy(a,b)        (a+b)
```

The preprocessor that is used can be modified in several ways. The default preprocessor, for instance, can be set to m4 by recompiling Spin itself with the compiler directive -DCPP=/bin/m4. The choice of preprocessor can also be changed on the command line, for instance, by invoking Spin as:

```
$ spin -P/bin/m4  model
```

Extra definitions can be passed to the preprocessor from the command line, as in:

```
$ spin -E-I/usr/greg -DMAX=5 -UXAM model
```

which has the same effect as adding the following two definitions at the start of the model:

```
#define MAX     5
#undef  XAM
```

as well as passing the additional directive -I/usr/greg to the preprocessor, which results in the addition of directory /usr/greg to the list of directories that the preprocessor will search for include files.

SEE ALSO
comments, **never**

NAME

mtype – for defining symbolic names of numeric constants.

SYNTAX

mtype [=] { *name* [, *name*]* }
mtype *name* [= mtype_name]
mtype *name* ' [' *const* ']' [= mtype_name]

DESCRIPTION

An mtype declaration allows for the introduction of symbolic names for
constant values. There can be multiple mtype declarations in a verification model. If multiple declarations are given, they are equivalent to a
single mtype declaration that contains the concatenation of all separate
lists of symbolic names.

If one or more mtype declarations are present, the keyword mtype can
be used as a data type, to introduce variables that obtain their values from
the range of symbolic names that was declared. This data type can also
be used inside chan declarations, for specifying the type of message
fields.

EXAMPLES

The declaration

```
mtype = { ack, nak, err, next, accept }
```

is functionally equivalent to the sequence of macro definitions:

```
#define ack      5
#define nak      4
#define err      3
#define next     2
#define accept   1
```

Note that the symbols are numbered in the reverse order of their definition in the mtype declarations, and that the lowest number assigned is
one, not zero.

If multiple mtype declarations appear in the model, each new set of symbols is prepended to the previously defined set, which can make the final
internal numbering of the symbols somewhat less predictable.

The convention is to place an assignment operator in between the
keyword mtype and the list of symbolic names that follows, but this is
not required.

The symbolic names are preserved in tracebacks and error reports for all
data that is explicitly declared with data type mtype.

In this example:

```
mtype a; mtype p[4] = nak;
chan q = [4] of { mtype, byte, short, mtype };
```

the `mtype` variable `a` is not initialized. It will by default be initialized to zero, which is outside the range of possible `mtype` values (identifying the variable as uninitialized). All four elements of array `p` are initialized to the symbolic name `nak`. Channel `q`, finally, has a channel initializer that declares the type of the first and last field in each message to be of type `mtype`.

NOTES

Variables of type `mtype` are stored in a variable of type `unsigned char` in their C equivalent. Therefore, there can be at most 255 distinct symbolic names in an `mtype` declaration.

The utility function `printm` can be used to print the symbolic name of a single `mtype` variable. Alternatively, in random or guided simulations with SPIN, the name can be printed with the special `printf` conversion character sequence `%e`. The following two lines, for instance, both print the name `nak` (without spaces, linefeeds, or any other decoration):

```
mtype = { ack, nak, err, next, accept }

init {
        mtype x = nak;

        printm(x);
        printf("%e", x)
}
```

The `printm` form is prefered, since it will also work when error traces are reproduced with the verifier, for models with embedded C code.

SEE ALSO

datatypes, printf, printm

NAME

nempty – predefined, boolean function to test emptiness of a channel.

SYNTAX

nempty (*varref*)

DESCRIPTION

The expression nempty(q), with q a channel name, is equivalent to the expression

```
(len(q) != 0)
```

where q is a channel name. The PROMELA grammar prohibits this from being written as !empty(q).

Using nempty instead of its equivalents can preserve the validity of reductions that are applied during verifications, especially in combination with the use of xr and xs channel assertions.

NOTES

Note that if predefined functions such as empty, nempty, full, and nfull are used in macro definitions used for propositional symbols in LTL formulae, they may well unintentionally appear under a negation sign, which will trigger syntax errors from SPIN.

SEE ALSO

condition, empty, full, len, ltl, nfull, xr, xs

NAME

never – declaration of a temporal claim.

SYNTAX

never { *sequence* }

DESCRIPTION

A never claim can be used to define system behavior that, for whatever reason, is of special interest. It is most commonly used to specify behavior that should *never* happen. The claim is defined as a series of propositions, or boolean expressions, on the system state that must become *true* in the sequence specified for the behavior of interest to be matched.

A never claim can be used to match either finite or infinite behaviors. Finite behavior is matched if the claim can reach its final state (that is, its closing curly brace). Infinite behavior is matched if the claim permits an ω-acceptance cycle. Never claims, therefore, can be used to verify both safety and liveness properties of a system.

Almost all PROMELA language constructs can be used inside a claim declaration. The only exceptions are those statements that can have a side effect on the system state. This means that a never claim may not contain assignment or message passing statements. Side effect free channel poll operations, and arbitrary condition statements are allowed.

Never claims can either be written by hand or they can be generated mechanically from LTL formula, see the manual page for ltl.

There is a small number of predefined variables and functions that may only be used inside never claims. They are defined in separate manual pages, named _last, enabled, np_, pc_value, and remoterefs.

EXAMPLES

In effect, when a never claim is present, the system and the claim execute in lockstep. That is, we can think of system execution as always consisting of a pair of transitions: one in the claim and one in the system, with the second transition coming from any one of the active processes. The claim automaton always executes first. If the claim automaton does not have any executable transitions, no further move is possible, and the search along this path stops. The search will then backtrack so that other executions can be explored.

This means that we can easily use a never claim to define a search restriction; we do not necessarily have to use the claim only for the specification of correctness properties. For example, the claim

```
never /* [] p */
{
        do
        :: p
        od
}
```

would restrict system behavior to those states where property p holds.

We can also use a search restriction in combination with an LTL property. To prove, for instance, that the model satisfies LTL property <>q, we can use the never claim that is generated with the SPIN command (using the negation of the property):

```
$ spin -f '!<> q'
```

Using the generated claim in a verification run can help us find counterexamples to the property. If we want to exclude non-progress behaviors from the search for errors, we can extend the LTL formula with the corresponding restriction, as follows:

```
$ spin -f '([]<> !np_) -> (!<> q)'
```

Alternatively, if we wanted to restrict the search to only *non*-progress behaviors, we can negate the precondition and write:

```
$ spin -f '(<>[] np_) -> (!<> q)'
```

The claim automaton must be able to make its first transition, starting in its initial claim state, from the global initial system state of the model. This rule can sometimes have unexpected consequences, especially when remote referencing operations are used. Consider, for instance, the following model:[1]

```
byte aap;

proctype noot()
{
mies:   skip
}

init {
        aap = run noot()
}
```

with the never claim defined as follows:

---

1. The example is from Rob Gerth.

```
never {
        do
        :: noot[aap]@mies -> break
        :: else
        od
}
```

The intent of this claim is to say that the process of type `noot`, with pid `aap`, cannot ever reach its state labeled `mies`. If this happened, the claim would reach its final state, and a violation would be flagged by the verifier. We can predict that this property is not satisfied, and when we run the verifier it will indeed report a counterexample, but the counterexample is created for a different reason.

In the initial system state the `never` claim is evaluated for the first time. In that state only the `init` process exists. To evaluate expression `noot[aap]@mies` the value of variable `aap` is determined, and it is found to be zero (since the variable was not assigned to yet, and still has its default initial value). The process with pid zero is the `init` process, which happens to be in its first state. The label `mies` also points to the first state, but of a process that has not been created yet. Accidentally, therefore, the evaluation of the remote reference expression yields *true*, and the claim terminates, triggering an error report. The simulator, finally, on replaying the error trail, will reveal the true nature of this error in the evaluation of the remote reference.

A correct version of the claim can be written as follows:

```
never {
        true;
        do
        :: noot[aap]@mies -> break
        :: else
        od
}
```

In this version we made sure that the remote reference expression is not evaluated until the process that is referred to exists (that is, after the first execution step in the `init` process is completed).

Note that it is not possible to shortcut this method by attempting the global declaration:

```
byte aap = run noot();   /* an invalid initializer */
```

In this case, with only one process of type `noot`, we can also avoid using variable `aap` by using the shorter remote reference:

```
noot@mies
```

To translate an LTL formula into a `never` claim, we have to consider first whether the formula expresses a positive or a negative property. A positive property expresses a good behavior that we would like our system to have. A negative property expresses a bad behavior that we claim the system does not have. A `never` claim is normally only used to formalize negative properties (behaviors that should never happen), which means that positive properties must be negated before they are translated into a claim.

Suppose that the LTL formula `<>[]p`, with `p` a boolean expression, expresses a negative claim (that is, it is considered a correctness violation if there exists any execution sequence in which eventually `p` can remain *true* infinitely long). This can be written in a `never` claim as:

```
never { /* <>[]p */
        do
        :: true /* after an arbitrarily long prefix */
        :: p -> break             /* p becomes true */
        od;
accept: do
        :: p        /* and remains true forever after */
        od
}
```

Note that in this case the claim does not terminate and also does not necessarily match all system behaviors. It is sufficient if it precisely captures all violations of our correctness requirement, and no more.

If the LTL formula expressed a positive property, we first have to invert it to the corresponding negative property. For instance, if we claim that immediately from the initial state forward the value of `p` remains *true*, the negation of that property is: `![]p` which can be translated into a `never` claim. The requirement says that it is a violation if `p` does not always remain *true*.

```
never { /* ![]p = <>!p*/
        do
        :: true
        :: !p -> break
        od
}
```

In this specification, we have used the implicit match of a claim upon reaching the final state of the automaton. Since the first violation of the property suffices to disprove it, we could also have written:

```
never {
        do
        :: !p -> break
        :: else
        od
}
```

or, if we abandon the correspondence with LTL and Büchi automata for a moment, even more tersely as:

```
never { do :: assert(p) od }
```

NOTES

It is good practice to confine the use of `accept` labels to `never` claims. SPIN automatically generates the `accept` labels within the claim when it generates claims from LTL formulae on run-time option `-f`.

The behavior specified in a `never` claim is matched if the claim can terminate, that is, if execution can reach the closing curly brace of the claim body. In terms of Büchi acceptance, this means that in a search for liveness properties, the final state of the claim is interpreted as the implicit acceptance cycle:

```
accept_all: do :: true od
```

The dummy claim

```
never {
        true
}
```

therefore always matches, and reports a violation, after precisely one execution step of the system. If a `never` claim contains no `accept` labels, then a search for cycles with run-time option `-a` is unnecessary and the claim can be proven or disproven with a simple search for safety properties. When the verifier is used in breadth-first search mode, only safety properties can be proven, including those expressed by `never` claims.

SEE ALSO

last, **accept**, **assert**, **enabled**, **ltl**, **notrace**, **np**, **pc_value**, **poll**, **progress**, **remoterefs**, **trace**

NAME

nfull – predefined, boolean function to test fullness of a channel.

SYNTAX

nfull (*varref*)

DESCRIPTION

The expression nfull(q) is equivalent to the expression

```
(len(q) < QSZ)
```

where q is a channel name, and QSZ the capacity of this channel. The PROMELA grammar prohibits the same from being written as !full(q).

Using nfull instead of its equivalents can preserve the validity of reductions that are applied during verifications, especially in combination with the use of xr and xs channel assertions.

NOTES

Note that if predefined functions such as empty, nempty, full, and nfull are used in macro definitions used for propositional symbols in LTL formulae, they may well unintentionally appear under a negation sign, which will trigger syntax errors from SPIN.

SEE ALSO

condition, empty, full, len, ltl, nempty, xr, xs

NAME

np_ – a global, predefined, read-only boolean variable.

SYNTAX

np_

DESCRIPTION

This global predefined, read-only variable is defined to be *true* in all global system states that are not explicitly marked as progress states, and is *false* in all other states. The system is in a progress state if at least one active process is at a local control state that was marked with a user-defined `progress` label, or if the current global system state is marked by a `progress` label in an event `trace` definition.

The np_ variable is meant to be used exclusively inside `never` claims, to define system properties.

EXAMPLES

The following non-deterministic `never` claim accepts all non-progress cycles:

```
never {  /* <>[] np_ */
        do
        :: true
        :: np_ -> break
        od;
accept: do
        :: np_
        od
}
```

This claim is identical to the one that the verifier generates, and automatically adds to the model, when the verifier source is compiled with the directive -DNP, as in:

```
$ cc -DNP -o pan pan.c
```

Note that the claim automaton allows for an arbitrary, finite-length prefix of the computation where either progress or non-progress states can occur. The claim automaton can move to its accepting state only when the system is in a non-progress state, and it can only stay there infinitely long if the system can indefinitely remain in non-progress states only.

SEE ALSO

condition, ltl, never, progress

NAME

pc_value – a predefined, integer function for use in never claims.

SYNTAX

pc_value (*any_expr*)

DESCRIPTION

The call pc_value(x) returns the current control state (an integer) of the process with instantiation number x. The correspondence between the state numbers reported by pc_value and statements or line numbers in the PROMELA source can be checked with run-time option -d on the verifiers generated by SPIN, as in:

```
$ spin -a model.pml
$ cc -o pan pan.c
$ ./pan -d
...
```

The use of this function is restricted to never claims.

EXAMPLES

```
never {
        do
        :: pc_value(1) <= pc_value(2)
        && pc_value(2) <= pc_value(3)
        && pc_value(3) <= pc_value(4)
        && pc_value(4) <= pc_value(5)
        od
}
```

This claim is a flawed attempt to enforce a symmetry reduction among five processes. This particular attempt is flawed in that it does not necessarily preserve the correctness properties of the system being verified. See also the discussion in Chapter 4, p. 94.)

NOTES

As the example indicates, this function is primarily supported for experimental use, and may not survive in future revisions of the language.

SEE ALSO

condition, **never**

NAME

`pointers` – indirect memory addressing.

DESCRIPTION

There are no pointers in the basic PROMELA language, although there is a way to circumvent this restriction through the use of embedded C code.

The two main reasons for leaving pointers out of the basic language are efficiency and tractability. To make verification possible, the verifier needs to be able to track all data that are part of reachable system states. SPIN maintains all such data, that is, local process states, local and global variables, and channel contents, in a single data structure called the system "state vector." The efficiency of the SPIN verifiers is in large part due to the availability of all state data within the simple, flat state vector structure, which allows each state comparison and state copying operation to be performed with a single system call.

The performance of a SPIN verifier can be measured in the number of reachable system states per second that can be generated and analyzed. In the current system, this performance is determined exclusively by the length of the state vector: a vector twice as long requires twice as much time to verify per state, and vice versa; every reduction in the length of a state vector translates into an increase of the verifier's efficiency. The cost per state is in most cases a small constant factor times the time needed to copy the bits in the state vector from one place to another (that is, the cost of an invocation of the system routine `memcpy()`).

The use of data that are only accessible through pointers during verification runs requires the verifier to collect the relevant data from all memory locations that could be pointed to at any one time and copy such information into the state vector. The associated overhead immediately translates in reduced verification efficiency.

See Chapter 17 for a discussion of the indirect support for pointers through the use of embedded C code fragments.

SEE ALSO

c_code, **c_decl**, **c_expr**

NAME

poll – a side effect free test for the executability of a non-rendezvous receive statements.

SYNTAX

name ? ' [' *recv_args* '] '
name ?? ' [' *recv_args* '] '

DESCRIPTION

A channel poll operation looks just like a receive statement, but with the list of message fields enclosed in square brackets. It returns either *true* or *false*, depending on the executability of the corresponding receive (i.e., the same operation written without the square brackets). Because its evaluation is side effect free, this form can be used freely in expressions or even assignments where a standard receive operation cannot be used.

The state of the channel, and all variables used, is guaranteed not to change as a result of the evaluation of this condition statement.

EXAMPLES

In the following example we use a channel poll operation to place an additional constraint on a timeout condition:

```
qname?[ack,var] && timeout
```

NOTES

Channel poll operations do not work on rendezvous channels because synchronous channels never store messages that a poll operation could refer to. Messages are always passed instantly from sender to receiver in a rendezvous handshake.

It is relatively simple to create a conditional receive operation, with the help of a channel poll operation. For instance, if we want to define an extra boolean condition P that must hold before a given receive operation may be executed, we can write simply:

```
atomic { P && qname?[ack,var] -> qname[ack,var] }
```

This is harder to do for rendezvous channels; see the manual page for cond_expr for some examples.

SEE ALSO

cond_expr, **condition**, **eval**, **receive**

NAME

`printf` – for printing text during random or guided simulation runs.

SYNTAX

`printf(` *string* `[` , *arg_lst* `]` `)`
`printm(` *expression* `)`

EXECUTABILITY

true

EFFECT

`none`

DESCRIPTION

A `printf` statement is similar to a `skip` statement in the sense that it is always executable and has no other effect on the state of the system than to change the control state of the process that executes it. A useful side effect of the statement is that it can print a string on the standard output stream during simulation runs. The PROMELA `printf` statement supports a subset of the options from its namesake in the programming language C. The first argument is an arbitrary *string*, in double quotes.

Six conversion specifications are recognized within the string. Upon printing, each subsequent conversion specification is replaced with the value of the next argument from the list that follows the string.

`%c`	a single character,
`%d`	a decimal value,
`%e`	an mtype constant,
`%o`	an unsigned octal value,
`%u`	an unsigned integer value,
`%x`	a hexadecimal value.

In addition, the white-space escape sequences \t (for a tab character) and \n (for a newline) are also recognized. Unlike the C version, optional width and precision fields are not supported.

The alternative form `printm` can be used to print just the symbolic name of an `mtype` constant. The two print commands in the following sequence, for instance, would both print the string `pear`:

```
mtype = { apple, pear, orange };
mtype x = pear;
printf("%e", x);
printm(x);
```

The method using `printf` works only when SPIN runs in simulation mode though, it does not work when an error trail is reproduced with the verifier (e.g., when embedded C code fragments are used). The alternative, using `printm`, always works.

EXAMPLES

```
printf("numbers: %d\t%d\n", (-10)%(-9), (-10)<<(-2))
```

NOTES

`Printf` statements are useful during simulation and debugging of a verification model. In verification, however, they are of no value, and therefore not normally enabled. The order in which `printf`s are executed during verification is determined by the depth-first search traversal of the reachability graph, which does not necessarily make sense if interpreted as part of a straight execution. When SPIN generates the verifier's source text, therefore, it replaces every call to `printf` with a special one that is called `Printf`. The latter function is only allowed to produce output during the replay of an error trace. This function can also be called from within embedded C code fragments, to suppress unwanted output during verification runs.

Special Notes on XSPIN: The text printed by a `printf` statement that begins with the five characters: "MSC: " (three letters followed by a colon and a space) is automatically included in message sequence charts. For instance, when the statement

```
printf("MSC: State Idle\n")
```

is used, the string `State Idle` will included in the message sequence chart when this statement is reached. A more detailed description of this feature can also be found in Chapter 12, p. 272.

It is also possible to set breakpoints for a random simulation run, when XSPIN is used. To do so, the text that follows the `MSC:` prefix must match the five characters: `BREAK`, as in:

```
printf("MSC: BREAK\n")
```

These simulation breakpoints can be made conditional by embedding them into selection constructs. For instance:

```
if
:: P -> printf("MSC: BREAK\n")
:: else /* no breakpoint */
fi
```

SEE ALSO

do, **if**, **skip**

NAME

priority – for setting a numeric simulation priority for a process.

SYNTAX

active ['[' *const* ']'] proctype *name* ([*decl_lst*]) priority *const* { *sequence* }
run *name* ([*arg_lst*]) priority const

DESCRIPTION

Process priorities can be used in random simulations to change the probability that specific processes are scheduled for execution.

An execution priority is specified either as an optional parameter to a
run operator, or as a suffix to an active proctype declaration. The
optional priority field follows the closing brace of the parameter list
in a proctype declaration.

The default execution priority for a process is *one*. Higher numbers indicate higher priorities, in such a way that a priority *ten* process is *ten*
times more likely to execute than a priority *one* process.

The priority specified in an active proctype declaration affects all
processes that are initiated through the active prefix, but no others. A
process instantiated with a run statement is always assigned the priority
that is explicitly or implicitly specified there (overriding the priority that
may be specified in the proctype declaration for that process).

EXAMPLES

```
run name(...) priority 3
active proctype name() priority 12 { sequence }
```

If both a priority clause and a provided clause are specified, the
priority clause should appear first.

```
active proctype name() priority 5 provided (a<b) {...}
```

NOTES

Priority annotations only affect random simulation runs. They have no
effect during verification, or in guided and interactive simulation runs. A
priority designation on a proctype declaration that contains no active
prefix is ignored.

SEE ALSO

active, proctype, provided

NAME

probabilities – for distinguishing between high and low probability actions.

DESCRIPTION

There is no mechanism in PROMELA for indicating the probability of a statement execution, other than during random simulations with prior- ity tags.

SPIN is designed to check the unconditional correctness of a system. High probability executions are easily intercepted with standard testing and debugging techniques, but only model checking techniques are able to reproducibly detect the remaining classes of errors.

Disastrous error scenarios often have a low probability of occurrence that only model checkers can catch reliably. The use of probability tags on statement executions would remove the independence of probability, which seems counter to the premise of logic model checking. Phrased differently, verification in SPIN is concerned with *possible* behavior, not with probable behavior. In a well-designed system, erroneous behavior should be impossible, not just improbable.

To exclude *known* low probability event scenarios from consideration during model checking, a variety of other techniques may be used, including the use of model restriction, LTL properties, and the use of progress-state, end-state, and accept-state labels.

SEE ALSO

if, **do**, **priority**, **progress**, **unless**

NAME

procedures – for structuring a program text.

DESCRIPTION

There is no explicit support in the basic PROMELA language for defining procedures or functions. This restrction can be circumvented in some cases through the use of either `inline` primitives, or embedded C code fragments.

The reason for this restriction to the basic language is that SPIN targets the verification of process interaction and process coordination structures, and not internal process computations. Abstraction is then best done at the process and system level, not at a computational level. It is possible to approximate a procedure call mechanism with PROMELA process instantiations, but this is rarely a good idea. Consider, for instance, the following model:

```
#ifndef N
#define N        12
#endif

int f = 1;

proctype fact(int v)
{
        if
        :: v > 1 -> f = v*f; run fact(v-1)
        :: else
        fi
}

init {
        run fact(N);
        (_nr_pr == 1) ->
        printf("%d! = %d\n", N, f)
}
```

Initially, there is just one process in this system, the `init` process. It instantiates a process of type `fact` passing it the value of constant N, which is defined in a macro. If the parameter passed to the process of type `fact` is greater than one, the value of global integer `f` is multiplied by `v`, and another copy of `fact` is instantiated with a lower value of the parameter.

The procedure of course closely mimics a recursive procedure to compute the factorial of N. If we store the model in a file called `badidea` and execute the model, we get

```
$ spin badidea
12! = 479001600
13 processes created
```

which indeed is the correct value for the factorial. But, there are a few potential gotcha's here. First, the processes that are instantiated will execute asynchronously with the already running processes. Specifically, we cannot assume that the process that is instantiated in a `run` statement terminates its execution before the process that executed the `run` reaches its next statement. Generally, the newly created process will start executing concurrently with its creator. Nothing can be assumed about the speed of execution of a running process. If a particular order of execution is important, this must be enforced explicitly through process synchronization. In the initially running `init` process from the example, synchronization is achieved in one place with the expression

```
(_nr_pr == 1)
```

The variable `_nr_pr` is a predefined, global system variable that records the number of current executing processes, see the corresponding manual page. Because there is initially just one executing process (the process of type `main` itself), we know in this case that all newly instantiated processes must have terminated once the evaluation of this expression yields *true*. Recall that a condition statement can only be executed in PROMELA if it evaluates to *true*, which gives us the required synchronization, and guarantees that the final value of `f` is not printed before it is fully computed.

A more obvious gotcha is that the maximum useful value we can choose for the constant `N` is limited by the maximum number of processes that can simultaneously be instantiated. The maximum value that can be represented in a variable of type `int` is more restrictive in this case, though. The size of an `int` is the same in PROMELA as it is in the underlying programming language C, which at the time of writing means only 32 bits on most machines. The maximum signed value that can be represented in a 32 bit word is $2^{31} - 1 = 2,147,483,648$, which means that the largest factorial we can compute with our model is an unimpressive $13! = 1,932,053,504$. To do better, we would need a data type `double` or `float`, but PROMELA deliberately does not have them. The only way we could get these would be through the use of embedded C code fragments. The more fundamental reason why these data types are not part of native PROMELA is that any need to represent data quantities of this size almost certainly means that the user is trying to model a computational problem, and not a process synchronization problem. The omission of the larger data types from the language serves as a gentle warning to the user that the language is meant for design verification, and not for design implementation.

If a procedural mechanism is to be used, the most efficient method would be to use a `macro` or an `inline` definition. This amounts to an automatic inlining of the text of a procedure call into the body of each process that invokes it. A disadvantage of a `macro` is that line-number references will be restricted to the location of the macro call, not a line number within a macro definition itself. This problem does not exist with an `inline` definition.

If a separate process is used to model the procedure, the best way to do so is to declare it as a permanent server by declaring it as an `active` `proctype`: receiving requests from user processes via a special globally defined channel, and responding to these requests via a user-provided local channel.

The least attractive method is to instantiate a new copy of a process once for each procedure call and wait for that process to return a result (via a global variable or a message channel) and then disappear from the system before proceeding. This is less attractive because it produces the overhead of process creation and deletion, and can add the complication of determining reliably when precisely a process has disappeared from the system.

SEE ALSO

_nr_pr, active, c_code, c_expr, hierarchy, inline, macros, proctype

NAME

proctype – for declaring new process behavior.

SYNTAX

`proctype` *name* ([*decl_lst*]) { *sequence* }
`D_proctype` *name* ([*decl_lst*]) { *sequence* }

DESCRIPTION

All process behavior must be declared before it can be instantiated. The `proctype` construct is used for the declaration. Instantiation can be done either with the `run` operator, or with the prefix `active` that can be used at the time of declaration.

Declarations for local variables and message channels may be placed anywhere inside the `proctype` body. In all cases, though, these declarations are treated as if they were all placed at the start of the `proctype` declaration. The scope of local variables cannot be restricted to only part of the `proctype` body.

The keyword `D_proctype` can be used to declare process behavior that is to be executed completely *deterministically*. If non-determinism is nonetheless present in this type of process definition, it is resolved in simulations in a deterministic, though otherwise undefined, manner. During verifications an error is reported if non-determinism is encountered in a `D_proctype` process.

EXAMPLES

The following program declares a `proctype` with one local variable named `state`:

```
proctype A(mtype x) { mtype state; state = x }
```

The process type is named A, and has one formal parameter named x.

NOTES

Within a `proctype` body, formal parameters are indistinguishable from local variables. Their only distinguishing feature is that their initial values can be determined by an instantiating process, at the moment when a new copy of the process is created.

SEE ALSO

_pid, active, init, priority, provided, remoterefs, run

NAME

progress – label-name prefix for specifying liveness properties.

SYNTAX

progress[a-zA-Z0-9_]*: *stmnt*

DESCRIPTION

A progress label is any label name that starts with the eight-character sequence progress. It can appear anywhere a label can appear.

A label always prefixes a statement, and thereby uniquely identifies a local process state (i.e., the source state of the transition that corresponds to the labeled statement). A progress label marks a state that is required to be traversed in any infinite execution sequence.

A progress label can appear in a proctype, or trace declaration, but has no special semantics when used in a never claim or in notrace declarations. Because a global system state is a composite of local component states (e.g., proctype instantiations, and an optional trace component), a progress label indirectly also marks *global* system states where one or more of the component systems is labeled with a progress label.

Progress labels are used to define correctness claims. A progress label states the requirement that the labeled global state must be visited infinitely often in any infinite system execution. Any violation of this requirement can be reported by the verifier as a non-progress cycle.

EXAMPLES

```
active proctype dijkstra()
{       do
        :: sema!p ->
progress:       sema?v
        od
}
```

The requirement expressed here is that any infinite system execution contains infinitely many executions of the statement sema?v.

NOTES

Progress labels are typically used to mark a state where effective progress is being made in an execution, such as a sequence number being incremented or valid data being accepted by a receiver in a data transfer protocol. They can, however, also be used during verifications to eliminate harmless variations of liveness violations. One such application, for instance, can be to mark message loss events with a pseudo progress label, to indicate that sequences that contain infinitely many message loss events are of secondary interest. If we now search for non-progress executions, we will no longer see any executions that involve infinitely many message loss events.

SPIN has a special mode to prove absence of non-progress cycles. It does so with the predefined LTL formula:

```
(<>[] np_)
```

which formalizes non-progress as a standard Büchi acceptance property.

The standard stutter-extension, to extend finite execution sequences into infinite ones by stuttering (repeating) the final state of the sequence, is applied in the detection of all acceptance properties, including non-progress cycles.

The manual page for `never` claims describes how the predefined variable `np_` can also be used to restrict a verification to precisely the set of either progress or non-progress cycles.

SEE ALSO
accept, end, labels, ltl, never, np_, trace

NAME

`provided` – for setting a global constraint on process execution.

SYNTAX

`proctype` *name* `(` `[` *decl_lst* `]` `)` `provided` `(` *expr* `)` `{` *sequence* `}`

DESCRIPTION

Any proctype declaration can be suffixed by an optional `provided` clause to constrain its execution to those global system states for which the corresponding expression evaluates to `true`. The `provided` clause has the effect of labeling all statements in the `proctype` declaration with an additional, user-defined executability constraint.

EXAMPLES

The declaration:

```
byte a, b;
active proctype A() provided (a > b)
{
        . . .
}
```

makes the execution of all instances of `proctype` A conditional on the truth of the expression `(a>b)`, which is, for instance, not true in the initial system state. The expression can contain global references, or references to the process's `_pid`, but no references to any local variables or parameters.

If both a `priority` clause and a `provided` clause are specified, the `priority` clause should come first.

```
active proctype name() priority 2 provided (a > b )
{
        . . .
}
```

NOTES

`Provided` clauses are incompatible with partial order reduction. They can be useful during random simulations, or in rare cases to control and reduce the complexity of verifications.

SEE ALSO

_pid, active, hidden, priority, proctype

NAME

rand – for random number generation.

DESCRIPTION

There is no predefined random number generation function in PROMELA. The reason is that during a verification we effectively check for all possible executions of a system. Having even a single occurrence of a call on the random number generator would increase the number of cases to inspect by the full range of the random numbers that could be generated: usually a huge number. Random number generators can be useful on a simulation, but they can be disastrous when allowed in verification.

In almost all cases, PROMELA's notion of non-determinism can replace the need for a random number generator. Note that to make a random choice between N alternatives, it suffices to place these N alternatives in a selection structure with N options. The verifier will interpret the non-determinism accurately, and is not bound to the restrictions of a pseudo-random number generation algorithm.

During random simulations, SPIN will internally make calls on a (pseudo) random number generator to resolve all cases of non-determinism. During verifications no such calls are made, because effectively all options for behavior will be explored in this mode, one at a time.

PROMELA's equivalent of a "random number generator" is the following program:

```
active proctype randnr()
{       /*
         * don't call this rand()...
         * to avoid a clash with the C library routine
         */
        byte nr;        /* pick random value  */
        do
        :: nr++         /* randomly increment */
        :: nr--         /* or decrement       */
        :: break        /* or stop            */
        do;
        printf("nr: %d\n")      /* nr: 0..255 */
}
```

Note that the verifier would generate at least 256 distinct reachable states for this model. The simulator, on the other hand, would traverse the model only once, but it could execute a sequence of any length (from one to infinitely many execution steps). A simulation run will only terminate if the simulator eventually selects the break option (which is guaranteed only in a statistical sense).

NOTES

Through the use of embedded C code, a user can surreptitiously include calls on an external C library `rand()` function into a model. To avoid problems with irreproducible behavior, the SPIN-generated verifiers intercept such calls and redefine them in such a way that the depth-first search process at the very least remains deterministic. SPIN accomplishes this by pre-allocating an integer array of the maximum search depth `maxdepth`, and filling that array with the first `maxdepth` random numbers that are generated. Those numbers are then reused each time the search returns to a previously visited point in the search, to secure the sanity of the search process.

The seed for this pre-computation of random numbers is fixed, so that subsequent runs will always give the same result, and to allow for the faithful replay of error scenarios. Even though this provides some safeguards, the use of random number generation is best avoided, also in embedded C code.

SEE ALSO

c_code, c_expr, if, do

NAME

`real time` – for relating properties to real-time bounds.

DESCRIPTION

In the basic PROMELA language there is no mechanism for expressing properties of clocks or of time related properties or events. There are good algorithms for integrating real-time constraints into the model checking process, but most attention has so far been given to real-time verification problems in hardware circuit design, rather than the real-time verification of asynchronous *software*, which is the domain of the SPIN model checker.

The best known of these algorithms incur significant performance penalties compared with untimed verification. Each clock variable added to a model can increase the time and memory requirements of verification by an order of magnitude. Considering that one needs at least two or three such clock variables to define meaningful constraints, this seems to imply, for the time being, that a real-time capability requires at least three to four orders of magnitude more time and memory than the verification of the same system without time constraints.

The good news is that if a correctness property can be proven for an untimed PROMELA model, it is guaranteed to preserve its correctness under all possible real-time constraints. The result is therefore robust, it can be obtained efficiently, and it encourages good design practice. In concurrent software design it is usually unwise to link logical correctness with real-time performance.

PROMELA is a language for specifying systems of asynchronous processes. For the definition of such a system we abstract from the behavior of the process scheduler and from any assumption about the relative speed of execution of the various processes. These assumptions are safe, and the minimal assumptions required to allow us to construct proofs of correctness. The assumptions differ fundamentally from those that can be made for hardware systems, which are often driven by a single known clock, with relative speeds of execution precisely known. What often is just and safe in hardware verification is, therefore, not necessarily just and safe in software verification.

SPIN guarantees that all verification results remain valid independent of where and how processes are executed, timeshared on a single CPU, in true concurrency on a multiprocessor, or with different processes running on CPUs of different makes and varying speeds. Two points are worth considering in this context: first, such a guarantee can no longer be given if real-time constraints are introduced, and secondly, most of the existing real-time verification methods assume a true concurrency model, which inadvertently excludes the more common method of concurrent process execution by timesharing.

It can be hard to define realistic time bounds for an abstract software system. Typically, little can be firmly known about the real-time performance of an implementation. It is generally unwise to rely on speculative information, when attempting to establish a system's critical correctness properties.

SEE ALSO
priorities, probabilities

NAME

receive statement – for receiving messages from channels.

SYNTAX

name ? *recv_args*

name ?? *recv_args*

name ?< *recv_args* >

name ??< *recv_args* >

EXECUTABILITY

The first and the third form of the statement, written with a single question mark, are executable if the first message in the channel matches the pattern from the receive statement.

The second and fourth form of the statement, written with a double question mark, are executable if there exists at least one message anywhere in the channel that matches the pattern from the receive statement. The first such message is then used.

A match of a message is obtained if all message fields that contain constant values in the receive statement equal the values of the corresponding message fields in the message.

EFFECT

If a variable appears in the list of arguments to the receive statement, the value from the corresponding field in the message that is matched is copied into that variable upon reception of the message. If no angle brackets are used, the message is removed from the channel buffer after the values are copied. If angle brackets are used, the message is not removed and remains in the channel.

DESCRIPTION

The number of message fields that is specified in the receive statement must always match the number of fields that is declared in the channel declaration for the channel addressed. The types of the variables used in the message fields must be compatible with the corresponding fields from the channel declaration. For integer data types, an equal or larger value range for the variable is considered to be compatible (e.g., a `byte` field may be received in a `short` variable, etc.). Message fields that were declared to contain a user-defined data type or a `chan` must always match precisely.

The first form of the receive statement is most commonly used. The remaining forms serve only special purposes, and can only be used on buffered message channels.

The second form of the receive statement, written with two question marks, is called a *random receive* statement. The variants with angle brackets have no special name.

Because all four types of receive statements discussed here can have side effects, they cannot be used inside expressions (see the manual page poll for some alternatives).

EXAMPLES

```
chan set = [8] of { byte };
byte x;

set!!3; set!!5; set!!2; /* sorted send operations   */

set?x;                   /* get first element        */
if
:: set?<x>               /* copy first element       */
:: set??5                /* is there a 5 in the set? */
:: empty(set)
fi
```

In this example we first send three values into a channel that can contain up to eight messages with one single field of type byte. The values are within the range that is expected, so no value truncations will occur. The use of the sorted send operator (the double exclamation) causes the three values to be stored in numerical order. A regular receive operation is now used to retrieve the first element from the channel, which should be the value two.

The selection statement that follows has three options for execution. If the channel is empty at this point, only the third statement will be executable. If the channel is non-empty, and contains at least one message with the value five, the second option will be executable. Because of the use of the random receive operator (the double question mark), the target message may appear anywhere in the channel buffer and need not be the first message. It is removed from the channel when matched. The first option in the selection structure is executable if the channel contains any message at all. Its effect when executed will be to copy the value of the first message that is in the channel at this point into variable x. If all is well, this should be the value three. If this option is executed, the message will remain in the channel buffer, due to the use of the angle brackets.

SEE ALSO
chan, **empty**, **eval**, **full**, **len**, **nempty**, **nfull**, **poll**, **send**

NAME

remote references – a mechanism for testing the local control state of an active process, or the value of a local variable in an active process from within a `never` claim.

SYNTAX

name [' [' *any_expr* ']'] @ *labelname*

name [' [' *any_expr* ']'] : *varname*

DESCRIPTION

The remote reference operators take either two or three arguments: the first, required, argument is the name of a previously declared `proctype`, a second, optional, argument is an expression enclosed in square brackets, which provides the process instantiation number of an active process. With the first form of remote reference, the third argument is the name of a control-flow label that must exist within the named `proctype`. With the second form, the third argument is the name of a local variable from the named `proctype`.

The second argument can be omitted, together with the square brackets, if there is known to be only one instantiated process of the type that is named.

A remote reference expression returns a non-zero value if and only if the process referred to is currently in the local control state that was marked by the label name given.

EXAMPLES

```
active proctype main () {
        byte x;
L:      (x < 3) ->
        x++
}
never { /* process main cannot remain at L forever */
accept: do
        :: main@L
        od
}
```

NOTES

Because `init`, `never`, `trace`, and `notrace` are not valid `proctype` names but keywords, it is not possible to refer to the state of these special processes with a remote reference:

```
init@label      /* invalid */
never[0]@label  /* invalid */
```

Note that the use of `init`, can always be avoided, by replacing it with an `active proctype`.

A *remote variable* reference, the second form of a remote reference, bypasses the standard scope rules of PROMELA by making it possible for the `never` claim to refer to the current value of local variables inside a running process.

For instance, if we wanted to refer to the variable `count` in the process of type `Dijkstra` in the example on page 77, we could do so with the syntax `Dijkstra[0]:count`, or if there is only one such process, we can use the shorter form `Dijkstra:count`.

The use of remote variable references is not compatible with SPIN's partial order reduction strategy. A wiser strategy is therefore usually to turn local variables whose values are relevant to a global correctness property into global variables, so that they can be referenced as such. See especially the manual page for `hidden` for an efficient way of doing this that preserves the benefits of partial order reduction.

SEE ALSO
_pid, active, condition, hidden, proctype, run

NAME

run – predefined, unary operator for creating new processes.

SYNTAX

run *name* ([*arg_lst*])

DESCRIPTION

The run operator takes as arguments the name of a previously declared proctype, and a possibly empty list of actual parameters that must match the number and types of the formal parameters of that proctype. The operator returns zero if the maximum number of processes is already running, otherwise it returns the process instantiation number of a new process that is created. The new process executes asynchronously with the existing active processes from this point on. When the run operator completes, the new process need not have executed any statements.

The run operator must pass actual parameter values to the new process, if the proctype declaration specified a non-empty formal parameter list. Only message channels and instances of the basic data types can be passed as parameters. Arrays of variables cannot be passed.

Run can be used in any process to spawn new processes, not just in the initial process. An active process need not disappear from the system immediately when it terminates (i.e., reaches the end of the body of its process type declaration). It can only truly disappear if all younger processes have terminated first. That is, processes can only disappear from the system in reverse order of their creation.

EXAMPLES

```
proctype A(byte state; short set)
{
        (state == 1) -> state = set
}

init {
        run A(1, 3)
}
```

NOTES

Because PROMELA defines finite state systems, the number of processes and message channels is required to be bounded. SPIN limits the number of active processes to 255.

Because run is an operator, run A() is an expression that can be embedded in other expressions. It is the only operator allowed inside expressions that can have a side effect, and therefore there are some special restrictions that are imposed on expressions that contain `run` operators.

Note, for instance, that if the condition statement

```
(run A() && run B())
```

were allowed, in the evaluation of this expression it would be possible that the first application of the `run` operator succeeds, and the second fails when the maximum number of runnable processes is reached. This would produce the value *false* for the expression, and the condition statement would then block, yet a side effect of the evaluation has occurred. Each time the evaluation of the expression is repeated, one more process could then be created.

Therefore, the SPIN parser imposes the restriction that an expression cannot contain more than one `run` operator, and this operator cannot be combined in a compound expression with other conditionals. Also, as a further precaution, an attempt to create a 256th process is always flagged as an error by the verifier, although technically it would suffice to allow the `run` operator to return a zero value.

SEE ALSO
_pid, active, priority, proctype, provided, remoterefs

NAME

scanf – to read input from the standard input stream.

DESCRIPTION

There is no routine in PROMELA comparable to the C library function scanf to read input from the standard input stream or from a file or device. The reason is that PROMELA models must be closed to be verifiable. That is, all input sources must be part of the model. It is relatively easy to build a little process that acts as if it were the scanf routine, and that sends to user processes that request its services a non-deterministically chosen response from the set of anticipated responses.

As a small compromise, PROMELA does include a special predefined channel named STDIN that can be used to read characters from the standard input during simulation experiments. The use of STDIN is not supported in verification runs.

SEE ALSO

c_code, printf, STDIN

NAME

send statement – for sending messages to channels.

SYNTAX

name ! *send_args*

name ! ! *send_args*

EXECUTABILITY

A send statement on a buffered channel is executable in every global system state where the target channel is non-full. SPIN supports a mechanism to override this default with option -m. When this option is used, a send statement on a buffered channel is always executable, and the message is lost if the target channel is full.

The execution of a send statement on a *rendezvous* channel consists, conceptually, of two steps: a rendezvous *offer* and a rendezvous *accept*. The rendezvous offer can be made at any time (see Chapter 7). The offer can be accepted only if another active process can perform the matching receive operation immediately (i.e., with no intervening steps by any process). The rendezvous send operation can only take place if the offer made is accepted by a matching receive operation in another process.

EFFECT

For buffered channels, assuming no message loss occurs (see above), the message is added to the channel. In the first form of the send statement, with a single exclamation mark, the message is appended to the tail of the channel, maintaining *fifo* (first in, first out) order. In the second form, with a double exclamation mark, the message is inserted into the channel immediately ahead of the first message in the channel that succeeds it in numerical order. To determine the numerical order, all message fields are significant.

Within the semantics model, the effect of issuing the rendezvous offer is to set global system variable **handshake** to the channel identity of the target channel (see Chapter 7).

DESCRIPTION

The number of message fields that is specified in the send statement must always match the number of fields that is declared in the channel declaration for the target channel, and the values of the expressions specified in the message fields must be compatible with the datatype that was declared for the corresponding field. If the type of a message field is either a user-defined type or chan, then the types must match precisely.

The first form of the send statement is the standard *fifo* send. The second form, with the double exclamation mark, is called a *sorted send* operation. The sorted send operation can be exploited by, for instance, listing an appropriate message field (e.g., a sequence number) as the first field of each message, thus forcing a message ordering in the target channel.

EXAMPLES

In the following example our test process uses sorted send operations to send three messages into a buffered channel named x. Then it adds one more message with the value four.

```
chan x = [4] of { short };

active proctype tester()
{
        x!!3; x!!2; x!!1; x!4;
        x?1; x?2; x?3; x?4
}
```

All four values are now receivable in numerical order; the last message only coincidentally, but the first three due to the ordering discipline that is enforced by the sorted send operators. A simulation confirms this:

```
$ spin -c tester.pml
proc 0 = tester
q    0
  1    x!3
  1    x!2
  1    x!1
  1    x!4
  1    x?1
  1    x?2
  1    x?3
  1    x?4
-------------
final state:
-------------
1 process created
```

NOTES

By convention, the first field in a message is used to specify the message type, and is defined as an mtype.

Sorted send operations and *fifo* send operations can safely be mixed.

SEE ALSO

chan, empty, full, len, nempty, nfull, poll, receive

NAME

separators – for sequential composition of statements and declarations.

SYNTAX

step   ;   step
step   ->   step

DESCRIPTION

The semicolon and the arrow are equivalent statement *separators* in PROMELA; they are not statement *terminators*, although the parser has been taught to be forgiving for occasional lapses. The last statement in a sequence need not be followed by a statement separator, unlike, for instance, in the C programming language.

EXAMPLES

```
x = 3;
atomic {
        x = y;
        y = x   /* no separator is required here */
};                /* but it is required here...    */
y = 3
```

NOTES

The convention is to reserve the use of the arrow separator to follow condition statements, such as guards in selection or repetition structures. The arrow symbol can thus be used to visually identify those points in the code where execution could block.

SEE ALSO

break, labels, goto

NAME

sequence – curly braces, used to enclose a block of code.

SYNTAX

{ sequence }

DESCRIPTION

Any sequence of PROMELA statements may be enclosed in curly braces
and treated syntactically as if it were a statement. This facility is most
useful for defining unless constructs, but can also generally be used to
structure a model.

EXAMPLES

```
if
:: a < b -> { tmp = a; a = b; b = a }
:: else  ->
        { printf("unexpected case\n");
          assert(false)
        }
fi
```

The more common use is for structuring unless statements, as in:

```
{ tmp = a; a = b; b = a; }
unless
{ a >= b }
```

Note the differences between these two examples. In the first example,
the value of the expression a < b is checked once, just before the brack-
eted sequence is executed. In the second example, the value of the
negated expression is checked before each statement execution in the
main sequence, and execution is interrupted when that expression
becomes *true*.

NOTES

The last statement in a sequence need not be followed by a statement
separator, but if the sequence is followed by another statement, the
sequence as a whole should be separated from that next statement with a
statement separator.

SEE ALSO

atomic, **d_step**, **unless**

NAME

show – to allow for tracking of the access to specific variables in message sequence charts.

SYNTAX

show *typename name*

DESCRIPTION

This keyword has no semantic content. It only serves to determine which variables should be tracked and included in message sequence chart displays in the XSPIN tool. Updates of the value of all variables that are declared with this prefix are maintained visually, in a separate process line, in these message sequence charts.

NOTES

The use of this prefix only affects the information that XSPIN includes in message sequence charts, and the information that SPIN includes in Postscript versions of message sequence charts under SPIN option -M.

SEE ALSO

datatypes, hidden, local, show

NAME

skip – shorthand for a dummy, nil statement.

SYNTAX

skip

DESCRIPTION

The keyword skip is a meta term that is translated by the SPIN lexical analyzer into the constant value one (1), just like the predefined boolean constant true. The intended use of the shorthand is stand-alone, as a dummy statement. When used as a statement, the skip is interpreted as a special case of a condition statement. This condition statement is always executable, and has no effect when executed, other than a possible change of the control-state of the executing process.

There are few cases where a skip statement is needed to satisfy syntax requirements. A common use is to make it possible to place a label at the end of a statement *sequence*, to allow for a goto jump to that point. Because only statements can be prefixed by a label, we must use a dummy skip statement as a placeholder in those cases.

EXAMPLES

```
proctype A()
{
L0:     if
        :: cond1 -> goto L1 /* jump to end   */
        :: else -> skip     /* skip redundant */
        fi;

        ...

L1:     skip
}
```

The skip statement that follows label L1 is required in this example. The use of the skip statement following the else guard in the selection structure above is redundant. The above selection can be written more tersely as:

```
L0:     if
        :: cond1 -> goto L1
        :: else
        fi;
```

Because PROMELA is an asynchronous language, the skip is never needed, nor effective, to introduce delay in process executions. In PROMELA, by definition, there can always be an arbitrary, and unknowable, delay between any two subsequent statement executions in a `proctype` body. This semantics correspond to the *golden rule* of concurrent systems design that forbids assumptions about the relative execution speed of asynchronous processes in a concurrent system.

When SPIN's weak fairness constraint is enforced we can tighten this semantics a little, to conform to, what is known as, Dijkstra's *finite progress* assumption. In this case, when control reaches a statement, and that statement is and remains executable, we can are allowed to assume that the statement will be executed within a finite period of time (i.e., we can exclude the case where the delay would be infinite).

NOTES

The opposite of `skip` is the zero condition statement `(0)`, which is never executable. In cases where such a blocking statement might be needed, often an assertion statement is more effective. Note that `assert(false)` and `assert(0)` are equivalent. Similarly, `assert(true)` and `assert(1)` are equivalent and indistinguishable from both `assert(skip)` and `skip`.

Because `skip` is intercepted in the lexical analyzer as a meta term, it does not appear literally in error traces. It will only show up as its numeric equivalent (1).

SEE ALSO

assert, condition, else, false, true

NAME
STDIN – predefined read-only channel, for use in simulation.

SYNTAX
```
chan STDIN; STDIN?var
```

DESCRIPTION
During simulation runs, it is sometimes useful to be able to connect SPIN to other programs that can produce useful input, or directly to the standard input stream to read input from the terminal or from a file.

EXAMPLES
A sample use of this feature is this model of a word count program:

```
chan STDIN;      /* no channel initialization */

init {
        int c, nl, nw, nc;
        bool inword = false;
        do
        :: STDIN?c ->
                if
                :: c == -1 ->   break   /* EOF */
                :: c == '\n' -> nc++; nl++
                :: else ->      nc++
                fi;
                if
                :: c == ' ' || c == '\t' || c == '\n' ->
                        inword = false
                :: else ->
                        if
                        :: !inword ->
                                nw++; inword = true
                        :: else /* do nothing */
                fi      fi
        od;
        printf("%d\t%d\t%d\n", nl, nw, nc)
}
```

NOTES
The STDIN channel can be used only in simulations. The name has no special meaning in verification. A verification for the example model would report an attempt to receive data from an unitialized channel.

SEE ALSO
chan, **poll**, **printf**, **receive**

NAME

timeout – a predefined, global, read-only, boolean variable.

SYNTAX

timeout

DESCRIPTION

Timeout is a predefined, global, read-only, boolean variable that is *true* in all global system states where no statement is executable in any active process, and otherwise is *false* (see also Chapter 7).

A timeout used as a guard in a selection or repetition construct provides an escape from a system hang state. It allows a process to abort waiting for a condition that can no longer become true.

EXAMPLES

The first example shows how timeout can be used to implement a watchdog process that sends a reset message to a channel named guard each time the system enters a hang state.

```
active proctype watchdog()
{       do
        :: timeout -> guard!reset
        od
}
```

A more traditional use is to place a timeout as an alternative to a potentially blocking statement, to guard against a system deadlock if the statement becomes permanently blocked.

```
do
:: q?message -> ...
:: timeout -> break
od
```

NOTES

The timeout statement can not specify a timeout interval. Timeouts are used to model only *possible* system behaviors, not detailed real-time behavior. To model premature expiration of timers, consider replacing the timeout variable with the constant value true, for instance, as in:

```
#define timeout true
```

A timeout can be combined with other expressions to form more complex wait conditions, but can not be combined with else. Note that timeout, if used as a condition statement, can be considered to be a system level else statement. Where the else statement becomes executable only when no other statements within the executing process can be executed, a `timeout` statement becomes executable only when no other statements anywhere in the system can be executed.

SEE ALSO
condition, **do**, **else**, **if**, **unless**

NAME

trace, notrace – for defining event sequences as properties.

SYNTAX

trace { *sequence* }
notrace { *sequence* }

DESCRIPTION

Much like a never claim declaration, a trace or notrace declaration does not specify new behavior, but instead states a correctness requirement on existing behavior in the remainder of the system. All channel names referenced in a trace or notrace declaration must be globally declared message channels, and all message fields must either be globally known (possibly symbolic) constants, or the predefined global variable _, which can be used in this context to specify don't care conditions. The structure and place of a trace event declaration within a PROMELA model is similar to that of a never claim: it must be declared globally.

An event trace declaration defines a correctness claim with the following properties:

- Each channel name that is used in an event trace declaration is monitored for compliance with the structure and context of the trace declaration.
- If only send operations on a channel appear in the trace, then only send operations on that channel are subject to the check. The same is true for receive operations. If both types appear, both are subject to the check, and they must occur in the relative order that the trace declaration gives.
- An event trace declaration may contain only send and receive operations (that is, events), but it can contain any control flow construct. This means that no global or local variables can be declared or referred to. This excludes the use of assignments and conditions. Send and receive operations are restricted to simple sends or receives; they cannot be variations such as random receive, sorted send, receive test, etc.
- Message fields that must be matched in sends or receives must be specified either with the help of symbolic mtype names, or with constants. Message fields that have don't care values can be matched with the predefined write-only variable _ (underscore).
- Sends and receives that appear in an event trace are called *monitored events*. These events do not generate new behavior, but they are required to match send or receive events on the same channels in the model with matching message parameters. A send or receive event occurs whenever a send or a receive statement is

executed, that is, an event occurs during a state transition.

- An event `trace` can capture the occurrence of receive events on rendezvous channels.
- An event `trace` causes a correctness violation if a send or receive action is executed in the system that is within the scope of the event `trace`, but that cannot be matched by a monitored event within that declaration.
- One can use `accept`, `progress`, and `end`-state labels in event `trace` declarations, with the usual interpretation.

An event `trace` declaration must always be deterministic.

A `trace` declaration specifies behavior that *must* be matched by the remainder of the specification, and a `notrace` declares behavior that may *not* be matched.

A `notrace` definition is subject to the same requirements as a `trace` definition, but acts as its logical negation. A `notrace` definition is violated if the event sequence that is specified can be matched completely, that is, if either a user-defined `end` state in the trace definition is reached, or the closing curly brace of the declaration.

EXAMPLES

An event `trace` declaration that specifies the correctness requirement that send operations on channel `q1` alternate with receive operations on channel `q2`, and furthermore that all send operations on `q1` are (claimed to be) exclusively messages of type `a`, and all receive operations on channel `q2` are exclusively messages of type `b`, is written as follows:

```
mtype = { a, b };
trace {
        do
        :: q1!a; q2?b
        od
}
```

NOTES

There are two significant differences between an event `trace` and a `never` claim declaration: First, an event `trace` matches event occurrences that can occur in the *transitions* between system states, whereas a `never` claim matches boolean propositions on system *states*.

A system state, for the purposes of verification, is a stable value assignment to all variables, process states, and message channels. The transitions of a `never` claim are labeled with boolean propositions (expressions) that must evaluate to *true* in system states. The transitions of an event `trace` are labeled directly with monitored events that must occur in system transitions in the order that is given in the `trace` declaration.

The second difference is that an event `trace` monitors only a subset of the events in a system: only those of the types that are mentioned in the `trace` (i.e., the *monitored events*). A `never` claim, on the other hand, looks at all global systems states that are reached, and must be able to match the state assignments in the system at every state.

An event `trace` automaton, just like a `never` claim automaton, has a current state, but it only executes transitions if one of the monitored events occurs. That is, unlike a `never` claim, it does not execute synchronously with the system.

It is relatively easy to monitor receive events on rendezvous channels with an event `trace` assertion, but very hard to do so with a `never` claim. Monitoring the send event on a rendezvous channel is also possible, but it would also have to match all rendezvous send *offers* that are made, including those that do not lead to an accepting receive event.

SEE ALSO
_, **accept**, **assert**, **end**, **ltl**, **never**, **progress**

NAME

`true` – predefined boolean constant.

SYNTAX

`true`

DESCRIPTION

The keyword `true` is a synonym of the constant value one `(1)`, and can be used in any context. Because of the mapping to `(1)`, `true` is also a synonym of `skip`. It supports a more natural syntax for manipulating boolean values.

NOTES

Because it is intercepted in the lexical analyzer as a meta term, `true` is always replaced by its numeric equivalent in error traces.

Semantically, `true`, `skip`, and `(1)` are indistinguishable. Which term is best used depends on context and convention.

SEE

condition, false, skip

NAME

`typedef` – to declare a user-defined structured data type.

SYNTAX

`typedef` *name* `{` *decl_lst* `}`

DESCRIPTION

`Typedef` declarations can be used to introduce user-defined data types. User-defined types can be used anywhere predefined integer data types can be used. Specifically, they can be used as formal and actual parameters for `proctype` declarations and instantiations, as fields in message channels, and as arguments in message send and receive statements.

A `typedef` declaration can refer to other, previously declared `typedef` structures, but it may not be self-referential. A `typedef` definition must always be global, but it can be used to declare both local and global data objects of the new type.

EXAMPLES

The first example shows how to declare a two-dimensional array of elements of type `byte` with a `typedef`.

```
typedef array { /* typedefs must be global */
        byte aa[4]
};

init {
        array a[8];      /* 8x4 = 32 bytes total */

        a[3].aa[1] = 5
}
```

The following example introduces two user-defined types named `D` and `Msg`, and declares an array of two objects of type `Msg`, named `top`:

```
typedef D {
        short f;
        byte  g
};

typedef Msg {
        byte a[3];
        int fld1;
        D    fld2;
        chan p[3];
        bit b
};
```

```
Msg top[2];
```

The elements of top can be referenced as, for instance:

```
top[1].fld2.g = top[0].a[2]
```

Objects of type Msg can be passed through a channel, provided that they do not contain any field of type unsigned.

```
chan q = [2] of { Msg };
q!top[0]; q?top[1]
```

If we delete the arrays from the declaration of type Msg we can also use objects of this type in a run parameter, for instance, as follows:

```
typedef D {
        short f;
        byte  g
};

typedef Msg {
        int fld1;
        D    fld2;
        bit b
};

Msg top[2];

proctype boo(Msg m)
{
        printf("fld1=%d\n", m.fld1);
}

init {
        chan q = [2] of { Msg };

        top[0].fld1 = 12;
        q!top[0]; q?top[1];
        run boo(top[1])
}
```

NOTES

The current SPIN implementation imposes the following restrictions on the use of typedef objects. It is not possible to assign the value of a complete typedef object directly to another such object of the same type in a single assignment. A typedef object may be sent through a message channel as a unit provided that it contains no fields of type unsigned. A typedef object can also be used as a parameter in a run statement, but in this case it may not contain arrays.

Beware that the use of this keyword differs from its namesake in the C programming language. The working of the C version of a `typedef` statement is best approximated with a macro definition.

SEE ALSO
arrays, **datatypes**, **macros**, **mtype**

NAME

`unless` – to define exception handling routines.

SYNTAX

stmnt `unless` *stmnt*

DESCRIPTION

Similar to the repetition and selection constructs, the `unless` construct is not really a statement, but a method to define the structure of the underlying automaton and to distinguish between higher and lower priority of transitions within a single process. The construct can appear anywhere a basic PROMELA statement can appear.

The first statement, generally defined as a block or sequence of basic statements, is called the *main sequence*. The second statement is called the *escape sequence*. The guard of either sequence can be either a single statement, or it can be an `if`, `do`, or lower level `unless` construct with multiple guards and options for execution.

The executability of all basic statements in the main sequence is constrained to the non-executability of all guard statements of the escape sequence. If and when one of the guard statements of the escape sequence becomes executable, execution proceeds with the remainder of the escape sequence and does not return to the main sequence. If all guards of the escape sequence remain unexecutable throughout the execution of the main sequence, the escape sequence as a whole is skipped.

The effect of the escape sequence is distributed to all the basic statements inside the main sequence, including those that are contained inside `atomic` sequences. If a `d_step` sequence is included, though, the escape affects only its guard statement (that is, the first statement) of the sequence, and not the remaining statements inside the `d_step`. A `d_step` is always equivalent to a single statement that can only be executed in its entirety from start to finish.

As noted, the guard statement of an `unless` construct can itself be a selection or a repetition construct, allowing for a non-deterministic selection of a specific executable escape. Following the semantics model from Chapter 7, the guard statements of an escape sequence are assigned a higher priority than the basic statements from the main sequence.

`Unless` constructs may be nested. In that case, the guard statements from each `unless` statement take higher priority than those from the statements that are enclosed. This priority rule can be reversed, giving the highest priority to the most deeply nested `unless` escapes, by using SPIN run-time option `-J`. This option is called `-J` because it enforces a priority rule that matches the evaluation order of nested `catch` statements in Java programs.

PROMELA `unless` statements are meant to facilitate the modeling of error handling methods in implementation level languages.

EXAMPLES

Consider the following `unless` statement:

```
{ B1; B2; B3 } unless { C1; C2 }
```

where the parts inside the curly braces are arbitrary PROMELA fragments. Execution of this `unless` statement begins with the execution of `B1`. Before each statement execution in the sequence `B1;B2;B3`, the executability of the first statement, or *guard*, of fragment `C1` is checked using the normal PROMELA semantics of executability. Execution of statements from `B1;B2;B3` proceeds only while the guard statement of `C1` remains unexecutable. The first instant that this guard of the escape sequence is found to be executable, control changes to it, and execution continues as defined for `C1;C2`. Individual statement executions remain indivisible, so control can only change from inside `B1;B2;B3` to the start of `C1` in between individual statement executions. If the guard of the escape sequence does not become executable during the execution of `B1;B2;B3`, it is skipped when `B3` terminates.

Another example of the use of `unless` is:

```
A;
do
:: b1 -> B1
:: b2 -> B2
...
od unless { c -> C };
D
```

The curly braces around the main or the escape sequence may be deleted if there can be no confusion about which statements belong to those sequences. In the example, condition `c` acts as a watchdog on the repetition construct from the main sequence. Note that this is not necessarily equivalent to the construct:

```
A;
do
:: b1 -> B1
:: b2 -> B2
...
:: c -> break
od;
C; D
```

if `B1` or `B2` are non-empty. In the first version of the example, execution of the iteration can be interrupted at *any* point inside each option sequence. In the second version, execution can only be interrupted at the start of the option sequences.

NOTES

In the presence of rendezvous operations, the precise effect of an `unless` construct can be hard to assess. See the discussion in Chapter 7 for details on resolving apparent semantic conflicts.

SEE ALSO

atomic, **do**, **if**, **sequence**

NAME

xr, xs – for defining channel assertions.

SYNTAX

xr *name* [, *name*] *
xs *name* [, *name*] *

DESCRIPTION

Channel assertions such as

```
xr q1;
xs q2;
```

can only appear within a proctype declaration. The channel assertions are only valid if there can be at most one single instantiation of the proctype in which they appear.

The first type of assertion, xr, states that the executing process has exclusive read-access to the channel that is specified. That is, it is asserted to be the *only* process in the system (determined by its process instantiation number) that can receive messages from the channel.

The second type of assertion, xs, states that the process has exclusive write-access to the channel that is specified. That is, it is asserted to be the only process that can send messages to the channel.

Channel assertions have no effect in simulation runs. With the information that is provided in channel assertions, the partial order reduction algorithm that is normally used during verification, though, can optimize the search and achieve significantly greater reductions.

Any test on the contents or length of a channel referenced in a channel assertion, including receive poll operations, counts as both a read and a write access of that channel. If such access conflicts with a channel assertion, it is flagged as an error during the verification. If the error is reported, this means that the additional reductions that were applied may be invalid.

The only channel poll operations that are consistent with the use of channel assertions are nempty and nfull. Their predefined negations empty and full have no similar benefit, but are included for symmetry. The grammar prevents circumvention of the type rules by attempting constructions such as !nempty(q), or !full(q).

Summarizing: If a channel-name appears in an xs (xr) channel assertion, messages may be sent to (received from) the corresponding channel by only the process that contains the assertion, and that process can only use send (receive) operations, or one of the predefined operators nempty or nfull. All other types of access will generate run-time errors from the verifier.

EXAMPLES

```
chan q = [2] of { byte };
chan r = [2] of { byte };

active proctype S()
{       xs q;
        xr r;

        do
        :: q!12
        :: r?0 -> break
        od
}
active proctype R()
{       xr q;
        xs r;

        do
        :: q?12
        :: r!0 -> break
        od
}
```

NOTES

Channel assertions do not work for rendezvous channels.

For channel arrays, a channel assertion on any element of the array is applied to all elements.

In some cases, the check for compliance with the declared access patterns is too strict. This can happen, for instance, when a channel name is used as a parameter in a run statement, which is counted as both a read and a write access.

Another example of an unintended violation of a channel assertion can occur when a single process can be instantiated with different process instantiation numbers, depending on the precise moment that the process is instantiated in a run. In cases such as these, the checks on the validity of the channel assertions can be suppressed, while maintaining the reductions they allow. To do so, the verifier pan.c can be compiled with directive -DXUSAFE. Use with caution.

SEE ALSO

chan, **len**, **nempty**, **nfull**, **send**, **receive**

EMBEDDED C CODE **17**

*"The purpose of analysis is not to
compel belief but rather to suggest doubt."*
(Imre Lakatos, Proofs and Refutations)

SPIN, versions 4.0 and later, support the inclusion of embedded C code into
PROMELA models through the following five new primitives:

```
c_expr, c_code, c_decl, c_state, c_track
```

The purpose of these new primitives is primarily to provide support for automatic model extraction from C code. This means that it is not the intent of
these extensions to be used in manually constructed models. The primitives
provide a powerful extension, opening SPIN models to the full power of, and
all the dangers of, arbitrary C code. The contents of the embedded code fragments cannot be checked by SPIN, neither in the parsing phase nor in the verification phase. They are trusted blindly and copied through from the text of
the model into the code of the verifier that SPIN generates. In particular, if a
piece of embedded C code contains an illegal operation, like a divide by zero
operation or a nil-pointer dereference, the result can be a crash of the verifier
while it performs the model checking. Later in this chapter we will provide
some guidance on locating the precise cause of such errors if you accidentally
run into them.

The verifiers that are generated by SPIN version 4.0 and higher use the embedded code fragments to define state transitions as part of a PROMELA model. As
far as SPIN is concerned, a c_code statement is an uninterpreted state trans-
former, deÞned in an external language, and a c_expr statement is a
user-deÞned boolean guard, similarly deÞned in an external language. Since
this ÔÔexternalÕÕ language (C) cannot be interpreted by SPIN itself, simulation
runs now have to be performed in a different way, as we will discuss. All ver-
iÞcations can be performed as before, though, with the standard C compiler

providing the required interpretation of all embedded code.

The primitives c_decl and c_state deal with various ways of declaring data types and data objects in C that either become part of the state vector, or that are deliberately hidden from it. The c_track primitive is used to instrument the code of the veriÞer to track the value of data objects holding state information that are declared elsewhere, perhaps even in in separately compiled code that is linked with the SPIN-generated veriÞer.

Because the SPIN parser does not attempt to interpret embedded C code fragments, random and guided simulation can no longer be done directly by SPIN itself. To account for this, the SPIN-generated veriÞers are now provided with their own built-in error trail playback capability if the presence of embedded C code is detected.

AN EXAMPLE

We will illustrate the use of these features with the example shown in Figure 17.1. The c_decl primitive introduces a new data type named Coord. To avoid name clashes, the new data type name should not match any of the existing type names that are already used inside the SPIN-generated veriÞers. The C compiler will complain if this accidentally happens; SPIN itself cannot detect these conßicts.

Because the new data type name may need to be referenced in other statements, we must secure that its deÞnition is placed high up in the generated code for the veriÞers. The c_decl statement accomplishes precisely that. The c_decl statement, then, is *only* meant to be used for the deÞnition of new C data types, that may be referred to elsewhere in the model.

The c_state primitive introduces a new global data object pt of type Coord into the state vector. The object is initialized to zero.

There is only one active process in this model. It reinitializes the global variable pt to zero (in this case this is redundant), and then executes a loop. The loop continues until the elements of structure pt differ, which will, of course, happen after a single iteration. When the loop terminates, the elements of the C data object pt are printed. To make sure an error trail is generated, the next statement is a *false* assertion.

Arbitrary C syntax can be used in any c_code and c_expr statement. The difference between these two types of statements is that a c_code statement is always executed unconditionally and atomically, while a c_expr statement can only be executed (passed) if it returns non-zero when its body is evaluated as a C expression. If the evaluation returns zero, execution is blocked. The evaluation of a c_expr is again indivisible (i.e., atomic). Because SPIN may have to evaluate c_expr statements repeatedly until one of them becomes executable, a c_expr is required to be free from side effects: it may only evaluate data, not modify it.

```
c_decl {
    typedef struct Coord {
        int x, y;
    } Coord;
}

c_state "Coord pt" "Global" /* goes inside state vector */

int z = 3;                   /* standard global declaration */

active proctype example()
{
    c_code { now.pt.x = now.pt.y = 0; };

    do
    :: c_expr { now.pt.x == now.pt.y } ->
                c_code { now.pt.y++; }
    :: else ->
                break
    od;
    c_code {
        printf("values %d: %d, %d,%d\n",
            Pexample->_pid, now.z, now.pt.x, now.pt.y);
    };
    assert(false)            /* trigger an error trail */
}
```

Figure 17.1 Example of Embedded C Code

DATA REFERENCES

A *global* data object that is declared with the normal PROMELA declaration syntax in the model (i.e., not with the help of c_code or c_state) can be referenced from within c_code and c_expr statements, but the reference has to be preÞxed in this case with the string now followed by a period. In the example, for instance, the global z can be referenced within a c_code or c_expr statement as now.z. (The name now refers to the internal state vector, where all global data is stored during veriÞcation.) Outside embedded C code fragments, the same variable can be referenced simply as z.

A process *local* data object can also be referenced from within c_code and c_expr statements within the same process (i.e., if the object is declared within the current scope), but the syntax is different. The extended syntax again adds a special preÞx that locates the data object in the state vector. The preÞx starts with an uppercase letter P which is followed by the name of the proctype in which the reference occurs, followed by the pointer arrow. For the data objects declared locally in proctype example, for instance, the preÞx to be used is `Pexample->`.

In the example, this is illustrated by the reference to the predeÞned local variable `_pid` from within the `c_code` statement as `Pexample->_pid`.

The `_pid` variable of the process can be referenced, within the `init` process itself, as `Pinit->_pid`.

Another way to write this particular model is shown in Figure 17.2. In this version we have avoided the need for the preÞxes on the variable names, by making use of the `c_track` primitive. The differences with the version in Figure 17.1 are small, but important.

We have declared the variable `pt` in a global `c_code` statement, which means that it gets included this time as a regular global variable that remains outside the state vector. Since this object holds state information, we add a `c_track` statement, specifying a pointer to the object and its size. SPIN will now arrange for the value of the object to be copied into (or out of) a specially reserved part of the state vector on each step. This is obviously less efÞcient than the method using `c_state`, but it avoids the need for the sometimes clumsy `now.` preÞxes that are required for references to objects that are placed directly into the state vector. Note that the reference to variable `z` still requires this preÞx, since it was declared as a normal global PROMELA variable, and similarly for the predeÞned local variable `_pid`. If we lifted the `printf` statement outside the enclosure of the `c_code` primitive, we could refer to variables `z` and `_pid` without a preÞx, as regular PROMELA variables, but we could not refer to the C variable `pt` at all; these external objects are only visible inside `c_code`, `c_expr`, and `c_track` statements.

EXECUTION

When a PROMELA model contains embedded C code, SPIN cannot simulate its execution in the normal way because it cannot directly interpret the embedded code fragments. If we try to run a simulation anyway, SPIN will make a best effort to comply, but it will only print the *text* of the `c_expr` and `c_code` fragments that it encounters, without actually executing them.

To faithfully execute all embedded C code fragments, we must Þrst generate the `pan.[chmbt]` Þles and compile them. We now rely on the standard C compiler to interpret the contents of all embedded code as part of the normal compilation process. For the Þrst example, we proceed as follows:

```
$ spin -a example
$ cc -o pan pan.c        # compile
$ ./pan                  # and run
values 0: 3, 0,1
pan: error: assertion violated 0 (at depth 5)
pan: wrote coord.trail
```

The assertion violation was reported, as expected, but note that the embedded

```
c_decl {
   typedef struct Coord {
        int x, y;
   } Coord;
}

c_code { Coord pt; }            /* embedded declaration */
c_track "&pt" "sizeof(Coord)"   /* track value of pt    */

int z = 3;                      /* standard global declaration */

active proctype example()
{
   c_code { pt.x = pt.y = 0; }; /* no 'now.' prefixes */

   do
   :: c_expr { pt.x == pt.y } ->
                c_code { pt.y++; }
   :: else ->
                break
   od;
   c_code {
        printf("values %d: %d, %d,%d\n",
           Pexample->_pid, now.z, pt.x, pt.y);
   };
   assert(false)               /* trigger an error trail */
}
```

Figure 17.2 Replacing c_state with c_track Primitives

printf statement was also executed, which shows that it works differently from a PROMELA print statement. We can get around this by calling an internal SPIN routine named Printf instead of the standard library routine printf within embedded c_code fragments. This causes the veriÞer to enable the execution of the print statement only when reproducing an error trail, but not during the veriÞcation process itself.

The counterexample is stored in a trail Þle as usual, but SPIN itself cannot interpret the trail Þle completely because of the embedded C code statements that it contains. If we try anyway, SPIN produces something like this, printing out the embedded fragments of code without actually executing them:

```
$ spin -t -p example
c_code2: {   now.pt.x = now.pt.y = 0;   }
   1: proc 0 (example) line  11 ... (state 1) [{c_code2}]
```

```
c_code3: now.pt.x == now.pt.y
  2: proc 0 (example) line  14 ... (state 2) [(({c_code3})]
c_code4: {  now.pt.y++;  }
  3: proc 0 (example) line  15 ... (state 3)  [{c_code4}]
  4: proc 0 (example) line  16 ... (state 4) [else]
c_code5: {  printf("values %d: %d %d,%d\n", \
        Pexample->_pid, now.z now.pt.x, now.pt.y);  }
  5: proc 0 (example) line  19 ... (state 9) [{c_code5}]
spin: line 20 ..., Error: assertion violated
spin: text of failed assertion: assert(0)
  6: proc 0 (example) line  20 ... (state 10) [assert(0)]

spin: trail ends after 6 steps
#processes: 1
  6: proc  0 (example) line  21 ... (state 11)
1 process created
```

The assertion is violated at the end, but this is merely because it was hard-wired to fail. None of the C data objects referenced were ever created during this run, and thus none of them had any values that were effectively assigned to them at the end. Note also that the text of the c_code fragment that is numbered c_code5 here is printed out, but that the print statement that it contains is not itself executed, or else the values printed would have shown up in the output near this line.

It is better to use the trail replay option that is now available inside the generated pan veriÞer. The additional options are:

```
$ ./pan --
  ...
  -C  read and execute trail - columnated output
  -PN read and execute trail - restrict output to proc N
  -r  read and execute trail - default output
  ...
```

With the Þrst of these options, the veriÞer produces the following information on the execution of the trail:

```
$ ./pan -C
1: example(0):[ now.pt.x = now.pt.y = 0; ]
2: example(0):[( now.pt.x == now.pt.y )]
3: example(0):[ now.pt.y++; ]
4: example(0):[else]
values 0: 3, 0,1
5: example(0):[ printf("values: %d,%d\n", \
        now.pt.x, now.pt.y); ]
pan: error: assertion violated 0 (at depth 6)
spin: trail ends after 6 steps
#processes 1:
```

```
    6: proc 0 (example)  line  20 (state 10)
                  assert(0)
 global vars:
        int    z:        3
 local vars proc 0 (example):
        (none)
```

Note that in this run, the print statement was not just reproduced but also executed. Similarly, the data object pt was created, and its value is updated in the c_code statements so that the Þnal values of its elements pt accurately reßect the execution. There is only one process here, with _pid value zero, so the columnation feature of this format is not evident.

More information can be added to the output by adding option -v. Alternatively, all output except the ones that are generated by explicit print statements in the model can be suppressed by adding option -n.

In long and complex error trails with multiple process executions, it can be helpful to restrict the trail output to just one of the executing processes. This can be done with the help of option -P, which should be followed by the pid number of the process of interest.

For a more detailed explanation of the special declarators c_decl and c_track, we point to the manual pages that follow at the end of this chapter.

ISSUES TO CONSIDER

The capability to embed arbitrary fragments of C code into a PROMELA model is powerful and therefore easily misused. The intent of these features is to support mechanized model extractors that can automatically extract an accurate, possibly abstract, representation of application level C code into a SPIN veriÞcation model. The model extractor (see Appendix D) can include all the right safeguards that cannot easily be included in SPIN without extending it into a full ANSI-C compiler and analyzer. Most of the errors that can be made with the new primitives will be caught, but not necessarily directly by SPIN. The C compiler, when attempting to compile a model that contains embedded fragments of code, may object to ill-deÞned structures, or the veriÞer may crash on faults that can be traced back to coding errors in the embedded code fragments.

If data that is manipulated inside the embedded C code fragments contains relevant state information, but is not declared as such with c_state or c_track primitives, then the search process itself can get confused, and error trails may be produced by the veriÞer that do not correspond to feasible executions of the modeled system. With some experience, these types of errors are relatively easy to diagnose. Formally, they correspond to invalid ÔÕabstractionsÕÕ of the model. The unintended ÔÕabstractionsÕÕ are caused by missing c_state or c_track primitives.

To see what happens when we forget to treat externally declared data objects as carrying state information, consider the following simple model:

```
c_code { int x; }

active proctype simple()
{
    c_code { x = 2; };
    if
    :: c_code { x = x+2; }; assert(c_expr { x==4 })
    :: c_code { x = x*3; }; assert(c_expr { x==6 })
    fi
}
```

We have declared the variable x in a c_code statement, but omitted to track its value. The veriÞer will therefore ignore value changes in this variable when it stores and compares states, although it will faithfully perform every assignment or test of this variable in the execution of the model.

At Þrst sight, it would seem obvious that neither one of the two could possibly fail, but when we perform the veriÞcation we see:

```
$ spin -a simple1.pr
$ cc -o pan pan.c
$ ./pan
pan: assertion violated (x == 6)
pan: wrote simple.pr.trail
...
```

To understand the reason for this error, consider for a moment how the depth-Þrst search process proceeds in this case. The veriÞer starts by executing the assignment

```
c_code { x = 2; };
```

Next, it has the choice between two executable statements. It can either increment the value of x by two, or it can multiply it by three. As it happens, it will choose to try the Þrst alternative Þrst. It executes

```
c_code { x = x+2; }; assert(c_expr { x==4 })
```

Not surprisingly, the assertion holds. The search now reaches the end of the execution: there are no further statements to execute in this model. So, the depth-Þrst search reverses and backs up to the point where it had to make a choice between two possible ways to proceed: at the start of the if statement. The veriÞer restores the state of the system to the control ßow point at the start of the if statement, but since the variable x is not treated as a state variable, its value remains unchanged at this point. The search now proceeds, with x having the value four. The multiplication that is now executed to explore the second option sequence

```
c_code { x = x*3; }; assert(c_expr { x==6 })
```

which results in the unexpected value of twelve for x. As a result, the second assertion fails. The counterexample that is generated will clearly show that there is confusion about the true value of x, which is the hint we can use to correct the model by supplying the missing c_track statement.

```
c_code { int x; }
c_track "&x" "sizeof(int)"

active proctype simple()
{
    c_code { x = 2; };
    if
    :: c_code { x = x+2; }; assert(c_expr { x==4 })
    :: c_code { x = x*3; }; assert(c_expr { x==6 })
    fi
}
```

Veriþcation now produces the expected result:

```
$ spin -a simple2.pr
$ cc -o pan pan.c
$ ./pan
(Spin Version 4.0.7 -- 1 August 2003)
        + Partial Order Reduction

Full statespace search for:
        never claim              - (none specified)
        assertion violations     +
        acceptance   cycles      - (not selected)
        invalid end states       +

State-vector 16 byte, depth reached 4, errors: 0
        8 states, stored
        0 states, matched
        8 transitions (= stored+matched)
        0 atomic steps
hash conflicts: 0 (resolved)
(max size 2^18 states)

1.573   memory usage (Mbyte)

unreached in proctype simple
        (0 of 8 states)
```

How does one determine which external data objects from an application contain state information and which do not? This is ultimately a matter of judgement, and lacking proper judgement, a process of discovery. The determination can be automated, to some extent, for a given set of logic properties. A data dependency analysis may be used to determine what is relevant and what is not. A more detailed discussion of this issue, though important, is beyond the scope of this book.

DEFERRING FILE INCLUSION

It is often convenient to include a collection of C code into a model with a preprocessor `include` directive, for instance, as follows:

```
#include "promela.h"     /* Promela data definitions */

c_decl {
#include "c_types.h"     /* C data type definitions */
}

c_code {
#include "functions.c"   /* C function definitions */
}

#include "model.pr"      /* the Promela model itself */
```

When SPIN invokes the C preprocessor on this model, the contents of the included Þles are inserted into the text before the model text is parsed by the SPIN parser. This works well if the Þles that are included are relatively small, but since there is a limit on the maximum size of a `c_code` or `c_decl` statement, this can fail if the Þles exceed that limit. (At the time of writing, this limit is set at 64Kbytes.)

There is an easy way to avoid hitting this limit. Because C code fragments are not interpreted until the veriÞer code is parsed by the C compiler, there is no need to actually have the body of a `c_code` or `c_decl` statement inserted into the text of the model before it is passed to the SPIN parser. We can achieve this by preÞxing the pound sign of the corresponding `include` directives with a backslash, as follows:

```
c_decl {
\#include "c_types.h"    /* C data type definitions */
}

c_code {
\#include "functions.c" /* C function definitions */
}
```

The SPIN parser will now simply copy the `include` directive itself into the generated C code, without expanding it Þrst. The backslash can only be used in this way inside `c_decl` and `c_code` statements, and it is the recommended way to handle included Þles in these cases.

NAME

c_code • embedded C code fragments.

SYNTAX

c_code { /* c code */ }

c_code ' [' /* c expr */ ']' { /* c code */ ; }

EXECUTABILITY

true

EFFECT

As deÞned by the semantics of the C code fragment placed between the curly braces.

DESCRIPTION

The c_code primitive supports the use of embedded C code fragments inside PROMELA models. The code must be syntactically valid C, and must be terminated by a semicolon (a required statement terminator in C).

There are two forms of the c_code primitive: with or without an embedded expression in square brackets. A missing expression clause is equivalent to [1]. If an expression is speciÞed, its value will be evaluated as a general C expression *before* the C code fragment inside the curly braces is executed. If the result of the evaluation is non-zero, the c_code fragment is executed. If the result of the evaluation is zero, the code between the curly braces is ignored, and the statement is treated as an assertion violation. The typical use of the expression clause is to add checks for nil-pointers or for bounds in array indices. For example:

```
c_code [Pex->ptr != 0 && now.i < 10 && now.i >= 0] {
        Pex->ptr.x[now.i] = 12;
}
```

A c_code fragment can appear anywhere in a PROMELA model, but it must be meaningful within its context, as determined by the C compiler that is used to compile the complete model checking program that is generated by SPIN from the model.

Function and data declarations, for instance, can be placed in global c_code fragments preceding all proctype deÞnitions. Code fragments that are placed inside a proctype deÞnition cannot contain function or data declarations. Violations of such rules are caught by the C compiler. The SPIN parser merely passes all C code fragments through into the generated veriÞer uninterpreted, and therefore cannot detect such errors.

There can be any number of C statements inside a c_code fragment.

EXAMPLES

```
int q;
c_code { int *p; };
init {
        c_code { *p = 0; *p++; };
        c_code [p != 0] { *p = &(now.q); };
        c_code { Printf("%d\n", Pinit->_pid); }
}
```

In this example we Þrst declare a normal PROMELA integer variable q
that automatically becomes part of the veriÞerÕs internal state vector
(called now) during veriÞcation. We also declare a global integer pointer
p in a global c_code fragment. Since the contents of a C code fragment
are not interpreted by SPIN when it generates the veriÞer, SPIN cannot
know about the presence of the declaration for pointer variable p, and
therefore this variable remains invisible to the veriÞer: its declaration
appears outside the state vector. It can be manipulated as shown as a regular global pointer variable, but the values assigned to this variable are
not considered to be part of the global system state that the veriÞer
tracks.

To arrange for data objects to appear inside the state vector, and to be
treated as system state variables, one or more of the primitives c_decl,
c_state, and c_track should be used (for details, see the corresponding manual pages).

The local c_code fragment inside the init process manipulates the
variable p in a direct way. Since the variable is not moved into the state
vector, no preÞx is needed to reference it.

In the second c_code fragment in the body of init, an expression
clause is used that veriÞes that the pointer p has a non-zero value, which
secures that the dereference operation that follows cannot result in a
memory fault. (Of course, it would be wiser to add this expression
clause also to the preceding c_code statement.) When the c_code
statement is executed, the value of p is set to the address of the PROMELA
integer variable q. Since the PROMELA variable is accessed inside a
c_code fragment, we need a special preÞx to identify it in the global
state vector. For a global variable, the required preÞx is the three-letter
word now followed by a period. The ampersand in &(now.q) takes the
address of the global variable within the state vector.

The last c_code statement in init prints the value of the process identi-
Þer for the running process. This is a predeÞned local variable.

To access the local variable in the init process, the required preÞx is
Pinit->. This format consists of the uppercase letter P, followed by the
name of the process type, followed by an arrow ->.

See also the description on data access in c_expr.

NOTES

The embedded C code fragments must be syntactically correct and complete. That is, they must contain proper punctuation with semicolons, using the standard semantics from C, not from PROMELA. Note, for instance, that semicolons are statement terminators in C, but statement separators in PROMELA.

Because embedded C code is not interpreted by the SPIN parser, inline parameter substitutions are not applied to those code fragments. In cases where this is needed, the inline deÞnitions can be replaced with macro preprocessor deÞnitions.

A common use of the c_code primitive is to include a larger piece of code into a model that is stored in a separate Þle, for instance, as follows:

```
c_code {
#include "someheaders.h"
#include "someCcode.c"
};
```

If the included code fragment is too large (in the current implementation of SPIN this means larger than about 64Kbyte of text), SPIN will complain about that and fail. A simple way to bypass this restriction, for instance, when generating the veriÞcation code with SPINÕs-a option, is to defer the interpretation of the include directives by the SPIN preprocessor, and to copy them through into the generated code unseen. This can be accomplished as follows, by placing a backslash before the pound sign of any include directive that appears inside a c_code primitive.

```
c_code {
\#include "someheaders.h"
\#include "someCcode.c"
};
```

Functionally, this is identical to the previous version, but it makes sure that the SPIN preprocessor will not read in the text of the included Þles when the model is parsed.

SEE ALSO

c_expr, **c_decl**, **c_state**, **c_track**, **macros**

NAME

c_decl, c_state, c_track • embedded C data declarations.

SYNTAX

c_decl { /* c declaration */ }
c_state string string [*string*]
c_track string string

EXECUTABILITY

true

DESCRIPTION

The primitives c_decl, c_state, and c_track are *global* primitives that can only appear in a model as global declarations outside all proc-type declarations.

The c_decl primitive provides a capability to embed general C data type declarations into a model. These type declarations are placed in the generated pan.h Þle *before* the declaration of the state-vector structure, which is also included in that Þle. This means that the data types introduced in a c_decl primitive can be referenced anywhere in the generated code, including inside the state vector with the help of c_state primitives. Data type declarations can also be introduced in global c_code fragments, but in this case the generated code is placed in the pan.c Þle, and therefore appears necessarily *after* the declaration of the state-vector structure. Therefore, these declarations cannot be used inside the state vector.

The c_state keyword is followed by either two or three quoted strings. The Þrst argument speciÞes the type and the name of a data object. The second argument the scope of that object. A third argument can optionally be used to specify an initial value for the data object. (It is best not to assume a known default initial value for objects that are declared in this way.)

There are three possible scopes: global, local, or hidden. A global scope is indicated by the use of the quoted string "Global." If local, the name Local must be followed by the name of the proctype in which the declaration is to appear, as in "Local ex2." If the quoted string "Hidden" is used for the second argument, the data object will be declared as a global object that remains *outside* the state vector.

The primitive c_track is a global primitive that can declare any state object, or more generally any piece of memory, as holding state information. This primitive takes two string arguments. The Þrst argument speciÞes an address, typically a pointer to a data object declared elsewhere. The second argument gives the size in bytes of that object, or more generally the number of bytes starting at the address that must be tracked as part of the system state.

EXAMPLES

The Þrst example illustrates how c_decl, c_code and c_state declarations can be used to deÞne either visible or hidden state variables, referring to type deÞnitions that must precede the internal SPIN state-vector declaration. For an explanation of the rules for preÞxing global and local variables inside c_code and c_expr statements, see the manual pages for these two statements.

```
c_decl {
        typedef struct Proc {
                int rlock;
                int state;
                struct Rendez *r;
        } Proc;

        typedef struct Rendez {
                int     lck;
                int     cond;
                Proc    *p;
        } Rendez;
}
c_code {
        Proc    H1;
        Proc    *up0 = &H1;
        Rendez  RR;
}

/*
 * The following two c_state declarations presume type
 * Rendez known the first enters R1 into state vector
 * as a global variable, and the second enters R2 into
 * proctype structure as local variable.
 */

c_state "Rendez R1" "Global"
c_state "Rendez R2" "Local ex2" "now.R1"

/*
 * The next two c_state declarations are kept outside
 * the state vector. They define H1 and up0 as global
 * objects, which are declared elsewhere.
 */

c_state "extern Proc H1" "Hidden"
c_state "extern Proc *up0" "Hidden"
```

```
/*
 * The following declaration defines that RR is to be
 * treated as a state variable -- no matter how it was
 * declared; it can be an arbitrary external variable.
 */

c_decl {
\#include "types.h"          /* declare type Rendez */
/* for the purpose of the backslash, see p. 504 */
}

c_track "&RR" "sizeof(Rendez)"

active proctype ex2()
{
        c_code { now.R1.cond = 1; };    /* global */
        c_code { Pex2->R2.lck = 0; };   /* local  */
        c_code { H1.rlock = up0->state; }; /* C */

        printf("This is Spin Version 4.0\n")
}
```

NOTES

SPIN instruments the code of the veriÞer to copy all data pointed to via c_track primitives into and out of the state vector on forward and backward moves during the depth-Þrst search that it performs. Where there is a choice, the use of c_state primitives will always result in more efÞciently executed code, since SPIN can instrument the generated veriÞer to directly embed data objects into the state vector itself, avoiding the copying process.

To get a better feeling for how precisely these primitives are interpreted by SPIN, consider generating code from the last example, and look in the generated Þles pan.h and pan.c for all appearances of variables R1, R2, P1, and up0.

Avoid using type-names that clash with internal types used within the SPIN-generated veriÞers. This includes names such as State, P0, P1, etc., and Q0, Q1, etc. Name clashes caused by unfortunate choices of type names are reliably caught by the C compiler when the veriÞcation code is compiled.

SEE ALSO

c_expr, **c_code**

NAME

c_expr • conditional expressions as embedded C code.

SYNTAX

c_expr { /* c code */ }
c_expr '[' /* c expr */ ']' { /* c code */ }

EXECUTABILITY

If the return value of the arbitrary C code fragment that appears between the curly braces is non-zero, then *true*; otherwise *false*.

EFFECT

As deÞned by the semantics of the C code fragment that is placed between the curly braces. The evaluation of the C code fragment should have no side effects.

DESCRIPTION

This primitive supports the use of embedded C code inside PROMELA models. A c_expr can be used to express guard conditions that are not necessarily expressible in PROMELA with its more restrictive data types and language constructs.

There are two forms of the c_expr primitive: with or without an additional assertion expression in square brackets. A missing assertion expression is equivalent to [1]. If an assertion expression is speciÞed, its value is evaluated as a general C expression *before* the code inside the curly braces is evaluated. The normal (expected) case is that the assertion expression evaluates to a *non-zero* value (that is to an equivalent of the boolean value *true*). If so, the C code between the curly braces is evaluated next to determine the executability of the c_expr as a whole.

If the evaluation value of the assertion expression is zero (equivalent to *false*), the code between the curly braces is ignored and the statement is treated as an assertion violation.

The typical use of the assertion expression clause is to add checks for nil-pointers or for possible array bound violations in expressions. For example:

        c_expr [Pex->ptr != NULL] { Pex->ptr->y }

Note that there is no semicolon at the end of either C expression. If the expression between square brackets yields *false* (zero), then an assertion violation is reported. Only if this expression yields *true* (non-zero), is the C expression between curly braces evaluated. If the value of this second expression yields *true*, the c_expr as a whole is deemed executable and can be passed; if *false*, the c_expr is unexecutable and blocks.

EXAMPLES

The following example contains a do-loop with four options. The first two options are equivalent, the only difference being in the way that local variable x is accessed: either via an embedded C code fragment or with the normal PROMELA constructs.

```
active proctype ex1()
{        int x;

         do
         :: c_expr { Pex1->x < 10 } ->
                 c_code { Pex1->x++; }
         :: x < 10 -> x++
         :: c_expr { fct() } -> x--
         :: else -> break
         od
}
```

The local variable x is declared here as a PROMELA variable. Other primitives, such as c_decl, c_state, and c_track allow for the declaration of data types that are not directly supported in PROMELA.

The references to local variable x have a pointer prefix that always starts with a fixed capital letter P that is followed by the name of the proctype and an pointer arrow. This prefix locates the variable in the local state vector of the proctype instantiation.

The guard of the third option sequence invokes an externally defined C function named fct() that is presumed to return an integer value. This function can be declared in a global c_code fragment elsewhere in the model, or it can be declared externally in separately compiled code that is linked with the pan.[chtmb] verifier when it is compiled.

NOTES

Note that there is no semicolon before the closing curly brace of a c_expr construct. It causes a C syntax error if such a semicolon appears here. All syntax errors on embedded C code fragments are reported during the compilation of the generated pan.[chtmb] files. These errors are not detectable by the SPIN parser.

Because embedded C code is not processed by the SPIN parser, inline parameter substitutions are not applied to those code fragments. In cases where this is needed, the inline definitions can be replaced with macro preprocessor definitions.

SEE ALSO

c_code, **c_decl**, **c_state**, **c_track**, **macros**

OVERVIEW OF SPIN OPTIONS **18**

"An error does not become a mistake
unless you refuse to correct it."
(Manfred Eigen, 1927–)

In this chapter we discuss all available SPIN options. The options are grouped into seven categories according to their primary use, as follows:

- Compile-time options, which can be used to compile the SPIN source itself for different platforms and for different types of use
- Simulation options, which can be used for customizing simulation runs of PROMELA models
- Syntax checking options, for performing a basic check of the syntactic correctness of PROMELA models
- LTL conversion options, describing various ways in which the conversion from LTL formulae to PROMELA never claims can be done
- Model checker generation options
- Postscript generation options
- Miscellaneous options

Except for the first category above, all these options are defined as run-time parameters to the SPIN tool. Since SPIN is an evolving tool, new options will continue to be added to the tool from time to time. An up-to-date list of these options in the specific version of SPIN that is installed on your system can always be printed with the command:

```
$ spin --
```

The discussion in this chapter covers all compile-time and run-time options that are available in SPIN version 4.

COMPILE-TIME OPTIONS

There are eight compile-time directives that can be used to change the default settings for the compilation of the SPIN sources. They are: `__FreeBSD__`, `CPP`, `MAXQ`, `NO_OPT`, `NXT`, `PC`, `PRINTF`, and `SOLARIS`.

These directives are typically set in the SPIN `makefile` at the time the tool is first installed on a system, and should rarely need modification later. The settings are typically included by changing the definition of the `CFLAGS` parameter in SPIN's `makefile`. As an example, to change the default location of the C preprocessor in the compiled version of SPIN, we could change the line

```
CFLAGS=-ansi -D_POSIX_SOURCE
```

into this new setting

```
CFLAGS=-ansi -D_POSIX_SOURCE -DCPP=/opt/prep/cpp
```

We first discuss the use of the `CPP` directive together with the two special cases `__FreeBSD__` and `SOLARIS`.

-DCPP=..., -DSOLARIS, -D__FreeBSD__

SPIN always preprocesses the source text of PROMELA models with the standard C preprocessor before it attempts to parse it. The preprocessor takes care of the interpretation of all `#include` and `#define` directives. On most UNIX systems, the location of the C preprocessor is `/lib/cpp`, so the default compilation of SPIN implies `-DCPP=/lib/cpp`.

On PCs the preprocessor is usually installed as a separate program, and therefore when SPIN is compiled with the directive `-DPC`, the default setting of the `CPP` parameter changes to `-DCPP=cpp`.

To override the default settings, an explicit value for the `CPP` parameter can be provided.

Two standard cases are predefined. By compiling SPIN with the directive `-D__FreeBSD__`, the default setting for the preprocessor changes to `cpp`, which matches the requirements on these systems. By compiling SPIN with the directive `-DSOLARIS`, the default setting for the preprocessor changes to `/usr/ccs/lib/cpp`, matching the location of the C preprocessor on Solaris systems.

These settings only affect the compilation of the `main.c` file from the SPIN sources.

There is also another way to define a switch to another preprocessor—by using SPIN's command line arguments `P` and `E`. For instance, on an OS2 system one might say:

```
$ spin -Picc -E/Pd+ -E/Q+ model
```

to notify SPIN that preprocessing is done by calling `icc` with parameters `/Pd+` `/Q+`. Similarly, on a Windows system with the Visual C++ compiler installed,

514

one can say:

```
$ spin -PCL -E/E model
```

independent of the settings for CPP with which SPIN itself was compiled. For more information on these run-time options, see the miscellaneous options section below.

-DMAXQ=N

The maximum number of message channels that can be created during a verification run is fixed to the value 255. This limit prevents both runaway models that may be attempting to create infinite numbers of channels, and it secures nicely that the identifying number, used internally by the verifier to keep track of channels, always fits within a single byte. In simulation, the requirements are less strict. In early versions of SPIN, the maximum number of channels that could be created in a simulation run was set at 2,500. In SPIN version 4.0 and later, the limit is set the same for both simulation and verification, which means that it is 255 in both modes. The default setting for simulations can be changed by compiling the SPIN sources with a different upper-bound, for instance, -DMAXQ=2500. This override only affects the compilation of the file mesg.c and it only affects the behavior of SPIN in simulation mode.

-DNO_OPT

In the conversion of LTL formulae into PROMELA never claims, SPIN uses a number of simple optimizations that are defined as rewrite rules on formulae. To study the effect of these rewrite rules, SPIN can be compiled without them. The rules are disabled if SPIN is compiled with the compiler directive -DNO_OPT. Clearly, it is not recommended to use this setting for normal use of SPIN.

-DNXT

In the syntax that SPIN accepts for the specification of LTL formulae, the standard LTL operator *next*, written X, is not allowed. The restriction secures that all LTL properties that can be expressed are necessarily compatible with SPIN's partial order reduction strategy. Technically, it means that the behavior expressed by these formulae is stutter invariant. Quite apart from this desirable closure property, one can also make a strong argument that the only types of properties that one can sensibly state about distributed system executions preclude the use of the next operator. (There is no real notion of a unique *next* step in a concurrent system.) The conversion algorithm for LTL formulae, though, can easily handle the next operator if the above concerns are not applicable. Furthermore, it is also possible to write LTL formulae that do include the next operator and that are still stutter invariant, but this is generally hard to determine.

If desired, therefore, SPIN can be compiled with the `next` operator enabled by adding the directive `-DNXT`.

-DPC

When the SPIN sources are compiled under Windows on a PC, a few UNIX-isms are not guaranteed to work. This, for example, includes calls to non-POSIX system library functions such as `sbrk()`. Also, the PC versions of parser generators such as `yacc` are likely to leave their output in files named `y_tab.c` and `y_tab.h`, rather then the multidotted file names used on UNIX systems `y.tab.c` and `y.tab.h`. Adding the compile-time directive `-DPC` will arrange for the right modifications in the compilation of the SPIN sources.

-DPRINTF

During verification runs, PROMELA `printf` statements are normally disabled. This means that execution of a print statement during the search that is performed by the verifier normally produces no output on the user's terminal. Such output would be of very little use. It would be generated in seemingly random order and it would noticeably slow down the verification process if it were not disabled. Nonetheless, for debugging purposes the execution of print statements during verification can be enabled by compiling the SPIN sources with the directive `-DPRINTF`. This change affects only the verification process; print statements are never disabled during simulation runs. The directive affects the compilation of only the source files named `pangen1.c` and `pangen2.c`.

SIMULATION OPTIONS

The command line options to SPIN that we discuss in this section are all meant to define or modify the type of output that is produced during a *simulation* run, that is, they do not affect any verification settings.

SPIN can be used for three main types of model simulation: random (default), interactive (option `-i`), and guided simulation (option `-t`).

When invoked with only a filename as an argument and no other command-line options, for instance,

```
$ spin model
```

SPIN performs a random simulation of the model that is specified in the file. If no filename is provided, SPIN attempts to read a model from the standard input. This can of course be confusing if it is unexpected, so SPIN gives a warning when it is placed in this mode:

```
$ spin
Spin Version 4.0.7 -- 1 August 2003
reading input from stdin:
```

Typing an end-of-file symbol gets the tool out of this mode again (control-d on UNIX systems, or control-z on Windows systems).

Also possibly confusing at first, even if a filename is provided, may be that a simulation run of the model by itself may not generate any visible output; for instance, when the PROMELA model does not contain any explicit print statements. At the end of the simulation run, though, if it does terminate, SPIN always prints some details about the final state that is reached when the simulation completes. By adding additional options (e.g., -c, or -p) more detail on a simulation run in progress will be provided, but only the information that the user explicitly requests is generated. Every line of output that is produced by the simulator normally also contains a reference to the source line in the model that generated it.

Summarizing: A random simulation is selected by default. If run-time option -i is used, the simulation will be performed in interactive mode, which means that the SPIN simulator will prompt the user each time that a non-deterministic choice has to be resolved. The user can then choose from a list of alternatives, and in this way interactively guide the execution towards a point of interest. If run-time option -t is used, the simulator is put into guided simulation mode, which presumes the existence of a trail file that must have been produced by the verification engine prior to the simulation.

ALPHABETICAL LISTING

-B

Suppresses the printout at the end of a simulation run, giving information on the final state that is reached in each process, the contents of channels, and the value of variables.

-b

Suppresses the output from print statements during a simulation run.

-c

Produces an ASCII approximation of a message sequence chart for a simulation run. For instance:

```
$ spin -c tpc6
proc 0 = :init:
proc 1 = user
proc 2 = local_tpc
proc 3 = manager
proc 4 = Session
proc 5 = Session
q   0   1   2   3   4   5
  4   .     tpc!offhook,0
  4   .   .   tpc?offhook,0
```

```
5    .    .    handler[0]!offhook
5    .    .      .    handler[0]?offhook
1    .    .      .    child[0]!start
1    .    .      .      .    me?start
1    .    .      .    child[0]!offhook
  . . .
```

For every process that is initiated, SPIN assigns a `pid` and prints it, together
with the name of the corresponding `proctype`. In the example, the simulation run starts with the initiation of six processes of the types listed. In the
remainder of the listing, the processes and message channels are only referred
to by their identifying numbers. The output for each process appears in a different column. Only message send and receive operations are printed in the
columnated format. If print statements are executed, the output from the
statement also appears within the column of the executing process (but see
options -b and -T). For send and receive operations, the left margin lists the
specific channel number that is used for the operation. See also options -M,
and -u.

-g

Shows at each time step the current value of global variables. Normally, this
only prints the value of a global variable when a new value was assigned to
that variable in the last execution step. To obtain a full listing of all global
variable values at each execution step, add options -v and -w.

-i

Performs an interactive simulation, allowing the user to resolve non-deterministic choices wherever they occur during the simulation run. The simulation
proceeds without user intervention whenever it can proceed deterministically.

-J

Reverses the evaluation order of nested `unless` statements, so that the resulting semantics conforms to the evaluation order of nested `catch` statements in
Java programs.

-jN

Skips the first N steps of a random or guided simulation. N most be a positive
integer value. See also option -uN.

-l

In combination with option -p, this shows the current value of local variables
of the process. Normally, this only prints the value of a local variable when a
value was assigned to that variable in the last execution step. To obtain a full
listing of all local variable values at each execution step, add options -v and
-w.

-m

Changes the semantics of send events. Ordinarily, a send action is unexecutable (blocked) if the target message channel is filled to capacity. When the -m option is used, send operations are always executable, but messages sent to a full buffer are lost.

-nN

Sets the seed for the random number generator that is used to guide a random simulation to the integer value N. There is no space between the -n and the integer N. Without this option, SPIN uses the current clock time as a seed. This means that to get a reproducible random simulation run, the use of the -n option is required.

-p

Shows at each execution step in the simulation run which process changed state, and what source statement was executed. For instance (using also a few other options discussed here):

```
$ spin -b -B -p -u5 tpc6
0: proc - (:root:) creates proc  0 (:init:)
1: proc 0 (:init:) line 213 "tpc6" (state 11) [i = 0]
2: proc 0 (:init:) line 219 "tpc6" (state 8)  [.(goto)]
3: proc 0 (:init:) line 215 "tpc6" (state 7)  [((i<1))]
4: proc 0 (:init:) creates proc  1 (user)
4: proc 0 (:init:) line 216 "tpc6" (state 3)  [run user(i)]
5: proc 0 (:init:) line 216 "tpc6" (state 4)  [i = (i+1)]
```

-qN

In columnated output (i.e., using option -c) and with options -s and -rthis suppresses the printing of output for send and receive operations on the channel numbered N. To discover which channel numbers correspond to which channels, it can be useful to first perform a straight simulation with just the -c option.

-r

Prints all receive statements that are executed, giving the name and number of the receiving process and the corresponding source line number. For each message parameter this shows the message type and the message channel number and name. For instance:[1]

---

1. For layout purposes, line and source file references that are normally part of the listings are omitted here.

```
$ spin -b -B -r -u99 tpc6
29:   proc 3 (manager) ... offhook <- q 5 (handler[0])
43:   proc 4 (Session) ... start   <- q 2 (me)
53:   proc 4 (Session) ... offhook <- q 2 (me)
62:   proc 3 (manager) ... number  <- q 5 (handler[0])
69:   proc 4 (Session) ... number  <- q 2 (me)
timeout
91:   proc 3 (manager) ... onhook  <- q 5 (handler[0])
-------------
depth-limit (-u100 steps) reached
```

-s

Prints all send statements that are executed in a format similar to that produced by the -r option. For instance:

```
$ spin -b -B -u99 -s tpc6
25:   proc 1 (user)      ... Sent offhook,0   -> q 1 (tpc)
27:   proc 2 (local_tpc) ... offhook -> q 5 (handler[0])
42:   proc 3 (manager)   ... start    -> q 2 (child[0])
43:   proc 3 (manager)   ... offhook  -> q 2 (child[0])
55:   proc 1 (user)      ... Sent number,0    -> q 1 (tpc)
56:   proc 2 (local_tpc) ... number -> q 5 (handler[0])
68:   proc 3 (manager)   ... number   -> q 2 (child[0])
86:   proc 1 (user)      ... Sent onhook,0    -> q 1 (tpc)
87:   proc 2 (local_tpc) ... onhook -> q 5 (handler[0])
88:   proc 1 (user)      ... Sent offhook,0   -> q 1 (tpc)
89:   proc 2 (local_tpc) ... offhook -> q 5 (handler[0])
96:   proc 3 (manager)   ... onhook   -> q 2 (child[0])
-------------
depth-limit (-u100 steps) reached
```

See also -c.

-T

Suppresses the default indentation of the output from print statements. By default, the output always appears indented by an amount that corresponds to the pid number of the executing process. With this option the output appears left-adjusted. See also -b.

-t[N]

Performs a guided simulation, following an execution trail that was produced by an earlier verification run. If an optional number N is attached (with no space between the number and the -t), a numbered execution trail is executed instead of the default unnumbered trail. Numbered execution trails can be generated with verification option -e.

-uN

Stops the simulation run after N steps have been executed. See also -jN.

-v

Performs the simulation in verbose mode, adding more detail to the printouts and generating more hints and warnings about dubious constructs that appear in the model.

-w

Enables more verbose versions of the options -l and -g.

SYNTAX CHECKING OPTIONS

-a

Normally, when simulation runs are performed, SPIN tries to be forgiving about minor syntax issues in the model specification. Because the PROMELA model is interpreted on-the-fly during simulations, any part of the model that is not executed may escape checking. It is therefore possible that some semantic issues are missed in simulation runs.

When SPIN option -a is used, though, a more thorough check of the complete model is performed, as the source text for a model-specific verifier is also generated. This means that, quite apart from the generation of the verifier source files, the -a option can be useful as a basic check on the syntactical correctness of a PROMELA model. More verbose information is generated if the -v flag is also added, as in:

```
$ spin -a -v model
```

-A

When given this option, SPIN will apply a property-based slicing algorithm to the model which can generate warnings about statements and data objects that are likely to be redundant, or that could be revised to use less memory. The property-based information used for the slicing algorithm is derived from basic assertion statements and PROMELA never claims that appear in the model.

-l

This option will cause SPIN to print the body text of each proctype specification after all preprocessing and inlining operations have been completed. It is useful to check what the final effect is of parameter substitutions in inline calls, and of ordinary macro substitions.

-Z

This option will run only the preprocessor over the model source text, writing the resulting output into a file named pan.pre. Good for a very mild syntax check only. The option is there primarily for the benefit of XSPIN.

POSTSCRIPT GENERATION

-M

Generates a graphical version of a message sequence chart as a Postscript file. A long chart is automatically split across multiple pages in the output that is produced. This representation is meant to closely resemble the version that is produced by XSPIN. The result is written into a file called `model.ps`, where `model` is the name of the file with the PROMELA source text for the model. The option can be used for random simulation runs, or to reproduce a trail generated by the verifier (in combination with option `-t`). See also option `-c` for a non-Postscript alternative.

MODEL CHECKER GENERATION

The following options determine how verification runs of PROMELA models can be performed. The verifications are always done in several steps. First, optimized and model-specific source code for the verification process is generated. Next, that source code can be compiled in various ways to fine-tune the code to a specific type of verification. Finally, the compiled code is run, again subject to various run-time verification options.

-a

Generates source code that can be compiled and run to perform various types of verification of a PROMELA model. The output is written into a set of C files named `pan.[cbhmt]`, that must be compiled to produce an executable verifier. The specific compilation options for the verification code are discussed in Chapter 19. This option can be combined with options `-J` and `-m`.

-N file

Normally, if a model contains a PROMELA `never` claim, it is simply included as part of the model. If many different types of claims have to be verified for the same model, it can be more convenient to store the claim in a separate file. The `-N` option allows the user to specify a claim file, containing the text of a `never` claim, that the SPIN parser will include as part of the model. The claim is *appended* to the model, that is, it should not contain definitions or declarations that should be seen by the parser before the model itself is read.

The remaining five options control which optimizations that may be used in the verifier generation process are enabled or disabled. Most optimizations, other than more experimental options, are always enabled. Typically, one would want to disable these optimizations only in rare cases, for example, if an error in the optimization code were to be discovered.

-o1

Disables data-flow optimizations in verifier. The data-flow optimization attempts to identify places in the model where variables become *dead*, that is, where their value cannot be read before it is rewritten. The value of such variables is then reset to zero. In most cases, this optimization will lower verification complexity, but it is possible to create models where the reverse happens.

-o2

Disables the elimination of write-only variables from the state descriptor. It should never be necessary to use this option, other than to confirm its effect on the length of the state vector and the resulting reduction in the memory requirements.

-o3

Disables the statement merging technique. Statement merging can make it hard to read the output of the pan -d output (see Chapter 19), which dumps the internal state assignments used in the verifier. Disabling this option restores the old, more explicit format, where only one statement is executed per transition. Disabling this option, however, also loses the reduction in verification complexity that the statement merging technique is designed to accomplish.

-o4

Enables a more experimental rendezvous optimization technique. This optimization attempts to precompute the feasibility of rendezvous operations, rather than letting the model checker determine this at run time. It is hard to find cases where the use of this option brings convincing savings in the verification process, so it is likely that this option will quietly disappear in future SPIN versions.

-o5

Disables the case caching technique. Leaving this option enabled allows the verifier generator to make smarter use of case statements in the pan.m and pan.b files, especially for larger models. This allows for a sometimes considerable speedup in the compilation of the generated verifier.

-S1 and -S2

Separate compilation options. If the size of the verification model is much larger than the size of a never claims, and there are very many such claims that need to be verified for a single model, it can be more efficient to compile the verification source text for the model separately from the source text for the claim automata. If the file model.pml contains both the main model specification and the never claim, in the simplest case the verifier is then generated and compiled in two separate steps

```
$ spin -S1 model.pml    # source for model without claim
$ spin -S2 model.pml    # source for the claim
```

This generates two sets of sources, with file names pan_s.[chmbt] and pan_t.[chmbt], respectively. These sources can be compiled separately and then linked to produce an executable verifier:

```
$ cc -c pan_s.c          # source for model without claim
$ cc -c pan_t.c          # source for the claim
$ cc -o pan pan_s.o pan_t.o            # link both parts
```

Alternatively, on a Windows machine using the Gnu C compiler, the command sequence might look as follows:

```
$ gcc -c pan_s.c          # source for model without claim
$ gcc -c pan_t.c          # source for the claim
$ gcc -o pan.exe pan_s.obj pan_t.obj    # link both parts
```

The idea is that the first part, generating and compiling the source for the main model without the claim, needs to be done only once, independent of the number of different never claims that must be verified. The second part, generating and compiling the source for the claim automata, can be repeated for each new claim, but is generally much faster, since the claim automata are typically much smaller than the model to be verified. Chapter 11, p. 261, contains a more detailed discussion of these options.

LTL CONVERSION

These two options support the conversion of formulae specified in Linear Temporal Logic (LTL) into PROMELA never claims. The formula can either be specified on the command line or read from a file.

-f formula

This option reads a formula in LTL syntax from the second argument and translates it into the equivalent PROMELA syntax for a never claim. Note that there must be a space between the -f argument and the formula. If the formula contains spaces, or starts with the diamond operator <>, it should be quoted to form a single argument and to avoid misinterpretation by the shell. The quoting rules may differ between systems. On UNIX systems either double or single quotes can be used. On many Windows or Linux systems only single quotes work. In case of problems, use the -F alternative below.

-F file

This option behaves like option -f except that it will read the formula from the given file and not from the command line. The file should contain the formula on the first line. Any text that follows this first line is ignored, which means that it can be used to store arbitrary additional comments or annotation on the formula.

MISCELLANEOUS OPTIONS

-d

Produces symbol table information for the PROMELA model. For each PROMELA object, this information includes the type, name, and number of elements (if declared as an array); the initial value (if a data object) or size (if a message channel), the scope (global or local), and whether the object is declared as a variable or as a parameter. For message channels, the data types of the message fields are also listed. For structure variables, the third field in the output defines the name of the structure declaration that contained the variable.

-C

Prints information on the use of channel names in the model. For instance:

```
$ spin -C tpc6
chan rtpc
    never used under this name
chan manager-child[2]
    exported as run parameter by: manager to Session par 3
    sent to by: manager
chan manager-parent
    exported as run parameter by: manager to Session par 4
    received from by: manager
```

In this example, the names Session, manager, parent, and child are the names of proctypes in the model. Local channel names are identified as the pair of a proctype name and a channel name, separated by a hyphen. A channel name is said to be *exported* if it appears as an actual parameter in a run statement. In effect, the channel is then passed from one process to another. The listing gives the number of the parameter in the call to run in which the channel name appears.

When combined with option -g, the output will also include information on known access patterns to all globally declared channels:

```
$ spin -C -g tpc6
chan handler
    received from by: manager
    sent to by: local_tpc
chan tpc
    received from by: local_tpc
    sent to by: user
chan rtpc
    never used under this name
chan Session-me
    imported as proctype parameter by: Session par 1
    received from by: Session
```

```
chan Session-parent
    imported as proctype parameter by: Session par 1
    sent to by: Session
chan manager-child[2]
    exported as run parameter by: manager to Session par 3
    sent to by: manager

chan manager-parent
    exported as run parameter by: manager to Session par 4
    received from by: manager
```

-Dxxx

Passes the argument -Dxxx in its entirety to the preprocessor that is used. This option allows one to leave the value of some symbolic constants unde-fined in the model, so that they can be defined on the command line. See also option -E.

-Exxx

Passes only the string xxx as an argument to the preprocessor.

-Pxxx

Replaces the compiled-in name of the preprocessor with xxx. By default, the program used here is the standard C preprocessor cpp, but with this option it can be replaced with any other, including user-defined programs.

-V

Prints the SPIN version number and exits.

```
$ spin -V
Spin Version 4.0.7 -- 1 August 2003
```

-X and -Y

These two options are reserved for use by the XSPIN interface. Their effect is limited to small changes in the formatting of the output that can be generated by the other options, such as the addition of blank lines to separate the output from different execution steps.

OVERVIEW OF PAN OPTIONS **19**

"The only reasonable way to get a program right
is to assume that it will at first contain errors
and take steps to discover these and correct them."
(Christopher Strachey, 1916–1975)

This chapter summarizes all verification options. The options apply to the verification code that is generated with SPIN's run-time option -a. Also included is an explanation of the information that is generated by the program at the end of a verification run (unless disabled with PAN run-time option -n).

The three main sections of this chapter cover:

- PAN Compile-Time Options:
  Options that are available at the time of compilation of the verifier source code.
- PAN Run-Time Options:
  Options that are available as command-line arguments to the executable PAN code that is generated by the compiler.
- PAN Output Format:
  An explanation of the information that is generated by the PAN verifiers at the end of a run.

The primary reason for the reliance of compile-time options for the automatically generated verifier code is efficiency: using compile-time directives allows for the generation of more efficient executables than if all options were handled through the use of command line arguments.

If the XSPIN user interface is used, most options are selected automatically by XSPIN (based on user preferences), so in that case there is no strict need to be familiar with the information that is presented in this chapter.

PAN COMPILE-TIME OPTIONS

There are quite a few compile-time options for the PAN sources. We will divide them into the following groups, depending on their main purpose:

- Basic options
- Options related to partial order reduction
- Options to increase speed
- Options to reduce memory use
- Options for use only when prompted by PAN
- Options for debugging PAN verifiers
- Experimental options

Usage of all compile-time directives is optional. In its most minimal form, the generation, compilation, and execution of the verification code would simply proceed as follows:

```
$ spin -a spec
$ cc -o pan pan.c
$ ./pan
```

The compile-time directive can modify the default behavior of the verifier to achieve specific effects, as explained in more detail shortly. For instance, to enable breadth-first search and bitstate hashing, the compilation command would change into:

```
$ cc -DBFS -DBITSTATE -o pan pan.c
```

BASIC OPTIONS

-DBFS

Arranges for the verifier to use a breadth-first search algorithm rather than the standard depth-first search. This uses more memory and restricts the type of properties that can be verified to safety properties only, but within these restrictions it is the easiest way to find a short error path. This option can be combined with the various methods for reducing memory use, such as hash-compact, bitstate hashing, collapse compression, and minimized automaton compression.

-DMEMCNT=N

Sets an upper-bound to the amount of memory that can be allocated by the verifier to 2^N bytes. This limit should be set as closely as possible to the amount of physical (not virtual) memory that is available on the machine. Without this limit, the verifier would pass this limit and start using virtual memory, which in this type of search can lead to a serious degradation of performance, and in the worst case (when the amount of virtual memory used exceeds the amount of physical memory used) to thrashing. For example,

```
$ cc -DMEMCNT=29 -o pan pan.c
```

sets the memory limit at $2^{29} = 512$ Megabyte. The next step up would bring this to 1 Gigabyte. Somewhat finer control is available with the directive MEMLIM.

-DMEMLIM=N

Sets an upper-bound to the amount of memory that can be allocated by the verifier to N Megabytes. For example,

```
$ cc -DMEMLIM=600 -o pan pan.c
```

sets the limit at 600 Megabyte.

-DNOCLAIM

If a PROMELA never claim is part of the model, the addition of this directive will exclude it from the verification attempt. It is safe to use this directive even if no never claim is present. The code that would ordinarily be used for the handling of the claim is disabled, which can also improve performance slightly.

-DNP

Includes the code in the verifier for non-progress cycle detection, which in turn enables run-time option -l and simultaneously disables run-time option -a for the detection of standard acceptance cycles.

-DON_EXIT=STRING

The name ON_EXIT can be used to define an external procedure name that, if defined, will be called immediately after the verifier has printed its final statistics on a verification run and just before the verifier exits. A possible use can be, for instance:

```
$ spin -a spec
$ cc -DON_EXIT=mycall() -o pan pan.c user_defined.c
$ ./pan
```

where the file user_defined.c contains the definition of procedure mycall().

-DPROV=file

If the name PROV is defined, the verifier will arrange to execute whatever code segment is defined in the file file into the verifier source text, at a point just before the search starts. The code segment should be a sequence of statements that will be inserted, via an include directive, at the start of the run() procedure. All variable access must be done with the proper local prefixes, using knowledge about the internal data structures used by the verifier, so the proper use of this option will require some knowledge of the internals of the verifier. The option can be used to set provisioning information, for instance, by assigning values to variables declared to be `hidden` that are used as constants in the model.

OPTIONS RELATED TO PARTIAL ORDER REDUCTION

-DNOREDUCE
Disables the partial order reduction algorithm and arranges for the verifier to perform an exhaustive full state exploration, without reductions. This clearly increases both the time and the memory requirements for the verification process. The partial order reduction method used in SPIN is explained in Chapter 9 (p. 191).

-DXUSAFE
Disables the validity checks on `xr` and `xs` assertions. This improves the performance of the verifier and can be useful in cases where the default check is too strict.

OPTIONS USED TO INCREASE SPEED

-DNOBOUNDCHECK
Disables the default check on array indices that is meant to intercept out-of-bound array indexing errors. If these types of errors are known to be absent, disabling the check can improve performance.

-DNOFAIR
Disables the code for the weak fairness algorithm, which means that the corresponding run-time option `-f` will disappear. If it is known that the weak fairness option will not be used, adding this directive can improve the performance of the verifier.

-DSAFETY
Optimizes the code for the case where no cycle detection is needed. This option improves performance by disabling run-time options `-l` and `-a`, and removing the corresponding code from the verifier.

OPTIONS USED TO DECREASE MEMORY USE

-DBITSTATE
Uses the bitstate storage algorithm instead of default exhaustive storage. The bitstate algorithm is explained in Chapter 9 (p. 206).

-DHC
Enables the hash-compact storage method. The state descriptor is replaced with a 64-bit hash value that is stored in a conventional hash table. Variations of the algorithm can be chosen by adding a number from zero to four to the

directive: HC0, HC1, HC2, HC3, or HC4 to use 32, 40, 48, 56, or 64 bits, respectively. The default setting with HC is equivalent to HC4, which uses 64 bits. The hash-compact algorithm is explained in Chapter 9 (p. 212).

-DCOLLAPSE
Compresses the state descriptors using an indexing method, which increases run time but can significantly reduce the memory requirements. The collapse compression algorithm is explained in Chapter 9 (p. 198).

-DMA=N
Enables the minimized automaton storage method to encode state descriptors. Often combines a very significant reduction in memory requirements with a very significant increase in the run-time requirements. The value N sets an upper-bound to the size of the state descriptor as stored. This method can often fruitfully be combined with -DCOLLAPSE compression.

-DSC
Enables a stack cycling method, which can be useful for verifications that require an unusually large depth-limit. The memory requirements for the stack increase linearly with its maximum depth. The stack cycling method allows only a small fraction of the stack to reside in memory, with the remainder residing on disk. The algorithm swaps unused portions of the search stack to disk and arrange for just a working set to remain in-core. With this method, the run-time flag -m determines only the size of the in-core portion of the stack, but does not restrict the stack's maximum size. This option is meant only for those rare cases where the search stack may be millions of steps long, consuming the majority of the memory requirements of a verification.

OPTIONS TO USE WHEN PROMPTED BY PAN
If the verifier discovers a problem at run time that can be solved by recompiling the verifier with different directives, the program prints a recommendation for the recompilation before it exits. This applies to two directives in particular: -DNFAIR and -DVECTORSZ.

-DNFAIR=N
Allocates memory for enforcing weak fairness. By default, that is, in the absence of an explicit setting through the use of this directive, the setting used is N=2. If this setting is insufficient, the verifier will prompt for recompilation with a higher value. The default setting can be exceeded if there is an unusually large number of active processes. Higher values for N imply increased memory requirements for the verification.

-DVECTORSZ=N

The default maximum size for the state vector (i.e., state descriptor) is 1,024 bytes. If this is insufficient, for unusually large models, the verifier will prompt for recompilation with a higher value. For example:

```
$ cc -DVECTORSZ=2048 -o pan pan.c
```

There is no predefined limit for the size of the state vector that can be set in this way. Often, a large state vector can successfully be compressed losslessly by also using the -DCOLLAPSE directive.

OPTIONS FOR DEBUGGING PAN VERIFIERS

-DVERBOSE

Adds elaborate debugging printouts to the run. This is useful mostly for small models, where a detailed dump of the precise actions of the verifier is needed to trace down suspect or erroneous behavior.

-DCHECK

Provides a slightly more frugal version of the -DVERBOSE directive.

-DSVDUMP

Enables an additional run-time option -pN to the verifier which, if selected, writes a binary dump of all unique state descriptors encountered during a verification run into a file named sv_dump. The file is only generated at the end of the verification run, and uses a fixed integer size of N bytes per recorded state. State descriptors shorter than N bytes are padded with zeros. See also -DSDUMP.

-DSDUMP

If used in combination with the directive -DCHECK this adds an ASCII dump of all state descriptors encountered in the search to the verbose debugging output that is generated.

EXPERIMENTAL OPTIONS

-DBCOMP

If used in combination with the directive -DBITSTATE, modifies the code to compute hash functions over not the original but the compressed version of the state descriptor (using the standard masking technique). In some cases this has been observed to improve the coverage of a bitstate run.

-DCOVEST

If used in combination with the directive -DBITSTATE, this option compiles in extra code for computing an alternative coverage estimate at the end a run. On some systems, the use of this code also requires linkage of the object code with the math library, for instance, with the compiler flag `-lm`.

The experimental formula that is used to compute the coverage in this mode was derived by Ulrich Stern in 1997. Stern estimated that when a run has stored R states in a hash array of B bits, then the true number of reachable states R' is approximately

$$R' = \frac{\ln (1 - R/B)}{\ln (1 - 1/B)}.$$

When the verifier is compiled with directive `-DCOVEST` it reports the estimated state space coverage as the percentage of states that was reached compared to the estimated total number of reachable states, that is:

$$\frac{R}{R'} \times 100\%$$

-DCTL

Allows only those partial order reductions that are consistent with branching time logics, such as CTL. The rule used here is that each persistent set that is computed contains either all outgoing transitions or precisely one.

-DGLOB_ALPHA

Considers process death to be a globally visible action, which means that the partial order reduction strategy cannot give it priority over other actions. The resulting verification mode restores compatibility with SPIN version numbers from 2.8.5 to 2.9.7.

-DHYBRID_HASH

Using this option can reduce the size of every state descriptor by precisely one word (4 bytes), but this benefit will only be seen in 25% of all cases. In the standard storage method, when the state descriptor is one, two, or three bytes longer than a multiple of four, the memory allocator pads the amount of memory that is effectively allocated with one, two, or three bytes, respectively. This padding is done to secure memory alignment. To avoid this in at least some of the cases, the `HYBRID_HASH` will consider state descriptors that exceed a multiple of four by precisely one byte, and truncate the state vector by that amount. The one byte that is removed is now added to the hash value that is computed. This can cause more hash collisions to occur, but it does preserve a correct search discipline, and it can save memory.

-DLC

If used in combination with the directive `-DBITSTATE`, this option replaces exhaustive storage of states in the depth-first search stack with a four-byte hash-compact representation. This option slows down the verification process, but it can reduce the memory requirements. There is a very small additional risk of hash collisions on stack states which, if it occurs, can affect the effective coverage achieved. This option is automatically enabled when -DSC is used in combination with -DBITSTATE.

-DNIBIS

Applies a small optimization of partial order reduction technique. The attempt is to avoid repeating the exploration of a successor state in cases where the exploration of the reduced set of transitions fails (e.g., because it closed a cycle). This requires extra testing to be done during the search to see if the optimization applies, which in many cases can more than cancel the benefit of the optimization.

-DNOCOMP

Disables the default masking of bits in the state vector during verifications. This can improve performance, but is not compatible with cycle detection or bitstate storage methods.

-DNOSTUTTER

Disables the rule that allows a never claim to perform stuttering steps. This is formally a violation of the semantics for LTL model checking. The stuttering rule is the standard way to extend a finite run into an infinite one, thus allowing for a consistent interpretation of Büchi acceptance conditions.

-DNOVSZ

This option removes four bytes from each state descriptor before it is stored in the state space. The field that is removed records the effective size of the state descriptor. In most cases, this information is indeed redundant, so when memory is tight and the exhaustive state space storage method is used, this option may give relief. The number of states stored that is reported at the end of a run should not change when -DNOVSZ is enabled. This option is not compatible with -DCOLLAPSE. Generally, the latter option will reduce the memory requirements by a more substantial amount, and in a safer way.

-DOHASH

Replaces the default hash function used in the verifier with an alternative one based on the computation of a cyclic redundancy check. In combination with run-time option -hN, a choice of 32 different hash functions can be used. The quality of these alternate function is often less than the built-in default.

-DPEG

Includes and enables code in the verifier for performing complexity profiling. With this option, the number of times that each basic statement is executed will be counted, and the counts are printed at the end of the run as a simple aid in identifying the hot spots in the code with respect to verification.

-DPRINTF

Enables the execution of `printf` statements during verification runs. Useful only for debugging purposes.

-DRANDSTOR=N

If used in combination with `-DBITSTATE`, this will randomly prune the number of states that are actually recorded in the hash array. The probability of storage is determined by the parameter N. For example,

```
$ cc -DRANDSTOR=33 -DBITSTATE -o pan pan.c
```

would reduce the probability of storage for each state from 100% to 33%. (Only approximately one out of every three unique states encountered is stored.) The value for N must be between 0 and 99. Low values will increase the amount of (duplicate) work that has to be done by the verifier, and thus increases the time requirements of a verification. Low values, however, can also increase the effective coverage of a bitstate verification for very large state spaces. This option can be useful also in sequential bitstate hashing runs to improve the cumulative coverage of all runs combined.

-DREACH

Use of this option changes the search algorithm in such a way that the absence of safety errors can be guaranteed within the run-time depth limit that is set by `-m`. The algorithm used is discussed in Chapter 8 (p. 171). This option cannot guarantee that the shortest path to a liveness error is found.

-DVAR_RANGES

Includes and enables code in the verifier for computing the effective value range of all basic (i.e., not PROMELA `typedef` structure) variables. To keep things manageable, all values over 255 are grouped under a single entry in the report that is generated at the end of the run.

PAN RUN-TIME OPTIONS

The following options can be given as command-line arguments to the compiled version of the verifiers generated by SPIN. They are listed here in alphabetical order.

-A

Suppresses the reporting of basic assertion violations. This is useful if, for instance, the verification process targets a different class of errors, such as non-progress cycles or Büchi acceptance cycles. See also -E.

-a

Arranges for the verifier to report the existence, or absence, of Büchi acceptance cycles. This option is disabled when the verifier is compiled with the directive -DNP, which replaces the option with -l, for non-progress cycle detection.

-b

Selecting this *bounded search* option makes it an error, triggering an error trail, if an execution can exceed the depth limit that is specified with the -m option. Normally, exceeding the search depth limit only generates a warning.

-cN

Stops the search after the Nth error has been reported. The search normally stops after the first error is reported. Using the setting -c0 will cause *all* errors to be reported. See also run-time option -e.

-d

Prints the internal state tables that are used for the verification process and stops. For the leader election protocol example from the SPIN distribution, the output looks as follows.[1] One state table is generated for each proctype that appears in the SPIN model, with one line per transition.

```
$ spin -a leader
$ ./pan -d
proctype node
  state  1 -(tr  8)-> state  3 [id  0 tp   2] [----L] \
        line 16 => Active = 1
  state  3 -(tr  9)-> state 30 [id  2 tp   5] [----L] \
        line 18 => out!first,id      [(3,2)]
  state 30 -(tr 10)-> state 15 [id  3 tp 504] [--e-L] \
        line 19 => in?first,number   [(2,3)]
  state 30 -(tr 17)-> state 28 [id 16 tp 504] [--e-L] \
        line 19 => in?second,number
  . . .
proctype init
  state 10 -(tr  3)-> state  7 [id 33 tp   2] [A---L] \
        line 49 => proc = 1
  state  7 -(tr  4)-> state  3 [id 34 tp   2] [A---L] \
        line 51 => ((proc<=5))
  state  7 -(tr  6)-> state  9 [id 37 tp   2] [A---L] \
        line 51 => ((proc>5))
  state  3 -(tr  5)-> state  7 [id 35 tp   2] [A---L] \
        line 53 => (run node(...))
  state  9 -(tr  1)-> state 11 [id 41 tp   2] [----L] \
        line 51 => break
  state 11 -(tr  7)-> state  0 [id 43 tp 3500] [--e-L] \
        line 58 => -end- [(257,9)]
  . . .
```

1. Not all transitions are shown. Long lines are split into two parts here for layout purposes.

```
Transition Type: A=atomic; D=d_step; L=local; G=global
Source-State Labels: p=progress; e=end; a=accept;
Note: statement merging was used. Only the first
   stmnt executed in each merge sequence is shown
   (use spin -a -o3 to disable statement merging)
```

The description of each transition specifies a series of numbers and strings. We refer to these with greek symbols, as follows:

```
state α -(tr γ)-> state β [id δ tp ε] [..λ..] \
    line φ => ..ν.. [..η..]
```

α is the source state of the transition.

β is the target state of the transition.

γ is a unique number that corresponds with the case number for the transition that appears in the two switch statements that are generated by SPIN in the files pan.m and pan.b. These two cases describe, respectively, the detailed precondition and effect of the execution of the forward and the backward move during the state space search for this specific transition.

δ is another identifying number for the transition that is used internally by the SPIN parser. This is also the identifying number used in the verbose printouts that are generated when the verifier is compiled with any one of the directives -DCHECK, -DDEBUG, or -DVERBOSE.

ε describes the type of the transition, assigning a classification that is used for enforcing the partial order reduction strategy. The number 2, for instance, indicates that the transition touches only local variables, and the number 3,500 indicates a process death operation. (The precise number assignments are not particularly interesting, but if needed, they can be found in the SPIN source file pangen2.c in procedure valTpe().)

In models that contain unless statements, the ε entry can be followed with some more information about the presence of an escape transition that would be taken in case the escape clause from the unless statement becomes executable.

λ is a string of dashes and symbols that interprets the type of transition encoded in ε. The lower and uppercase letters that can appear here are explained at the bottom of the printout as the *transition types* and *source-state* labels, which is meant to be self-explanatory.

ϕ is the line number at which the original text for the transition can be found in the source file for the model. (To avoid too verbose outputs, the file name is not included here.)

ν reproduces the source text for the transition.

η appears on only transitions that are marked by SPIN as conditionally safe transitions for the partial order reduction strategy. The numbers indicate the types of conditions that apply and are also included in the printout only for debugging purposes.

The state tables are optimized in three separate steps by the verifier before the verification process begins. The original and intermediate versions of the tables can be generated by using the -d argument two, three, or four times in a row (e.g., by typing the command pan -d -d -d).

-E
Suppresses the reporting of invalid end-state violations. See also -A.

-e
Creates a numbered error trail for all errors that are encountered during the search up to the bound set by the -cN argument. By default, only one single error trail is produced per run. The maximum possible number of error trails is therefore generated by the combination:

```
$ ./pan -e -c0
```

-f
Uses the weak fairness restriction in the search for either acceptance cycles (in combination with option -a) or non-progress cycles (option -l). The weak fairness algorithm is discussed in Chapter 8 (p. 182).

-hN
If the verifier is compiled with the directive -DOHASH, this option replaces the default hash function with an alternative function. The value N must be greater than zero and less than 33. The default hash function corresponds to the setting -h1.

-i
Enables a fine-grained iterative search method to look for the shortest path to an error. After each error that is found, the verifier will set a new depth limit that is one step smaller than the length of the last error trail. The use of this method can increase complexity. For the method to reliably identify the shortest possible error path, the verifier must be compiled with -DREACH. The option is only guaranteed to work for safety properties. Given a safety property, there is also an alternative way to home in on the shortest possible error path, also at increased resource requirements (memory and time). That alternative option is to compile the verifier with option -DBFS. In this case, the -DREACH option is not needed.

-I
An alternative to run-time option -i. Instead of reducing the search depth to one step below the length of the last error trail that was generated, this option reduces it to half that size, in an effort to reduce the number of iterations that has to be made. This will not necessarily find the shortest possible error

sequence, but it often gets reasonably close. This option also requires compilation with -DREACH for best performance.

-J

Reverses the evaluation order of nested unless statements so that the resulting semantics conforms to the evaluation order of nested catch statements in Java programs. This option matches command-line option -J to Spin itself, where it applies to simulation instead of verification runs. To play back an error trail that was generated with the -J verification option requires the use of the -J option during guided simulation.

-l

Arranges for the verifier to report the existence, or absence, of non-progress cycles. This option is not enabled unless the verifier source code is compiled with -DNP and disables the search for acceptance cycles (option -a).

-mN

Sets the maximum search depth for a depth-first search verification to N steps. The default value for N, that is, in the absence of an explicit -m argument, is 10,000. See also -b.

-n

Suppresses the default listing of all unreached states at the end of a verification run.

-q

Adds an extra restriction on end states. Normally a valid end state is one where each process has reached the end of its code or has stopped at a state that was marked with an end-state label. By default, message channels are not required to be empty for a state to be considered a valid end state. The use of this option adds that requirement.

-s

Changes the bitstate search algorithm to use 1-bit hashing instead of the default 2-bit hashing method. The use of this option requires compilation with -DBITSTATE.

-V

Prints the Spin version number that was used to generate the verifier code and stops.

-wN

The default size of the hash table that is used for exhaustive (i.e., non-bitstate) verifications is $2^{18} = 262, 144$ slots. For bitstate verifications, the default size of the hash array is 2^{18} bits, which means $2^{15} = 32,768$ bytes. This default corresponds to the setting -w18. The default size can be changed, with currently an upper-limit of -w32.

-X

Option reserved for use by XSPIN. It causes the UNIX standard error output to be printed onto the standard output stream.

-Y

Causes the end of the output to be marked with a special line that can be recognized by postprocessors such as XSPIN.

PAN OUTPUT FORMAT

A typical printout of a verification run is shown in Figure 19.1 This is what each line in this listing means:

```
(Spin Version 4.0.7 -- 1 August 2003)
```

Identifies the version of SPIN that generated the pan.c source from which this verifier was compiled.

```
+ Partial Order Reduction
```

The plus sign means that the default partial order reduction algorithm was used. A minus sign would indicate compilation for exhaustive, non-reduced verification with option -DNOREDUCE. If the verifier had been compiled with the breadth-first search option, using compiler directive -DBFS, then this fact would have been noted here as well.

```
Full statespace search for:
```

Indicates the type of search. The default is a full state space search. If the verifier is instead compiled with one of the various types of state compression enabled (e.g., collapse compression, bitstate search, or hash-compact storage), this would be noted in this line of output.

The next line in the output reads:

```
never claim            - (none specified)
```

The minus sign indicates that no never claim or LTL formula was used for this run. If a never claim was part of the model, it could have been suppressed with the compiler directive -DNOCLAIM. If a trace assertion is used instead of a never claim, this would also be reflected in this line of output.

```
assertion violations    +
```

The plus indicates that the search checked for violations of user-specified assertions, which is the default.

540

```
$ ./pan
(Spin Version 4.0.7 -- 1 August 2003)
        + Partial Order Reduction

Full statespace search for:
        never claim             - (none specified)
        assertion violations    +
        acceptance   cycles     - (not selected)
        invalid end states      +

State-vector 32 byte, depth reached 13, errors: 0
      74 states, stored
      30 states, matched
     104 transitions (= stored+matched)
       1 atomic steps
hash conflicts: 2 (resolved)
(max size 2^18 states)

1.533   memory usage (Mbyte)

unreached in proctype ProcA
        line 7, state 8, "Gaap = 4"
        (1 of 13 states)
unreached in proctype :init:
        line 21, state 14, "Gaap = 3"
        line 21, state 14, "Gaap = 4"
        (1 of 19 states)
```

Figure 19.1 Example Output Generated by Pan

```
        acceptance   cycles     - (not selected)
```

The minus indicates that the search did not check for the presence of acceptance or non-progress cycles. To do so would require a run-time option -a or compilation with -DNP combined with the run-time option -l.

```
        invalid end states      +
```

The plus indicates that a check for invalid end states was done (i.e., for absence of deadlocks).

```
State-vector 32 byte, depth reached 13, errors: 0
```

The complete description of a single global system state required 32 bytes of memory. The longest depth-first search path contained 13 transitions from the root of the tree (that is, 13 statement executions, starting from the initial system state). Of course, this depth is typically smaller when breadth-first search is used than with the default depth-first search. No errors were found in the search, as reflected in the zero error count.

Normally, the number of errors reported is either zero or one, since by default the search will stop when the first error is found. The verifier can be run in several different modes, though, where it would be allowed to continue the search beyond the first error. The run-time flags -c and -e can be used for this purpose.

```
74 states, stored
```

This line indicates that a total of 74 unique global system states were stored in the state space (each represented effectively by a state vector of 32 bytes).

```
30 states, matched
```

In 30 cases the search returned to a previously visited state in the search tree.

```
104 transitions (= stored+matched)
```

A total of 104 transitions were explored in the search, which can serve as a statistic for the amount of work that has been performed to complete the verification.

```
1 atomic steps
```

One of the transitions was part of an atomic sequence; all others were outside atomic sequences.

When breadth-first search is used, in addition to these numbers, the verifier also reports a count for the number of *nominal* states. This number is derived by subtracting all states that would not have to be stored in a *depth*-first search from the reported number of stored states. This includes all states inside atomic sequences, and all states that record the point of execution in the middle of attempted rendezvous handshakes. Some of those handshake attempts will succeed, and some will fail (if, for instance, the intended recipient of the rendezvous offer is not ready to accept it), so separately, the number of successful rendezvous handshakes will also be reported in this case. These additional numbers are meant to make it easier to compare the performance of breadth-first searches with depth-first searches.

The next line in the output from Figure 19.1 reports:

```
hash conflicts: 2 (resolved)
```

In two cases the default hashing scheme (a weaker version than what is used in bitstate hashing) encountered a collision and had to resolve this collission by placing states into a linked list within the hash table.

```
(max size 2^18 states)
```

The (perhaps default) argument that was specified for the size of the hash table was 2^{18} equivalent to a run-time option -w18. If this had been a bitstate search, the size would give the number of bits in the memory arena, rather than the number of slots in the hash table.

```
1.533    memory usage (Mbyte)
```

Total memory usage was 1.533 Megabytes, including the stack, the hashtable, and all related data structures. Choosing smaller values for run-time options `-m` and `-w` than the defaults, would allow memory use to decrease. In this case, with only 74 reachable states of 32 bytes each, this could result in considerable savings.

When the verifier is compiled with directive `-DCOLLAPSE` for memory compression, some extra statistics are printed on how many elements there turned out to be in each of three main groups that are stored and indexed separately. For instance, the report

```
nr of templates: [ globals chans procs ]
collapse counts: [ 3262 18 20 3 ]
```

says that there were 3,262 different versions of the portion of the state descriptor containing global variables values, 18 different versions of the portion containing all channel states, 20 different versions of local process states for processes created from the first `proctype` declaration in the model, and two for processes created from the second `proctype` declaration. If more `proctype` declarations are present in the model, more numbers will follow in this list.

```
unreached in proctype ProcA
        line 7, state 8, "Gaap = 4"
        (1 of 13 states)
unreached in proctype :init:
        line 21, state 14, "Gaap = 3"
        (1 of 19 states)
```

A listing of the state numbers and approximate line numbers for the basic statements in the specification that were not reached. Since this is a full state space search that ran to completion, this means that these transitions are effectively unreachable and constitute dead code in the model.

In bitstate searches the output also contains an estimate for the coverage that was realized in a verification run. This estimate is based on a statistical argument about the likelihood of hash collissions and the number of reachable system states that may have been missed because of this. The coverage estimate is expressed as the so-called *hash factor*, which measures the relative number of bits in the bitstate space that remained unused. This hash factor is computed as the number of bits that was available for the search in the bitstate space (which can be set with run-time parameter `-w`), divided by the number of states that was reached.

For the default double-bit hashing method, a value for the hash factor over one hundred normally correlates with high confidence with an exhaustive, or nearly exhaustive, coverage. Lower values correlate with lower confidence, with values near one corresponding to near certainty that only a very small fraction of the true state space was visited in the run. See also the compile-time directive -DCOVEST, which can be used to add the computation of an alternative coverage estimate to the search results.

LITERATURE

*"I find that a great part of the information I have
was acquired by looking up something
and finding something else on the way."*
(Franklin P. Jones, 1853–1935)

Abadi, M., and L. Lamport. [1991]. "The existence of refinement mappings." *Theoretical Computer Science.* May 1991. Vol. 82, No. 2, pp. 253–284.

Alpern, B. and F.B. Schneider. [1985]. "Defining liveness." *Information Processing Letters.* Oct. 1985. Vol. 21, No. 4, pp. 181–185.

Alpern, B. and F.B. Schneider. [1987]. "Recognizing safety and liveness." *Distributed Computing.* Vol. 2, pp. 117–126.

Ball, T., R. Majumdar, T. Millstein, and S.K. Rajamani. [2001]. "Automatic Predicate Abstraction of C Programs." *SIGPLAN Notices.* Vol. 36, No. 5, pp. 203–213.

Bang, K-S., J-Y. Choi, and C. Yoo. [2001]. "Comments on "The Model Checker Spin." *IEEE Trans. on Software Engineering.* June 2001. Vol. 27, No. 6, pp. 573–576.

Bartlett, K.A., R.A. Scantlebury, and P.T. Wilkinson. [1969]. "A note on reliable full-duplex transmission over half-duplex lines." *Comm. of the ACM.* May 1969. Vol. 12, No. 5, pp. 260–261,265.

Berard, B., M. Bidoit, A. Finkel, et al. [2001]. *Systems and Software Verification: Model-Checking Techniques and Tools.* Springer Verlag.

Bloom, B.H. [1970]. "Spacetime trade-offs in hash coding with allowable errors." *Comm. of the ACM.* July 1970. Vol. 13, No. 7, pp. 422–426.

Bosnacki, D. [2001]. *Enhancing state space reduction techniques for model checking.* Ph.D Thesis. Eindhoven Univ. of Technology, The Netherlands.

Brat, G., K. Havelund, S.J. Park, and W. Visser. [2000]. "Java PathFinder: Second generation of a Java model checker." *Proc. Workshop on Advances in Verification.* July 2000. Chicago, Illinois.

Büchi, J.R. [1960]. "On a decision method in restricted second order arithmetic." *Proc. Intern. Congr. on Logic, Methodology and Philosophy of Science.* Stanford, CA. Stanford Univ. Press. pp. 1–11.

Carter, L., R. Floyd, J. Gill, G. Makowsky, and M. Wegman. [1978]. "Exact and approximate membership testers." *Proc. 10th Annual ACM Symp. on Theory of Computing.* San Diego, CA. pp. 59–65.

Chechik, M. and W. Ding. [2002]. "Lightweight reasoning about program correctness." *Information Frontiers.* Dec. 2002. Vol. 4, No. 4, pp 363–379.

Chou, C-T. and D. Peled. [1999]. "Formal verification of a partial order reduction technique for model checking." *Automated Reasoning.* Nov. 1999. Vol. 23, No. 3, pp. 265–298.

Choueka, Y. [1974]. "Theories of automata on ω-tapes: A simplified approach." *Journal of Computer and System Science.* April 1974. Vol. 8, No. 2, pp. 117–141.

Clarke, E.M., E.A. Emerson, and A.P. Sistla. [1986]. "Automatic verification of finite-state concurrent systems using temporal logic specifications." *ACM Trans. on Prog. Lang. and Systems.* April 1986. Vol. 8, No. 2, pp. 244–263.

Clarke, E.M., O. Grumberg, and D.E. Long. [1994]. "Model checking and abstraction." *ACM-TOPLAS.* Sept. 1994. Vol. 16, No. 5, pp. 1512–1542.

Clarke, E.M., O. Grumberg, and D. Peled. [2000]. *Model Checking,* Cambridge, MA. MIT Press.

Corbett, J.C., M.B. Dwyer, J.C. Hatcliff, S. Laubach, C.S. Pasareanu, Robby, and H. Zheng. [2000]. "Bandera: Extracting finite-state models from java source code." *Proc. 22nd International Conf. on Software Engineering.* June 2000. Limerick, Ireland. ACM Press. pp. 439–448.

Courcoubetis, C., M.Y. Vardi, P. Wolper, P., and M. Yannakakis. [1990]. "Memory efficient algorithms for the verification of temporal properties." *Proc. 2nd Conf. on Computer Aided Verification,* Rutgers Univ., NJ. Also in: *Formal Methods in Systems Design.* Oct. 1992. Vol. 1, No. 2/3, pp. 275–288.

Cousot, P. and R. Cousot. [1976]. "Static determination of dynamic properties of programs." *Proc. Colloque sur la Programmation.* Apr. 1976. Paris, France. Dunod Publ. pp. 106–130.

Dams, D. [1996]. *Abstract Interpretation and Partition Refinement for Model Checking.* Ph.D Thesis. Eindhoven Univ. of Technology, The Netherlands.

Dams, D., R. Gerth, and O. Grumberg. [1997]. "Abstract interpretation of reactive systems." *ACM Trans. on Programming Languages and Systems.* March 1997. Vol. 2, No. 19, pp. 253–291.

Dams, D., W. Hesse, and G.J. Holzmann. [2002]. "Abstracting C with abC." *Proc. Conf. on Computer Aided Verification.* July 2002. Copenhagen, Denmark. Springer Verlag, LNCS 2404, pp. 515–520.

Das, S., D.L. Dill, and S. Park. [1999]. "Experience with Predicate Abstraction." *Conf. on Computer-Aided Verification.* Trento, Italy. Springer Verlag, LNCS 1633, pp. 160–171.

Dillon, L.K., G. Kutty, L.E. Moser, P.M. Melliar-Smith, and Y.S. Ramakrishna. [1994]. "A graphical interval logic for specifying concurrent systems." *ACM Trans. on Softw. Eng. and Methodology.* Apr. 1994. Vol. 3, No. 2, pp. 131–165.

Doran R.W. and L.K. Thomas. [1980]. "Variants of the software solution to mutual exclusion." *Inf. Proc. Letters.* Vol. 10, No. 4, pp. 206–208.

Dijkstra, E.W. [1965]. "Solution of a problem in concurrent programming control." *Comm. of the ACM,* Sept. 1965. Vol. 8, No. 9, p. 569.

Dijkstra, E.W. [1968]. "Co-operating sequential processes." In: *Programming Languages.* Ed. F. Genuys. New York, Academic Press, pp. 43–112.

Dijkstra, E.W. [1972]. "Notes on Structured Programming." In: *Structured Programming.* Eds. O.-J. Dahl, E.W. Dijkstra and C.A.R. Hoare. London, Academic Press, pp. 1–82.

Dijkstra, E.W. [1975]. "Guarded commands, nondeterminacy and formal derivation of programs." *Comm. of the ACM.* Aug. 1975. Vol. 18, No. 8, pp. 453–457.

Dwyer, M.B., G.S. Avrunin, and J.C. Corbett. [1999]. "Patterns in Property Specifications for Finite-state Verification." *Proc. 21st Int. Conf. on Software Eng.* May 1999. ACM Press. pp. 411–420.

Emerson, E.A. [1990]. "Temporal and model logic." In: *Handbook of Theoretical Computer Science.* Elsevier. Vol. B, pp. 997–1072.

Etessami, K. and G.J. Holzmann. [2000]. "Optimizing Büchi automata." *Proc. Proceedings of 11th Int. Conf. on Concurrency Theory.* Aug. 2000. Springer Verlag, LNCS 1877, pp. 153–167.

Etessami, K., T. Wilke, and R. Schuller. [2001]. "Fair simulation relations, parity games, and state space reduction for Büchi automata." *Proc. 28th Int. Col. on Automata, Languages, and Programming.* Springer Verlag, LNCS 2076, pp. 694–707.

Gastin, P. and D. Oddoux. [2001]. "Fast LTL to Büchi automata translation." *Proc. 13th Int. Conf. on Computer Aided Verification.* Springer Verlag, LNCS 2102, pp. 53–65.

Gerth, R., D. Peled, M.Y. Vardi, and P. Wolper. [1995]. "Simple on-the-fly automatic verification of linear temporal logic." *Proc. Symposium on Protocol Specification, Testing, and Verification.* Warsaw, Poland. Chapman & Hall Publ. pp. 3–18.

Godefroid, P. and G.J. Holzmann. [1993]. "On the verification of temporal properties." *Proc. Int. Conf on Protocol Specification, Testing, and Verification.* Liege, Belgium. North-Holland Publ. pp. 109–124.

Godefroid, P., G.J. Holzmann, and D. Pirottin. [1995]. "State space caching revisited." *Formal Methods in System Design.* Nov. 1995. Vol. 7, No. 3, pp. 1–15.

Gödel, K. [1931]. "Uber Formal Unentscheidbare Sätze der Principia Mathematica und Verwandter Systeme." *Monatshefte für Math. u. Physik.* Vol. 38, pp. 173–198.

Goldstein, H.W. and J. von Neumann. [1947]. *Planning and coding problems for an electronic computing instrument.* Part II, Vol. 1. Apr. 1947. In: John von Neumann. *Collected Works.* Vol. V, p. 92. Ed. A.H. Taub. Pergamon Press, N.Y. 1963.

Graf, S. and H. Saidi. [1997]. "Construction of abstract state graphs with PVS." *Proc. Conf. on Computer Aided Verification.* Haifa, Israel. Springer Verlag, LNCS 1254, pp. 72–83.

Harel, D. [1987]. "Statecharts: A visual formalism for complex systems." *Sci. Comput. Program.* June 1987. Vol. 8, No. 3, pp. 231–274.

Havelund, K. and T. Pressburger. [2000]. "Model Checking Java Programs Using Java PathFinder." *Int. Journal on Software Tools for Technology Transfer.* Apr. 2000. Vol. 2, No. 4, pp. 366–381.

Heijenoort, J. van. (Ed.) [2000]. *From Frege to Gödel: A Source Book in Mathematical Logic, 1879–1931.* New York, toExcel.

Hoare, C.A.R. [1978]. "Communicating sequential processes." *Comm. of the ACM.* Aug. 1978. Vol. 21, No. 8, pp. 666–677.

Holzmann, G.J. [1981]. *PAN - a protocol specification analyzer.* Bell Laboratories Technical Memorandum. May 1981. TM81-11271-5.

Holzmann, G.J. [1987]. "Automated protocol validation in Argos: Assertion proving and scatter searching." *IEEE Trans. on Software Engineering.* June 1987. Vol. 13, No. 6, pp. 683–697.

Holzmann, G.J. [1988]. "An improved reachability analysis technique." *Software Practice and Experience.* Feb. 1988. Vol. 18, No. 2, pp. 137–161.

Holzmann, G.J. [1991]. *Design and Validation of Computer Protocols.* Englewood Cliffs, NJ, Prentice Hall.

Holzmann, G.J., P. Godefroid, and D. Pirottin. [1992]. "Coverage preserving reduction strategies for reachability analysis." *Proc. 12th Int. Conf on Protocol Specification, Testing, and Verification.* Orlando, FL. June 1992. Springer Verlag, LNCS, Vol. 663, pp. 178–191.

Holzmann, G.J. and D. Peled. [1994]. "An improvement in formal verification." *Proc. 7th Int. Conf. on Formal Description Techniques.* Berne, Switzerland. Oct. 1994. Chapman & Hall Publ. pp. 197–211.

Holzmann, G.J., D. Peled, and M. Yannakakis. [1996]. "On nested depth-first search." *Proc. Second Spin Workshop.* Aug. 1996. Rutgers Univ., New Brunswick, NJ. American Math. Society. DIMACS/32, pp. 23–32.

Holzmann, G.J. [1997]. "State Compression in SPIN." *Proc. Third SPIN Workshop.* Apr. 1997. Twente Univ., The Netherlands. pp 1–10.

Holzmann, G.J. [1997b]. "The Model Checker Spin." *IEEE Trans. on Software Engineering.* May 1997. Vol. 23, No. 5, pp. 279–295.

Holzmann, G.J. [1998a]. "An analysis of bitstate hashing." *Formal methods in system design.* Nov. 1998. Vol. 13, No. 3, pp. 287–307.

Holzmann, G.J. [1998b]. "Designing executable abstractions." *Proc. Formal Methods in Software Practice.* Clearwater Beach, FL. ACM Press. pp. 103–108.

Holzmann, G.J. [1999]. "The engineering of a model checker: The Gnu i-protocol case study revisited." *Proc. of the Sixth Spin Workshop.* Toulouse, France. Sept. 1999. Springer Verlag, LNCS 1680, pp. 232–244.

Holzmann, G.J. and A. Puri. [1999]. "A Minimized Automaton Representation of Reachable States." *Software Tools for Technology Transfer.* Nov. 1999. Vol. 2, No. 3, pp. 270–278.

Holzmann, G.J. and M.H. Smith. [1999]. "Software model checking: Extracting verification models from source code." *Formal Methods for Protocol Engineering and Distributed Systems.* Oct. 1999. London, England. Kluwer Publ. pp. 481–497.

Holzmann, G.J. and M.H. Smith. [2000]. "Automating software feature verification." *Bell Labs Technical Journal.* April–June 2000. Vol. 5, No. 2, pp. 72–87.

Holzmann, G.J. [2000a]. "Logic Verification of ANSI-C Code with Spin." *Proc. of the 7th SPIN Workshop.* Sept. 2000. Springer Verlag, LNCS, Vol. 1885, pp. 131–147.

Holzmann, G.J. [2000b]. "Software model checking." Course notes for NATO Summer School. Aug. 2000. Marktoberdorf, Germany. IOS Press. *Computer and System Sciences.* Vol. 180, pp. 309–355.

Holzmann, G.J. and M.H. Smith. [2002]. "An automated verification method for distributed systems software based on model extraction." *IEEE Trans. on Software Engineering.* Apr. 2002. Vol. 28, No. 4, pp. 364–377.

Huth, M. and M. Ryan. [2000]. *Logic in Computer Science: Modelling and Reasoning about Systems*. Cambridge Univ. Press.

Ip, C.N. and D. Dill. [1996]. "Verifying systems with replicated components in Murphi." *Proc. 8th Conf. on Computer Aided Verification*, Springer Verlag, LNCS 102, pp. 147–158.

Jenkins, B. [1997]. "Hash functions." *Dr. Dobbs Journal*. Sept. 1997. Vol. 22, No. 9.

Kernighan, B.W. and D.M. Ritchie. [1978]. *The C Programming Language*. First edition. Englewood Cliffs, NJ, Prentice Hall.

Kernighan, B.W. and R. Pike. [1999]. *The Practice of Programming*. Reading, MA, Addison-Wesley.

Kesten, Y. and A. Pnueli. [1998]. "Modularization and abstraction: The keys to practical formal verification." *Mathematical foundations of Computer Science*. Springer Verlag, LNCS 1450, pp. 54–71.

Kesten, Y., A. Pnueli, and M.Y. Vardi. [2001]. "Verification by augmented abstraction: The automata theoretic view." *Journal of Computer and System Sciences*. Vol. 62, No. 4, pp. 668–690.

Kupferman, O. and M.Y. Vardi. [1999]. "Vacuity detection in temporal model checking." *Proc. Conf. on Correct Hardware Design and Verification Methods*. Springer-Verlag, LNCS 1703, pp. 82–96.

Kurshan, R.P. [1993]. *Automata-Theoretic Verification of Coordinating Processes*. Princeton, NJ, Princeton Univ. Press.

Kwiatkowska, M., [1989]. "Event fairness and non-interleaving concurrency." *Formal Aspects of Computing*. Vol. 1, No. 3, pp. 213–228.

Lakatos, I., [1976]. *Proofs and Refutations: The Logic of Mathematical Discovery*. Cambridge Univ. Press.

Lamport, L. [1983]. "What good is temporal logic?" *Proc. IFIP Conf. on Information Processing*. Paris, France. North-Holland Publ. pp. 657–668.

Lamport, L. [1986]. "The mutual exclusion problem—parts I and II." *Journal of the ACM*, Apr. 1986. Vol. 33, No. 2, pp. 313–347.

Levitt, J.R. [1998]. *Formal verification techniques for digital systems*, Ph.D Thesis, Stanford Univ., Stanford, CA.

Manna, Z. and A. Pnueli. [1995]. *Temporal Verification of Reactive Systems: Safety*. Springer Verlag.

Mazurkiewicz, A. [1986]. "Trace Theory." In: *Advances in Petri Nets*. Springer Verlag, LNCS 255, pp. 279–324.

McIlroy, M.D. [1982]. "The development of a spelling list." *IEEE Trans. on Communications*. Jan. 1982. Vol. COM-30, No. 1, pp. 91–99.

Morris, R. [1968]. "Scatter storage techniques." *Comm. of the ACM*. Jan.

1968. Vol 11, No. 1, pp. 38–44.

Peled, D., T. Wilke, and P. Wolper. [1996]. "An algorithmic approach for checking closure properties of ω-regular languages." *Proc. Proceedings of 7th Int. Conf. on Concurrency Theory.* Aug. 1996. Springer Verlag, LNCS 1119, pp. 596–610.

Peled, D. [1994]. "Combining partial order reductions with on-the-fly model checking." *Proc. 6th Int. Conf. on Computer Aided Verification.* Stanford, CA. June 1994. Springer Verlag, LNCS 818, pp. 377–390.

Peled, D. and T. Wilke. [1997]. "Stutter-invariant temporal properties are expressible without the next-time operator." *Information Processing Letters.* Vol. 63, No. 5, pp. 243–246.

Peterson, G.L. [1981]. "Myths about the mutual exclusion problem." *Inf. Proc. Letters.* Vol. 12, No. 3, pp. 115–116.

Perrin, D. [1990]. "Finite automata." *Handbook of Theoretical Computer Science.* Ed. J. van Leeuwen, Elsevier. Vol. B, pp. 1–57.

Pike, R., D. Presotto, K.L. Thompson, and G.J. Holzmann. [1991]. "Process Sleep and Wakeup on a Shared-memory Multiprocessor." *Proc. of the Spring 1991 EurOpen Conf..* Tromso, Norway. pp. 161–166.

Pnueli, A. [1977]. "The temporal logic of programs." *Proc. 18th IEEE Symposium on Foundations of Computer Science.* Providence, RI. IEEE Press. pp. 46–57.

Prior, A.N. [1957]. *Time and Modality.* Oxford, England, Clarendon Press.

Prior, A.N. [1967]. *Past, Present, and Future.* Oxford, England, Clarendon Press.

Raynal, M. [1986]. *Algorithms for Mutual Exclusion.* Cambridge, MA, MIT Press,

Rescher, N. and A. Urquhart. [1971]. *Temporal Logic.* Library of Exact Philosophy. Springer Verlag.

Ruane, L.M. [1990]. "Process synchronization in the UTS kernel." *Computing Systems.* Vol. 3, No. 3, pp. 387–421.

Russell, B. [1903]. *The Principles of Mathematics.* Cambridge Univ. Press. Vol. 1, par. 78 and Ch. X.

Ruys, T.C. [2001]. *Towards Effective Model Checking.* Ph.D Thesis. Twente Univ., The Netherlands.

Schlor, R. and W. Damm. [1993]. "Specification of system-level hardware designs using timing diagrams." *Proc. European Design Automation and ASIC Design.* Feb. 1993. IEEE Press. pp. 518–524.

Schoot, vander H. and H. Ural. [1996]. *An improvement on partial order model checking with ample sets.* Computer Science Technical Report,

TR-96-11. Sept. 1996. Univ. of Ottawa, Canada.

Shankar, N. [2002]. "Verification by Abstraction." *Proc. 10th Anniversary Colloquium*, March 2002, United Nations Univ., Int. Inst. for Software Technology. Lisbon, Portugal.

Stern, U. and D.L. Dill. [1995]. "Improved probabilistic verification by hash compaction." *Proc. IFIP WG 10.5 Advanced Research Workshop on Correct Hardware Design and Verification Methods*. IFIP. pp. 206–224.

Strachey, C. [1965]. "An impossible program." *Computer Journal*. Jan. 1965. Vol. 7, No. 4, p. 313.

Telcordia [2000]. *LATA Switching Systems Generic Requirements, Section 11: Service Standards*. A Module of LSSGR, FR-64, GR-511-CORE, Issue 1. June 2000. Telcordia Technologies.

Thomas, W. [1990]. "Automata on infinite objects." *Handbook of Theoretical Computer Science*. Ed. J. van Leeuwen, Elsevier. Vol. B, pp. 133–187.

Tarjan, R.E. [1972]. "Depth first search and linear graph algorithms." *SIAM J. Computing*. Vol. 1, No. 2, pp. 146–160.

Tip, F. [1995]. "A survey of program slicing techniques." *Journal of Programming Languages*. Sept. 1995. Vol. 3, No. 3, pp. 121–189.

Turing, A.M. [1936]. "On computable numbers, with an application to the Entscheidungs problem." *Proc. London Mathematical Soc.* Ser. 2-42, pp. 230–265.

Vardi, M.Y. and Wolper, P. [1986]. "An automata-theoretic approach to automatic program verification." *Proc. Symp. on Logic in Computer Science*. Cambridge, England. June 1986. pp. 322–331.

Vardi, M.Y. [2001]. "Branching vs. linear time: Final showdown." *Proc. Tools and Algorithms for the Construction and Analysis of Systems*. Springer Verlag, LNCS 2031, pp. 1–22.

Villiers, P.J.A. [1997]. *Validation of a micro-kernel: A case study*. Ph.D Thesis. University of Stellenbosch, S. Africa.

Wolper, P., Vardi, M.Y., and Sistla, A.P. [1983]. "Reasoning about infinite computation paths." *Proc. 24th IEEE Symposium on Foundations of Computer Science*. Tucson, AZ. IEEE Press, pp. 185–194.

Wolper, P. [1986]. "Specifying interesting properties of programs in propositional temporal logic." *Proc. 13th ACM Symposium on Principles of Programming Languages*. St. Petersburg Beach, FL. Jan. 1986. ACM Press, pp. 148–193.

Wolper, P. and Leroy, D. [1993]. "Reliable hashing without collision detection." *Proc. 5th Int. Conf. on Computer Aided Verification*. Elounda, Greece. Springer Verlag, LNCS 697, pp. 59–70.

AUTOMATA PRODUCTS A

"Beyond each corner new directions lie in wait."
(Stanislaw Lec, 1909–1966)

SPIN is based on the fact that we can use finite state automata to model the behavior of asynchronous processes in distributed systems. If process behavior is formalized by automata, the combined execution of a system of asynchronous processes can be described as a product of automata.

Consider, for instance, a system A of n processes, each process given in automaton form, say: A_1, A_2, $\cdots$, A_n. Next, consider an LTL formula f and the Büchi automaton B that corresponds to its *negation* $\neg f$. Using the automata theoretic verification procedure, we can check if A satisfies f by computing the global system automaton S

$$S = B \otimes \prod_{i=1}^{n} A_i$$

We use the operator Π here to represents an *asynchronous product* of multiple component automata, and $\otimes$ to represent the *synchronous* product of two automata.

The result S of this computation is another finite state automaton that can now be analyzed for its acceptance properties. If formula f can be violated (that is, if $\neg f$ can be satisfied), then S will have accepting ω-runs that demonstrate it. We can check if S has accepting runs with the algorithms discussed in Chapter 8.

The definition of the component automata that are used in the computation of the asynchronous product are derived from `proctype` declarations, and the Büchi automaton B is defined by a `never` claim.

We have so far taken for granted how the asynchronous and synchronous products of automata are computed and how properties such as Büchi acceptance, non-progress, and the existence of invalid end states can be expressed within this framework. We will discuss those details here.

For each finite state automaton $A = (S, s_0, L, T, F)$ that is derived from a `proctype` declaration or a `never` claim we can identify three interesting subsets of $A.S$ that capture the assignment of the special label-types used in PROMELA. We will name them as follows:

> $A.A$ is the set of states marked with accept-state labels,
> $A.E$ is the set of states marked with end-state labels,
> $A.P$ is the set of states marked with progress-state labels.

We present the definition of asynchronous and synchronous product first within the standard automata theoretic framework. Within this framework we reason about ω-runs (infinite runs) that do or do not satisfy standard Büchi acceptance conditions. The set of final states $A.F$ for each component automaton is in this case identical to set $A.A$: the set of local states that is explicitly labeled with an accept-state label.

SPIN also has separate verification modes for verifying the absence of non-progress cycles and for verifying pure safety properties, including the verification of absence of deadlock. At the end of this Appendix we will show how the definitions can be modified slightly to also capture these other types of verification.

ASYNCHRONOUS PRODUCTS

The asynchronous product of n component automata is defined as follows:

Definition A.1 (Asynchronous Product)

> The asynchronous product of a finite set of finite state automata $A_1, ..., A_n$ is another finite state automaton $A = (S, s_0, L, T, F)$, where
>
> $A.S$ is the Cartesian product $A_1.S \times ... \times A_n.S$,
>
> $A.s_0$ is the n-tuple $(A_1.s_0, ..., A_n.s_0)$,
>
> $A.L$ is the union set $A_1.L \cup ... \cup A_n.L$, and
>
> $A.T$ is the set of tuples $((x_1, ..., x_n), l, (y_1, ..., y_n))$ such that
> $\exists i, 1 \leq i \leq n, (x_i, l, y_i) \in A_i.T$, and $\forall j, 1 \leq j \leq n, j \neq i \rightarrow (x_j \equiv y_j)$,
>
> $A.F$ is the subset of those elements of $A.S$ that satisfy the condition
> $\forall(A_1.s, \cdots, A_n.s) \in A.F, \exists i, A_i.s \in A_i.F$.

Note that not all the states in this product automaton are necessarily reachable. Their reachability depends on the semantics we attach to the labels in set $A.L$ (cf. p. 129).

Recall that the labels from the sets $A_i.L$ in each component automaton record basic PROMELA statements, such as assignment, assertion, print, condition, send, and receive statements. The intended interpretation of these labels is given by the semantics of PROMELA, as outlined in Chapter 7. Because PROMELA statements can manipulate data objects, when we interpret the semantics on the labels, we really expand automata into *extended* finite state automata. The automata still remain finite-state under this extension, due to the fact that in PROMELA all data types can have only finite domains. Each extended automaton can be converted fairly trivially into a pure finite state automaton by expanding out the data values. When SPIN computes the asynchronous product, it does this expansion on the fly.

Another interesting aspect of Definition A.1 is that it states that the transitions in the product automaton are the transitions from the component automata, arranged in such a way that only *one* of the component automata can execute one transition at a time, indivisibly. This corresponds to the standard interpretation of the semantics of concurrency based on the *interleaving* of process actions. This is of course not the only possible interpretation. Some of the alternatives are discussed in Appendix B (The Great Debates).

ENCODING ATOMIC SEQUENCES

PROMELA has a notion of atomic sequences that allows a sequence of transitions from a single process component to be executed indivisibly. In effect, the interleaving of transitions is temporarily disabled in this case. This feature can easily be captured within the automata framework we have discussed, as also shown in Chapter 7. To do so, we can introduce a special global integer data object named **exclusive**, with initial value 0. The component processes (represented by automata) are assigned unique positive integer numbers (pids) to distinguish them. We can now add a clause to the precondition of each transition in component **p** that makes the executability of the transition dependent on the truth if: $\text{exclusive} \equiv 0 \lor \text{exclusive} \equiv \text{p.pid}$. The first transition in each atomic sequence in component **p** now gets an extra side effect **exclusive = p.pid**, and the last transition gets an extra side effect **exclusive = 0**. These few changes suffice to produce the desired semantics.

RENDEZVOUS

PROMELA also has a notion of synchronous rendezvous that is not directly addressed by Definition A.1. These types of operations can also be encoded within the given framework with relatively little effort.

In a rendezvous event, matching send and receive operations from different processes meet in a single event that is executed atomically. Since we do not have simultaneous executions, we must be able to secure in some other way that synchronous send and receive operations indeed execute atomically in that order.

One way to accomplish this is to define another special global integer data object, call it **handshake**, with initial value 0. Each rendezvous port in the system is now assigned a unique positive integer number.

We now again add some new clauses to the preconditions of transitions in the system. For all receive operations on rendezvous port **i**, this extra condition is handshake $\equiv$ i, to restrict the states in which they are enabled to those in which a rendezvous operation on port i has been initiated. For all non-rendezvous transitions, and all send operations on rendezvous ports, the extra clause is handshake $\equiv 0$, to prevent their execution when a rendezvous action on any queue is currently in progress.

Next, we add some side effects to the transitions that correspond to rendezvous send or receive operations. For each send operation on rendezvous port i, we add the side effect handshake = i, and to each rendezvous receive operation we add the side effect handshake = 0.

The additions guarantee that as long as handshake $\equiv 0$, all transitions, except the receive halves of rendezvous operations, are executable as before. Whenever the send half of a rendezvous operation is initiated, however, the value of handshake becomes positive, and it allows only a *matching* receive handshake to take place. Once that happens, the value of handshake returns to its default initial value. (In the SPIN implementation this handshake variable is called boq, which was originally chosen as an acronym for "blocked on queue.")

SYNCHRONOUS PRODUCTS

The synchronous product of two finite state automata is defined as follows:

Definition A.2 (Synchronous Product)

The synchronous product of finite state automata P and B is a finite state automaton A = (S, s_0, L, T, F), where

A. S is the Cartesian product P'. S $\times$ B. S, where P' is the stutter-closure of P in which a nil self-loop is attached to every state in P that has no successor,

A. s_0 is the tuple (P. s_0, B. s_0),

A. L is P'. L $\times$ B. L,

A. T is the set of pairs (t_1, t_2) such that $t_1 \in$ P'. T and $t_2 \in$ B. T,

A. F is the set of pairs (s_1, s_2) $\in$ A. S where $s_1 \in$ P. F $\lor s_2 \in$ B. F.

The intuition expressed here is that one of the two automata, say, automaton B, is a standard Büchi automaton that is, for instance, derived from an LTL formula, or directly given as a PROMELA never claim. As in Definition A.1, we again assume that sets of final states P. F and B. F in the component automata are identical to the corresponding sets of acceptance states P. A and B. A.

The main difference between an asynchronous and a synchronous product is in the definition of sets L and T. In a synchronous product, the transitions in the product automaton correspond to *joint* transitions of the component automata. The labels on the transitions now also consist of two parts: the combination of the two labels from the original transitions in the components. The semantics of a combination of two labels is defined in SPIN as the logical

```
#define N           4
#define p           (x < N)

int x = N;

active proctype A()
{
        do
        :: x%2 -> x = 3*x+1
        od
}

active proctype B()
{
        do
        :: !(x%2) -> x = x/2
        od
}

never {     /* <>[]p */
T0_init:
        if
        :: p -> goto accept_S4
        :: true -> goto T0_init
        fi;
accept_S4:
        if
        :: p -> goto accept_S4
        fi;
}
```

Figure A.1 Example PROMELA Model

---

and combination of the preconditions of the two original statements, and the concatenation of the two actions. (Hence, P⊗B is not necessarily the same as B⊗P.) When SPIN computes the synchronous product of a system and a claim automaton, the labels in the claim automaton B define only conditions (i.e., state properties) and no actions. Since one of the actions is always nil, the catenation of actions from the two automata is now independent of the ordering, and we have P⊗B ≡ B⊗P.

AN EXAMPLE

Consider the PROMELA model of two asynchronous processes and a `never` claim derived from the LTL formula <>[]p, shown in Figure A.1.

The control-flow graph of each of these three components can be formalized as a finite state automaton, as illustrated in Figure A.2.

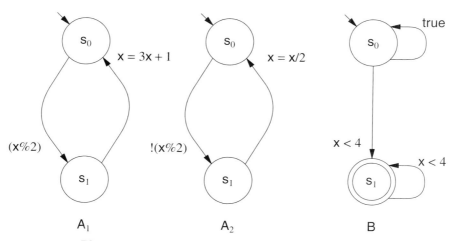

Figure A.2 Finite State Automata A_1, A_2, and B

The full asynchronous product of A_1 and A_2 is shown in Figure A.3. The states in the product automaton have been marked with pairs of statenames p, q with p the name of the corresponding state in component automaton A_1, and q the corresponding state in component automaton A_2. State s_0, s_0 is the initial state. Since neither A_1 nor A_2 contained accepting states, the product automaton has no accepting states either.

The initial state of the product is s_0, s_0. If we apply PROMELA semantics and interpret the labels on the transitions, it is clear that all paths leading into state s_1, s_1 are infeasible, since they require both the condition (x%2) and its negation to evaluate to *true* without an intervening change in the value of x. State s_1, s_1 is therefore effectively unreachable under the intended label semantics.

Applying PROMELA semantics, we can compute the expanded version of the asynchronous product from Figure A.3 (fully expanding all possible values of integer data object x) which can now be interpreted as a pure finite state automaton. This automaton is shown in Figure A.4. The states are marked with a triple p, q, v, with p and q referring to the states of component automata A_1 and A_2 as before, and v giving the integer value of variable x at each state.

The *synchronous product* of the automaton in Figure A.4 and the property automaton B is illustrated in Figure A.5.

The states are now marked with a tuple p, q, v, r, with the first three fields matching the markings from Figure A.4, and the last field recording the state from component property automaton B. All transitions in the automaton from

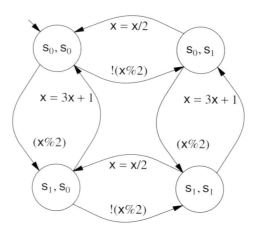

Figure A.3 Asynchronous Product of A_1 and A_2

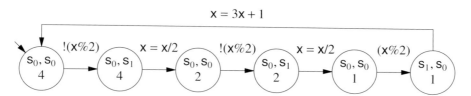

Figure A.4 Expanded Asynchronous Product for Initial Value $x = 4$

Figure A.5 are now joint transitions from the automaton in Figure A.4 and the property automaton B. The transitions from B are not explicitly indicated in Figure A.5, since they will be clear from context. All transitions in the top half of the figure correspond to self-loop labeled *true* on $B.s_0$; all transitions in the bottom half similarly correspond to the self-loop labeled $x < 4$ on $B.s_1$, and all transitions between top and bottom half correspond to the transition from $B.s_0$ to $B.s_1$ labeled $x < 4$ in B. Note that some transitions are not possible, and not drawn in the figure, because the property automaton B forbids them once it has reached state $B.s_1$.

If the automaton in Figure A.5 allows any ω-accepting runs, they correspond to executions that satisfy the LTL formula $<>[]p$. The automaton has four reachable accepting states, but it is easy to see that none of these states is

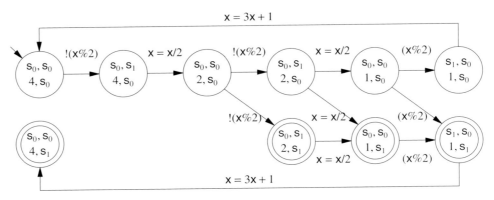

Figure A.5 (Expanded) Synchronous Product
of Figure A.4 and Automaton B

reachable from themselves (i.e., part of a cycle or a strongly connected component in the reachability graph). Hence, the sample PROMELA model we started this example with does *not* satisfy the LTL formula given.

NON-PROGRESS CYCLES

SPIN uses a simple mechanism to encode the detection of non-progress cycles in terms of standard Büchi acceptance, thus avoiding the need for a special algorithm. When the verifier sources are compiled with the directive -DNP, a predefined never claim is included in the model that corresponds to the LTL formula ($\Diamond \Box$ np_), which states that it is impossible for the system to eventually ($\Diamond$) reach a point its execution from which it always ($\Box$) traverses only *non*-progress (np_) states (cf. page 447).

In a synchronous or asynchronous product of component automata, the product automaton is considered to be in a progress state if and only if at least one of the component automata is in a progress state (that is, a state within set A. P as defined on page 554). A never claim in PROMELA syntax corresponding to the predefined formula can be written as follows:

```
never {     /* <>[] np_ */
        do
        :: np_ -> break
        :: true
        od;
accept:
        do
        :: np_
        od
}
```

This claim defines a non-deterministic Büchi automaton. Note, for instance, that in the initial state of the automaton the option `true` is always executable. The only accepting runs are the infinite runs in which eventually no more progress states are reached. The `true` self-loop in the initial state allows the automaton to remain in its initial state for an arbitrary number of initial steps in the run. When a non-progress state is reached, the automaton can, but need not, switch to its accepting state. It is, for instance, possible that the first few non-progress states encountered in a run do not immediately lead to a point in the run where a return to a progress state is impossible. The structure of the automaton as given allows us to skip over such states, in a hunt for the real violations.

DEADLOCK DETECTION

Absence of deadlock is system property that cannot be expressed directly in LTL, and hence it does not easily fit within the standard framework of ω-automata that we have sketched here.

To define a notion of acceptance that captures precisely the set of deadlocking runs of a finite state automaton, we have to reconsider the definitions of set $A.F$ for the asynchronous and synchronous product computations.

To do so, we start with the assumption that set $A.F$ in each component automaton is now defined to contain only the normal termination state of automaton A (i.e., the state that corresponds to the point immediately before the closing curly brace of a PROMELA `proctype` or `never` claim body declaration).

For the asynchronous product, we now redefine the set of final states $A.F$ from Definition A.1 as follows, using the definition of $A.E$ that was given on page 554:

$A.F^s$ is the subset of those elements of $A.S$ that satisfy the condition
$\forall (A_1.s, \cdots, A_n.s) \in A.F, \exists i, (A_i.s \in A_i.F \ \lor \ A_i.s \in A_i.E)$,
further, we require that $\forall (s, l, t) \in A.T, s \notin A.F$.

That is, the product state is in set $A.F$ if and only if all component automata are either in their normal termination state, or in a specially marked end state, and further if the state has no successors. This precisely captures the notion of an *invalid end state*, which is SPIN's formalization of a system deadlock state.

We can do something similar for Definition A.2. Note that we may still want to make use of the SPIN machinery to compute synchronous products also if we perform a verification of only safety properties, because we can make good use of `never` claims as a pruning device: the `never` claim can be used to *restrict* a verification run to a subset of behaviors that is deemed to be of primary interest.

To make this possible, it suffices to redefine the set of final states of a synchronous product from Definition A.2 as follows:

A. F^s is the set of pairs $(s_1, s_2) \in$ A. S where $s_1 \in$ P. F.

The only change from the version used in Definition A.2 is that the criterion for determining if a state is in A. F now uniquely depends on the system automaton P, and is independent of the state of the never claim (i.e., Büchi automaton B).

THE GREAT DEBATES **B**

"It is not necessary to understand things
in order to argue about them."
(Pierre Augustin Caron de Beaumarchais, 1732–1799)

Quite a few issues in formal verification have sparked heated debates over the years, without ever coming to a clear resolution. Perhaps the first such issue came up when temporal logic was first being explored, in the late seventies, as a suitable formalism for reasoning about concurrent systems. The issue was whether it was better to use a branching-time or a linear-time logic. Much later, the debate was between symbolic or explicit verification methods. Many of these issues directly relate to design decisions that have to be made in any verifier, including SPIN. We discuss the more important ones here, briefly motivating the rationale for the choices that were made in the design of SPIN. The issues we discuss are:

- Branching Time versus Linear Time
- Symbolic Verification versus Explicit Verification
- Breadth-First Search versus Depth-First Search
- Tarjan's SCC Algorithms versus SPIN's Nested Depth-First Search
- Events versus States
- Realtime Verification versus Timeless Verification
- Probabilities versus Possibilities
- Asynchronous Systems versus Synchronous Systems
- Interleaving Semantics versus True Concurrency
- Open versus Closed Systems

BRANCHING TIME vs LINEAR TIME

The two main types of temporal logic that are used in model checking are CTL, short for Computation Tree Logic, and LTL, short for Linear Temporal Logic. CTL is a *branching* time logic, and is almost exclusively used for applications in hardware verification. LTL is a *linear* time logic, and is almost exclusively used for applications in *software* verification. The main issues that have been debated concern the relative expressiveness of the two logics and the relative complexity of verification.

Perhaps one reason why the debate has persisted for so long is that the two logics are not really comparable: their expressiveness overlaps, but each logic can express properties that are outside the domain of the other. The standard examples that are used to illustrate the difference are that LTL can express *fairness* properties and CTL cannot, but CTL can express the so-called *reset* property and LTL cannot. Fairness properties are often used as constraints on cyclic executions, stating, for instance, that every cyclic execution either must traverse or may not traverse specific types of states infinitely often. The reset property expresses that from every state there exists *at least one* execution that can return the system to its initial state. Not surprisingly, this type of property is more important in hardware than in software specifications. The overlap between CTL and LTL is sufficiently broad that most properties of interest can easily be expressed in both logics. A notion of fairness, though not expressible in CTL, can be embedded into the verification algorithms, so this is also not much of an issue.

This leaves the issue of complexity, which continues to be a source of confusion. The main argument here is based on an assessment of the theoretical worst-case complexity of verifying either CTL or LTL formulae. Consider a system with R reachable states and a formula of "length" n, where the length of a formula is the number of state subformulae it contains. The standard procedure for CTL model checking can visit every reachable state up to n times, giving a worst-case complexity of $O(R \cdot n)$. The standard procedure for LTL model checking, however, first requires the conversion of the LTL formula into an ω-automaton of, say, m states, and then computing the synchronous product of that automaton and the system, which in the worst case can be of size $R \cdot m$. This gives a complexity of $O(R \cdot m)$. The focus of the argument is now that in the worst case m can be exponentially larger than n. This argument leads to the statement that CTL model checking is "of linear complexity," while LTL model checking is "of exponential complexity." Those who read this and try to find a significant difference between the run-time or memory requirements of CTL model checkers and LTL model checkers are often surprised: there is no such difference and in many cases LTL model checkers like SPIN have been shown to significantly outperform CTL model checkers when presented with the same verification problem. So what is going on?

Let us first consider the worst-case complexity of converting an LTL formula into an ω-automaton. As a simple example, consider the formula `[] (p -> (q U r))`. The CTL equivalent[1] of this formulae is `AG((!p) || A(q U r))`, where `A` is the universal path quantifier, `G` is the equivalent of the LTL box operator `[]`, and `||` is the logical or operator. There are six state

subformulae (properties that can be true or false in any given state): `p`, `q`, `r`,
`A(q U r)` , `((!p) || A(q U r))`, and `AG((!p) || A(q U r))`. The
standard CTL model checking algorithm marks each system state with the
truth value of the propositional symbols `p`, and`q`, `r` in a first pass, and then in
three new passes it will mark those states in which the remaining state subformulae hold. In the worst case, this requires four visits to each state.

The worst-case ω-automaton generated from the LTL version of the formula
would have $2^6 = 64$ states. A good implementation of an LTL converter, however, generates an equivalent ω-automaton of only *two* states. The size of the
synchronous product of this automaton and the system is somewhere between
R, the original system size, and $2 \cdot R$. With SPIN's nested depth-first search
algorithm, in the worst case we would visit every state four times to perform
the verification. Whether the CTL verification method or the LTL verification
method performs better depends entirely on the unpredictable specifics of the
system structure being verified: there is no predetermined winner.

A few things are worth observing.

1. The worst-case behavior of LTL converters is rare. In most cases, the
   converters perform significantly better than worst-case.
2. Temporal logic formulae of practical interest very rarely have more
   than two or three temporal operators in them. It can be hard to develop
   a good intuition for the true meaning of more complex formulae. Even
   experienced people can easily be confused by them. The shorter formulae translate into small automata, achieving very low multiplication
   factors for both CTL and LTL verification alike.
3. What affects complexity is not really the number of *potentially* reachable states in the automaton that is generated from an LTL formula, but
   the number of *effectively* reachable states.

The memory and run-time requirements of the two types of searches for identical multiplication factors are, of course, identical. LTL verification algorithms, however, can more easily be implemented with an on-the-fly verification strategy: they do not require the whole system graph to be computed
before the verification procedure can begin.

As many have observed by simply running verification tasks with both CTL
and LTL-based model checkers, in practice there is no measure that can reliably tell which method can solve a given problem more efficiently. It is clear,
though, that CTL model checkers have been a powerful force in the development of the early tools for hardware verification, while LTL model checkers
have become dominant in applications of software verification. The

---

1. The equivalence assumes that there are no states without outgoing transitions in the system
being verified.

difference in logic, however, is not the only factor that sets these types of model checkers apart, so the relative success of each type of tool within a given domain may well be due, at least in part, to other factors as well.

A further discussion of these issues, with an extensive list of references, can be found in Vardi [2001].

SYMBOLIC VERIFICATION vs EXPLICIT VERIFICATION

Symbolic verification algorithms, or BDD-based methods, offer an ingenious strategy to combat state-space explosion problems. They are, of course, not the only such strategy, but in the domain of hardware verification they are often extremely effective. When applied to software verification problems, they tend to perform more poorly, but in that domain strategies such as partial order reduction often perform exceptionally well. There are no guarantees in either domain, though. The performance of the symbolic verification methods depends critically on the variable ordering that is chosen for the BDDs. Choosing an optimal variable ordering is an NP-complete problem, so in practice only heuristic methods are used. Similarly, in applications of partial order reduction methods, computing the optimal reduction is an NP-complete problem, so heuristics are used here as well. The method implemented in SPIN, for instance, is based on a fairly conservative static approximation of data independence relations that tends to give the majority of the benefits of the reduction at a very small run-time cost.

Because of the conservative approximation used in SPIN, it is hard to construct a case where a verification attempt with partial order reduction enabled behaves worse than one without it. The difference in even the worst case is limited to a few percent of run-time. With the use of BDDs in hardware verification, the odds are less favorable. Undeniably, the best-case performance of these methods is outstanding, but it is relatively easy to find or construct cases where the symbolic verification methods behave significantly worse than explicit state methods. Worse still, it is often unpredictable when this happens, and there is very little that can be done about it when it is encountered (short of solving the NP-hard problem of variable ordering).

When symbolic verification and partial order reduction methods are compared, some popular statistics tend to be misused a little. The memory use of a BDD-based method is ultimately determined by the number of nodes in the BDD structures, and for an explicit state method it is determined by the number of states stored. It can be very misleading, though, to compare the number of potentially reachable states that is captured by a BDD structure with the number of states that is explored with an explicit state method based on partial order reduction. First, of course, potentially reachable does not mean effectively reachable. Secondly, and more importantly, the states explored in an explicit search based on partial order methods are equivalent to a possibly exponentially larger set of effectively reachable states. It is the very purpose of the partial order reduction method to make this difference as large as possible. If memory use is compared between the two methods, the only valid metric is to compare true memory use: bytes. The results of such comparisons can be very surprising, and can contradict the artificial counts that are meant to show a disproportionally large benefit for symbolic methods.

Neither method is necessarily superior to the other. Some trends seem fairly generally agreed upon, though. Within the domain of software verification, partial order methods tend to give better performance, and within the domain of hardware verification, the symbolic methods tend to perform better. There are reasons for the difference. Binary or boolean data, often bit-vectors, tend to dominate in hardware verification problems: structures that favor BDD representations. More complex, and highly correlated, higher-level data structures tend to dominate in software verification problems, and are not easily exploited with BDDs. Asynchronous process execution tends to dominate in software applications, a phenomenon exploited by partial order techniques; while synchronous, clocked, operation is more the rule in hardware applications, not easily exploited by partial order reduction.

BREADTH-FIRST SEARCH vs DEPTH-FIRST SEARCH

Perhaps even an older point of debate is whether, in explicit state model checkers, it is better to use a breadth-first or a depth-first discipline as the default search algorithm. SPIN uses depth-first search as its default algorithm, and contains a breadth-first search only as a user-defined option, which is effective only for safety properties. The main advantage of a breadth-first search algorithm is that for safety properties it can find the shortest path to an error state, while the depth-first search often finds a longer path. For liveness properties, or properties of infinite sequences, the advantages disappear. There are two well-known and efficient variants of the depth-first search that can be used to demonstrate the existence of strongly connected components in a reachability graph: Tarjan's classic depth-first search algorithm, and the more recent nested depth-first search method that is implemented in SPIN.

We can think of a variant of the nested depth-first search method that is based on breadth-first search. Starting the breadth-first search from the initial system state, we proceed with the search normally. Each accepting state found in this process would be placed on a special watch list. We are interested in identifying at least one accepting state that is reachable from itself. To solve that problem is harder. We can consider performing a second breadth-first search (the nested search step) from each of the states on the watch list, but an essential property of the nested depth-first search is missing: the second search can no longer be done in post-order. Therefore, we may need to create as many copies of the state space as there are reachable accepting states. This increases the worst-case complexity of the search from linear to quadratic.

Quite apart from this technical problem in constructing an effective algorithm for proving liveness properties with a breadth-first search, is the issue of memory requirements. Even if we could manage to restrict the state space to just a single copy of each reachable state, we no longer have the depth-first search stack to fall back on for reconstructing counterexample error paths. The breadth-first search needs a queue to store each new generation of states that are to be explored further, which fulfills a similar role as the stack in a depth-first search. To be able to construct error paths, though, the breadth-first search needs to store links (pointers) at each state, pointing to at least one of the state's predecessors in the reachability graph. Each such pointer takes at least 32-bits of memory. The nested depth-first search method does not need to store such links between states, trading the inconvenience of longer error paths for a savings in memory.

SPIN has an option to find a shorter error path that is based on depth-first search that works for both safety and liveness properties. In this variant of the search we store with each reachable state also the distance from the initial system state at which that state was found. If a shorter path to the state is found later in the search, its successors are re-explored, up to a user-defined maximum search depth. Clearly, finding the shortest possible error path is almost always more expensive than just plain proving the existence any error path.

TARJAN SEARCH vs NESTED SEARCH

The automata theoretic verification procedure as implemented in SPIN relies on our ability to detect the presence of infinite accepting runs in a finite reachability graph. The classic way of doing so would be to use Tarjan's depth-first search algorithm to construct the strongly connected components of the graph, and then analyze each such component for the presence of accepting states. The memory and time requirements of this procedure are well-known. In the worst case, we may have to visit every reachable state twice: once to construct the reachability graph, and once in the analysis of a strongly connected component. The storage requirements for each reachable state increase with two, typically 32-bit wide, integer values: one to store the so-called depth-first number and one to store the lowlink number. Further, to be able to reconstruct an accepting path through a strongly connected component, at least one 32-bit pointer to a predecessor state would need to be stored at each reachable state, bringing the total to three 32-bit values of overhead per state. The benefit of Tarjan's algorithm is clearly that it can produce all accepting runs.

The innovation of the nested depth-first search algorithm lies in the fact that it is not necessary to produce all accepting runs. The search is set up in such a way that an accepting run corresponds to a counterexample of a correctness claim. Any one counterexample suffices to invalidate the claim. The nested depth-first search algorithm has the property that it is able to detect at least one accepting run, if one or more such runs exist. It does so at the same worst-case time complexity (maximally visiting every state twice), but at a lower memory overhead. Only two bits of memory need to be added to each state, instead of three 32-bit values. No pointers between states need to be stored, making it possible to also support very memory-frugal approximation algorithms such as the supertrace or bitstate hashing method, which are among SPIN's main features.

One point in favor of Tarjan's algorithm is that it makes it easier to implement a range of different fairness constraints, including the strong fairness option that is currently not supported by SPIN.

EVENTS vs STATES

SPIN is an *explicit state* model checker. To perform verification, the system builds a global state reachability graph, which can be stored in various ways in memory. The focus on states, rather than transitions or events, also extends to the way in which correctness properties are formalized. A correctness property, such as a temporal logic formula, is built up from simple boolean properties of system states. That means, to express the property that after an off-hook event a telephone subscriber will always receive a dial tone signal, we have to find a way to express the occurrence of the related events as state properties, rather than directly as events. An off-hook condition, for instance, will likely be registered somewhere in a status field, and similarly the generation of dial tone by the system will be recorded somewhere. This strict adherence to the notion of a state as the single mechanism to support correctness arguments is sometimes clumsy. For instance, we may want to state the correctness property that always within a finite amount of time after the transmission of a message the message will be received at its destination. Clearly, the state of a message channel will change as a result of both types of events, provided that the message is sent through a buffered channel. If send and receive events are rendezvous handshakes, however, it becomes much harder, and we have to find more subtle ways of recording their execution in a way that is observable to SPIN during verification.

In principle, it would be possible to switch to a purely event-based formalism for expressing correctness requirements. That too would have limitations, because many types of properties lend themselves more easily to state-based reasoning. A hybrid approach may be the most attractive, shifting some of the ensuing complexity into the model checker itself. To date, we have not explored this extension for SPIN yet.

REALTIME VERIFICATION vs TIMELESS VERIFICATION

One of the most frequently asked questions about SPIN concerns the preferred way of modeling time. Verification of system properties is based on the fundamental assumption that correctness should be independent of performance. As Edsger Dijkstra first articulated, under no circumstances should one let any argument about the relative speed of execution of asynchronous processes enter into correctness arguments. PROMELA has only a rudimentary way for modeling the concept of a timeout, through the use of a predefined and read-only global boolean variable named timeout. The timeout variable is *true* only when all processes are simultaneously blocked, and it is *false* otherwise. This allows us to model the functional intent of a timeout condition: it takes effect to relieve the system from an apparent hang state. There is a pleasing analogy with the predefined read-only local boolean variable else in PROMELA (yes, this is a variable, and not a control-flow keyword, as in most implementation languages). The else variable becomes *true* only when the process that contains it cannot make any other transitions.

If we replace an occurrence of timeout with skip we can capture the assumption that timeouts may also happen when the system is not actually stuck, and we can verify the validity of our correctness claims under those much more severe conditions. Generally, though, this will cause a flood of pseudo error scenarios that are of only marginal interest to a designer. All this reinforces the notion that SPIN is not meant to be used as a performance analysis tool.

There are indeed algorithms for doing real-time analysis with model checkers, but the penalty one pays for this additional functionality is almost always severe: typically an increase in computational complexity of several orders of magnitude. By focusing on only functional and logical correctness issues, SPIN can gain significant efficiency, and handle a broader class of problems.

PROBABILITY vs POSSIBILTY

This issue is very similar to the previous one. It is possible to modify the standard model checking algorithms to take into account a notion of probability. One could, for instance, tag the options in every selection construct with relative probabilities to indicate their relative likelihood of occurrence.

There are many problems with this approach. First, it can increase the verification complexity, depriving us of the ability to verify properties of larger systems. Second, it can be difficult to correctly interpret the results of a verification run that is based on probability estimates. We could, for instance, compute the combined probability of occurrence of an error scenario, but that would be meaningless as a metric. Almost all error scenarios, including the devastating ones that can cause huge damage, have an exceedingly low probability of occurrence. Errors almost always have a low probability of occurrence, since the normal design practices will easily shake out the higher probability bugs. It is the very goal of model checking to find the low probability scenarios that cause systems to fail. It would be a grave error to restrict a verification to only higher probability behaviors. Finally, it can be hard to come up with a realistic estimate for the relative probability of different options for execution. More often than not, if such tags have to be assigned, they will be guessed, which undermines the validity of the verification process.

ASYNCHRONOUS SYSTEMS vs SYNCHRONOUS SYSTEMS

Most hardware model checkers have adopted a synchronous view of the world where in principle all process actions are clock-driven. In such a system, at every clock-tick every process takes a step. One can model asynchronous process behavior in such systems by including a non-deterministic pause option at every move in every process. At each step, then, a process can choose to either pause or to advance with its execution. SPIN is one of the few systems that adopts an asynchronous view of the world. Since in a distributed system different processes cannot see each other's clock (and clock synchronization in a distributed system is actually a pretty difficult task in its own right), the speed of execution of processes is fundamentally asynchronous and cannot be controlled by any device or process: it is beyond the control of the programmer, just like it is in the real world of distributed computing.

This choice has both advantages and disadvantages. The main disadvantage is that it is hard to model synchronous system behavior with an asynchronous model checker. Then again, it is precisely the point of the choice to make this hard, so this is not too surprising. Yet it does, for all practical purposes, eliminate SPIN as an effective candidate for doing hardware verification. There are very good systems for addressing that problem, so this is not a significant loss.

Apart from a better fit for the types of design problems that SPIN targets, there is also an unexpected benefit of adopting the asynchronous view of the world: greater verification efficiency. Assume a model with N asynchronous processes. Modeling these processes in a synchronous tool with non-deterministic pause transitions to emulate asynchronous behavior incurs an N-fold overhead: at every step the model checker must explore N additional pause transitions compared to the SPIN-based graph exploration. This efficiency argument, though, applies only to explicit state verification methods; it disappears when symbolic verification algorithms are used.

INTERLEAVING vs TRUE CONCURRENCY

Sometimes a distinction is made between *true concurrency* semantics and the interleaving semantics we have described. In addition to the interleaving of actions, a true concurrency semantics allows also for the simultaneous execution of actions. In Definition A.1 (p. 554), this would mean the introduction of many extra transitions into set T of the product automaton, one extra transition for each possible combination of transitions in the component automata.

In distributed computer systems, it is indeed possible that two asynchronous processes execute actions in the same instant of time, at least as far as could be determined by an outside observer. To see how such events can be modeled, we must consider two cases.

First, consider the case where the process actions access either *distinct data objects*, or none at all. In this case, the simultaneous execution of these actions is indistinguishable from any arbitrarily chosen sequential interleaving. The interleaving semantics, then, gives a correct representation. The addition of the simultaneous transitions cannot add new functionality.

Secondly, consider the case where two or more process actions do access a *shared data object*. Let us first assume that the object is a single entity that resides at a fixed location in the distributed system, and is accessed by a single control unit. That control unit obviously can do only one thing at a time. At some level of granularity, the control unit wil force an interleaving of atomic actions in time. If we pick the granularity of the actions that are defined within our labeled transition systems at that level, the interleaving semantics will again accurately describe everything that can happen.

But, what if the data object is not a single entity, but is itself distributed over several places in the distributed system where it can be accessed in parallel by different control units? Also in this case, the same principles apply. We can represent the data objects in our automata model at a slightly lower level of granularity, such that each distinct data object resides in a fixed place.

The important thing to note here is that automata are modeling devices: they allow us to model real-world phenomena. The theoretical framework must allow us to describe such phenomena accurately. For this, interleaving semantics offer the simplest model that suffices.

OPEN vs CLOSED SYSTEMS

Traditionally, model checking is based on two requirements: the model must be finite and it must be closed. The benefit of the finiteness assumption will need few words here, although it does mean that we can only reason about infinite state systems if we can make finitary abstractions of them.

To be closed, a model must include all possible sources of input and it must include explicit descriptions of all process behaviors that could affect its correctness properties. The most often quoted benefit of an open systems description, where not all elements of a system are necessarily specified, is that of convenience. In most cases, though, it is not very hard to extend a system's model with a minimal set of worst case assumptions about the environment in which it is meant to execute. These worst case assumptions can effectively match the defaults that would be presumed in an open systems model.

In the design phase, it can be quite helpful to a designer to focus explicitly on the otherwise hidden assumptions. There is also significant extra power in the use of a closed systems model. The designer can, for instance, modify the environment assumptions to see what effect they can have on critical correctness properties. The assumptions can also be used to focus a verification task more precisely on the correct operation of a system under a specific set of conditions. The convention of working with closed system models, finally, naturally matches a standard assume-guarantee style of reasoning.

EXERCISES WITH SPIN   **C**

"I hear and I forget;
I see and I remember;
I do and I understand."
(Confucius, 551–479 BC)

C.1.

How many reachable states do you predict the following PROMELA model will generate?

```
init {   /* example ex1 */
         byte i = 0;
         do
         :: i = i+1
         od
}
```

Try a simulation run:

```
$ spin -p -l -u100 ex1
```

Will the simulation terminate if the `-u100` argument is omitted? Try it.

C.2.

Estimate the total number of reachable states that should be inspected in an exhaustive verification run. Is it a finite number? Will a verification run terminate? Try it as follows, and explain the result.

```
$ spin -a ex1
$ cc -o pan pan.c
$ ./pan
```

C.3.

What would happen if you had declared local variable `i` to be a `short` or an `int` instead of a `byte`?

C.4.

Predict accurately how many reachable states there are for the following model. Write down the complete reachability tree for N equal to two, as specified.

```
#define N 2

init {   /* example ex2 */
         chan dummy = [N] of { byte };
         do
         :: dummy!85
         :: dummy!170
         od
}
```

Check your prediction by generating, compiling, and running the verifier as follows:

```
$ spin -m -a ex2
$ cc -o pan pan.c
$ time ./pan
```

(Option -m defines that messages appended to a full buffer are to be lost.)

C.5.

What happens to the number of reachable states if you set N to three? Express the number of states as a function of N. Use the formula to calculate how many states there will be if you set N equal to 14. Check your prediction by running the verification, and write down:

T: the *sum* of user time plus system time for the run,
S: the number of states *stored* in the state space,
G: the number of *total* number of states generated and analyzed,
V: the vector size, that is, the state descriptor size, which is the amount of memory needed to store one state.

Compute G/T as a measure for the efficiency of the run. The product of S and V gives you the minimal amount of memory that was needed to store the state space. This is of course not the only place where memory is used during a verification (the stack, for instance, also consumes memory), but it is often the largest memory requirement.

The efficiency of a standard exhaustive verification run is determined by the state space storage functions. To study this, repeat the last run first with a smaller and then with a bigger hash table than the predefined default:

```
$ time ./pan -w10     # hash table with 2^10 slots
$ time ./pan -w20     # hash table with 2^20 slots
```

Explain the results. [Hint: Compare the number of hash conflicts.]

C.6.

Estimate how much memory you would need to do a run with N equal to 20? (Warning: Both the number of reachable states and the number of bytes per state goes up with N. Estimate about 30 bytes per state for N equal to 20.) If you have about 8 Megabytes of physical memory available to perform the verification, what maximal fraction of the state-space would you expect to be able to reach?

Now set N to 20 and perform a bitstate verification, as follows:

```
$ spin -m -a ex2
$ cc -DBITSTATE -o pan pan.c
$ time ./pan
```

If you did the calculation, you probably estimated that there should be 2,097,151 reachable system states for N equal to 20. What percentage of these states was reached in the bitstate run? How much memory was used? Compare this to the earlier estimated maximal coverage for a standard exhaustive verification and explain the difference.

C.7.

The default state space in the bitstate verification we performed in the last exercise allocates a hash array of 2^{22} bits (i.e., one quarter Megabyte of memory). Repeat the run with larger amount of memory and check the coverage. Check what percentage of the number of states is reached when you use the 8 Megabyte state space on which your first estimate for maximal coverage in a full state space search was based (2^{23} bytes is 2^{26} bits, which means a run-time flag -w26). You should be able to get reasonably good coverage and between 40,000 and 400,000 states *stored* per second, depending on the speed of the machine that is used. Note that the actual number of states *reached* is about twice as large as the number of states *stored* in this experiment: The number of states reached equals the number of transitions that were executed.

On a 2.5 GHz Pentium 4 Windows PC, for instance, the run reaches 99% coverage at a rate of 400,000 states per second.

```
$ spin -a ex2
$ cl -DPC -DSAFETY -O pan.c
$ time ./pan -w26
(Spin Version 4.0.7 -- 1 August 2003)
        + Partial Order Reduction

Bit statespace search for:
        never claim              - (none specified)
        assertion violations     +
        cycle checks             - (disabled by -DSAFETY)
        invalid end states       +
```

```
State-vector 38 byte, depth reached 20, errors: 0
2.07474e+006 states, stored
2.07474e+006 states, matched
4.14948e+006 transitions (= stored+matched)
        0 atomic steps
2.07223e+006 lost messages
hash factor: 32.3456 (expected coverage: >= 98% on avg.)
(max size 2^26 states)

Stats on memory usage (in Megabytes):
87.139  equivalent memory usage for states
16.777  memory used for hash array (-w26)
0.280   memory used for DFS stack (-m10000)
17.262  total actual memory usage

unreached in proctype :init:
        line 8, state 6, "-end-"
        (1 of 6 states)

real    0m5.247s
user    0m0.015s
sys     0m0.000s
$
```

If enough memory is available, also perform an exhaustive (non-bitstate) verification and compare the total actual memory usage for the two runs.

C.8.

How many states should the following program generate?

```
#define N   20

int     a;
byte    b;

init {
        do
        :: atomic { (b < N) ->
                if
                :: a = a + (1<<b)
                :: skip
                fi;
                b=b+1 }
        od
}
```

Run a bitstate analysis, using the command

```
$ time ./pan -c0 -w26
```

and explain all numbers reported.

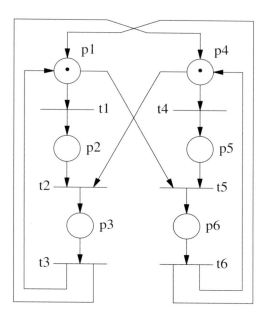

Figure C.1 Petri Net with Hang State

C.9.

It is often much easier to build an little validation model and mechanically verify it than it is to understand a manual proof of correctness in detail. Petri Nets are relatively easy to model as PROMELA validation models. A PROMELA model for the net in Figure C.1, for instance, is quickly made.

```
#define Place    byte    /* < 256 tokens per place */

Place p1, p2, p3;
Place p4, p5, p6;

#define inp1(x)              (x>0) -> x--
#define inp2(x,y)            (x>0&&y>0) -> x--; y--

#define out1(x)              x++
#define out2(x,y)            x++; y++

init
{       p1 = 1; p4 = 1; /* initial marking */
```

```
        do
/*t1*/  :: atomic { inp1(p1)     -> out1(p2) }
/*t2*/  :: atomic { inp2(p2,p4) -> out1(p3) }
/*t3*/  :: atomic { inp1(p3)     -> out2(p1,p4) }
/*t4*/  :: atomic { inp1(p4)     -> out1(p5) }
/*t5*/  :: atomic { inp2(p1,p5) -> out1(p6) }
/*t6*/  :: atomic { inp1(p6)     -> out2(p4,p1) }
        od
}
```

For this exercise, consider the following PROMELA model of a Petri Net taken from a journal paper that was published in 1982 and proven to be dead-lock-free in that paper with manual proof techniques.

```
#define Place   byte

Place P1, P2, P4, P5, RC, CC, RD, CD;
Place p1, p2, p4, p5, rc, cc, rd, cd;

#define inp1(x)        (x>0) -> x--
#define inp2(x,y)      (x>0&&y>0) -> x--; y--
#define out1(x)        x++
#define out2(x,y)      x++; y++

init
{       P1 = 1; p1 = 1; /* initial marking */
        do
        :: atomic { inp1(P1)     -> out2(rc,P2) }
        :: atomic { inp2(P2,CC) -> out1(P4)     }
        :: atomic { inp1(P4)     -> out2(P5,rd) }
        :: atomic { inp2(P5,CD) -> out1(P1)     }
        :: atomic { inp2(P1,RC) -> out2(P4,cc) }
        :: atomic { inp2(P4,RD) -> out2(P1,cd) }
        :: atomic { inp2(P5,RD) -> out1(P1)     }

        :: atomic { inp1(p1)     -> out2(RC,p2) }
        :: atomic { inp2(p2,cc) -> out1(p4)     }
        :: atomic { inp1(p4)     -> out2(p5,RD) }
        :: atomic { inp2(p5,cd) -> out1(p1)     }
        :: atomic { inp2(p1,rc) -> out2(p4,CC) }
        :: atomic { inp2(p4,rd) -> out2(p1,CD) }
        :: atomic { inp2(p5,rd) -> out1(p1)     }
        od
}
```

See if SPIN can find a deadlock in the model.

DOWNLOADING SPIN   D

> *"On two occasions I have been asked, 'Pray, Mr. Babbage,*
> *if you put into the machine wrong figures, will the right*
> *answers come out?' I am not able rightly to apprehend the*
> *kind of confusion of ideas that could provoke such a question."*
> *(Charles Babbage, 1792–1871)*

SPIN can be run on most systems, including most flavors of UNIX and Windows PCs. The only strict requirement is the availability of a standard, ANSI compatible, C preprocessor and compiler. If these programs are not already installed on your system, good quality public domain versions can be readily found on the Web. A recommended source for these tool, plus a host of other UNIX applications, is

```
http://www.cygwin.com
```

Instructions for installing SPIN, documentation, test cases, and the complete set of SPIN sources, are maintained and kept up to date at

```
http://spinroot.com/spin/index.html
```

The SPIN package has been freely available in this form since 1991. Officially, the SPIN sources are not considered to be in the public domain, since they are protected by a copyright from Bell Labs and Lucent Technologies. In effect, though, the software is very widely distributed and for all practical purposes treated as freeware. The tool is used for educational purposes, for research in formal verification, and has found considerable use in industry.

Commercial use of SPIN requires the acceptance of a standard license agreement from Bell Labs, which can be done by clicking an *accept* button, and entering some contact information, at URL

```
http://cm.bell-labs.com/cm/cs/what/spin/spin_license.html
```

The commercial license also requires no fees. SPIN continues to evolve, with new releases appearing every few months. The changes made in each new release of the tool—bug fixes, extensions, and revisions—are documented in update files that are part of the distribution.

Perhaps the best way to stay up to date on new developments related to SPIN is through the SPIN Workshop series. International SPIN Workshops have been held annually since 1995. The proceedings of the workshops are published by Springer Verlag in their series of Lecture Notes in Computer Science.

LTL CONVERSION

Etessami's `eqltl` tool, for the conversion of extended LTL formulae, containing precisely one existential quantifier that we discussed in Chapter 6, can be downloaded from:

```
http://www.bell-labs.com/project/TMP/
```

The alternative converter developed by Denis Oddoux and Paul Gastin for the conversion of standard LTL formulae into PROMELA `never` claims is available from the SPIN Web site at:

```
http://spinroot.com/spin/Src/ltl2ba.tar.gz
```

The original package can also be obtained from the authors of this software via:

```
http://verif.liafa.jussieu.fr/ltl2ba/
```

MODEL EXTRACTION

In Chapter 10 we discussed the use of a model extraction tool to facilitate the mechanical construction of SPIN verification models from implementation level code. The model extractor is available from Bell Labs via URL

```
http://cm.bell-labs.com/cm/cs/what/modex/index.html
```

The distribution package includes documentation, as well as the *FeaVer* graphical user interface that can facilitate the use of the model extraction software.

TIMELINE EDITOR

The timeline editor tool, discussed in Chapter 13, is part of the *FeaVer* interface for the model extractor (see above). It can also be run as a stand-alone tool. This stand-alone version of the tool can be downloaded via URL

```
http://cm.bell-labs.com/cm/cs/what/timeedit/index.html
```

TABLES AND FIGURES

*"An undetected error [...] is like a sunken rock
at sea yet undiscovered, upon which it is impossible
to say what wrecks may have taken place."*
(Sir John Herschel, 1842)

TABLES

FIGURES

INDEX

*"Not everything that can be counted counts,
and not everything that counts can be counted."
(Albert Einstein, 1879–1955)*

585